THE WILD TURKEY
Its History and Domestication

By A. W. SCHORGER

The Chemistry of Cellulose and Wood (New York, 1926)
The Passenger Pigeon (Madison, 1955)
The Wild Turkey: Its History and Domestication (Norman, 1966)

LIBRARY OF CONGRESS CATALOG CARD NUMBER: 66–13426

THE
WILD
TURKEY
ITS HISTORY AND
DOMESTICATION

A. W. Schorger

UNIVERSITY OF OKLAHOMA PRESS : NOR

Dedicated to my grandchildren since they, like this book, are hostages to fortune.

PREFACE

When the Spanish explorers brought the turkey to Spain from Central America, North America made its most important avian contribution to the economy of our globe. The instantaneous changes of color of the fleshy neck, coupled with a peafowl pomposity, fascinated even an East Indian emperor. Novelty soon faded upon recognition that, as a bird for the table, the turkey had no equal. As is to be expected, it first graced the feasts of royalty. Today, in the United States, no economic status is a bar to its enjoyment.

Although the turkey has nearly five centuries of recorded history, there is much in the behavior of the wild bird that requires verification. It is doubtful if more than a small number of the wild birds east of the Mississippi are without a degree of admixture with the domestic form. This complicates the problem. It is uncertain to what extent the bird has changed its habits as a result of civilization. The early accounts of the behavior of the turkey when crossing a large stream are contradictory. It is questionable if, in the future, any person will be so fortunate to see turkeys attempt to cross the Ohio or the Mississippi. There are many papers on the changes in color of the head and neck, but they do not leave the conviction that exact reasons for these changes have been found. It is possible in some of the early descriptions of behavior to state that they are incorrect or improbable, but not in others. There have been some fundamental investigations in recent years, particularly those of A. S. Leopold on wildness and those of E. B. Hale and M. W. Schein on behavior. More basic studies of this nature are needed.

Although the literature on the wild turkey is extensive (approximately six thousand references), all phases of its life history are not covered.

Where information is lacking it has been necessary to resort to our knowledge of the domestic breeds. The native bird, on account of its wildness, is not amenable to some kinds of investigation. The turkey is an adaptable species. The domestic turkey in some countries became feral unexpectedly and again became a game bird.

An attempt has been made to provide a comprehensive history of the species. Management has been treated very briefly as it is aside from our direct objective.

The wild turkey reached its nadir about the year 1900. Its present abundance is a great tribute to management. Essential is a suitable habitat, but this is of no avail unless accompanied by a law-abiding public conscience. Happily, the day has passed when any game animal can be killed out of season with impunity. Few, if any, of our game birds have been studied with more intensity than the turkey, not only to perpetuate the species, but to provide hunting of the highest quality. If this book will aid research on so fine a species, its purpose will have been accomplished.

I am indebted to the following persons for various favors: A. S. Leopold, H. S. Mosby, R. W. Bailey, H. L. Stoddard, O. J. Gromme, Levon Lee, Caleb Glazener, J. H. Herriott, E. R. Mulvihill, Kathryn S. Reierson, Marguerite A. Christensen, and Helen F. Northup. My debt is especially great to Patricia Murrish for typing the manuscript, and to my wife for assistance in checking it.

A. W. Schorger

Madison, Wisconsin
May 20, 1966

CONTENTS

ILLUSTRATIONS

PLATES

FIGURES

TABLES

THE WILD TURKEY
Its History and Domestication

1

Discovery of the Turkey
in Central America and Mexico

AMERICA has the distinction of having provided the world with the largest domestic gallinaceous bird, the turkey. Long thought to have been of Asiatic or African origin, it received extremely inappropriate common and scientific names. Following its introduction into Spain early in the sixteenth century, the domestic bird was brought back to America by the English colonists of the Atlantic seaboard. It was then only a puny representative of the wild bird. Its meat was found to be of superior quality and continued in favor for festive occasions. Subjected to human persecution, the wild ancestor became very wary and developed into a gamebird which has no equal. Aesthetically, it has a strong appeal. Familiarity tends to diminish appreciation, but I do not know of a more entrancing sight in nature than a group of wild gobblers in mating display.

We are confronted with the fact that the word *turkey* was in use long before the present bird was known in Europe. During the reign of Edward III (1312–77), William Yoo of the county of Devon had on his coat-of-arms "three Turkey-cocks in their pride proper" (Izacke, 1681). There is little probability that the birds were other than peafowl (*Pavo*). Any large bird that spread its tail was a peafowl, or a turkey. Cambrensis (1602:47), who lived 1146?–1220?, completed his *Topographia* in 1187. He stated that wild peafowl (*pavones silvestris*) were abundant in Ireland. The only bird that could be intended was the capercaillie (*Tetrao urogallus*). The wild turkeys in Ireland protected by an act (1787) of George III must have been capercaillies (Longfield, 1868:3, 143, 238). As late as the middle of the eighteenth century, the capercaillie in Scotland was sometimes called a wild turkey (Burt, 1818:71).

The turkey was confused with the guinea fowl (*Numida meleagris*) in the sixteenth century. Elyot (1552) wrote: "Meleagrides, birdes, which we doo call hennes of Genny, or Turkie henne." A similar definition is given by Thomas Cooper (1584). Francis Bacon (1670:183) had the true turkey in mind when he wrote that in the pheasants, peacocks, and turkeys, the male is larger than the female, and, "The turkey-cock hath great and swelling Gills, the Hen hath less." Without diagnostic information, it is not always certain that the "turkey" of the sixteenth century was the turkey.

The loose terminology of the Spanish explorers renders it difficult at times to determine to which bird they refer. *Gallina* and *pavo* usually meant turkey, but these names at times, apparently, were applied to the curassow (*Crax rubra*), crested guan (*Penelope purpurascens*), horned guan (*Oreophasis derbianus*), chachalacas (*Ortalis* and *Penelopina*), and the ocellated turkey (*Agriocharis ocellata*) of the Yucatán Peninsula. Assurance that the bird referred to was a turkey must sometimes be based on information obtained subsequent to the original reports.

There is a possibility that Columbus was the first European to see the turkey. During his fourth voyage, he discovered a group of islands off the coast of Honduras, one of which he called Guanaja. There was nothing of importance on these islands, so on August 14, 1502, he landed at Point Caxinas (Cabo de Honduras). Here he was hospitably received by the natives, who brought food consisting in part of native fowls (*gallinas de la tierra*) which were better than those of Spain (Colón, 1947:278; Beretta, 1945:564). This is the first use of *gallina de la tierra*, a name that subsequently was commonly applied to the turkey. There is supporting evidence. The Cuban name for the turkey, *guanajo*, is believed to have been derived from the turkey seen by Columbus at or near the Guanajas. Furthermore, when Cortés arrived at Trujillo, Point Caxinas, in 1525, the natives gave him fish and turkeys (*gallinas*) (Díaz, 1933: II, 188). Christopher Columbus himself is silent regarding the birds at Point Caxinas; however, when on the Costa Rican coast, he saw some very large fowls (*gallinas*) with feathers like wool (Major, 1847:193). What he saw is difficult to determine. The young of vultures have plumage of this description.

The Third Decade of Martyr (1944:229) was published in 1516. Regarding the visit of Columbus to Cape Honduras, he wrote that here were birds like peafowls in color, size, taste, and savour. It is difficult to identify the *pavos* of Enciso (1897:*xxiii, xxvii, xxix*), writing in 1519. For Santa Marta, Colombia, he mentions feathers of parrots, *pavos*, and other birds. There were in the woods at Darien, Panama, many *pavos* of different kinds. The domesticated *pavos* along the coast from Cabo Gracias a Dios, Nicaragua, northward may well have been turkeys.

An unquestionable opportunity for seeing the turkey (*Meleagris*) was in 1517 when Yucatán was discovered by Francisco Hernández de Córdoba. None of the members of his expedition wrote an account mentioning the turkey. Las Casas (1951:159, 161, 163) came to Cuba in 1511 and remained in the New World until 1547. His history was not finished until about 1561. He states that when members of the Córdoba expedition landed near Cape Catoche, the natives presented, roasted, two of the large turkeys (*gallinas*) of this country. The birds were as large as peafowls. At Campeche they were given many fowls with a dewlap (*gallinas de papada*), as large and perhaps better than peafowls. These birds were unquestionably turkeys. Many turkeys were also seen at a large farm near Champotón.

The nearest contemporaneous account is that of Martyr (1944:311), secretary to the Council of the Indies. In addition to having access to the reports from the Indies, he was industrious in interviewing returning Spaniards. He states that at the banquet given by the Cacique of Campeche, turkeys (*pavos*) were served. This statement appeared in his Fourth Decade, written in 1520, and printed in Basle in 1521.

According to Oviedo (1851: I, 497), the natives at Campeche supplied many good birds as large as peafowls and no less tasty. Here the Spaniards obtained *gallinas*, like peafowls, according to Santa Cruz (1920). Gómara (1554:61) says that at this town the Spaniards were given ducks and "gallipavos." The Grijalva expedition of 1518 covered much the same ground. The Indians of Cozumel, according to Oviedo (1851: I, 507), brought the captain certain *gallinas* of the island, as large as peafowls. He also speaks of them as peafowls or large fowls. Díaz (1933: I, 26), a member of the expedition, mentions that at the Río Tabasco (Grijalva) the Indians brought fish and *gallinas*; and at Cozumel, according to Las Casas (1951: III, 159), the Indians gave Grijalva turkeys (*gallinas de papada*). Concerning this island, Cervantes de Salazar (1914–36: I, 150, 152, 159) wrote that there was a large number

5

Fig. 1.—*Localities where turkeys were raised in Mexico and Central America in the sixteenth century. (After Schorger.)*

of birds called *gallinas de la tierra* (turkeys). The Spaniards subsequently obtained turkeys at Champotón and the Río Grijalva.

The Cortés (1932: I, 29) expedition of 1519 revealed that the turkey was widely distributed as a domesticated bird (Fig. 1). He wrote on July 10, 1519, that the people along the coast from the island of Cozumel to Veracruz raise many *gallinas* like those of Tierra Firme which are as large as peafowls. When the expedition landed at Cozumel, the Indians abandoned their homes, from which Pedro de Alvarado ordered forty *gallinas* to be taken (Díaz, 1933: I, 47). The Indians at the Río Grijalva gave presents of *gallinas* and other foods. Gómara (1554: 105v), after the battle of Pontochán (Champotón) in 1519, states that the Spaniards received *gallipavos*. Some lords at Tabasco came carrying turkeys, which,

6

according to Tápia (1939:53), a member of the expedition, were here called *gallinas de las Indias*.

The history of the turkey in the Yucatán Peninsula is complicated by the presence of the handsome, native ocellated turkey. It occupied the peninsula from northern British Honduras to southern Tabasco. In coloration it is much closer to the peafowl than the common turkey. The Mayas called Yucatán the land of the turkey (*pavo silvestre*) and deer (Pech, 1939:211). Landa (1937:2), who came to Yucatán in 1549, states that the natives called it *Umil cu[t]z yetel ceh*, land of the turkey and the deer. The orthography of Espinoza (1948:114) is at variance but the meaning is the same. In the province of Guaymil, Yucatán, there is an abundance of deer and turkeys (*pavos*), hence the natives call it *Yetelzeh y Vnunuýz*, meaning land of deer and turkeys. Since he is discussing game, the turkeys in question must be the ocellated.

It is difficult to decide in some cases if the stylized figures in the Mayan codices represent the common or the ocellated turkey. Tozzer and Allen (1910) decided that all belonged to the latter species. Seler (1909) believes that both species are represented. His criteria for the common turkey are the tubercles on the naked skin of the head and neck (colored blue and red), the long, pendant frontal caruncle, the dark, banded feathers, and the long beard on the breast. The markings relied upon for the ocellated turkey are the white edges of the primaries, the inner ones being crossed sharply with narrow white bands, and the clearly marked tips of the tail feathers. The male of the common turkey in Nahuatl was called *uexolotl*, and the female, or the family in general, *totolin*. The Zapotecs called the female *pète* or *père*, the native hen: and to distinguish it from the introduced Spanish hen, *pète hualache*, *pète zaa*. The male was *pète nigòla*. In Guatemala the male was *mama col* or *mam col*. The Mayas of Yucatán called the male of the domesticated turkey *ulum*, the female *tux* or *ixtux*, while the wild ocellated turkey was *cutz*. At the present time in the Yucatán Peninsula, the ocellated turkey is called *pavo de monte*, and *ḵuts* (Paynter, 1955:84). Leopold (1959:275) adds *guajalote de Yucatán*, *guajalote brilliante*, and *cūt*.

The natives of Yucatán never domesticated the ocellated turkey. It was the wild turkey of the region and was captured by trapping. A figure in the *Codex Borgia* (1904) shows a turkey in a noose, and another in the *Codex Troano* (1939) in a net. The bird was also taken alive by a wicker basket that dropped over it (Tozzer and Allen, 1910). The ocellated turkey is difficult to raise.[1]

It is of special interest that none of the bones found at archeological sites in Yucatán have been definitely assigned to the common turkey. Mercer (1896:168) found beneath a layer of human culture some bones identified by E. D. Cope as *Meleagris*, an identification that at that time could have applied to either the common or ocellated turkey. The bones found in the caves Actun Spukil and Actun Coyok were identified by Harvey I. Fisher (Hatt *et al.*, 1953:83–85), as those of the ocellated turkey (*Agriocharis ocellata*). A large number of bones was unearthed in the ruins of Mayapán, dating for the most part from the thirteenth to the fifteenth century A.D. (Pollock and Ray, 1957:636, 644–45). There were found 1,268 turkey bones, representing 196 individuals, all of which were identified as those of the ocellated turkey. Their location suggested that the birds were consumed by the priests and the aristocracy. Surprisingly, no bones of the crested guan (*Penelope*) were found, and those of the great curassow (*Crax*) and chachalaca (*Ortalis*) occurred in only trifling numbers. It is possible that domesticated turkeys were not raised until shortly before the arrival of the Spaniards since turkeys were far less numerous than in the Mexican domain.

The Indians were very skillful in capturing wild birds and in domesticating some of them. The chachalaca can be tamed easily and probably was domesticated prior to the turkey. It is still a common bird in Mexican homes. The *gallina de la tierra* and the *ave de la tierra* in the Spanish literature may at times have been applied to this bird. In Yucatán in 1588, Ponce (1932:325) was offered chachalacas by the natives, and he

---

[1] Beebe (1939) stated that it had never laid an egg in captivity. This appears to be incorrect. The director of the Zoological Garden, Berlin, obtained a cock and two hens in the fall of 1881 (Dürigen, 1906:294). The next spring the hens laid forty eggs. The first sixteen eggs, eight of which were infertile, gave a small number of beautiful poults. This appears to be the first time that the species bred in captivity. The experience of Dr. Gaumer in raising this turkey in Yucatán has been described by Chapman (1933:148). About 430 eggs of the wild bird were purchased from the natives. About four hundred of these eggs hatched, but at the end of six months only thirty-seven young survived. During the following eight months this number was reduced to fourteen. With these, Gaumer started for Paris but on arriving in New York only two of the turkeys remained alive. Successful breeding was attained in 1948, at the gardens of the Zoological Society of San Diego, California, by Lint (1952), using artificial insemination. In 1950 nine turkeys were raised by the natural mating of birds of the second generation.

mentions that two of them lived with the turkeys at the convent of Ichmul. In 1580 many wild birds, like Castilian chickens and called *chachalacas*, were being raised by the natives in southern Oaxaca (Paso y Troncoso, 1905:237).

There are numerous references to turkeys in Central and South America by the early navigators. Only one indicates that the domestic turkey and not the curassow may have been found. According to Martyr (1944:173), when Vicente Yáñez Pinzón was at the Gulf of Paria, Venezuela, in 1500, the Indians gave him some fowls (*pavos*) differing from the peafowl in color. There were live hens to be taken to Spain for propagation and males for immediate consumption. If the birds could be raised in quantity, it is probable they were turkeys. Their ultimate fate is unknown. Eden (1885:129) assumes that they were turkeys for he has the marginal note: "Peacockes which we caule Turkye Cockes." Cárcer y Disdier (1960) recently discovered documents showing that turkeys were brought to Spain from Tierra Firme for breeding purposes, by royal decree, by at least 1511.

Judging from a modern account of the Tarahumaras, taming of the wild turkey was no problem: "The turkey (*siwí*) in a domesticated state is not often seen among the Tarahumaras. However, plenty of turkeys are found wild in the Sierra and brought home by the Indians. They are fed and carefully raised until they become quite tame and do not try to run away. It is not even necessary to clip their wings. The Tarahumaras value a turkey at about two pesos. At night the turkeys sleep on top of the houses or in nearby trees. If the Indians come across the eggs of a turkey, they often put them under a setting hen" (Bennett and Zingg, 1935:23, 113).

Outside the Yucatán Peninsula, the first turkeys seen in the territory controlled by the Aztecs was during the Grijalva expedition in 1518. Landing at the Río de Banderas (Jamapa), just south of Veracruz, the expedition was provided turkeys (*gallinas de la tierra*) and maize by the natives (Díaz, 1933, I:28). At Isla San Juan de Ulúa, opposite present Veracruz, the Indians brought *gallinas de papada* (Las Casas, 1951: III, 214); and at the Isla de los Sacrificios they brought bread, *tortillas*, and well-done turkey pies (Juan Díaz, 1939:32). The Cortés expedition of 1519 found turkeys abundant in Mexico. At the Port of San Juan de Ulúa, according to Díaz (1933: I, 70), many Indians appeared carrying

9

turkeys. Pedro de Alvarado, with some soldiers, went on a foraging expedition to some towns subject to Cotaxtla, on the Atoyac River, and returned with turkeys. The Indians of Quiahuitztlán brought turkeys and maize bread. While Cortés was camped at the hill of Zumpango in 1519, some Tlaxcalans arrived with five Indians saying: "If you are gods who eat blood and flesh, eat these Indians and we will bring you more; and if you are good gods here are incense and feathers; and if you are men here are turkeys, bread and cherries" (Tápia, 1866:569). During the march to the City of Mexico, turkeys were reported at nearly every town.

ABUNDANCE

Turkeys were raised in large numbers in the Mexican states. A good idea of their abundance is obtained from the tribute exacted by the Mexican lords. About 1430, Netzahualcoyotzin, lord of Texcoco, required among other provisions one hundred turkeys (*coqs*) daily (Ixtlilxochitl, 1840: XII, 240). This would be 36,500 turkeys yearly. Torquemada (1943: I, 167) states that this ruler exacted six to eight thousand turkeys annually. These numbers are within reason; however, when four million *fanegas* of maize are included in the tribute, some doubt is thrown on the accuracy of the data. Every person in Misquiahuala had to contribute to Montezuma one turkey every twenty days (Cook, 1949:38). The population of the town in 1519 was estimated at 7,500 persons, thus the annual contribution would reach the enormous number of 135,000 turkeys. Assuming that only adults were intended to contribute and that they formed two-fifths of the population, the number of turkeys would be 54,000. In some towns at least, as at Tepeucila, only the lords were permitted to eat turkeys (Nuttall, 1926:70).

The food required from each *señor* for the fiesta of the Tlaxcalan god Camaxtli was great and was consumed entirely. Of *gallinas de la tierra* alone there were provided fourteen to sixteen hundred daily. Torquemada (1943: II, 365) says that the number is not as surprising as that these were turkeys (*gallos de papada*). Large numbers of turkeys were required just to feed the carnivores and raptors in Montezuma's menagerie. Cervantes de Salazar (1914: II, 21) and Clavigero (1787:214) state that to feed the raptors, five hundred turkeys were used daily. Gómara (1554:105v) gives the same number and adds that three hundred men were required to attend the aviary. The carnivores were also fed turkeys, in addition to deer and dogs. According to Motolinía (1914:132, 188), one of the large eagles in Montezuma's menagerie required a turkey daily. The Indians at the opening of the Hospital of the Incarnation at Tlaxcala in 1538 made an offering of 140 turkeys and an infinite number of Castilian chickens. Montezuma's raptors were fed turkeys and nothing else, while the carnivores were fed many turkeys, according to Cortés (1932:109). Between Montezuma's menagerie and his large household, it seems safe to assume that his levy was one thousand turkeys per day, or 365,000 yearly. Gómara (1554:300) mentions that at one of the Mexican feasts, between one thousand and fifteen hundred turkeys were consumed.

Cortés (1932: I, 87), with his usual modesty, requested Montezuma to provide him with an estate. The monarch in a short time had four good houses constructed. In one of them, in addition to the living quarters, there was a pool in which were placed five hundred ducks. He added fifteen hundred turkeys (*gallinas*). Martyr (1944:385, 470) was told that the number of turkeys was fifteen hundred, some being for propagation and others for the table. During the Indian uprising, everything on the estate was carried off.

Prior to the battle of September 5, 1519, between the Spaniards and the Tlaxcalans, the latter, according to Ixtlilxochitl (1840: XIII, 189), brought the Spaniards turkeys, maize, and cherries. The food was provided so that when the Spaniards were defeated, they could not claim it was because of hunger. Torquemada (1943: I, 423) gives the number of turkeys as three hundred and is copied verbatim by Herrera (1944: III, 150). Gómara (1943: III, 165) has the same story. This would be an extraordinary example of Indian chivalry. Cortés and Díaz are silent on the subject. The Anonymous Conqueror (1917:36) wrote that the Mexicans raised many turkeys very good to eat. They were the most conspicuous and cheapest source of meat in Mexico (Prescott, 1843: II, 111).

The Mexicans were terrified when they saw horses for the first time and believed they were carnivorous. They consequently provided turkeys for the horses as well as for the Spaniards (Martyr, 1944:585). During the Cortés expedition to Honduras in 1524, a sick horse was left with the Indians at Lake Petén-Itzá. Believing the horse to be a rational animal, they tried to cure it by feeding it turkeys and other meats, according to Villagutierre (1933:82). When it died, they made a statue of the horse and worshiped it to appease the potential wrath of Cortés. When some missionaries arrived at the lake in 1618, the image was still in one of the temples. The incident was first mentioned by Cogolludo (1867:93), but he is silent on the offering of turkeys.

COMMERCE

The markets in the city of Mexico were described by several writers. Cortés (1852:32) in his letter of 1520 states: "There is a street for game in which are sold all kinds of native birds such as turkeys, partridges, quails, wild ducks. . . ." Díaz (1933: I:184) mentions that they sold hen and cock turkeys (*gallinas* and *gallos de papada*), rabbits, hares, deer, and other game. In the great market, the eggs of turkeys, geese, and many other birds were for sale in large amounts (Lorenzana, 1770:104). All transactions consisted in exchanging one product for another, the cocoa bean being the closest approach to money. Gómara (1943: I, 240) gives as an example that a turkey was exchanged for a bundle (*haz*) of maize. Just what constituted a bundle is uncertain. The modern Guatemalan Indian, in harvesting corn, transports it in a globular net apparently holding about two bushels of corn on the ear (Weatherwax, 1954: Fig. 27). In 1628 a turkey or a Spanish chicken sold for a real in Yucatán (Espinoza, 1948:115). Oviedo (1950:173) gives the price of a *pavo*, in this case a curassow, as a *castellano*, or gold peso, worth a real in purchasing power in Spain. Motolinía (1914:142) gives a more lucid value, one turkey being worth three or four Spanish chickens.

Cooked turkeys were available in the markets. There is little information on how the turkeys were prepared by the natives for eating. The first Spaniards to reach Yucatán were supplied with the roasted birds. Cobo's history (1890: I, 345) was written in 1653. He states that during extraordinary festivals a tamale containing an entire turkey was prepared. There were no leaves large enough to cover it, so it was wrapped in a mat made of palm leaves.

EARLY DESCRIPTIONS

A brief but diagnostic description of the turkey was published by Martyr (1587:351 [365]) in 1530 in his Fifth Decade: "The Mexicans raise this bird (*pauonum*) as chickens (*gallinas*) are raised in Spain. Turkeys resemble peafowl in size and in the color of their plumage. The females lay from twenty to thirty eggs. The males are always in rut so that their flesh is indifferent. Like peacocks they display before the females, spreading the tail in the form of a wheel. They parade before them, take four or more steps, then shiver as if affected with a strong fever. On the neck are displayed feathers of various colors (*diuersos ad sui libitum inter colli plumas colores ostentant*), sometimes blue, green, or purplish according to the movement of the feathers." There follows a fanciful tale, which he was unwilling to believe, related to him by a priest, Benito Martín, who had traveled extensively in the New World and had reared large flocks of turkeys. The male, said Martín, has obstacles on his feet (presumably the spurs), so that he has difficulty in approaching the hen for coition. If someone holds the hen, the cock will run to her without fear. The Fifth Decade appears to have been completed in 1523. It seems that Martyr had not seen a turkey up to this time or he would have noticed that the neck is practically devoid of feathers and that the changes in color enumerated are undergone by the bare skin.

Some peafowl, or turkeys, described by Oviedo (1950:172) in 1526 are unquestionably curassows. When he comes to the true turkey he writes: "Other turkeys (*pavos*) larger, better tasting, and more beautiful have been found in New Spain, many of which have been taken to the islands and to Castilla del Oro, and are raised domestically under supervision of the Christians. Of these the females are ugly and the males handsome, and very often they spread their tails although these are not as large or as beautiful as those of [the peafowl of] Spain. However, with respect to the remainder of their plumage it is all beautiful. The neck and head are covered with a fleshy skin, without feathers, which at their desire changes to different colors. Especially when they display it turns a very bright red and when they cease it becomes yellow and other colors, blackish, and sometimes a brown and white color. On the forehead above the bill the turkey has a short protuberance which when he displays enlarges and extends more than the width of a palm; and from the middle of the breast there grows and persists a tuft of hairs as thick as a finger, and these hairs are neither more nor less than those in the tail of a horse, very black and longer than the width of a palm. The flesh of these turkeys is very good and incomparably better and more tender than that of the peafowls of Spain."

The first details on the Mexican turkeys obtained by direct observation

13

are given by Sahagún (1938: III, 190). He came to New Spain in 1529 and his manuscript was completed about 1570. He is one of the few Spanish writers to mention the wild bird. He states that they have wild hens (*gallinas monteses*) and cocks which are like the domestic hens and cocks in size, plumage, and in all other respects. These birds are found in the forests.

The modern domesticated turkey occurs in a number of colors, and Sahagún informs us that this condition existed among the turkeys of the Aztecs. Color Plate LXXXIV, from his *Códice Florentino* evidently represents the brown phase. He writes: "The native hens and cocks are called *totollin*. These are well-known domestic birds having a round tail, and feathers in the wings but they do not fly. They are very good to eat, having the best meat of all the birds. They eat corn as mash when small, also cooked, ground pigweed, and other plants. They lay eggs and hatch poults. They are of various colors, some white, others red, others black, and others brown. The males are called *huexólotl* and have a large dewlap, a large breast and a large neck which has red tubercles. The head is blue, especially when angry, *se sejunto*. It has a fleshy appendage which hangs above the bill. It puffs up, swells or shrinks. Those people who dislike others, give them to eat or drink that bit of soft flesh above the bill, so that they may not get an erection.

"The female fowl is smaller than the cock, stands lower, and has tubercles on the head and throat. She submits to the cock, lays eggs, sits upon them and hatches the poults. Her flesh is very savory and fat. She is corpulent. She puts her poults under her wings and feeds her little ones worms and other things which she finds. The eggs which she conceives first thicken and develop a membrane and while inside grow a tender shell. Afterwards the hen lays them, and after the eggs are laid the shell hardens."

Motolinía (1914:83) came to Mexico in 1524. He mentions that the cock has a tuft of bristles on the breast stiffer than horse hair, and on some old birds more than a hand-breadth in length. This beard, used as a hyssop, lasts a long time. One of these cocks has as much meat as two Spanish peacocks. The turkey resembles a peafowl more than any other bird because it spreads its tail in the same manner. The plumage is less beautiful, and the voice is as unpleasant as that of the peacock.

Salazar (1914: I, 20), writing of the domestic turkey (*cuzcacahtl*), says that it is colored white and blackish only. The head is red. On the forehead is an ugly fleshy protuberance used for dressing the plumage. It shows a certain vanity and ostentation like a peacock when it spreads its tail. It is greatly esteemed among the Indians. Gómara (1554:335) remarks briefly that it has a large chin or swelling of the throat which changes to many colors. It is gentle enough to be caught even with the hands. Its appetite is great.

The Spaniards found that the Mexicans were making a dye from the cochineal insects and they soon developed a large European trade in this product. Gómez de Cervantes (1944:172, 202), in a manuscript dated 1599, states that turkeys are very harmful since they eat the cochineals and puncture the cacti so that the sap runs out and the plants can no longer support the insects. Among the illustrations of the enemies of the cochineal, the turkey appears.

Little is added to our knowledge by Hernández (1651:27): "There is an Indian cock, which some call *gallipavo*, known to all. There are also found wild ones which are twice as large as the domestic ones, tougher and inferior food, otherwise similar, which are sometimes killed with arrows and sometimes with crossbows." He then states that there are females of this species, called *cihuatotolin*, that feed on carrion and are disgusting to the palate. He refers to either the black vulture (*Coragyps atratus*) or the turkey vulture (*Cathartes aura*). In view of the time in which he wrote, there is no excuse for this error.

About a century ago, Blasquez (1868:337) compared the Mexican wild and domestic races. The wild turkeys were larger than the domestic ones, weighing ordinarily from sixteen to twenty pounds. The plumage and colors were the same, the only difference being that the frontal caruncle and fleshy tubercles of the head and neck were very small in the wild species, which gave the impression that the neck was much longer. The beard, or *xelhuastle*, on the breast measures sometimes more than a third of the Castilian yard (280 mm.).

The domestic turkey of the Mexicans had most of the color phases of the modern bird. An unknown Franciscan friar (Anon., 1903:159), about 1538–39, prepared a manuscript on the customs of the natives of Michoacán. The Chichimecas made banners of white turkey feathers. Chichimeca was a vague name sometimes applied to any of the wildest tribes of Mexican Indians.

Common Names

There is little doubt that our bird derived its name from Turkey. In the Middle Ages nearly everything exotic was obtained in or through Turkish, or Arabian, territories. Even our maize is still known in the Near East and India as Turkey wheat. The belief that the turkey came from Turkey persisted long after it was known that the New World was its origin. Willughby (1678:160) wrote that the English call the bird *turkey* because it was thought to have been brought from Turkey. Samuel Johnson (1755) says: "Turkey [gallina turcica Lat.]. A large domestick fowl brought from Turkey."

There are numerous suggestions on the origin of the name *turkey*, most of which are exercises in imagination. The most logical is that it was derived from Turkey. Newton (1881) thought that the name was derived from the turkey's call notes *turk, turk, turk*. Turquoise was once called Turkey stone. This led Broderip (1849:131) to hint that the blue on the head of the bird led to the name *turkey*.

The Hebrew name for the peafowl, *tāūas*, is similar to the Hindustani *taus*. Solomon permitted ships to sail from the Gulf of Aqaba to India whence they returned with ivory, monkeys, sandalwood, and peacocks (*togi*), (Barnett, 1956:92). Buckton (1866) gives authority for the statement that in the dialect of Malabar the name of the peafowl is *togei*. This name followed the peacock westward and it has been suggested that turkey was derived from it.[2]

Few birds have been burdened with as many names in the same language as the turkey. Most of those used by the Spaniards have been mentioned previously. When, and from what locality the turkey was

---

[2] The turkey was favored above the bald eagle for our national emblem by Franklin since it was respectable and a native of America. His plea ran in part: "Others object to the *bald eagle* as looking too much like a *dindon*, or turkey. For my own part, I wish the bald eagle had not been chosen as the representative of our country; he is a bird of bad moral character; he does not get his living honestly; you may have seen him perched on some dead tree, where, too lazy to fish for himself, he watches the labor of the fishing-hawk; and when that diligent bird has at length taken a fish, and is bearing it to his nest for the support of his mate and young ones, the bald eagle pursues him and takes it from him" (Sparks, 1882, 10:63). He failed to draw the moral that if the osprey would keep its mouth shut, instead of screaming, after capturing a fish, the eagle would not be made so aware of possible booty. It would have been highly incongruous to have selected a bird with so foreign a name as *turkey*.

16

brought to Cuba is unknown. Rodrigo Ranjel (Oviedo, 1851: I, 556), in his narrative of the De Soto expedition in 1539, mentions that while on the way to the Georgia towns they breakfasted on turkeys, called *guanaxas*. Since the expedition started from Cuba, the name must have been in use on this island. Gómara (1554:335) was partial to *gallipavo* and thought that the turkey was so named because it resembled both a peacock and a rooster. Two names are distinctive, *gallo de papada* (Díaz, 1933, I:184), and *gallina por barba* (Gómara, 1943: I, 192). The former is "cock with a throat wattle," and the latter, "fowl with a beard." It has been shown by Termer (1951) that the chicken did not exist in the New World prior to Columbus and that the *gallina* of the Spaniards in the Western world was the turkey. Gemelli-Careri (1719: VI, 116, 122, 138), while in Mexico in 1698, wrote of the turkey as *guaxalote, galli d'India, galli d'India silvestri,* and *gallo de la tierra.*

TABLE 1

INDIAN NAMES OF THE TURKEY IN CENTRAL AMERICA AND MEXICO

Name	Tribe	Area	Reference
Guanajo		Central America	Cobo (1890–91, II:238)
Chumpìpe		Central America	Cobo
Heuheucho		Central America	Cobo
Toú	Zapotec	Isthmus of Tehuantepec	Covarrubias (1946)
Totóli	Nahuat	Isthmus of Tehuantepec	Covarrubias
Lapump	Chontal	Isthmus of Tehuantepec	Covarrubias
Tulú	Chontal	Isthmus of Tehuantepec	Covarrubias
Tunuk	Popoloca	Isthmus of Tehuantepec	Covarrubias
Tutk	Mixe	Isthmus of Tehuantepec	Covarrubias
Túnuk	Zoque	Isthmus of Tehuantepec	Covarrubias
Tu:l	Huave	Isthmus of Tehuantepec	Covarrubias
Tunuk (male)	Jacalteca	Chiapas	La Farge and Byers (1931:328)
Äetsok (female)	Jacalteca	Chiapas	La Farge and Byers
Ahtsok (female)	Jacalteca	Chiapas	La Farge and Byers
Chiqui	Opata	Sonora	Anon. (1894)
Tóva	Papago	Sonora	Lumholtz (1912:373)
Urút	Cocopa	Sonora	Lumholtz

Cuvis	Cahita or Yaqui	Sonora	Beals (1943:16)
Tshīví	Tarahumara	Sonora	Lumholtz (1902:212)
Siwí	Tarahumara	Sonora	Bennett and Zingg (1935:23)

The display of the turkey is so like that of the peacock that it was entirely logical for the Spaniards to consider it a kind of peafowl. Martyr (1587:351), writing in Latin, called it *pavo*, as did Oviedo (1950: IV, 49), writing in Spanish. The old Castilian-Mexican dictionary of Molina (1944) gives for the turkey *pauo, paua o pauon*, and *quetzaltototl*. The latter name is derived from one of the trogons. It could be inferred that *pavo* was the most popular name for the turkey in Mexico in the sixteenth century; however, the Christians, according to Oviedo (1851: III, 300), called it *pavo de la papada*. In spite of the statement of García (1945:363) that the turkey (*pavo*) was called *gallo de Indias*, preserved in the Catalan *galldindi*, this name was uncommon in the western hemisphere.

The usual name for the turkey today is *guajalote* or *guajolote*, a corruption of the Aztec, *huexolotl*. Cobo (1890–91: II, 237) wrote in 1653: "The *guajalote* is now so familiar in all Europe that there is no region without knowledge of it. In New Spain, domestic and wild, it is so-called by the Mexican Indians. Because of its resemblance to the peacock (*pavo real*) in its display, the Spaniards applied the name *gallopavo* to embrace the two names by which it was called in different parts of the Indias, since in New Spain it had the name *gallina* and *gallo de la tierra*, in other parts being called *pavo*, and in Spain *gallopavo* in order to distinguish it from our chickens and peacocks, and this name has prevailed for more than 60 years."

Some names for the wild turkey used in recent years are: *guajalote del monte, guajalote salvaje* (Blasquez, 1868:329); *guajalote, pavo común* (Cubas, 1884:158), *guajolote monte, gallopavo* (López, 1911:379, 381), *guajalote silvestre*, and *cocono* (Leopold, 1959:268). Southwest of the city of Durango is the Bajía de los Coconos, the "Valley of the Turkeys" (Bailey and Conover, 1935:422). The use of *gallina silvestre* dates back to at least 1579 (Paso y Troncoso, 1905.1).

The Mayan and Aztec names of the turkey have been given previously. Some of the modern Indian names are given in Table 1.

2

The Domestic Turkey in the Early Southwest

THE PASSION of the Spaniards for precious metals rendered them gullible to rumors of great riches. Fray Marcos in 1539 came supposedly in sight of Hawikuh, one of the Seven Cities of Cibola. His entirely false report of the wealth of Cibola led to the famous Coronado expedition of 1540–42 to New Mexico. Coronado, on arriving with his famished companions at Hawikuh in 1540, found the natives hostile, and in order to secure food he was obliged to take the pueblo by force. Here he found a few turkeys. An anonymous participant (Anon., 1896:565) wrote: "We found in it what we needed more than gold and silver, and that was much corn and beans and turkeys, better than those of New Spain, and salt, the best and whitest I have seen in all my life." The Spanish text reads *larger*, not *better* as in Winship's translation. The Spaniards, prior to colonization, were forced to depend upon the natives for food; hence, turkeys and other provisions are frequently mentioned as available at the pueblos visited.

The Spaniards, disappointed over the anticipated wealth of the Southwest, left the country in peace for forty years. The Rodríguez expedition of 1581 followed the Río Grande from its junction with the Conchos. On entering the first inhabited pueblos in Doña Ana County, New Mexico, they found turkeys. Continuing up the river as far as Puaray, the expedition saw many turkeys at the numerous pueblos. The Espejo expedition of 1582–83 followed the same route. When considerably below El Paso, an Indian pointed westward and stated that at a distance of fifteen days' journey was a large lake with tall houses where the inhabitants had large supplies of maize and turkeys. Casas Grandes, in Chihuahua, was then in ruins and did not have a lake, so he must have meant the Pima pueblos at the salt marshes in southern New Mexico. Sosa (1865:331), during his brief raid into New Mexico in 1590, was content to say that the inhabitants had turkeys and made robes of their feathers.

Archeologists have provided much information on the probable time when the turkey was domesticated.[1] Amsden (1949:131) states that the domestic turkey has not been found outside of the range of the wild Merriam's turkey from which it descended. He adds that it has not been found at the Basket-Maker and early Pueblo sites in the hot arid lowlands of Nevada nor in the similar environment of the Hohokam territory of southern Arizona. This is only partially true. The Hohokam culture began about the time of Christ and centered on the Salt and middle Gila rivers. Although the tribe was well within the range of the wild turkey, so few turkey bones have been found that decidedly limited usage is indicated. The Basket Makers were concentrated where the state of Utah, Colorado, Arizona, and New Mexico join. Although turkey-feather blankets have been found in their graves, these may have been made from the wild birds since turkey pens and dung are absent from Basket-Maker sites.

The earliest appearance of turkeys is reported by Martin *et al.* (1952:483) for the Pine Lawn Phase (*ca.* 150 B.C. ± 160 years to *ca.* 500 A.D. by carbon 14 dating) in Tularosa Cave near Reserve, New Mexico. On tracing the history of a desiccated turkey (Plate 1) on exhibit at Mesa Verde, I was informed by Paul A. Berger, superintendent of the Canyon de Chelly National Monument, Arizona, that the specimen was found in 1947 in a Basket-Maker cave near the mouth of Canyon del Muerto. It was estimated to be about seventeen hundred years old (250 A.D.). During the modified Basket-Maker period (*ca.* 500–700 A.D.), turkeys were kept in captivity in northeastern Arizona and northwestern New Mexico and were very probably domesticated. These birds were definitely domes-ticated during Pueblo I (*ca.* 700–900 A.D.). Turkeys were not domesticated during the Hohokam culture of central and southern Arizona (Martin, Quimby, and Collier, 1947:171, 202). The Mogollon-Mimbres people had turkeys, but whether wild or domesticated is uncertain.

[1] It is possible that the turkey was tamed rather than domesticated. A domesti-cated animal conforms readily to an alien environment while, with a tamed one, some restraint is necessary.

There is considerable difficulty in dating the various cultures, so agreement among writers is not to be expected. Where structural timbers are available, dating by the growth rings is far more reliable than by the carbon 14 method. The type of pottery found is frequently used for dating. According to McGregor (1941:234, 248, 266), turkeys were domesticated by the Basket Maker III people, 500–700 A.D., in the San Juan River area, north of Kayenta, Arizona. During Pueblo I, 700–900 A.D., turkeys were certainly domesticated, as they probably were also during Pueblo II and III, 900–1100 A.D. The turkey appears in the earliest ceramic levels of the Mimbres phase of the Mogollon culture (*ca.* 1090 A.D.) in southwestern New Mexico and southeastern Arizona (Wheat, 1955:157). It is represented frequently on the pottery. So few bones of the bird have been unearthed that domestication was very unlikely. The domestication of the turkey is placed by Morris (1939:120) as far back as middle Basket Maker III. Bones of the turkey are found in the refuse deposits of Pueblo III. According to Wormington (1947:55, 70), turkey feathers were utilized during the modified Basket-Maker period (400–700 A.D.), but it is not certain that turkeys were then domesticated; however, during the developmental Pueblo period (700–1100 A.D.), turkeys and dogs were domesticated.

It has been stated that the Indians allowed their turkeys to run loose about their villages (Plate 2). I find nothing in the early literature in substantiation. Hough (1903:356) wrote: "The writer has copied numerous pictographs in the valley of the Little Colorado River [Arizona] showing unmistakably the herding of turkeys and deer by men." There certainly was no herding of deer. The pictographs undoubtedly represented hunting drives which so many of the Indian races were accustomed to make. Hodge (1912: II, 321) states that there is evidence that large flocks of turkeys were herded as are sheep and goats in the present day. It is also said that the Queres at Laguna and Acoma formerly had large flocks of turkeys which were herded (Gunn, 1917:26). Bandelier and Hewett (1937:36) thought that domesticated wild turkeys were "allowed to run loose about the villages." Charles C. Mason, who was one of the first to dig in the ruins of Mesa Verde, inferred that the turkeys were at liberty during the day (McNitt, 1957:326). He wrote: "Almost every house has its turkey pen in which the birds were probably fastened at night." There may have been some freedom within the village, but little beyond its walls.

The pueblos were so subject to raids by Navahos and Apaches that all possessions, except growing crops, were kept within the walls. It would have been impossible to herd the turkeys away from the pueblos and return them to safety at night because of physical barriers. Access to the houses built in caves and on mesas was frequently to be had only by scaling a nearly vertical wall. Acoma at the time of its discovery had many turkeys. The entire mesa has an area of about seventy acres, cleft by a canyon. The southern portion of the mesa was never built upon. Prior to 1629 the only trail to the top of the northern section was on the northwest side. Here the Ladder Trail consisted of finger and toe holes cut in the rock (Sedgwick, 1926:28). The pueblos built on more or less level ground had no openings in the walls of the first story.

The only privilege, apparently, that the turkeys had was close confinement. Judd (1925:241) was close to the truth when he wrote that in pre-Spanish days at Pueblo Bonito the "imprisoned turkeys begged crumbs and sunflower seeds." There is confirmation in the statement of Gallegos (1927:26) regarding San Miguel: "There is not an Indian who does not have his *corral* in which he keeps his turkeys. Each one holds a flock of one hundred birds." When the Spanish soldiers entered the pueblo of Malagón, the Indians threw dead turkeys down the corridors to them. Although the turkeys were in the pueblo at the time, there is the possibility that they were brought in because the Spaniards were in the neighborhood. Numerous turkey pens have been found within the confines of the villages. Here the droppings of the birds accumulated to a considerable depth. The deposits contained feathers and fragments of egg shells. Some pens had nests made of adobe.

Confirmation of confinement has been attained recently (Schorger, 1961). I have examined a turkey found by W. Hough in Tularosa Cave near Reserve, New Mexico, in 1905. The specimen dates back to at least 1100 A.D. The contents of the crop consisted of 190 cc. of corn kernels perfect in shape except for attack by insects. It is to be assumed that the inhabitants abandoned the cave suddenly, leaving the confined bird to die of thirst. A sick turkey would not have eaten the corn. Dung from the cave contained large amounts of leguminous starch. Some dung collected at the turkey pen at Balcony House, Mesa Verde, contained remains of corn and a legume in quantity. It must be concluded that the turkeys were held in confinement and fed corn and beans.

The extensiveness of the deposits of dung was first brought to the attention of archeologists by the young Swedish nobleman, Baron Nordenskjöld (1893:95). In 1891 with the assistance of the Wetherill brothers, he examined some of the ruins in Mesa Verde National Park. He wrote: "Several circumstances lead us to the conclusion that the cliff-dwellers kept some bird, probably the turkey, in a domesticated state. Huge layers of excrement occur in the open space already mentioned on several occasions, which lies at the back of the cave in the more extensive cliff-dwellings. At Step House, where these deposits lay beside the ruin, their depth was 0.6–2 m., their breadth 13 m. and their length 40 m. In this instance the entire mass of turkey droppings mixed with all kinds of refuse probably contains between 200 and 300 cubic m., a quantity which must have taken a long time to collect. The brothers Wetherill, who are experienced ranchers, consider these excrements, which are in a very good state of preservation, to be turkey droppings. That this bird occupied an important place in the domestic economy of the cliff-dwellers is shown by the fact that most of the bone awls are made of turkey bones. This bird probably supplied the down of which the so-called feather cloth or rather down cloth, was made, for the material consists of the humeral quill coverts of a gallinaceous bird." In the back of Cliff Palace and other ruins, during their restoration, excrement of turkeys to a depth of several feet was encountered.

Merriam's turkey, like the other "white rumped" races, appears to have offered no particular difficulty to domestication. It should be stated, however, that there is no proof that the turkey being raised was identical with Merriam's turkey. In 1716, Velarde (1931:129) wrote concerning the Sobaipuris and other Pimas living in southern Arizona that "they raise chickens of Castile (there are countless turkey in the mountains, although they are easy to domesticate)." In spite of the abundance of the wild turkey in the territory of the Pimas, they never domesticated the bird. Manje's statement that in some places in southern Arizona there were thousands of turkeys, known as "chickens of the Indias," must refer to the wild birds (Karns, 1954:238). The number of turkeys to be found varied with the time and place. Escalante (1871:148) was with the Rodríquez expedition of 1581. Beginning with the first pueblos on the Río Grande, they went upstream fifty leagues and passed sixty-one pueblos. Turkeys were raised at the pueblos, but whether at every one is

23

not stated specifically. The abundance of domesticated turkeys in New Mexico is mentioned often. Benavides (1945:39) asserted that in 1630 the number was limitless.

The raising of turkeys fell to a minimum at the beginning of the nineteenth century. Barreiro (1832:21) remarked that although there was in New Mexico an infinite number of wild turkeys, called *gallinas de la tierra*, few people hunted them and no one was interested in capturing and domesticating them for propagation. In 1849, according to J. A. de Escudero, there was still little hunting of turkeys (Carroll and Haggard, 1942:99). Gregg (1844: I, 191), in the 1830's, found domestic fowls scarce except for chickens. He doubted if there were more than half a dozen turkeys in the territory. Some were seen at the Zuñi Pueblo in 1853 by Möllhausen (1858: II, 98).

The places where the Spaniards found turkeys being raised will be shown on accompanying maps. Included are archeological sites where turkey pens and bones have been found. It is impossible, when only individual bones of the turkey are found, to determine if they belonged to the wild or domesticated bird.

ARIZONA

Since the Anasazis domesticated the turkey and the Hohokams did not, remains of the turkey are usually absent in the southern half of Arizona (Fig. 2) (Roberts, 1939:14). Haury (1945:160) failed to find turkey bones at Los Muertos, about twelve miles southeast of Phoenix. He thought the place too far out of the bird's range. Negative results were also obtained at Ventana Cave, Papago Indian Reservation, Pima County (Haury, 1950:160). No turkey bones were found at the Babocomari site on the Babocomari River, twelve miles west by southwest of Fairbank, Cochise County (Di Peso, 1951:14).

Turkey pens and the skeleton of a turkey were found in Tseahatso Cave, Canyon del Muerto, just east of Chinle, Apache County (Morris, 1933:196–97). In Painted Cave (36° 33′ N, 109° 15′ W), Haury (1945.1:26) found a turkey pen with a nest and three eggs. The specimen found in 1947 in a cave in the Canyon del Muerto has been mentioned.

During excavations in the Whitewater district eight miles southwest of Lupton, Roberts (1939:118, 230; 1940:112, 126, 134) found plentiful remains of the turkey. It is doubtful if the bird was eaten since most of

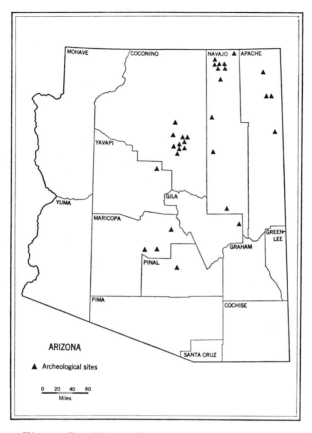

Fig. 2—*Localities where remains of turkeys were found in Arizona.*

the finds were articulated skeletons which had been buried, at times with children. One child was buried with a turkey on one side and a dog on the other. Roberts suggests that these were possibly pets. Regarding turkey pens he wrote (1939:118): "The fill in house 13a indicated that the pit had not been used as a habitation for some time previous to the construction of 13b. On the floor was a thick layer of turkey droppings. Several broken eggs were found near the north post and the skeleton of one bird was lying near the center of the chamber. This indicates that the enclosure was used as a turkey pen."

No proof for the domestication of the turkey in the Flagstaff region,

Coconino County, has been found. Bones of the deer and turkey were discovered in the middens at the Elden Pueblo, six miles from Flagstaff (Hargrave, 1929:1). Turkey bones were also found at the following localities in the Flagstaff area: one bone at Medicine Cave, ten miles northeast of Flagstaff; one at Wupatki Pueblo, twenty-eight miles northeast of Flagstaff; two at Grand Falls, thirty miles northeast of Flagstaff; one at Winona village, twelve miles east of Flagstaff; two at Walnut Canyon, ten miles southeast of Flagstaff; and one at Baker's Bluff, twenty miles north of Flagstaff (Hargrave, 1939:208). Owing to their small number, the bones were probably from the wild bird.

Perfectly preserved tarsi, dating from 1000 to 1100 A.D. were found in dwellings thirty-five miles north of Flagstaff (Miller, 1932). Five bones of the turkey were unearthed at two sites a short distance northeast of Winona, fourteen miles east of Flagstaff (McGregor, 1941.1:258). There is a rather vague statement of the finding of a turkey during excavations at Cinder Park, twenty-one miles northeast of Flagstaff (De Laguna, 1942:56). Since the bird is said to have been killed for its feathers and not eaten, it is to be assumed that an articulated skeleton was found. No bones were found during the excavations at Nalakihu, a Pueblo III site, at the foot of Citadel Butte (King, 1949:141). There was no evidence of turkeys having been domesticated in the Pueblo III cliff dwellings in northeastern Arizona. Wild turkeys were abundant, but their bones have not been found. The scarcity of refuse about Pueblo II sites in the San Francisco Mountains may be the reason for the absence of remains, but two bone whistles found may have been made from the bones of this bird (Bartlett, 1934:68). No bones of the turkey were found during excavations in Big Hawk Valley, Wupatki National Monument, thirty miles north by northeast of Flagstaff (Smith, 1952.1:183). Trees are absent here.

Awls made from turkey bones were found at the prehistoric pueblo of Kinishba, Gila County, four miles west of Fort Apache (Cummings, 1940:64, 65).

A few bones of the turkey were found in the refuse heaps at Snaketown, Maricopa County, a Pima settlement twelve miles southwest of Chandler (Gladwin et al., 1937:156, 157). The scarcity of these bones indicates that the turkey was not domesticated. Turkey bones were found frequently during excavations at the cave and cliff dwellings in the valleys of the Verde and Salinas rivers (Mearns, 1896:397).

The first mention of domestic turkeys in Arizona was during the Coronado expedition in 1540. Reports of pueblos at Tusayan, Navajo County, having been received, Pedro de Tovar and Fray Juan de Padilla were sent to investigate. Castañeda reported: "The people of the whole district came together that day and submitted themselves...." They gave him some dressed skins and cornmeal, and pine nuts and corn and birds of the country (*abes de la tierra*) (Winship, 1896:489). Tusayan was the area occupied by the Hopis or Moquis. Regarding the Espejo expedition in 1582–83, Aranda (1871:120) reported that there were no turkeys at Aguato (Awatovi), a now extinct pueblo about nine miles southeast of Walpi. Numerous remains of the turkey have been found in the northern part of the county. Not one identifiable turkey feather was found in the Basket-Maker caves near Kayenta, Navajo County (Guernsey and Kidder, 1921:44). Evidently, the turkey was not then domesticated and was seldom hunted. Remains of the turkey were found at two sites in Segi (Tsegi) Canyon, ten miles west by north of Kayenta. Bones were found in the lower Segi, while Turkey Cave was so named from the "enormous amounts of turkey droppings in the refuse" (Guernsey, 1931:21, 57).

Turkey bones were found at several other pueblos in the northern part of the county (Hargrave, 1939:208). One bone was found at Betatakin Pueblo, fifteen miles southwest of Kayenta; seventy-seven at Kiet Siel (Keet Seel), fifteen miles west by north of Kayenta; three at Turkey Cave; seven at Kacody Pueblo; and one at Awatobi Pueblo, fifty-eight miles north of Winslow. The large number of bones found at Kiet Siel is weighty evidence that the people living in the Kayenta area around 1300 A.D. had domestic turkeys. While exploring Kiet Siel in 1895, Richard Wetherill noted on the ceiling of the cave a painting showing three turkeys perched on the heads of as many men (McNitt, 1957:82).

Some ruins in the valley of Laguna Creek, a few miles west of Kayenta, were examined by Kidder and Guernsey (1919:39, 52), who stated regarding Ruin 4: "Thirty feet eastward from the kiva, and, like it set against the cliff, there was found a grass-lined hollow 18 inches in diameter and one foot deep, surrounded on three sides of a square by a wattled fence. This last was burned off at the old ground level, so that its former height could not be determined. It was suggested by Clayton Wetherill that this might have been a nest for setting turkey hens. He informs us that nests very similar to this one, sometimes containing egg-shells, were found by him and his brothers in the Mesa Verde ruins. Although no bits of shell were recovered here, there were some turkey droppings and feathers in and about the inclosure; not more, however, than were found in the general digging throughout the cave." Turkey nests were found in Ruin 7. A hollow had been formed in the rubbish and faced with adobe to form a cavity about eight inches deep and twelve inches in diameter. There were more than the usual quantities of feathers and droppings about these nests. So many bones were found that the conclusion was drawn that the birds were kept for food as well as for making feather blankets.

In 1895, Fewkes (1898:627, 733) found artifacts of turkey bones at ruins in the Jeditoh Valley, Antelope Mesa, and necklaces of turkey bones at the Sikyati ruin. W. Hough (1903:356) stated that the bones of dogs and turkeys were found in nearly every Hopi ruin. The numerous mural decorations on the kivas at the ancient Hopi pueblos of Awatovi and Kawaika-a were studied by Watson Smith (1952). I do not believe that any of the bird illustrations unquestionably represent the turkey. These pueblos are on the southern edge of Antelope Mesa, about six miles east of Keams Canyon.

Many turkey bones, including those from young birds, as well as artifacts of turkey bones were found at the pueblo ruins three miles from Winslow (Fewkes, 1904:27, 94, 110). A bone of a turkey was found during excavations in the Forestdale Valley, extreme southern part of Navajo County, twenty miles west of Cooley (Haury, 1940:15, 16). The site was dated as the seventh century A.D. The single bone indicates that turkeys were not domesticated at the time and that the wild birds were seldom utilized.

Judd (1930:62) has reported finding at Betatakin an awl made from the tibiotarsus of a turkey, and a humerus from which the condyles had been removed. A cave (36° 55′ N, 110° 8′ W) in Hagoe Canyon, a tributary of Gypsum Wash, Monument Valley, was examined by Kidder (1917:110) who stated that the turkey was domesticated. On the time scale, the culture appears to be between the Basket Makers and the later Cliff Dwellers. At ruins in the Segi Canyon drainage area, egg shells, apparently from the turkey, were found (Beals *et al.*, 1945:36, 46). One burial included a turkey beside a man. The bones of the turkey were in an articulated position, and gravel from the crop was found in its proper place. Feathers of the turkey were found in Woodchuck Cave, a Basket Maker II site. The latter lies northeast of Betatakin in Water Lily Canyon, a branch of Degozhi Canyon which connects with Segi Canyon (Lockett and Hargrave, 1953:20, 30). The feathers were thought to have been from the wild bird since the domesticated turkey was believed to be unknown for Basket Maker II period.

Turkey bones were found by Di Peso (1958:115) in the trash at the Reeve Ruin near Redington, Pima County. There was no evidence that the Reeve people penned or otherwise domesticated the turkey.

Among the bones found at Casa Grande (33° N, 111° 35′ W), Pinal County, were those of the antelope, turkey, rabbit, and bear (Fewkes, 1912:146). A perforated tube, probably used as a whistle, was made from a turkey bone.

Fewkes (1898:627, 733) found awls made from the leg bones of the turkey in Yavapai County at the ruins of Palatki and Honanki, twenty-five miles southwest of Flagstaff. The Tuzigoot ruin on the Verde River near Clarkdale did not yield any turkey bones (Caywood and Spicer, 1935:93). This is an indication that turkeys were neither raised nor hunted.

COLORADO

Pre-Columbian remains of the turkey are limited to the southwestern corner of the state (Fig. 3) and are most numerous in Montezuma County. Excavations in the Piedra River area, Archuleta County, yielded a few identifiable bones of the turkey (Roberts, 1930:144). Most of the awls found at an excavation about ten miles west by south of Red Mesa, La Plata County, were made from the tibiae of turkeys (Morris, 1939:120, 123). Beads and tubes made from turkey bones were also found.

The cliff dwellings of the Mesa Verde National Park, most of which lie in the southern part of Montezuma County, have been particularly productive of remains of the turkey. According to Chapin (1892:149),

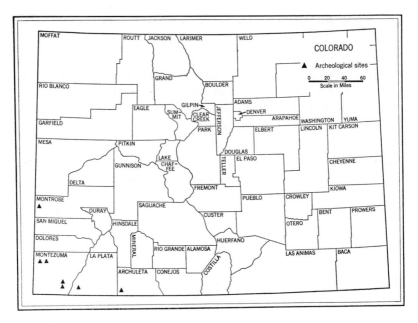

Fig. 3.—*Localities where remains of turkeys were found in Colorado.*

there was on the wall of a ruin in Navajo Canyon a crude picture representing two turkeys fighting. Navajo Canyon runs north and south near the center of the park.

Regarding excavations in the Mesa Verde National Park, O'Bryan (1950:101) wrote: "Turkey bones were plentiful in all ruins, with the exception of Site 145. In the villages at Sites 102 and 1, only turkey burials were found, no turkey bone implements or scattered bones; probably the birds were kept only for their feathers. A few stray turkey bones were recovered from the pueblos at Sites 102 and 1, a single awl from the first-mentioned ruin. The commonest type of awl from Site 34 was made from the upper portion of a turkey tibiotarsus." The refuse heaps in the Spruce Tree Cliff ruin in the Mesa Verde National Park contained many turkey bones (Fewkes, 1909:4, 7). The abundance of turkey guano at places in the cave shows where the turkeys were kept.

Martin (1929:8) investigated the ruins in Townships 38 and 39, Ranges 18 and 19 west. Those in Little Cow Canyon were named "Turkey House Ruins because of the number of pictographs of turkeys and men wearing what appeared to be turkey masks." The ruins on the north rim of Ruin Canyon, Township 38 north, Range 19 west, yielded bones of the turkey, deer, and quail, and awls made from the bones of the turkey (Martin, 1930:4, 39). Awls made from turkey bones were found also at the Lowry ruin nine miles west of Ackmen (Martin *et al.*, 1936:69).

At Mesa Verde on June 17, 1960, Dr. Douglas Osborne showed me a turkey (Plate 3) found buried beside a child in Long House the summer of 1959. It is an immature bird in an excellent state of preservation. The complete defeathering was attributed to dermestids. A second specimen, less well preserved, was found in the same cave.

Alice Hunt (1953:178) found a pendant 4.5 cm. in length, probably made from the leg bone of a turkey, at the Fremont dwelling site, La Sal Mountain area. She has informed me that the site is just inside Montrose County.

NEVADA

The Indians of Nevada apparently did not have domestic turkeys. No bones of this bird were found at two localities in Clark County, Pueblo Grande de Nevada (Lost City) near St. Thomas (Harrington, 1927:272), and the Virgin River site near Logandale (Harrington, 1930:12).

NEW MEXICO

New Mexico, because of the large number of pueblos near fertile soil, had the greatest number of domestic turkeys (Fig. 4). There are many general references in the Spanish literature to the abundance of turkeys and maize at the pueblos. It is advisable to mention that many of the Spanish texts are corrupt in places. This applies particularly to *Colección de documentos inéditos* by Pacheco and Cárdenas. Superior, though limited in scope, is *Colección de varios documentos para la historia de la Florida y tierras adjacentes* by Buckingham Smith. Some of the English translations are misleading and confusing. For example, Castañeda wrote: "*Auia en estas prouincias grā cantidad de gallinas de la tierra y gallos de papada sustenabanse muertos sin pelar ni abrir sesenta dias sin mal olor.*" Winship's (1896:521) translation is: "There are a great many native fowl in these provinces, and cocks with great hanging chins. When dead, these keep for sixty days, and longer in winter, without losing their feathers or opening, and without any bad smell." The passage should

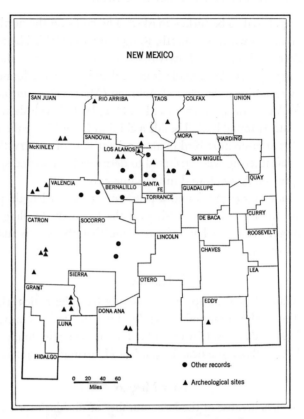

NEW MEXICO

Fig. 4.—*Localities where remains of turkeys were found in New Mexico.*

read: "There were in these provinces a great many turkey hens and cocks with throat-wattles, which, without plucking or drawing, could be kept after death for sixty days without a bad odor."

The Tigua pueblos extended up the Río Grande from Isleta to Bernalillo. The Tiguas called the turkey *dire* (Gallegos, 1927:28). At one of the Tigua pueblos, Bernalillo County, the Espejo expedition found provisions, including turkeys, abundant (Luxán, 1929:79).

Information on the domestication of the turkey in Catron County is entirely archeological. Turkey bones were comparatively common in the rubbish at the Mogollon village site, ten miles north of Glenwood (Haury, 1936:6, 93). Martin and his associates (1940:76; 1943:235)

32

have excavated several sites in the Apache National Forest, west of Reserve. The SU site yielded some turkey bones in 1939, and twenty fragments of bones from at least five individuals in 1941. Subsequent work at the site yielded additional bones (Martin and Rinaldo, 1947:288, 358). Eight fragments in all were found in houses on Turkey Foot Ridge, and also in caves (Martin *et al.*, 1949:176; Martin and Rinaldo, 1950:350). Through 1950 the Pine Lawn area yielded 419 fragments of unworked turkey bones (Martin and Rinaldo, 1950.1:492; Martin *et al.*, 1954:155). There was no concrete evidence of domestication of this bird. The Sawmill Site (Sec. 14, T7S, R20W) in Pine Lawn Valley yielded five fragments of bones of the turkey (Bluhm, 1957:67).

The best evidence for the domestication of the turkey was obtained by Hough (1914:5, 72). Tularosa Cave, on Tularosa Creek near Reserve, contained at one end a pen where were found a desiccated adult turkey, desiccated poults, and eggs. Droppings of the birds were present in great quantity. Subsequently, Martin *et al.* (1952:456) found loose and tied turkey feathers in Tularosa and Córdova caves. He thinks that turkeys appeared in the Pine Lawn Phase several centuries earlier than in the Anasazi culture, late Basket-Maker times.

Conkling Cavern, at Bishop's Cap, twelve miles southeast of Las Cruces, Doña Ana County, yielded two bones of the turkey (Conkling, 1932:18). Howard and Miller (1933:16) state that Conkling Cavern lies on the eastern slope of Pyramid Peak, and Shelter Cave on the western. Bones of the turkey were found in both caves. Whether the deposits were Pleistocene or Recent was not determinable.

Burnet Cave, Rocky Arroyo, Eddy County, lies on the eastern slope of the Guadalupe Mountains west of Carlsbad. Among the bones excavated were the metatarsal and metacarpal of the turkey (Wetmore, 1932:8; E. B. Howard, 1932:10; Schultz and Howard, 1936:277).

The site of the Cameron Creek village, Grant County, two miles northwest of Hurley and two miles directly south of Central, yielded bones of the deer, rabbit, and wild turkey (Bradfield, 1931:11). Implements made from turkey bones were found at a site two miles south of Mimbres (Nesbitt, 1931:92). A recovered bowl has a fair representation of a turkey, while another shows an antelope with the spread tail of a turkey. Turkey bones were found also at the Harris village site, one-fourth mile east of Mimbres (Haury, 1936:6, 93). The Swarts Ruin lies on the

Mimbres River about midway between Mattocks and the Luna County line. Since only the fragment of a tarsometatarsus was found in the ruin, it appears that the turkey was not used for food (Cosgrove and Cosgrove, 1932:4). Remains of the turkey were not found by Cosgrove (1947:46) in Greenwood, Steamboat, Dove Mountain, or Doolittle caves. This was considered evidence that the Basket Makers did not use the bird.

Coronado (1896:559) in 1540 arrived at Hawikuh, McKinley County, the first of the Seven Cities of Cibola entered by the Spaniards. Actually, there were only six pueblos, which lay within a radius of ten miles. They are commonly known as the Zuñi pueblos. Hawikuh lies twelve miles southwest of present Zuñi. On August 3, Coronado wrote to Mendoza: "We found fowls, but only a few, and yet there are some. The Indians tell me that they do not eat these in any of the seven villages, but keep them merely for the sake of procuring the feathers. I do not believe this, because they are very good and better than those of Mexico." This is a translation by Winship of an Italian version by Ramusio (1606:302), the original letter having been lost. The word *maggiori* should have been translated *larger*, not *better*.

An anonymous companion of Coronado wrote in a similar vein of Cibola: "For food they have an abundance of maize . . . [and] some turkeys like those of Mexico, which they keep more for their feathers than for eating as they make robes of them since they do not have cotton" (Anon., 1870:320). Bandelier (1892:48) has translated *gallinas de las de Mexico*, "fowl obtained from Mexico," which cannot be correct. Another writer (Anon., 1873:532) stated that Cibola (Hawikuh) had much corn, beans, and turkeys.

The inhabitants of Hawikuh, during the Espejo expedition (1583), presented *tortillas*, turkeys, and rabbits (Obregón, 1924:292). Oñate (Bolton, 1916:235), during his stay at the pueblo in 1598, noted that the inhabitants were offering turkey feathers to their idols, showing that turkeys were still being raised. Apparently, the few turkeys found by the Spaniards were kept mainly for their feathers for religious purposes, and hares and rabbits furnished the main sources of meat and skins for the fur blankets.

The mortar used in constructing a wall of Kiva I near Hawikuh contained some leg bones of the turkey as well as gravel from the gizzard. There is no explanation for this unusual placement. Regarding Kiva II,

Hodge (1923:26) wrote: "Immediately beneath the floor of the domicile ... were some turkey bones and the small gravelly contents of a gizzard. ... So highly regarded was the turkey by the Zuñi that a skeleton of this bird was found in the cemetery of Hawikuh accompanied with an earthenware food vessel, the remains having been deposited in much the same manner as the human interments surrounding it." Numerous artifacts of turkey bones, beads, "bird callers," and awls were found at Hawikuh (Hodge, 1920:79, 121, 127).

The village of the Great Kivas lies about twenty miles northeast of Zuñi. A long narrow corridor, containing the skeleton of a turkey, was believed by Roberts (1932:47) to have served as a turkey pen. He wrote: "The most satisfactory explanation for the long, narrow corridor desig- nated 13 is that it may have functioned as a pen for keeping turkeys. There was plentiful evidence around the village that the people had had considerable numbers of such fowl, and the birds may on occasion have been confined in an enclosure of this kind. Beyond the fact that the skeleton of a turkey was found in it, the place itself gave no indication that it had functioned in that capacity. ... Pens of this kind, stone walls, and brush tops, are not unknown among the present Pueblos, and may well have been employed in the past."

Jeançon (1923:25, 27, 68) excavated the Po-shu adobe ruin near Abiquiu, Rio Arriba County. It is located on the southern side of the Chama River, twenty-two and a half miles above the junction of this stream with the Río Grande. Aside from artifacts of turkey bones, frag- ments of egg shells were numerous. One egg was almost entire and still contained the yolk. Many pieces of pottery were found with fragments of egg shells adhering to them. The author considers the eggs to have been from the wild bird, but this is open to doubt. A large number of sites in Governador Wash in San Juan and Rio Arriba counties were examined by Hall (1944:28, 78). Most of the ruins are in northwestern Rio Arriba County. The turkey was represented by 273 bones, identified by Dr. Alexander Wetmore. A human burial place contained three skulls of dogs and an apparently articulated skeleton of a turkey.

Shufeldt (1914:13) examined the turkey bones, including twelve crania, found at Puyé in 1907 by E. L. Hewett. He thought that all the bones represented at least fifty individuals. The bones were found in association with human remains in an old burying ground. It is probable that the turkeys were interred with the dead. Puyé lies ten miles west of Espanola.

The Queres pueblos in the eastern part of Sandoval County were visited by the Espejo expedition in 1583. Luxán (1929:79, 81, 83, 85, 117) mentions that while members of the expedition were still among the Tigua Indians, people from eight or ten leagues up the river came with presents of turkeys. Among the Queres, nearly every pueblo seems to have contributed the birds, Cochiti and Sia being specifically mentioned. Cochiti was on the west bank of the Río Grande, twenty-three miles southwest of Santa Fe. Sia was on the Río de las Vacas, sixteen miles northwest of Bernalillo. The pueblo of La Tiete (not located), in the province of the Queres, provided many turkeys. Espejo (1871:113) mentions the province of the Tigua, which contained sixteen pueblos, one of them being Pualas (Puaray), at present Bernalillo. The Spaniards entered this pueblo, from which the inhabitants had fled, and found much maize, beans, pumpkins, and many turkeys. In 1598 the pueblos near Puaray still had great flocks of turkeys (Villagrá, 1933:169).

Bones of the turkey were found in Jemez Cave, six miles north of Jemez Springs, by Alexander and Reiter (1935:35). Concerning a pre-Spanish site seven miles south of Los Alamos, in the canyon of the Rito de Los Frijoles, Hendron (1946) wrote: "To the side of the dwellings, situated near the back wall of the cave, was a turkey pen of little cleanliness. When I discovered this pen hundreds of years later, the floor was covered with human feces, turkey, and rodent droppings."

The Pueblo Indian civilization reached its peak in Chaco Canyon, San Juan County. The canyon is approximately thirty miles long. The houses had been abandoned long before the arrival of the Spaniards. The numerous ruins have yielded remains of the domesticated turkey. The bones of this bird represented 8.7 per cent of all of the animal bones found at the small pueblo of Tseh So, about fifty miles northeast of Gallup. With one exception, the turkey bones were found associated with human burials. Complete skeletons were found except that the heads were missing. Also found were fragments of egg shells, and awls made from the tibiae of turkeys. The region is at present devoid of oak and piñon pine mast, and the inference is that the turkeys were originally imported (Brand et al., 1937:94, 101, 106). The vegetation of the canyon is known to have deteriorated markedly; also, if the Indians raised corn, as they certainly did, turkeys could have been kept. The presence of egg shells indicate that the birds were raised locally. Bones and fragments of egg shells were also found at the ruin of Leyit Kin (Dutton, 1938:36, 48, 55). Bones and egg shells of the turkey were prominent in all the kivas at Sites Bc 50–51, which are within one half of a mile of Pueblo Bonito. Bones were also found in the refuse heaps. There was no evidence of burial of the birds (Kluckhohn *et al.*, 1939:148, 150).

The famous Pueblo Bonito has been extensively explored. It is located in Chaco Canyon at approximately 36° N, 108° W. This pueblo originated in the ninth or early tenth century and was abandoned about 1100 A.D. Here Pepper (1909:245) found smooth pieces of chalcedony believed to have come from the gizzard of a turkey. Feathers of the bird were also found (Pepper, 1920:109). The extensive investigations by Judd (1954:66, 72, 140) at this pueblo leave no doubt that the turkey was domesticated. Egg shells and many bones were found. In the refuse heaps, unworked bones were conspicuous. The bones were used extensively for making awls. The tibiotarsus was usually selected, but the tarsometatarsus, radius, and ulna were also utilized. Individual bones, incomplete skeletons, and awls made from turkey bones were found at Pueblo Arroyo (Judd, 1959:62, 126, 127). This pueblo is approximately one-half mile west of Pueblo Bonito. The structural timbers date from 1052–1117 A.D.

The Pecos ruin lies about one and a half miles northeast of Rowe, San Miguel County. It was founded about 1350. A member of the Coronado expedition stated that the people of Cicuique (Pecos) did not raise either cotton or turkeys since the buffalo country lay only fifteen leagues to the eastward (Anon., 1857:150). The buffalo supplied both food and clothing. This may have been a temporary condition. Later, 1582–83, Aranda (1871:122) reported that the Ubates (Tanos) had five pueblos where the Spaniards were given provisions, including turkeys. The archeological investigations of Kidder (1932:195, 196, 217) at Pecos revealed many turkey bones as well as awls and flutes made from them. A ruin on Tecolote Creek, about ten miles south by west of Las Vegas, contained numerous broken bones of the buffalo, deer, antelope, and turkey (Holden, 1931:48).

In Santa Fe County, the Rodríguez expedition found four Tano pueblos in the Galisteo Valley: Malpartida, Malagón, Piedrahita (Piedra

Ita), and Galisteo, all within short distances of each other. The inhabitants of Piedrahita were intimidated into furnishing supplies, and their example was followed by the other pueblos. Gallegos (1927:38, 39) wrote: "Together with the supply of corn and flour which they had given us they gave us large numbers of turkeys, for they have large flocks of them and do not value them highly." The inhabitants of Malagón having killed three of the Spanish horses, five soldiers entered the pueblo seeking redress: "To placate us they threw many dead turkeys down the corridors to us, but we decided not to take them that they might know we were angry." This had the desired effect for the following day Malagónians appeared in the Spanish camp with supplies, including many turkeys. Meacham (1926:283) identifies Malagón with the ruined pueblo, San Lázaro, twelve miles southwest of Lamy. Espejo (1871:122) went twelve leagues east of the Queres into the province of the Ubates, who had five pueblos well provided with food such as turkeys and maize. This must have been the group of pueblos mentioned by Gallegos. Hodge (1912: II, 686) identifies the Ubates with the Tanos and their pueblos in southern Santa Fe County, and mentions San Lázaro as one of them. Their principal village was Ximena, present Galisteo. Twitchell (1911:282) thinks that the pueblos of the Ubates lay north of Santa Fe.

Turkeys, according to Whitman (1940:401), were once raised for their feathers at San Ildefonso, a Tewa pueblo twenty-two miles northwest of Santa Fe. The Pindi pueblo in the village of Agua Fria, six miles south of Santa Fe, yielded turkey bones in such abundance that there can be no doubt that the birds were used for food as well as for their feathers. No site in the Río Grande Valley is known to have contained as many bones. The outlines of the original turkey pens could be traced. Here the fill consisted of soft, yellowish, decomposed turkey droppings and wind-blown sand (Stubbs and Stallings, 1953:47, 126).

Turkeys were first mentioned as occurring in the pueblos of the lower Río Grande by the Fray Agustín Rodríguez expedition under the command of Francisco Sánchez, commonly called Chamuscado. According to the testimony given by Piedro de Bustamente (1871:84), a soldier in the expedition, they entered the province of San Felipe in 1581. Here was a group of pueblos belonging to the Piros Indians. The inhabitants of the first occupied pueblo, San Marcial, Socorro County, gave them maize, turkeys, and other supplies. Proceeding up the river, they found numerous pueblos where there were many fields of maize, beans, and pumpkins, and many turkeys were raised. The Gallegos (1927:24) relation adds that the Piros fled from San Miguel (San Marcial) and in their houses was found an abundance of turkeys, cotton, and corn. The expedition marched four days through the Piros territory that contained large numbers of turkeys.

The Espejo expedition, in February, 1583, arrived at or near San Marcial. Luxán (1929:72) wrote: "Most of them have especially for sleeping, quilts made from feathers of turkeys because they raise cocks and hens in quantities. The women wear their hair tied to the head and cover their privy parts and body with cotton blankets and tanned deerskins, and above these their feather quilts in place of cloaks." All the Piros pueblos provided turkeys.

Turkeys were not raised at Yurabi (Taos), Taos County, according to an anonymous member of the Coronado expedition (Anon., 1857:150). On the other hand Jaramillo (1857:309) states that at Taos there were robes made of feathers, presumably turkey, like those at the other pueblos. These may have been made from the wild birds or obtained in trade.

Bones of the turkey were found in deposits north and south of Taos, and since associated with the bones and hair of deer, must have been recent. Formerly, turkeys were not kept in the pueblo, but are now bred by one family there (Parsons, 1936:20, 23).

The inhabitants of Acoma (34° 54' N, 107° 35' W), Valencia County, were of Keresan stock. This famous pueblo could be reached in 1540 only by ascending three hundred steps cut in the rock and finally climbing a vertical wall twelve feet high by means of holes cut for the hands and feet. Alvarado (1857:65) thought it one of the strongest places that he had seen and regretted that the ascent had been made. The inhabitants were well supplied with maize, beans, and fowls (turkeys) like those of New Spain. A member (Anon., 1857:150) of the Coronado expedition wrote that the Spaniards were given cotton mantles, skins of deer and buffalo, turquoises, and turkeys. Castañeda (Winship, 1896:521) adds that the inhabitants provided a great number of large turkey cocks with wattles.

During the Espejo (1871:117) expedition, the Spaniards were also given large supplies of maize and turkeys. The cultivated, irrigated fields of the Indians were two leagues from the mesa. In December, 1598, Zaldívar and ten companions were killed at Acoma when they demanded blankets and provisions. The pueblo was conquered the following January and the Indians gave the blankets, turkeys, and other provisions requested (Hammond, 1926:460). Formerly, according to Gunn (1917:26), the Queres Indians of Laguna and Acoma had large flocks of turkeys.

Utah

There is no satisfactory reference to the natural occurrence of the wild turkey in Utah (Fig. 5) or for that matter north of the Grand Canyon, which was an effective barrier. The Indians did have domestic turkeys. Any turkeys found must have been imported originally.

No bones of the turkey or dog were found during the excavations in Nine Mile Canyon, Duchesne County, thirty-eight miles northeast of Price (Gillin, 1955:23). Steward (1941:319) investigated several ruins in the Johnson Canyon and Paria River region, Kane County. Site 2 yielded several turkey feathers and Site 4 several bones thought to be those of the turkey. These sites are about four miles west of the Paria River and six miles northwest of Pahreah. Droppings, feathers, and pieces of egg shell are reported to have been found in a cliff dwelling, dated 1200 A.D., near Kanab (Thomas, 1957:5).

Turkey feather cloth from Basket-Maker sites was found by Richard Wetherill in 1893 in Cottonwood Wash, San Juan County, about thirty miles north of Bluff (McNitt, 1957:65, 159). Four years later while exploring caves in Grand Gulch, about thirty miles west by north of Bluff, he discovered formalized petroglyphs of turkeys, mountain sheep, and snakes. Bones of the turkey dating from 775 A.D. were found in all parts of the archeological site on Alkali Ridge, ten miles east of Blanding. One turkey had received a formal burial for it was accompanied by a large fragment of a pottery jar. This bird was probably a pet because a femur had been broken and had so healed that one leg was considerably shorter than the other. Beads and awls made from turkey bones were also found (Brew, 1946:115, 121, 243). Four bones of the turkey were found at Poncho House, lower Chinle Wash (Hargrave, 1939:208). The latter joins the San Juan River at 37° 14′ N, 109° 44′ W.

The Temple Square Museum, Salt Lake City, has a desiccated turkey found in San Juan County. The date and locality are unrecorded. A cave

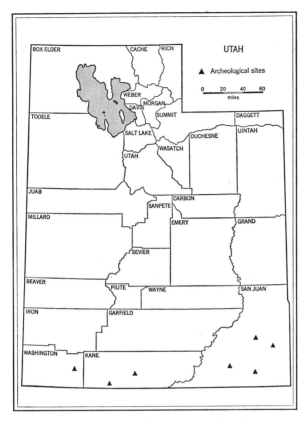

Fig. 5.—*Localities where remains of turkeys were found in Utah.*

on the north side of Parunuweap (Arunuweap) Canyon, Washington County, approximately a mile west of the eastern boundary of Zion National Park, yielded turkey feathers, droppings, and fragments of egg shells (Schroeder, 1955:159).

Excavations on the Fremont River, in the western part of Wayne County, failed to yield evidence of the turkey (Morss, 1931:58).

3

Original Distribution and Numbers

O NE OF THE EARLY ATTEMPTS to map the range of the wild turkey in
the United States was by Boyer (1930). He placed the range much
too far northward. A decided improvement was the map by McClanahan
(1940). Mosby (1949) published a map showing the original ranges of
the eastern and Florida turkeys. It is probable that the eastern race did
not range as far west as the Texas Panhandle. At the same time, Walker
(1949) outlined the range of the turkey west of the Mississippi. The map
of Ligon (1946) shows Merriam's turkey meeting the races eastward
along the Platte, the Arkansas, and the Canadian rivers. A gap exists
along the Cimarron in Oklahoma. The most reliable of the published
maps is that of Aldrich and Duvall (1955).

Original Range in the United States

The distribution map (Fig. 6) has been prepared from the detailed
maps of the border states. No particular problem in distribution arises
until the 95th degree of longitude is reached. Beyond this line it is
impossible to map accurately the ranges of the three indigenous races
because of a lack of specimens.

The demarcation of the Florida turkey (*M. g. osceola*) from the eastern
turkey is uncertain. Specimens north of a line drawn from southern
Wakulla County to northeastern Nassau County are far closer to the
eastern turkey than to the Florida race. Williams (1904:453) lists *silvestris*
for Leon and Wakulla Counties. The Academy of Natural Sciences of
Philadelphia has a female eastern turkey, No. 136731, collected February
4, 1936, by Francis Harper, near Coleraine (originally Colerain), Georgia.
The old town of Colerain is in extreme southwestern Camden County.

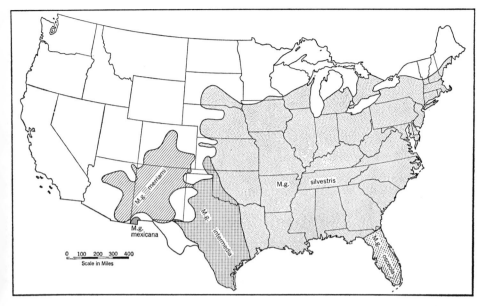

Fig. 6.—*Original range of the wild turkey in the United States and Canada.*

This bird had flown across the St. Mary's River from Nassau County, Florida. According to Hebard (1949), the turkeys on his mother's place, Coleraine Plantation, were nearly pure eastern birds with some characteristics of the Florida form. They flew freely back and forth across the St. Mary's River.

Howell (1932:195) considered specimens from the mouth of the Aucilla River, Jefferson–Taylor counties, and Gainesville, Alachua County, intermediate between *osceola* and *silvestris* but closer to the former.

John T. Emlen kindly examined the twenty-one specimens from Wakulla County in the Philadelphia Academy of Natural Sciences, collected 1913–19. All but two are clearly the eastern race. Nos. 72837 and 72857, having slightly barred secondaries, approach *osceola*. George Lowery has informed me that the adult male from northern Leon County, in the Louisiana State University collection, is indistinguishable from Louisiana specimens of *silvestris*. Specimens 269274–5 from New River, Bradford County, in the U. S. National Museum, are definitely *osceola*.

43

The Florida turkey extended south to Royal Palm Hammock, ten miles southwest of Homestead, Dade County, where it was a rare resident (Howell, 1921:255). It is very doubtful if it was to be found on the "wooded keys" of the Florida Keys as stated by Johnson (1918:95). Ellis (1917), writing from Chokoloskee in extreme southwestern Collier County, stated that the turkey was not nearly as plentiful as a decade earlier.

The eastern turkey (*M. g. silvestris*) extended from northern Florida to the southern parts of Maine, New Hampshire, Vermont, New York, Ontario, Michigan, Wisconsin, Minnesota, and South Dakota. In the West there were narrow extensions of range along the large streams on account of the presence of trees and permanent water. The turkey in Nebraska followed the Niobrara to Cherry County and the Platte to its fork in western Lincoln County. From the fork, along the South Platte, to Adams County, Colorado, no reference to turkeys has been found. There are many statements by travelers on the scarcity of timber along this portion of the stream until southwestern Weld County was reached.

Turkeys were plentiful in the eastern half of Kansas. In the western part they were confined mainly to the valleys of the Republican, Smoky Hill, and Arkansas rivers. The eastern turkey followed the Smoky Hill to Wallace County, and the Arkansas probably to Ford County. A different race was found in southwestern Kansas. In 1815 the party of De Mun (1928:206), starting from St. Louis, shot some turkeys in the sandhills south of the Arkansas in Kearny County. These hills establish the locality. He made this significant entry in his journal: "Here we killed several turkeys, the plumage of which differs from that of our wild turkeys." To one familiar with the eastern turkey, the amount of white on the upper tail coverts of the Río Grande turkey would be striking. This appears to be the northern limit for this race. Merriam's turkey must be excluded since, for a distance of eighty miles up the Arkansas from the sandhills, there is no mention of a turkey by any of the numerous travelers who followed the Arkansas to Bent's Fort and on to Santa Fe. Cooke (1909:411) assumed that the eastern form extended into southeastern Colorado. Later (1913), Cooke decided that it never reached this state. His map shows a long gap without turkeys along the Arkansas River in western Kansas and southeastern Colorado.

It was thought by Duck and Fletcher (1945:85) that the eastern turkey may have extended the entire length of the Cimarron. This is doubtful. From north central Beaver County, Oklahoma, to north central Cimarron County, a distance of 110 miles, no record of a turkey could be found. The much traveled Santa Fe Trail struck the Cimarron at the Lower Spring and ran up the river to Cold Spring, a distance of 85 miles. If turkeys existed along this stretch of the river, it is to be expected that mention would have been made of them. As for the Canadian River, turkeys occurred along its entire length.

The division between the Río Grande and the eastern turkey is based mainly on probability since few early specimens are available. The only early Texas specimen of the eastern turkey of which I have knowledge is No. 20338 in the U. S. National Museum taken in Newton County in 1906. Cahn (1921:172) listed this form for Harrison County. Nehrling (1882:175) thought that the birds occurring in Harris, Montgomery, Galveston, and Fort Bend counties were eastern. This is the form given by Simmons (1915:322) for Harris County. Wolfe (1956:24) stated that *silvestris* is not now found except in the "southeastern part of area 8" of his map. "Eight" should read "three."

Jordan (1879) mentioned that the eastern turkey extended west to the Colorado River and farther west was replaced by the "Mexican" race. A map of the original range of the eastern turkey is given by Newman (1945:281). He believed that this race was confined mainly to the pine belt east of the Trinity River and up the Red River to Childress County. Southward it extended into Harris and Chambers counties. Walker (1954:12) states that the eastern turkey was once common from the Brazos River eastward, its apparent western limits being the junction of the East Texas Timber Country and the Blackland Prairie. The various soil areas are shown in Plate 4. The rainfall for the areas, taken from Carter (1931), is given in Table 2.

The western limit of the eastern turkey seems to be more dependent on rainfall than soil. It does not appear to occur where the annual rainfall is below 25 inches. The western boundary may be represented by a line drawn from the mouth of the Brazos to Clay County, Texas, thence northwest through Cotton and Beaver counties, Oklahoma, and north through western Clark County, Kansas. Early specimens of the eastern turkey exist for Dewey, Major, Payne, Pawnee, and Haskell counties, Oklahoma.

TABLE 2
RAINFALL IN TEXAS SOIL AREAS

A. East Texas Timber Country	35 to 50 inches SW to NE
B. Gulf Coast Prairie	35 to 50 inches west to east
C. Blackland Prairie	30 to 40 inches SW to NE
D. Grand Prairie	30 to 35 inches west to east
E. West Cross Timbers	26 to 30 inches west to east
F. Central Basin	25 inches
G. Rio Grande Plain	20 to 30 inches west to east
H. Edwards Plateau	20 to 30 inches west to east
I. Rolling Plains	22 to 27 inches west to east
J. High Plains	15 to 17 inches west to east
K. Mountains and Basins	14 to 17 inches

The winter of 1882–83, L. L. Dyche collected three turkeys in the Indian Territory for the University of Kansas. Since these are the westernmost turkeys of the eastern race extant, it is necessary to show that they were taken in Major and Dewey counties, and not in Woodward County as supposed. This can be done from the information taken from Dyche's field notes by Edwords (1894:97). The specimens were taken on the ranch of G. A. Thompson on December 29, 1882, and on that of the Dickey brothers on January 3, 1883. The map (Fig. 7) by Milman (1931) shows that the greater part of the Thompson ranch was on Indian Creek, Major County, and that the Dickey Brothers Ranch was in Major and Dewey counties. The Loco Camp and Wolf Creek mentioned were undoubtedly in the northern part of Dewey County.

The eastern range of the Rio Grande turkey is somewhat better defined. According to Carroll (1900:341), it occurred in Refugio County in 1900. This race is given by Simmons (1925:84) for Travis County. Under *mexicana*, Singley (1893:368) lists it for Lee County, and Lloyd (1887:187) lists it for Tom Green and Concho counties. According to Sutton (1940:178), it occurred formerly in Tarrant County. He has informed me that he must have assumed that this race was present formerly. Native stock still exists in Shackelford County. The Rio Grande turkey has been planted so widely since 1930 that any specimen taken since that date must be ruled out so far as the former range is concerned. Walker (1954:12) states that, in general, the species is confined to that portion of the state where the annual rainfall is between 20 and 30 inches.

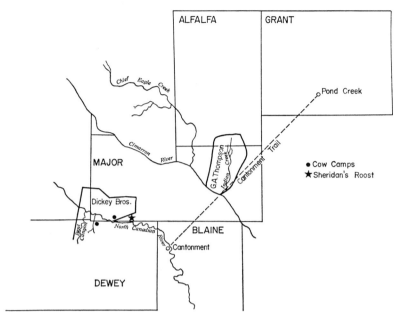

Fig. 7—*Ranches in Oklahoma where L. L. Dyche collected turkeys.*

Recently, Ligon (1961:102) expressed the opinion that the Rio Grande turkey entered New Mexico by way of the Canadian and Cimarron rivers. I know of nothing to substantiate this belief. Lee (1959:1), however, states that considerable evidence exists that fifty to seventy-five years ago the Rio Grande turkey occurred along the streams in northeastern New Mexico. The present population of this race in the area is due to transplants. In view of the available information, I would confine the northern range of this subspecies to Kearny County, Kansas, and on the Cimarron to Beaver County, Oklahoma.

Merriam's turkey ranged from northern Colorado, south through the center of the state and along the southern border. It also occupied suitable areas in Arizona and New Mexico, where it was more abundant than in Colorado. It was considerably more widely distributed in New Mexico than at present and occupied all but seven counties. This race entered Cimarron County, Oklahoma, along the Cimarron, but went no farther eastward. The extent to which this race penetrated Texas along the Canadian is conjectural in the absence of specimens, but probably as far as Carson County. Originally, it was less of a mountain bird than at present. In extreme western Texas it occurred in the Guadalupe Mountains and, apparently, in the Franklin Mountains also.

There is no valid reason to believe that the wild turkey ever occurred in Montana. Some of the very fragmentary bird bones found at Late Prehistoric Indian sites, the Hagen Site five miles southeast of Glendive, Dawson County (Mulloy, 1942:90), and the Pictograph Cave a few miles southeast of Billings, Yellowstone County (Olson, 1958), have been tentatively identified as those of the turkey. Professor Olson has informed me that the identification was the "best guess."

Gould's turkey (*M. g. mexicana*) entered southwestern New Mexico and inhabited the Animas and Hatchet mountains. A specimen has been taken recently in the Peloncillo Mountains (Bohl and Gordon, 1958). The map of Ligon (1946: op. 30) shows this race as also occupying the Chiricahua Range and the region about Nogales, Arizona. The Natural History Museum, San Diego, California, has a specimen taken by Frank Stephens in the Chiricahua Mountains in 1881, long before the native population became extinct. A. S. Leopold has examined this specimen for me and has pronounced it to be definitely *merriami*. Swarth (1904:4) has *merriami* occupying the Huachuca Mountains on the Mexican border, but no specimens were taken. There is, accordingly, no proof for the former presence of *mexicana* in Arizona.

Original Range in Mexico

The wild turkey in Mexico was confined largely to the mountains (Fig. 8). Its occurrence was rare in the Central Plateau desert, extending approximately from latitude 21° to the Río Grande. The Rio Grande turkey ranged from the Río Grande through eastern Coahuila down the Sierra Madre Oriental and the Gulf Coastal Plain to Guanajuato, latitude 21°. The area occupied in northern Veracruz is uncertain.

The south Mexican turkey (*M. g. gallopavo*) is known with certainty to have extended as far north in Veracruz as Zacualpán, and west to northern Jalisco, latitude 21°. It extended southward to latitude 19°, thence southwest to latitude 17° on the coast of Guerrero.

Leopold (1948:395) said he did not know of any reference to the occurrence of wild turkeys in the vicinity of the Valley of Mexico, and his range map shows a gap for this area. For a celebration in Mexico

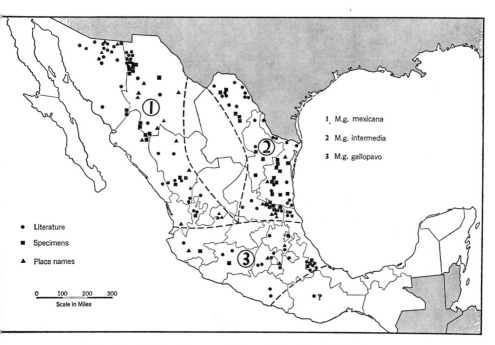

Fig. 8.—*Original range of the wild turkey in Mexico.*

City in the middle of the fifteenth century, the inhabitants of Tenancingo, Ocuilan, Coatepec, and neighboring pueblos were required to provide wild turkeys (*gallos y gallinas monteses*), deer, hares, and other game (Tezozomoc, 1943:145). These pueblos lay about thirty miles southwest of Mexico City. Tepeapulco had wild turkeys and many tame ones (*gallos y gallinas de la tierra monteses, y cantidad dellas mansas*). There were also wild turkeys, which are native peafowl (*en los montes gallinas que son pavos de la tierra*), in the forests at the mines of Tamazcaltepec (Anon., 1905: VI, 301; VII, 26). In 1698, Gemelli-Careri (1719: VI, 116) hunted at the village of St. Jerome near Mexico City. This was apparently modern San Jerónimo Tepetlacalco. He found an abundance of turkeys (*guaxolotes*, or *galli d'India*) which traveled the woods in flocks. These were the best fowls that the Spaniards discovered, and some were taken to Europe. They roosted on dead trees and were shot easily during a new moon. When one fell, the noise of the gun did not cause the others to fly.

49

Gould's turkey occupied the western and eastern slopes of the Sierra Madre Occidental south to northern Jalisco. It was absent from the Pacific Coastal Plain. It is possible that Merriam's turkey entered northern Sonora by way of the Santa Cruz River, Arizona.

Estimates of Original Abundance

There are few specific data on which to base an estimate of the original population of the turkey. The early general statements of abundance, however, are supported by some present population densities. In southwestern Maine in 1638–39, Josselyn (1860:39) saw three score broods of young turkeys sunning themselves in a morning. Morton (1838: II, (v), 48) mentions great flocks of turkeys that sometimes passed the doors of the colonists in eastern Massachusetts and adds: "I have asked them [Indians] what number they found in the woods, who have answered Neent Metawna, which is a thousand that day; the plenty of them is such in those parts."

In the woods of Maryland, Alsop (1880:41) saw "whole hundreds in flights." Much later, Browning (1928:362) wrote of the glades of Garrett County, Maryland: "From fifty to one hundred young turkeys, in one large glade of perhaps a hundred or more acres, all engaged in catching grasshoppers, flying, running, and in every sort of action, was a sight pleasant to the eye of the beholder." Strachey (1849:125), writing in 1612, reported a "great store" of turkeys, forty in a flock, in Virginia. Flocks of several hundred birds were observed by Lawson (1937:22, 156) to leave a swamp at sunrise in North Carolina. Some flocks numbered five hundred. As late as 1905, Neill Spence of Raleigh informed Olds (1905) that he had killed over seven hundred wild turkeys. The Elvas manuscript of De Soto's expedition into Georgia in 1540 mentions the abundance of turkeys. In one Indian town, De Soto was given seven hundred of these fowls (Smith, 1866;67). This number is open to doubt. There were plenty of turkeys in Florida according to Stork (1769:20). Kenworthy (1882) stated that Jack Brown of Rosewood, Levy County, killed 416 turkeys in the Gulf Hammock over a period of eight years.

Turkeys were very abundant in Kentucky. At Rockcastle River in 1775 they were "so numerous that it might be said they appeared but one flock, universally scattered in the woods" (Ranck, 1901:164). They could be seen by the scores and hundreds in the Barrens in 1769 (Altsheler,

Plate 1.—Turkey found at Canyon del Muerto (Canyon de Chelly), Arizona, in 1947, dating to A.D. 250. (Courtesy Gordon Vivian, National Park Service.)

Plate 2.—Developmental Pueblo diorama showing turkeys at large, Mesa Verde National Park, Colorado.

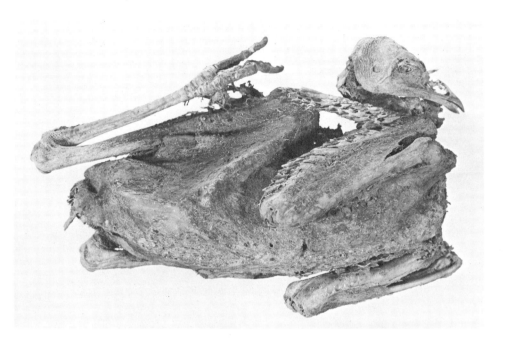

Plate 3.—Defeathered turkey found in 1959 in Long House, Mesa Verde National Park, Colorado. (Courtesy Douglas Osborne, National Park Service.)

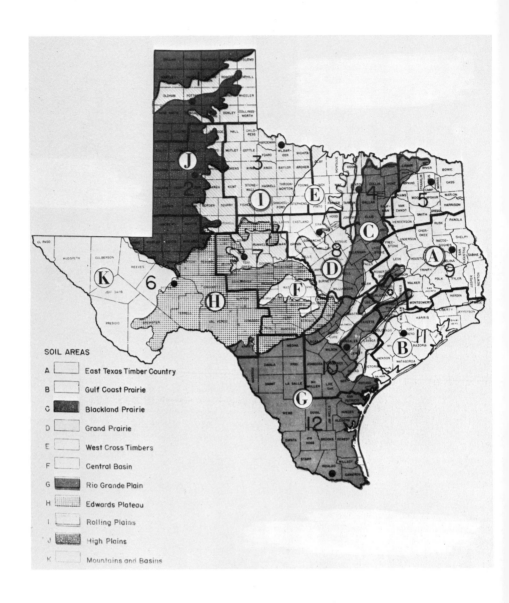

Plate 4.—The soils of Texas. (After M. K. Thornton and E. H. Templin.)

SOIL AREAS

A   East Texas Timber Country

B   Gulf Coast Prairie

C   Blackland Prairie

D   Grand Prairie

E   West Cross Timbers

F   Central Basin

G   Rio Grande Plain

H   Edwards Plateau

I   Rolling Plains

J   High Plains

K   Mountains and Basins

Plate 5.—Restoration of *Parapavo*. (Los Angeles County Museum.)

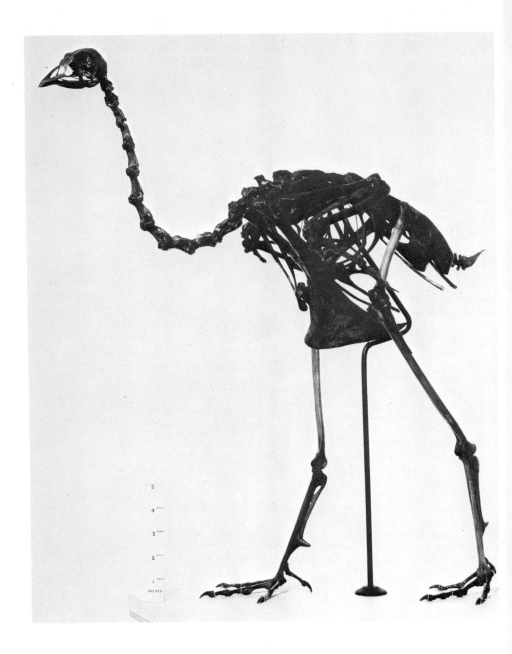

Plate 6.—Skeleton of *Parapavo*. (Los Angeles County Museum.)

Plate 7.—Eastern wild turkeys, March, 1961. (Courtesy W. H. Turcotte, Mississippi Game and Fish Commission.)

Plate 8.—Eastern wild turkeys displaying. (Courtesy Allan D. Cruick-shank.)

1931:172). Ashe (1808:134, 173) wrote that turkeys were so abundant during the early settlement of Kentucky that he was a poor sportsman who could not shoot a dozen in a day. Had he been so inclined he could have killed forty one July day, 1806, at the mouth of the Big Sandy.

The valley of the Ohio was a haven for turkeys. Smyth (1784:337) wrote that on the upper Ohio, turkeys were numberless, sometimes as many as five thousand in a flock. At the Big Kanawha River, West Virginia, on October 13, 1785, General Butler (1848:447) wrote in his journal that his party had nothing to do but spring from the boats among flocks of turkeys and kill as many as desired. He had just killed two fine ones in a single shot. About 1800, numerous flocks of hundreds of birds could be found in the Kanawha Valley (Hildreth, 1836:85). The abundant beech mast in the bottom lands in the fall of 1790 brought the turkeys in countless numbers. The inhabitants were so cloyed with turkey that one could not be sold for six cents (Hildreth, 1848:496). The fall of 1845, Perry (1899:71) was hunting along the Maumee River in northwestern Ohio after a fire had swept an area six to twenty miles wide and sixty miles long. Here he saw over five hundred turkeys leave a strip of unburned woods after rain had quenched the fire.

During the early days of the settlements in Licking County, Ohio, turkeys could be seen in flocks of one to five hundred. A good idea of their numbers can be gotten from the following account by Bushnell (1889:63): "A pedler from Chillicothe stopped at Oren Granger's tavern one Monday noon, where he saw several fine turkeys. He bargained with Leveret Butler for one hundred such, to be delivered at Mr. Granger's the next Saturday noon. Butler went home, run his bullets, went out in the afternoon and in two hours killed twenty-nine. A rain came up and wet the guns, and he was obliged to stop. He hung up the turkeys after the Indian fashion, sticking the head of one through a slit in the neck of another, and balancing them across a limb. Next day it rained. Wednesday he went again with one Nickols, and camped out the rest of the week. They carried in 130. The wild cats spoiled six for them. Selecting one hundred of the best, he delivered them to Mr. Granger and received his pay."

Approximate data on the density of turkeys in Ohio can be obtained from the accounts of the circular hunts. During a hunt enclosing five square miles in Licking County, Ohio, in 1817, 350 turkeys were surrounded (Beers & Co., 1880:239). This gives a population of seventy birds to the square mile. Bushnell (1889:126) had access to a paper written by Rev. Timothy Howe of a hunt in the same county in 1823, the area driven consisting of four square miles of deadened timber. Soon after the drive began, turkeys started flying over the lines in flocks. Only sixty or seventy birds were killed. The kill was accordingly fifteen to eighteen per square mile. Schaff (1905:148) cites Howe on a circular hunt that took place in the county in 1825. It appears to be the same hunt mentioned above since, again, sixty to seventy turkeys were killed. Schaff states that the area driven comprised fifteen hundred acres that had been deadened for fifteen to sixteen years, so that the kill was twenty-six to thirty per square mile. During an undated hunt in Sharon Township, Franklin County, five hundred turkeys were taken (Hist. Publ. Co., 1901:67). Assuming that the entire township of twenty-five square miles was driven, twenty turkeys were killed per square mile. A circular hunt in Portage County in December, 1818, resulted in taking four hundred turkeys. On one hunt a year later, over three hundred were shot (Beers & Co., 1885:199); the areas of the drive are not given. As late as 1876, E. H. Ray saw ten hens with an average brood of ten poults on an area of twenty-four square miles in Lucas County, Ohio (Campbell, 1940:65).

A British officer was with a band of Indians moving to attack Fort Recovery. On June 28, 1794, they organized in eastern Indiana a hunt that yielded two hundred deer and an equal number of turkeys (Chew, 1890:386). Brown (1817:79) stated that in traveling seven miles through the woods of Dearborn County, Indiana, he counted about one hundred turkeys, of which more than one-half were young just able to fly. Making the liberal assumption that this transect was one-fifth of a mile, there were about seventy turkeys to the square mile. Faux (1823:272) was at Harmony, Indiana, in 1819 when turkeys were in "sickening abundance." A young hunter who in 1832 supplied New Harmony with turkeys often had ten to fifteen hanging at one time on his horse (Maximilian, 1906: I, 168). When Indiana was first settled, a hunter could see daily many flocks numbering fifty to seventy-five turkeys to the flock (Cockrum, 1907:436). In the early days it was not uncommon for a hunter to kill from fifteen to twenty turkeys daily in the vicinity of Indianapolis (Butler, 1913:63).

Rale (1900:169) wrote of Illinois in 1723: "We can hardly travel a league without meeting a prodigious multitude of Turkeys, which go in troops, sometimes to the number of 200." This state is reputed to have had "thousands upon thousands" of turkeys prior to the winter of 1831–32 when most of them perished (Walker, 1911:113). A man named Short fired into a flock of about fifty turkeys, killing sixteen by aiming at their necks (Onstot, 1902:137). James R. Brown stated that in White County it was considered a fair night's work to kill six to fifteen turkeys (Inter-State Publ. Co., 1883:801). Crossing the Mississippi, we have this statement for Clayton County, Iowa, around 1836: "At stated times during the year a regular trail was formed by the wild turkeys crossing the [Turkey] river, which from this fact, took its name. I have seen a train of them, two to four abreast, extending from the river's bank to the forest a quarter of a mile away" (Dickens, 1903).

The winter of 1810–11, Audubon (1942:163) saw innumerable flocks of turkeys at Cape Girardeau, Missouri. Subsequently he wrote: "What would be said to a gang of Wild Turkeys,—several hundred trotting along a sand-bar of the Upper Mississippi" (Audubon, 1900: I, 243). According to Goebel (1889:128), when turkeys were little hunted, it was not uncommon to find flocks containing several hundred birds in the large bottoms along the Missouri, Meramec, and Bourbeuse rivers. The first morning after arriving in Lincoln Township, Nodaway County, Joseph Hutson went hunting and saw fully five hundred turkeys (Nat. Hist. Co., 1882:234). The head of every hollow where the snow had melted had been scratched over. W. C. Atkinson shot 180 turkeys between July, 1837, and the beginning of March, 1838, in Daviess County (Birdsall & Dean, 1882:155). This number does not show very extensive hunting. Two men in Scotland County had their rifles with them while husking corn and killed 132 turkeys in one day (Goodspeed Publ. Co., 1887:414). The best day that Bogardus (1879:239) ever had was on Shoal Creek, which rises in Clinton County, after a fresh fall of seven to eight inches of snow. He and a companion killed fourteen turkeys by noon. These birds were not hunted especially except after a freshly fallen snow, but during a period of three weeks in camp between fifty and sixty were killed. According to information furnished by J. L. Smith, president of the Missouri Sportsmen's Association, 8,942 turkeys were killed during the year ending March 1, 1886 (West, 1886). How the datum was obtained is not stated. The kill was one bird to 7.8 square miles.

There are no data on the turkey in eastern Kansas where the state population should have been highest. The winter of 1868 about forty turkeys were killed by Alfred Cory in Cloud County. None was shot more than one quarter of a mile from Cory's house (Crèvecoeur, 1902:73). In October of 1868, while camped in Ford County, General Sheridan wrote that eighty turkeys were killed in one day (Custer, 1890:12). In the early fall of 1870, Bertram (1902:201) saw as many as one thousand turkeys daily over a period of ten days to two weeks in and about the junction of the North and South Forks of the Solomon River. During a blizzard in December of the same year, turkeys in flocks of three to four hundred birds were to be found along the Solomon. Any number could have been taken, but the snow so retarded travel that hunters killed only enough for food (Hollibaugh, 1902:92).

No section of the country contained such multitudes of turkeys as the Oklahoma-Texas area. Dodge (1877:232) saw flocks which he was certain contained several hundred turkeys. Révoil (1875:53) mentioned that while in the west with a party of 280 Indians, they pursued a flock of about two hundred turkeys on the prairie. After being flushed five times, the birds were so exhausted that they could be caught by the neck and killed. The Indians returned to camp with 160 of them.

While returning to camp at the head of Coal Creek, Pittsburg County, Oklahoma, on August 8, 1853, Whipple (1856: III [Part 1], 15) encountered the largest flock of turkeys that had been seen: "There must have been many hundreds." The winter of 1868–69, Sheridan was camped in the vicinity of the Antelope Hills, Ellis County, where the trees were black with turkeys. They were so plentiful that the soldiers had all they wanted (Custer, 1890:32). According to Lane (1926:496), flocks containing three thousand turkeys each were seen as late as 1877 by hunters. Knott (1888) thought that one thousand turkeys occupied a roost near his camp in Kingfisher County in 1879. In February, 1878, Strong (1960:15, 31) hunted with General Sheridan at two especially large roosts on the Canadian River southwest of Fort Reno. Each roost was about one-fourth of a mile in width and one mile in length.

Fort Sill in Comanche County had turkeys in abundance. Neal Evans, the first post trader at the fort, stated: "One can hardly imagine now the size of the enormous droves of wild turkey that roamed the country in the late fall. In the Deep Red, below Fort Sill, I am confident that I have seen as many as 10,000 in a single drove. The ground in the oak forest would be torn up as if plows had passed over it, where the turkeys scratched for acorns. In a single night a small detail of men had gone from the post to a turkey roost on Deep Red and killed an army wagon full. . . ." (Griswold, 1958:6). Some of the bags made near the fort in 1873 were: a party of twelve men killed 156 turkeys; a group of officers, 60; another party of officers with a small detail of men, 130 odd; and three officers at Christmas brought in 50 odd ("Basso," 1874). In 1880 it was stated that turkeys could still be had by the cartload by hunting on moonlit nights (G. W. S., 1880). Drains of these magnitudes on the avian population could not last. The winter of 1884–85 about 400 turkeys were eaten at Fort Sill, and the next winter about 225 (Crane, 1886).

Doolin (1913) relates that, in the 1880's, two men found a flock of five to six hundred turkeys digging for acorns through the snow on Rock Creek, Osage County, Oklahoma. After being fired at, many of the birds remained in the vicinity, hiding under the tall grass that had been pressed down by the snow. These birds were "jumped" and forty-three killed during the morning's hunt. Two men in 1881 killed over one hundred turkeys in one night in the Indian Territory ("Crocus," 1881). The following year one man estimated that there were ten thousand turkeys in an unnamed area ten miles by twenty miles in the Territory (W. J. D., 1882). This gives a density of fifty birds to the square mile. Murphy (1882:52) wrote that four men in two nights shot seventy-five turkeys. In December of 1882, a hunting party that had been in the Indian Territory returned to Wichita, Kansas, with about five hundred birds (Bentley, 1883). In Noble County, the winter of 1883–84, Cooke (1888:106) saw flocks of two to five hundred in number. He had seen a lumber wagon "piled up" with the birds killed in a single night. Whitney (1887) stated that he and four companions killed 230 turkeys. The place and length of time hunted were not given. About 1888, near Crescent, Logan County, four men killed forty-nine turkeys in one night (Chambers, 1945:402).

Wright (1913) saw flocks of turkeys, numbering thousands, coming to roost on the Canadian River and its timbered affluents. They covered the prairies for miles. The terrain of Oklahoma was conducive to seeing nearly all the turkeys that inhabited a given area. Coming from the prairies where they had been feeding, they were readily visible as they

55

concentrated for roosting in the timber which was generally limited to the borders of the streams. As late as about 1896, according to Askins (1931:63), five hundred turkeys could be seen in a day near Ames, Major County.

TABLE 3

MODERN DENSITIES OF TURKEYS TO THE SQUARE MILE

State	Year	Area	Turkeys to Sq. Mi.	Reference
Alabama	1941	Occupied area in state	1.4	Wheeler, 1948:44
Alabama	1945	Salt Springs Game Sanctuary	23.7	Wheeler, 1946.1:141
California	1951	Castro Valley	40.0	Burger, 1954:198
Florida	1948	Orange County	7.1	Newman & Griffin, 1950:Table 1
Georgia	1935	1 to 20 acres of managed land	32.0	Stoddard, 1935:327
Louisiana	1941–42	Small separated units	1.3	Bick, 1947:132–33
Louisiana	1946	Small separated units	1.2	Hollis, 1950:15
Mississippi	1953	Coahoma County, occupied habitat	21.0	Havard, 1953
Mississippi	1951	16 counties	8.3	Loveless, 1951
Mississippi	1951	29 counties	4.2	Loveless, 1951.1
Missouri	1946	Drury Refuge	6.21	Dalke et al., 1946:20
Missouri	1945	Caney Mountain Refuge	3.3	Dalke et al., 1946:20
Missouri	1942	Taney County	1.13	Dalke et al., 1946:11
Missouri	1942	Entire range	0.62	Dalke et al., 1946:12
Oklahoma	1953–54	Wichita Wildlife Refuge	3.5	Thomas, 1954
Texas	1948	Blanco River Study Area	4.0	Walker, 1948
Texas	1948	Turtle Creek Area	8.3	Walker, 1948
Texas	1948	Luckenbach Area	6.8	Walker, 1948
Texas	1951	Norias Division, King Ranch	94.1	Colbath, 1951
Texas	1957	Edwards County	8.5	Thomas and Green, 1957:24
Texas	1957	Medina County	13.0	Thomas and Green, 1957:24
Texas	1962	Welder Refuge, San Patricio County	30.0	Glazener, 1962

Virginia	1937 Buckingham County, occupied	2.8	Mosby and Handley, 1943:30, 33
Virginia	1937 Occupied area of state	1.7	Mosby and Handley, 1943:31, 34
West Virginia	1949–50 Occupied area	1.26	Bailey et al., 1951:2, 3
West Virginia	1949–50 Morgan County, small part	3.26	Bailey et al., 1951:8
West Virginia	1950 Greatest density county wide	2.5	Uhlig, 1950
West Virginia	1950 Occupied forest land on refuge	7.7	Uhlig, 1950
West Virginia	1955 Forested area	2.0	Bailey, 1957:2

A graphic account of the abundance of turkeys in Alfalfa County in 1881 is given by Nelson (1953:131): "About a mile above the cabin on the creek was a bunch of timber we called Elm Mott. The turkeys would come there; then afraid to pass the new barn, they would leave the creek and run east nearly three-quarters of a mile across an open space to a bunch of timber on a branch. Three different days in October there were turkeys in sight all the time crossing that open space, sometimes in a line halfway across and thirty or forty feet wide. The boys would stand and watch, saying 'Now come and just look at the turkeys.' There was a turkey roost down the creek about six miles southeast of camp in a heavy grove that we called the Big Timber. A path in the snow ten feet wide led from this roost to the blackjacks [*Quercus marilandica*] two miles east." In the spring of 1882, the turkeys collected opposite the mouth of Eagle Creek in Major County. Some forty acres were so covered with the birds that it was thought that "every turkey on earth was in that bunch."

Turkeys were about as abundant in Texas as in Oklahoma. In 1848, Bracht (1849:77) encountered a flock of between four and five hundred birds three miles north of Béxar (San Antonio). Strong (*ca.* 1926:24), in 1871 with three other army officers, camped at the mouth of Cambren (Cameron) Creek, Jack County. In two nights they filled two army wagons with turkeys which were sent to Fort Richardson. "Saxet" (1884), in the fall of 1872, hunted in the county eighteen miles from

Fort Richardson with twelve men from the post. From 3:00 P.M. on Monday to 11:00 A.M. on Wednesday, 181 turkeys were killed. All the birds were shot on the ground, there being no roost shooting.

Turkeys were present formerly by the thousands in Denton County and almost covered the trees along the streams (Bates, 1918:294). J. R. Cook (1907:115) had a camp in the fall of 1874 on the Salt Fork of the Brazos in western Stonewall County. Below the camp was a large roost where in the evenings the turkeys arrived by thousands from every direction. By shooting at the roosts near Fort Mason, Mason County, Texas, "two or three hundred pounds of meat" could be obtained in an evening ("Old Scout," 1874).

Bingham (1878) hunted in Frio County, Texas, in November, 1878, and states: "I will assert that I saw in one roost, the night before we left, in five hundred yards distance, over a thousand turkeys. I killed at least twenty-five turkeys in thirty minutes. Our whole kill of turkey on the tramp was over a hundred. . . ."

In December, 1881, "Wilhelm" (1882) saw a wagon load of turkeys for sale in the plaza of San Antonio. He was assured that three men killed all of them in one night on the Frio River. From fifty to sixty turkeys were killed in a night at a roost by "Almo" (1886). He thought that this type of hunting should be discontinued. In the 1890's, hunters killed as many as five hundred turkeys in one night in Frio County (Anon., 1945:18). There is the following facetious statement regarding the former abundance of turkeys in Mitchell County: "He [Dave Pool] said that whenever the people of Colorado City wanted wild turkeys they hitched a team to a wagon, drove to some stream where there was timber, ran the wagon under a turkey roost, and fired; and that they never took the trouble to pick up the birds that did not fall into the wagon!" (Douthit, 1942:33).

The abundance of turkeys along the upper Brazos River, Texas, in December, 1872, is well described by Elgin (1938:86): "All the evening long we saw great droves of turkeys, all going apparently to the same point. These droves would have from twenty to thirty turkeys to several hundred. As we quit work and started to camp I heard an immense number of turkeys gobbling and strutting, and the dog I had rushed into their midst, but in a few moments came rushing back with his tail stuck between his legs. Just then I rode upon the mass of turkeys. There was an opening of ten or twelve acres in the shinnery and it was covered with turkeys as thick as they could stand. I was riding a gun-shy horse and just then the boys in the party spied the turkeys and turned loose a volley of shots into them. My horse dashed into middle of them and the turkeys closed in around us. I began to yell, trying to get out of the way, and as badly scared as my dog had been—not at the turkeys but at the bullets singing around me from the guns of my men. How many thousands or millions of turkeys there may have been I would not attempt to say. This, the first real cold day of winter, was driving them into the shinnery for protection." (A shinnery is a dense growth of shrubby trees consisting especially of shin oak, *Quercus havardii*.)

Examples of Present Densities

Probably few areas at present have the turkey populations that once existed under primitive conditions. Stoddard (1935:327) states that in Georgia he has known as many as one hundred turkeys to use a planted food patch of three acres in late winter, and as many as five hundred to range over an area of 2,500 acres. On well-managed grounds, heavily

TABLE 4
Estimated Pre-Columbian Turkey Populations in the United States

State	Square Miles Occupied	Turkeys to Sq. Mi.	Population
Alabama	51,078	10	510,780
Arizona	42,770	1	42,770
Arkansas	52,675	10	526,750
Colorado	16,740	1	16,740
Connecticut	4,899	5	24,495
Delaware	1,978	5	9,890
Florida	47,980	8	383,840
Georgia	58,483	10	584,830
Illinois	55,935	5	279,675
Indiana	36,205	8	289,640
Iowa	47,470	5	237,350
Kansas	47,230	5	236,150
Kentucky	39,864	10	398,640
Louisiana	45,162	10	451,620
Maine	700	1	700

Maryland	9,881	8	79,048
Massachusetts	7,867	5	39,335
Michigan	18,753	5	93,765
Minnesota	500	0.5	250
Mississippi	47,248	10	472,480
Missouri	69,226	6	415,356
Nebraska	6,180	1	6,180
New Hampshire	2,760	2	5,520
New Jersey	7,522	5	37,610
New Mexico	42,790	1.5	64,185
New York	30,905	2	61,810
North Carolina	49,097	10	490,970
Ohio	41,000	8	328,000
Oklahoma	69,031	10	690,310
Pennsylvania	45,045	7	315,315
Rhode Island	1,058	5	5,290
South Carolina	30,305	10	303,050
South Dakota	3,470	1	3,470
Tennessee	41,797	8	334,376
Texas	201,460	10	2,014,600
Vermont	500	1	500
Virginia	39,893	8	319,144
West Virginia	24,080	8	192,640
Wisconsin	14,640	0.5	7,320
Total	1,354,177		10,274,394

planted for food, and well patrolled, it should be possible to have a concentration of one turkey to fifteen to twenty-five acres. I have been informed by W. C. Glazener (1962) that on the Welder Refuge, San Patricio County, Texas, the winter concentration is thirty birds per square mile for the entire area. Since only one-half or less of the refuge is used by the turkeys, the actual density is sixty-five to seventy to the square mile. Thomas (1954) estimated that 322 turkeys utilized only 17,584 of the 59,099 acres in the Wichita Mountain Wildlife Refuge. This gives a population of 11.7 turkeys per square mile for the occupied area, or 3.5 birds per square mile for the entire refuge. Western Maryland has approximately 150,000 acres of first-class turkey habitat, the goal for which, according to Arner (1954:5), should be one turkey to every one hundred acres, or 6.4 birds per square mile. Most states by management have been able to increase the population considerably. In 1951, Mississippi had an estimated population of ten thousand turkeys in forty-nine counties (Loveless, 1951.2:11). Seven years later there were an estimated twenty thousand turkeys in sixty-nine counties (Ryan, 1958).

Modern densities of turkeys in various states are given in Table 3. An estimate of the pre-Columbian populations in the United States is given in Table 4. The total population, approximately ten million, is believed to be conservative. Leopold (1931:191) estimated that each square mile of available range in Missouri might carry five birds. Bennitt and Nagel (1937:57) thought this density moderate. Based on fifty thousand square miles of forest and five birds per acre, Missouri a century previously had at least 250,000 turkeys. In estimating the primitive populations, only the land areas of the states have been included. Occupied areas in the border states have been taken from the respective range maps. Some of the early and modern densities reported lead me to believe that an original density of ten turkeys per square mile for the good turkey states is a safe assumption. Some states such as Illinois, Iowa, Kansas, and Michigan contained so much prairie in the occupied range that the density was probably only five birds per square mile. The range in Wisconsin consisted so much of prairies and oak openings that it is doubtful if there was a density greater than one turkey to two square miles. Also, the winters are severe.

4

Taxonomy and Description

IT WAS LONG THOUGHT that turkeys were most closely related to pheasants and so were accordingly placed in the Phasianidae rather than in the separate family Meleagrididae. This opinion still lingers. Gilliard (1958:121) writes that turkeys are so similar to pheasants that they must have descended from Old World stock. Turkeys, however, are unquestionably of North American origin. The two living genera, *Meleagris* and *Agriocharis*, as well as the extinct *Parapavo*, have never been found elsewhere (Mayr, 1946:22). J. A. Allen (1893:109) expressed the opinion that *Meleagris* originated in Mexico. Although turkeys were thought to have been common in the West during the Miocene and Pliocene (Wetmore, 1936:325), Howard (1950:2) has stated that they are known with certainty only from Late Pliocene and Pleistocene. Howard's time scale is shown in Table 5.

TABLE 5
GEOLOGIC TIME SCALE USED BY HOWARD

Period	Epoch	Approximate Age at Beginning
Quaternary	Recent	15,000 years
	Pleistocene	1,000,000 years
Tertiary	Pliocene	10,000,000 years
	Miocene	30,000,000 years
	Oligocene	40,000,000 years
	Eocene	60,000,000 years

FOSSIL TURKEYS

The fossil turkeys which have been recorded are:

Meleagris gallopavo.—Pleistocene. Ninety-eight bone fragments from the Seminole area, Pinellas County, Florida; also, remains from Hog Creek, near Sarasota, Sarasota County, and near Lecanto, Citrus County (Wetmore, 1931:32). The *Ardea sellardsi* of Shufeldt (1917:19) from Vero, Florida, is synonymous with *M. gallopavo.* The deposit is believed to be Recent (Wetmore, 1956:57). Remains have been found at Ocala, Marion County (Shufeldt, 1918:358); Rock Spring, six miles north of Apopka, Florida (Woolfenden, 1959:185); caves of Tennessee (Shufeldt, 1897:648); Conard Fissure near Willcockson, northern Newton County, Arkansas (Brown, 1909:206; Shufeldt, 1913:299; Hay, 1924:252); a left tibiotarsus from the Rexroad Fauna, Upper Pliocene, Meade County, Kansas (Wetmore, 1944:198); the distal half of an ulna-radius from Pleistocene gravels near Ashmore, Coles County, Illinois (Galbreath, 1938:311); left humerus, Pleistocene, near North Liberty, St. Joseph County, Indiana (Wetmore, 1945); caves at Carlisle, Cumberland County, Pennsylvania—"birds in great quantities, particularly wild turkeys, and some of these of an enormous size, probably weighing thirty or forty pounds" (Baird, 1850:355); Hartman's Cave, near Stroudsburg, and Durham Cave, near Riegelsville, Bucks County, Pennsylvania (Leidy, 1880:348; 1889:6, 19); caves in Pyramid Peak, Doña Ana County, New Mexico, Pleistocene or Recent (Howard and Miller, 1933:16); parts of the humerus, ulna, and radius, tentatively placed in Late Pliocene, but indistinguishable from modern bird, gravel deposit three and a half miles northeast of San Antonio, Socorro County, New Mexico (Needham, 1936). A. Wetmore, who identified the latter bones, has told me that the remains are without doubt Pleistocene.

Meleagris antiqua Marsh.—Distal end of humerus found by George B. Grinnell in supposedly Miocene clay deposits of the White River formation, northern Colorado (Marsh, 1871:126). The label reads: "Type *Mel. antiquus.* G. Ranch. Col[orado]. G. B. G. August 6, 1870." It was later placed in the Oligocene by Wetmore (1956:57). The bone has been considered too fragmentary to decide with certainty that it represents a turkey (Howard, 1950:13; Shufeldt, 1914.1:35). The bone has been identified as belonging to one of the Cracidae, *Paracrax* Brodkorb (Brodkorb, 1964.1).

Meleagris alta Marsh.—*M. altus* (Marsh, 1870; 1871.1; 1872:260) from the Lower Pleistocene marl, Monmouth County, New Jersey; cave at

Frankstown, Blair County, Pennsylvania (Holland, 1908:232; Peterson, 1926:254); cave at Port Kennedy, Merion Township, Montgomery County, Pennsylvania (Wheatley, 1871; Mercer, 1899:280). Synonyms: *Meleagris superba* Cope (Cope, 1871:239; Shufeldt, 1915:66); *Meleagris celer* Marsh (Marsh, 1872; Shufeldt, 1913.1:21; Brodkorb, 1964:325).

Meleagris tridens Wetmore.—Pleistocene, metatarsus with three spurs, Seminole area, Pinellas County, Florida (Wetmore, 1928:157; 1931:34). This is the only known example of multiple spurs in the New World.

Agriocharis progenes Brodkorb.—Rexroad formation, Uppermost Pliocene, Meade County, Kansas (Brodkorb, 1964.1).

Agriocharis leopoldi Miller and Bowman.—Described by Miller and Bowman (1956:42) as *Meleagris leopoldi*. Tarsometatarsus, Late Pliocene, three and a half miles south and thirteen miles east of Cita Canyon, Randall County, Texas; described as *Parapavo californicus* (Miller and Johnstone, 1937).

Agriocharis crassipes Miller.—*Meleagris crassipes*, tarsometatarsi, Pleistocene, San Josecito Cave, Nuevo León, Mexico (Miller, 1940); broken tarsometatarsus, Late Miocene, San Pedro Valley, Cochise County, Arizona (Wetmore, 1925; 1927:181).

Agriocharis anza Howard.—Middle Pleistocene, Arroyo Tapiado, San Diego County, California (Howard, 1964:19); Middle Pleistocene, Seymour Formation, near Gilliland, Knox County, Texas (Brodkorb, 1964.1.).

Parapavo californicus (Miller).—The tar pits of Rancho La Brea, Los Angeles, California, are famous for the perfect preservation of the bones of extinct animals. More than seven hundred individuals of this extinct turkey have been found (Stock, 1953:62). It approached the wild turkey in size and had long, somewhat heavier spurs (Plate 5). A mounted skeleton is 60 cm. in height. About 150 bones of the young of *Parapavo* have been found (Howard, 1930:83, 86), and the tarsometatarsi studied (Howard, 1945).

In 1909, L. H. Miller (1909) described the bird as a fossil peacock, *Pavo californicus*. This led Osborn (1925:542) to suggest that the bird was of Asiatic origin. Further study revealed that the skeleton differed from *Pavo* so that a new genus, *Parapavo* (peacock-like), was created (Miller, 1916). Howard (1927:30) believes that *Parapavo* occupied a position between *Meleagris* and *Agriocharis*, but was closer to the latter. Sushkin

64

(1928), working wtih K. Lambrecht in Budapest in 1927, came to the same conclusions. *Parapavo* differed widely from *Pavo* and was so close to *Agriocharis* that generic separation was questionable. The beak of *Parapavo* is decidedly broader and flatter than that of its living relatives as is shown by the following measurements (Howard, 1928):

Species	Breadth of Beak
Meleagris gallopavo	11.7 mm.
Agriocharis ocellata	12.8 mm.
Parapavo californicus	14.7–15.1 mm.

Parapavo californicus (Plate 6) has been found in the following localities: Late Pleistocene, Rancho La Brea and Carpinteria asphalts, California, but not from the McKittrick asphalt; gravel beds southwest of La Habra, near Los Angeles, Orange County line (Howard, 1936); a coracoid, Highland Park district, and two bones, Workman Street, Los Angeles (Miller, 1942).

Meleagris richmondi (Shufeldt, 1915:67) is a synonym. A fragmentary sternum was found near Mission San Jose, Alameda County, California.

Parapavo oklahomaensis (Sandoz and Stovall, 1936), represented by a left tarsometatarsus with a complete spur core from a gravel pit at Chickasha, Oklahoma, has not been described and remains a *nomen nudum*.

Turkey Hybrids

It is a common assumption that two species are related if they produce hybrids, and closely so if the hybrids are fertile. Hybrids between gallinaceous birds are common. Sperling (1661:369) painted the turkey as a libidinous creature. He believed it to be a cross between the peahen and a rooster. He was probably misled by the name *gallopavo*. The gobbler, in the absence of female turkeys, would court the common hen, while, in similar circumstances, the turkey hen would accept the rooster. There was also coupling between the gobbler and the peahen. The first mention of a hybrid offspring is by Edwards (1761). The bird, shot in Dorsetshire in October, 1759, was supposed to be a cross between a turkey and a pheasant. Subsequently, Edwards published a colored plate of the specimen (1806). Buffon (1771:159) thought the hybrid was between a turkey and a grouse for the following reasons: the bird had only sixteen rectrices while both the turkey and pheasant have eighteen; the possession of "double" feathers was a character absent in the supposed parents, but present in the grouse. It should be mentioned that both turkeys and pheasants do have aftershafts. Temminck (1813:387) agreed with Buffon, but Suchetet (1890:355) believed that Edwards was correct.

Pheasants and turkeys were mated by artificial insemination by Asmundson and Lorenz (1957). The fertility of the eggs was 37.3 per cent and their hatchability 17.1 per cent. The cross, male pheasant x female turkey, gave 82.5 per cent males, and male turkey x female pheasant, 55.1 per cent males. All the hybrids were sterile and relatively silent. Their heads resembled those of the pheasant and were fully feathered except around the eyes. There was no frontal caruncle or beard. The tail feathers were intermediate in length and were never spread. The feathering of the head of some of the hybrids, when not fully grown, had a great resemblance to the illustration of Edwards' hybrid (Asmundson and Lorenz, 1955).

The chromosomes of the turkey and the pheasant are more nearly alike than those of the latter and the domestic fowl (Sokolow et al., 1936:482). This seems to be supported by the hybrids. Serebrovsky (1935) crossed a female turkey with a male leghorn. Only one egg hatched, the time required being twenty-four days. The chick's down was white with no traces of the stripes characteristic of the young turkey. On the head was a bare spot where the frontal caruncle should have been. The chick weighed more than the chick of either species. Live crosses are also mentioned by Ogorodny (1935) and Kondo (1947). In studying the reciprocal crosses, using artificial insemination, Warren and Scott (1935) found that fertility of the eggs was much higher crossing a female turkey x male chicken. Although one embryo survived for twenty-two days, none of the eggs hatched. Some eggs developed young to the feather stage.

Quinn and associates (1937) had little better success. Only one embryo survived to the point of hatching. This chick, though having characters intermediate between the turkey and the chicken, was more like the latter. Asmundson and Lorenz (1957) obtained very low fertility and zero hatchability.

The young hybrids obtained by Olsen (1961) from turkey hens artificially inseminated with semen from chickens resembled the latter more than turkeys. A supposed cross, Wyandotte male x turkey female, is shown by Hachisuka (1928). Hopkinson (1934:324) mentions that there are crosses from a female Rhode Island Red in the Natural History Museum, London. Induced immunological mutual tolerance of the turkey and chicken to their antigens failed to indicate enhanced chances for interbreeding (Ryle and Simonsen, 1956). Ryle (1957) has suggested that one of the difficulties in hybridization between species may be due to injury of heterologous spermatozoa by normal heteroantibodies.

A supposed cross between the curassow (*Crax*) and turkey is mentioned by Przibram (1910:84).

Crosses between the turkey and the capercaillie, obtained by using captive male capercaillies one to two years of age and female turkeys, was reported by Gloger (1834:517). Never reaching full growth, they attained the size of chickens and died during molting.

A cross, *Numida* male x *Meleagris* female, is mentioned by Poll (1920:368). The specimen, of unknown origin, in the Berlin Zoological Museum was examined without comment by Serebrovsky (1929:327). An illustrated article on a hybrid from a turkey and a guinea fowl was published by E. Díaz (1901). It was intermediate in size between the two species. On the throat was a bulky tuft of feathers. A supposed cross between a turkey and a guinea fowl lived for several years in Pullen Park, Raleigh, North Carolina. Three of the four in the brood died. Olds (1909) described the survivor as having a head like a turkey and mottled plumage.

A note by Mowbray (1922), containing a photograph, mentions a cross between a turkey and a peacock (*Pavo*) at Miami, Florida. Antonius (1933) was unable to obtain a cross between the two species. Hybrids were obtained by Randall (1934) by crossing a peahen with a bronze domestic gobbler. Five of the six eggs laid were hatched. Four of the young nearly reached maturity, and one lived for several years. He states that the gobbler to be used should be very tame and raised apart from other turkeys.

The ocellated turkey (*Agriocharis ocellata*) was formerly in the genus *Meleagris*. Bartlett (1898:217) makes the bare statement that fertile hybrids between the two species were obtained in the London Zoological Gardens. J. J. Yealland of the London Zoological Society informs me that one hybrid was obtained in 1865, and that "a number bred in 1868." Further information is lacking. Hybrids are mentioned by Ghigi and Delacour (1931). Professor Ghigi has written to me that at

Rovigo, near Venice, a female ocellated turkey was bred with a male domestic turkey. The female laid nine eggs, all of which hatched. One of the young survived for two years, the others dying within a brief time. A note in Taibell (1934:102) states that Ghigi raised several hybrids by crossing a peahen with a male *wild* turkey.

Artificial insemination was used successfully by Lorenz and associates (1956; Asmundson, 1957) to produce hybrids. Female Broad-Breasted Bronze turkeys were inseminated with sperm from the male ocellated turkey. The F_1 progeny was intermediate in size, head furnishings, and all observed traits except the voice, which was similar to *ocellata*. The frontal caruncle, small in *ocellata*, was well developed, but the fleshy knob on top of the head of *ocellata* was absent. There was a well-developed beard which is absent in *ocellata*. The F_1 males were fertile when crossed with female turkeys. The single F_1 female laid well but the eggs were soft-shelled and infertile. In view of these results, it was thought that *Agriocharis* should be returned to *Meleagris*. Direct crossing of the two species, held in captivity in Yucatán, has been reported (Smithe and Paynter, 1963:261). Paynter (1955:84) does not recognize *Agriocharis* as generically distinct from *Meleagris*. Doubt that *Agriocharis* should be retained had been previously expressed by Ridgway and Friedmann (1946:458). On the other hand, Ghigi (1936:355) thinks that the ocellated turkey should be in a separate genus.

We are again plagued with the question of what constitutes a genus. Chapman (1896) placed the ocellated turkey in a new genus, *Agriocharis*. The decision was based on the differences in the head and neck furnishings, plumage (especially the tail), absence of beard in the male, and the presence of spur knobs in the female. The spurs in the male are longer and more slender than in *Meleagris*. There are two marked differences in habits. Leopold (1959:278) mentions that in winter there is no segregation of the sexes as in *Meleagris*. The ocellated turkey takes to wing readily when a threat of danger is even two hundred yards distant. F. Gaumer (1897:111) wrote: "It flies with the greatest rapidity at the sight of man, regardless of distance." As is well known, the common wild turkey places more trust in its legs. The Indians of Yucatán, with all their skill with animals, were never able to domesticate the ocellated turkey.

The feathers of the two turkeys are totally different in markings. The tips of the rectrices in the ocellated turkey are more rounded than in the common turkey. When the ocellated turkey displays, there are some gaps between the rectrices while in the common turkey there are none in the "fan." Through the courtesy of K. C. Lint, I received a colored slide of the head and neck of an ocellated turkey taken during the mating season at the San Diego Zoological Garden. The small caruncles on the summit of the eminence on the crown and a row of the same extending from the base of the frontal caruncle posteriorly over the eyes are cream-colored. The tip of the frontal caruncle and a few scattered caruncles on the neck are red. All the remainder of the head and neck are deep blue.

There is no doubt, states Shufeldt (1914:47), that the ocellated turkey "belongs to a perfectly distinct genus"; however, its skeleton is so similar to that of *Meleagris* that osteologically it can be accorded only specific rank. Griscom (1932:104) wrote: "The generic distinctness between it and other members of its family show that it is a relict from a relatively ancient past and could not possibly have originated in the area where it now occurs, a region primarily of Pleistocene age, which in times past has been almost completely submerged."

The eggs of the ocellated and eastern turkeys are practically indistinguishable in size and coloration. I have compared the downy young of both species. *Agriocharis* (length 135 mm.) was very pale yellow below, including the throat; the crown was clay brown with a single narrow fuscous black streak extending to the rump; back and rump were ochraceous streaked with fuscous black. *M. g. silvestris* (length 130 mm.) was tinged with yellow below; the crown was cinnamon with three blackish streaks, one being median; back and rump were heavily marked with dark brown.

Systematics is still guided by personal opinion. No cross has yet been obtained between free-living *Agriocharis* and *Meleagris*. Although crosses have been obtained by artificial insemination, it is a question of how much value should be given to human assistance. Even hybrids obtained in the wild are not always used as a basis for placing the parents in the same genus. A case in point is the fairly common hybrid between the prairie chicken (*Tympanuchus cupido*) and sharp-tailed grouse (*Pedioecetes phasianellus*). There is evidence that some of the crosses are fertile (Ammann, 1957:111). In view of the external characters and habits of the ocellated turkey, it would seem preferable to retain the genus *Agriocharis*.

CLASSIFICATION

A satisfactory method for classifying birds has yet to be devised. Stresemann (1959) has reminded us that, after nearly two hundred years of effort, comparative morphology, physiology, and ethology have failed as tools for determining the relationships of the higher categories of birds. Some ornithologists have considered the gallinaceous birds to be very primitive. Beebe (1918:*xxiii*) wrote: "Considering the group as a whole, the Galliformes, or fowl-like birds, are unquestionably low in the scale of avian evolution. In spite of their fine feathers and elaborately specialized plumage characters, neither anatomically nor mentally are they of high rank." Portmann (1938) studied the postembryonic development of gallinaceous birds and came to the conclusion that they are very primitive. Growth is isometric, i.e. all parts develop uniformly in length and weight. Of present living birds, the megapodes are the most primitive followed by other members of the Galliformes.

The turkey is a plastic species, and it has been recommended for study to determine heritable characters and formation of subspecies (Osgood, 1921). Inbreeding in the turkey does not lead to extinction as with the chicken. Asmundson (1934) writes: "This difficulty would probably not arise with turkeys since brother-sister matings have been found to give satisfactory results in the hatchability of the eggs, viability of the young to eight weeks of age and in rate of growth. It should, therefore, be possible to build up homogenous lines of turkeys through inbreeding that would prove useful for genetic and other research." The existence of parthenogenesis in the eggs of the turkey (Olsen and Marsden, 1954) indicates that the bird is very primitive. In the arrangement of families by various writers, the rank of the Meleagrididae is as follows: The American Ornithologists' Union, pertaining to North American families only (1957:148), ranks it twenty-fourth; Berlioz (1950:916), retaining it under Phasianidae, forty-eighth; Mayr and Amadon (1951:34), thirty-third, Van Tyne and Berger (1959), thirty-ninth; and Stresemann (1927–34), listing subfamily Meleagrinae under Phasianidae, tenth. Some allowance must be made for the number of families recognized by the writers. It is evident that most classifications do not list Galliformes as a particularly low order.

Long ago, Parker (1866:234) called attention to the similarity of the skulls of the Galliformes and the Anseriformes. When it comes to the electrophoretic mobility of the egg whites, it is easy to distinguish between the two orders (Landsteiner *et al.*, 1938); however, the chromosome numbers have been reported to be the same for a duck and a turkey (Werner, 1931).

A decision to place the turkeys among the pheasants or in a separate family depends upon whether the approach is anatomical, physiological, morphological, or otherwise. Ridgway and Friedmann (1946:63, 436) placed the turkeys in the separate family Meleagrididae under the superfamily Phasianoidea on the basis of the head furnishings, the truncated contour feathers, the acetabulum, and the weak, straight furcula. Hudson *et al.* (1959:56) write that, except for the loss of the femorocaudal portion of the pyriform muscle, the turkey is essentially a pheasant.

A new taxonomic approach involves examination of the proteins of the blood serum and egg whites. Bain and Deutsch (1947) examined the egg white proteins of several species of birds and concluded that the electrophoretic pattern of the turkey was closer to the chicken than to the guinea hen or pheasant. The same technique previously applied to the blood serum of the turkey and related birds had given less satisfactory results (Deutsch and Goodloe, 1945). The first serious use of the electrophoretic method as a tool in avian taxonomy was by McCabe and Deutsch (1952). They decided that the guinea hen was more closely related to the peafowl than to the turkey. The patterns of the three species show closer relationship to each other than to the pheasants. Mainardi (1958), using immunology and chromatography, concluded that the turkey and guinea fowl are more closely related to each other than to the chicken. Recently, Sibley (1960:239) stated that from the electrophoretic patterns, the turkey is a pheasant and might be included properly in the subfamily Phasianinae. The egg whites from individual domestic turkey eggs showed appreciable variations in the electrophoretic profiles. On the basis of immunology, Mainardi (1959) considers *Phasianus, Numida,* and *Meleagris* as closely related while "*Gallus* and

Coturnix, which belong with *Phasianus* to the same family, are rather remote from one another, and from all other species." He would place Numididae and Meleagrididae under Phasianidae.

NOMENCLATURE

The nomenclature of the turkey has followed a tortuous path. The bird was confused with the guinea fowl, the *Meleagris* of the ancients, for two centuries; and this in spite of the fact that some of the early writers gave it an American origin. Gyllius (Aelianus, 1533:455), e.g. described the turkey correctly under the name *Gallo peregrino* and stated that it came from the New World. To Belon (1555:248) the turkey and guinea fowl were identical. He used for the turkey the following names: *Coc d'Inde* (French); *Meleagris* (Greek); and *Gibber* (Latin). Both Gesner (1555:464) and Aldrovandi (1599:36) believed the turkey to be the *Meleagris* of Africa. The synonymy of the turkey as given by Charleton (1677:81) is: *Gallopavo, Gallus Indicus, Meleagris,* Turkey-Cock, *Gallina Africana,* and *Gallina Numidica.* The names given by Rzaczynski (1721:301), *Gallus Indicus vulgo, Meleagris, Gallopavo, Avis Lybica,* and *Avis Numidica,* show continued confusion with the guinea fowl. Buffon (1771:157) showed beyond the shadow of a doubt that the turkey came from America. With less judgment than polemical skill, Barrington (1781:127) subsequently insisted that the bird was of African or eastern origin.

The name *Meleagris* arose in mythology. Homer, in the *Iliad*, mentions that Meleager (Meleagros), son of Oeneus, king of Calydon, killed a boar that was ravishing the land. The tale was subsequently expanded by various writers. On the death of Meleager, his sisters who mourned for him were transformed into birds, *meleagrides*. Aristotle (1862:139), who lived 384–322 B.C., knew of the guinea fowl for he wrote that *meleagris* and *phasianus* lay spotted eggs. The normal eggs of both species, however, are unspotted. Varro (1533:61), writing about 36 B.C., states that the African fowls were called *meleagrides* by the Greeks. Owing to their rarity, they were expensive in Italy. According to Pliny (1826:1880) (ca. 77 A.D.), *meleagrides* in Boetia were taught to battle like fighting cocks.

A preference for *Meleagris* over *Gallopavo* was expressed by Barrère

(1745:75) since the turkey had nothing in common with the peacock except the habit of spreading the tail; the only justification for *Gallopavo* would be the belief that it was a cross between a rooster and a peafowl. In order to avoid confusion with the guinea fowl, Moehring (1752:51) placed the turkey in a new genus, *Cenchramus*. Brisson (1760:162) selected *Gallo-pavo* and called the wild turkey *Gallo-pavo sylvestris* after Ray. Since no type was designated, under the International Code of Zoological Nomenclature, *Gallo-pavo* was merely a substitute for *Meleagris*. In 1828, Billberg (1828:4) proposed *Pseudotaon* for *Meleagris*.

When Linnaeus (1746:60) used *Meleagris* for the turkey, a mistake was made that is now beyond correction. Whether or not he was influenced by Sibbald (1684:16), who called the turkey both *Gallopavo* and *Meleagris*, it is unfortunate that *Gallopavo* was not chosen. The tenth edition of the *Systema* (Linnaeus, 1758) has the accepted binomial [*Meleagris*] *gallopavo*. In the twelfth edition, Linnaeus (1766) states, following the brief description, that the name is based on the *Gallopavo* of Gesner (1555:464) and the "Gallo Pavo *Sylvestris*" of Ray (1713:51), who in turn relied on the New England wild turkey of Josselyn (1860:39). There is no reason to believe that any of the authors except Josselyn had ever seen a wild turkey. Linnaeus' name was originally based on the domestic bird.

An unacceptable binomial applied to a wild turkey is the *Meleagris occidentalis* of Bartram (1791:83, 290). On the St. John's River, Florida, the turkeys were "expanding their silver-bordered train." This was within the range of the Florida turkey. *Occidentalis* is a *nomen nudum* since the description is not only inadequate but inaccurate. The tips of the tail feathers of this race are brown or buff. In McIntosh County, Georgia, Bartram observed a gobbler raised from an egg taken in the wild: "his head was above three feet from the ground when he stood erect; he was a stately beautiful bird, of a very dark dusky brown colour, the tips of the feathers of his neck, breast, back, and shoulders, edged with a copper colour, which in a certain exposure looked like burnished gold, and he seemed not insensible of the splendid appearance he made." It differed from the European turkey in being three times the weight and size. The feathers of both sexes were of a dark brown color, no black ones being present. This bird was the basis of his *Meleagris Americanus* that bred and was resident in Pennsylvania.

73

Nomenclature of Races of the Turkey

Considerable confusion was caused by Vieillot (1817:447) in giving two names to the wild turkey. His description is based primarily on *Le dindon sauvage* of the French edition (1799) of Bartram's travels. The copies of the *Dictionnaire* published in March, 1817, contain a description of *Meleagris silvestris*, while those issued in June, 1817, contain revised sheets, tipped in, with the name *Meleagris fera* (Sherborn, 1902; McAtee, 1947). Possibly he dropped *silvestris* because of the prior use of *sylvestris* by Ray and others. Vieillot and Outart (1825:10) used *fera*, and this usage was followed by Lesson (1836:359), Coues (1899), Elliot (1893:387; 1902:237) used *americana* in 1893 and in 1902 stated that he eliminated by emendation, so that Vieillot's *silvestris* must be accepted.

The *Meleagris americana* of Bartram ran a good race for supremacy. It was used by Gray (1870:262) and consistently by Coues in his various publications from 1872 to 1899, when *fera* was preferred. Ogilvie-Grant (1893:387; 1902:237) used *americana* in 1893 and in 1902 stated that he could see no objection to its employment. Harper (1942) has contended that *americana* has precedence over *silvestris* and has suggested Chester County, Pennsylvania, as the type locality. I am in full agreement with his position. Vieillot adds nothing to Bartram's description of the wild turkey which he uses. In fact, when he describes *Meleagris silvestris*, he falls into error or had the domestic bird in mind: "The pinions of the wings and the feathers which cover the tail underneath are of a silvery white at their ends; the bill and the feet are black." It does not seem valid to reject the *americana* of Bartram on the assumption that he was not a binomialist.

The name *Meleagris palawa*, suggested by Barton (1805) to distinguish the wild from the domestic turkey, is unaccompanied by a description. *Palawa* is a variant of the Delaware Indian name for the turkey. Lesson (1831:489) introduced a new name, *Gallo-pavo primus*, for the wild turkey. The American Ornithologists' Union (1903), after using *Meleagris gallopavo* for years, in 1903 settled on *Meleagris gallopavo silvestris* Vieillot for the eastern turkey.

Florida turkey.—At the turn of the century a new subspecies was described. The Florida wild turkey was named *Meleagris gallopavo osceola* by Scott (1890) after the Seminole chief, Osceola. Elliot (1899:232) preferred *M. fera osceola*.

Rio Grande turkey.—The turkeys of southern Texas were originally blanketed under *M. gallopavo* or *M. mexicana*. In 1879, before trinomials became respectable, Sennett (1879:428) named the turkeys of the lower Río Grande *Meleagris gallopavo* variety *intermedia*. His description of the specimens taken at Lomita Ranch, Hidalgo County, seven miles up the river above Hidalgo, is so slight that a *nomen nudum* is as much in order as in the case of Bartram. He (Sennett, 1892:167) subsequently published an adequate description and named the bird *Meleagris gallopavo ellioti* after his friend D. G. Elliot; however, *intermedia* has priority. Different specimens were used by Sennett in describing *intermedia* and *ellioti*.

Merriam's turkey.—The turkeys of western Texas, the Rocky Mountains, New Mexico, Arizona, and the tableland of Mexico were assigned by Baird (1858:618; 1874:410) to *Meleagris mexicana* Gould, but he suspected that they might belong to a new species. Since Merriam's turkey has so much white in the plumage, it is rather surprising that recognition as a new subspecies was so long in coming. The early travelers in the Southwest noted that it differed from the eastern turkey with which they were familiar. While near Rabbit Ear Creek, northeastern New Mexico, G. C. Sibley (Gregg, 1952:99) recorded on October 13, 1825: "The hunters killed some Turkies this Morning, which are the first we have seen since leaving the Waters of the Osage River. These are different in their Plumage from the Wild Turkies of the Missouri, having more white about them & resembling somewhat our Tame Turkies." Woodhouse (1853:94) wrote that he could see no difference between the turkeys seen at Santa Fe and "our common species," but his guide, Leroux, told him that the turkeys along the Gila River had much more white upon them than those found east of the Río Grande. It was mentioned by J. G. Cooper (1870:523) that the turkeys of Arizona and New Mexico were strikingly lighter in color than the eastern birds. The light color of the turkeys shot in the Wet Mountains of Colorado was noted also by Campion (1878:133).

In February, 1860, Henry Bryant wrote to Baird (Dall, 1915:336) that in his opinion the New Mexican turkey was a variety and not a species.

It was thought by Coues (1866:93) to be entirely proper to separate the western and eastern turkeys. It remained for Nelson (1900) to show that the southwestern turkey was a distinct subspecies, *M. g. merriami*. It was named after C. Hart Merriam.

South Mexican turkey.—The original *Meleagris gallopavo* of Linnaeus, although a domestic bird (Newton, 1868:102), must be the starting point for the various subspecies. The Mexicans domesticated the native turkey, which extended from Veracruz westward, and it is the domestic bird that was introduced into Europe. The wild bird, accordingly, must be *Meleagris gallopavo gallopavo*. When Gould (1856) described his Mexican turkey (*Meleagris mexicana*), he contended that Linnaeus based his *Meleagris gallopavo* on the wild turkey found north of Mexico. This led to the use of *M. gallopavo* for the eastern turkey in the AOU Check-Lists until the turn of the century. Characteristic of the native Mexican race are the white tips of the tail feathers and the upper tail coverts. Bonaparte (1825:98) used these characteristics to identify the tame turkeys sold as wild ones in the Philadelphia and New York markets. The white "rump" has been eliminated in nearly all of the modern domestic turkeys, but the white tips of the tail feathers persist. Baird (1867) stated that the domestic turkey is unquestionably of Mexican origin. Coues (1897), after discussing the nomenclature, came to the only proper solution, i.e. naming the Mexican bird *M. g. gallopavo*.

Gould (1856:63) described a turkey as follows: "In size this new Turkey exceeds that of the largest specimens of the North American species; but it has shorter legs, a considerably larger and more broadly expanded tail, conspicuously zoned with brown and black, and terminated with white; the tail coverts are very profusely developed, largely tipped with white, and bounded posteriorly with a narrow line of black, their basal portions being rich metallic bronze. The same arrangement of colouring also prevails on the feathers of the lower part of the flanks; and on the under tail coverts, where it is particularly fine; the centre of the back is black, with green, purplish and red reflexions: the back of the neck, upper part of the back, and shoulders, are in some lights bronzy, in others the colour of fire; the greater wing coverts are uniform bronzy brown, forming a conspicuous band across the wing; all the primaries are crossed by mottled bars of blackish brown and white, freckled with brown; all the under surface is fiery copper, intensely brilliant in certain lights, and becoming darker towards the flanks.

"Total length 4 feet 4 inches [1,320 mm.]; bill 2½ inches [73], wing 21¾ inches [552], tail 16 inches [406], and when spread, about 24 inches across; tarsi 6¾ [171]."

It is uncertain, because of the brief description, if Gould's *mexicana* is synonymous with *gallopavo* or represents the at-present accepted *mexicana*. Attempts have been made to settle the point on a geographical basis. Gould stated that his specimen came from Mr. Floresi, Real del Monte Mines, Mexico. Floresi worked for an English mining company at Bolaños, Jalisco, which also operated mines at Real del Monte, Hidalgo. Nelson (1900:123) gives reasons for believing that Gould's specimen came from Bolaños, northern Jalisco. He had two specimens from El Salto, Durango, that matched Gould's description. Hellmayr and Conover (1942:294) prefer Real del Monte Mines as the type locality. Only three of Gould's measurements are useful. The lengths of the wing, tail, and tarsus fit those of *mexicana* better than those of the smaller *gallopavo*.

Moore's turkey.—Moore (1938) described a new subspecies, *onusta*, as occurring in southeastern Sonora and Sinaloa. It was so named on account of its heavy body. Nelson (1900:123) considered the turkeys of northern Chihuahua to be intermediate between *merriami* and *mexicana*. Moore did not recognize *mexicana*. He examined specimens from Durango to Bonito Creek, northern Sonora, and arrived at the same conclusion as did Nelson. If *onusta* is a good subspecies, it is remarkable that it should occur in the territory of the "intermediates."

Variations In Plumage

The turkey instead of the widgeon should have been used by John Ray (Willughby, 1678:376) when he wrote: "Mr. Willughby in this and other Birds is, in my opinion, more particular and minute in describing the colours of each single feather of the Wings and Tail than is needful; sith in these things nature doth as they say sport her self, not observing exactly the same strokes and spots in the feathers of all Birds of the same sort."

According to Le Conte (1858:179), "In the tame bird, the colours vary infinitely, and in the wild one, very considerably." There is the further complication of admixture with the domestic turkey, so that there is no assurance that the specimen in hand represents a pure race. To add to the problem, game managers in recent years have stocked turkeys of two subspecies in the same area. Presumably, old specimens taken in wild areas are closest to the original stock; however, of the 359 specimens of all races in three of the largest collections in the United States, only 4 per cent were taken prior to 1886, the year the first AOU Check-List appeared.

The fine markings of the feathers differ so between individuals, even from the same locality, that it seems almost superfluous to describe them. A coarse example in point is the barring of the primaries of the eastern turkey. Ridgway and Friedmann (1946:440) wrote: "... primaries clove brown barred with white, the white bars nearly, if not quite, as wide as the dusky interspaces, and touching the shaft of the quills." Equality of the white bars and dusky spaces had been previously mentioned by Elliot (1872: Plate XXX). Audubon's famous plate shows the light bars nearly equal to the dark interspaces. Baird (1858:616) was more realistic in giving the width of the white bars as one-half of that of the dark interspaces. I have examined forty-five specimens of the eastern turkey, and only two of them show this condition. The bars on the ninth primary of fifteen males collected in the period 1886–1913 were measured. The width of the dark interspaces varied from 8 to 15 mm. (average 10 mm.), and that of the white bars from 3 to 8 mm. (average 5 mm.). A female, Museum of Comparative Zoology, No. 202684, taken at Mount Carmel, Illinois, May 8, 1878, has the white bars extremely variable in width, and not all of them run to the shaft. Other specimens examined are similar. Ridgway and Friedmann (1946:448) mention a specimen from Kissimmee, Florida, in the center of the range of *osceola*, having the wing quills in agreement with those of *silvestris*. Baird *et al.* (1874:410) state that the tips of the upper tail coverts of specimens of *silvestris* from Arkansas are "rufous-chestnut instead of dark maroon-chestnut, as in typical *gallopavo* from Pennsylvania and Virginia."

Descriptions of Races

The turkey has a heavy body and stout legs, which in the male are provided with spurs (Fig. 9). The head and neck are furnished with wattles and unprepossessing caruncles, the colors of which can be changed at will. Most of the feathers are banded and truncated. The body plumage is dark, in part velvety black, with brilliant metallic reflections of coppery bronze and green. In some races there is much white in the wings and upper tail coverts. The designation of the metallic hues of the feathers is dependent on the incidence of the light. The subterminal band of the back feathers of an eastern turkey, e.g., is green at one angle, and pale bronze and golden bronze at other angles.

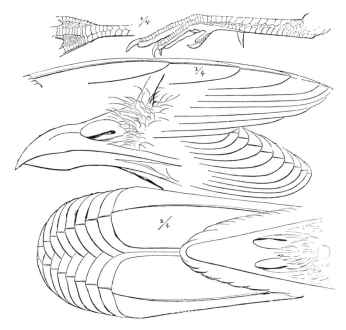

Fig. 9.—*Members of turkey. (After J. G. Cooper* [*1870*].)

The descriptions given below are limited to the principal characteristics distinguishing the various races. Detailed descriptions of the plumage are given by Ridgway and Friedmann (1946:436–58). I have used their measurements.

Meleagrididae
Soft parts.—Head and neck are naked except for scattering bristle-like feathers. Females have more or less contour feathers on the hind neck

extending to the nape. In the male there are prominent caruncles, largest on the lower part of the neck. The loose skin of the throat forms a wattle that is considerably less prominent in the female. Both sexes have an erect frontal caruncle about 25 mm. long, capable of distention in the male to a long flabby appendage, especially during the breeding season. In the male, according to mood, the skin may be red, purple, blue, or creamy white.

The bill is yellow with orange at the base. The tarsi are coral red, the color being dull prior to shedding of the scales.

The spurs of the male vary in length and in shape. If present in females, they are merely nubs.

The feathers composing the beard, or pectoral appendage, are hairlike, not round, and sooty black to black in color. The length depends partly on age. Although characteristic of the males, a short beard is occasionally found on females.

Meleagris gallopavo silvestris Vieillot
Eastern Turkey (Plates 7 and 8)

Adult male.—General color of plumage is dark brown with glittering metallic reflections of coppery bronze, appearing metallic red and green at certain angles. Feathers of breast, back, sides, flanks, scapulars, and lesser upper wing coverts truncate, terminating in a narrow band of velvety black.

Upper tail coverts are *chestnut* tipped with a narrow band of velvety black preceded by broad bands of pinkish-bronze and greenish-black.

Tail feathers are rounded, russet to brown in color, vermiculated and barred with black. Inner webs of outer rectrices are most prominently barred. Rectrices are broadly tipped with *deep buff* to *cinnamon brown* and have a subterminal black band.

Primaries are clove brown crossed with white bars generally reaching the shaft, the bars occasionally as wide as the dark interspaces, but usually narrower. Secondaries are edged with white, the white bars more or less triangular, so that they appear conspicuously light in color.

Adult female.—Similar to male but browner, and metallic reflections are less brilliant. Feathers of the breast, flanks, and sides are *tipped with brown.*

Adult male.—Wing, 480–550 mm. (average, 512.9 mm.); tail, 370–440

(397.2); culmen from cere, 31–38 (34.8); tarsus, 146–181.5 (162.6); middle toe without claw, 73–87 (81.4); length of tarsal spur, 14.5–23 (18.5); diameter of tarsal spur, 10–13.5 (11.6).

Adult female.—Wing, 382–438 mm. (414.3); tail 306–345 (329.3); culmen from cere, 28–35.5 (31.7); tarsus, 126–143 (131.8); middle toe without claw, 61.5–68 (65.4).

Type locality.—Pennsylvania

Meleagris gallopavo osceola Scott
Florida Turkey

Adult male.—Similar to *silvestris* but smaller. The white bars of the primaries and outer secondaries are more irregular and narrower than the dark interspaces, and generally *not reaching the shaft.* The inner secondaries are *without distinct bars* and have brownish vermiculations on the inner edge. *Silvestris* and *osceola* are the only races with chestnut upper tail coverts.

Adult female.—Similar to the male but duller.

Adult male.—Wing, 430–487 mm. (462); tail 345–390 (362.8); culmen from cere, 30.5–35.5 (32.9); tarsus, 159.5–174 (169.8); middle toe without claw, 70–82.5 (76.4); length of tarsal spur, 17–32 (25.1); diameter of tarsal spur, 9.5–13 (11.6).

Adult female.—Wing, 354–390 (368.7); tail, 268–304 (291); culmen from cere, 26.8–31 (29.1); tarsus, 125.5–135.5 (132.3); middle toe without claw, 59–68 (63.2).

Type locality.—Tarpon Springs, Florida.

Meleagris gallopavo intermedia Sennett
Rio Grande Turkey (Plate 9)

Adult male.—Similar to *silvestris* but smaller. Upper tail coverts, lower tail coverts, and rectrices are *tipped with cinnamon-buff.* White bars of primaries are irregular, sometimes not reaching the shaft and interrupted or streaked with black. Those of innermost secondaries are indistinct, as in *osceola.* Back and rump are black, the feathers at a certain angle showing a subapical band of gray.

Adult female.—Similar to the male but duller. Feathers of the breast, sides, and flanks are tipped with pale pinkish buff.

Adult male.—Wing, 462–468 mm. (465); tail, 346–385 (369.3); culmen from cere, 35–37 (35.8); tarsus, 162–171 (166.3); middle toe without claw,

78–81.5 (80.2); length of tarsal spur, 11.5–17 (14.7); diameter of tarsal spur, 11.5–12.5 (12.2).

Adult female.—Wing 385–405 mm. (392.3); tail, 277–302 (290.3); culmen from cere, 26.5–32.5 (30.3); tarsus, 126–138.5 (130.4); middle toe without claw, 61.5–71 (65).

Type locality.—Lomita, Texas.

Meleagris gallopavo merriami Nelson
Merriam's Turkey (Plate 10)

Adult male.—Similar to *intermedia* but larger. Tips of rump feathers, upper tail coverts, and rectrices are pale *buff to almost white*. Feathers of flanks and under tail coverts are tipped with pale rufous or white, with a rusty tinge.

Middle tail feathers are *distinctly barred*, black and chestnut. Tail is *more rufous* than *intermedia, mexicana*, or *gallopavo*.

Velvety black lower back almost devoid of iridescence.

Adult female.—Similar to *intermedia* but *larger*, and with tips of upper tail coverts and rectrices paler; innermost secondaries are mottled more strongly with dusky.

Adult male.—Wing, 502–524 mm. (511); tail, 373–427 (398.4); culmen from cere, 34.5–40 (37.2); tarsus, 159–175 (166.6); middle toe without claw, 78–88 (83.5).

Adult female.—Wing 400–463 mm. (435.9); tail, 325–360 (345); culmen from cere, 31–34 (32.3); tarsus, 124–159 (133.6); middle toe without claw, 66–73 (68.8).

Type locality.—Forty-seven miles southwest of Winslow, Arizona.

Meleagris gallopavo gallopavo Linnaeus
South Mexican Turkey

Adult male.—Similar to *merriami* but smaller. Tail blackish and *less rufescent.* Incomplete russet bars on basal two-thirds of outer tail feathers.

Tips of rectrices, feathers of rump, upper tail coverts, lower tail coverts, and flanks are *pale pinkish buff*, similar to *merriami*. Feathers of lower back and rump are blackish with narrow bluish tips and with subterminal blue-green reflections.

Outer secondaries have white margins.

Adult female.—Similar to *merriami* but upper body plumage has pronounced greenish and reddish metallic reflections.

Adult male.—Wing, 465–513 mm. (489); tail, 345–400 (372.5); culmen from cere, 34–38.5 (35.8); tarsus, 162–176 (168.4); middle toe without claw, 74–85 (79.9); length of tarsal spur, 14.5–16.5 (15.5); diameter of tarsal spur, 11.5–14 (12.8).

Adult female.—Wing, 396–416 mm. (405.6); tail, 311–323 (319.8); culmen from cere, 32.5–36 (34.6); tarsus 130–140 (135); middle toe without claw, 65–71.5 (68.6).

Type locality.—Mirador, Veracruz.

Meleagris gallopavo mexicana Gould
Gould's Turkey

Adult male.—Similar to *gallopavo* but larger. Lower back and rump have *coppery* and *greenish-golden* reflections, not bluish black as in *gallopavo* or faintly iridescent velvety black as in *merriami*.

Tips of upper tail coverts and rectrices are a faint *pinkish cast, almost white.*

Rectrices are more dusky and less evenly barred than in *merriami* and more vermiculated as in *gallopavo*.

Outer secondaries have broader white edgings than in *merriami* and much less rufescent inner secondaries.

Adult female.—Similar to *gallopavo* but feathers of upper body have less pronounced metallic greenish and reddish sheen, being more purplish.

Adult male.—Wing, 465–545 mm. (504.1); tail, 363–437 (396.1); culmen from cere, 34.5–41 (38.7); tarsus, 168–182 (173.8); middle toe without claw, 84–93 (87.6); length of tarsal spur, 13.5–17.5 (16.1); diameter of tarsal spur, 11–13 (12).

Adult female.—Wing, 402–436 mm. (419.6); tail, 318–362 (334.9); culmen from cere, 33.5–35 (34.4); tarsus, 132–139.5 (134.5); middle toe without claw, 68–73 (70.1).

Type locality.—Bolaños, Jalisco.

Meleagris gallopavo onusta Moore
Moore's Turkey

Adult male.—A doubtful subspecies. Similar to *mexicana*. Rump black without iridescence.

Differs from *mexicana* (for which Moore [1938] gives the range from Jalisco to southern Chihuahua east of the Sierras) in having the median rectrices barred instead of mottled or vermiculated. Less cinnamon from anterior to white tips of rectrices and upper tail coverts.

Nearest to *merriami*. On upper tail coverts and rectrices, the subterminal narrow cinnamon bar of *merriami* is absent; black bar immediately anterior to it is usually or always absent; iridescence both above and below is darker, less brilliantly green and coppery.

Adult female.—Differs from *mexicana* as the male.

Adult male (one specimen).—Wing, 505 mm.; tail, 421; culmen from cere, 38.4; tarsus, 173.7; middle toe without claw, 89.5.

Adult female (four specimens).—Wing, 417–448 mm. (434); tail 331–347 (339); culmen from cere, 32–38.4 (34.5); tarsus, 140–149 (145.5); middle toe without claw, 71–75.9 (73.5).

Type locality.—Guayachi, Chihuahua.

Weights

The early literature on North America gives some fantastic weights for the wild turkey. A few examples will suffice. An anonymous (1906) author gives the weights of Maryland wild turkeys as running from forty to sixty-three pounds. He killed one that weighed forty-three pounds with the feathers and entrails removed. Lawson (1937:156) never weighed a turkey, but he was informed of one that weighed nearly sixty pounds. Catesby (1754:*xliv*) wrote: "It is commonly reported that these Turkeys weigh sixty Pounds a piece, but of many hundred that I handled, I observed very few to exceed the Weight of thirty Pounds." The high weights cannot be attributed to hybridization since there was universal agreement that the domestic turkey was much smaller than the wild one.

The breeding of heavy turkeys is a relatively recent pursuit. It was stated in 1752 that in France (*Dictionnaire universal*, 1752) a turkey sometimes weighed more than twenty pounds. By 1876 in Scotland, the Norfolk and Cambridge turkeys were the same size as the eastern wild turkey (Gilmour, 1876:15). Domestic turkeys of enormous size are now being raised. The prize turkey shown at the meeting of the National Turkey Federation in 1960 weighed fifty-eight pounds, two ounces. Some growers are aiming to produce birds weighing one hundred pounds.

The large weights attributed to wild turkeys must be from estimates. A hunter killed a large gobbler on Cache River, Arkansas, and the lowest estimate of its weight by any member of the party was twenty-five pounds. The actual weight was twenty-one pounds. He (J. E. R., 1881) gave this sage advice: "When you kill a gobbler of twenty-five or thirty pounds do not weigh him; they generally resent such a proceeding by falling off from five to ten pounds."

The average weight of the hen, according to Audubon (1831:15), is nine pounds, although he shot one that weighed thirteen pounds. Males weighed fifteen to eighteen pounds. These data are acceptable, but he overreaches by mentioning one in the market of Louisville that weighed thirty-six pounds. Even Bent (1932:334) lost his customary caution by stating that a fully grown gobbler in good condition seldom weighs more than twenty or twenty-five pounds, but that there are apparently authentic records of birds weighing thirty to forty pounds. A turkey killed in Dinwiddie County, Virginia, weighed twenty-seven pounds, but it was believed to be a hybrid since it had some white feathers (Lewis, 1885). Godsey (1930) wrote that Missouri wild turkeys are hybrids and attain a large size. One was killed that weighed twenty-nine pounds. Bogardus (1879:232, 234), in Illinois, killed two "very large" turkeys weighing twenty pounds each. He describes killing a quite fat gobbler weighing twenty-seven pounds. This must have been a hybrid. Some of the published weights are difficult to evaluate. Jordan (1879), for the turkeys in Montgomery County, Texas, gives the weights of old males in good condition at twenty to twenty-six pounds, but specimens of the latter weight were exceedingly rare. A weight of twenty-one pounds was a "big average." Hens weighed eleven to fourteen pounds. According to A. H. Rutledge (1936:492), the male rarely weighs more than twenty pounds; however, he weighed one of twenty-three pounds. Previously (1919), he described the killing of a gobbler weighing twenty-five pounds. The record gobbler for a Mississippi hunting club was 23.5 pounds (Dalrymple, 1957). Without stating the race, Nelson and Martin (1953:41) give the following weights: average for the male, 16.3 pounds, and maximum, 23.8 pounds; average for the female, 9.3 pounds, and maximum, 12.3 pounds.

Eastern turkey (*M. g. silvestris*).—Within recent years weights have been obtained, particularly by game managers, that are reliable. H. E. Davis (1931), during his long experience as a hunter, never saw more than five old gobblers weighing more than seventeen pounds, the maximum being twenty-one pounds. Subsequently, he stated that he had records of two birds weighing 22.5 pounds each. Any bird weighing more must be considered a hybrid (Davis, 1937). The largest turkey ever shot by Johenning (1940) in Virginia was a male weighing twenty pounds. A male trapped by Bailey (1950:7) in spring in West Virginia weighed 20.75 pounds. Herbert Stoddard has informed me (*in litt.*) that on February 13, 1957, President Eisenhower shot on the Greenwood Plantation, Thomas County, Georgia, a gobbler weighing 22.25 pounds. In his opinion, if the bird had not been excessively fat, it would have weighed about eighteen pounds.

The weights of 181 turkeys shot in Pennsylvania (Bowers, 1958) are shown in Table 6.

TABLE 6

Number of Specimens	Age	Range in Pounds	Average Weight in Pounds
36	Juvenile male	4.5–14	10.06
36	Juvenile female	4–10.5	7.25
65	Adult male	12–28	17.00
44	Adult female	7.5–16	11.06

Only two of the turkeys weighed twenty-eight pounds, showing that they were hybrids. Few Pennsylvania turkeys are without some domestic crossing.

The heaviest turkey handled by Mosby and Handley (1943:98) in Virginia weighed 20.56 pounds. Few turkeys in the state reach this weight. The heaviest male among the turkeys killed in two of the state forests in 1945 weighed 17.1 pounds. The ranges in weights of eighty-two turkeys shot in Virginia (McDowell, 1956:18; *cf.* Tuttle, 1946) in November, 1953, are shown in Table 7.

TABLE 7

	Range in Pounds
Old males	14.44–17.10
Juvenile males	6.5–13
Old females	8–10.5
Juvenile females	5–8

Only one male trapped by Wheeler (1948:46) in Alabama weighed as much as 20.13 pounds. Table 8 shows the weights by months for adult males.

TABLE 8

| No. of Birds | Month | Weight in Pounds | | |
		Average	Minimum	Maximum
5	Sept.	12.00*	7.50	14.38
2	Dec.	16.50	16.13	16.87
2	Jan.	17.75	17.25	18.25
3	Feb.	16.87*	14.81	20.13
2	Mar.	16.75	15.75	17.75
1	Apr.	17.25	—	—

*Approximate weight.

Wheeler believed that a gobbler attained its maximum growth when about three years of age. Adult turkeys have the lowest weight in late summer, and the highest in late winter and early spring.

It may be concluded that any weight over twenty-three pounds for any eastern turkey is open to suspicion.

Florida turkey (*M. g. osceola*).—Allen (1871:343) was informed by George A. Boardman that very fat gobblers often weigh 25 to 28 pounds; however, the average weight of the males was 18 to 20 pounds, and of the females, 6 to 10 pounds. The hens collected by Kennard (1915:6) in February in the Big Cypress Swamp weighed 5.75 to 8.5 pounds, and the gobblers 15 to 18 pounds. Friends furnished weights of 22, 23, and 25 pounds. The largest turkey handled by "Osceola" (1924) weighed 19 pounds. W. E. D. Scott (1892:215) weighed in excess of 70 turkeys. The males ranged from 12 to 22 pounds, with an average of 16 pounds; the females, 4.75 pounds to 9.5 pounds. Scott's weights are acceptable.

Rio Grande turkey (*M. g. intermedia*).—The heaviest turkey that Bracht (1849:77) weighed at San Antonio in 1848 was about 20 pounds. He was told of weights of 25 to 30 pounds. An unusually fat bird shot by Dresser (1866:26) near San Antonio in 1863 weighed close to 16 pounds with the entrails removed. Two hens collected in spring in the Sierra del Carmen, Coahuila, Mexico, weighed 8 and 9.5 pounds respectively (Miller, 1955:162). Birds trapped in Texas by Glazener (1945) in

January and February, 1945, weighed as follows: adult males, 18 to 21 pounds; adult females, 8 to 10 pounds; young females, 6 to 7.5 pounds. Cox (1948) gives the average weights of turkeys in the one, two, and three year or over classes as: females, 6.05, 7.21, and 7.78 pounds; males, 10.64, 13.6, and 15.8 pounds.

Merriam's turkey (*M. g. merriami*).—Some of the weights given for this race are as exaggerated as those for the eastern turkey in colonial times. Bendire (1892:117) shot a bird that weighed twenty-eight pounds after being drawn; and he saw tracks five and six inches in length. Weights of sixteen to forty pounds are given by Bailey (1928:231). Ligon (1946:6) wrote: "Sizes and weights of wild turkeys vary considerably according to age and with the availability of fat-producing food. Mature, fat gobblers range from 18 to 35 pounds and even heavier in exceptional cases." Adult hens weigh eight to twelve pounds.

A turkey shot by Schultz (1909) in central Arizona was estimated to weigh thirty pounds, but on the scales the weight was twenty-two pounds. The two heaviest turkeys shot during the 1952 hunting season in Arizona weighed eighteen pounds each (Hall, 1952:2). The maximum weights for the turkeys shot on the Kaibab Plateau during the seasons of 1956 and 1957 were 17.75 pounds for a male and 9.5 pounds for a female (Russo, 1959:177). The average weights of seventy-three turkeys shot on the Gila National Forest, New Mexico were: mature males, 13.77 pounds; mature females, 10.11 pounds; young males, 8.91 pounds; young females, 7.3 (Gordon and McClellan, 1952). The difference between the sexes is less than should be anticipated.

The average weights of turkeys trapped in winter in Wyoming (Crump and Sanderson, 1951:9) were: mature gobblers, 16.06 pounds; mature hens, 9.31 pounds. The heaviest gobbler, trapped February 16, 1951, weighed 19.69 pounds. A gobbler captured on January 24 weighed 12.75 pounds. When recaptured twenty-three days later, it weighed 11.88 pounds, a loss of 0.87 pound.

The heaviest turkeys trapped by Burget (1946:10) in Colorado were a male weighing 20.25 pounds, and a female weighing 11.75 pounds. During the hunting season of 1953, the three largest gobblers shot in the Stahlsteimer Creek Area weighed 17.5, 18.5, and 19.0 pounds respectively (Burget, 1954:30). Burget (1957:20) weighed 133 trapped turkeys, and the results are shown in Table 9.

TABLE 9

Average Weight—Pounds

22 mature gobblers	16.53
7 yearling gobblers	12.25
4 juvenile gobblers	10.00
46 mature hens	10.08
31 yearling hens	8.41
23 juvenile hens	6.75

An exceptionally large turkey weighing 22 pounds was taken near Pagosa Springs. The specimen is in the Denver Museum. The data show that Merriam's turkey is no heavier than the eastern race.

Gould's turkey (M. g. mexicana).—I am indebted to Starker Leopold for the weights, given in Table 10, of turkeys collected in northwestern Chihuahua in summer.

TABLE 10

No. of Specimens	Age	Sex	Weight in Pounds Range	Average
5	adult	male	15.1–16.6	15.7
3	yearling	male	9.0–13.75	11.4
2	adult	female	9.4– 9.7	9.6
4	yearling	female	6.0– 9.5	7.7

5

Anatomy and Physiology

A STUDY of the skeleton of a bird, or of its parts, will reveal the order, family, and usually the genus and the species to which it belongs. There are excellent drawings of bird bones, with nomenclature, in a publication by Howard (1929). The skeleton of a wild turkey is shown in Plate 11. Daudin (1800) published an illustration of the skeleton of the domestic turkey with the names of the various bones. A recent paper on the skeleton by Passantino (1938) is marred by poor illustrations. The pneumaticity of the bones was studied by Camper (1773).

Osteology

Several osteological features peculiar to the turkey were found by Huxley (1868). The postacetabular length of the ilium is greater than the preacetabular length; and the length of the postacetabular area is greater than the width. The slender furcula, viewed laterally, is straight and provided with a rodlike hypocleidium. The acromiom of the scapula is peculiar in shape.

The skulls of wild and domesticated turkeys have been studied extensively by Shufeldt (1887; 1887.1). He states: (1) In the wild bird the nasals fuse with the frontals while a suture persists in the domesticated one; (2) the parietal prominences of the wild bird are more conspicuous than those of the domesticated one, and the median longitudinal from the parietal prominences to the occipital ridge is shorter in the wild bird; (3) the postnasal and preparietal depressions are greater in the wild bird; (4) the pterygoids are longer and more slender in the wild bird; (5) the interorbital septum is entire in the wild bird and perforated in the tame; (6) the skull of the domesticated turkey is thicker and more rounded than in the wild bird, and this difference is usually perceptible at a glance; and (7) the tibiotarsus is more massive in the tame turkey. As Shufeldt states, exceptions to these criteria are numerous.

The presence of two foramina in the orbital septum of the tame turkey was mentioned by Eyton (1867:171). All skulls, apparently, have a narrow foramen at the summit of the septum. The presence of two foramina appears to be independent of race. I have the skulls of two Río Grande turkeys, one with two foramina, the other with a single foramen. The skull of a broad-breasted bronze turkey has only the summit foramen.

There are twenty-six vertebrae in the turkey: fifteen cervical, five dorsal (of which one, the twentieth, is free), and six free caudal vertebrae, plus a pointed pygostyle. Four of the dorsal vertebrae are fused. In the sternum the keel is broad. The posterior lateral processes are long and slender, resulting in deep sternal notches. Posterior to the carinal apex, the border of the keel widens and is depressed where the keel rests upon a limb while the bird is roosting. The deformations are caused by the weight of the body. Wild birds have the "roost dent" but rarely crooked keels, which occur commonly in domestic turkeys.

Considerable attention has been paid to this deformity. In Great Britain, five male turkeys out of sixteen which had been using flat roosts had crooked keels (Anderson, 1900). The prevailing opinion was that the deformity was produced by roosting. North (1939) experimented with roosts of various sizes and shapes, and set at different angles, and concluded that poles four inches in diameter produced the least indentation. The keels of males had larger indentations than those of the females, but within sexes there was no relation between weight and the depth of the indentation. The principal cause of crooked keels appears to be due to faulty nutrition rather than to the type of roost (Marsden and Martin, 1945:594). I have seen deformed sternums of native wild turkeys.

The quadrate in the skull of the wild turkey is distinctly reptilian in character (Lowe, 1926). An ossified aponeurotic lamella extending from the hypotarsus to the spur, or hallux, in the tarsometatarsus may be present or absent. Lowe (1933:342) had no explanation for the lack of uniformity. Regarding the circulatory system in the femur of the domestic turkey, Foote (1921:6) states: "The section is composed of concentric laminae separated and crossed by vascular canals. The wall of the bone is divided into nearly equal segments by large radiating canals extending from the medullary canal to the periosteal surface. From these canals are sent off small, lateral, parallel canals which divide the wall of the bone into laminae. The laminae are interrupted in the anterior wall and posterior ridge by incompletely differentiated Haversian systems."

Some curious malformations in domestic turkeys have been reported. Pennant (1781:81) illustrates a toe with a sharp curved claw growing upward on the tibia of a bird raised in his poultry yard. At the March 3, 1875, meeting of the Boston Society of Natural History, "Dr. J. B. S. Jackson (1875) exhibited a curiously malformed sternum of a turkey, containing a large cavity through which the intestine passed."

I have counted nineteen calcified tendons, or "splints," in the muscles of the tibiotarsus of the eastern wild turkey. The vesicular structure of the calcified tendons of the turkey was examined by Lieberkühn (1860) a century ago. He found rings of true ossified tissue surrounding the Haversian canals. Retterer and Lelièvre (1911) worked with the calcified tendons in the toes of a three-year-old turkey. The principal amount of the so-called ossified tissue consists of tendinous tissue, the cells of which are hypertrophied and hyperplasied. The conjunctive fibers are likewise hypertrophied and calcified. Only a very thin perivascular zone shows a true osseous structure.

An extensive description of the eye of the turkey was published by Du Petit (1738). Home (1796:18) reported that the marsupium (pecten) in the back of the eye was joined to the crystalline lens by a transparent membrane. There are twenty-two pecten plications (*Fächerfalten*) according to Wagner (1837:208). Jegorow (1887) found that the sympathetic nerve in the neck was without influence on the movement of the iris or the lower eyelid. The muscular structure of the eye has been examined more recently by Bland-Sutton (1920). The nictitating membrane is moved by the pyramidalis and quadratus muscles. The quadratus arises from the sclerotic above the optic nerve and nearest the optic nerve, where its border is the narrowest, and forms a sling (Fig. 10). The pyramidalis, or nictator muscle, arises from the sclerotic on its nasal side, and ends in a long tendon playing in the loop of the quadratus, and after winding about the globe, ends in the lower angle of the nictitating membrane. Contraction of the pyramidalis pulls over the eye the nictitating membrane that retracts and refolds through its inherent elasticity.

The roof of the mouth of the turkey is shown by Sippel (1908:505).

Veinous System and Blood

A comprehensive study, with good illustrations, of the veinous system of the turkey has been made by Neugebauer (1845). Plates 12 and 13 show the veins in the head and intestines. No such study of the arterial system exists. Garrod (1873:468) states that both carotids are present in the turkey.

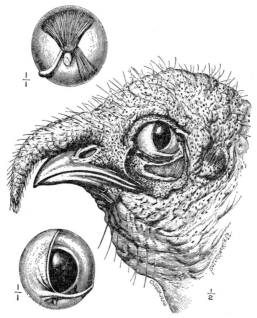

Fig. 10.—*Head and eye of the domestic turkey. (After Bland-Sutton [1920].)*

The arterial blood of the turkey has a specific gravity of 1.061, and the serum of 1.021 (Davy, 1839:24). The hemoglobin crystallizes in cubes, rarely in octahedral plates (Krukenberg, 1882:94). Malassez (1872:530) reported that a cubic centimeter of the blood contained 2,700,000 erythrocytes, the dimensions of which were 15 x 6.5 microns. Other dimensions given are: 12.5 x 7.1 microns (Gulliver, 1875:489); 13.4 x 7.4 microns (Wormley, 1885:733). Cullen (1903:354) found that the blood of the turkey, like that of most birds, contains leucocytes of four different forms.

93

The iron content of the hemoglobin of various animals is quite uniform, running about 0.333 per cent. Pelouze (1865) found that 100 grams of blood from the turkey contained 0.03345 gram of iron. Recent analyses show considerable variation in the number of grams of hemoglobin in 100 cc. of blood. Scott *et al.* (1933) found an average of 13.87 grams for female turkeys and 15.04 grams for males, and Wolterink *et al.* (1947:431) found 14 grams for females and 13.7 grams for males. Rhian *et al.* (1944:225, 228) found only 10.5 per cent hemoglobin in the blood of females. Apparently, the hemoglobin content decreases after the breeding season. The blood of males contained 15.4 per cent hemoglobin on June 14 and only 12.6 per cent on August 13. The examination of blood has been of considerable aid in taxonomy but has not reached the fineness anticipated. Reichert and Brown (1909:29) made the prediction that "the blood of each family, genus, species, and individual will be found to be absolutely specific."

The average blood pressure in the carotid of a male turkey weighing 8,750 grams was 193 mm. of mercury (Stübel, 1910:257, 261). In some cases the pressure rose to 226 mm. The heart beats were ninety-three per minute. This figure is exceptionally low for birds.

DIGESTIVE SYSTEM

Concerning the digestive system of the turkey, Audubon (1839:197) says: "Oesophagus dilated into a very large crop; stomach transversely elliptical, extremely muscular; intestines long and wide; caeca very large, oblong." This statement must be credited to William MacGillivray. The digestive organs are shown in Plate 13. It has been long recognized that birds that eat coarse vegetable matter of low nutrient value have the longest intestines in proportion to weight. Buffon (1771:145) reported that the intestines of the turkey were nearly four times as long as the distance from the tip of the bill to the end of the rump. Leopold (1953:198) examined two male wild turkeys from Colonia Pacheco, Chihuahua, and obtained the following data: large intestine, 20 cm.; caeca, 42 (41–43); small intestine, 224 (223–25).

The ptarmigan (*Lagopus*), which is not primarily a seedeater like the turkey, has longer caeca (47 cm.) than the turkey, though weighing only one-fourteenth as much. There is no clear understanding of the function of the caeca. Groups of birds with similar food habits may show considerable diversity in the development of the caeca (Newton and Gadow, 1893–96:68). The measurements given by Beddard (1898:293) for the ocellated turkey are: large intestine, 14 cm.; caeca, 34; small intestine, 168. Unfortunately, the sex is not given so that it is impossible to draw a direct comparison with the common turkey.

The gizzard of seed-eating birds is a powerful organ for crushing (Plate 14). The turkey being one of the largest of the gallinaceous birds and readily available, it is natural that it would be selected for experiments in digestion. After Borelli (1681:395) had concluded that the comminution of food by the gizzard, in conjunction with sharp stones, was of great importance in the process of digestion, he was requested by the Grand Duke Ferdinand II of Tuscany to present experimental proof. Among the objects introduced into the stomachs of turkeys through the mouth were glass balls, hollow cubes of lead, and pyramids of wood. The following day the glass objects were found to be crushed to a powder, the lead cubes flattened, and the wooden pyramids worn down. Réaumur (1756:272, 291) gave a turkey glass balls such as were used for imitation pearls. These were crushed completely. Also, he used tubes of tin plate with covers soldered on the ends. These required a load of eighty pounds to deform. They were crushed flat within twenty-four hours. Next he fed turkeys English walnuts, starting with one nut and gradually increasing the number to twenty-four at one feeding. Although the nuts were ordinary size, with some being quite large, all passed into the gizzard within twenty-four hours. The use of turkeys for digestion experiments was continued by Spallanzani (1787:401).

The forced feeding of English walnuts (*Juglans regia* L.) to fatten turkeys has been practised in Europe for at least two centuries and continues in some of the Mediterranean countries. Trebeden (1902) expressed surprise on finding the procedure in vogue at a country house in France. Sacc (1863) reported that not all of his domestic turkeys would voluntarily eat English walnuts but those that did became fat more readily. In the gizzard, the nut was ground so finely that within fifteen to twenty minutes not a trace was to be found. He thought that a chemical reaction on the shell was involved.

The temperament of the wild turkey is such that experiments on digestion cannot be conducted successfully with it. Adult Merriam's turkeys, trapped with a full crop, were so badly frightened that digestion ceased, the birds eventually dying (Ligon, 1946:13). Because trapped wild turkeys are unable to digest food properly, it is desirable to take them as soon as possible to the place selected for release (Sylvester and Lane, 1946:341). Female Broad-Breasted Bronze turkeys, sixteen months old, were used by Schorger (1960) to determine the time required for the gizzard to crush *Carya* nuts. When the crop is empty, a nut passes almost immediately to the gizzard, the turkey apparently having no control over the passage. The birds were force-fed the nuts after being deprived of food for twenty-four hours and were killed at intervals to determine the condition of the nuts. Wild pecans (*Carya pecan*) required one hour for crushing; however, one pecan, except for smoothing, was recovered unchanged after seven hours in the gizzard. Hickory nuts (*Carya ovata*) required thirty to thirty-two hours. A hickory nut is first worn thin, then an indented fracture is made by the gravel (Plate 15).

The gizzard of the turkey was figured by Home (1807:178). In spite of the powerful muscles, the gizzard would be inefficient without the presence of gravel. This should be highly siliceous. Salgues (1934) obtained the following weights in grams, based on thirty-four specimens, of inert material in the gizzard: average, 23.200; minimum, 14.040; maximum, 45.895.

Any chemical action resulting in the softening of the shell of nuts can be ruled out. Bent coins given to ostriches with their food had the imprint worn on the convex side while that on the concave side was intact. This showed that the stomach fluids had no effect, the erosion being purely mechanical (Marshall, 1895:314). The numerous glands opening into the mouth and gullet of the turkey appear to have no digestive function. According to Blount (1947:142), the crop has a pH of 4.0 because of lactic acid produced by bacteria. The glands of the proventriculus secrete a protein-splitting enzyme. Food remains in this organ for only a relatively brief period. The gizzard has a pH of 2.0 to 3.5 from the presence of hydrochloric acid, which seems to be essential for the proper functioning of the pepsin enzyme from the proventriculus. The pH of the digestive tract of the domestic turkey was determined by Farner (1942:446): crop, 6.07; proventriculus, 4.72; gizzard, 2.19; duodenum, 5.82–6.52; jejunum, 6.67–6.95; ileum, 6.85; colon, 6.46; caeca, 5.86; and bile, 6.01. In common with data from other birds, the gizzard is more acid than other parts of the digestive tract. Worden (1956:33) gives a pH of 2.0–3.5 for the gizzard and about 4.0 for the crop.

WEIGHTS OF PARTS AND ORGANS OF DOMESTIC TURKEY

The weights of the parts and organs of female bronze domestic turkeys, using twelve birds twenty-four to thirty-three weeks of age, were determined by Latimer and Rosenbaum (1926), and Latimer (1927). The results are given in Table 11.

TABLE 11
AVERAGE WEIGHTS OF PARTS AND ORGANS OF THE FEMALE DOMESTIC TURKEY

	Weight in grams	Per cent of body weight
Body weight	4125.2	—
Head	67.0	1.67
Integument	383.3	9.6
Feathers	214.3	5.6
Musculature	2364.7	58.5
Ligamentous skeleton	388.5	9.7
Digestive tube (empty)	184.7	4.6
Crop and esophagus (empty)	24.8	0.70
Stomach (empty)	7.0	0.17
Gizzard (empty)	95.8	2.40
Intestines (empty)	57.0	1.42
Liver	92.3	2.25
Pancreas	6.13	0.15
Lungs and trachea	25.6	0.64
Heart	21.3	0.53
Thyroid	0.293	0.0076
Thymus	2.26	0.06
Spleen	1.97	0.48
Suprarenals	0.311	0.0077
Hypophysis	0.0189	0.00048
Kidneys	22.26	0.55
Ovary	29.0	0.68
Oviduct	36.4	0.78
Brain	6.31	0.16
Spinal cord	5.40	0.14
Eyeballs	9.79	0.24

The above data on the heart do not agree with those of Löer (1911:309). He used five female domestic turkeys of fairly uniform weight, the average being 3,324 grams, and obtained an average weight for the heart of 37.4 gr., or 1.12 per cent of the body weight. He found that, on the whole, birds living in the wild have a relatively larger heart than the domestic ones, that sex has essentially no influence on size, and that in the young the heart is proportionally larger than in the old. Long (1939:44) found that the percentage weights of the hearts of two wild poults varied with age as follows: fourteen days, 0.725 per cent; sixty days, 0.536 per cent. Recently, Hartman (1955:228) determined the percentages for two wild female Florida turkeys to be 0.39 and 0.40. Disregarding Löer's data, it is apparent that the weight of the heart of the turkey is low in comparison with that of other birds.

The weight of the brain in relation to that of the body is very low in the turkey in comparison with other birds. This indicates a low degree of 'intelligence.' A male eastern wild turkey, weighing 6,340 gr., had a brain weighing 12 gr., or 0.19 per cent (Fox, 1923:399). The weight of the brain of a female domestic turkey was 0.16 per cent of the weight of the body (Latimer and Rosenbaum, 1926; Latimer, 1927).

No complete study of the myology of the turkey has been made.

CHROMOSOMES

The elements of the chromosome complex in the amnion and in the spermatogonia of the turkey varied in size from 0.4 to 6 microns (Shiwago, 1929:108). The somatic chromosome number, according to Werner (1931:157), is the same, apparently, as for the duck (seventy-six for the male and seventy-seven for the female). The chromosomes have the shapes of a J, a rod, and a globe. In the male the group consists of six pairs of large chromosomes, three pairs of short rod-shaped chromosomes, and twenty-nine pairs of globe-shaped chromosomes. The female differs essentially in having one odd chromosome which is the largest in the group. Shiwago (1929:108) got a chromosome count of 46. Sokolow et al. (1936:486) state that the turkey has rod-shaped chromosomes with a terminal spindle fiber attachment. The evolution of the various forms of gallinaceous birds is attributed to mutation of the genes rather than to morphological changes in the chromosomes.

Sense of Smell

There is no reason to believe that the sense of smell in the turkey is any less rudimentary than in other birds. Caton (1873) has discussed the keen sight and hearing of the turkey and its lack of ability to smell. Nevertheless, some hunters have attributed their failure to bag a turkey to having been "smelled." Dodge (1877:233) advised the hunter to approach against the wind for: "All his senses are exquisite, and in sense of smell he is scarcely excelled by the elk." Jones (1898:197) wrote that the turkey scented the hunter, and Rutledge (1941) claimed that it would be difficult to offer any other explanation for the detection of a well-hidden man.

A pair of turkeys was found by Hill (1905) to be indifferent to asafetida, oil of anise, oil of lavender, camphor, chloroform, and carbon bisulphide. Regarding a gobbler fed from a sieve under which hydrocyanic acid was generated, he wrote: "For some minutes the cock turkey fed with his usual eagerness; then, suddenly, he began to stagger round the enclosure, crossing his legs and holding his beak straight up in the air. He made his way back into the pen, where he stood with head down and wings outstretched. After ten minutes he returned to the enclosure, but did not eat any more grain. His comb and wattles were deeply suffused with blood." Balls of napthalene scattered about the traps set for turkeys prevented the deer from taking the corn used as bait, but had no apparent effect on the turkeys (Wheeler, 1946).

The olfactory nerve of the turkey was examined by Owen (1837). He states: "The olfactory nerve does not form a ganglion at its commencement but is continued as a small round chord from the anterior apex of each hemisphere, and is ramified on a small middle spongy bone, there being no extension of the pituitary membrane over a superior turbinated bone as in the *Vulture*. In this bird [turkey] the olfactory nerves are compressed within a narrow interorbital space, which would not admit the lodgement of ganglions; the olfactory nerves after passing through this space then diverge to the nasal cavity."

Body Temperature

The body temperature of the domestic turkey is about 106° F. Marsden and Martin (1945:685) give the following data: "At hatching time turkeys of both sexes have a body temperature of approximately 103° F. Within a week it rises to about 106°, and by the sixth week it reaches 106½°. At other times the average is approximately 1° lower, or 105½°. Except at the day-old stage, variations of as much as 1½° either way from the average given are within the normal range."

Heat regulation in the domestic turkey has been studied by Robinson and Lee (1946). They found the mean normal rectal temperature to be 105.4°. When the temperature is hot, the bird ruffles its feathers and spreads its wings. The mouth is open and the tongue vibrates. The body movement accompanying panting increases the circulation of the air. At a temperature of 113° F., there occurs a heat stroke and collapse of the legs. There is no external use of water to aid cooling. During hot weather in southern Texas, turkeys will spend the middle of the day standing on the ground or on a limb of a tree with the wings extended.

FAT

The "breast sponge," so named by Audubon (1831:5), is a thick mass of fibrous tissue overlying the breast and crop of the male. In spring, prior to the mating season, it becomes so permeated with fat that it weighs as much as two pounds. As a result, the adult gobbler loses for the time being his trim appearance. The fat is a source of energy during the mating season, when the male eats but little. According to Jordan (1914:104), the yearling male does not possess the breast sponge and is in no condition to mate. This is not true of the young domestic gobbler.

The factor causing accumulation of fat in birds prior to migration, and in some non-migratory birds before the breeding season, is incompletely understood. Wolfson (1945:108) states: "Concomitant with the recrudescence of the testes, large deposits of fat occur in the migrants, and this change in metabolism is no doubt related to a change in the functioning of the thyroid gland. In addition, other endocrine glands are probably involved."

Wild turkeys also become very fat in late fall and early winter when mast is abundant. Most of the fat is deposited beneath the feather tracts on the back and around the gizzard. Herbert Stoddard, who mounted the bird shot by President Eisenhower, informs me that it had approximately four pounds of fat. According to Montule (1821:73), the fat of the wild turkey is not confined to a particular part as in the domestic one, and its being spread throughout the flesh of the wild bird renders it considerably more savory.

Turkeys, according to Jordan (1898:247), are in their very best condition from the beginning of the gobbling season to April 1. After this date, weight is lost rapidly. May (1873:69, 89) recorded in his journal at Marietta, Ohio, on June 19, 1788, that turkeys were available in any quantity "but it is the season when they are not fat"; and on July 25, that turkeys are now good. Draper (1851) interviewed Colonel Nathan Boone, son of Daniel, who obtained from his father the following information of conditions in Kentucky about 1775: "Turkies were very poor in summer from ticks, and poor food; fatten rapidly on beech and other small mast—good eating in fall, winter, and spring." Because of leanness and ticks, turkeys were not in good condition in Montgomery County, Texas, except from November to April (Jordan, 1879). They were in prime condition during January, February, and March.

The birds at times accumulated so much fat it impeded their flight. When this occurred they were run down with horses (Brown, 1924:11). It was a common occurrence for fat turkeys, when shot from a tree, to split open on striking the ground. There were numberless wild turkeys at Mays Lick, Mason County, Kentucky, in 1788: "The latter were often so fat that in falling from the tree when shot their skins would burst" (Drake, 1820:21). Schultz (1810: I, 122) wrote of turkeys so overburdened with fat that they flew with difficulty. He adds: "It frequently happens, that after shooting one on a tree, you will find him bursted by falling on the ground." The split on the back could be six inches or more in length (Bushnell, 1889:64). Similar instances are recorded for Indiana (Blanchard, 1884:113; Goodspeed Bros. & Co., 1884:290).

Excessive fatness seems to have been a common phenomenon throughout much of the range of the turkey. Beechnuts and pecans, because of their high oil content, were especially conducive to fatness. Turkeys using a roost on the Llano River, Texas, had been feeding on pecans and were excessively fat (Holden, 1932:37). One spring in Linn County, Kansas, George W. Hinds (Mitchell, 1928:160) killed thirty-nine wild turkeys, some of which were so fat they burst after falling. Sage (1860:312) mentions that two hunters on the upper Cimarron River killed ten turkeys, several having on their backs an "inch thickness of pure fat." The fat of the domestic turkey has the following properties:

specific gravity at 37.8° C. is 0.9090; melting point, 31°–32°; and iodine number, 66.4 (Ross and Race, 1911). The composition of the fat will vary depending upon the kind of food eaten.

ENERGY METABOLISM OF POULTS

The physiology of poults has been investigated by Long (1939). He experimented with two strains of wild poults, one derived from game farm stock (GF), the other from game farm females mated with wild males (WM). A poult with high activity was selected from each class for the determination of the energy metabolism (Table 12). The higher CO_2 and heat production of the WM poult showed that it was the more active of the two poults. This is corroborated by data on activity.

TABLE 12

THE ENERGY METABOLISM OF TWO TURKEY POULTS NINETEEN DAYS OLD
(24 hours after feeding and at 32.2° C. environmental temperature)

Type and sex of poult	Body temp.	Body weight	CO_2 per day	Heat production per 24 hours	
				Total per day	Per square meter body surfaces
Males	°C.	Grams	Grams	Calories	Calories
GF	40.7	95.6	5.49	18.25	873
WM	40.8	88.8	7.55	25.09	1261
Experimental difference		6.8	2.06	6.84	388

COLOR CHANGES OF HEAD AND NECK

The most striking and elusive physiological phenomenon of the turkey is the change at will of the colors of the head and of the neck of the gobbler. It would be incorrect to assume that any one color is normal unless one can be assured that the bird is in complete repose. Aside from the skin, certain appendages are involved in the change of color: the frontal caruncle, the caruncles on the neck, and the throat wattle. The frontal caruncle, which can be expanded or contracted at will, may be extended to six inches in a large domestic gobbler. When contracted it may not be more than one to one-half inches. About the greatest extension in hens is one and one-half inches. Concerning the marked difference between the domestic and wild turkey, Le Conte (1858:179) wrote: "The great mark of distinction is in the enormous palear [palea] or dewlap of the former, which extends from the base of the lower mandible to the large caruncles on the lower part of the neck. Whatever alterations may have been produced by long domestication, this palear could not have been formed by an enlargement of the rather loose skin of the neck. It is a specific character, which as in our own [wild] bird is not found in the Meleagris ocellata of Honduras." However, the frontal caruncle and the throat wattle of the tame turkey are simply excessive developments of the same organs in the wild bird.

The changes in color, so peculiar and so prominent, were mentioned by Oviedo (1950:174) in 1526. Googe (1577:167v) favors us with more detail: "The colour of that wrinkled skinne about his head (which hangeth ouer his byll and about his necke, al swelling as it were with little blathers) he changeth from time to time like the *Chamaelon*, to al colours of the Rainebowe, sometimes white, sometimes red, sometimes blewe, sometimes yellowe, which colours euer altring, the byrd appearth as it were a myracle of nature."

The Emperor Jahangir (1909:216), in 1612, was so impressed by the color changes that he recorded them in his memoirs. The colors, changing momentarily, were red like coral, white like cotton, or like turquoise. When the bird was in heat, the frontal appendage extended the length of a span and resembled the trunk of an elephant. When deflated it was like the horn of a rhinocerous and, in length, only the breadth of two fingers. The color around the eyes was turquoise and never changed. Audubon's (1831:17) description of the head and neck of the male is brief: "Frontal caruncle blue and red. Rugose and carunculated skin of the head and neck of various tints of blue and purple, the pendulous anterior caruncles of the latter, or the *wattles*, bright red, changing to blue." Baird (1858:616) merely states that the naked skin of the head and neck is blue, while the caruncles are purplish red.

Few observers have recorded the season, or the stimulus, when the color undergoes changes. Baines (1890:343) wrote that the heads of wild turkeys, especially of gobblers in spring, are a light bluish color, more frequently white than blue. Catchings (1898), a doctor of medicine at Woodville, Mississippi, has this comment: "The head and neck of a wild gobbler is of a blue color, with the exception of a little white spot on top of his head and the caruncles low down on his neck near where the feathers begin, and they are white at all times; only when the turkey is in full strut, then they are red; as soon as he stops strutting these caruncles turn white again. Now, no one ever saw a tame or domesticated gobbler with a blue head. Their heads and necks are red all over when they strut, and stay red for some time afterwards."

The head of the wild turkey, according to Mosby and Handley (1943:89), may be a brilliant red and the "skull cap" practically white. If the bird is frightened, the head turns blue immediately. Following death, the characteristic color of the head is bluish.

The most complete description of the changes is given by Leopold (1944:181). The colors are most stable during the midwinter season. The frontal caruncle, throat wattle, and smooth skin of the head and neck of an adult male eastern turkey are blue; the caruncles on the lower part of the neck are bright red. The throat wattle of first-year males, when present, is blue, as is the smooth skin of the head and neck; the scattered caruncles on the sides and back of the neck, and the small caruncles on the lower throat are red. On females the frontal caruncle is wartlike; the throat wattle is absent on first-year birds, and if present in older birds, is blue; head and neck are blue; scattered, small red caruncles may appear in adults on the neck and lower throat. The seasonal and momentary change of color of the head, according to Leopold, is due to both pigments and blood. The bright turquoise blue is certainly a pigment. The red color is due to blood circulating under the skin. The red wattles and throat caruncles fade at once to whitish blue after death, indicating that the blood has drained away.

The wattles of males of all types expand during the mating season. The heads of adult wild gobblers show a small wattle and some red on the throat. These changes correspond with the increase in size of the gonads and are caused by increased secretion of testicular hormones. A strutting male can change at will the color of the pate and frontal region of the head, and the shape of the frontal wattle. While the turkey is strutting, the red of the crown may turn in a few seconds to whitish blue, then revert to red. Without doubt, these changes are produced by alterations in the supply of blood. The frontal caruncle becomes elongated, turgid, and red by an increase in the blood pressure, and blue when the blood drains away. The wattles and head coloring revert slowly to a winter condition. The head of an adult male may remain primarily red until September.

The red color produced by the blood streaming through the head of the turkey, according to Schjelderup-Ebbe (1932:206), is a defense mechanism giving the bird a much more martial and terrifying appearance. Since the male will produce this color even when there is no rival in the vicinity, it is preferable to attribute it to sexual display. He (1924:110) has described the changes in color in the domestic male as follows: "The colours of the bare head ornaments of the turkey-cock when he is calm are grey or grey-red, the lower ones almost grey-white, the tap over the beak is grey-red, the skin at the nape of the neck has a pale blue tint. When the effective state sets in, the changing colourings pass through degrees of vividness, but the stages vary directly with the degree of excitement. The tap turns a purplish red, the chin adornment bright red, the cheeks likewise, the front of the skin of the head a dark red, the skin of the back part of the head and of the neck increases in blueness."

Not much is known regarding the differences, if any, in the change of color in the heads of the various races of the wild turkey. According to Ligon (1946:5), the hens and first-year males of Merriam's turkey of pure strain, particularly in winter, have blackish heads and necks. The throat wattle and bare skin of the neck show little sign of any other color, while in the eastern and Rio Grande turkeys the heads are conspicuously blue. His description of the mating display is as follows:

"A mature Merriam's gobbler in his mating conduct displays such effulgent beauty as to defy adequate description. The successive emotional phases as mirrored in varying coloration of the upper head and neck have rarely been described. They begin with enlargement of the wattles and caruncle and in heightened coloration from the dominant pink or pale red of the relaxed individual to a flaming red, followed by pale blue about the eyes that deepens into a striking purple; the pale front of the head varies to azure blue, while the extreme top of the head fades to a pale blue with the slightest infusion of salmon pink. As if to accentuate the vividness of the head embellishments, the folds of the neck may assume a whitish cast and a velvet-like texture. The color succession pattern is not always the same; for example, a diminution of the urge to display may cause the bare skin of the head and neck to assume an entirely uniform, creamy-white color. Further, blending and fading in the color patterns may occur rapidly. When the bird reverts to total relaxation, the dominant pale red of the base parts is, normally, restored quickly." The frontal caruncle extends three inches.

The color of the head of a Merriam's gobbler, according to Burget (1957:13), is greenish-blue except under excitement when it becomes red about the neck and reddish-blue in the cheeks. During the mating season the caruncles on the neck become brighter. The elongated frontal caruncle retains its greenish-blue color.

The mechanism whereby the turkey expands and contracts the frontal caruncle and other appendages has been investigated by many workers. The swelling of the frontal caruncle proceeds so rapidly and strongly that Vulpian (1875:166) compared it with the swelling of the cavernous bodies of the sex organ of man and assumed participation by the vasomotor nerve fibers. An anatomical investigation by Jegorow (1890) agreed with this assumption (Plate 16). The appendages of the turkey, according to Marshall (1895:160), have a superficially located network of blood vessels with a complicated irregular course and with enlargements here and there. Smooth muscles as well as elastic binding tissues are found. From sexual excitement, a constriction of the veins occurs in the frontal caruncle so that blood continues to enter through the arteries but none can flow out. The blood dams up in the caruncle and enlarges it, since the elements of which it is composed are elastic. The turgescence was explained by Pangalo (1906) as due to arteries with thick walls, which on dilation extend the appendage. The assumption of Moser (1906:220) that the lymph tracts play a role in the change of color has never been confirmed. Little more research was done for two decades.

The literature on the histology of the caruncles was reviewed by Oswald (1924) and some direct investigation made of the tissues, including those of turkeys injured by fighting. On the head and neck of a domestic gobbler are found about fifty caruncles from the size of a hazelnut to that of a walnut. On most of the caruncles are still smaller tubercles the size of hemp seeds. The enlargement of the frontal caruncle is due to increased blood pressure in the cavernous tissue.

The frontal caruncle is present in both sexes at hatching, that of the male on the average being considerably less developed (Champy, 1924).

Champy and Kritch (1926) described the frontal caruncle as a cone consisting of large bundles of smooth muscles surrounding a compact crescent-shaped conjunctive axis. Few of the capillaries are sinuous but a number of the arterial vessels, surrounded by a very muscular wall, are helical arteries. Mucoelastic tissue was absent in the adult birds examined. The mechanism of the blood stasis is peculiar, being unlike that known for ordinary erectile organs. The turgescence in the comb of the rooster is permanent and not influenced by nerve phenomena although the latter play a primary role in the functioning of erectile organs with vascular sphincters when the turgescence is not permanent.

There is in the caruncles a base of dense fibrous tissue which appears white when no other color intervenes and which seems to play the role of a reflector (Champy et al., 1929). Color results in two ways: (1) The caruncles at the base of the neck are supplied with blood by the erectile arteries; (2) also, in the dorsal region there are, in the skin, pigmented cells surrounding the vessels and containing a rose-colored, apparently carotinoid pigment. Some cells have a melanin pigment, and also a blue one, which appears to be localized in the superficial epidermic layers. The carotinoid pigment is easily removable with fat solvents, the blue pigment less easily so for it seems to be a combination of a carotinoid substance with proteins.

A detailed examination of the skin on the head and neck of the turkey was made by Wodzicki (1929). According to his definitions, the appendices consist of the frontal appendix, the fleshy caruncles, and the eminence from which the beard arises. The other parts of the skin of the head and the upper part of the neck are verrucose and distinguishable by the presence of small dermal papillae, by copious vascularization, finally by scattered filoplumes. The papillae on the posterior part of the head are of small dimensions but become a little larger on the lateral and upper parts of the neck. They attain their largest dimensions on the lower anterior part of the neck, where they form large fleshy caruncles in adult males.

The frontal appendix appears prior to hatching, the other excrescences much later. Their growth is preceded by local vascularization and with loss of the contour feathers. The caruncles then appear in the form of small dermal papillae. The sexual dimorphism in the development of the papillae appears at this time. In the female, the frontal appendix and the caruncles continue to be small and weakly vascularized while those of the male are well developed and much larger. The excrescences and appendages in the male, as well as the bare skin, have the power to change color. When the gobbler displays or becomes angry, the appendages swell and become various shades of red, changing to blues. During display, the frontal caruncle, normally 1 to 2 cm. in length, extends to 10 cm., the largest diameter being 2.5 to 3.5 cm.

The verrucose skin of the gobbler has the appearance of being richly vascularized. There are found in the dermis all the layers of the skin with the exception of the subcutaneous tissue. The complete absence of this layer, as well as the considerable development of the blood vessels of the dermis, tends to give sections of the skin from this region a characteristic appearance. Beneath the basal germinative layer of the epidermis are found many layers of cells separated from clearly visible intercellular spaces. The corneous layer is relatively thin and slightly developed. The dermis consists of two layers, a superficial and a deeper one. The superficial layer is distinguished by the presence of bundles of conjunctive fibers which run in every direction and extend into the dermic papillae. The conjunctive tissue of the deeper layer is more loose and contains, besides numerous vessels, muscular fibrillae and a few feather follicles. The arrangement of the blood vessels in this part is as follows: the deeper part of the dermis is provided with well-developed vessels, and there are in this layer numerous arterio-veinous anastomoses. The anastomotic part is very short, and the veins into which the arteries empty have a spongy appearance. The vessels of the deeper layer ramify into branchlets which run towards the epidermis, there to form the loops of the subepidermic capillaries. The branchlets which traverse the deeper part of the papillary layer of the dermis to provide the subepidermic capillaries are characterized by the presence of muscular fibers in their walls.

The verrucose skin of the head of the gobbler being completely devoid of pigment, the red or blue color of the excrescences is explained solely by the action of the subcutaneous vessels. While the blood vessels in the comb of a rooster give it a uniform red color, the structure of the vessels in the appendages of the gobbler permits them to change from red to blue. Under excitement, the muscles in the walls of the vessels cause their contraction, producing a stasis of veinous blood in the subcutaneous vessels and changing the color from red to blue.

The verrucose skin of the head of the gobbler has large papillae, semi-oval in shape and provided with nerve branchlets and loops of blood vessels. The caruncles, especially on the upper fourth of the neck, differ structurally from the papillae. They are distinguished by the great thickness of the skin, 7 to 10 mm., while the verrucose skin of the head has a thickness of 2.0 to 2.5 mm. Anteriorally, the thickness attains 25 mm. This increase in thickness is due in the first place to the development of a deep network of subcutaneous vessels. The arrangement of the blood vessels in the caruncles is as follows: the caruncles of the anterior part of the neck are provided with branchlets of the *Arteria oesophagea descendeus*; in the center of each papilla is found an artery and several efferent veins which, after a winding course, empty into the external jugular veins. This papillary artery is divided into numerous branches of which the greater part form the layer of subepidermic capillaries. Other branches communicate directly with the veins. These arterio-veinous anastomoses are distinguished by the length of the anastomotic part and the very pronounced epitheliodal modification of the muscular fibrils of their walls. They empty obliquely into the veins, the walls of which are thin and delicate.

The histological structure of the frontal appendix is almost identical with that of the caruncles (Plate 17). The epidermis is of slight thickness, the dermis being composed of a superficial layer and a deeper one. The superficial layer has small epitheliodal eminences. The deeper part is composed of large vessels, nerves, and a spongy body which occupies the center of the appendix. It consists of large veinous cavities and afferent arterial branches which travel in a very homogenous, compact conjunctive tissue. Fibromucoid tissue is absent.

According to Schneider (1931:252), no growth of the frontal caruncle takes place during the first two months after hatching, then the appendage gradually grows to full size. He considers it erroneous to speak of swelling tissue and erectility in the caruncle since the lengthening results from increased flow of blood in cooperation with the circular musculature of the arteries, without any stoppage of blood. Contraction takes place only by the longitudinal musculature. The red color is due to blood, all other colors being optical, i.e. interference colors.

The color problem is discussed in a further paper by Champy and Demay (1930). The papillae of the head of the turkey frequently contain carotinoid pigments. They are a vivid red or orange-red color more or less mixed with lipoids. The pigment is generally found in the deep layer of the epidermis where the cells have a peculiar appearance. The red color is not always due to pigment, as in the dorsal caruncles, but is also due to dilated blood vessels. The white areas are due sometimes to cholesterol, sometimes to densification of the conjunctive tissue, which becomes white and dense like sclerotic tissue. The blue color is remarkable in that it is absent except during the sexual period. The cause of the blue color is uncertain. He considers the theory of cerulescence, i.e. the Tyndall effect, improbable, since there is no melanin at all in the blue areas in the guinea fowl and turkey. The blue color is produced especially in the conjunctive tissue, apparently, but its presence depends upon the time of the year.

The mechanism of the turgescence of the frontal appendix is explained in this way. In a state of repose the blood is directed almost exclusively into the capillaries of the superficial layer of the skin. During sexual excitement, and especially during display, the spiral small arteries open widely. The muscles of the walls act as a sphincter and supply a sufficient quantity of blood to fill the vessels and render the organ turgescent. The increase in volume affects the length of the appendix but not its width, the cavities being elongate in shape. Turgescence proceeds slowly, but the return to the state of repose is very rapid. This peculiarity is explained by the facility with which the blood, filling the cavities, empties directly into the veins once the influx of arterial blood from the spiral arteries is arrested. The result is that the blood producing the turgescence empties rapidly through the veins to produce a state of repose.

The red and blue colors of the head, as explained by Wodzicki (1929), are entirely due to the colors from veinous and arterial blood, pigments being absent. He makes no reference to the presence or absence of pigments in the skin of the neck.

A recent study by Laruelle *et al.* (1951) is essentially in agreement with Wodzicki. When the gobbler is in repose, the entire caruncular system becomes red—pure red in the lower part of the head, and violet-red around the eyes. The caruncles covering the head, with the exception of the frontal appendix, are of the pigmented type while those on the neck are vascular. Characteristic of the first is the presence beneath the epidermis of either a layer of chromatophores (rose-colored in the fresh state), or of a layer of melanophores in proximity. The caruncles with chromatophores (dorsal caruncles in which there is little change of color) have only a few vessels in their central region, while the second (corresponding to the bluish or violet regions) have a vascular axis along which the melanophores are chiefly located. This deep vascular layer is separated from the epithelium by a conjunctive tissue, milky in appearance and poor in cellular elements. The second type of color change is entirely vasuclar and depends on the presence or absence of blood in the subepidermal vessels.

The following conclusions were reached by Laruelle:

1.—The changes in color shown by the vascular caruncles of the gobbler are due to changes in the passage of blood through the arterial subepidermal network of the caruncles;

2.—The changes in the vascular passage which can affect the interior of the subepidermal network of the gobbler appear to result from several factors—first, anastomoses providing direct communication between the arteries and veins of the central region, and, second, an external longitudinal musculature situated in the wall of the central and radial arteries of the caruncles;

3.—The reduced modifications of color shown by the vascular caruncles of the female turkey appear to be due to the small number of anastomoses found between the central arteries and veins, and to the almost complete absence of the external longitudinal musculature in the walls of the central and radial arteries.

4.—The severing of the cutaneous branches of the cervical nerves of the spine in the gobbler is accompanied by a permanent blanching and by a partial regression of the corresponding caruncles resulting from the muscular constriction of the central arteries, and by a permanent diversion of the blood of the arteries towards the central veins, by reason of the wide openings of the anastomoses located between these vessels.

Total castration of the turkey leads to far greater regression of the functioning of the caruncles than the severing of the cervical nerves (Laruelle *et al.*, 1952). The longitudinal musculature of the arteries disappears almost completely while the other elements remain unchanged. The longitudinal and spiral muscles surrounding the arteries are of great importance in producing the changes of color. Their almost complete absence in the female is a striking difference between the sexes (Laruelle *et al.*, 1952.1).

The entire subject of changes of color remains in an unsatisfactory state, especially with respect to the role of pigments. It appears quite certain that between the domestic and wild birds the changes are not identical.

The role of the sympathetic nervous system in producing the changes in the color of the head furnishings was studied by Jegorow (1890). His paper has colored illustrations of the head and neck of a gobbler in repose and after severing the sympathetic nerve. The sympathetic nervous system contains the fibers producing contraction of the vessels of the furnishings. Plate 16 illustrates the subepidermal blood vessels colored blue in the original. Nerves, particularly the sympathetic, are very abundant in the head furnishings of the rooster (Coujard, 1941).

Sex Organs

The sex organs of the male turkey and the male chicken are quite similar, and the sex is discernible at all ages (Hammond and Marsden, 1937). The day-old male has two small genital papillae, one on each side of the ventral surface of the everted vent. In the female these papillae are either lacking or less conspicuous. Ninety per cent accuracy in determining the sex may be expected with experience. After the turkeys have reached an age of twelve to sixteen weeks, it is usually simple to determine the sex by examination of the color of the feathers of the breast. The tips are black in the male and brown in the female.

All female birds have two ovaries, the right one being rudimentary usually. Should the left ovary be removed surgically or destroyed by disease, the right ovary will develop into a testis. The bird may then function as a male, having acquired the plumage and other characters of this sex. This change in the female is known as *virilism* and is apparently due to the secretion of a hormone by the adrenal glands. Assumption of female characters by a male is decidedly uncommon. Isolation of a female turkey led her to adopt male behavior (Lack, 1941:422).

Weights of the testes of the domestic turkey were determined by Law and Kosin (1958), who found that the right testis was heavier than the left. Asymmetry of the testes in birds is not common. Friedmann (1927) examined the testes of 104 species of breeding males, *not* including the turkey. In all, the testes were of equal size. The data on weights in Table 13 were provided by I. L. Kosin (*in litt.*).

TABLE 13

RANGE OF WEIGHTS OF TESTES OF DOMESTIC TURKEYS DURING MAY–JUNE.

	Indoor Environment		Outdoor Environment	
	Left	Right	Left	Right
Killing Date	Grams	Grams	Grams	Grams
May 6	12.00	29.21	31.71	28.43
	12.12	22.03	19.94	24.32
May 20	21.66	27.84	7.91	21.13
	18.79	37.84	18.91	30.62
June 1	17.56	17.56	13.82	30.89
	17.59	32.32	10.60	14.37
June 17	11.40	26.47	3.96	5.16
	22.42	26.49	8.45	10.05

The maximum weight of the two testes appears to be about 90 gr., but may be higher early in spring at the height of the breeding season.

SEMEN AND FERTILIZATION

The average volume of semen collectable from the domestic male is 0.33 cc. The average number of sperms per cubic millimeter was 8.4 millions, giving 2.8 billions of sperms for each ejaculation (Parker[1], 1946). This is a good example of nature's prodigality since in the case of the wild bird only about twelve spermatozoa will perform their function. The minimum optimum dose of semen for artificial insemination was found by Lorenz (1950:24) to be 0.025 cc. The maximum fertility was reached soon after the second day of insemination and remained at this level for six weeks. Some of the eggs were fertile after the second day, and some were fertile after eight to ten weeks. Little difference in the percentage of fertility was obtained when the insemination was performed at intervals of one, two, three, and four weeks (Burrows and Marsden, 1938). Females artificially inseminated at intervals of thirty days laid eggs which were 83 per cent fertile. The quantities of semen obtainable from the males varied from 0.1 cc. to 0.7 cc., but from the majority of the males was 0.3 to 0.4 cc.

[1] The author has informed me that in Table 2 of his paper, cubic centimeters should read cubic millimeters.

The shapes of the spermatazoon of the turkey as shown by Ballowitz (1888) (Plate 18a), and by Wakely and Kosin (1951) (Plate 18b) have only a general resemblance. The latter authors found many parts of the spermatazoon to be abnormal.

Stimulated by light, the hypophysis, or pituitary gland, secretes hormones which act upon the gonads. Hypophysectomy of an adult male turkey resulted in the fading of the brilliant colors of the wattles and atrophy of the frontal caruncle. Three weeks after the operation, the testes weighed only 3.9 gr. It was assumed that their normal weight would reach 100 gr. (Hill and Parkes, 1934:231).

Copulation prior to laying is assumed to be sufficient to fertilize all of the subsequent eggs. The sperm is retained in the oviduct and fertilizes the eggs as they mature (Mann, 1883). One copulation has been stated to be sufficient for the purpose (Ghigi and Delacour, 1931). Shepard (1883) mentions that a female confined in a chicken yard where there was no possibility of contact with a male soon began to lay, depositing thirteen eggs. All of the nine eggs allowed to remain under her hatched, indicating that all of the eggs were fertilized by a gobbler prior to her confinement. The number of unions among wild turkeys is unknown but the domestic turkeys are as lustful as house sparrows (*Passer domesticus*). Active spermatazoa are produced when the domestic male is seven months old (Margolf *et al.*, 1947:27). Mating, egg production, and reproduction can be induced at this age by suitable exposure to light. Prior to egg production, the females copulated from one to sixteen times and from four to forty times for the entire breeding season. The fertility of the eggs was not influenced by the frequency of copulation before or after laying began. The seven males mated seven to thirty-five times prior to the period of egg laying, five of them over thirty times. The period of egg production ran from January 21 to March 18. Sexual activity was highest three to four weeks prior to peak egg production.

It is now thought that repeated copulations are essential to obtain eggs with high fertility. Semen capable of fertilization may be retained in the oviduct for as long as eight weeks, but this is unusual (Kosin and Wakely, 1950:261). Lorenz (1950:25) found that fertility declined after the first three weeks and reached almost zero in 57 days. Fertile eggs were rarely observed as late as 72 days. Eggs laid 60 to 224 days after removal of the males were examined by Olsen and Marsden (1953:639).

Of 934 eggs, 16.7 per cent showed embryonic development. It was suggested that parthenogenesis may have played a part. The first day after removal of the male, Albright (1930–32) found that 66.66 per cent of the eggs were fertile. This figure declined to 33.33 per cent on the nineteenth day and to zero on the thirty-second day. According to H. M. Scott (1937:20), copulation takes place two to three weeks in advance of oviposition. Although fertility persists for thirty days, a single copulation is insufficient to secure good fertility. Both egg production and fertility generally declined after April (Parker, 1947:120).

Fertility depends upon the frequency of copulation and its efficiency. The mating efficiency of domestic males varied from 44.3 to 87.5 per cent (Smyth and Leighton, 1953:1,009). The initiation of copulation, and its frequency, depends upon the female. If receptive, she will squat on the approach of the male. Females vary widely in sexual activity. During a period of seven weeks, one group of females averaged 10.7 "matings" while another group was content with 4.8 (Smyth, 1955). It was stated by Bechstein (1807:1,127) that one male can serve ten to fifteen hens. This ratio is essentially the same recommended today. Platt (1925) suggests using one male, two years of age, to twelve to fifteen females. There is a tendency to lower the age of the males. Marsden and Martin (1945:123) state that the male should be at least 8.5 months old. A mature, vigorous male can fertilize from fourteen to twenty females. Approximately fifteen minutes elapse between ovulation and entrance of a spermatazoon into the ovum.

<h2 style="text-align:center">PARTHENOGENESIS</h2>

It is interesting that parthenogenesis exists in the turkey, indicating that it is low in the scale of avian development. M. W. Olsen has written me that the trait for parthenogenesis is better developed in turkeys than in chickens. Dixon (1853:366) mentions two cases savoring of parthenogenesis. A female mated in July or August of one year produced fertile eggs the following April. One Christmas he disposed of all of his turkeys, including a fine gobbler, but kept one female. The latter laid eleven eggs from which eight strong poults were hatched. The hatchability was unusually high for parthenogenesis.

A series of papers on parthenogenesis in the turkey have been published by Olsen and Marsden. They reported in 1953 that 16.7 per cent of 934 eggs laid by hens 60 to 224 days after removal of the males showed delayed and retarded embryonic development (1953:639). This was suggestive of parthenogenesis. Of the 1,400 eggs laid by virgin Beltsville Small White Turkey hens, 14.1 per cent showed the same phenomenon, the incidence of which varied from 0 to 49.1 per cent, depending upon the individual (Olsen and Marsden, 1954:342). Development began while the eggs were still in the oviduct. The investigators kept virgin Beltsville Small White Turkeys separate before they became six weeks of age. Artificial light, used in addition to daylight, was turned on at 6:00 A.M. and off at 8:00 P.M. The first eggs were laid eight months after isolation. The incubated eggs showed 22.4 per cent parthenogenetic development (Olsen and Marsden, 1954.1). In 1956, Olsen and Marsden (1956:676) reported the hatching of a live parthenogenetic poult. For the year 1954, Kosin and Nagra (1956:606) found up to 80 per cent parthenogenetic development in the unincubated eggs laid by virgin turkey hens.

Highly important is the announcement of the raising of a fertile parthenogenetic male at Beltsville, Maryland. A news release (Anon., 1959) states that a parthenogenetic male sired thirty-seven poults that showed normal growth. True parthenogenesis produces males only. Since two of the poults were females, this is strong indication that the male was actually the father.

Seven virgin and seven previously mated females were artificially inseminated with semen from a parthenogenetic male by Olsen (1960). Of the 189 eggs laid by the virgin females, 94 were fertile, and 80 poults hatched; and of the 131 eggs laid by the previously mated females 51 were fertile and 42 produced poults. On incubating over 8,000 unfertilized eggs, 722 (9.0 per cent) were found to contain embryos of which 20 survived to twenty-nine days of incubation and were assisted from the shell. The hatching of a parthenogenetic poult has been described by Kosin et al. (1962:52).

EFFECTS OF GONADECTOMY

It is only within the last thirty years that studies have been made on the effect of gonadectomy on the secondary sexual characters of the turkey. The differences between sexes, aside from the sexual glands, are known as the secondary sexual characters. The principal ones which have been accepted for the turkey are:

1. *Head and neck furnishings.*—The frontal caruncle is longer and capable of much greater extension in the male than in the female. The other caruncles are larger in the male, especially on the dorsal surface of the head and the frontal base of the neck. The throat wattle is larger in the male;

2. *Size of body.*—The male weighs about twice as much as the female;

3. *Plumage.*—The plumage of the male has a higher sheen. The breast feathers of the male are tipped with black, but of the female, white or tan;

4. *Beard.*—Present in the male but usually absent in the female. In some races of the domestic turkey, a beard is common in the female;

5. *Spur*—Present in the male, but unknown in a normal female except as a scale or small knob;

6. *Voice.*—The male has a resonant gobble, the female a plaintive piping;

7. *Display.*—The spreading of the tail, dragging the primaries on the ground, emission of a puffing sound, turgescence of the head and neck furnishings, erection of the contour feathers, and stamping the ground are characteristically male performances. Display by the female is unusual and lacks fullness;

8. *Belligerency.*—Fighting is typical of the male during the breeding season. Individual domestic males may show belligerency at any time;

9. *Breast sponge.*—The breast sponge, filled with fat prior to the mating season, is found only in the male.

The effects of gonadectomy on the secondary sexual characters are inconsistent. Lack of agreement among workers may be owing to a number of causes: (1) The difficulty in complete removal of the testes and the ovary, particularly the latter; (2) the age of the subjects at the time the gonadectomy was performed; (3) the length of time the experimental birds were kept under observation; and (4) the breed of turkeys used in the experiments.

The head and neck furnishings regress following gonadectomy. Athias (1928), in his pioneer work, found that during the first few days following removal of the testes, extrusion of the frontal caruncle was normal, but the ability to expand it was gradually lost. At the same time, the throat wattle and the papillae of the head and neck became smaller and less red. Eventually, the frontal caruncle could not be extended beyond the length of the bill. The red color diminished greatly. The heads of the males acquired the appearance of those of the females, the red masses of the neck remaining larger and more colored in two individuals.

Females ovariectomized at an age of three or four months showed an increased development of the furnishings of the head and neck (Athias, 1931). The frontal caruncle became longer and was capable of extension to a maximum length of 3 to 4 cm. The red color increased in the area and was as vivid as in males. Oordt (1933), on the other hand, noted no change in the frontal caruncle of females ovariectomized at the age of five months and held under observation for eighteen months.

The size of the bodies of the male and female are not influenced by gonadectomy, hence are independent of a sex hormone.

The plumage of the male is not affected by castration. Athias (1928, 1929, 1931), and Padoa (1931) reported that ovariectomy produced no change in the plumage of the female. Subsequently, in personal communications, Athias informed Oordt (1936) that his poulards acquired the plumage of the adult cock. Oordt (1933) had four ovariectomized females, and Scott and Payne (1934) one female, that assumed the male plumage. It seems clear therefore that the female plumage is dependent on a sex hormone.

I do not believe that the beard can be considered a secondary sexual character since it occurs too frequently in females both wild and domestic (Schorger, 1957:445). Approximately a year after ovariectomy, one of Athias' (1931) poulards had a beard almost 2 cm. in length while bristles had begun to grow on another bird. Oordt and Maas (1929) had some females with well-developed beards. Scott and Payne (1934) had an ovariectomized poulard that developed a beard but they considered this of doubtful significance. They commented that no beard had been observed on a female of their strain of bronze turkeys for eight years, but that a black beard was common in female Holland Whites. Padoa (1933) thought the presence of a beard in normal females might be a racial character. The ten females he ovariectomized did not show a beard during the first year of life. Within two to three years, six had a normal beard, two had a mediocre one, one a very small beard, and in one it was lacking.

There is agreement that castration has no effect on the growth of the beard of the male whether the operation is performed before or after puberty. The beard appears during the first year and develops as well in capons as in normal males.

The growth of spurs is generally not retarded by castration. Athias (1928, 1929) reported that castration did not affect spur growth. Later, he informed Oordt (1936) that some of his capons developed spurs and some did not, but that he also had normal males over three years old that had not grown spurs. The young males castrated by Oordt and Maas (1929) and by Oordt (1931) did not develop spurs. Padoa (1931) reported that a capon, nine months after castration, had not developed spurs. Later (1933), he added that the capons of A. Taibell showed development of spurs. Padoa also found that some of his capons, two to three years after castration, had fully developed spurs. Scott and Payne (1934) castrated poults nine weeks old. No difference was noted in the growth of the spurs between the capons and normal males, and no spurs developed on the poulards; however, the observations extended over a period of only thirty-eight weeks. Over a period of three months, ending in April, Oordt (1931.1) injected a testicular hormone preparation, Hombreol, into two females. One bird showed a slight development of spurs after four weeks. Growth ceased at the beginning of the breeding period. Both females started to lay eggs the beginning of April. There is no satisfactory explanation for discrepancies. Oordt (1936) believes that spur growth is dependent on a male hormone but that individuals in some breeds of turkeys may not be dependent on it. Athias (1947) in his last paper considered the growth of spurs to be independent of a sex hormone. It is difficult to conceive that the presence of spurs is not due to some male factor at present undiscovered. Cells for producing spurs may be performed at birth and continue to function in spite of castration.

All investigators agree that when the left ovary is removed in the turkey, there is no development of the right ovary. This is a striking difference from the female chicken where under the same operation the right ovary develops into a testicle and there is growth of spurs. According to Athias (1931), the complete removal of the left ovary in adults is difficult to accomplish. A tiny, loose fragment will graft and develop into an ovary. The operation is most successful with birds two and a half to three months old, the ovary then being less fragile and diffuse. The ovary regenerates in nearly all females operated on after puberty. If the gonadectomy is incomplete, there is no variation from the normal in either sex except in degree.

In the incompletely castrated turkey the development of the eusexual characters, i.e. characters dependent on sex hormones, is less rapid than in normal animals (Athias, 1931.1). The decrease in growth of the frontal caruncle is especially marked.

The characteristic call of the male reappears in spring in some castrates, but not in others (Athias, 1929). In the castrates of Athias (1928), in a period of three months, the spreading of the tail and the fighting ardor disappeared. Some birds had the feathers almost constantly erect, especially in spring (Athias, 1929). The mock display (*Scheinbalz*) which is made in a few cases by total castrates is considered by Oordt and Maas (1929) to be the result of very strong stimulation. Some females ovariectomized at the age of five months also indulged in mock display. Athias (1931) noted that females from which the ovaries were completely removed often raised the body feathers and spread the tail.

The fighting instinct disappears or is greatly reduced by castration. The defense posture is brief and accompanied by plaintive cries. The castrates remain indifferent towards the females and so timid as not to attack other animals in the normal way (Athias, 1928). Several months after castration there is an increase in combativeness. One individual showing an increase of the fighting instinct and spreading of the tail did not have a trace of testes as shown by anatomical investigation (Athias, 1929). Complete spreading of the tail did not take place.

TARSI

The appearance of the tarsi varies with age and season. Prior to shedding, the scales are silvery, the new ones coral red. The scales of large adults are thick, horny, and rough (Petrides, 1942:324). Pirnie (1935:260) states that the tarsi of old males are slender and over six inches long. They are the same length in captive stock but bulkier. The color is brighter after the old scales are shed in autumn and much brighter in the second year than in the first. The tarsi of males are more highly colored than those of females. In domestic birds the color varies from silvery gray to black.

The only significant differences found by Leopold (1944:177) between wild eastern, domestic, and hybrid turkeys were in weight and in the diameter of the tarsi. The wild birds were least heavy and had tarsi with the smallest diameters. The lengths of the tarsi of the three classes were nearly equal. The small diameter was measured laterally at the middle point of the tarsus, and the large diameter anteroposteriorly. Leopold's measurements are given in Table 14.

TABLE 14

AVERAGE TARSAL MEASUREMENTS (MM.) OF
WILD, DOMESTIC, AND HYBRID TURKEYS

Type	Number of Specimens	Tarsal Length	Tarsal Diameter Greatest	Least
ADULT MALES				
M. g. silvestris	24	167	19.1	11.0
Hybrid	5	162	21.0	13.5
Domestic	1	169	23.0	13.5
FIRST-YEAR MALES				
M. g. silvestris	8	158	17.0	10.5
Hybrid	17	158	20.0	12.8
Domestic	9	156	21.5	13.5
ADULT FEMALES				
M. g. silvestris	14	130	15.5	9.0
Hybrid	18	125	17.1	10.5
Domestic	6	126	18.0	11.5*
FIRST-YEAR FEMALES				
M. g. silvestris	8	128	15.0	9.0
Hybrid	26	124	16.8	10.3
Domestic	12	125	18.7	11.0

*One specimen.

I have the tarsus of a male broad-breasted bronze turkey, fourteen months old and weighing thirty-three pounds, which has the following measurements (in mm.): length, 159; greatest diameter, 23; least diameter, 16.

Measurements of the greatest width of the tarsi of wild turkeys in South Carolina were made by W. P. Baldwin (1947:35). They are shown in Table 15.

The form and arrangement of the plates on the tarsus of the domestic turkey were studied by Grafe (1948). Clearly formed banded plates in two rows, overlapping like shingles from the proximal to the distal end, cover the dorsal surface of the tarsus. In the middle third of the tarsus

TABLE 15

DIAMETER (MM.) OF TARSI OF EASTERN WILD TURKEYS

Age and sex	Number of birds	Greatest Diameter Range	Average
1st-year male	1	—	18
Adult male	8	19–21	19.6
1st-year female	2	14–15	14.5
Adult female	4	16–17	16.2

they are especially well developed and stand at uniform angles to each other. The number of plates in the two rows is not always the same, the lateral having about nine to ten and the inner eight to ten plates. No diagnostic difference in arrangement from that of the guinea fowl (*Numida meleagris*) or the chicken (*Gallus domesticus*) could be detected.

SPURS

Spurs are comparatively rare in female turkeys and when present are usually mere protuberances. The shape and dimensions vary with age and in some cases with race. The spurs are used in fighting but no serious injury is inflicted. Devoe (1953:223) wrote that a fighting bird has been known to drive a spur almost an inch into an oak board. This is drawing the long bow. The spur is present in all domestic turkeys, according to Grafe (1948), being 1 to 2 mm. long in females and 10 mm. or more in males. In old birds, its distance from the proximal end of the tarsus is over 60 mm. and in the young, 50 to 60 mm. The specimens he examined were only six to fifteen months old.

The length of the spur is indicative of age but it is not a safe criterion. Jones (1922) wrote: "The first thing an old turkey hunter does after killing a gobbler is to examine his spurs to see how old he is. . . . Some claim you can tell best by the length of the beard, but that is not so; the spurs are the best indication of age. A turkey's spurs never come to a keen point until he is three or four years old. After four years they take on a slight curve. About twenty-five years ago I killed them with spurs an inch and a half long and as keen as any rooster's spurs you ever saw. Not so now." Alexander (1888) killed a turkey in Bossier Parish, Louisiana, that weighed 21.5 pounds and had spurs 1.5 inches (38 mm.)

long. A turkey shot in Virginia had spurs 1.25 inches (32 mm.) long (Johenning, 1940).

Measurements of the spurs of the various races are given in Table 16.

TABLE 16

LENGTHS OF SPURS GIVEN BY RIDGWAY AND FRIEDMANN (1946)

Race	Number of Specimens	Range mm.	Average mm.
M. g. silvestris	9	14.5–23	18.5
M. g. osceola	11	17–32	25.0
M. g. gallopavo	4	14.5–16.5	15.5
M. g. mexicana	9	13.5–17.5	16

LENGTH OF SPURS MEASURED BY SCHORGER

M. g. silvestris	21	15–32	22
M. g. osceola	19	17–34	23
M. g. intermedia	17	19–30	24
M. g. merriami	3	18–27	22
M. g. mexicana	1	19	—

The average length given by Mosby and Handley (1943:250) for twelve eastern turkeys over two years old is 24 mm. with a range of 16–29 mm. Leopold (1944:177) obtained a mean of 24 mm. for twenty-four specimens. A length greater than 32 mm. is exceptional. Well-developed spurs on eastern, Florida, and Rio Grande turkeys show little difference in length, shape, and sharpness. They curve upward in all races. The spurs of Merriam's turkeys are conspicuous for their poor development. In most cases they are blunt triangles, and in some specimens with lengthy beards are mere nubs.

The unusual state of the spurs in Merriam's turkey was recognized by early ornithologists. A letter from C. Bendire, dated December 29, 1872, is quoted by Coues (1873.1:326): "The males do not all have spurs; in fact, I thought at first that the variety of turkey we have in Arizona never had any, and I have been so informed by Mexicans and Indians. But I killed two gobblers myself a few days ago, and both were spurred, though the largest bird I ever killed, a male weighing twenty-eight pounds, had no spurs." The same condition was observed in southwestern New Mexico by Henshaw (1874:435), who wrote: "A few of the gobblers had spurs; in one instance these took the form of a blunt,

rounded knob half an inch long. In others, however, it was much reduced, and in others still the spur was wanting, though my impression is
that all the old males had this weapon."

Beard

The turkey is noted for a long hairlike appendage on the breast commonly called a beard. The bristles of which the beard is composed are
primitive feathers, not "hairs," as they are sometimes called. True hairs
are covered with scales of a characteristic shape. Ficalbi (1891:241)
thought that the bristle was intermediate between a feather and a hair,
a conclusion with which Meijere (1895:572) correctly disagreed. The
morphology of the bristles and the histology of the prominence to which
they are attached has been studied by Bulliard (1926).

The beards of several races of the wild turkey were examined by
Schorger (1957). The structural units are crescent-shaped and arranged
in circles. The melanin, to which the dark color of the bristle is due, is
concentrated at the points of overlap. The medulla is much smaller than
in a normal feather. The bristles are usually in bundles that issue from a
single follicle (Plate 19a); however, intergrowth between two bristles
(Plate 19b) is unusual. No uniformity in the shape of the cross section
(Plate 20) of a bristle exists between races, or even within a single bristle.
Apparently, the bristles are primitive contour feathers. Pirnie (1935:261)
makes the qualified statement that the beard may be shed completely at
moulting time. In actuality, the beard is not shed but grows continuously.
As long ago as 1879, Jordan (1879) stated that the beard attains a length
of ten to thirteen inches, and "never grows shorter or sheds out."

The beard, on technical grounds at least, is considered to be an orna-
ment. Darwin (1896:110) could see no aesthetic value, for he wrote: "The
tuft of hair on the breast of a wild turkey-cock cannot be of any use, and
it is doubtful whether it can be ornamental in the eyes of the female
bird; indeed, had the tuft appeared under domestication, it would have
been called a monstrosity."

Beards on Females

Regarding beards on females, Audubon (1831:15) wrote: "Some
closet naturalists suppose the hen Turkey to be destitute of the append-

age on the breast, but this is not the case in the full-grown bird. The young males, as I have said, at the approach of the first winter, have merely a protuberance in the flesh at this part, while the young females of the same age have no such appearance. The second year, the males are to be distinguished by the hairy tuft, which is about four inches long, whereas in the females that are not barren, it is yet hardly apparent. The third year, the male Turkey may be said to be adult, although it certainly increases in weight and size for several years more. The females at the age of four are in full beauty, and have the pectoral appendage four or five inches long, but thinner than in the male. The barren hens do not acquire it until they are very old. The experienced hunter knows them at once in the flock, and shoots them by preference. The great number of young hens destitute of the appendage in question has doubtless given rise to the idea that it is wanting in the female Turkey." In his technical description of the female, he gives the length of the beard as four inches. With age there is an increasing tendency towards maleness in female birds (Young, 1955:453), but it must not be assumed that all female turkeys four years or more in age will have beards.

Data on the occurrence of a beard in wild females are limited except for the eastern turkey, but a beard has been found on the females of several races. In the spring of 1942, five out of seventy-five yearling female wild turkeys raised in captivity in Pennsylvania had beards (Keiser and Kozicky, 1943:10). An old female shot in Pennsylvania in 1957 had a beard eight inches long (Bowers, 1958). Wunz (1962) reported three females with beards in this state. In 1881 a female killed in Virginia had a beard approximately eight inches in length, this being the longest beard ever seen on a hen by the hunter (M., 1881). Mosby (1940) reported that in Virginia females have beards rather frequently. The beards of five females exceeded 7.5 inches (190 mm.) and two exceeded 9 inches (229 mm.). The number of bristles was less than in the average male. Mosby and Handley (1943:95) observed that even the rudiments of a beard were seldom seen the first fall, and that a visible beard does not appear until the third year. Six of thirteen captive hens had beards averaging 65 mm., while one adult hen (over a year old) had a beard of 184 mm. McDowell (1954:45), in Virginia, found only four bearded females among 557 turkeys of both sexes killed during the 1953–54 season.

Examination of 230 females, fourteen months old, at the Cumberland State Game Farm, revealed that 17 (7.4 per cent) had beards protruding from the breast feathers. If the eminence from which the beard arises had been examined, the percentage undoubtedly would have been higher. The beards of these females varied in length from 39 to 107 mm. In South Carolina, beards have been reported for both sexes (Wayne, 1910:65). Davis (1949:57) has seen a number of old females with beards, the maximum length being six inches (152 mm.). During trapping operations in Alabama, two hens with beards 6.50 (165 mm.) and 7.25 inches (184 mm.) long were captured (Wheeler, 1946.2). An old female taken by Maximilian (1858:427) had a beard 6.75 inches long. Goebel (1889) stated that although beards are common on domestic females, he never saw one on a wild female in Missouri; however, Leopold (1944:177) reported one 65 mm. long.

The hunting by Jordan (1898:330) in Texas was within the range of the eastern race. He stated: "Hens have beards only in rare cases. I have seen and killed a few hens with beards, but not in one case out of a hundred will a hen be found with one. I have seen thirty or forty hens together and not one with a sign of a beard." On the Trinity River he killed one with a five-inch beard. Baines (1890:344) reported that beards on females were not very common, but on his last hunt two of the three females killed had beards.

The female Florida turkey, according to information given to Scott (1892), sometimes has a small beard. McLaurin (1957:35) adds that "substantiated reports of kills of hen turkeys with beards have been surprisingly numerous."

Writing of the Rio Grande turkey, Walker (1950:3) adds: "Many hunters believe that a gobbler always has a beard, while a hen has none. This is entirely false. Many young gobblers, hatched in June, have no beards by the following November, while bearded hens are common." In March, 1959, while I was going over the Hopper Ranch, Brooks County, Texas, with Caleb Glazener, Frank Hopper told me that a short time previously members of the Texas Game and Fish Commission had trapped seven hens, three of which had beards. He and Glazener thought that 10 per cent of the females have beards. A flock of two males and eight females near the road had one bearded female.

Merriam's turkey has been stocked in Wyoming. It has been stated that a mature male has a beard nine inches long, while that of a mature female attains a maximum of three inches (Anon., 1955:27). Of thirty-five females trapped in New Mexico, four were found to have beards (MacDonald, 1961).

An adult female Gould's turkey taken in Hidalgo County, New Mexico, had a beard five to six inches long (Bohl and Gordon, 1958). Its largest ovum measured 11 mm.

A beard is fairly common among domestic female turkeys, especially on Holland Whites. S. J. Marsden informed me (Schorger, 1957:445) that he examined 1,373 Beltsville Small White females six to eleven months old and found that 122 (8.9 per cent) had beards. They ranged from 3 to 63 mm. in length, the average being 26 mm. The beard on a white turkey is always black. For unknown reasons, there is an increase in bearded females among pen-reared wild turkeys. McDowell (1954:46) has suggested that a nutritional or genetic factor is involved.

BEARDS ON MALES

The beard reaches its perfection in the male. Audubon (1929:54) wrote in 1820: "The Beard of the Turkey shows about one Inch Long the 1st year, and one of the Male in full growth and plumage must be 3 years old." One of the better early descriptions of the beard is by Jordan (1898:226). He states that in the domestic turkey the beard is crinkled, giving a "bunchy" appearance, while in the wild bird it is long and entirely straight. It does not show on the young gobblers until late October or November. Full growth to eleven or twelve inches is attained in three or four years. It does not appear that the length is limited by wear but rather to cessation of growth. The beard on a young gobbler is two inches by November of the first year of life. By March it is three inches and projects an inch from the feathers. It is five inches long at the age of two years, and about eight inches at the age of three years.

The tip of the beard does wear off, and in the wild bird it is sometimes crinkled. The beard is not always present on the male. Maximilian (1858:426) mentions a male forty-four inches long, the beard being absent entirely. Wheeler (1946.1:142) trapped a beardless adult gobbler in Alabama. The growth of the beard is not uniform in the various races. It is retarded particularly in the Florida turkey. Specimens of males that I have examined with spurs present and a beard absent are shown in Table 17.

TABLE 17

RETARDED GROWTH OF BEARD IN THE MALE TURKEY

Race	Museum	Specimen Number	Date of Collection	Spurs Length mm.	Beard
osceola	AMNH*	10,946	March 28	23	absent
osceola	AMNH	354,183	March	10	absent
osceola	MCZ**	5,289	February 25	4	absent
osceola	MCZ	181,151	March 10	3	absent
osceola	MCZ	244,265	February 28	2	absent
intermedia	MCZ	187,257	March 6	4	absent
merriami	MCZ	213,556	November 30	8	trace

*American Museum of Natural History.
**Museum of Comparative Zoology.

The color of the beard is black. Old specimens in museums may have a tinge of gray. Exceptions are infrequent. The beard of a turkey killed in Arkansas is stated to have had a "ring" around it (J. G. S., 1882). Presumably, the ring represented a change in color. Jordan (1898:246) wrote: "The gobblers of these Brazos bottoms [Texas] were also distinguished by their peculiar beards. In other varieties of turkeys three inches or less of the upper end of the beard is grayish, while those of the Brazos bottoms were more bunchy and the black ran up to the skin of the breast." I may add that the proximal ends of the bristles are usually loosely coated with gray scales. When these are removed, the bristles are black. Frank Hopper informed me that one fall two gobblers with "yellow" beards were shot on his Texas ranch. These examples were unique in his experience. A turkey shot by Baines (1888) had white legs and a nearly white beard. This must have been at least a partial albino.

The rate of growth of the beard is shown in Table 18. McDowell (1954:49) examined for beards twenty-seven juvenile males of which only twelve had beards ranging from 0.5 to 3 inches, the average being 0.98 inch (25 mm.). The beards of sixteen old gobblers varied from 7 to 12.25 inches with an average of 10 inches (254 mm.). The beards of eight adult males measured by Baldwin (1947:35) varied from 227 to 263 mm., the average being 248 mm.

TABLE 18

GROWTH OF THE BEARD IN MALE TURKEYS

Race	Number of Specimens	Age in Months	Range in m.m.	Average in m.m.	
sylvestris, wild	6	under 12	11–55	33	Mosby and Handley (1943:249–52)
sylvestris, captive	9	under 12	32–67	43	
sylvestris, wild	3	12–24	30–122	71	
sylvestris, captive	4	12–24	77–164	108	
sylvestris, wild	11	over 24	228–315	269	
sylvestris, captive	2	over 24	233–257	245	
sylvestris	8	12	—	33	Leopold (1944:177)
Hybrid	17	12	—	91	
Domestic	9	12	—	33	
sylvestris	24	adult	—	261	
Hybrid	5	adult	—	210	
Domestic	1	adult	—	205	

Additional measurements of long beards are given in Table 19.

TABLE 19

LENGTHS OF BEARDS OF SEVERAL RACES

Race	State	Length in Inches	Length in Mm.	Reference
M. g. silvestris	Pa.	10–11	254–279	Bowers (1958)
M. g. silvestris	N.C.	12	305	Anon. (1900)
M. g. silvestris	S.C.	13, 14	330, 356	Davis (1949:57; 1937)
M. g. silvestris	Ga.	11	279	"Old Subscriber" (1893)
M. g. silvestris	Ala.	11.5	292	Jones (1887)
M. g. silvestris	Ind.	12	305	A., J. (1877)
M. g. silvestris	La.	13	330	Jones (1922)
M. g. silvestris	N. Tex.	12	305	Baines (1890:344)
M. g. silvestris	Kan.	12.5	318	R., G. B. (1887)
M. g. osceola	Fla.	11	279	"Osceola" (1924.1)
M. g. osceola	Fla.	13	330	Grant (1911)
M. g. osceola	Fla.	11.7	297	Schorger
M. g. intermedia	Tex.	10.3	262	Schorger
M. g. mexicana	Chihuahua	8.2	208	Schorger
M. g. merriami	N.M.	10–12	254–305	Ligon (1946:6)

MULTIPLE BEARDS

The occurrence of multiple beards is an interesting phenomenon. Double beards are fairly common. Vieillot and Outart (1825:Pl. 201), and Jardine (1853:Pl. I) have illustrations of turkeys with triple beards. As a rule, the length decreases from the upper to the lower beard. Marsden and Martin (1945:54) mention a white domestic turkey with seven distinct beards arranged in a row and varying in length from normal to very small. Multiple beards on females are uncommon. Recently, Marsden (Schorger, 1957:446), in examining Beltsville Small White females, found three with two, three, and five beards respectively.

A wild gobbler, according to Rutledge (1936), often has two to three beards. Goebel (1889) killed a male in Missouri with four beards of decreasing length, the lowest being "a short curled-up stump." A male shot in Virginia carried two beards, 8.5 and 2.5 inches in length (Johenning, 1940). More turkeys with multiple beards have been reported from Texas than elsewhere. Jordan (1898:330) writes: "I have seen gobblers with two or three beards. I saw one at Eagle Lake, Texas, with five separate, long and distinct beards." A gobbler with three beards is mentioned by Baines (1890:344). One shot in Bee County, Texas, is stated to have had four beards measuring 5.5, 6.5, 7.5, and 6 inches respectively (Anon., 1940). Recently, a gobbler was shot in Edwards County that had four beards (Anon., 1956). A quintuple beard from a bird shot in Sutton County in 1954 is shown in Plate 21. All records are surpassed by a gobbler with nine beards killed in Kerr County, Texas (Anon., 1961).

LONGEVITY

It was stated by Flower (1925:1,410) that he had failed to find a longevity greater than ten years for either the wild or domestic bird. Oustalet (1899) mentions that Leseur gave to the Jardin des Plantes, Paris, a turkey on July 18, 1834, which died on December 7, 1846. The period of captivity was accordingly twelve years, four months, and nineteen days. Its age at the time of presentation is unknown. A maximum age for the domestic bird is given by Cuenot (1911:106) as sixteen years. Of two turkeys in the London Zoological Gardens, one was killed six years, two months, and ten days after birth; the other died at an age of eight years, six months, and five days (Flower, 1938:227).

Doyle (n.d.:216) mentions a Norfolk black turkey which weighed thirty-six pounds at fourteen years of age.

According to Brown (1928:347), an eastern wild turkey, received at the Philadelphia Zoological Garden on May 29, 1919, died December 21, 1924, a captivity period of nearly five years and seven months. Mann (1930:244) states that of the 114 wild turkeys kept at the National Zoological Park, Washington, the greatest longevity was six years and eight months, this age applying to birds at liberty in the park. Two of the male wild turkeys kept by Randall (1930) were still breeding strongly at ten years of age. A male "wild" turkey, hatched at the Poynette Game Farm in the spring of 1952, was received at the Vilas Park Zoo, Madison, Wisconsin, May 25, 1953. It died February 7, 1961, approximately eight years and eight months old.

Data on the survival of native turkeys are meager and generally indefinite. Alford (1940) began hunting a gobbler in Sabine County, Texas, in the spring of 1898. Judging from its size and unusually long beard, it was old at the time. It was not killed until 1907, at an estimated age of twelve to fifteen years. Mosby and Handley (1943:175) mention hens kept for propagation which lived more than five years. In their opinion the average life of a wild turkey is five years; however, field reports indicated that some birds may live for ten to twelve years. The average life span was estimated by Davis (1949:60) to be eight years. A few hermits in the Pee Dee swamp in South Carolina were at least ten years old when last observed. A huge gobbler killed by S. A. Graham in South Carolina in the Santee swamp was probably over fifteen. It was mature when first observed and defied capture for ten years.

In Ligon's opinion (1946:6), the maximum age of Merriam's turkey in the wild is ten years. A gobbler, whose history was known, died in good flesh and physical condition at nine and a half years. Accurate data on age can seldom be obtained without marking. A wild bird retrapped by Bailey and Rindell (1960:2) in West Virginia was five and a half years old. Band returns on Florida turkeys showed a survival up to ten years (Powell, 1961:15). A crippled male shot in March, 1958, in Alabama was thought to be at least four years old. Its range did not exceed twelve hundred yards from the point of original observation in April, 1955 (Kennamer, 1959).

6

Characteristics

THE TURKEY HAS CERTAIN innate characteristics that cause it to react in definite ways under the proper stimuli. Habits on the other hand are both variable and changeable. Its fear of man is acquired, but seldom will it remain undisturbed in the presence of a large predator. Curiosity is a strong trait, and reaction to loud sounds equally so. The wild bird is pugnacious during the breeding season, while the domestic bird may show irascibility towards humans at any time.

FEAR OF PREDATORS

The instinctive solicitude of the female turkey for her young impressed Erasmus Darwin (1809). At the sight of a kite hovering in the air, she conveyed her agitation to her young, who sought concealment in the grass. The fears shown by gesture and deportment were accompanied by a warning *koe-ut, koe-ut*, which sent the young into hiding whether the mother was visible or not. The inborn fear of raptors has been cleverly demonstrated by the use of a cardboard decoy having a short neck and a long tail (Lorenz, 1939:93; Tinbergen, 1939:24; Schleidt, 1961:542). When the decoy was pulled in one direction to simulate a hawk, then in the opposite direction so that the long tail resembled the neck of a goose, young turkeys showed no fear of the goose but manifested pronounced flight reactions towards the hawk. While fear of raptors is innate, Ramsay (1951) found that factors for familial recognition in young turkeys were largely acquired.

The behavior of a wild female and her young has been described by Gilmour (1876:14): "While the young birds were thus busily engaged, the old hen would stand like a sentinel in the midst, her neck stretched to its full extent and her head turned sharply from side to side, while with her quick keen eye she watched, not only her brood, but also for any approaching danger. If you approached near, and there was not sufficient cover for her to hide in, she crouched almost level with the ground with her head and neck stretched out straight in front of her, and, at a warning chuck from her, the young ones disappeared as if by magic, and were by no means easy to discover in the tufts of grass, etc., in which they had taken refuge." The extent to which the mother will subject herself to danger has its limits. In Indiana County, Pennsylvania, a female with three young appeared near the home of Stewart (1913) in 1892. The poults were captured and placed in the barn as decoys, but the mother refused to enter.

PRIMITIVE UNWARINESS TO MAN

The turkey has inherited the capacity for wildness, but under primitive conditions it was quite unsuspicious of man. In 1810, Joynes (1902) saw turkeys in large flocks near Point Pleasant, West Virginia, sometimes so near that one could be killed with a pistol. Three men in a canoe took successive shots at a turkey standing on the bank of the Ohio River, but "it walked away very composedly" (Nourse, 1925:137). Adair (1775:360) wrote: "At many unfrequented places of the Mississippi, they are so tame as to be shot with a pistol, of which our troops profited, in their way to take possession of the Illinois-garrison." Michaux (1805:216) wrote similarly of the birds in the uninhabited parts. In the east, however, and particularly near the seaports, they could not be approached without difficulty. Indifference to gunfire at times may have been because of reasons other than lack of wariness. Möllhausen (1858: II, 201) wrote of his experience with the turkeys in the Aztec Mountains of western Arizona in 1853 as follows: "The very turkeys seemed to be suffering from cold, and cowering between the rocks and bushes took little notice of the shots with which they were saluted as the hunters came up."

Turkeys that had arrived at or that were already on a roost were notoriously indifferent to disturbance. This made night shooting very popular. In 1699, Penicaut (1869) camped under some trees on Lake Pontchartrain where great numbers of turkeys were roosting. When the moon rose, as many turkeys were killed as desired since they were not afraid of the guns. They were even indifferent to a fire built at the roost.

While in the Raton Mountains, on the Colorado–New Mexico border, on January 19, 1851, Bennett (1947) wrote: "Snow from 4 to 30 feet deep. . . . At night killed some wild turkeys which appeared to hover about our fire." Caton (1877:323) and a companion built a fire and camped under a very large tree. Several hours later they discovered a turkey roosting in the top of it. In July, 1898, in Durango, Nelson (1891–1904) had the experience of seeing an old male turkey continuing to walk towards his campfire though it was not killed until several shots had been fired. The camp was under a large pine in which the bird was probably accustomed to roost.

The Duke of Württemberg (Paul Wilhelm, 1828:81, 88) considered the wild turkey a stupid, unwary bird. Concerning the large flocks observed on the sandy or stony areas along the Mississippi River above the mouth of the Ohio, he remarked that even the rumbling noise of the steamers seldom disturbed their repose. Schultz (1810: II, 19) thought that "wild" could not be attached to the turkey with full propriety. He frequently passed within thirty yards of flocks drinking along the Ohio with no sign of disturbance. Palmer (1818) was near Mt. Vernon, Kentucky on July 27, 1817, when "on our road we saw a flock of wild turkies feeding on the ground, they paid but little attention, letting us get within twenty yards of them, and then running into the thicket." In the Western Reserve, Ohio, when a flock was encountered suddenly, the birds flew into trees and waited for him to pass by (Griffiths, 1835). Halsell (1948:21) states that at his home in Wise County, Texas, in 1870, wild turkeys would come to the house and roost in the trees with the chickens and domestic turkeys. Cook (1907:114) camped in western Stonewall County, Texas, the fall of 1874. He wrote: "I had killed turkeys in southwest Missouri, also in southeastern Kansas, and had always looked upon them as a wary game bird. But here, turkey, turkey! Manifesting at all times and places a total indifference to our presence." While living in Montgomery County, Missouri, Duden (1834:175) was visited daily by wild turkeys with their young. They often sat on his fences so trustingly that he found it difficult to bring himself to shoot at them.

Regarding an experience with turkeys south of St. Augustine, Florida, Elliot (1897:177) wrote: "As I dismounted from my horse there was a sudden rush and commotion in front, and a flock of Turkeys started away, some to run and a few to take wing. The runners soon disappeared, but the flying birds took refuge in the trees near at hand, and standing motionless, or else slowly walking on the large limbs, looked down upon us as if wondering what kind of intruders we were. They evinced no particular alarm, certainly nothing like that which one of these birds would be apt to show at the present time under similar circumstances."

Merriam's turkey originally showed no more wariness than its eastern relative. Concerning this race in southwestern New Mexico, Henshaw (1874:433) wrote that it appeared to be entirely unsuspicious and showed no knowledge of man as a potential enemy; if not shot at it was possible to approach within a few yards. Flight was rare except when the birds were hard pressed, but when sensing danger they ran with great speed to the steep sides of the ravines, which they ascended easily.

Turkeys could be so trusting that an observer might believe they were domestic. When Woods (1822:122) was in Perry County, Indiana, he passed fourteen or fifteen wild turkeys in a field. Since they slowly walked into the woods, he did not suspect that they were wild; however, at the cabin, he was told there were no tame turkeys for many miles, but there were plentiful wild ones. Wheaton (1882) states: "The few which remain exhibit great intuitive or acquired cunning in avoiding detection. As if aware that their safety depended on their preserving an incognito when observed, they effect the unconcern of their tame relatives so long as a threatened danger is passive or unavoidable. I have known them to remain quietly perched upon a fence while a team passed by; and on one occasion knew a couple of hunters to be so confused by the actions of a flock of five, which deliberately walked in front of them, mounted a fence, and disappeared leisurely over a low hill before they were able to decide them to be wild. No sooner were they out of sight than they took to their legs and then to their wings, soon placing a wide valley between them and their now amazed and mortified pursuers." This indicates more guile than I believe the turkey is capable of mustering.

The turkey was least wary when there was concern for food. Hildreth (1836) wrote that turkeys were so slightly alarmed by the presence of man that they entered his fields and fed on the corn given to the hogs. A flock of thirty birds came to feed daily at the hogpen of a settler who, from his cabin, shot one daily until twenty-seven were killed. They were neither greatly alarmed by the report of the rifle, nor frightened away by those which had been killed. In Fairfield County, Ohio, wild turkeys approached the cabins close enough to look into the windows. While John Eric was loading corn into a wagon, the turkeys pecked at the corn from the opposite side of the vehicle. He tried to kill them by using ears of corn as missiles (Scott, 1877:217, 222). Blair (1915:234) states that in 1857, in Kansas, wild turkeys ran behind the wagons looking for food.

The inclination of the turkey, when fully protected, to disregard man as an enemy is pronounced. Dimock (1926:255) mentions that the turkeys on a citrus plantation in Florida were protected. At the sound of a felled tree, the birds came promptly to collect the insects in the upper branches. A recent report by Jantzen (1956.2) is illuminating: "The turkey on the Kaibab North shows little or no concern for the presence of humans. Two separate attempts were made to run a turkey down; they were not successful. However, the turkey showed little concern other than to remain safely out of reach. On one occasion, they did not fly but out-distanced pursuit uphill. On another occasion, the flock scattered and flew. Some birds flew up to 200 yards, but immediately started calling to regroup the flock and began feeding again."

Merriam's turkey has been restored to Mesa Verde, Colorado, and has become tame. When I was in the park, Douglas Osborne remarked to me: "I think that the turkey domesticated the Pueblos rather than that the Pueblos domesticated the turkey."

WILDNESS

None of our native animals is more wary than the "educated" wild turkey. The eastern turkey has been well described by Thorpe (1846:61): "It's game head and clear hazel eye, the clean firm step, the great breadth of shoulder, and deep chest, strike the most superficial observer. Then there is an absolute commanding beauty about them, when they are alarmed or curious, when they elevate themselves to their full height, bringing their head perpendicular with their feet, and gaze about, every feather in its place, the foot upraised at an instant, to strike off at a speed, that, as has been said of the ostrich, 'scorneth the horse and his rider.' " And, "the turkey never speculates, never wonders; suspicion of danger prompts it to immediate flight, as quickly as a reality."

Ligon (1946:10) has given us this picture of Merriam's turkey at the present time: "Probably no other bird or mammal excels the turkey in alertness. It can instantly detect the slightest movement of an object in the scope of vision. When it notes evidence of danger, as a crouching cat, sneaking coyote, or an observer in a blind, the entire group is instantly made aware of the danger, through actions or the alarm signal 'put-put.' If the threat does not appear serious, all are likely to investigate in order to satisfy themselves. If the danger proves real, the skill and speed with which all disappear is astonishing. . . . the turkey takes greater advantage of the warnings of its associates than any of the other dwellers of the forest. Even the shriek of a chipmunk, chatter of a chickaree, or the scolding of chickadees or tiny bush tits is sufficient to cause all turkeys within hearing to snap to attention."

It was insisted by Le Conte (1858:181) that the true wild turkey had never been tamed. Birds hatched from eggs obtained in the woods showed a degree of adaptation to domestication, but when about one year of age, they took to the woods and never returned. He states further that these wild birds will not mix with the domestic turkeys and will not interbreed. These claims, unfortunately, are not in accord with the usual habits of the two races. The eastern Indians did not domesticate the turkey but did raise captured wild poults. Barton (1805) stated that it is certain that the turkey was not generally domesticated by the eastern Indians before the arrival of Europeans. The statement that Hernando de Soto on entering Alabama found the Indians raising captured wild poults by the thousands is a gross exaggeration (Federal Writers' Project, 1941:118). Swanton (1946) was correct in writing that it was rarely tamed in the Southeast.

When the La Salle expedition of 1682 reached an Arkansas village, Membré (1852) says that the inhabitants had large numbers of turkeys and tamed bustards (Canada geese). The Indian slave of Du Pratz (1758:125) told him that his nation raised turkeys as easily as the French did chickens. Solis (1931), in 1767–68, crossed the San Pedro River, Texas, from the south and came to a village of the Tejas Indians where there were young chickens, young turkeys, and some dogs. The activities of the Indians were limited to raising young turkeys captured in the wild.

The Indians of upper Chesapeake Bay, according to Strachey (1849:36), had tame turkeys about their houses, but these birds were not raised by those living on the James River. Kalm (1772:163) also mentions that the Indians tamed turkeys and kept them near their huts. These turkeys were raised for use as decoys to attract the wild birds (Lawson, 1937:157). Byrd (1940:72) wrote: "Some Indians and Virginians raise expressly this wild breed, in order to decoy the completely wild ones by this means, so that they come to rest near their houses or huts. They then shoot them down from the trees in which they always roost." No reference was found on the raising of turkeys by the Indians of New England.

There are opinions to the contrary, but in general, it was difficult—or impossible—to domesticate the eastern turkey. Byrd (1940:71) states: "If one takes the eggs from the wild ones and places them under the domesticated ones, they still preserve their wild nature, and will never go into a house to roost, but will always roost in a high tree near the house, and thus separate themselves from the domesticated birds, despite the fact that they hatch and run with them." The statement of Dale, quoted by Klein (1750:112), indicates that the early colonists attempted to domesticate the wild turkey: "The wild Turkees are now kept by a great many of our English Gentlemen, and seem to do very well, where there (in Nova Anglia) are Small Woods and Copses in Parks or other enclosed places for them." Kalm (1772:163) writes that when the eggs were taken from the woods and hatched under a domestic turkey, the young became tame; however, when they were grown it was necessary to keep their wings clipped to prevent them from flying away.

About 1864 a Mr. Townsend, of Lockport, New York, raised sixteen turkeys hatched from the eggs of a wild bird. All of them went wild and were shot eventually (Davison, 1894). Bachman (1855:14) found that wildness disappeared from generation to generation, "until they acquired all the docility—the dependence and stupidity of the common domesticated breeds." "Aztec" (1889) claims that he was unable to tame the eastern wild turkeys that he raised, and Nehrling (1882) states that young hatched under a domestic hen became very wild when grown. One writer (N. A. T., 1886) mentions an acquaintance in Taylor County, Texas who raised wild turkeys from eggs found in the woods. When hatched, they were so wild that they were confined in a coop with the mother, whereby they became partly tame. As they grew up, they roosted in the tops of the tallest trees, and fought with the domestic turkeys. Their uncontrollable wandering habits led eventually to their final disappearance. In June, 1903, Professor R. L. Blanton captured five wild poults that were raised with domestic turkeys. It is reported that when they bred the following year, they became wary as soon as the eggs hatched (Stone, 1908).

The wild turkey had become rare at Scarborough, Maine, by 1663 because of overhunting by the English and the Indians. Josselyn (1860:39) wrote: "But some of the English bring up great store of the wild kind, which remain about their homes as tame as ours in England." The wild race was sometimes raised in New Hampshire. Blood (1860:177) states that some were tamed by Theodore Barker between 1785–90. Archelaus Cummings also had a flock, the gobbler of which had a bell fastened to its neck. The birds instinctively took to the woods but would return home. Timothy Adams (Leonard, 1855:120) found a nest containing fourteen eggs on which a wild hen was sitting. The incubation was completed under a hen and every egg hatched. The entire brood was raised, then sent to the Boston market. On December 23, 1798, Bentley (1905–14, II:292; IV:108) wrote in his diary that he dined with Captain Hodges on a wild turkey raised by one Mr. Breed at Nahant, Massachusetts. Mr. Breed's turkeys roosted in trees throughout the winter. The birds were in demand by gourmets but success in raising them diminished.

Avery (1886), in Alabama, had little difficulty in domesticating wild turkeys hatched from eggs. His yard was recognized as a haven: "Whenever they were threatened by danger, even when a mile from the house, they rose with their loud cry of alarm 'put! put!' which they never ceased to utter 'till they found themselves safely alighted in the yard." One hen flew at least one-half mile from the yard every morning before alighting to go to her nest two miles distant. Both Peck (1853) and Duden (1834:175) wrote that wild turkeys hatched from the eggs were easily domesticated. This statement does not mean much since the writers fail to state how long the birds were kept. While at Chouteau's Post, Mayes County, Oklahoma, Irving (1944:108) recorded on October 6, 1832, the presence of chickens, wild turkeys, and tamed geese.

Races of wild turkeys with "white rumps" can develop as much wildness as the eastern forms, yet they appear to be more easily domesticated. Dresser (1866) noted that the Mexicans along the lower Río Grande sometimes domesticated the Rio Grande turkey. At Piedra Negra he saw two turkeys that had been caught when young and had become quite tame. At the time, the female was sitting on a nest. Regarding Gould's turkey among the Tarahumaras of Chihuahua and Sonora, Bennett and Zingg (1935:23) write: "The turkey (*siwi*) in a domesticated state is not often seen among the Tarahumaras. However, plenty of turkeys are found wild in the Sierra and brought home by the Indians. They are fed and carefully raised until they become quite tame and do not try to run away. It is not even necessary to clip their wings. The Tarahumaras value a turkey at about two pesos. At night the turkeys sleep on top of houses or in nearby trees. If the Indians come across the eggs of a turkey, they often put them under a setting hen."

Wildness is essential for the survival of the turkey. Leopold (1944:191) gives this definition: "Wildness is the inherited condition by which turkeys as individuals, and collectively as populations, are adapted to live successfully in a natural environment." The turkey, though inheriting wildness, retains it only by constant external stimulation. Caton (1877:324), from years of experience, found that the great timidity of the wild turkey disappears very slowly, but diminishes with each succeeding generation.

Physiology of Wildness

The first attempt to obtain physiological data for wildness was made by Gerstell and Long (1939). A comparison was made between poults from game farm (GF) stock and wild mated (WM) birds. The GF turkeys were hybrids between wild and domestic turkeys. Although in appearance they could pass for wild stock, adequate wildness was lacking. The WM chicks were obtained by mating the GF hens with wild gobblers. The WM poults were better coordinated, more alert, and more shy than the GF poults. The respiratory rate and metabolism were also higher for the WM poults. Some of the birds, after sixteen weeks of age, were released for stocking. When the crates were opened, the WM birds flew out while the GF birds walked out. After dark, one could walk under the roost of the GF birds without disturbing them, while the WM birds flew in all directions.

Some fundamental reasons for wildness were found by Leopold (1944:186). As compared with the domestic turkey, the brain of the wild bird is 35 per cent heavier, the pituitary 50 per cent, and the adrenals 100 per cent. Theoretically, starting with a hybrid female that is 50 per cent wild, by mating with a pure wild gobbler and back crossing, the seventh generation should be 99 per cent wild. By this method, even the eleventh generation of birds from the Lost Trail Game Farm failed to have sufficient wildness, apparently because of some hybrid blood in the wild gobblers. Complete elimination of the taint of hybridism is extremely difficult. The hybrids tended to settle down where released and an observer could approach within one hundred feet of them without causing alarm. Some of them roosted on low limbs or on logs on the ground and fell prey to predators. Survival until spring was only 23 per cent. They tended to form larger winter flocks, averaging fourteen in comparison with eight for the native stock. There was little segregation of the sexes. In early spring the hybrid flocks broke up much earlier than the native ones. Gobbling began a month earlier and the peak was reached much earlier than with the wild birds. The color of the plumage bore no apparent relation to wildness, but Leopold adds: "For those who seek external manifestations of wildness in turkeys, I would suggest the limited molts and the limited development of the secondary sex characters of the head as the most likely criteria. At least, these are visible characters which I have found consistently associated with wild behavior."

The findings of Knoder (1959) are essentially in agreement with those of Leopold. The body weight of his Waterloo hybrids was 20 to 25 per cent higher than that of the wild birds. Based on percentage of body weight, the brain and endocrine glands of the hybrids were intermediate between those of the wild and domestic birds. Yearling wild gobblers were unable to produce fertility in the eggs of laying hens, while Waterloo yearling gobblers produced 34.8 to 75.5 per cent fertility. This suggests that the Waterloo birds were hybrids. It should be pointed out that the mating of yearling wild gobblers with hens in the wild has resulted in fertile eggs.

DOMESTICATION OF THE EASTERN TURKEY

The wild turkey was much superior to the early tame bird in size and appearance. Priest (1802:90) wrote: "Why do not the Americans domesticate this noble bird? They are much better adapted to bear this climate than the puny breed their ancestors imported from England." As early as 1614, Hamor (1860:21) mentioned that the wild turkey in Virginia was much larger than the English bird. Catesby (1754:*xliv*) commented that it surpassed the European tame turkey in stature, shape, and beauty of plumage. The superior size of the wild bird is mentioned also by Loskiel (1794:91) and Dwight (1821:55). The praise of the wild bird by Kalm (1772:163) was limited. In his opinion, it differed from the tame turkey only in its larger size, and redder, tastier flesh. It puzzled Byrd (1940:71) why the domestic turkey never attained the size of the wild one although both were given the same food. The development of a heavy domestic turkey was slow in coming. Clinton (1815) wrote: "As to comparative size, it may be observed that the largest wild turkey does not exceed the largest tame turkey one half in weight. . . . The wild turkey has been frequently tamed and his offspring is of a larger size."

Although many attempts have been made to domesticate the wild eastern turkey, most of them ended in failure. The autumn after hatching, the birds, if left at large, wandered away and did not return. Considerable success was attained by crossing the domestic and wild birds by design or accident, the resulting hybrids being larger and hardier. Lawson (1937:156) states: "Sometimes the wild breed with the tame ones, which they reckon makes them very hardy, as I believe it must. I see no manner of Difference betwixt the wild Turkies and the tame ones; only the wild are ever of one Colour, viz: a dark gray or brown. . . . The Eggs taken from the Nest and hatched under a Hen will yet retain a wild Nature, and commonly leave you and run wild at last, and will never be got into a House to roost but always perch on some high Tree hard by the House, and separate themselves from the tame sort, although, at the same time, they tread and breed together." He was informed that if the eggs of the wild bird were soaked in "milk-warm" water for a time the wildness would be removed! The wild gobbler raised by Audubon (1831:14) would never roost with the tame turkeys.

The wild poult is considerably hardier than the domestic one. In 1834, Featherstonhaugh (1844:205) stopped at a home on the banks of the Ouachita River, Arkansas, where he saw young wild turkeys hatched from eggs running with tame turkeys. They had a darker, glossier plumage, a quicker and brighter eye, and were more active than the tame ones. The woman of the house told him that the wild young were as hardy as young chickens and easier to raise than tame poults. On this subject, Caton (1877.1:306) wrote: "My experiments with the wild turkey show that the wild birds reared in domestication are remarkably vigorous and healthy, much more so than the common domestic turkey, while they are equally prolific, though in many instances both the male and female are a year later in breeding than the domestic bird."

The progeny from wild eggs, according to Crèvecoeur (1925:131), was crossed with the domestic race to secure a hardier and heavier bird. He had often killed some weighing twenty-seven pounds. Concerning crosses in New York, De Kay (1844:200) stated that the domesticated and the wild birds were frequently crossed, producing a highly prized variety, scarcely inferior to the wild turkey in brilliancy of plumage. Dr. Henry Bryant wrote to Baird (Dall, 1915:336) from Boston in 1860 that from his own experience the offspring from mating wild and domestic turkeys were more vigorous and fertile, and healthier than the domestic bird alone could produce. Bryant (1859) cited the statement of Gould (1856:62) that the eastern turkey does not readily associate or mate with the domestic bird. He adds that this is not true in America for, "It is an ordinary occurrence for the tame hen to prefer the wild gobbler to the domestic ones. I have in my own possession wild hens that bred with a tame gobbler, a fact much stranger than that of the wild gobbler breeding with the tame hen." It had been noted long before by Audubon (1831:13) that in Kentucky wild gobblers sometimes paid their addresses to domestic females. Because of frequent mingling of the two breeds, crossing could scarcely be avoided. Hudson (1942) mentions that twice in Attala County, Mississippi, his father killed wild turkeys that were fraternizing with a tame flock in their orchard. Allen (1918), who was born in 1848 and lived in Fannin County, Texas, states that it was quite common for wild turkeys to come close to his home and mingle with the domestic turkeys. In 1895 two wild hens with about twenty young were associating with tame turkeys in Stephens County, Oklahoma (L. D. W., 1895).

Wild turkeys were still common in Calhoun County, Michigan, in 1869, and there were large flocks of halfbreeds, according to information given to Allen (1871:349) by D. D. Hughes. A further proof of crossing is shown by the weights of the "wild" turkeys handled by Hubbard (1875), a game dealer in Lansing, Michigan. The largest birds shipped during a period of four years were: 34.5 pounds, 1871; 29.5 pounds, 1872; 26.5 pounds, 1873; and 24 pounds, 1874. Cushman (1893:99) reported that crossing domestic female turkeys with a wild or partially wild gobbler improved the breed greatly. Gobblers one-half wild were found best for mating. Turkeys having one-fourth to one-third wild blood grew the largest. A wild gobbler mated a month later than the domestic gobblers usually did. The Nittany turkey was developed at Pennsylvania State College by P. H. Margof and H. H. Kauffman by selection from the native wild turkey (Marsden and Martin, 1945:59). The objective was to produce a docile variety, similar to the wild bird in color and size, with better ability to produce eggs and "take on finish." The adult male weighed twenty pounds, and the female twelve pounds. The experiment was discontinued for undisclosed reasons.

It is generally assumed that the American bronze turkey was obtained by crossing the domestic bird with the wild one. Robinson (1924:282) states: "The earliest American race of turkeys given the distinctive appellation 'Bronze' was the Point Judith Bronze turkey, a local race developed about 1830–40, in the vicinity of Point Judith, Rhode Island, from crosses of wild and domestic turkeys." Some of Caton's (1877:328) hybrids wandered and never returned. Individuals were recognized in the yards of neighbors miles distant. The hybrids grew larger than either parent.

REVERSION TO THE WILD

It is not uncommon for domestic turkeys to revert to the wild. Darwin (1868, I:190) wrote that at one time the turkey was almost feral along the Paraná River, South America. The existence of feral turkeys in the Hawaiian Islands, particularly on Niihau, is well known. Hallock (1905) reported that there was excellent shooting of feral birds at Buncombe, North Carolina. Tame breeds, even Holland Whites according to Thompson (1926), when kept in a timbered region where there are wild turkeys, will frequently go wild and remain so in fall when the ground is covered with mast. A wild turkey that remained all winter with a domestic flock in Bates County, Missouri, was shot in the spring since it sought to entice away the tame turkeys (Tathwell and Maxey, 1897:137). A resident of Nodaway County, Missouri, stated that the tame turkeys would fight the wild ones but sometimes go away with them. He lost four flocks this way (National Hist. Co., 1882:324). Hampton (1900) suggested stocking preserves with domestic turkeys, selecting the "old-fashioned black turkey" as this variety becomes wild most quickly, particularly when some wild turkeys are about. Several people who have allowed their turkeys to wander at will have told me some birds became so wary that they could be recovered only by shooting.

The feral turkeys of the Hawaiian Islands, according to Caton (1887), had a marked tendency to assume the characters of the wild turkey: "At Haiku I found two hens in confinement which Mr. Dickey had purchased from a native who had caught them. I studied them with great interest. . . . On approaching them they showed about as much alarm as our wild turkey would, similarly situated. A very decided tendency was shown to revert to the color of our wild turkey. The legs had already assumed a lightish color with a pink shade, not so brilliant as in the wild ancestor, but quite unlike the black leg of the black tame turkey. The color of the plumage had also undergone a marked change. The ends of the tail feathers and of the tail coverts had assumed a tawny or russet shade, hardly so pronounced as in our wild turkey, but a great departure from all tame turkeys. My observations in domesticating the wild turkey show that they first degenerate in their coloring in these two points. The white bars on the wing feathers were there, but they are not always absent on the domesticated turkey.

"In form, too, a change was manifest; the legs were longer and the body was longer and more erect than in the tame bird. Altogether the tendency to revert to the form, coloring, and habit of their wild ancestors was very marked."

Effects of Domestication on the Wild Turkey

The effects of domestication on the wild turkey in Illinois were observed by Caton (1877:322). There was no diminution in size or reproductiveness after the eleventh generation but some profound alternations were obtained. He wrote: "They have changed in form and in length of the legs. The body is shorter and more robust, and its position is more horizontal; but most especially have they varied in color. These changes I have constantly watched. In the first and even second generation but little change was observed. After that the tips of the tail feathers and of the tail coverts began to lose the soft, rich chestnut brown so conspicuous on the wild turkey of the woods, and to degenerate to a lighter shade; the beautiful, changeable purple tints on the neck and breast became marked with a greenish shade; the bristles on the naked portions about the head became more sparse or altogether disappeared;

the blue about the head and the purple of the wattles were replaced by the bright red observed on the tame turkey-cock; the beautiful pinkish-red of the legs became dull or changed to brown. The next year, or when the bird was in its second year's growth, say the third generation, these marks of degeneration would on most of the specimens, especially of the cocks, disappear, and the plumage would show the thorough-bred wild turkey. Each succeeding generation shows these changes to be more pronounced, but each year as the bird gets older, the shades of color of the wild parent become more distinct. The change of form keeps pace with the change of color, which is much more manifest on the hen than on the cock. I have hens now three or four years old with brown legs, though still showing the pink shade, and on whose feathers the white has very considerably replaced the cinnamon shades. In fact I have many specimens that would readily pass for the bronze domestic turkey, even in the view of an expert. I am satisfied that without a fresh infusion of wild blood, in the course of fifteen or twenty years more but few individuals would show the distinctive marks of the wild turkey to any considerable extent, and the whole would be pronounced the bronze domestic turkey."

The habits of the wild turkey, continues Caton, change less rapidly than its form and coloring. By the time the wild male is five months old, it seeks a high perch in a tall tree and as it grows older it gradually perches higher until the tip is reached; then it reverses the procedure until it roosts no higher than the domestic bird. The flesh of the young wild bird is as white as that of the domestic one until midwinter. It continues to darken for several years. Domestication, however, results in white flesh for turkeys of wild stock that are two or three years old. Of the two suggested reasons for the change, difference in food and lessened activity, the latter should be the more important.

HIDING TRAIT

The male is credited with a somewhat greater mental capacity than the female (Schjelderup-Ebbe, 1924). No one will claim that either has much intelligence. The opinion of one hunter (D. C., 1880) runs: "The wild turkeys are plenty here, and I think most of those who have given their attention to this bird will agree with me, that they have [are] the wildest and the tamest, the most cunning and wary, and the most stupid

Plate 9.—Male Rio Grande turkey. (Texas Game and Fish Commission.)

Plate 10.—Flock of Merriam's turkeys. This race has much white in the plumage. (Colorado Fish and Game Department.)

Plate 11.—Skeleton of eastern wild turkey. (U. S. National Museum.)

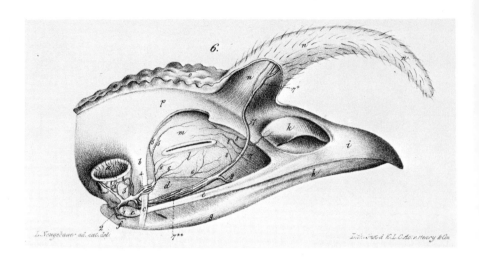

Plate 12.—Veins in the head of the turkey. (After Neugebauer [1845].)

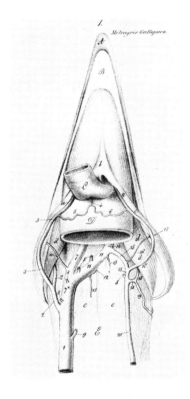

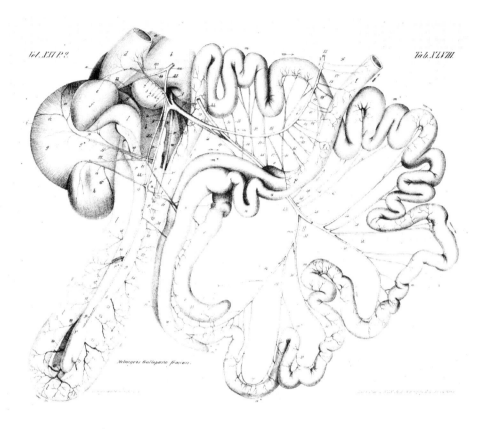

Plate 13.—Intestines with veinous system of a female domestic turkey.
(After Neugebauer [1845].)

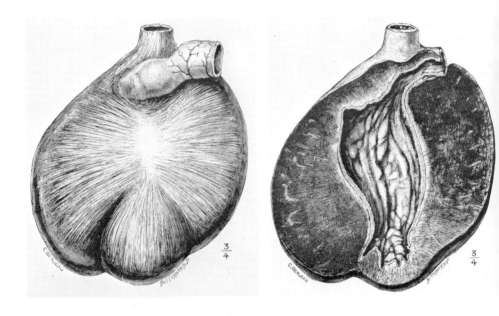

Plate 14.—External and internal views of the gizzard of a turkey. (After Bland-Sutton [1920].)

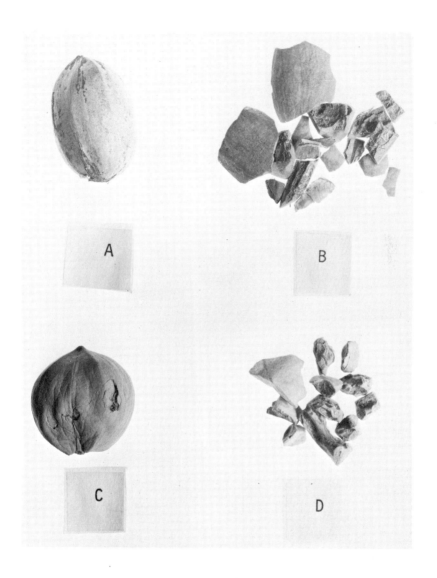

Plate 15.—Crushing of *Carya* nuts in the gizzard of the turkey: A. natural pecan; B. pecan after remaining in the gizzard one hour; C. hickory nut showing incipient fracture; D. hickory nut after remaining in the gizzard for thirty-one hours. (After Schorger [1960].)

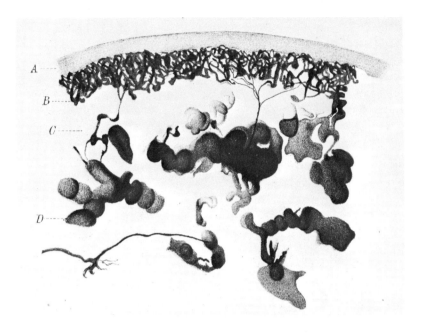

Plate 16.—Section of a caruncle from the neck of a gobbler. The vessels are filled with a "blue substance." A. Outer epithelial layer; B. first cavernous layer; C. [description missing]; D. second cavernous layer with slender and enlarged vessels. (The vessels are colored blue in the original.) (After Jegerow [1890].)

and foolish of all birds. The first two or three times starting him, he will put himself in the air the moment he hears or sees you, if half a mile away. Shoot at him every time you see or hear him, and he will soon become demoralized and then find some tree-top, or place to hide, and if his head is out of sight, all right, he will permit the dog to point him, and be kicked out within fifteen or twenty steps of the hunter."

A turkey may hide or "freeze" at the first sign of danger, or after it has been pursued. Maynard (1881:346) landed from his boat on a pile of debris along the St. John's River when a large gobbler flushed so close to him that he could feel the air current produced by the beat of its wings. A dog is greatly feared. When a flock is flushed, the birds may alight in trees or seek concealment on the ground. Jones (1898:193) wrote: "Old logs, fallen tree-tops, piles of old brush, blackened limbs, tufts of weeds and spots of dead prairie grass grown in small openings among timber, afford attractive points for concealment." Six turkeys were shot in Ohio in a small prairie, thickly overgrown with boneset, where they had hidden ("Splasher," 1881). In Iowa, turkeys followed for some time usually hid and were pointed by dogs (Anon., 1882). A turkey tracked by a dog at Wooster, Ohio, took refuge in a hollow, burnt stump (M., 1878). In Trumbull County, Ohio, a female on being flushed alighted in a marsh. Here she was found so concealed in the grass of a hummock that only the tail was visible (Underwood, 1894).

Some unusual captures have been reported. Thinking itself safe, a turkey was shot in Michigan after it had stuck its head and neck into a brush heap (De Land, 1903:225). Askins (1931:62) mentions that in St. Clair County, Illinois, a gobbler was so pressed by hunters during a tracking snow that it took refuge in a brush pile and was killed by a dog. In the early days of Columbus, Ohio, a wild turkey pursued by a dog entered the open door of a cabin, took refuge on a bed, and was captured (Lee, 1892:296).

THE WIRE FENCE PROBLEM

The success of the tunnel pen in capturing turkeys depends upon the trait that the birds do not look downward for an opening through which they might escape. The most charitable way of putting it is that they are confused by their situation. A mesh wire fence offers almost as serious a problem. Stoddard (1935:332) advises against enclosing food patches although turkeys will eventually learn to fly over wire fences. He states that they are incapable of distinguishing the difference between the wire strands and smilax and other vines common to their habitat, and may spend hours poking their heads through the meshes of the fence.

The fence as an obstacle has been described by Blakey (1937:23) as follows: "No wild turkey, in fact no turkey, seems to cross a wire fence readily. It will pace a beaten path along the fence, mechanically sticking its head through every part of the wire but making no effort to cross over. Where ordinary low field fencing is used, crossing may be induced by leaning poles against each post, at a gradual incline, in the direction of the desired crossing.

"This procedure has been improved in the recent use of higher wire fences by constructing an ordinary rail fence immediately against the wire fence on the side of crossing. This prevents the approaching bird from getting up to the wire near the ground, limits its visibility through the fence, and encourages it to fly onto the rail fence, whence it will readily hop or fly over the few feet remaining of higher fence. The two fences must be in direct contact, however, or the bird will get down between them and the purpose of the rail fence will be defeated."

A mile of old hog-wire fence at the Caney Mountain Refuge, Missouri, according to Leopold (1941:12; 1942) had one path 250 feet in length, and sixteen other well-defined paths, 10 to 50 feet in length formed by the turkeys pacing the fence. When coming down a hill, the birds will not hesitate to fly over the fence, but on going uphill, particularly if the fence is brushy, they will pace it. This conforms with the habit of the turkey to run up a hill and fly down it. Captured wild turkeys will run the fences by which they are confined until reduced to "sheer skin and bones." When alarmed they will go to any hole in the fence that will admit the head and often strangle or break their necks (Steinhart, 1936:53). This difficulty has been overcome with confined turkeys by boarding the base of the fence to a height of four feet so that they cannot see through (Randall, 1934.1:128).

A mesh fence was erected March 20, 1959, at the Welder Wildlife Foundation close to a blind from which I observed turkeys going to roost. At 5:50 P.M., I went into the blind placed thirty-eight paces from roosting trees. Four gobblers came west along the fence at 6:15. On reaching the blind, two ran past while the remaining two stopped, uttering a low, querulous *whur-r-r-r*, then proceeded east and went out of sight. The fence bothered them. At 6:56, I heard a turkey fly into the roost east of the blind followed by two more. I then opened a slit in the blind on the east side and there stood two gobblers on the inside of the fence, about 12 feet from the fence and 150 feet from the blind. One ran three or four steps, cleared the fence, and went up into a tree. The other bird soon followed, taking a running start, but hit the fence with a resounding bang. I thought that it had surely killed itself. But no! It bounced back about five feet, landed on its feet and stood there as if dazed for about a minute. It then walked away from the fence about twenty feet, took a run and over it went.

Curiosity

It is difficult to find a logical explanation for some of the traits of the turkey. Suspicion, or curiosity, is highly developed. Clothes on the line or a pail in the yard were sufficient to arouse it (Beyers, 1939). Concerning the domestic turkeys of Charley Baker, a ranchman in McLennan County, Texas, Smith (1946:64) wrote: "Whenever Baker hears a commotion he investigates. He never knows what he will find. The animals become incensed over all manner of objects—old bones, birds and bird nests, skunks, oddly-shaped rocks, *et cetera, ad infinitum*." Rutledge (1946:23) had a Negro on his place who, after concealing himself carefully, could induce wild turkeys to come within range by waving a red handkerchief, or by slapping a felt hat against his boots to simulate the fighting of gobblers. Barnard (1958) found that cannibalism among wild turkey poults could be averted by arousing their curiosity. A bright tin can, a wad of paper, a bright glass dish, or anything new placed *daily* in the enclosure would absorb their attention.

A large gobbler was shot by John Garrison near Gainesville, Missouri. The wing beats of the turkey brought a flock that stopped beside the dying bird (Turnbo, 1904:132). It is to be expected that when one or more members of a flock fall from gunfire, the others would depart with celerity, but Audubon (1831:11) writes: "The gobblers continued yelping in answer to the female, which all this while remained on the fence. I looked over the log and saw about thirty fine cocks advancing rather cautiously towards the very spot where I lay concealed. They came so near that the light in their eyes could easily be perceived, when I fired one barrel, and killed three. The rest, instead of flying off, fell a strutting around their dead companions, and had I not looked on shooting again as murder without necessity, I might have secured at least another." Caton's (1886) wild turkeys could be driven from his grounds in a brief time by shooting; however, "the flock will hold a great wake over a fallen companion instead of running away."

REACTION TO NOISES

It is peculiar that some members of the family of gallinaceous birds are stimulated into calling by various noises. This is a common phenomenon with the ring-necked pheasant. In India a noise will start to calling every peafowl within hearing (Beebe, 1922:168). This trait in the wild turkey did not escape notice by Audubon (1900:329, 507). He mentions that on the felling of a live oak every turkey within hearing would gobble; and whenever there was a burst of laughter from a sugar camp in the woods, a turkey or an owl would respond. Often when corn meal was being prepared for breakfast in Effingham County, Illinois, in 1830, turkeys would gobble in response to the pounding (Baskin and Co., 1883). Jordan (1914:108) mentions a case of a turkey gobbling every time a plowman called to his mules. Turkeys, according to Rutledge (1941:94), dislike noises. A sawmill on his place drove away the turkeys but not the deer. A man was dismantling some old mine cars at Bear Swamp, Clinton County, Pennsylvania. The screeching resulting from the removal of nuts from rusted bolts attracted a wild turkey so he went home for his gun. When the work was continued, the turkey called, approached within range, and was killed (Tobias, 1950). Ruha (1958) wrote that in spring males may be induced to gobble by the sound of a tractor, chain saw, clapping of the hands, whistling like a hawk, and striking the side of a car. One old male paid no attention to these sounds but gobbled whenever a jet plane flew over. A warden in Pennsylvania had a flock of nine wild turkeys come to his car, attracted by the music from his radio (Milford, 1961). In Mississippi I was told that the low of a cow, the alarm call of a crow, the hoot of an owl, and the drumming of a woodpecker would always cause a turkey to gobble.

Observations made in April by Brandt (1951:621) give a good illustration of the reaction of Merriam's turkey to noises: "When a sharp noise suddenly brings to attention his well-hidden ear, he sends forth a deep, rolling gobble which causes to tremble the very earth that he measures, and which a hundred pines with wild rejoicing echo. . . . Almost any sudden sound will touch him off, and when there are several toms in a group, they all seem to respond to this impulse at the same, precise instant. The Wild Turkeys that stayed around our cabin were good watchdogs. Whenever a car or a stranger either afoot or on horseback appeared, instantly they issued forth a series of loud gobbles. Early in the morning they were inclined to answer the noisy flickers, but as the day wore on, gradually they paid this bird less heed. However, any sharp, unusual noise, like the blowing of a horn, the slamming of a door, or a shrill whistle invariably caused them to burst forth with wild notes. Many a time I halloed a good night to them, when they had gone to roost high in the pines beyond the park, and almost invariably there came back a clear-cut, courteous answer. The turkey gobbler is a 'dawn buster.' Magnificent is his lordly morning roll; the first challenge is released just as day turns out the candlets in a paling eastern sky, and shortly thereafter the various toms make the giant tree shafts reverberate at close intervals with vigorous, daybreak matins unequalled."

It is generally assumed that it is an unusual sound that moves the turkey to gobble. This cannot be true of the hoot of an owl, a sound which has been familiar to many generations of turkeys. Hunters have placed great faith in hooting to elicit a response from turkeys. According to Jordan (1914:199): "If satisfied that gobblers are in the vicinity, wait until dawn approaches, and if then you do not hear them, hoot like the barred owl. If there is an old gobbler within hearing, nine times out of ten he will gobble when the owl hoots." The guide of a hunter in Florida imitated the call of the barred owl. This, he asserted, usually produced a gobble if there were any turkeys in the neighborhood. The time was about daylight. Without any warning, two turkeys flew from a pine twenty feet distant ("Meleagris," 1889). Turpin (1928:614), while hunting in Arkansas, had a guide who "owled" to get the turkeys to gobble. My limited experience does not permit me to affirm or deny the effectiveness of the hoot. I was near a creek bottom in Mississippi, where turkeys were roosting, on a March morning near daybreak. A barred owl was in the vicinity. The owl was hooting and the turkeys were gobbling, but the timing did not indicate that the owl was stimulating the turkeys. The latter continued to gobble long after the owl became silent. The barred owls at the Welder Wildlife Foundation brought no response from the turkeys. Some of the hooting took place in broad daylight.

The mechanism whereby sounds release the gobbling was studied by Schleidt (1954). No difference in reaction between wild and domestic turkeys could be detected. The effective stimuli are tones, sounds, and noises having frequencies between 200 and 6,000 cycles per second. More frequent gobbling is obtained by a quick repetition of the same stimulus. In bad weather the effectiveness of the stimulus is lowered. If a strong and a feeble stimulus are given alternately, the threshold for the feeble one is raised. In a certain individual, duration and intensity of gobbling are always the same. Gobbling follows the all-or-none law. The number of reactions which can be released in sequence is variable and depends upon stimuli and internal factors. Gobbling is considered to be a sub-drive of the urge to procreate and is a consummatory act. Concerning the characteristic simultaneous gobbling of several birds, Schjelderup-Ebbe (1932:110) writes: "Noteworthy is the pronounced degree of simultaneous and mutual beginning and ending of 'bubbling' so charac-teristic of gobblers when several of them occur in the same place. On first reflection it appears that the animals reacted to the same stimulation as a unit. The explanation is to be found in the fact that one animal having begun gobbling the others follow him so quickly that it is im-possible for the human ear to detect an interval; and it is also impossible to determine which animal first produced the sound. Likewise this holds true for the cessation of gobbling. One must note with astonishment the great speed of the transplanting of sound from animal to animal." This phenomenon pales in comparison with the machine-like precision with which a compact flock of shorebirds will twist and turn.

PLAY

Some actions of turkeys are best defined as play. Burget (1957:9) writes: "The flocking habit also has a definite social aspect. On cold mornings after the birds have fed well they will play together. Frequent-ly as many as eight or ten will participate in a sort of chase during which they will run at each other, then dodge suddenly, missing a collision by inches. Sometimes they will duck through or around a patch of brush to put their companians off guard." The behavior of a turkey at times is unpredictable and often difficult to understand. Schmid (1937:39) considers the domestic bird of lower intelligence than a chicken and possessed of an "impervious" character. He mentions that a turkey will begin to run around a tree and that the remainder of the flock will get into line and follow the leader, moving rhythmically about the tree. When the leader leaves the ring, the play discontinues. Any reason for this peculiar performance could not be discovered.

An interesting description of the behavior of a flock of wild turkeys prior to going to roost is given by Rutledge (1941.1:149): "I heard a flock of wild turkeys calling. . . . They were not calling strayed members of the flock. They were just having a twilight frolic before going to roost. They kept dashing at one another in mock anger, stridently calling all the while, almost playing leapfrog in their antics. Their notes were bold and clear, and some that they gave would defy imitation; indeed, had they given none but the queer notes, and had I not seen them, I should have been unable to identify the callers. For about five minutes they played on the brown pine-straw floor of the forest, then as if at a signal, they assumed a sudden stealth and stole off in the glimmering shadows. I stole after them. In a few minutes I heard them flying up to the roost; maneuvering nearer, I had the pleasure of watching sixteen take to the trees."

Sense of Sight

The keenness of sight of the turkey is proverbial. Latham (1956:239) doubts if any other member of the animal kingdom is better endowed. At times it appears to be unable to recognize an animate object unless it moves; however, the slightest movement is sufficient for detection. Dorman (1873) states that although a turkey will approach very near to a person if he remains perfectly motionless, it is very quick to discover the least movement, and also will hesitate if there is the least suspicion about the call note. Whenever it stops to look, should there be a tree about, it will probably stop behind it and with just the head and neck extended peer cautiously ahead. Drane (1899) was informed by an old hunter in Bledsoe County, Tennessee, that in spite of the acuteness of vision of the wild turkey, the best way to get a shot was to sit down in the open with back to a tree. The turkey will then approach within ten steps without detecting the hunter.

PUGNACITY

Turkeys are pugnacious. Among birds where the male is much larger than the female, as with the turkey, the male is the despot (Schjelderup-Ebbe, 1931:97). Both sexes have periods of irritability. Fighting takes place most extensively in spring during the mating period (Plate 22). According to Burget (1957:10), the young males usually open the season. Grabbing each other by the cheeks or wattles, a pair moves in a circle beating each other loudly with their wings. Sometimes several birds will join in a general melee to which the old males usually pay no attention; however, at times a degree of irritability is aroused that causes them to disperse the combatants with a few pecks. The adult males, as the season advances, begin combats that are audible at a considerable distance and so absorb their attention that no watch is kept for potential predators. Females fight also, their necks being so twisted around each other in the circling movements that they would be expected to break. In fall when the flocks are assembling for the winter, the local females appear to resent the intrusion of outside hens. Lively struggles between the females take place until the flocks become settled on a wintering ground.

It is mentioned by Kalm (1772:163) that tamed wild turkeys are more irascible than the domestic birds. Le Fort (1891:564) had a fine, large wild gobbler that attacked the children of the farm and the wife of the keeper so vigorously with wings and beak that it was sent to the *rôtissoire*. At Everglades, Florida, near the Big Cypress Swamp, two tamed wild turkey gobblers would attack an insect net waved at them and pursue the operator when he ran (Davis, 1912:342). Caton (1877:321) adds: "The young bird from the egg of the wild turkey, when brought up in close intimacy with the human family becomes very tame, and when grown the males become vicious and attack children and even grown persons." On the Mt. Mitchell wildlife management area in western North Carolina, a female wild turkey with a partially hatched clutch of eggs attacked Clodfelter (1943) several times while he was attempting to take a photograph.

During the vicissitudes of the siege of Khartoum, General Gordon (1885:45, 172) made some interesting observations on September 18, 1884: "In the serail, we have a Turkey cock and five Turkey hens. They were all very tame, but having put the turkey cock's head under his wing, and swung him into sleep on one occasion, he is now shy to come near me; however, if one goes to his wives and scratches them he is furious, and comes up with his neck of all colours, but keeps out of range. I am sorry to say that one of his wives, having sat with patience for three weeks on eggs, and brought forth two chicks, *he killed them*; such is the accusation lodged against him by the cook. I think a Turkey cock, with every feather on end, and all the colours of the rainbow on his neck, is the picture of physical strength; his eye is an eye of fire, and there is no doubt of his being angry when he sees his wives touched." Later, he mentioned that it was dangerous to pass the gobbler in the yard. In his opinion a turkey-cock excelled all other birds for pluck.

Both wild and domestic turkeys are belligerent and can be destructive. Concerning the turkeys of the Hopi Indians of northeastern Arizona, Hough (1915:172) says they roamed the villages without restraint and became household pets. Occasionally they gave a stranger much annoyance by their attacks, usually an unexpected one from the rear. Doyle (n.d.:216) has described the behavior of a Norfolk black turkey that weighed thirty-six pounds when fourteen years of age. It was extremely truculent. Among its misdemeanors was the killing of poults by cracking their skulls with his bill and then attempting to devour them. A wild gobbler kept by Gilmour (1876:12) attacked people with beak and spur: "The cock behaved very well for a short time, but fell into bad ways, and after he had decapitated several fowls of one kind and another, we were compelled to put him once more under lock and key." A man in Pennsylvania on investigating the unusual behavior of a bronze gobbler found that it had nearly killed a large rabbit (Smith, 1932). Gillmore (1874:229) tied to a tree his cat which had followed him into the forest. On his return he found nine wild turkeys taking turns at trying to peck the cat. It must be said that wanton destruction of animals by wild turkeys in nature is practically unknown.

It has long been recognized that red antagonizes the turkey. Willughby (1678:160) wrote: "The antipathy this Fowl hath against a red colour, so as to be much moved and provoked at the sight thereof, is very strange and admirable." A half-blood Frenchman living on the Embarrass River, Illinois, whenever he wanted a turkey, tied a piece of scarlet cloth around the neck of a domestic gobbler and set him free. The wild turkeys in attacking it were so fearless that they afforded easy marks (Gillmore,

1874:230). It is recorded that in New Hampshire a woman wearing a red dress was set upon by two wild turkeys. One of them was shot (Kidder and Gould, 1852:20). Advantage was taken of the repugnance to red in driving turkeys. According to Latham (1823:128): "It is pleasing to see with what facility the drivers manage them by means of a red rag, fastened to the end of a stick; which from their antipathy to it as a colour, acts on them as a scourge to a quadruped." Red to a gobbler probably means a rival in anger or in mating display.

It is not red alone that produces antipathy. Goldsmith (1855:62) wrote: "But there is another method of increasing the animosity of these birds against each other, which is often practised by boys, when they have a mind for a battle. This is no more than to smear over the head of one of the turkeys with dirt, and the rest run to attack it with all the speed of impotent animosity; nay, two of them, thus disguised, will fight each other till they are almost suffocated with fatigue and anger." The abnormal appearance in this case must have been the cause of resentment.

EFFECTS OF COMBAT

The truculence of the gobblers is at its height during the breeding season. Writers differ greatly on the injury, if any, that fighting males receive at this time. There is even difference of opinion on the use of spurs. Audubon (1831:4) states that if during the fierce struggle an exhausted bird loses its hold, its rival strikes him to the ground. When one is dead, the victor caresses the body as though it were a female. The extensive experience of Jordan (1914:131) was entirely contrary to that of Audubon. He had never seen a wild gobbler show affection towards a fallen foe but had many times seen a domestic gobbler behave in this way to a dead wild gobbler that he placed before him on the ground. At the sight of the dead bird, the domestic gobbler would bristle with rage and even pound Jordan if he held the bird. After venting his rage he would strut and gobble, the red of his head becoming more intense, then proceed with the caressing motions. Usually, however, the domestic gobbler would retire from the dead wild bird and strut furiously for an hour or two. Jordan had tried this experiment many times in many places with the same results.

In all his life Jordan (1898:310) never saw an old gobbler kill another, never found one dead, or even in a serious condition, from fighting in the woods. He had killed many old gobblers with their heads and necks covered with blood, and with spur punctures on their breasts, but these injuries did not prevent gobbling. Because of the thick coat of feathers, the wounds from the spurs were only skin deep.

One writer (J. D. H., 1879) states that two wild gobblers fought for about thirty minutes, using spurs and claws, and when he fired at them they were clinched with their bills. One turkey was killed and the other, though severely wounded, continued to peck at the dead antagonist. Heilborn (1930:61) shows two hostile domestic turkeys with their bills crossed, each bird grasping a mandible.

The spurs, according to Brandt (1951:625), are useless weapons as he never saw them used in fighting. In combat when the males flew at each other, the toes were held wide apart, the effect being to give a vigorous kick or push. An adversary seeks to grasp the loose skin on the head of its opponent so that when a hold has been produced, the necks become twisted like serpents. He adds: "Such fighting does not seem to inflict serious wounds, yet when one bird grasps another there is produced an apparent spasm of pain which overcomes the unfortunate one, and he immediately becomes meek and docile, only to break away in time and renew the conflict with his previous fire. As soon as the head skin is seized, it almost immediately changes color from various deeper hues to almost white, which shows the effect of pain on the nervous system." Although a combat may last all day, Brandt was unable to find an authentic record of an opponent being killed; however, turkeys have been known to die from combat exhaustion. When one of a flock of gobblers becomes sick and his head droops, the remaining gobblers pounce upon the unfortunate one until it expires. The latter statement by Brandt requires confirmation.

There is very little in the literature to support Audubon regarding the fatal endings of combats. However, Randall (1930:106) states that the gobblers sometimes fight to death. It is also said that during the mating season wild gobblers sometimes invade farmyards to seek a combat and occasionally kill domestic gobblers (Luttringer and Gerstell, 1952:10). According to Barnes (1936), whenever a wild gobbler joined his domestic turkeys, there would be a bitter battle with the tame gobbler lasting for hours at a time. Heads and necks became bloody and torn, even the wattles torn off. The wild bird was generally the better fighter. No fatality was mentioned.

I have been unable to discover, through interviews and correspondence, a single case of disability even. On this subject Mosby and Handley (1943:106) write: "The senior author has observed several fights among wild gobblers and these observations would indicate that, although skirmishes are not unusual at any season of the year, mortal combats between gobblers are rare. Such observations as have been made in the field show that as soon as one of the fighting gobblers displays a definite supremacy over the other, the defeated male quickly retreats and leaves the field to the victor. Experience with closely confined, captivity-reared adult wild gobblers strengthens this belief. Fighting is common among penned gobblers, and also hens, until a 'pecking order' is established. Skirmishes may continue for days, but once a bird is defeated, it seldom puts up any further resistance and is primarily interested in attempting to escape its victor."

The gobbler believes that all fighting should take place under meleagrid rules. When one combatant has had enough, he lies on the ground with outstretched neck, and this attitude of submission is respected. When a combat occurs between a gobbler and the more agile peacock, the latter usually wins by attacking from the air. This maneuver is so foreign to the gobbler's ancestral experience that he proceeds to the state of submission, which is not understood by his rival. Death of the gobbler will then follow unless there is human intervention (Lorenz, 1952:194). It is to be noted that the submissive position is due to fear since it is identical with that assumed for concealment.

DESTRUCTION OF POULTS AND EGGS BY THE GOBBLER

There is a persistent belief that the old gobblers will sometimes destroy eggs and young. Audubon (1831:4) stated that the female secretes her nest carefully to prevent the male from breaking the eggs for the purpose of prolonging his period of sexual pleasure; and that they will destroy the young, even when two-thirds grown, by repeated blows on the head. Concerning this statement Jordan (1898:310) wrote: "This assertion of the great author I feel obliged to criticize. From my vast experience and sources of observation I have never met with anything to justify such a statement. I have never seen an old gobbler attempt to fight a young one from the egg to maturity." Keeler (1893:263) makes the farfetched suggestion that the white wing bars of the turkey serve as recognition marks "to enable the female to keep her brood out of the way of her fierce mate." The hens, according to Ligon (1927:113), evidently keep the young away from the gobblers.

Caton's (1877:325) experience was as follows: "I have never noticed any disposition of the old cocks to interfere with a setting hen, or her nest, or her young brood, only when a half-grown flock comes home they are simply treated as strangers, as already stated." Mosby and Handley (1943:136) state that two reliable reports of gobblers killing poults were received in Virginia; however, they thought that losses of this kind must be extremely rare. F. V. Hebard has informed me of his conviction that the gobbler destroys both eggs and poults. I have talked with several men with long experience with turkeys in the wild and none had witnessed either destruction of eggs or young by a gobbler.

A case of destruction of poults by the mother under highly abnormal conditions has been reported (Schleidt et al., 1960). Two of a number of poults, deafened by a surgical operation, reached maturity and incubated normally, but killed their young as they hatched. The reason assigned was that the mother could not hear the peeps of the young and therefore looked upon them as enemies.

Cases of predation on eggs by turkeys are few. Stoddard (1946:191) mentions four instances of the destruction of nests of the bobwhite by domestic turkeys and one by a wild bird. The best evidence that the turkey occasionally destroys its eggs and young is given by Mosby and Handley (1943:115–16). A wild gobbler was seen to eat an egg by pecking a hole in the side and tilting the egg on its bill so that the contents ran into its mouth. One clutch of eggs, smashed but none of the contents eaten, appeared to have been destroyed by a gobbler mounting a sitting hen. They add: "The wild turkey has an insatiable curiosity and will peck at any object which catches its eye; it is possible that some eggs are destroyed more out of curiosity than to obtain food." Similar statements on the destruction of the eggs are made by Bailey et al. (1951:11). Between the care with which the hen conceals her eggs when off the nest and her isolation after the young appear, there can be only a slight chance of destruction of eggs and young by the gobbler.

The peck order exists among turkeys as well as other fowls. On this subject Brandt (1951:626) wrote: "The flock appeared to lack definite leadership, and the peck order was not well established except in the case of one somewhat underdeveloped bird. . . . The gobblers seemed to have established a normal peck order, although there were few indications of it when they strutted about in the clearing. . . . At the feeding area the females were more insistent than their larger mates in asserting their social position, and often an old hen would rush briefly at a smaller, younger female."

Some peculiar reactions have been reported for the turkey. It has long been known that if the wings of a gobbler are pulled down to simulate the strutting posture, the tail will automatically spread into a fan. This I can confirm. MacQuin (1820:60) wrote: "This bird is so stupid, or timorous, that if you balance a bit of straw on his head, or draw a line with chalk on the ground from his beak, he fancies himself so loaded or so bound, that he will remain in the same position till hunger forces him to move. We made the experiment." Gordon (1885:176) wondered why only the male turkey was "mesmerised" by the chalk line.[1]

[1] A valuable contribution by Hale and Schein on the ethology of the domestic turkey has appeared recently (1962). It covers display, feeding and drinking, courtship, sexual behavior, parental care, fighting, communication, and response to predators.

7

Habits

THE TURKEY MAY BE EXPECTED to behave in certain ways. Habits are changed for survival when conditions render it necessary; hence, some of the performances of earlier days would be difficult to observe at the present time.

ROOSTING

The turkey, when it is time to retire, is possessed of a single purpose—to rise to a suitable perch. During the days when turkeys were driven to market, they could not be forced onward once they had decided to go to roost. Sheridan's troops camped on the Washita River, Oklahoma, the evening of December 15, 1868. The insistence of the turkeys in going to roost at the proper time and at an accustomed place is shown graphically by the following account by Keim (1870:154):

"On the night of the fifteenth, upon the column going into camp in a heavy timber on the river, it was discovered that we were in the midst of a favorite roost of immense numbers of wild turkeys. The traces were everywhere visible, and some lively sport was anticipated when the droves returned from their rambles after food. Towards sunset, about fifty fine birds, headed, as usual, by a noble cock, appeared on the bluff overlooking the camp. With an air of surprise at the intrusion, the flock gathered in full view, apparently holding an inspection, and resolving what to do. At this moment, another immense flock came floating down from another direction, and lit in the trees within the lines of the camp. In an instant about fifty shots were fired, killing several.

"As the daylight drew nearer to a close, the turkeys, having failed to look out for other accomodations, were bent upon taking possession of their customary haunts. The numbers also increased. It was now impossible to cast the eye any where along the heavens without getting a glimpse of turkeys sailing about in the air. One drove entered the camp, running amongst the tents and wagons. It was decidedly amusing to witness the scene which ensued. Soldiers, teamsters, and dogs joined in the pursuit. One moment dashing under a wagon, and the next amongst the horses and mules. In the early part of the race, the turkeys had the best [of it], but, bewildered and headed off, soon became exhausted. A number were caught in this way.

"While this exciting chase was going on, a party of soldiers occupied themselves with shooting at the birds as they settled in the trees, or as they approached the ground. During this fusilade, one of the volunteers, tying his horse to the picket, was somewhat astounded to find the animal jerk away from him and instantly fall to the earth. A stray bullet had finished him. Considering all the firing and confusion, it was a matter of great surprise that no other casualties occurred."

Movement towards the roosting place, which is usually the same as that used the night before, takes place at 3:00 or 4:00 P.M. (Jordan, 1898:370). If sundown, by miscalculation, finds them a mile or so from the roost, they will break into a run. The lead is taken by the old hens. On arriving at the roost after a long run, they will form a close group and utter a low purring sound. When an old hen rapidly gives several loud clucks, ending in a gutteral cackle, the entire flock takes to the air, alighting in different directions in the tallest trees. Seldom more than two or three birds alight in the same tree. They will shift until a satisfactory perch is found. There is a decided preference, evidently due to a feeling of greater safety, for roosts over water such as cypress swamps and flooded river bottoms.

Following the breeding season, turkeys form flocks of males and females with their young. Obviously, at this time flocks going to roost will be headed by a male or female. In mixed flocks leadership does not appear to be confined to either sex.

Turkeys show no regularity in using a given tree or locality for roosting, or in the number of birds sleeping in the same tree. At times a roost will be used many nights in succession. If shot at on the roost or otherwise disturbed, they may abandon a roost for a long time. There are positive statements that only one turkey will roost in a tree, but there are many cases to the contrary. Sometimes so many birds have selected the same limb that it was broken by their weight. There have been fixed opinions on the species of trees that turkeys select for roosting, yet a wide variety has been used. A tall, bare tree standing in water is especially favored. The roosts on the Edwards Plateau, Texas, are in trees only twenty-five to thirty feet high since taller ones are seldom to be found.

It is stated by Jordan (*l.c.*) that turkeys dislike roosting in the same trees on two or more successive nights. He had known them to use three or four different roosts within a week. Frequently, they would roost near a given site for many nights. Old gobblers were prone to roost in the same place, if not in the same tree, night after night.

The procedure of going to roost is a noisy affair (Goebel, 1889). The alighting of a turkey in a tree top, when there is no wind, can be heard at the distance of a quarter of a mile. The birds do not fly up in unison but one or more at a time, and seldom more than one bird is seen in a tree. The roost may cover eight to ten acres. It is almost dark before all the birds settle down quietly. Jones (1898:185) writes that they will go to roost wherever night overtakes, disperse themselves widely, and seldom use the same roost two nights in succession. He had great faith in the turkey's understanding of camouflage. When leaves were still present, the bird alighted on the topmost branch of the highest tree, the weight of its body so folding the foliage that it could not be seen from above or below. When the leaves fell, choice was made of old deformed trees having knots, humps, or crooks, near which it rested. However, credulity is strained by the tale of the bird that, lacking these devices, flattened its body on a limb along which it stretched its legs and neck to resemble an arboreal deformity.

The eastern turkey, according to Rutledge (1941.1:149), follows a definite route and arrives at the roost on schedule. Little noise is made in flying up but more is made as the wings strike limbs and branches on alighting. Contrary to the general opinion, they do not roost high. A preference is shown for evergreens over bare trees, and he found them in the dense tops of yellow pines not over forty feet high; occasionally the birds roosted as low as twenty feet. Regarding the use of bare trees, he also believes that the turkey selects one having old squirrel nests or bunches of mistletoe or Spanish moss for the purpose of camouflage. The bird is distinguishable, however, by the extended neck and head moving

163

against the sky, and the tail which appears exceptionally long when the bird is at roost. When flushed at night, a turkey will usually alight in a bare tree, not on the ground. The flight is generally only one hundred yards even though the same bird is flushed five or six times.

Concerning the roosting of Merriam's turkey in the Mogollon Mountains, Arizona, Goldman (1902:123) wrote: "A few minutes later I cautiously approached the place where probably over 150 turkeys, all females and young of the year, were noisily trying to settle themselves for the night. They occupied the tops of tall pines for about 200 yards along one of the steep walls of the cañon. In many of the trees there were only two or three turkeys, but some of the larger ones, and especially those with many dead branches, contained from five to ten birds. Many of them sat as closely together as possible and constantly craned their necks about, squawking, crowding each other and struggling for places. They flew frequently from tree to tree and sometimes a bird, alighting clumsily on a crowded branch would knock off one or two others and all would fly off noisily to other places. At first the disorder seemed to be general and most of the birds were crowding or being crowded and were uttering loud cries of 'quit, quit, quit,' with many modulations depending apparently upon the degree of excitement. They rapidly became quieter, however, until by the time it was dark they were settled for the night." At 9.00 P.M. he fired into the roost. There resulted great commotion but no outcries. On leaving the roost at daylight the following morning, the turkeys usually flew two to three hundred yards, then ran rapidly out of sight. A flock of fifteen males flew to branches of dead trees. There was no sound except from the wings, and, in contrast to the females and young, there was no crowding and no confusion.

Roosting in tall pines in mid-May in Arizona has been described also by Brandt (1951:628). Before rising, a turkey would stretch its neck, peer in the direction of the roost, and utter low sounds. The hen was the more reluctant to fly up and its yelps were answered by a gobbler in the tree. Regardless of the length of the limb, there would be but one turkey on it. The bird always alighted near the trunk of the tree, walked out on the limb, or jumped to a higher one. After having selected a place, each turkey preened itself, then settled down with the tail directed at an angle towards the ground. The head dropped backward in repose, and finally disappeared from sight. The light was too dim to determine definitely if the head was tucked under a wing.

The fourteen turkeys observed by Brandt roosted in four trees, there being five in one, four in another, three in another, and two in the fourth tree. As soon as he left the blind, the necks of all of the birds protruded but there was no sound from them. When a powerful electric light was flashed upon them, there was craning and peering and occasional low alarm notes, but no bird rose to a standing position or showed other signs of fear. Only seven birds returned to the roost the following evening, and none the third night.

The method of going to roost in the southwest shows that the turkey has difficulty in making up its mind:

"They frequent the valleys of streams along which is a fringe of heavy trees, on the branches of which they roost at night. They are very choice in their selection of a roosting place, preferring a dense mass of trees not far from a bluff bank, from the top of which they can easily pitch into the branches. The turkey flies strongly and well, but his great weight makes it difficult for him to rise from the ground; consequently, he takes the wing very reluctantly. . . .

"Every one who has kept tame turkeys must have noticed the dilatory and ridiculous performances attendant on getting to roost each night.

"Though each has roosted on the same branch for months and knows exactly the best way to get to it, he will go round and round the tree, noting each branch and favourable alighting place with critical eye, and seemingly intent on finding some new way to arrive at the old end. Now he thinks he has found it, squats and almost stretches out his wings, when he thinks better of it, and walks on to do the same thing over and over again. The wild turkey has the same peculiarity and makes as much 'to-do' about getting to bed as a spoiled child" (Dodge, 1877:232).

The wild turkey watched by McNeale (1925) settled down to roost in a large, dead chestnut and craned its neck in all directions as if searching for an enemy. Its position was shifted half a dozen times to different limbs before being satisfied with one. Even then it thrust its head about, particularly below, as if danger was to be expected from that quarter. At dusk it finally thrust its head beneath a wing.

Several writers have stated that the wild turkey puts its head under a wing as a final act in settling down for the night. The general opinion is that the neck and head rest between the shoulders. I was told in New Mexico that the head is not placed under a wing even during a blizzard. I was at the Meadow Valley Reserve, Juneau County, Wisconsin, on April 9, 1957. Stanley Plis informed me that although the Pennsylvania game farm turkeys had roosted all winter long—even during the severest weather—in the very tops of two oaks, when the snow disappeared they began to roost in a dense clump of Norway pines about twenty feet high. There is no accounting for this vagary. The instant that I flashed a light into the pines, three or four turkeys flew out but did not go far. The light was turned off so as not to disturb the remainder of the flock. I tried repeatedly to settle this question in the South, but by the time all was quiet it was so dark that it was impossible to determine the position of the head. The illustration of sleeping wild turkeys in Davis (1949:Op. 278) shows the head resting between the shoulders. Under date September 23, 1960, Stanley J. Marsden wrote that domestic turkeys will place the head under a wing in cold weather. This is shown by the matting of the feathers under the wing from the moisture in the bird's breath. In case of respiratory trouble, mucus is deposited on the feathers under the wing. I have been informed by Kenton C. Lint that both adult ocellated turkeys and their poults have been observed with head under wing at night.

It is stated by Hebard (1941:41–43) that in southern Georgia the old gobblers roost alone on tall pines on a hill. Others roost in the center of a hammock in tall hardwoods from the first to the topmost branch. At the edge of a hammock they appear to select the very top of a pine. The birds arrive at the roost from 4:00 P.M. to sundown, and the head is placed under a wing. It is possible to walk beneath the turkeys while talking without causing them to fly. Near daylight even a whisper will result in flight. Undisturbed, they often remain on the roost until well after sunrise.

A roost may be used over a long period: "Frequently the birds will travel several miles to a good roosting site. In the winter the same roosting area may be used continuously for months at a time. In a single roosting area in southern Colorado, where some twenty pines were used, droppings accumulated to a depth of twelve to fifteen inches. A second roost, some miles distant, showed almost as heavy use" (Burget, 1957:11). These roosts were in dry areas where the weathering of the droppings would be slow. The hens and poults flew into the pines at an angle. A flock of mature gobblers was the last to go to roost. They chose a tree that had an open top and was bare of limbs for the first fifty feet. After craning their necks in various directions, they flew perpendicular to their perches.

I examined two roosts on the Encino Division of the King Ranch in Texas in the month of March. Some of the heaps of dung beneath the trees were sixteen inches in diameter and four inches in height. This showed that some turkeys had roosted on exactly the same places on the limbs for long periods of time. I watched turkeys go to roost several evenings at the Welder Wildlife Foundation. The first roost was in a grove of live oaks with large, nearly horizontal limbs. At 6:55 the first turkey flew up, followed by eleven others within the space of one minute. At this time it was so dark that the birds could not be seen on the ground, and they arrived so quietly that I was not aware of their presence until hearing the wing beats. The turkeys usually alighted on the lower limbs first, then reached a perch in the top of the tree in three or four stages. In this process some of the birds were clearly outlined against the sky. The angle of flight from the ground was about 30°. There was no sound other than the beating of wings and this was less loud than would be anticipated. Within ten minutes all was quiet in the roost. A last distant gobble was heard at 7:15, but there was none from this roost. The following evening, roosting was a disjointed affair. The first turkey flew up at 7:00 and was followed by four others at 7:06, 7:07, 7:08, and 7:10 P.M. No other turkeys appeared. At 7:20 a distant male gobbled and was answered by one on the roost.

The blind was moved to a roost in which were two oaks with few limbs and placed on the eastern side to take advantage of the evening light in the western sky. It is said that the gobblers run a few steps before taking wing for the roost and that the females take off from a standing position. This may be true in general. At 6:59 four gobblers appeared within twenty feet of the blind and I could hear another strutting. It was just out of the angle of vision. Three of the birds erected their necks in the alarm attitude and eyed the blind rigidly for half a minute. I was very much afraid that they would leave suddenly; however, they started feeding. All but the strutting gobbler fed up to rising to the roost. This I did not expect.

167

At 7:03 the first bird took off from a standing position. The other four soon followed. Of the five, three ran a few steps before taking wing; the remaining two flew from a standing position. There was no fuss about deciding to fly up. The situation was different once they were in the trees. The first place they alighted was never the right one, and they had to shift two or three times. Three birds went into one tree, selecting top-most positions. One decided finally not to remain and flew to a small limb on an adjoining tree, a distance of about twelve feet, where he balanced precariously with tail partly spread, then settled down. There was much standing up on the perches, craning of necks, then settling down and repeating the performance all over again. I left at 7:15, at which time it was so dark that the heads were not distinguishable. Of the five birds, finally, two trees held two turkeys each, and one tree one.

These turkeys left the ground about one hundred feet from the trees. The take-off angle was about 25°, then the birds rose rather sharply at an angle of about 70°. There was not much more than a swish of the wings to be heard.

I have seen turkeys alight on limbs less than an inch in diameter and maintain their balance. Two wild turkeys in Oklahoma were seen to alight on wires where they rocked precariously back and forth (Anon., 1960).

Number Roosting in a Single Tree

The number of turkeys that will roost in a single tree is highly variable. In South Carolina, Davis (1949:87) never knew two turkeys to settle for the night in the same tree or occupy the same trees two nights in succession. According to Josserand (1938), only one turkey to a tree is the rule and a roosting flock may extend as much as a quarter of a mile. In Florida it was considered unusual to find two birds in the same tree ("Osceola," 1927:59). Allen and Neill (1955) state that there is usually only one turkey to a tree, rarely two to three, and that the flock covers a distance of one to two hundred yards. In southern Florida they inhabit the prairie, but with few big trees they will roost in buttonbushes and custard apples only five or six feet from the ground. Old gobblers usually go to cypress "heads." In northern Florida, turkeys are most common at the edges of swampy forests and hammocks.

In Texas in fall and winter a flock would roost in a single tree or in several adjacent ones (Jordan, 1881). Prior to Christmas, 1878, Rollie Burns (Holden, 1932:63) hunted at a roost on the Llano River where there were thousands of turkeys. Occasionally, a limb would break from their weight, and about an hour was required for the birds to settle down: "As a rule the turkeys on the same limb turn their heads in the same direction. I have seen as many as fifteen or twenty turkeys on one limb." Regarding a night ride with General R. S. Mackenzie's troops in northern Texas in 1871, Carter (1935:74) commented that "the loud crashing of the pecan limbs heavily loaded with their weight of wild turkeys—and the loud gobbles g-o-b-b-l-e-s of the big gobblers, made the blood fairly dance and tingle in the veins." In southern Texas the turkeys roosted as high as possible on tall cottonwoods. On the Medina River, eleven were counted on one large limb (Dresser, 1866:25).

Roosting over Water

There is a general agreement that, wherever possible, turkeys will roost over water. One writer (J. E. R., 1881) states: "It is a fact known to hunters that wild turkeys that live in a low swampy country nearly always roost in the cypress or other timber that grows in the sloughs and along the edges of shallow lakes or sluggish streams. They seem to love to roost over water. In mountainous or hilly countries it is said that they generally roost in the timber on the sides of the steepest hills. Safety is perhaps the ruling motive in both cases." In South Carolina turkeys roost about 85 per cent of the time over water. If the weather is cold and windy, they choose large pines on ridges. Old gobblers generally roost higher than females and young.

Next to roosting trees standing in water, trees surrounded by cane-brakes are preferred (Davis, 1949:84–85). Mestier (1877) found a cypress swamp full of roosting turkeys on Cache River, northeastern Arkansas. At Cardwell, Dunklin County, Missouri, the turkey was not known to roost elsewhere than over water in the cypress swamps (Widmann, 1896:221). Kennard (1915:5) was in the Big Cypress Swamp, Florida, in February. He wrote: "The hens usually roost in a tall cypress near the edge of the swamp, while the old gobblers at this season seem exclusive and prefer to roost alone, usually in some tall pine on the nearby ham-mock. Then when morning comes, after a few preliminary gobbles when the hens have flown down and begun to feed, the old gobbler comes down and is supposed to pay his respects to each of his consorts, or for that matter any other consort that happens to be near."

Selection of Roosting Sites

Turkeys make use of the best roosting places within their range. Tall trees growing along streams are used in the Southwest. A preference is shown for trees growing in canyons and ravines, the turkeys flying down to the trees from adjacent heights. Turkeys on the lower Río Grande roosted on the large limbs of hackberry and huisache (*Vachellia farnesiana*) trees in the bottom of arroyos ("Texas," 1891). Chapman (1891:321) reported that along the Nueces River most of the turkeys spent the night in the trees on the banks but some occupied the hackberry mottes (groves) of the chaparral. Hough (1898) mentions an article in the Dallas (Texas) *News* in which the writer stated that the turkey has been exterminated in many regions in Texas because of shooting at the roosts. Where trees for roosting were scarce, the concentration of turkeys in the small patches of timber made the birds an easy prey.

Walker (1954:22) writes: "The old gobblers in East Texas seem to prefer the almost impenetrable bottoms, roosting in some of the taller trees, but occasionally are found roosting on the sides of post oak ridges. In either case, East Texas birds shift roosting sites more often than do their western counterparts." The turkeys in the mountains at the heads of the Medina, Sabinal, and Frio rivers had no regular roosting places (Sharpe, 1889). Wherever sundown happened to find them, they flew down to trees along some water course. Roosts on consecutive nights might be miles apart. Usually a roost will be abandoned if disturbed. When turkeys roost where night overtakes them, food is generally scarce and they wander great distances.

Turkeys usually select the best trees available for roosting regardless of species although the reason for choosing some roosts is not apparent. Henshaw (1874:434) reported that in southeastern Arizona the Mexican (Merriam's) turkey roosted in large cottonwoods by the streams. Ligon (1946:15, 27) found Merriam's turkeys roosting in cottonwoods so rarely, particularly in winter, that he considered it a change in habits, and that the use of cottonwoods instead of pines for roosting by the turkeys of southeastern Colorado during the 1860's and 1870's was an indication that they belonged to the eastern race. It is extremely doubtful that any turkey other than Merriam's occurred in Colorado. During the winter of 1944–45, southwest of Kim, Los Animas County, a flock was using a grove of broad-leaved cottonwoods (*Populus deltoides*) (Burget, 1957:12). There were no other large trees in the area. In the Spanish Peaks, turkeys were roosting in cottonwoods in preference to pines presumably because of the undergrowth of the latter.

Merriam's turkey usually roosts in pines because they are the most abundant large trees within its range. Preference is shown in Colorado for pines with large open tops with small, nearly horizontal limbs (Burget, 1957:11). A roost at Devil Creek, western Archuleta County, has been in use for at least fifty years. The limbs of the trees are worn smooth from the gripping action of the feet of the turkeys. As many as two hundred birds have used the roost with as many as thirty in one tree. Most of the roosting trees in pine forests in Arizona were mature (Jantzen, 1956:7). They were in open stands and were free of limbs twenty feet from the ground. Occasionally the birds roosted in partly dead pines and, during snowstorms, in junipers. On the other hand, Tooker (1933:92) states that in Arizona, when gobblers are in flocks, they invariably select dead pines for roosts.

East of the Rockies many species of trees have been utilized. In the evening near Fort Sill, Oklahoma, turkeys assembled from near and far in some bottomland with large cottonwoods to go to roost ("Basso," 1874). Occasionally, a hundred or more were to be found within a space of two hundred yards. A flock of eighteen to twenty-five wild turkeys roosted in an old elm on the farm of Nauman (1924:134) in Keokuk County, Iowa. Gillmore (1872:309) failed to get within gunshot of a flock of at least thirty turkeys that had gone to roost in the top of a dead sycamore along the Embarrass River in Indiana. Turkeys, according to Rutledge (1936:532), prefer conifers to bare trees "for obvious reasons." He once saw a large tree, in which the birds were roosting, blown down during a storm. They stayed in the tree while it fell, and the next morning none were missing or injured. In Virginia, a decided preference is shown for conifers, especially pines. Occasionally, hardwoods are used for roosting (Mosby and Handley, 1943:166). Burleigh (1931), in April, 1919, observed two turkeys go to roost in the top of a large white pine in a secluded ravine in Center County, Pennsylvania. There is no consistency in the use of available conifers. At Horse Cove, North Carolina, turkeys roosted in trees bare of foliage instead of in adjacent pines and hemlocks (Clifton, 1883).

Turkeys generally roost high, and frequently in bare trees. Loskiel (1794:91) wrote that they usually perch so high that they cannot be killed except by a ball. Referring to his hybrid turkeys, domestic x wild, Crévecoeur (1925:132) states that during the most severe winter weather, they roosted in the tips of the tallest trees and faced the northwest wind. The wild turkeys kept by Johnson (1930) in North Dakota roosted as high as they could get. He advised against going near a roost at night for if once disturbed they will not roost in the same place again. Domestic turkeys have retained this wild trait. Adams (1873:126) informs us: "I have seen broods of turkeys . . . perched on the topmost branches of tall trees during exceedingly cold weather when they might have roosted in barns. Indeed, farmers stated to me that when left to themselves they infinitely prefer out of doors at all seasons, and usually select prominent and exposed situations."

Early Indifference to Shooting at the Roost

Turkeys that have had slight experience with man will not leave the roost sometimes despite shooting. This makes it possible to kill the birds in large numbers. Ashe (1808:144), near Marietta, Ohio, came upon a flock of turkeys which had gone to roost: "They rose up with much perturbation and noise, and again descended to rest. The whole gang occupied four trees, and still they rose, fell and acted with one accord. I resolved to fire on them. I had heard, that whenever wild turkies settled to roost, there they remained in despite of all opposition." He fired three shots and in each case the birds rose above the trees about thirty yards and descended again. The account is imaginative. No flock of turkeys ever rose and fell as a unit in the manner described.

Reaction to Fire

Roosting turkeys appear to be fascinated or bewildered by fire. Byrd (1929:150) wrote in 1728: "They roost commonly upon very high Trees, Standing near some River or Creek, and are so stupify'd at the Sight of Fire, that if you make a Blaze in the Night near the Place where they roost, you may fire upon them several times successively, before they will dare to fly away." A Navaho Indian informed Hill (1938:174) that if a fire was built under roosting turkeys, all of them could be killed since they would not fly away. Concerning a camp on the Ohio River near the mouth of the Wabash, Brackenridge (1834:35) stated: "Once, having encamped somewhat later than usual in the neighborhood of a beautiful grove of sugar trees, we found, after kindling our fires, that a large flock of turkeys had taken up their night's lodgings over our heads: some ten or twelve of them were soon taken down for our supper and breakfast." A ground fire was something to which turkeys were long accustomed because of frequent burnings by the Indians. In November, 1818, the forest near Herculaneum, Missouri, was on fire. Flocks of turkeys rose ahead of the fire and alighted in the trees (Babcock, 1864:117).

Morning Roosting Schedule

Under normal weather conditions, turkeys will remain on the roost until it is broad daylight. Gobbling begins before daybreak (Lewis, 1863:140). On a clear, warm morning, turkeys leave the roost about sunrise, but on cold, rainy mornings they have been known to remain on the roost until nine o'clock. When there is much rain and snow, they will remain in trees (Rutledge, 1946:49). Jordan (1914:228) writes: "In the South they are unprepared for much cold, and at such times will likely be found grouped together on the sunny slopes of hills, or behind some log or fence, to avoid the bitter winds, especially if the sun is not shining. They will then often remain on their roosts half a day rather than alight on the cold snow." During heavy storms, Merriam's turkey will remain on the roost for days at a time. It is very reluctant to travel in soft snow (Burget, 1946:5). Bedichek (1950:139) was informed by a friend that in winter he had seen turkeys roosting with their tails to a "tugging norther." This is most unusual. A turkey has at least sense enough to face a strong wind or a driving snow.

Loafing

Turkeys usually loaf during the middle of the day: "During the daytime the turkey likes to roost on the ground, and because its breast is long and deep, it usually takes an attitude different from others of the galline tribe. When it squats, instead of resting on the keel of its breast-bone like most birds, it tilts forward and sits on the breast muscles surrounding the wishbone, which position elevates the tail" (Brandt, 1951:624). After feeding they will lounge on sunny slopes if the weather is cool or seek a shady place if it is hot. They may remain quiet, preen their feathers, or dust themselves (J. E. R., 1881).

While on the White River, Arkansas, Schoolcraft (1819:36) noted that turkeys were found during the heat of the day in open post oak woods. The resting period in Alabama is generally from 10:30 A.M. to 2:30 P.M. (Wheeler, 1948:28). Each flock has a loafing ground that is used regularly. In hot weather the males select a thick stand of young hardwoods free from underbrush and with a nearly closed canopy. Here there are numerous wallows, made apparently so the turkeys can rest their bodies on the cool, damp earth. There is no indication of their use for dusting. Numerous feathers imply considerable time spent in preening. At midday hens and their broods rested under an isolated tree or in a grove in the open.

Turkeys in hilly or mountainous country, after feeding at a low elevation, will walk to the top of a ridge to rest. In case of danger they can fly quickly down either slope. Koch (1889:129), writing of his experience with turkeys in Pennsylvania, said: "Our turkeys spend only a few hours of the day in the 'bottoms' (level forests at the foot of the mountains), going there on account of the food and the springs. Often they come to the borders of the corn and buckwheat fields, but soon return again to the mountains where with their vigilance there is less danger."

A brief description of the daily routine in Texas follows: "The Comanche county birds resorted to the brooks at about ten o'clock every morning. From that time they would sit in the shade until late in the day, and then they would feed until their roosting time, which was just before dark, when all start for the trees. The hunter could easily tell the roost by examining the large trees along the margin of the streams and pond holes, and noticing the large quantity of manure that had accumulated under the trees. I have known the entire flock to be killed while roosting on the same tree" (P. M. S., 1882). They were noisy before flying to the roost.

BATHING

Bathing in water by turkeys, if it occurs at all, is very rare. Rutledge (1930) mentions finding a hen turkey taking a bath but remarks that this is unusual. The wading of turkeys into the water to drink or to secure aquatic vegetation should not be confused with bathing.

DUSTING

Turkeys take dust baths at frequent intervals. Audubon (1831:7) wrote that the mother takes the poults to deserted ant hills where they dust to remove the scales from the growing feathers and to suppress the attacks of ticks and other vermin since the odor from the ants is repulsive to these insects. The old birds also dust to remove ticks and mosquitos. The statement of Sharp (1914:65) on this subject paraphrases Audubon. This is not "anting" in the usually accepted sense as assumed by McAtee (1947.1). It is doubtful that the earth from any ant hill, deserted or occupied, will serve as an insect repellant because of its odor. Any formic acid secreted by the ants would soon evaporate. I have placed in the nests of tree swallows, swarming with mites, powdered earth from an occupied ant hill. The mites were indifferent to it. When crushed ants were placed in a nest, mites on encountering them would back away. This treatment had no perceptible effect in reducing their number.

A very complete discussion of insects in relation to dusting is given by Jordan (1898:330): "It is a well-known fact that turkeys and all other feathered species have a habit of rolling themselves in dust and ashes to remove vermin from the skin and feathers, but that the dust or clay or sand from an ant bed operates as any special factor I have yet to learn; but I believe a bath of dry wood ashes, where an old log or stump was burned, is preferred by them on account of the cleansing effect of the ashes.

"The lice or parasite which troubles the turkeys is much larger than those that infest chickens. . . . One peculiar feature about ticks, redbugs, chiggers, etc. on turkeys, they do not inflame the skin by their poison as they do the human skin. A hundred ticks or redbugs may get on a turkey in the space of half an inch and bite a week and not irritate or inflame the parts as much as one redbug will the human skin. The redbug is scarcely large enough to be seen with the naked eye, but on the human skin will inflame a place as large as the palm of one's hand and cause the most excrutiating pain. The ticks when full of blood soon drop off, or are pulled off by the beak of the turkey. I do not think the dust affects the ticks at all, but it worries the lice, especially ashes which the birds prefer to roll in. I have known turkeys to scratch up and wallow in wet ash piles where an old log or stump has been burned in the woods, and have killed them with the lumps of wet ashes clinging to the feathers. Mosquitos, buffalo and car gnats, and sand flies torment the wild turkey terribly in the spring about the river swamps by biting their naked heads and necks. I have seen them so annoyed that they would go to an old burning log or stump and stand in the smoke to avoid these pests, and at night roost as high as they could climb. There they enjoy peace from their tormentors all night, but the annoyance is renewed on alighting from the trees in the morning. Sometimes the poor birds will repair to open fields or prairies and get the sunshine, which at once drives the pests away."

Dusting in Alabama generally begins the middle of March, which is two or three weeks prior to laying, and extends to the last of August (Wheeler, 1948:27). The incubating hen goes to a dusting place, lies on her side and raises clouds of fine, hot sand by shuffling her legs and moving her wings so as to pull up the dust and force it through the feathers. The dry soil is also pecked against the neck and breast. After dusting for some minutes, the bird rises and shakes herself vigorously to expel the excess dirt. Hens dust more frequently than do males. Favored dusting places are open areas in woods where logs and brush have burned. This is in agreement with Jordan.

The dusting behavior of Merriam's turkey has been described as follows: "The Wild Turkey enjoys dusting itself more than any creature that I have ever seen. It lies in languor, first on one side, then on the other, throwing fine earth over itself, also between its partly spread wings, and tosses the dusting cloud to a height of two or three feet. While thus engaged the bird does not sit on its breastbone, but lies forward on the wishbone, with its tail elevated, and by its expression appears to enjoy a sensation of lassitude. The glossy plumage becomes dull as the bird lazily prolongs its bathing, often for 30 minutes at a time. Hens seem to indulge in this refresher more than their larger mates, although both frequently thus bepowder themselves. After dusting, a bird often walks away a short distance, and finally shakes itself and thereby causes the particles to rise in a small cloud. Usually after shaking the bird does not preen, but resumes feeding at once. Wheresoever I went in the steep environs of Rustler and Barfoot parks the dusting basins of the turkeys were in evidence" (Brandt, 1951:624).

There is no proof for any of the reasons advanced for dusting. Burget (1957:18) believes that the chief purpose of dusting is to clean the body and feathers. After dusting and shaking, every feather is straightened and cleaned to remove the remainder of the dust. A second purpose of dusting is the removal of parasites from the body. Thirdly, moulting, from July into October, appears to produce an itching in the skin. Frequently the birds have been observed reaching in and deliberately pulling out a feather. It is possible that dusting gives relief from itching since the dusting beds are used most frequently during these months.

It is stated that nesting hens visit the dusting places regularly, apparently to secure relief from parasites (Mosby and Handley, 1943:117). Newman (1950:7) thinks they dust to remove lice and for "the sheer fun of it." In Florida dusting is performed the middle of the morning, and the most dusting is done by laying hens. Dusting is also closely associated with moulting. It appears, however, that dusting places are not essential for the establishment of a permanent range. Hens have been observed to dust in Alabama during the first week in March and this action is considered to be a good indication of the beginning of laying (Wheeler, 1944).

DRINKING

Water is an important requirement for turkeys. They usually drink twice a day, in the morning and in the afternoon. According to Wheeler (1948:26), they generally drink early in the morning after leaving the roosting trees, and this may explain in part why the birds roost over or near water. Harris (1897) killed two turkeys from a flock of sixteen as they arrived at a pool to drink about 3:00 P.M. Where watering places are limited, hunters lie in wait for the turkeys to come to drink. Goebel (1889:128) stated that turkeys are seldom found more than one to two miles from water. During the mating and nesting seasons of 1955 and 1956 in New Mexico, Spicer (1959:24) found that 71.4 per cent of the turkeys were within a half mile of water and 93.6 per cent were within one mile. He concluded that permanent water supplies need not be less than one and a half to two miles apart. Adults apparently do not place much dependence on dew and food as a source of water. Two nesting hens with soaked plumage were observed traveling to a spring to drink during a shower.

Nests are usually close to water (Blakey, 1937:6). In Alabama all nests were placed within 350 feet of water (Wheeler, 1948:36). It is thought by Walker (1954:22) that during the first days of the life of the poults, they obtain sufficient water from dew and insects. After two weeks of age, they follow the mother to water. Poults appear to require a regular and close supply of water. In Colorado a nest was placed within ten feet of a spring seepage (Burget, 1957:18). Prior to hatching of the eggs, the spring went dry, leaving the nearest source of water a half mile distant.

Swimming Ability

There is some difference of opinion on the swimming ability of the turkey. According to McNight (1917:80), it is a good swimmer and will cross water a mile in width. No example is given. Guyon (1879:209) considered it an excellent swimmer, while Sandys and Van Dyke (1904:265) state that it performs poorly in the water, merely flapping its way to shore. There is no doubt that the turkey can swim sufficiently well to save itself when an emergency arises. A frightened domestic turkey once flew into the Erie Canal in an attempt to escape. It swam quite rapidly for a distance of about seventy-five feet before taking to the bank (Johnson, 1897). In connection with the crossing of streams, Audubon (1831:2) wrote: "The old and fat birds easily get over, even should the river be a mile in breadth; but the younger and less robust frequently fall into the water,—not to be drowned, however, as might be imagined. They bring their wings close to their body, spread out their tail as a support, stretch forward their neck, and, striking out their legs with great vigour, proceed rapidly towards the shore; on approaching which, should they find it too steep for landing, they cease their exertions for a few minutes, float down the stream until they come to an accessible part, and by a violent effort generally extricate themselves from the water. It is remarkable that immediately after crossing a large stream, they ramble about for some time, as if bewildered. In this state they fall an easy prey to the hunter."

A gobbler was seen to swim from a ridge in a flooded area, rather than fly, to escape detection (A. H. Rutledge, 1936:492). A turkey feeding in shallow water at the edge of a lake in Arizona chanced to step into deep water. In place of turning back, it swam across a narrow space of deep water. Walking out, it shook the water from its feathers and began feeding (Tooker, 1933:36). Turkeys in Florida, and elsewhere (Plate 23), do not hesitate to walk in shallow water, and will walk across a log over a stream (Allen and Neill, 1955:38).

Poults swim surprisingly well. The attempted crossing of the Iowa River, where it was one hundred yards wide, by poults only a few days old, was witnessed by Dupont (1888). The hen flew across the river and, in response to her loud calls, twelve to fourteen young ran quickly down the bank and entered the water. Just before they reached the opposite bank the hen became frightened and, giving the alarm notes, flew back across the stream. The poults immediately turned back. On reaching the strongest part of the current, about half of them gave up and floated with the stream. These young were rescued from a boat and released after they became dry.

On May 14, 1954, at the Little Shoal Creek embayment of Bankhead Lake, Alabama, a hen was observed calling excitedly to two poults in the water. Their age was estimated at ten days. The water was at least one hundred yards wide. The hen had evidently flown across and was calling the poults to her (Martin and Atkeson, 1954). Taber (1955) on June 9, 1951, came upon a pair of adult turkeys with six poults three or four days old. The birds scattered and one of the poults walked along a fallen tree extending into a pond. On reaching the end of the tree, it entered the water and swam a distance of about thirty yards to the opposite shore. When picked up, it was cold and exhausted. One adult, apparently the mother, remained in sight "but showed a minimum amount of agitation."

Crossing Streams and Lakes

The crossing of large streams in autumn seems to have been a very deliberate affair. According to Audubon (1831:2): "When they come upon a river, they betake themselves to the highest eminences, and there often remain a whole day, or sometimes two, as if for the purpose of consultation. During this time, the males are heard *gobbling*, calling, and making much ado, and are seen strutting about, as if to raise their courage to a pitch befitting the emergency. Even the females and young assume something of the same demeanour, spread out their tails, and run round each other, *purring* loudly, and performing extravagant leaps. At length, when the weather appears settled, and all around is quiet, the whole party mounts to the tops of the highest trees, whence at a signal, consisting of a single *cluck* given by a leader, the flock takes flight for the opposite shore." While on the lower Ohio on October 17, 1820, Audubon (1929:8) recorded in his journal that turkeys were extremely plentiful and crossing hourly from the north side. Many weak birds perished by falling into the stream.

The method of crossing the Mississippi as described by Thorpe (1854:11) is very similar to that of Audubon. The few flocks seen by Sandys and Van Dyke (1904:263) to cross streams flew from the ground, not trees, without any fuss. On reaching the opposite shore, they continued onward, making in all a flight of about one-half mile. In commenting on the statement of Audubon, Jordan (1898:312) wrote: "I will say in this connection, that turkeys may so act in rare instances if the stream be exceptionally wide, delaying their progress for an hour. Turkeys do not like to fly under any conditions, nor use their wings save when necessary, but I have never seen a river that they could not easily fly across, starting at the water's edge, arising, and alighting in the top of the trees on the opposite bank. J. K. Renaud, of New Orleans, and I once, while paddling a skiff up a large lake in Alabama, counted a flock of sixteen turkeys flying across the lake some distance ahead of us. We noticed that these turkeys just barely skimmed over the water by sailing with set wings and rose to the top of a higher ridge on the side where they alighted than the one whence they started; not one even touched the water. The lake was probably 300 yards wide."

Accounts of the turkey's behavior on reaching a stream vary widely. Dodge (1877:232) mentions a flock that spent several hours deciding to cross a stream fifty or sixty yards wide. There was much running up and down the bank, piping, and feints of flying. When one turkey flew, the others followed and crossed with ease. Audubon's account of the crossing of rivers has been used without credit being given (Anon., 1877). Woodward (1877) after reading the article, denied that turkeys fly to the tops of the tallest trees and fuss for a considerable time before crossing. He had seen an old gobbler rise from the edge of the Missouri River and cross where it was one-half to three-fourths of a mile wide. An entire flock performed the same feat before he could get near enough for a shot. In his opinion the turkey could rise from the ground and fly almost as strongly as a quail.

The following contradictory appendix was added by Charles Hallock, editor of *Forest and Stream*: "The above strictures are true in part; but did the writer ever see a flock of turkeys on their travels and just previous to crossing a river? We have, and on that very Missouri River, too, and the fuss they made before taking wing put us much in mind of the barnyard species, who, though he uses the same perch to roost on each night, goes round and round, all but flying, and then hesitating, walking off to take a new survey as if in hopes of finding some newer and easier way of accomplishing the feat. Wild turkeys can take wing with very rapid flight when startled, but they are a lazy bird, and when strutting at their leisure, like some other bipeds, always take the greatest trouble to accomplish a little matter. When crossing rivers wild turkeys are given to the very acts stated in the article to which our correspondent takes exception."

Turkeys, states Goebel (1889:128), are reluctant to cross rivers under any circumstance. They cannot fly across a stream as wide as the Missouri when the sandbars are submerged by high water and will not even attempt to do so except under the pressure of immediate danger. On the other hand, Burtt (1876), who was Secretary of the Jefferson City Shooting Club, mentions that in November, 1876, a flock of eight wild turkeys flew across the Missouri when it was about a mile wide. The birds landed exhausted in the center of Jefferson City and were captured. In December, 1839, H. G. Reese (Union Hist. Co., 1881:113) took the ferry from Kansas City, Kansas, to Harlem, Missouri. As he was about to enter the boat, a flock of turkeys came across the Missouri and alighted near him. A flock of exhausted wild turkeys dropped into the streets of Caruthersville, Missouri, in November, 1913. The anonymous writer (1913) stated that there was no timber for their shelter closer than the Tennessee side of the Mississippi, the width of which was given as three miles. It was a bold assumption that the flock crossed the river since no turkey could fly the distance stated.

There are many examples of turkeys flying across streams or lakes, but rarely is the width of the water given. A flock of turkeys was frightened from Long Point on Lake Maxinkuckee, Indiana. A portion of the flock dropped into the water before reaching the eastern shore (Evermann and Clark, 1920:537). A map of the lake shows that the distance flown was about 3,800 feet. A large flock of wild turkeys entered the city limits of Keokuk, Iowa, on October 23, 1883. About half the flock flew from the bluffs to the islands in the Mississippi. A young bird dropped into the water and was captured while swimming to an island (Scott, 1883). Sennett (1878:53) frequently observed turkeys flying across the lower Río Grande in Texas. In January, 1822, a flock of turkeys flew across the Brazos River, Texas, a mile above its mouth. A single turkey flew over first, then the remainder straggled across (Lewis, 1899:26). Maximilian (1858:429) saw flocks fly across the Wabash and the broad Ohio, but he never saw turkeys in the water as mentioned by Audubon.

Turkeys had their limits in flying the Ohio as shown by the following: "One day a large flock going down the bottom was met by another flock coming in the opposite direction, and the result was a furious battle of the gobblers. The Griffin boys, attracted by the commotion, formed a semi-circle and drove them all across the [Ohio] river, but so fat and heavy were they that they could not rise to the top of the Kentucky bank. Their only alternative was to return to the Indiana shore, from which the boys frightened them away again, and before they could reach any landing place many of them were so exhausted that they sank [dropped] into the water. The boys returned to their cabin with eleven which they had captured with their skiffs" (Weakley, Harraman and Co., 1885:432).

It is stated by Bonaparte (1825:97) that a wild turkey flew across the Susquehanna at Clearfield, Clearfield County, Pennsylvania. In October, 1875, two turkeys that flew from Dauphin County, Pennsylvania, across the Susquehanna River, were found floundering in the water near the Perry County shore, one and a half miles below Duncannon. They were captured easily. The river was stated to be nearly a mile wide at this point (Anon., 1875). This width is doubtful. A hunter mentions seeing a turkey attempting to fly across an unnamed creek in Surry County, Virginia. It fell into the water a few yards from the shore ("Old Man,"

1889). Chippoak, Sunken Marsh, and Grays creeks widen appreciably at their lower ends but at no place much exceed a width of one thousand feet.

Sikkem (1921) on January 24, 1921, flushed two hens on the bank of Aquia Creek, apparently at the wide lower end, Stafford County, Virginia. One bird struck the ice on the opposite shore and ran towards the woods. The other bird fell in the water and was dead by the time it was recovered with the aid of a boat. This bird, a female, was fat and weighed 8.5 pounds. Fisher (1894) was informed that turkeys had been seen frequently to fly across the Potomac near Weverton, Washington County, Maryland. Several times birds were unable to reach the Virginia shore and fell into the swift water. F. V. Hebard informed me that he had frequently seen turkeys fly across the St. Mary's River in southern Georgia where it was one hundred feet wide, but in one case the distance was over three hundred feet.

FLIGHT

The flight of the turkey is powerful, and the size of the bird lends deception to its speed. It can rise easily from a standing position, and the first wing beat is sufficient to raise leaves or other light forest debris. In winter an impression of the wings is left on the snow. Once in the air it proceeds with strong wing-beats for a hundred yards or so then sails smoothly. The heavy body is under perfect control, but on touching land it runs for some distance. This seems to be a matter of convenience rather than necessity for it is capable of alighting in a tree after a long flight. Audubon (1929:173) likened the alternate flapping and sailing of the carrion crow to the flight of the turkey.

If the bird starts from a sufficient elevation, the flight is a long glide with little flapping of the wings. Rutledge (1923:26) wrote of his hunting in Pennsylvania: "This sailing of wild turkeys down the long slope of a mountain is one of the sights of nature which affects me deeply. Launching forth on their great wings, these proud and stately birds volplane roaring down over the tree-tops at cyclone speed."

An unknown Frenchman (J. C. B., 1941:34), writing of the turkey near Presque Isle, Pennsylvania, stated that the flocks travel on an elevation so they can take wing readily. When surprised on the ground, they will run to an opening on an elevation before flying. Bartram (1751:9) in 1743 ascended the Flying Hill, Berks County, Pennsylvania, and mentioned that its name was derived from the great numbers of wild turkeys which formerly flew from it to the plains.

When flying from one high tree to another, or at a certain altitude in the forest, the turkey, according to Maximilian (1858:429), makes a splendid, rapid flight, straight and steady, its long neck outstretched. It usually alights on a high limb and turns its head in all directions to look about. A turkey rising from the ground in woods sometimes does so at a small angle from the perpendicular. A hunter in Arkansas stated that the turkeys always started "straight up," rising well above the trees before gliding. Their altitude was enough to soon put them out of range (Hough, 1903). Brewster (1950:15) flushed a gobbler from an opening and likened its flight to that of the ruffed grouse. It passed through a thicket easily and crossed the opening with rapidly whirring wings. After towering over the tops of the forest trees beyond, it set its wings and glided like a grouse. There was a tremendous noise on rising, but the wings made more of a flapping than a whirring sound.

An excellent description of the flight is given by Mosby and Handley (1943:171): "The wings of the wild turkey are powerful. Considering its weight and size, the wild turkey can leave the ground quickly and fly with truly remarkable speed. For example, it is possible for a wild turkey to clear a fifty- to sixty-foot tree even when flushed within 100 feet of the base. In getting on the wing, several short, rapid steps are taken followed by two or more hops and then a leap upward, accompanied by vigorous strokes of the wings. . . . Once off the ground, the turkey is capable of rising at a sharp angle and the bird usually makes a mighty effort, with rapidly beating wings, until it has cleared the tree tops. Once having cleared the tree tops, the turkey usually glides or sails and seldom resorts to more than an occasional wing beat. In full glide, the neck is fully extended, the feet are extended backward beneath the tail and the tail is manipulated to control the direction of flight. In landing in trees, the feet are thrown forward, the body is pitched upward at about a 45-degree angle, the tail is fully expanded and curved and the wings 'backwater' rapidly to check the descent. Should the flying turkey come to the ground rather than alighting in a tree after its flight, its actions are similar except that the body is not pitched at such a sharp angle. . . . It is amazing to observe the adroitness with which this great bird can maneuver on the wing when its flight carries it through thick vegetation or between branches or trees as it takes off or lands." Turkeys usually run before taking flight, but they are perfectly capable of taking wing from a standing position. Rutledge (1959) mentions that a gobbler "exploded" from the base of a myrtle bush where it had squatted.

The altitude above the ground and the distance which a turkey flies depends upon circumstances. Yorke (1890:97) states that the bird will fly one-half mile at an altitude of not more than 40 to 60 feet above the ground. The altitude given by Askins (1931:59) for flying over open fields between woodlands is 150 feet. In Arizona, Brandt (1951:625) observed turkeys flying over pines at more than 100 feet from the ground. When taking off from a broom sedge opening, "they seem to fly in a straight line to a point over the tallest tree in the nearby wooded area whether it be 50 or 100 feet high" (Hebard, 1941:42).

The maximum distance a turkey can fly in a single flight is one mile. Usually it is much less. Repeated flights are exhausting. Murray (1841: II, 58) was told that on a prairie an active Indian or white could run down a turkey in about an hour. When Kelly (1851) was at the Big Blue River, Kansas, in the spring of 1849, some men ran down a turkey but ended about as exhausted as the bird. He remarked that a fat turkey cannot rise on the wing more than once. In Barry County, Michigan, in 1839 some girls "ran down a full grown young wild turkey" prior to Thanksgiving (Hayes, 1896:239).

According to Crane (1897:431), the first flight of turkeys, even when thin, is one-half to three-fourths of a mile, and if fat, the distance is much less. Succeeding flights are shorter. Turkeys have been run down and caught after landing and running one-half to two miles. When the birds were run down with a horse in Wise County, Texas, their first flight was usually four to five hundred yards, and the next one about two hundred yards (Halsell, 1948:43). Mershon (1923:28) mentions that an old gobbler once flew three hundred yards. He states that, after running rapidly for five steps, a turkey will then fly in so straight a line that a track in the snow can be easily picked up again. Rutledge (1936:492) watched a gobbler fly across water from a pine ridge to the mainland a mile distant.

Speed of Flight

The flight speed of the turkey has been estimated to be as high as sixty miles an hour (Rutledge, 1941.1:97). Kanoy (1936) in a car followed a turkey along a stretch of road for nine-tenths of a mile in North Carolina. The gobbler flew about eight feet above the highway, and during the entire distance the speedometer did not vary from fifty-five miles per hour. A large gobbler, flushed by the car of Glover (1947) along a mountain road in West Virginia, ran several steps, and after a few wing strokes progressed by alternate gliding and beating of wings. Its speed was thirty-eight to forty-two miles an hour over a distance of approximately one-half mile. Other observations by him showed speeds of twenty-nine to thirty-six miles per hour.

Mosby and Handley (1943:174) give some speeds obtained with a stopwatch and by pacing. A second-year gobbler flew at the rate of 42.8 miles over a distance of 352 feet; and two hens, six months old, flew 32.5 and 33.5 miles respectively over distances of 379 and 396 feet. Neither hen appeared to be alarmed. Wesley E. Lanyon has informed me that when a flock of feeding turkeys was fired upon at Tallahassee, Florida, he determined by radar that the maximum flight speed of a hen was 31.7 miles per hour. The wing area per gram of weight of a small female eastern turkey was found by Poole (1938:517) to be 0.962 cm. The areas for some other gallinaceous birds are: eastern bobwhite, 1.09 cm.; ruffed grouse, 1.02 cm., and ring-necked pheasant, 0.70 cm.

Running

The turkey puts more faith in its legs than in its wings. If the source of disturbance is not too close, the head and neck are extended forward and it is gone like a streak. The running ability of the turkey was the first trait to impress the early colonists. Wood (1865:32) wrote quaintly: "He hath the use of his long legs so ready, that he can runne as fast as a Dogge, and flye as well as a Goose." Clayton (1844:30) informs us: "They have very long Legs, and will run prodigiously fast. I remember not that ever I saw any of them on the Wing, except it were once." The turkeys in New York ran so extraordinarily fast, according to Rasieres (1849:354) that the Dutch usually took along Indians when they went to hunt them. A winged bird could not be secured unless the legs were also hit. And we have Byrd's statement (1929:150) that they run very fast and, like the ostrich, spread their wings as sails to increase their speed.

The neck outstretched is a characteristic attitude for the running turkey and has been mentioned by several writers. When Möllhausen (1858: I, 139) was in Oklahoma in 1853, he noted that the turkeys "fled incontinently, with outstretched necks, and hid themselves among the bushes." Concerning a flock of turkeys scattered widely by the Indians, Judge Banta (1881:46) wrote that the birds "sped on with long, outstretched necks, half on foot, half on wing." The outstretched neck forms a single plane with the back (Taber, 1955). One writer (I. N. deH., 1905) informs us that his wild turkeys opened their wings halfway when alarmed and folded them again before starting to run. Partial opening of the wings may be a precaution taken if immediate flight becomes necessary. Flocks commonly run in single file. According to O'Hanlon (1890:154), they usually run through the brakes and shrubs in a long line of a dozen or more individuals. At Boerne, Texas, Taylor (1936:127) wrote: ". . . there goes a flock of turkeys before me, dashing up the steep mountain in a long, black line, with the fleetness of race-horses."

RUNNING SPEED

The speeds given for running turkeys show considerable variation. A visitor (Anon., 1836:171) to southern Texas in 1831 gave chase on horseback and found that the turkeys could run more swiftly than wolves and almost as fast as horses. Davis (1949:60) considered the fox one of the fastest mammals on foot that he knew. He once saw a fox dash into a flock of turkeys and they outran him for a distance of fifty or sixty yards before flying. According to Mosby and Handley (1943:174), an undisturbed hen ran at a speed of twelve miles per hour. It was estimated that if the bird were alarmed, the speed would be fifteen to eighteen miles. The Florida turkey can run fifteen to eighteen miles per hour and can attain thirty miles in short spurts (McLaurin, 1957:23). Amundson (1957:8) states that it can reach a speed of thirty miles per hour but the average is fifteen miles. While in a car in Arizona, Brandt (1951:625) timed the running speed of a turkey at nineteen miles per hour.

The strides of an adult gobbler chased by a dog were found by Mosby and Handley (1943:174) to be 43.5 to 46.7 inches long. I measured the strides of a flock of Rio Grande gobblers that ran across a dusty road at apparently normal speed. They measured 22.0 to 34.5 inches with an average of 28 inches.

Thayer (1909:88) believed that the gleam on the back of a running turkey is protective. He writes: "For instance, the gleaming high-light, the central point of shine on the back or side of an iridescent bird, say a turkey gobbler or a peacock, may move backward on the bird's surface while the bird himself moves forward, so that to the observer's eye it seems to be standing still, and since by virtue of its very brightness this spot will hold the attention, it must often happen that the bird seems to be motionless when he is in fact slipping away. It may be objected, and truly, that such deceptions as this are of only momentary effect. But the reader should realize, in this case and in all kindred ones, that it is just these tiny, trivial seeming moments that often tip the balance toward escape or capture, toward life or death, in an animal's career." This seems farfetched.

SEASONAL MOVEMENTS

The turkey is not a true migrant. There are spring and fall altitudinal movements in mountainous country, and wanderings when there is a shortage of food. Emigrations do take place. The undependable Ashe (1808:135) states that it is migratory, spending the winter southward and returning in spring. Audubon (1831:8) thought it probable that in August "all the Turkeys now leave the extreme north-western districts, to remove to the Wabash, Illinois, Black River, and the neighborhood of Lake Erie." In 1821 or 1822, according to Tucker (1882:89), a great movement of turkeys, squirrels, raccoons, and bears passed the West River settlement in Randolph County, Indiana. A large part of the settlers' crops was destroyed. The movement was southward across the Ohio River.

Regarding a trek of turkeys in Johnson County, Indiana, Banta (1881:64) wrote: "In the spring of 1823 a drove passed over the after-site of Franklin, numerous enough to make a well marked trail a hundred yards in width, but they were extremely poor and were, no doubt, migrating in search of food." In 1822 there was a complete failure of mast in southern Ohio and Indiana (Schorger, 1949). The dearth of food would have continued through the spring of 1823 so the turkeys may have been more or less constantly on the move. Great migrations of turkeys are said to have occurred in Daviess County, Kentucky, in early times (Inter-State Publ. Co., 1883.1). No reason is suggested.

Animals naturally gravitate towards a region rich in food. Hildreth (1843:126) mentions that turkeys, bears, and other game came from afar to Chestnut Ridge in western Pennsylvania to partake of the bountiful crop of mast. Sears (1920:123), probably in the 1850's, saw great numbers of turkeys moving eastward somewhere between Muskegon and Saginaw, Michigan. There were turkeys as far as he could see. It was a fall with a large crop of mast. A movement of wild turkeys was once witnessed by Thompson (1926:145) when he was living between the Little Black and Current rivers in southeastern Missouri. He wrote: "Our farm boasted the only watering pond during drought between the two rivers. The acorn crop along the Little Black River had been a complete failure. In the hardwood, mountainous region, acorns of all kinds were abundant. One Saturday afternoon I discovered the migration; hundreds and hundreds of turkeys heading straight for our pond in the timber. It was during the month of October, and for three days I saw myriads of turkeys near the pond. They came, then drank and moved off into the northwest hills."

It is difficult to evaluate the statement of Ketchum (1865:78) that Point Pelee, Ontario, was an important point of departure for turkeys and several other species of animals. They passed from island to island by flying or swimming in summer or traveling on the ice in winter. Since it is eight miles from the tip of Point Pelee to Pelee Island, no turkey could make the crossing except on the ice. It may have been assumed that turkeys seen on the end of the Point intended to depart over the water. There are numerous references in the literature to flocks of turkeys seen on sand spits projecting into lakes and streams. The use of these places is logical. The turkeys could get grit and water, and loaf while having an almost uninterrupted view of approaching enemies.

Burning could cause a migration of turkeys by destroying food and cover. One writer ("X," 1886) states that burning of the region around Fort Sustly [Camp Supply], Oklahoma, in 1884 and 1885, destroyed the food supply. The turkeys left in large numbers going southward and eastward. The burnings occurred in late fall and the turkeys did not return. In January, 1886, he went south to the Canadian to hunt. Here the country had also been burned, and turkeys were scarce.

Turkeys will leave in fall areas inhospitable for wintering even though the food supply is still ample. Concerning the turkeys of Garrett County, Maryland, Browning (1928:142) said: "During the winter, the turkeys used to leave the glades, and go to the Potomac and Cheat Rivers to feed on the steep hills, where the ground was less covered with snow; and as soon as the snow melted, they returned to the glades in immense numbers. There they remained, and fed on the grasshoppers until cold weather came on again."

Turkeys in New Mexico and Arizona spend the summer at an altitude of 7,000 to 9,500 feet, then move downward in autumn. Food was plentiful on the Coconino National Forest in Arizona in the fall of 1947, but the turkeys started for their winter ranges about September 4 (Hall, 1948). The same fall, on the Apache National Forest, turkeys began their departure on August 25 although some remained on the summer ranges until October 15 (Hall, 1948). At this time, the wind, sleet, and snow were responsible for their departure. Food plots failed to hold the birds. Acorns and piñon nuts were abundant on most of the winter ranges in Arizona in the fall of 1948, yet the migration started the middle of September (Hall, 1949). The wintering and nesting ranges of Merriam's turkey may be twenty-five to forty miles apart (Ligon, 1946:8). In winter, according to Reeves (1954), the turkeys will remain as close to their summer range as the condition of the snow will permit.

Turkeys have been seen in the Mount Eden area, five miles north of Flagstaff, Arizona, in December only. This indicates that Mount Eden is on a migration route (Pugh, 1954:122). In the fall of 1948, turkeys in Colorado moved south and returned in the spring of 1949. One flock of twenty-five birds moved northwest for seven miles in late February or early March (Burget, 1949). Turkeys began moving to higher elevations in Arizona on March 3, 1949, and, by March 31, were found over a large part of the White Mountains where few, if any, wintered (Hall, 1949.1). On the Apache National Forest, return to the summer range began on March 10, 1950, the turkeys having been on their winter range less than five months (Hall, 1950). Walker (1951:12) states that in southern Texas a flock wintering within a radius of five miles may spread out eighteen to twenty miles to rear young and spend the summer. The Turtle Creek area of Kerr County is one of the most productive of turkeys. Here the shift from the winter roost to the summer range is not over five miles (Walker, 1951.1:30). In Menard and Kimble counties the shift is seven to eighteen and a half miles.

Many of the "islands" occupied by Merriam's turkey must have been reached by emigration across deserts or semideserts. Water would be the most essential requirement during the emigration. If this took place during the summer rains, or when there was snow, there was a good chance for a successful passage. The uniformity of this race suggests that interchange between the islands must have been quite frequent formerly. Spicer (1957) was informed by Levon Lee that a cowboy saw a flock of turkeys traveling in a desert near the Animas Mountains in southwestern New Mexico.

In the fall of 1932, Richard Wetherill, formerly with the U.S. Forest Service, traced a flock of turkeys for several miles in Sandoval County. The birds were moving west to Mount Taylor from San Ysidro.

One of the clearest cases of true emigration is described by Spicer (l.c.). In November and early December, 1955, about 1,000 of the 1,500 turkeys resident on Mount Taylor, New Mexico, dispersed in all directions. During the winter of 1955–56 there were numerous reports of turkeys being seen in submarginal territory ten to thirty miles from Mount Taylor, to reach which they had to cross desert or semidesert. The male to female ratio of the resident population was 70 to 100 in 1954, 74 to 100 in 1955, and 170 to 100 in 1956. The latter ratio shows that the females were more prone to migrate than the males. The average flock size in May of 1954 was 2.75; in 1955, 5.87; and in 1956, 2.42. Food and water were not factors. About the only logical reason for the emigration was the high density of the population.

An apparent emigration of turkeys in 1951 from the Graham Mountains, Arizona, is mentioned by Knopp (1959:17). Turkeys—hens only— were seen in the nearby Gila and Galiuro mountains that had no native population. To reach them the birds had to cross at least ten miles of desert grassland. The habitat of the new areas was no better than that which the birds had left.

Some experimental wandering is normal for the turkey. This trait has enabled it to reoccupy areas from which the original population had been extirpated because of weather or other causes. The severe winter of 1842–43 virtually exterminated the turkey in Wisconsin. A party of Milwaukee hunters in December, 1852, killed seven wild turkeys on

Rock Prairie, Rock County. The birds were stated to have come in from Illinois (Schorger, 1942:180). Their presence could scarcely be explained otherwise. It is well known that the present turkey population in southwestern New York is due to birds that emigrated from Pennsylvania. Recently, a flock of about two hundred turkeys appeared in Cowley County, Kansas, where they had long been extinct (Hanzlick, 1960). The logical conclusion is that they drifted in from Oklahoma.

The best examples of "colonization" are to be found in the discontinuous range of the turkey in the Southwest. For example, Merriam's turkey formerly occurred in the Guadalupe Mountains, Texas. There would be no special difficulty for turkeys to move eastward from the Sacramento Mountains in New Mexico to the Guadalupes and follow them southward into Texas. Ligon (1946:21) was apparently mistaken in his belief that the turkeys found at Valverde (near modern Elmendorf) were only winter residents and had drifted down from the Magdalena Mountains. They were once permanent residents here. Wislizenus (1848:37) was just below Valverde on July 31, 1846, when he recorded that there were many turkeys in the cottonwoods.

8

Feeding Habits and Foods

THE TURKEY CONSUMES a great variety of animal and plant foods. By far the greater part is from plants. Mast is consumed in the largest quantity when procurable, but some succulent plant material is essential. The food eaten depends largely on what is available. The yield of mast, e.g., is dependent upon the geographical area and the season. It may be abundant one year and practically absent the next. Test plots in Missouri yielded 574 pounds of seeds and mast per acre in 1938 and only 128 pounds in 1939 (Dalke, 1953). There may be a large crop of acorns but if they are heavily infested with the larvae of weevils (*Balaninus*), edibility will be of short duration. The bear oak (*Quercus ilicifolia*), though having an abundance of acorns in autumn, has its disadvantages (Howard, 1938). It grows in dense stands to the exclusion of herbaceous plants, hence it is lightly used by turkeys and other game except at the edges. Openings made with a bulldozer provided a variety of foods. In Pennsylvania, openings made with this machine were thought to be of little value to turkeys (Forbes and Harney, 1952:74). The desirability of making clearings will depend upon ecological conditions.

Deer, rodents, hogs, and other animals compete with the turkey for mast. Catesby (1754:x) wrote that turkeys in some winters become very lean from the shortage of food caused by the passenger pigeons (*Ectopistes migratorius*) that devoured the acorns and other mast. But competition from pigeons is a thing of the past. Secondary foods are usually so abundant that Bailey *et al.* (1951:22) doubt if turkeys starve directly from a mast failure.

TIME AND METHOD OF FEEDING

Turkeys usually feed in the morning and late afternoon, and rest during the middle of the day, but some feeding is done at any time. The method of feeding is well described by Jordan (1898:350) : "In the early morning, all things favorable, their first movement is in search of food, which search they undertake with characteristic vigor and energy, scratching up and turning over the dry leaves and decaying vegetation if in the late fall and winter. A double purpose is gained in turning over the dry leaves, that of gathering various seeds or mast, and of obtaining all manner of insects, of which they are very fond, and which constitute a large part of their food supply. There is no fowl of the gallinaceous order that requires and destroys more of the insects than wild turkeys. They are as omnivorous as the human race. They will scratch with great earnestness over a considerable space, then all at once, by a peculiar sort of espionage or system, start off and move rapidly, sometimes raising their broad wings and flapping them against their sides, as if to stretch or yawn, while others leap and skip and waltz about. Then they will all march off in one direction for 100 to 300 yards. Suddenly when one finds a morsel of some kind to eat and begins to scratch up the leaves, the whole flock will do likewise, and they will keep it up until another large space, perhaps half an acre or an acre of land is so gone over. What induces them to scratch up one place so thoroughly and leave others untouched would seem a mystery to the inexperienced; but close observation will show such scratching indicates the presence of some kind of food hidden under the leaves."

Most of the food is obtained on or close to the ground. In Florida, turkeys occasionally fly into the oaks to secure acorns (Allen and Neill, 1955:38). Obtaining food from shrubs is described by Burget (1957:27). They fly into tall shrubs, such as thornapple (*Crataegus*) and skunkberry (*Rhus trilobata*), and alight. If pricked by a thornapple spine they yelp but continue to feed industriously. On the tough and limber branches of the skunkberry, they teeter up and down and pick the fruit rapidly. They do not fly into rose bushes but secure the hips by jumping upward three or four feet. When the snow is deep in Arizona, turkeys have been known to fly into juniper trees (*Juniperus scopulorum*) and feed on the berries (Reeves, 1950:10).

194

The seeds of grasses are obtained by stripping the heads, the sound of which can be heard at a considerable distance. A wild gobbler raised by Rutledge (1941.1:84) would fly to the top of stacks of rice and, standing on a sheaf, would strip the heavy heads.

On January 5, 1961, Hayden (1961:5) observed a flock of fifteen to twenty turkeys feeding on grapes. They were very noisy and flew from vine to vine. The birds feeding in the top of a vine dislodged fruits, which were eaten quickly by the birds on the ground. Gradually the turkeys on the ground replaced those feeding in the vines. Following a storm on December 31, 1960, tracks in the snow had indicated that the flock, during a period of five days, had not moved more than three hundred yards, which was the extent of the grape tangle. The same method of feeding was observed in three different areas.

EATING BUDS

Budding is resorted to in an emergency. Randall (1933:71) states that when acorns are abundant, turkeys will feed upon them almost entirely; but in the Adirondacks when snow covered the ground his wild turkeys budded to a limited extent. When there is a mast failure or flooding, especially in the South where large areas of land are frequently covered with water, the turkeys live on buds (Jordan, 1898:350). They fly into the trees instead of moving to dry land and will persist in remaining in these trees for two or three months, with the water five to twenty-five feet deep beneath them. During this period they subsist upon the green buds of the trees and the few grape and brier seeds that remain on the vines and that can be reached from the limbs on which they are perched. If the overflow occurs in December, January, or February, they must move to dry land or starve because the buds are not sufficiently developed to be utilized. No birds were known to have starved to death, but at times they were greatly emaciated. The trees are covered with buds and blossoms in March and April, and if the overflow occurs at this season, the turkeys have an easy living. The buds of the ash (*Fraxinus*), hackberry (*Celtis*), pin oak (*Quercus*), and the yellow bloom of the birch (*Betula*) are preferred by the turkeys. With the beech (*Fagus*) and some other trees, it is the bloom which is eaten. Turkeys keep in fair flesh on a bud diet, but it is not as palatable as when mast or grain is eaten. Jordan knew a flock in Alabama to feed for two months on hackberry buds although a flight of three hundred yards would have taken them to dry land. Robinson (1921) discusses budding but all of his information appears to have been taken from Jordan.

FEEDING IN SNOW

Deep snow makes it difficult for turkeys to obtain sufficient food. Opinions differ as to the depth of the snow through which turkeys will scratch to reach the ground. Mershon (1923:33) has stated that they were so fond of buckwheat that they would scratch off the snow "no matter how deep." On the other hand, Bailey *et al.* (1951:19) write: "Observations during the winter of 1947–48 showed conclusively that a six-inch snow cover for a period of only three days was sufficient to cause turkeys to strip the needles and buds from hemlock and beech seedlings." During cold weather and snowstorms in January in West Virginia, the feeding radius of the turkeys was reduced to one-half to three-fourths of a mile (Glover, 1948). They scratched through snow twelve inches deep under the beech trees. During extended periods of soft snow the turkeys did considerable flying. They would fly to the ground from the roost, walk a few yards, then fly to the feeding grounds. When the snow was less than ten inches deep, or crusted, they walked. North of Mancos, Colorado, in the winter of 1948–49, when deep snows prevailed, the turkeys fed for three weeks exclusively on rose hips (Burget, 1957:28). They flew from the roost to the rose thicket and back again.

Turkeys, to secure food, take advantage of the pawing ability of deer. In Pennsylvania they follow the deer and feed where they have pawed through the snow (Grahame, 1953). Merriam's turkey in South Dakota is stated to forage successfully in snow that is four inches deep (Anon., 1958:27). If deeper, they will follow the deer and, when a hole is made in the snow, jump in and take what the deer has uncovered.

Turkeys will take advantage of deer at any season. The following incident is recorded: "As I looked into my melon patch one day I discovered that a number of deer and wild turkeys had taken possession of it and that after they had dined on melons at my expense were engaged in a little innocent dance among the vines. The turkeys would flap their wings and strike and jump against the deer, while the latter danced and jumped around the turkeys like lambs at play" (Tathwell and Maxey, 1897:137). This was not play but a contest for food. In March, 1956, Quenton Breland took me to a chufa patch on the Leaf River Cooperative Wildlife Management Area, Mississippi. Several wild turkeys and deer ran from the field on our approach. He explained that the deer will paw out the chufa plants to expose the nuts and eat those in sight. The recovery, however, is small. The turkeys then take over and by scratching secure nearly every nut. Turkeys, when feeding, will not only attempt to drive other turkeys from their immediate vicinity but young deer as well. He had seen yearling deer driven away by turkeys. The latter would beat the legs of the deer with their wings. The deer would attempt to butt the turkeys or strike them with their front feet, but the birds were too nimble to be touched.

Dominance by individual turkeys persists during feeding. Regarding a flock of wild turkeys in his cornfield, Browning (1928:143) stated that one gobbler feeding at a corn shock would not allow another to feed at it. While feeding on an ear, if another turkey was heard on the opposite side of the shock, he would run around and drive the bird away.

Distance Traveled in Feeding

The turkey in northern Florida is likely to be regular and pass a certain point daily at a given time. Less regularity is shown in southern Florida, and the course is not always circular (Allen and Neill, 1955:38). A flock in Missouri while feeding traveled at the rate of one mile in five hours and twenty minutes from 1:40 to 3:00 P.M., and one mile in one hour and twenty-five minutes from 3:00 to 4:15 P.M. (Dalke et al., 1946:27). The speed of travel while feeding, according to Burget (1957:27), is two miles per hour. The distance that turkeys travel in a day depends upon the supply of food. If plentiful, a mile would be the maximum (Jordan, 1898:350). A flock under the observation of Steele (1957) in Oklahoma spent most of its time on one square mile along a river but did use temporarily lands five or six miles distant. Askins (1931:71) gave the cruising range for turkeys in southern Illinois as a circuit of about ten miles. They fed until about 10:00 o'clock, then went for water. He thought that the greatest weakness in the turkey was its habit of following the same path in feeding, rendering it much more vulnerable to the hunter. During fall and winter in Missouri, turkeys came into the cornfields to feed at certain hours of the day, arriving and departing by regular trails (Goebel, 1889:129).

During the first snow of the season, a warden in Augusta County, Virginia, tracked a flock 5.5 miles from its roost to the point where the birds left the road. This distance was covered between 7:00 and 10:00 A.M. (Mosby and Handley, 1943:231). The average daily range in the Kentucky Woodlands Refuge is ten to fifteen miles in fall and winter (Baker, 1943:27). When food is abundant in Alabama, a flock may range over less than four hundred acres. By late fall and early winter this may increase to one thousand acres. Gobblers during the height of the breeding season may range over 25,000 acres (Wheeler, 1946.1:141). Davis (1949:64) states that turkeys range widest in upland forests. One flock was known to cover an area over a mile in width and six to eight miles in length.

Regarding feeding activities, A. C. Martin *et al.* (1939:571) wrote: "During a single day of undisturbed feeding, a bird may often travel 2 miles or more, yet field observations indicate that while feeding there is a minimum of waste motion; a turkey seldom takes a step except to pick up a fragment of food that appears more desirable than any within its reach." Turkeys may feed industriously at one place then move one-half mile or more before resuming feeding. A flock is scattered while feeding but any laggard quickens its pace to join the loose assembly. There is frequent lifting and crossing of the wings on the back. It was found that there was no regularity in timing in moving over the range. One flock under observation for a period of two weeks arrived in the same locality at times varying from 7:30 A.M. to 4:00 P.M. (Mosby and Handley, 1943:152).

SCRATCHING

Much of the food of the turkey is located in fall and winter by scratching. Following a short step forward, one foot is placed about six inches ahead of the other, drawn backwards and outwards, then the other foot is brought into action. The result is a V-shaped mark about eighteen inches long. According to Davis (1949:70), old gobblers scratch at the base of large trees, especially pines, where food is most plentiful. The entire surface is laid bare and the covering materials thrown well back. If scratching is general over an area, it is the work of hens and young. Along the Roanoke River, Virginia, in December, Judd (1905:49) found places where turkeys had scratched in the dry oak leaves to a depth of two or three inches. The scratched places were circular and fifteen to eighteen inches in diameter. Among the white oaks where the turkeys had been searching for acorns, there were fully fifty scratching places, as many as five occurring on one square rod.

ALERTNESS WHILE FEEDING

There is an old and persistent belief that turkeys when feeding have one of their members on guard. Kester (1928:127) wrote in 1827 that feeding flocks have sentinels on a fence or stump. A female with out-stretched neck in the top of a piñon pine in northern New Mexico was thought by Sheldon (1919) to be a sentinel. Nicholson (1928) observed five gobblers feeding on a burned savannah in Florida. One bird stood with head and neck erect as if on guard. According to Rutledge (1941.1:101), a pair of gobblers while dusting kept guard alternately.

The experience of Guthrie (1926) on a December day in the White Mountains, Arizona, is given as follows: "I was riding along through the lower reaches of the foothills, and began to hear a great noise of turkeys, as if hundreds were yelping. I got off my horse and walked cautiously ahead, the noise becoming clearer and louder. . . . Below was a wonderful sight. Scattered through the swale must have been nearly a hundred turkeys. Some were scratching; some busily picking off red-caps from wild rose clumps; several young gobblers fighting, with their necks twisted around each other; and several standing on logs or fallen timber. Very soon, however, I heard a distinct 'putt, putt, putt' to one side, and looking that way saw a big gobbler, on a slight rise to the left, and quite a little higher than the flock in the swale, standing perfectly erect and alert. He was the lookout, and was giving the alarm, for no sooner had he begun to 'sound off' than every bird 'came to attention,' as it were, and in a few seconds [they] were running and half-flying over the next ridge and out of sight."

No one turkey has an assignment to stay on guard. Nearly every member of a flock will at some time or other raise its head and become alert. As Mosby and Handley (1943:151) state, it is difficult to approach a flock of wild turkeys without detection even though the birds are feeding and scratching noisily. At least one turkey will be surveying the surroundings, and any unusual movement or noise causes it to issue a warning "putt-putt" or "quit" note that places the flock on the alert. A hen with poults is on guard constantly.

Insects form the most important food of young turkeys. Stevenson (1915:59) mentions that the Zuñi Indians feed the blossoms of wild four-o'clocks (*Quamoclidion multiflorum*) to newly hatched turkeys. If there is a sound reason for this, it remains unknown. Audubon (1831:7) wrote that turkeys are scarce in rainy seasons since the poults rarely survive a thorough wetting. The mother overcomes this danger by plucking the buds of the spicebush (*Benzoin*) and feeding them to her young. This statement has the flavor of folklore. Brooks (1933) found that domestic male turkeys grow considerably faster than the females. They also show an efficiency in the utilization of food 25 to 50 per cent greater than the females for each pound of weight acquired between eighteen and twenty-eight weeks of age.

Amount of Food Eaten

The crop is capable of great distension. It may hold 400 cc. but may appear full when containing only 50 to 60 cc. of food (Martin *et al.*, 1939:571). According to Burget (1957:27), a large gobbler will consume a pound of food at one meal. During the hunting season more than a pint (473 cc.) of food has been taken from a single crop. In Virginia several crops contained slightly more than one pound of food. The largest volume was 386 cc. (Mosby and Handley, 1943:153). When a turkey is killed, there is no way to determine that it had satisfied its hunger. The volume of food in the crop depends upon the time of day; it is usually smallest when the bird leaves the roost in the morning.

It is stated by Kozicky and Metz (1948:30) that, contrary to the prevailing opinion, turkeys feed longer and more regularly in March and April than at any other time of the year. During these months the females eat more than the males.

The amount of food necessary to keep a wild turkey in good condition is not known with accuracy. It has been postulated that if three-fourths of a turkey's diet is acorns, and half a pound of acorns is the daily con-sumption, then fifty pounds of acorns will be required to support the bird for one hundred days. To do this, estimating one turkey per fifty acres, each acre must provide one pound of acorns (Reid and Goodrum, 1957:Table 10).

Animal Foods

Most gallinaceous birds will eat small reptiles, but they form a minor item in the diet of the turkey. A dusky salamander (*Desmognathus fuscus*) was eaten in West Virginia (Bailey and Rindell, 1960:[37]). In New Mexico a horned toad (*Phrynosoma*) was devoured (Ligon, 1946:62). Audubon (1831:9) found lizards in the crops of turkeys. Instances of lizards being devoured are also recorded for Missouri (Woodruff, 1908) and Alabama (Good and Webb, 1940).

The eating of snakes is not uncommon. Hay (1892:527) states that the gartersnake, *Eutainia* (*Thamnophis*) *sirtalis*, was preyed upon by turkeys in Indiana. A small snake (*Natrix*) was found in the crop of a turkey collected at Holopaw, Florida (Howell, 1932:196). The swallowing of a snake, judging from Caton's (1877:327) account, has its tribulations: "I once saw a half-grown turkey acting very strangely, and stopped a little way off to notice his actions. I soon observed that he was in conflict with a snake about ten inches long. He would pick it up and throw it, and again seize it as soon as it struck the ground. At length, after the snake seemed pretty well disabled, he seized it by the head and began to swallow it. The part of the snake yet in sight thrashed around vigorously, sometimes winding itself around the head and neck of the bird. This was too much for the turkey, and he threw it up and went at it again to make it more quiet, and then another attempt was made to swallow it; but it was not till the third effort was made that success was achieved, and then the process occupied several minutes, the tail of the snake being all the time active till it finally disappeared."

The utilization of crustaceans is fairly extensive, especially in the Southeast. Of New England, Wood (1865:32) wrote that when snow covered the ground, the wild turkeys resorted to the seashore in search of shrimps and other aquatic animals at low tide. Barton (1805) reminds us that it was not generally known that wild turkeys feed on shellfish and various species of reptiles. Parenthetically, he states that turkeys will survive for a considerable length of time on crushed brick and water without apparent ill effects. He was apparently unaware of the bird's strong resistance to starvation.

Fiddler crabs (*Uca*) are consumed in quantity. Lyell (1845:133) wrote of the domestic turkey: "A planter of this country [Georgia] told me it was amusing to see a flock of turkeys driven down for the first time from the interior to feed on the crabs in the marine marshes. They, at first, walk about in a ludicrous state of alarm, expecting their toes to be pinched, but after a time, one bolder than the rest is tempted by hunger to snap up a small fiddler after which the rest fall to and devour them by thousands." In the coastal swamps and rice fields of South Carolina, fiddler crabs and shad frogs (*Rana spenocephala*) are important items in the food of the wild turkey (Davis, 1949:72). Crayfish were eaten in Alabama (Good and Webb, 1940), and in Mississippi where the turkeys waded into the water "feather deep" in order to secure them ("Southern," 1900).

Grasshoppers form the largest item among the animal foods of turkeys. Roberts (1901) dwells on their fondness for these insects. Death of domestic turkeys has been attributed to the eating of grasshoppers (*Melanoplus femur-rubrum* and *M. mexicanus*), the distended crop actually being punctured by the spines of the legs (Wickware, 1945). No mortality among wild birds from this cause has been recorded. The condition of the grasshoppers fed to poults was of marked effect (Milby and Penquite, 1940). The grasshoppers, mainly *Melanoplus differentialis*, had an average crude protein content of 62.8 per cent on the dry basis. When one-half of the protein content of the ration fed was supplemented with one-fifth of a pound of frozen whole grasshoppers, the poults grew faster than on the control ration. All of the protein, largely vegetable, in the starting mash could be replaced with grasshoppers killed by cooking in a steam pressure cooker or by freezing, then sun dried, without affecting normal growth. When these insects were killed by exposure to the sun under glass, then sun dried, and fed to the poults, heavy mortality and poor growth resulted.

There is so much variation in the foods reported, even within the same state, that it is preferable to give the principal foods by states. Several hundred food items have been eaten by turkeys but most of them are of minor value. For example, drupes of moonseed (*Menisperum canadense*) were utilized by only one turkey according to A. L. Nelson, Patuxent Research Refuge, cited by Breiding (1946). Only a seed or two of broom sedge (*Andropogon virginicus*) was found in 20 of 350 turkey stomachs examined (Davison and Van Dersal, 1941).

The seeds of *Crotalaria spectabilis* are toxic to chickens, quail, and doves, but as many as a thousand seeds did not poison turkeys according to experiments made in Florida (Thomas, 1934).

Mast is one of the most desirable of foods for turkeys, especially during the winter months. When there is a failure of mast, the secondary foods become important. Succulent foods, such as blades of members of the grass family, are essential in the diet of the turkey, particularly during the breeding season, on account of their vitamin content. In parts of the Southwest, grasses and their seeds form the main food of the turkey. Hundreds of plant items are consumed. In the last analysis, it is availability that determines what will be eaten.

Alabama.—In winter the thirty-eight crops and gizzards examined contained 84.55 per cent by volume of plant and 15.45 per cent of animal matter (Webb, 1941).

	Per cent
Acorns (Principally *Quercus stellata* and *Q. falcata*)	63.20
Beechnuts (*Fagus*)	4.61
Dogwood (*Cornus*) fruit	3.19
Hickory (*Hicoria* [*Carya*] spp.) fruit	2.95
Gum (*Nyssa*) seed	2.31
Grape (*Vitis*) fruit	1.42
Miscellaneous	6.87

The animal matter consisted chiefly of the grasshopper, *Schistocera americana*, and a few of *Melanoplus*.

In spring the stomachs collected March 15–April 15 contained 88.29 per cent plant and 11.71 per cent animal matter (Good and Webb, 1940).

	Per cent
Oaks (*Quercus*), acorns, leaves, catkins	40.13
Gum (*Nyssa*) seed	3.91
Beech (*Fagus*), fruit, bracts, buds and twigs	3.79
Dogwood (*Cornus florida*) fruit	3.16
Papaw (*Asimina*) fruit	1.91
Sedges, seeds, flowers, stems, leaves	5.30
Herbs and forbs, leaves, seeds, and flowers	4.74

The animal matter consisted chiefly of Coleoptera (*Phyllophaga*, *Passalus cornutus*, *Sitophilus granarius*) and Orthoptera, with small numbers of roaches, ants, spiders, millipedes, ticks, crayfishes, snails, and a lizard.

Arizona.—In August in the San Francisco Mountain region, turkeys fed on gooseberries (*Ribes rusbyi*), and in September on piñon nuts (*Pinus edulis*) (Merriam, 1890:89). The turkeys collected by Goldman (1902:127) had been feeding largely on piñon nuts. Though he was told by old hunters that turkeys feed on berries of the cedar (*Juniperus utahensis*), none were found in the crops even though the berries were very abundant. (It is doubtful if these berries would be eaten in quantity where piñon nuts were available.) Kennerly (1856:7) found them to be feeding on the berries of the rough-barked cedar (*Juniperus pachydermata*) and other cedars.

An examination of twenty-four crops and forty-three droppings collected in the fall from the San Carlos Indian Reservation, was made by Murie (1946). The seed heads of at least eight kinds of grasses were eaten, the most important being *Muhlenbergia phleoides*. Ragweed (*Ambrosia psilostachya*), mainly seeds, was found in more crops than any other item. Goldeneye (*Viguiera*), sunflower (*Helianthus annus*), and *Eriogoneum pharnaceoides* were also important, as were the seeds of yellow pine (*P. ponderosa*), and acorns when available. They are fond of the fruits of wild mulberry, prickly pear, and giant cactus (Bendire, 1892:119).

Extensive data are given by Reeves (1950, 1951) on the food habits by month from March, 1950, through October, 1951. A few crops were examined but the analyses were made mainly on droppings. Grasses and forbs form the chief food items throughout the year, their green leafage being utilized extensively during the summer. Otherwise, the principal foods in March were acorns, juniper berries, pine needles, and insects. April through October, turkeys ate: acorns, juniper berries, florets of pinegrass (*Blepharoneuron tricholepsis*) and love grass (*Eragrostis* sp.), achenes and green foliage of dandelion (*Taraxacum* sp.), achenes of sunflower (*Helianthus* sp.), seeds of sedges (*Carex* sp., *Cyperus* sp.), wheatgrass (*Agropyron* sp.), bluegrass (*Poa* sp.), panic grass (*Panicum* sp.) wild millet (*Echinochloa* sp.), dropseed (*Sporobolus* sp.), knotweed (*Polygonum* sp.), muhlygrass (*Muhlenbergia* sp.), drupes of sumac (*Rhus glabra*), beetles (*Coleoptera*), lamellicorn beetles (Scarabaeidae), grasshoppers (Locustidae). November through February, items in the turkeys' diet included: Juniper berries, seeds of sweet clover (*Melilotus alba*), cultivated oat (*Avena sativa*), love grass (*Eragrostis* sp.), dropseed (*Sporobolus* sp.), grama grass (*Bouteloua* sp.), sedge (*Cyperus* sp.), tarweed (*Madia* sp.), rose hips (*Rosa* sp.), drupes of sumac (*Rhus glabra*), seeds and needles of pine (*Pinus* sp.), and fragments of insects.

Arkansas.—Acorns of pin and white oaks were eaten, also "hickory" nuts on which turkeys grow fat (Geombeck, 1890).

The crops and gizzards of twenty-two turkeys taken in April and 1,026 droppings collected throughout most of the year, from the White River bottoms of the southeastern part of the state, were examined by Meanley (1956). Based on frequency of occurrence, the principal plant foods were: in April, hackberries (*Celtis laevigata*), pecans (*Carya illinoensis*), fruit and seeds of tupelo gum (*Nyssa sylvatica*), acorns (*Quercus*), seeds of hawthorns (*Crataegus*), grapes (*Vitis*), seeds of rattan vine (*Berchemia scandens*), fruit and seeds of poison ivy (*Toxicodendron radicans*), and seeds of Solomon's seal (*Polygonatum*); in June, berries (*Rubus*), achenes of sedge (*Carex*), acorns, seeds of panic grass (*Panicum*), seeds of swamp privet (*Forestiera acuminata*), and leaves of sorrel (*Rumex acetosella*); in summer, seeds of crab grass (*Digitaria sanguinalis*), hackberry, storax (*Styrax americana*), spangletop grass (*Leptochloa panicoides*), and grapes; in fall, seeds of crab grass, barnyard grass (*Echinochloa crus-galli*), spangletop grass, panic grass, buckthorn (*Bumelia*), and grapes; in winter, acorns, grass blades (Gramineae), seeds of poison ivy and of hawthorn. The principal animal foods were: stinkbugs (*Nezara viridula* and *Solubea pugnax*), wheel bug (*Arilus cristatus*), fall armyworm (*Laphygma frugiperda*) and spotted cucumber beetle (*Diabrotica undecimpunctata*).

California.—Staples in the turkey's diet are insects and green plants in spring, grasshoppers and seeds in summer, and acorns and other mast in winter (Burger, 1954:199). In autumn, acorns and fruits of the manzanita (*Arctostaphylos*) and coffeeberry (*Rhamnus*) are generally available (Burger, 1954.1:144).

Colorado.—Turkeys eat acorns and pine seeds (*Pinus edulis* and *P. ponderosa*). There is little evidence of eating juniper berries in quantity. Also eaten are seeds of grasses and oats, rose hips, fruits of snowberry, skunk bush (*Rhus trilobata*), barberry (*Berberis* sp.), and kinnikinnick (also leaves), and, in winter, succulents at open springs, alfalfa shoots, and grasses. Pine needles are not taken during regular feeding, dry grass being preferred (Burget, 1946:5). In midsummer and fall, seeds of oat grass (*Danthonia intermedia*), wheat grass (*Agropyron* spp.), and awnless brome grass (*Bromus inermis*) are important, and elk sedge (*Carex geyeri*) in winter (Burget, 1948).

Food based on 126 crops taken in early fall, 1949–54 inclusive, in per cent by volume, consisted of: miscellaneous vegetable matter, 26 per cent; cultivated oats, 25; barley, 10; grass leaves, 6; acorns, 6; dandelions, 5; bristle grass, 5; fruit of kinnikinnick, 5; and grasshoppers, 12 (Burget, 1957:21).

Florida.—A specimen collected in January on the Aucilla River had eaten: acorns (65 per cent); 172 wax-myrtle berries; 79 seeds of hornbeam (*Carpinus caroliniana*); 63 seeds of poison ivy (*Rhus radicans*); 18 seeds of rattan vine (*Berchemia scandens*); and 3 per cent insect remains. An April specimen from Osceola County had eaten: 77 seeds of black gum (*Nyssa biflora*); 33 seeds of greenbrier (*Smilax*); 65 seeds of blue-eyed grass (*Sisyrinchium*); 625 seeds of rush grass (dropseed) (*Sporobolus*); 5 per cent of huckleberries; a small snake, and a few insects and spiders (Howell, 1932:196). For another specimen, Judd (1905:51) reported: seeds of the longleaf pine; seeds of *Panicum minimum*; berries of the spicebush (*Benzoin benzoin*), wax myrtle (*Myrica cerifera*), and false Solomon's seal (*Polygonatum* sp.); tubers of the groundnut (*Apios apios*); seeds of tupelo gum; and acorns.

The principal winter foods are acorns, pine seeds, sweet gum (*Liquidamber styraciflua*) seeds, cabbage palm (*Sabal palmetto*) seeds, partridge peas, and seeds of "brown-heads" (Allen and Neill, 1955:7).

The contents of thirty-two crops in winter consisted of 53.8 per cent by volume of acorns, mainly *Quercus virginiana*. The number of acorns in a crop varied from 1 to 137.5, and weight from 2 to 225 gr. Other items were: slash pine (*Pinus caribea*) seeds, 11.6 per cent; grass (*Paspalum* sp.) seeds, 10.3 per cent; and cabbage palm seeds, 10.3 per cent. The 2,775 droppings contained chiefly leaves of Gramineae, and remains of seeds of *Paspalum, Panicum, Quercus, Ilex opaca, Zea mays,* and *Myrica* (Schemnitz, 1956). Gainey (1954) thinks the most important winter foods are provided by the oaks, wax myrtle (*Myrica cerifera*), gums (*Nyssa*), holly (*Ilex glabra*), and carpet grass (*Axonopus compressus*).

The crops of ten turkeys taken during 1954 on the Collier Wildlife area showed a high utilization of green vegetation and the berries of wax myrtle (Garrison, 1954). This was attributed to the slight fruiting in 1953 of the cabbage palm, which is normally an important source of food. Shortage of high quality foods led to the consumption of the seeds of hard-head (yellow-eyed grass, *Xyris* sp.) to the extent of 46.7 per cent. Normally, they are rarely eaten. Cypress mast is an important food. The crops of thirty-two turkeys from four areas contained mainly berries of the wax myrtle, acorns, carpet grass seeds, gum fruit, and berries of ink-berry (*Ilex glabra*).

Georgia.—Little has been published. Long ago, Hawkins (1848:21) wrote that wild turkeys ate the fruit of the dwarf saw palmetto (*Serenoa repens*). The acorns of *Quercus pumila* are an important food according to Stoddard (1941:151).

Illinois.—In Fulton County in the fall, turkeys like pecans, wild grapes, and insects (Strode, 1893).

Indiana.—Turkeys eat all kinds of forest mast, the different kinds of walnuts, chestnuts, fruit of the papaw (*Asimina*), various fruits as those of "*Symphoria*" (*Symphoricarpos?*), *Rosa*, insects, caterpillars and pupae, beetles, bugs, young twigs, leaves and sprouts, and grass blades (Maximilian, 1858:429).

Iowa.—On the bottom lands at the mouth of Turkey River, there was a rank growth of "horse-weed" producing a black, oily seed of which wild turkeys were very fond (Sherman, 1913:88). The horseweed referred to may be a species of *Polygonum*. In addition to the seed of the horseweed, Peterson (1943) mentions the fruit of the hackberry.

Kansas.—Two legumes, both known as "turkey pea," are mentioned by Hunter (1823:392). One plant grew to a height of eight to ten inches, producing small tubers the size of a hazelnut that the turkeys ate. The other plant grew twelve to eighteen inches high, blossomed profusely in July, and produced a bountiful supply of "small peas" of which turkeys were very fond. The first legume is undoubtedly the hog peanut (*Amphicarpa bracteata*), which does not produce a true tuber but an underground seed. Professor R. L. McGregor, of the University of Kansas, has identified the second plant as hoary pea (*Tephrosia virginiana*).

Kentucky.—Most of Audubon's experience (1831:7, 9) with the habits of the wild turkey was obtained in Kentucky. The food consisted of dewberries, blackberries, strawberries, corn, and grass, with preference for pecans and grapes. Among the animal foods were grasshoppers, beetles, tadpoles, and small lizards.

A hunter killed a turkey with some thirty chestnuts in its crop. He believed that they improved in flesh better when mast was abundant than when feeding only on scattered corn in the fields (J. D. H., 1879). Baker (1943.1) found a dead wild turkey with sixty-four small acorns and a quantity of grass in its crop.

Louisiana.—Turkeys ate oak, chinquapin, beech, and pecan mast; seeds and fruits of dogwood, holly, black gum, and huckleberry; and insects (Kopman, 1921:86).

Maryland.—Acorns were scarce in the winter of 1944–45 (Wilson, 1945:27–33). Analyses of droppings by months were made. For July, 1944, turkeys ate: blackberry (*Rubus* spp.), 50 per cent; wheat, 30 per cent; some domestic cherry, 10 per cent; and in all, twenty-nine identifiable food items. August results were: millet (*Setaria italica*), 40 per cent; wheat (*Triticum*), 30 per cent; blackberry, 10 per cent. September showed: crab grass (*Digitaria*), 30 per cent; grape, 10 per cent; greens, 10 per cent; and flowering dogwood 10 per cent. For October, crab grass was 40 per cent; flowering dogwood, 30 per cent; grape, 20 per cent. In November, green vegetation accounted for 60 per cent; grape, 30 per cent; acorn, 10 per cent. December was mostly grape. January, 1945, turkeys ate: poison ivy (*Toxicodendron*), 30 per cent; greenbrier (*Smilax*), 20 per cent; summer grape (*Vitis aestivalis*), 10 per cent. February showed: grape, 40 per cent; greenbrier, 20 per cent; poison ivy, 10 per cent; and green vegetation, 10 per cent. In March, with the snow gone, green vegetation, mostly wheat, made up 40 per cent of the diet, supplemented by a few acorns. In April, green vegetation rose to 50 per cent, of which bluegrass (*Poa*) and buttercup (*Ranunculus*) formed 20 per cent each. May results were: buttercup, 40 per cent; bluegrass florets, 20 per cent; violet, 10 per cent. For June, wheat was 60 per cent; domestic cherry, 20 per cent.

Analyses of 1,979 droppings, collected June-September, but mainly in August (Wilson, 1946) showed these results: in June the turkeys ate oat grass (*Danthonia spicata*), raspberry (*Rubus*), and panic grass (*Panicum*); in July. wheat and blackberry; in August, wheat, snail, black cherry (*Prunus serotina*); and in September, wheat, crab grass, and flowering dogwood.

Michigan.—Turkeys sometimes wintered on corn left in the shock (Beal, 1903:236). Mershon (1923:33) mentions buckwheat, beechnuts, acorns, and grass seeds. Typical food plants in the Allegan Forest are: white oak (*Quercus alba*), black oak (*Q. velutina*), red oak (*Q. rubra*), beech (*Fagus grandifolia*), black cherry (*Prunus serotina*), flowering dogwood (*Cornus florida*), wild grape (*Vitis* spp.), and greenbrier (*Smilax rotundifolia*) (Wilson and Lewis, 1959:211).

Mississippi.—On December 2, 1820, below the Chickasaw Bluffs, Audubon shot three turkeys, the crops of which were filled with winter grapes. The food of the wild turkey in this state is probably very similar to that in Alabama.

Missouri.—Wild grapes are relished (Goebel, 1889:128). In early summer, turkeys are fond of the shoots of "wild onions" (leeks), according to O'Hanlon (1890:154).

Some of the preferred foods are: panicum (*Panicum barbulatum*), leaves; sedge (*Carex cephalophora*), fruit; hop hornbeam (*Ostrya virginiana*), fruit; oaks, particularly post (*Quercus stellata*) and blackjack (*Q. marilandica*), acorns; hackberry (*Celtis*), fruit; strawberry (*Fragaria virginiana*), fruit; wild rose (*Rosa*), fruit; tick clover (*Desmodium rotundifolium*), flowers, fruit; various species of *Lespedeza*, flowers, leaves, fruit; *Croton capitatus* and *C. monanthogynus*, fruit; flowering spurge (*Euphorbia nutans*), flowers, leaves, fruit; sumac (*Rhus*), fruit; summer grape (*Vitis aestivalis*), young tendrils, fruit; frost grape (*Vitis cordifolia*), leaves, fruit; black gum (*Nyssa sylvatica*), fruit; blueberry (*Vaccinium*), leaves, fruit; bedstraw (*Galium*), fruit; longleaf bluet (*Houstonia longifolia*), fruit. Preferred insect foods are: spiders (Araneida), walking stick (*Diapheromera*), grasshoppers (*Melanoplus*), stinkbug (Pentatomidae), caddis fly (Phryganeidae), robber fly (Asilidae), ground beetle (Carabidae), blister beetle (Meloidae), weevil (*Balaninus*), ichneumon fly (Amblytelinae), and ants (Formicinae) (Blakey, 1937:12, 28–31).

The year-round diet, based on 3,244 droppings, consisted of 76 per cent plant and 24 per cent animal food (Dalke *et al.*, 1942; 1946:27–35). In all, 136 species of plants were utilized. Buttercup (*Ranunculus*), wood sorrel (*Oxalis*), sheep sorrel (*Rumex*), and bluegrass (*Poa*), were favored in spring and early summer, as well as fruits of blackberry (*Rubus*), cherry (*Prunus*), mulberry (*Morus*), and, especially, flowering dogwood (*Cornus florida*.). The diet included insects of forty-three families, principally Acrididae, Pentatomidae, Phasmidae, Carabidae, Curculionidae, Scarabaeidae, and Formicidae.

Nebraska.—During the plagues of Rocky Mountain locusts (*Caloptenus* [*Melanoplus*] *spretus*), wild turkeys fed almost exclusively on them (Aughey, 1878:46). Wild plums (Anon., 1916:225) and acorns are also mentioned (Leach, 1909:22).

New Mexico.—The crop of a turkey taken in the Manzano Mountains in November contained a half pint of the fruiting panicles of a grass (*Muhlenbergia* sp.), grass blades, seeds of cheat, piñon nuts, and other pine seeds (Judd, 1905:51). According to Bailey (1928:233), the diet of turkeys was: "In winter pinyon nuts, acorns, and juniper berries; in summer, flower buds, grass and other seeds, wild oats, wild strawberries, manzanita berries [*Arctostaphylos pungens*], rose haws, fruit of wild mulberry and prickly pear, grasshoppers, crickets, beetles, caterpillars, ants, and other insects."

A turkey killed in the Black Range in February had eaten 76 berries of the alligator juniper (*Juniperus pachyphloea*), 25 piñon nuts, 6 acorns, 30 worms each an inch long, and green grass blades (Ligon, 1946:60–62). Another turkey killed on Black Mountain in late March had consumed 30 piñon nuts and 215 berries of the alligator juniper. Other foods included: blades of bluegrass; foxtail; brome grass; florets and stem fragments of grama grass (*Bouteloua gracilis*); seeds of dropseed grasses (*Sporobolus microspermus* and *Blepharoneuron tricholepsis*), wild rye, wild oats, pine grass, sunflower, Rocky Mountain bee plant (*Cleome serrulata*), ground cherry, and wild buckwheat; fruit of wild grape, sumac (particularly *Rhus trilobata*), and bearberry or kinnikinnick (*Arctostaphylos uvai-ursi*); wild peas; lily buds; rose hips; and tubers of nut grass (*Cyperus*).

A turkey killed in the Pecos Mountains on July 27 at an elevation of over 11,000 feet had eaten mainly grasshoppers and crickets (Bailey, 1904:352). Also eaten were grass seeds, buds of the mariposa lily, strawberries, and beetles.

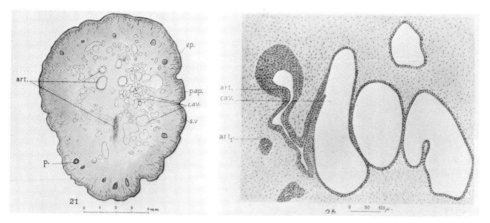

Plate 17a.   Plate 17b.

Plate 17a.—Cross section of frontal caruncle of a male turkey: *ep.*, epidermis; *pap.*, papillae; *sv.*, layer of subepidermic vessels; *p.*, flioplumes; *art.*, branching small arteries; *cav.*, cavernous sinuses. (After Wodzicki [1929].)

Plate 17b.—Direct communication between an artery and a cavernous sinus, *cav.*; oblique section of a helical artery, *art.* (After Wodzicki [1929].)

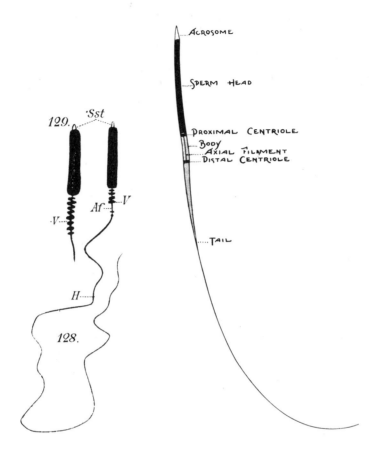

Plate 18a.—Spermatozoon of turkey. (After Ballowitz [1888].)

Plate 18b.—Spermatozoon of turkey. (After Wakely and Kosin [1951].)

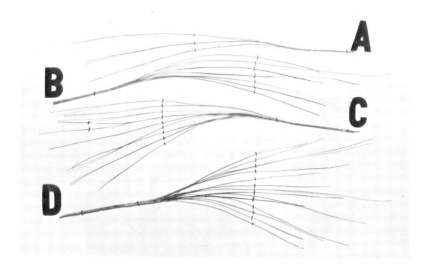

Plate 19a.—Bundles of bristles from the Florida wild turkey. (After Schorger [1957].)

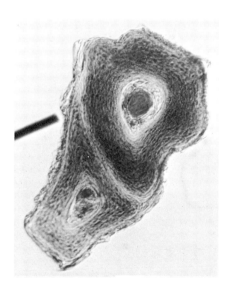

Plate 19b.—Intergrowth of two bristles of the domestic bronze turkey. (After Schorger [1957].)

BASE   MIDDLE   TIP

M. G. MERRIAMI

M. G. SILVESTRIS

M. G. OSCEOLA

M. G. INTERMEDIA

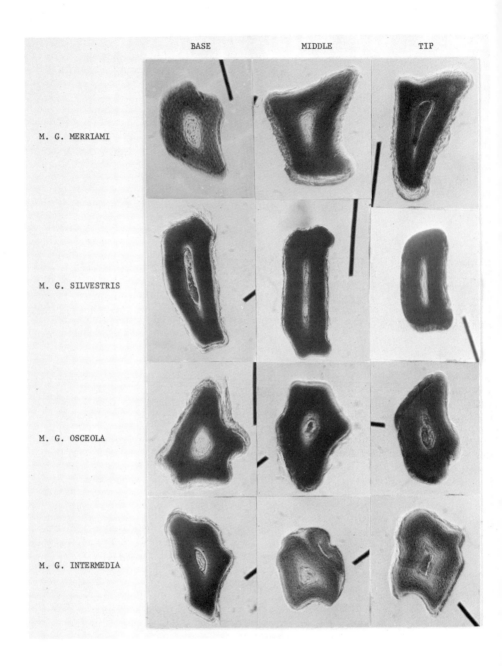

Plate 20.—Cross sections of bristles from four races of the wild turkey. (After Schorger [1957].)

Plate 21.—Quintuple beard
from a Rio Grande turkey
shot in Sutton County,
Texas, in 1954.
(Courtesy James G. Teer.)

Plate 22.—Battle between two wild turkey gobblers during the mating season in the Wichita Mountains National Wildlife Refuge, Oklahoma. (Photograph by Ernest J. Greenwalt, U. S. Fish and Wildlife Service.)

Plate 23.—Rio Grande turkey wading. (Courtesy Allan D. Cruick-shank.)

Plate 24.—Nest and eggs of eastern turkey. (Courtesy Wayne Bailey, West Virginia Conservation Commission.)

New York.—The principal foods in fall and early winter are beech-nuts, acorns (*Quercus borealis*), and black cherries (*Prunus serotina*). From January 15 to March 21, the main items are: leaves of sedge (*Carex pedunculata, C. arctata,* and *C. gracillima*); seeds of broad-leaved dock (*Rumex obtusifolia*); burdock (*Arctium*), and grasses; leaves of wood fern (*Dryopteris spinulosa*), Christmas fern (*Polystichum acrostich-oides*), and *Polypodium*; fertile fronds with spores of sensitive fern (*Onoclea sensibilis*); beech buds; leaves and young stems of hemlock (*Tsuga canadensis*); blackberry (*Rubus*) seeds remaining on canes; and pulp and seeds of apples in February. In spring and fall, besides mast, turkeys ate tubers of spring beauty (*Claytonia caroliniana*), and in spring, blossoms of violets (*Viola* spp.). The data are based on approximately three hundred droppings collected from October to April [Stephen W. Eaton (*in litt.*)].

Turkeys released in the Lake George area in February, 1960, when the snow was three to four feet deep, subsisted largely on juniper berries (Bailey and Rinell, 1960.1). Eating the seeds of burdock (*Arctium* sp.) in winter is also mentioned (Dayhart, 1963).

North Carolina.—The crop of one turkey collected in December contained dipterous larvae, white oak acorns, and berries of the flowering dogwood. Another had eaten half a pint of dogwood berries and a few pine needles (Judd, 1905:49, 51). According to Everitt (1928:19), the food consists of "all varieties of wild seeds, such as acorns, beechnuts, gumberries, grape and pine seeds, together with grasshoppers and other insects."

Ohio.—Beechnuts abounded in southeastern Ohio in the fall of 1790, and they attracted the turkeys in great numbers (Hildreth, 1848:496). Loskiel (1794:69) wrote that turkeys feed avidly on the fruit of the mulberry (*Morus ruba*) and on its leaves when they drop in autumn. It is doubtful if the leaves were eaten. This impression may have come from seeing the birds scratching in the leaves. They became very fat from eating acorns, chestnuts, and beechnuts (Taylor, 1890:440). Wheaton (1875:571) mentions grain, nuts, acorns, berries, grasshoppers, and some large insects.

Oklahoma.—"Pecans, acorns, grass seeds, berries, and green grass constitute their diet in Texas and the Indian territory" (Crane, 1897:431). A turkey on the Ponca Reservation had eaten persimmons, chinquapins, and acorns of the white oak (W. R., 1901). Turkeys are said to be fond of the red berries of the "winter mulberry" (Barde, 1914:65).

In winter most of the wild turkeys have access to cultivated grains standing in the fields and to sorghum grains and cottonseed meal fed to livestock. The berries of the false buckthorn (*Bumelia lanuginosa*) form one of the principal natural winter foods; also acorns and hackberries. Flocks may feed exclusively for a week or more on the blades of rye and wheat. In summer and fall, sand plums, mulberries, wild grape, and persimmons are consumed. Grass heads are stripped in fall. Grasshoppers form the most important summer food and are taken almost exclusively by the poults [Ralph J. Ellis (*in litt.*)].

Pennsylvania.—Beechnuts and hemlock buds are mentioned as food items (W. R. T., 1889). The crop of a turkey taken in Juniata County in November contained sixty-eight large acorns of the white oak, seven wild grapes, three seeds of dogwood, a few grass blades, five needles of the white pine, many seeds of the white snakeroot, a small millepede, larvae of the carabid beetle, and the body of a squash bug (Christy and Sutton, 1929:114). Berries of jack-in-the-pulpit (*Arisaema*) are taken frequently.

The crops of fifteen turkeys shot in November contained 97.7 per cent plant matter: wheat (*Triticum aestivum*) kernels, 39.1 per cent; corn (*Zea mays*) kernels, 23.6; acorns, 10.2; grass (Gramineae) leaves, 7.2; wild grape (*Vitis* spp.) fruit, 4.2; panic grass (*Panicum* spp.) leaves, 3.1; wild cherry (*Prunus* spp.) fruit and stones, 2.1; and miscellaneous, 8.2. The 2.3 per cent animal matter consisted chiefly of millepedes (Diplopoda), stink bugs and assassin bugs (Hemiptera), crickets, grasshoppers and walking sticks (Orthoptera), beetles (Coleoptera), spiders (Arachnida), wasps and ants (Hymenoptera), and centipedes (Chilopoda); and one lizard (Reptilia) (Bennett and English, 1941).

The crops and stomachs collected in November by Kozicky (1942) contained mainly acorns and wild grapes with small amounts of corn, seeds of black gum (*Nyssa sylvatica*), and seeds of sedge (*Carex intumescens*). The results of analysis of 770 droppings are given in per cent by volume. April through May, turkeys ate: acorns, those of *Quercus alba* preferred, 27.8; Gramineae and Cyperaceae, 17.6; cultivated grains, 7.3. June-September showed: grass and sedge leaves, 27.8; huckleberry, 15.1; wild grape, 11.7; acorns, 11.4. October-December results were: acorns, 56.9; grass and sedge leaves, 10.8. For January-March, acorns were 53.8; wild grape, 19.8; cultivated grains and supplied feed, 18.4.

In the fall of 1960, turkeys utilized the abundant mast of blue beech (*Carpinus caroliniana*) when not covered with snow. When snow came they fed extensively on wild grapes (*Vitis aestivalis*) (Hayden, 1961).

South Carolina.—In the Pee Dee Swamp, berries of the American holly (*Ilex opaca*) are preferred to those of the dogwood. The fruit of the turkey berry or green haw (*Crataegus viridis*) is important in some seasons. The post oak (*Quercus stellata*), water oak (*Q. nigra*), laurel oak (*Q. laurifolia*), and swamp red oak (*Q. pagoda* = *rubra* var. *pogodaefolia*) are the most important producers of acorns. Acorns of the swamp chestnut oak (*Q. prinus*) and overcup oak (*Q. lyrata*) are stated to be too large to be swallowed by turkeys. In some areas fiddler crabs and shad frogs are important food items (Davis, 1949:72, 74). Rutledge (1946:144) in late February killed a gobbler whose crop contained only the blades of marsh grass and the leaves of wampee (*Pontederia cordata*).

South Dakota.—General D. L. Magruder in December, 1855, found turkeys eating wild grapes, rose hips, cottonwood buds, and hackberries. The last were apparently their favorite food, judging from the quantity in their crops (Grinnell, 1909.1:854). There are many references by the early travelers to the abundance of wild grapes along the Missouri in autumn.

Texas.—Marcy (1866:220) states that the beans of the mesquite (*Prosopis*) were a food for wild horses, deer, antelope, and turkeys. William Lloyd wrote to Bendire (1892:117): "Their principal food being acorns they were most abundant where there was much mast, migrating considerable distances, but in this case only governed by food supply. I have seen them freely eating mesquite beans when they fall in the late summer, and pecan nuts are also a favorite food. They also feed on grasshoppers and other insects during April and May, running after them in the same way as the Chaparral Cock."

In spring, turkeys will eat leaves of the leek (*Allium*) (Roemer, 1849:288; Holden, 1932:38). According to Nehrling (1882:175), when pecans and acorns became scarce, turkeys ate the berries of the myrtleholly (*Oreophila myrtifolia*) in eastern Texas. John W. Thomson informs me that *Ilex cassine* was probably misidentified as *Oreophila myrtifolia* (*Pachystima myrsinites*) which does not occur in Texas. Elm samaras (Dobie, 1929:209) and fruit of the chinaberry (probably *Sapindus*) are mentioned (Cook, 1907:114). The latter is usually known as soapberry. In northwestern Texas, although pecans are the principal winter food, fruits of buckthorn (*Bumelia*) and red haw (*Crataegus*) are also important (Jackson, 1945). Grasshoppers form the main food in summer.

Croton seeds form the chief food through December in southern Texas (Glazener, 1944–45). Analyses of droppings showed that blades and seeds of grasses were the most important foods throughout the year. Bristle grasses (*Setaria* spp.) and Paspalum (*Paspalum plicatulum*) are used most extensively. Acorns formed 47.3 per cent of the contents of seven crops collected in November and December, 1944, and one in April, 1946. Grasshoppers, available throughout the year, are the important source of animal food. Chemical analyses have been made of thirty-nine food items found in the crops of wild turkeys from the King Ranch, southeastern Texas (Beck and Beck, 1955). Some of the plants furnishing seeds of particularly high food value were the crotons (*Croton glandulosus, C. lindheimeri, C. texensis*), groundsel (*Senecio ampullaceous*), crownbeard (*Verbesina encelioides*), and prickly ash (*Zanthoxylum clava-herculis*).

Acorns of live oak (*Quercus virginiana*), shin oak (*Q. brevilobia*), blackjack oak (*Q. marilandica*), post oak (*Q. stellata*), Spanish oak (*Q. texana*), seeds of prickly ash (*Zanthoxylum* sp.), and fruits of the prickly pear (*Opuntia atrospina*) and the trujillo cactus (*O. leptocaulis*) are important foods in part of the Edwards Plateau (Walker, 1951.1). In fall and winter, important items are: acorns, seeds of the rough-leaved elm, fruits of two sumacs, hackberry, pecan, grass and weed seeds, cedar berries, and fruit of cacti (Walker, 1951). Acorns usually disappear by December 15. Cedar berries and fruit of cacti are utilized mainly from December 15 to March 15.

The nuts of the pecan have a high oil content, and turkeys became very fat on them (Dresser, 1866:25). It was observed at an early date that these nuts formed the favorite food of wild turkeys (Taplin, 1955:84). Elgin (1938:84) states that in Brown County in 1872 there was a huge crop of pecans, and "The woods were alive with turkeys, and they were as fat and oily as the pecans." A "double handful" of pecans has been taken from the crop of a single turkey (Holden, 1932:37).

Virginia.—There is an old statement that in Virginia the planters used turkeys to remove the larvae of the tobacco moth from the plants and that the birds throve on them (Anon., 1832). A turkey taken in winter had consumed 90 per cent vegetable and 10 per cent animal matter (Judd, 1905:50). The vegetable matter consisted of wild black cherries, grapes, berries of the flowering dogwood and sour gum, a few chestnuts, twenty-five acorns (*Quercus palustris* and *Q. velutina*), a few alder catkins, seeds of jewelweed, and five hundred seeds of tick trefoil (*Meibomia = Desmodium nudiflora*). The animal matter comprised one harvest spider (Phalangidae), one centipede, one millepede (*Julus*), one ichneumon fly (*Ichneumon unifasiculata*), two yellow jackets (*Vespa germanica*), one grasshopper, and three katydids (*Cyrtophyllus perspiculatus*).

The crops and gizzards of 114 turkeys taken on the George Washington National Forest during the hunting seasons of 1935, 1936, and 1937 contained 93.26 per cent vegetable and 6.74 per cent animal matter (Martin *et al.*, 1939). The principal foods were: grapes (*Vitis*, chiefly *aestivalis*), 18.68 per cent; acorns (*Quercus* spp.), 14.82; corn (*Zea mays*), 10.72; fruit of dogwood (*Cornus florida*), 10.02; samaras of ash (*Fraxinus* spp.), taken only in 1935, 4.23; and seeds of *Eupatorium* (principally *urticaefolium*), 2.68. The animal matter comprised grasshoppers, crickets (Gryllidae), walking sticks (Phasmidae), and larvae of March flies (*Bibio* sp.).

The food habits have been treated thoroughly by Mosby and Handley (1943:147–51) who include the investigations of Rivers (1940). Of the 537 stomachs examined, 487 were collected in November and December. The food consisted of 94.74 per cent vegetable and 5.25 per cent animal matter. While the turkeys had taken parts of 354 species of plants, only a few were of importance: oaks (*Quercus* spp.), 27.84 per cent; dogwoods (*Cornus* spp.), 14.35; grasses other than corn (Gramineae), 7.56; grapes (*Vitis* spp.), 6.18; greenbriers (*Smilax* spp.), 1.94; poison ivy (*Rhus toxicodendron*), 1.91; gums (*Nyssa* spp.), 1.82; beech (*Fagus grandifolia*), 1.43; ash (*Fraxinus* spp.), 1.21; and sumac (*Rhus* spp.), 1.01. The animal matter consisted chiefly of Orthoptera and Diptera.

A summary of a nine-year study of winter foods is given by Culbertson

215

(1948) as follows: Fagaceae (oak and beech), 44.8 per cent; Cornaceae (dogwood and black gum), 15.6; Gramineae (grasses), 10.6; Caprifoliaceae (honeysuckle), 8.2; others, 14.8; and animal matter, 6.

West Virginia.—The seeds of the "pea vine" (possibly *Vicia*) are said to have been formerly an important food of the turkey (Bishop, 1927:27). Brooks (1943) had evidence that the fruit of *Ilex collina* was utilized by turkeys.

Analysis of 4,279 droppings collected from July, 1946, to April, 1947, but mainly in winter, showed 98.32 per cent vegetable matter distributed as follows (Glover and Bailey, 1949): oats (*Avena sativa*), 21.46 per cent; corn (*Zea mays*), 16.23; grasses (*Poa, Danthonia, Muhlenbergia, Digitaria, Festuca, Setaria*), 12.30; beechnuts (*Fagus grandifolia*), 11.05; beech buds, 9.90; ferns (Pteridophyta), 9.72; hemlock (*Tsuga canadensis*) needles, 3.66; bryophytes (mostly *Lycopodium*), 3.19; wild grape (*Vitis* sp.), 2.80; dogwood (*Cornus florida* and *C. amomum*), 2.20; blackberry (*Rubus* sp.), 2.14; and wild cherry (*Prunus* sp.), 0.96. The winter of 1946–47 was severe, and corn and oats were provided foods. Only a few acorns were produced in 1946.

Ferns, mosses, hemlock needles, and lichens are rarely taken by turkeys except when starving. As the snow and cold increased, they fed at springs and open creeks on grasses (Gramineae), brake fern (*Pteris aquilina*), hepatica (*Hepatica triloba*), violet (*Viola* sp.), and strawberry (*Fragaria americana*) (Glover, 1948:418).

R. W. Bailey has informed me that in the middle of October, 1956, the dogwood was without fruit and turkeys were feeding heavily on fruit of the witch hazel (*Hamamelis virginiana*). The crop of an adult turkey killed at this time contained fifty-six walking sticks, thirty-six stink bugs, and other items.

Wyoming.—In the Laramie Peak area, turkeys not descending to agricultural lands in winter are assumed to live on berries of junipers, bitterbush (*Purshia tridentata*), and skunkbush (*Rhus trilobata*) (Coughlin, 1943:6). Here winter sometimes lasts until July 4. Food items known to be taken in other areas are acorns, seeds of ponderosa pine, weeds and grasses, chokecherries, rose hips, and ants and their eggs (Anon., 1955:26).

Mexico

Chihuahua.—Turkeys ate wild oats, seed balls of the sycamore, leaves of grass, *Artemisia*, and "trifolium grass" (clover?), and a caterpillar. The crop of a female contained 100 per cent vegetable matter: fruiting panicles of *Muhlenbergia* (fully one-half pint); a few seeds of *Bromus* and some grass blades, 55 per cent; one seed of the piñon pine (*Pinus edulis*), and other pine seeds, 45 per cent (Nelson, 1891–1904). For April-August, important food items were acorns, manzanita berries, grasses, clover (*Desmodium*), other greens, and ants and other insects [A. S. Leopold (*in litt.*)].

Coahuila.—Information on the turkey's food habits in northern Coahuila has been supplied by General Miguel S. Gonzalez, Rancho El Jardin. The scientific names have been taken largely from Van Dersal (1938). I wish to express my thanks to W. C. Glazener for checking the scientific names against the Spanish.

Food items available at 6,000 to 8,000 feet elevation were: piñon nuts (*Pinus cembroides*); madroño berries (*Arbutus texana*); chilipiquin del monte (*Capsicum annuum*); sprouts; and insects. Food is abundant at 3,000 to 6,000 feet: madroña berries; granjeno (*Celtis pallida*); chapote (black persimmon, *Diospyros texana*); prickly pear (*Opuntia*); acorns; pecan nuts (*Carya pecan*); palo blanco seeds (*Celtis* sp.); huisache seeds (*Acacia farnesiana*); guajillo seeds (*Acacia berlandieri*); mesquite pods (*Prosopis* sp.); and insects.

Michoacán.—Several turkeys had their crops filled with seedling cacti (*Opuntia*) an inch in length exclusive of the roots, and scattered corn, other seeds, fruits, and grasshoppers (Nelson, 1891–1904).

Tamaulipas.—Foods in August were: seeds of panic grass (*Panicum xalapense*), lantana berries (*Lantana velutina*), leaves and shoots of crownbeard (*Verbesina microptera*), and grasshoppers and other insects [A. S. Leopold (*in litt.*)].

Destruction of Agriculture Crops

Wild turkeys were frequently destructive to the crops of the early settlers. In Lowndes County, Alabama, deer and turkeys ravaged the young crops, but during the first year of settlement, a good crop of corn was raised in spite of the turkeys (Russell, 1951:9). According to Hughes

(1932:64), both passenger pigeons and turkeys were so abundant in West Virginia as to be very destructive to grain. Atkinson (1876:75) was informed that turkeys were so numerous at the beginning of the nineteenth century that in the fall it was necessary to have a guard on duty daily to prevent destruction of the crops. Colonel W. Clapham settled near West Newton, Westmoreland County, Pennsylvania. On December 22, 1761, Kenny (1938:92) recorded in his journal that he understood that the Colonel "rais'd many Hundrd Bushell Corn this Sumer, but ye Turkeys like to destroy much of it, they were so thik about in his Corn fields, that they shot a Heap of them—." In Lawrence County, Pennsylvania, they were especially destructive to buckwheat in the fall (Durant and Durant, 1877:74).

Ohio was particularly plagued by turkeys. In Montgomery County in 1801 and 1802, the birds were so injurious to the growing corn that the crop was gathered early in order to save it (Beers & Co., 1882: I, 294). A settler who began farming in Washington County in 1804 had his wheat field black with turkeys after it had been sown (Williams & Bro., 1881:648). Up to 1819 the birds were so abundant in Morgan County that corn had to be harvested early and stacks of small grain protected by a covering of brush (Robertson, 1886:104). There were instances when a sower of wheat had to interrupt his work to drive the turkeys away with a club (Bushnell, 1889:63). Aaron Davis mentions that boys had to guard the buckwheat and other fields of grain and that he had driven away hundreds of turkeys in a day (Anon., 1876:448). Regarding early conditions in Huron County, Lewis (1858:34) stated: "In the autumn of 1827, it seemed to me that the wild turkeys were more numerous than I have ever seen them before or since. . . . I had one ten-acre field sown to wheat, upon which the turkeys had commenced feeding. One day I went to the field and what a sight did I behold; one half of the field was literally filled with these famous birds of the forest, and it really looked more like a field of turkeys than a field of wheat."

Turkeys in Wayne County, Michigan, tramped down the buckwheat and ate the grain (Nowlin, 1882:491). Prior to the destructive deep snow of 1835, they were a menace to crops in Fountain County, Indiana (Beckwith, 1881:290). Banta (1881:156) informs us that the birds scratched up the newly planted corn, ate it after it matured, and trod down smaller grain. In White County it was necessary to protect the crops (Battey & Co., 1883:202). In Crawford County, Illinois, hunts were organized to exterminate turkeys and prairie chickens because they destroyed so much corn ("Ignis Fatuus," 1885). Concerning a circular hunt in the Sangamon River bottoms of Illinois, Waters (1937) wrote: "One of my earliest and most vivid recollections was of the day when everybody combined to slaughter the last immense flock of Wild Turkeys. They enticed so many tame Turkeys away and were so destructive to crops, that their extermination was decreed by the grange, churches, and general public."

The birds were numerous enough in Taney and Christian counties, Missouri, to be a nuisance. They scratched up the planted corn or ate it from the stalk when ripe (Spears, 1889:490). There were similar complaints from Schuyler County (Swanson and Ford, 1910:21), and Ray County (Missouri Hist. Co., 1881:203). Peck (1853:29), during the time of early settlements, saw over one hundred turkeys at one time being driven from a single cornfield in winter. When a boy, Judge John English was assigned the task of killing squirrels at a cornfield in Moniteau County, Missouri, the winter of 1863–64. In addition to squirrels, he killed fifty turkeys (Ford, 1936:69). In Duval County, Texas, the wild turkeys ate both corn and melons (Hughes, 1884:94).

The domestic turkey has also been recorded as a nuisance. The town records of Cambridge, Massachusetts, for April 14, 1636, read: "Ordered, That whosoever finds a cock, hen, or turkey, in a garden, it shall be lawful for them to require three pence of the owner; and if they refuse to pay, then to kill the same" (Paige, 1877:39).

9

Habitat

T HE WILD TURKEY has flourished in such diverse terrains as the low, moist, and hot coastal plain of Veracruz, the swamps of our Southeast, the semiarid mountains of the Southwest, and the plains and forests of the northern states. It is not safe to go beyond the general statement that a suitable habitat is one that provides cover, food, water, and has a temperate winter. There is an advantage to turkeys living in hilly or mountainous country, since from the elevations they can glide instantly out of danger. Most of the eastern turkeys lived at low altitudes, but it is reasonable to suppose that if there had been in the East mountains of sufficient altitude, they would have ascended them in summer to the tree line.

Habitats of the Eastern Turkey

Writing of turkey hunting in Hampshire County, West Virginia, in 1893, Smith (1894) stated that the birds must be sought on the open benches, necessitating a climb of at least 2,000 feet. Waldo (1901) went to extremes in stating that he had never seen the wild turkey in the southern Appalachians below 2,500 feet. The best hunting area of which he was aware was at 5,000 feet. Brewster (1886:103) reported that turkeys ranged over the highest mountains in the region of Asheville, North Carolina, and nested above 5,000 feet. At Tray Mountain, Georgia, turkeys were observed at elevations of 2,100 to 3,400 feet (Denton and Neal, 1951:26). A turkey was seen by Wetmore (1940:184) at 6,100 feet on June 27, 1937, on Old Black Mountain in the Great Smokies. Clingmans Dome, 6,642 feet, is the highest peak in the group. According to Thornborough (1937:35), turkeys are rarely seen in the Great Smokies below

3,000 feet. Formerly, the turkey occurred as low as tidewater along the Atlantic Ocean and was abundant on the low level lands of the north central states.

Under primitive conditions, trees were not essential to turkeys except for roosting. The open prairies were used extensively for feeding. Thick grass also offered protection. A flock of forty to fifty turkeys, flushed from a cornfield, took refuge in a strip of prairie along the Scioto River in Ohio (Jones, 1898:198). In Stafford Township, Greene County, Indiana, turkeys "sought the treeless marshes very often for food, or to hatch their young" (Goodspeed Bros. and Co., 1884:289). In the spring of 1830 in Edwards County, Illinois, Stuart (1833: II, 235) followed a road that ran entirely over a prairie where there were many deer and turkeys. Anderson (1882:152), in the winter of 1801–1802, walked from his post on the Des Moines River, Van Buren County, Iowa, to the Missouri River. The small groves dotting the "boundless plains" were swarming with wild turkeys. Regarding the stretch of the Missouri River from the Sioux River, Iowa, to the mouth of White River, Lyman County, South Dakota, Lewis (1905:311) wrote: ". . . a greater quantity of turkeys than we had before seen, a circumstance which I did not expect in a country so destitute of timber." Hunting eventually made the birds less venturesome. In Missouri, "Turkeys would never go far out into the larger prairies; but they were frequently found in the prairies along the edges of the woods when they were grasshopper-hunting. . . ." (Goebel, 1889:128). After the rice harvest at Heyward's plantation in South Carolina, the birds would feed in the field, but never more than one or two hundred yards from the edge of the jungle (Heyward, 1937:121).

The use of prairie is mentioned by James (1823:107): "Near the sources of Grand River [Iowa], we discovered as we thought several large animals feeding in the prairie, at a distance of half a mile. These, we believed, could be no other than bisons; . . . and creeping with great care and caution, about one-fourth of a mile through the high grass, arrived near the spot, and discovered an old turkey, with her brood of half-grown young, the only animals now to be seen." On May 14, 1859, Patterson (1942:128) hunted to a distance of seven miles from his camp on Plum Creek, Nebraska. He saw on the plains eight wild turkeys, two antelopes, and three wolves. While in present Noble County, Oklahoma, Boone (1929:68) recorded that hundreds of turkeys were found on the open prairie. Gregg (1844:II, 232) wrote of northeastern Texas: "About the Cross Timbers and indeed on all the brushy creeks, especially to the southward, are great quantities of wild *turkeys*, which are frequently seen ranging in large flocks in the bordering prairies." One observer reported seeing hundreds of turkeys feeding at one time on the prairies near Fort Sill, Oklahoma ("Basso," 1874).

The prairies and creek bottoms in Oklahoma were sometimes burned to drive out the turkeys (Askins, 1931:61). Inman (1881:101), who is not always reliable, states that in 1836 the Indians burned the prairie at Pawnee Rock, Kansas, the fire traveling at the rate of eight miles in fifteen minutes. Turkeys and other animals were burned to death. No references have been found to show that turkeys wandered more than a mile from timber. The Tonkawa Indians, according to James B. Bailey, who settled in the Brazoria District, Texas, in 1818, would wait until the turkeys had wandered about a mile into the prairie from the woods, then run them down on horseback (Golson, 1950:24).

The eastern turkey was found mainly in open hardwoods having mast-bearing trees. Thickets and woods with a dense undergrowth were generally avoided because they reduced the bird's field of vision and speed of escape. The type of soil may influence the turkey population, but its importance is not nearly as great as has been thought. Albrecht (1944) thought the fertility of the soil has a direct effect on the quality and abundance of wildlife. In Missouri the heaviest turkey populations occur on limestone soils with frequent open-faced hillsides, and the lowest on granite soils, which are deficient in calcium and phosphorus. The Clarksville stony loam supported 79 per cent of the turkeys in the state, and it was thought that it would continue to do so (Leopold and Dalke, 1943:432; Leopold, 1943.1:65). On the other hand, ponds, constructed on many dry ridges to give a permanent supply of water, attracted deer and turkeys which were formerly absent (Leopold, *l.c.*:64). Uhlig and Bailey (1952:26) in West Virginia, and Latham (1958:16) in Pennsylvania could not find a relation between the type of soil and the abundance of turkeys. In Texas turkeys prefer sandy country (Tabor, 1920). These birds are most successful in Oklahoma on sandy loams along streams (Steele, 1959).

It was stipulated by Mason (1958) that for the restoration of the wild turkey in New York, the release area should be a semi-wilderness of at least 3,000 acres, mainly woodland, having a considerable amount of beech, oak, and black cherry of an age sufficient to produce mast. Other requirements were the availability of water throughout the year, and a depth of snow rarely exceeding one foot. The Allegheny State Park, in which the restoration of the turkey is being attempted, was inspected by Bailey and Rinell (1960.1) in the fall of 1960. The area comprises 58,000 acres with elevations of 1,332 to 2,375 feet. Snow accumulates to a depth of three feet or more and covers the ground from the middle of November to the last of March or early April. Prior to its acquisition in 1921, the area had been logged and burned repeatedly. The woods are open and park-like from overgrazing by deer and consist of young trees. The only common understory is hornbeam (*Carpinus*). The principal trees are beech, black cherry, ash, magnolia, aspen, red oak, maple, and hemlock. Turkeys have been established also in woodlot areas in Chautauqua County near the Park. The land is used mainly for pasture and the few woodlots are small, 25 to 200 acres. Here the turkeys winter in the wooded swamps but in feeding do not hesitate to travel in the open from one woodlot to another.

It is considered in Pennsylvania that a management area should comprise 10,000 to 15,000 acres to be effective. Kozicky and Metz (1948:27) add: "Cover composition is as important as the individual forest cover types that compose a range. The area should be from 60 to 80 per cent in oak forest cover, 10 to 15 per cent in coniferous growth, and the remaining habitat in small (one-half to two acres in size), scattered, grassy openings. The timber should be middle-aged, that is, in the pole stage (4 to 12 inches in diameter at 4½ feet above the ground). The white oak–black oak–red oak forest cover type (Society American Foresters Type number 49) is the most desirable of all forest cover to wild turkeys in Pennsylvania. A limited amount of the range (10 to 15 per cent) should be maintained in a sapling stage (3 feet in height to 4 inches in diameter at 4½ feet above the ground) of growth as escape cover. However, a sanctuary refuge may be substituted. Fortunately, the required cover conditions are found in varying degrees of the optimum throughout the wild turkey range. But, the timber in some areas is in the mature or standard stage (1 foot to 2 feet in diameter at 4½ feet above the ground) and is beyond the optimum carrying capacity for wild turkeys." Additional requirements are food-producing trees, shrubs and vines, and running water.

Three basic types of turkey habitat for West Virginia are given by Uhlig and Bailey (1952:25–26): (1) The Eastern Panhandle section containing the primary forest types, red oak, hard pine-oak, white oak, and chestnut oak; (2) the Mideastern section containing northern hardwoods, red oak, and white oak; (3) the Southeastern section containing red oak and northern hardwoods. After a study of the various forest types, they concluded: "All of these facts would seem to indicate that northern hardwoods are more attractive to turkeys on the basis of type alone. However, when an area by area study is made, it appears more likely that elevation, topography, accessibility, and general location of the forest types are more important in regard to the capacity of the area to support turkeys than are the forest types themselves." The difficult terrain now occupied by turkeys is largely not a matter of choice but of necessity. Even the response to the hunter has changed. Brooks (1943.1:39) states that, in the Cheat ranges of West Virginia, the food of the turkeys is down in the comparatively open beech forests where they gather in the morning and evening. After feeding, or being disturbed, they move up the mountains to the laurel and rhododendron thickets. Previously when alarmed, turkeys usually flew down a mountain or across to another ridge. Now they baffle the hunters by refusing to do so.

Ideal requirements for the habitat of the turkey in Virginia are given by Mosby and Handley (1943:206): (1) The area should contain 50,000 acres or more, the minimum being 15,000 acres. (2) The forest cover should comprise 50 to 90 per cent of the area, the remainder being well-dispersed open spaces; also, the forest should consist of mixed species and not extensive, pure stands. (3) Food requirements are to be met by having at least 25 per cent of the forest in hardwoods, preferably oaks, with a fairly abundant, well-distributed supply of mast, seeds, and berries. There should be no competition for food from the presence of domestic animals or deer in excessive numbers. Openings to provide grasses and succulent vegetation should be available from early spring to far into the winter. (4) Water should be well distributed. (5) Large areas of swamp or other lands subject to flooding are to be avoided. The terrain should be rolling to precipitous with streams, swamps, or other barriers to facilitate escape from enemies. (6) There should be refuges of 1,000 acres or more. (7) Area should have suitable roosting trees, preferably conifers. Heavy snowfall should not last more than a month, and the rainfall should not be excessive during the breeding season.

Turkeys in South Carolina are at present confined largely to swamps. In the early part of the present century, according to Davis (1949:37–38), the highest turkey populations were in the Pearce preserve, Pee Dee Swamp, Florence County; the swamps of the Black and Santee rivers, Williamsburg County; the Okeetee preserve, Savannah River Swamp, Jasper County; and Britton's Neck between the junction of the Little Pee Dee and Great Pee Dee rivers, Marion County.

Concerning habitat, Rutledge (1941:94) wrote: "There are certain essentials for the habitat of the wild turkey. These may vary in different localities, but in the main they are much the same. The birds like abundant water. They like the shores of lakes and lagoons, of streams and rivers, and they are very fond of flooded swamps. In many places they become almost semiaquatic. On the great delta of the Santee River, near my home, they haunt the old marshy ricefields, coming to the highlands only to roost. I think they like to throw off pursuers by flying across some considerable body of water. Throughout the southeastern states most of the wild turkeys are found in swamps and wildwoods adjacent to the great rivers, especially in the areas where the rivers approach the coast." Big timber is required for roosting and the woods should be open. Rutledge (1923.1:247) mentions two nearly identical ridges, one of which was frequented by hundreds of turkeys, but none was to be found on the other. The one ridge was not used since it contained a thick growth of laurel that facilitated the approach of predators. The Francis Marion National Forest Wildlife Preserve on the coast of South Carolina has a varied terrain consisting of dense bays, gum and cypress swamps, hardwood territories, and pine uplands (Holbrook, 1958:2).

Turkeys in Georgia are found in much the same habitat as in South Carolina. Preserves as small as 2,000 acres, when adjacent to heavily timbered bottomlands, have developed good stocks of turkeys. The birds have ranged out of areas as large as 15,000 acres in search of favored foods, in spite of efforts to hold them in the center through plantings and artificial feeding. As Stoddard (1935:22) points out, turkeys inhabit swamps not from choice, but from persecution. They are naturally not wild and lose their wariness towards man under close protection.

In Alabama a public hunting ground should not have less than 50,000 acres and a refuge not less than 5,000 acres (Wheeler, 1948:21). The timber should not be of uniform composition. Extensive pine forests with only a few hardwoods growing along widely separated stream bottoms, and river swamps with heavy, continuous stands of hardwoods support very few turkeys. Optimum range will be well watered and contain timber of various types, of which 50 per cent is hardwood, one half of which is oak. The forest should be broken with scattered clearings that produce a luxuriant growth of native grasses, legumes, and plants with succulent fruits. Wheeler (1946.1:140) considered the Salt Springs Sanctuary, comprising 5,500 acres in southern Clarke County, an ideal turkey range. The fenced area, 2,200 acres, contains 13 per cent open pine timber, 42 per cent mixed pine and hardwood, 39 per cent oak-hickory, and 6 per cent fields.

An area of 6,000 to 16,000 acres is considered desirable in Mississippi to hold one or more flocks of turkeys. According to Cook (1945:75): "Large swampy bottoms with ridges extending above high water level provide one of the best types of ranges; but no range is more desirable or more popular than a hill range where small spring-fed creeks course through the rough terrain covered by a mixed hardwood, pine forest." There should be sufficient hardwood trees and shrubs to provide food. Openings and food patches improve the range.

The ideal habitat in Louisiana is a mixed forest with hardwoods, mainly oaks, predominating (Hollis, 1950:35). There should be food-producing shrubs and types of vegetation producing green foods. The understory of the forest should be open. Plants characteristic of the occupied range are: oaks (*Quercus*), hawthorn (*Crataegus* spp.), sweet gum (*Liquidambar styraciflua*), holly (*Ilex* spp.), magnolia (*Magnolia* spp.), greenbrier (*Smilax* spp.), black gum (*Nyssa* spp.), grape (*Vitis* spp.), rattan (*Berchemia scandens*), and dogwood (*Cornus* spp.).

Concerning the Ozark Range in Missouri, Blakey (1937:2) wrote: "A preliminary study of range factors on the Missouri Ozarks indicates that conditions are highly desirable there for supporting a reasonable concentration of wild turkeys. The topography is ideally suited to the adaptable characteristics of the birds in feeding and in scaling-escape flight, to their requirements for gobbling and roosting grounds, and to their needs as regards properly located cover for nesting and ranging.

Water, as the turkey needs and uses it, is thoroughly adequate, even in the driest season. The open and cut-over condition of the entire Ozarks affords ideal dispersion to cover and open areas, with a diversification of food supply impossible under heavily forested conditions. The annual mast crop far exceeds the possible need, choice varieties of fleshy fruits much used by turkeys are abundant, and repeated firing of the range has assisted in developing an exceedingly rich leguminous flora." The best turkey habitat in the state consists of 49 per cent timber, 21 per cent woods pasture, 18 per cent permanent pasture, and 12 per cent fields in crops. For management purposes there should be 70 per cent timber and 30 per cent open land (Lewis, 1958:93).

HABITATS OF THE FLORIDA TURKEY

The highest elevation in Florida is about 300 feet. Shallow lakes, swamps, and sluggish streams with marshy banks are numerous. It would be difficult for the Florida turkey to avoid wet places even if it chose to do so. The birds were formerly abundant along all the wooded streams and on the hammocks. Concerning the St. Johns River in 1562, Ribaut (1927) wrote that turkeys occurred in marvelous number. The early literature mentions turkeys as abundant along the following streams: Alligator Creek, Caloosahatchee River, Fisheating Creek, Halpatiokee (St. Lucie) River, Homosassa River, Indian River, Kissim-mee River, and Myakka River and its lakes. Other favored habitats were the Kissimmee prairies, Big Cypress Swamp, and Turnbull Swamp at the head of Indian River. Travel in the early days was mainly by water so that if turkeys were seen at all they would be along the streams. As to the large prairie at Peas (Peace) Creek, near New Fort Center, there were "numberless turkeys on the banks of the creek, or in the adjoining islands" (Hallock, 1876:310). Ober (1874) stated that the shore of Lake Okeechobee was unsuitable for turkeys.

The types of habitats suitable for turkeys in Florida, as given by New-man and Griffin (1950:13) are:

Clay Pine Land.—The typical trees are the longleaf pine (*Pinus palustris*) and loblolly pine (*Pinus taeda*). Areas covered with live oak (*Quercus virginiana*) are common. Magnolia (*Magnolia*), bay trees (*Persea*), some bald cypress (*Taxodium distichum*), water oak (*Quercus nigra*) and other hardwood mast trees occur along the stream bottoms and bayheads. The value of this formerly excellent turkey habitat has been reduced greatly by extensive agricultural development.

Rolling Sandy Pine Land.—Longleaf pine and a variety of oaks, including turkey oak (*Quercus laevis*), are the characteristic trees. The frequent lakes and hollows with bayheads to be found in the hills support cyrilla, or titi (*Cyrilla*), and buckwheat tree (*Cliftonia*), and some cypress and water oak.

Flat Pine Land.—Characteristic trees in the northern part of the state are the longleaf pine, slash pine (*Pinus elliottii*), and gallberry (*Ilex glabra*); in the south, Caribbean pine (*Pinus caribaea*) and saw palmetto (*Serenoa repens*). The value of this type and the previous one for turkeys depends largely upon the number and dispersal of swamps, hammocks, and bayheads.

Red Clay Hammock Land.—This was formerly turkey habitat of high quality, but only a small portion remains untouched by agriculture. Water oak, live oak, and laurel oak (*Quercus laurifolia*) are the principal trees.

Calcareous and Phosphatic Hammock Land.—The characteristic trees are loblolly pine, live oak, southern red oak (*Quercus falcata*), and sweet gum (*Liquidambar styraciflua*). Though excellent turkey habitat, it has been reduced to minor importance by cultivation and improved pasturing. Where there is ranching, the turkey population remains high.

Low Marl Hammock Land.—Typical trees are laurel oak, swamp chestnut oak (*Quercus prinus*), loblolly pine, Florida maple (*Acer floridanum*), sweet gum, and cabbage palmetto (*Sabal palmetto*). This type of land is very good for turkeys, but only the Gulf Hammock section, e.g. Levy County, contains an area of sufficient size to maintain a satisfactory game population.

Sandy Prairie Land.—This type consists of open grassland containing saw palmetto and having islands of cabbage palm, Caribbean pine, and live oak. Where these islands are numerous, there is turkey habitat of high value.

Swamp.—The trees of the northern swamps comprise cypress, cabbage palm, laurel oak, black gum (*Nyssa sylvatica*), and tupelo gum (*Nyssa aquatica*). The swamps of the Everglades contain almost pure stands of stunted cypress. The principal value of a swamp habitat is in providing a refuge for remnant populations.

228

Within a single state, turkeys can live in so great a variety of habitats that it is impossible to define habitat succinctly and comprehensively. The general statement has been made that the Florida turkey thrives in a mixture of heavy hardwoods and open pasture. The optimum range has well-distributed forest clearings in which are rank growths of native grasses, legumes, and plants producing succulent fruits. The forested land should contain a plentiful supply of water and a variety of trees producing mast (Anon., 1950:13).

Habitats of the Rio Grande Turkey

In south central Kansas, according to a communication from William Peabody, the Rio Grande turkey occupies the narrow strips of cover along the streams. These strips vary in width from several hundred yards to one-half mile. The greatest density of birds occurs in areas consisting of approximately equal parts of grazing and cropland. The best habitat appears to be the grass-cottonwood association with interspersion of various shrubs. Preference is shown for an open understory.

There are three requirements for the turkey in northwestern Oklahoma (Steele, 1959). Aside from water and open-topped trees for roosting, there should be in winter an ample supply of succulent vegetation such as weeds, wheat, or rye. The best habitat is sandy land along streams.

The Rio Grande turkey in Texas made much use of the prairies and plains. Concerning turkeys coming to roost on the North Fork and Canadian Rivers, Wright (1913:72) wrote: "Several times, at a distance, we mistook them for large herds of buffalo. They literally covered the prairies for miles with their immense flocks, and, more than once, we saddled our horses to make a run for them, thinking they were buffalo." Brigadier General Johnson was stationed at Fort Terrett in 1852. He described the country for miles around the fort as devoid of timber except some bordering the streams. Here the birds roosted by the thousands at night within a mile of the post and could be killed in any desired number (Fisher, 1937).

The use of the prairies near Corpus Christi is mentioned by Hancock (1887:14): "On the evening of March 26th [1884] several were put to flight from some tall oak trees . . . where they had settled down for their night's rest. The next morning while riding over the prairies our dog flushed many from the tall grass.

"After being frightened from their roosts at night, they make for the open prairies; here they remain but a short time, as the wild animals, especially of the cat tribe, are a troublesome foe, continually on the alert to capture them.

"From the many enemies of this bird, and the exposed situation of the nests, which are built on the open prairies, but a small average [of the young] ever attain the mature state."

The Rio Grande turkey formerly occupied the Mexican coastal plain along the Gulf of Mexico as far as the state of Veracruz and the mountains of the Sierra Madre Oriental to which it is at present largely confined. Miller (1955:162) states that this turkey is a lowland race which in the Sierra del Carmen, Coahuila, apparently does not range above 7,500 feet.

Texas has a terrain varying from the coastal flats to the high Trans-Pecos region where in the Guadalupe Mountains, El Capitan reaches a height of 9,020 feet. Owing to the presence within the state of three races of the turkey, the physiography of the state will be given in some detail. The soils have been described by Carter (1931). The entire area east of the High Plains was once occupied by turkeys. The principal types of terrain (Plate 4) are the following:

1. East Texas Timber Country.—This area, extending southward from the Red River 150 miles, includes the East Texas Timber Country in the northeast and East Cross Timbers. Westward it terminates sharply at the edge of the Blackland Prairie. The timber is a mixture of pine and hardwood, pine predominating in the southeastern section. Westward adjoining the prairie there is a border of post oak twenty to fifty miles wide. The surface is rolling and hilly, deeply carved by stream dissection. The elevations of 100 to 200 feet in the southern part increase to 300 to 600 feet in the northern part. The annual rainfall of 40 to 50 inches in the east decreases to 35 inches on the western border.

It was the opinion of old residents interviewed by Walker (1953.1) that the great increase in density of the post oak belt during the past fifty years resulted in the disappearance of the native turkeys. The Rio Grande turkeys stocked in Freestone, Robertson, and Anderson counties avoided the dense woods and moved through open woods, on pasture roads, and along right-of-ways for power and pipe lines. Walker concluded that the ranges should contain a minimum of 30 to 35 per cent open terrain and that 50 per cent of well-spaced open country was much more desirable.

2. *Gulf Coast Prairie.*—The coastal prairie is but a few feet above sea level, the land rising to 100 feet in the northern section. The vegetation consists of coarse grasses and timber along the streams on some of the slopes of the uplands. In passing from the eastern to the western border, the annual rainfall decreases from 50 to 35 inches.

3. *Blackland Prairie.*—This treeless prairie is over three hundred miles in length and varies from seventy-five miles in width at the north to twenty miles in the southwest. Smaller black prairies lie within the East Texas Timber Country. The native grasses are chiefly andropogons, grama, and buffalo. In the north small amounts of hackberry and elm occur, and in the south are scattered growths of mesquite and shrubs. Owing to the former presence of turkeys, there must have been timber along the streams prior to extensive settlement. Elevations vary from 300 to 800 feet. The annual rainfall is 35 to 40 inches. The native turkey was the eastern form.

4. *Rio Grande Plain.*—The area under consideration is subhumid. Most of the region is covered with small mesquite trees, thick in some areas and scattered in others. Chaparral, consisting of various thorny shrubs, is abundant in some sections. Prickly pear and thickets of scrub oaks are common in places. In others are mottes of live oak. Along the streams can be found a heavy growth of mesquite, oak, hackberry, elm, and some pecan. The grasses are andropogons, needle, grama, buffalo, and mesquite. Most of the land is at an elevation of 200 to 700 feet but reaches 1,000 feet on the northern border. The annual rainfall is variable, however it averages 30 inches on the eastern border and 20 inches on the western. The Rio Grande turkey is the resident bird.

5. *Edwards Plateau.*—The eastern part of the plateau is subhumid and the western semiarid. The area is a limestone plain, greatly dissected, lying at elevations of 2,000 to 4,000 feet. The annual rainfall decreases from 25 to 30 inches in the eastern part to 15 inches in the semiarid west. The mineral region, confined mainly to Mason and Llano counties, is characterized by an extrusion of granite. The Plateau has a high population of Rio Grande turkeys.

The eastern part of the Plateau has thickets of small oaks consisting mainly of live oak (*Quercus virginiana*), shin oak (*Q. breviloba*), post oak (*Q. stellata*), and Spanish oak (*Q. texana*). Some mesquite (*Prosopis juliflora*) is present. Proceeding westward, trees decrease until on the western border there are only small numbers of stunted oaks and mesquites. Dense cedar (*Juniperus ashei*) breaks are characteristic of the broken lands of the eastern and central sections. The central section, especially, has many species of shrubs and thorny bushes such as cat-claw (*Acacia*), sumacs (*Rhus*), buckthorn (*Bumelia*), and agrito (*Mahonia*). Plants common to the Stockton Plateau in the western section are sotol (*Dasylirion texanum*), lechuguilla (*Agave lecheguilla*), yucca (*Yucca*), cenizo (*Atriplex canescens*), catclaw, prickly pear (*Opuntia*), and various other species of cactus. The principal grasses are buffalo (*Buchloë dactyloides*), curly mesquite (*Hilaria*), gramas (*Bouteloua*), needle (*Stipa*), and three awn (*Aristida*). The valleys of the eastern and central sections contain a considerable amount of timber such as sycamore (*Platanus occidentalis*), hackberry (*Celtis reticulata*), ash (*Fraxinus texensis*), elms (*Ulmus*), walnut (*Juglans major*), pecan (*Carya pecan*), and oaks. The vegetation of Kerr County has been covered by Buechner (1944) and that of the Kerr Wildlife Management Area by Hahn (1951.1).

6. *West Cross Timbers.*—This timbered area is about two hundred miles long and has a maximum width of about fifty miles. The trees, of rather small size, are mainly post and blackjack oaks. There are small numbers of other hardwoods. The grassy prairies within the area have scattered mesquites. The surface is rolling and generally 1,000 to 1,200 feet above sea level. The annual rainfall of 30 inches in the eastern part decreases to 26 inches in the western. The area was formerly occupied by the eastern turkey.

7. *Rolling Plains.*—The plains have an elevation of about 1,500 feet in the eastern part and rise to 2,500 feet along the High Plains on their western boundary. Because of cutting by the streams, some of the valleys in the eastern part drop to 1,000 feet. A tongue penetrating the High Plains along the Canadian River attains an elevation of 3,000 feet. Except after rains, most of the streams are dry. The rainfall is irregular and varies annually from 25 to 27 inches in the east to 22 inches in the west. The Rio Grande turkey is the native bird.

The vegetation is typical of a subhumid climate and varies with the soil and topography. Most of the area is covered with grama, buffalo, and mesquite grasses. The grasses on the sandy soils are needle, andropogon, and grama. The sandy soils also support shin oaks and sage (*Artemisia*). Except on the loose sandy soils, mesquite is widely distributed over most of the area. Many of the valleys contain mesquite, oak, elm, and hackberry. Along some of the streams in the eastern section there are superior growths of pecan trees.

8. *High Plains (Staked Plains, or Llano Estacado)*.—These plains having an elevation of 3,000 to 4,500 feet are devoid of trees and permanent surface water. Very small shin oaks form thickets. Turkeys (Rio Grande) occurred only in some of the river valleys.

9. *Mountains and Basins (Trans-Pecos Region)*. The western part is mountainous. The entire area is either arid or semiarid. On account of the lack of permanent water, turkeys do no occur in the Big Bend although they are to be found across the Río Grande in Coahuila.

Habitats of Merriam's Turkey

Merriam's turkey has occurred in the Guadalupe Mountains of Texas having descended this chain from New Mexico. Bailey (1905:35) lists the plants of the Upper Sonoran zone, some of which follow: piñon pine (*Pinus edulis*), Mexican piñon (*Pinus cembroides*), alligator juniper (*Juniperus pachyphloea* = *J. deppeana*), drooping juniper (*Juniperus flaccida*), one-seed juniper (*Juniperus monosperma*), mountain juniper (*Juniperus sabinoides* = *J. ashei*), gray oak (*Quercus grisea*), Emory oak (*Quercus emoryi*), wavyleaf oak (*Quercus undulata*), Texas oak (*Quercus texana*), netleaf hackberry (*Celtis reticulata*), Texas mulberry (*Morus microphylla*), adolphia (*Adolphia infesta*), catclaw (*Mimosa biuncifera*), birchleaf cercocarpus (*Cercocarpus parvifolius* = *C. betuloides*), silk-tassel (*Garrya lindheimeri*), syringa bush (*Philadelphus microphyllus*), skunkbush (*Schmaltzia* [*Rhus*] *trilobata*), redbud (*Cercis occidentalis*), agaves (*Agave wislizeni* and *A. applanata*), and yucca (*Yucca baccata*).

The principal plants of the Transition Zone of the Guadalupe Mountains are: ponderosa pine (*Pinus ponderosa*), limber pine (*Pinus flexilis*), Douglas fir (*Pseudotsuga mucronata*), bigtooth maple (*Acer grandidentatum*), hop hornbeam (*Ostrya baileyi* = *O. knowltonii*), chinquapin oak (*Quercus acuminata* = *Q. muhlenbergii*), Gambel oak

233

(*Quercus novomexicana* = *Q. gambelii*), gray oak (*Quercus grisea*), wavyleaf oak (*Quercus undulata*), black cherry (*Prunus* sp.), serviceberry (*Amelanchier alnifolia*), buckthorn (*Rhamnus purshiana*, probably *R. betulaefolia*), wild tea bush (*Ceanothus greggii*), New Mexican locust (*Robinia neomexicana*), barberry (*Berberis repens*), snowberry (*Symphoricarpos* sp.), wild potato (*Solanum tuberosum boreale*), and flax (*Linum perenne*).

Merriam's wild turkey was found originally in New Mexico along all the wooded streams, the only other suitable habitat being the mountains. Mitchell (1898:307) reported turkeys plentiful in the mountains, San Miguel County, from an elevation of 8,000 feet to the timber line. Ligon (1929:12) states that the first turkeys were trapped in January, 1927, in the White Mountains, Lincoln County, in traps set at 9,000 feet. Turkeys, as Bailey (1904:352) was informed, were common in the Pecos Mountains at 11,000 feet. One was collected on July 27, 1903, at over 11,000 feet.

The turkey in 1888 was common along the Los Pinos River, La Plata County, Colorado, below 7,000 feet (Morrison, 1888). Drew (1885:17) stated that it spent the summer and winter up to 7,000 feet in Colorado. The summer range is raised to 10,000 and 11,000 feet by Burget (1946:5).

The altitudes given for the turkey in Arizona are comparable to those for New Mexico and Colorado. In late November, 1884, Scott (1886:389) found turkeys common in the pine woods at the highest elevations of the Catalina Mountains, northeastern Pima County, though the ground was covered with snow. Guthrie (1926), in December, encountered a flock of seventy-five to one hundred turkeys on a north slope of the White Mountains at about 7,500 feet. On the west side of San Francisco Mountain, Mearns (1890:52) observed turkeys nearly up to the timber line at 11,500 feet. Jenks (1931:12) states that turkeys are found in the Transition (7,000–8,200 feet) and Canadian (8,200–9,200 feet) zones on the Mogollon Plateau and San Francisco Mountains. In the Chiricahua Mountains, Tanner and Hardy (1958:3) found turkeys at elevations of 5,400 to 9,795 feet. Two adults with at least twelve young able to fly were seen at 8,800 feet on July 2, 1956.

The climate of New Mexico is semiarid. The annual rainfall in the northwestern part of the state is about 7 inches and in the central and lower Río Grande Valley about 9 inches. Precipitation is greatest in the mountains, the highest peak generally receiving the greatest fall of rain and snow. The Pinos Altos range in Grant County has a precipitation of more than 25 inches. There are about forty mountain ranges with peaks reaching elevations of 8,500 to over 13,000 feet. Between the mountains occur arid valleys and mesas frequently gashed by deep canyons. Accordingly, turkeys are to be found only in isolated mountainous areas at the present time. The most favorable habitat for these birds is in the Transition Zone, about one-twentieth of the area of the state, at elevations of 7,500 to 9,500 feet. The vegetation of the state has been covered in considerable detail by V. Bailey (1913:28). Turkeys frequently winter in the foothills and rough borders of the valleys of the Upper Sonoran Zone. Here the prominent plants are: piñon pine (*Pinus edulis*), one-seed juniper (*Juniperus monosperma*), alligator juniper (*Juniperus pachyphloea*), Rocky Mountain juniper (*Juniperus scopulorum*), Arizona white oak (*Quercus arizonica*), Emory oak (*Quercus emoryi*), skunkbush (*Schmaltzia* [*Rhus*] *trilobata*), velvet-leaved sumac (*Schmaltzia pumila*), mountain mahogany (*Cercocarpus parvifolius*), silk-tassel (*Garrya goldmanii* and *G. wrightii*), grama grasses (*Bouteloua* spp.), and cacti (*Opuntia* spp.).

The legumes are well represented by several species of *Lupinus*, *Meibomia*, *Phaseolus*, *Petalostemum*, and *Astragalus*. In addition to the grama grasses there are several species of dropseed grasses (*Muhlenbergia*), feather grasses (*Stipa*), love grasses (*Eragrostis*), and panic grasses (*Panicum*).

The principal trees and shrubs of the Transition Zone are: ponderosa pine (*Pinus scopulorum* = *P. ponderosa*), Chihuahua pine (*Pinus chihuahuana* = *P. leiophylla*), Apache pine (*Pinus mayriana* = *P. engelmannii*), oaks (eleven species, *Quercus* spp.), cherry (*Prunus* spp.), Arizona madroño (*Arbutus arizonica*), buckthorns (*Rhamnus* spp.), Utah serviceberry (*Amelanchier oreophilus* = *A. utahensis*), thornapples (*Crataegus* spp.), wild roses (*Rosa fendleri* and *R. maximiliani*), bearberry (*Arctostaphylos uva-ursi*), and mountain snowberry (*Symphoricarpos oreophilus*). Many of the genera of herbaceous plants and grasses mentioned for the Upper Sonoran Zone are also found in the Transition Zone.

The largest part of Arizona is arid or semiarid. Turkeys at present are to be found principally in the San Francisco Mountains, the Mogollon Mesa, and the following mountain chains in the southeast: Santa

Catalina, Pinaleno, Graham, and Chiricahua. The annual rainfall in the state varies from 3.6 inches at Yuma to 28.3 inches at Crown King, Yavapai County. Turkeys are limited mainly to the Transition and Canadian zones. According to Merriam (1890:10), the principal trees of the Canadian Zone, altitude 8,200 to 9,200 feet, are the Douglas fir, mountain pine, and aspen. Characteristic of his Pine (Transition) Zone, altitude 7,000 to 8,200 feet, is the ponderosa pine. The principal trees of the Piñon (Upper Sonoran) Zone, altitude 6,000 to 7,000 feet, are the piñon pine, one-seed juniper, and alligator juniper.

The principal plants are given in more detail by Shreve (1926:565):

Upper Sonoran Zone.—The dominant plants are *Pinus cembroides, Juniperus pachyphloea, J. monosperma,* and *J. utahensis.* In the southern part of the state, associated trees are the evergreen oaks, *Quercus emoryi, Q. oblongifolia,* and *Q. arizonica.* In parklike areas occur the shrubs, *Arctostaphylos, Garrya, Cercocarpus, Rhamnus,* and *Fallugia,* and many species of bunch grasses.

Transition Zone.—The principal tree is *Pinus scopulorum* (=*P. ponderosa*). In northern Arizona the commonest undershrubs and small trees are *Quercus gambelii, Robinia neomexicana, Arctostaphylos pungens, Cercocarpus parvifolius, Fallugia paradoxa, Rhus trilobata, Ceanothus greggii,* and *Artemisia tridentata.* In the southern part of the state the most common low trees and shrubs are *Quercus hypoleuca, Q. reticulata, Arbutus arizonica, Ceanothus fendleri,* and *Robinia neomexicana.* Compositae and legumes are abundant.

Canadian Zone.—Pines are represented by *Pinus flexilis* and *P. strobiformis,* a variety of *flexilis.* The dominant trees are *Abies concolor, Pseudotsuga taxifolia,* and *Picea engelmannii. Populus tremuloides* covers old burns. Along streams and in openings are *Alnus oblongifolia, A. tenuifolia, Acer grandidentatum,* and *A. brachypterum,* a variety of *grandidentatum.* Shrubs are represented by the genera *Symphoricarpos, Ribes, Cornus, Jamesia, Sorbus,* and *Pachystima.*

In the Graham Mountains, some turkeys live the year round at elevations of 5,000 to 7,000 feet, but most of the birds were found above 8,000 feet (Knopp, 1959:26). Some turkeys were seen in January above 9,000 feet. Above 8,000 feet the vegetation consists mainly of open ponderosa pine forest. There are many small meadows with a luxuriant growth of grasses, *Bromus* spp., *Blepharoneuron tricholepis, Muhlenbergia montana,* and *Sitanion hystrix.* Dense fir and aspen were used for nesting. Grasses formed a more important source of food than mast. Below 8,000 feet the terrain was dominated by evergreen oaks, junipers, and piñon pine. Its limited use by turkeys was attributed to lack of water and grass.

The following conclusions were reached by Reeves (1954:8): "Optimum turkey habitat is found in the ponderosa pine or subalpine type. Gambel oak is abundant and the climax grasses for the plateau area (Arizona fescue, beardless bunch, and mountain muhly) are dominant. Adjacent to the pine or subalpine type are juniper or piñon-juniper belts which form ideal emergency winter ranges. Water is an important aspect of optimum range, preferably in the form of running streams and springs. Rugged topography is ideal."

Elevations in Colorado vary from 3,386 to 14,402 feet. The average elevation of the timber line is 11,500 feet. The eastern half of the state is subhumid, the western semiarid. The annual precipitation varies from 7 inches at Garnett, Alamosa County, to 37.4 inches at Savage Station, San Miguel County. Turkeys were formerly common in the eastern plains area along the Arkansas River and its tributaries, the Purgatoire and Fountain; also along the South Platte and Cherry Creek. They are now found mainly in the southern mountains.

On the eastern slope of the high mountains a chaparral belt lies between the grassland and the ponderosa pine forest of the foothills. In the southern part of the state the chaparral consists chiefly of a scrub growth of oaks (*Quercus gambelii, Q. turbinella, Q. undulata*) and snowberry (*Symphoricarpos*). Some of the plants associated with ponderosa pine are grasses (*Bromus, Bouteloua, Festuca, Agropyron, Muhlenbergia, Danthonia, Sporobolus, Koeleria,* and *Poa*), strawberry (*Fragaria*), northern bedstraw (*Galium boreale*), fringed sagebrush (*Artemisia frigida*), bitter brush (*Purshia tridentata*), chokecherry (*Prunus virginiana*), aspen (*Populus tremuloides*), rose (*Rosa macounii*), ninebark (*Opulaster intermedius*), serviceberry (*Amelanchier alnifolia*), and bearberry (*Artostaphylos uva-ursi*) (Curtis and Lynch, 1957). The mountain golden pea (*Thermopsis montana*) grows abundantly in places at this altitude. It is unknown if its seeds are an attractive food. The vegetation of the Transition Zone (ponderosa pine type) is also described by Cary (1911:34).

Habitats of Turkeys in Mexico

Gould's turkey (*Meleagris gallopavo mexicana*) is confined mainly to the Sierra Madre Occidental mountains of Mexico. The occupied area corresponds with the northern half of the Sierra Madre Occidental Biotic Province of Goldman and Moore (1946). The Animas Mountains of New Mexico and the bordering San Luis Mountains of Mexico form the northern end of the Sierra Madre. The timber line of the San Luis Mountains begins at 5,250 feet and extends to the summit with an elevation of 7,874 feet (Mearns, 1907:90). The important plants of the mountains are:

Trees:—*Pinus strobiformis* (= *P. flexilis*), *Pinus cembroides, Pinus ponderosa, Pinus mayriana* (= *P. engelmannii*), *Pinus chihuahuana* (= *P. leiophylla*), *Juniperus monosperma, Juniperus pachyphloea, Quercus gambelii, Quercus oblongifolia, Quercus arizonica, Quercus reticulata, Quercus emoryi, Quercus chrysolepsis, Quercus hypoleuca* (*hypoleucoides*), *Celtis occidentalis, Morus celtidifolia, Prunus salcifolia* (= *P. serotina*), *Prosopis juliflora, Rhamnus purshiana,* and *Arbutus arizonica.*

Shrubs and Large Plants:—*Yucca baccata, Yucca glauca, Agave palmeri, Rhus toxicodendron, Rhus trilobata, Rhamnus californica, Vitis arizonica, Opuntia lindheimeri, Rubus deliciosus, Lonicera ciliosa, Berberis wilcoxii, Holodiscus dumosus, Ribes viscosissimum, Fallugia paradoxa, Mimosa biuncifera, Mimosa dysocarpa, Erythrina flabelliformis, Garrya wrightii, Symphoricarpos oreophilus,* and *Arctostaphylos pungens.*

The Sierra Madre Occidental, Transverse Volcanic, Veracruz, Sierra Madre Oriental, and Tamaulipas biotic provinces of Goldman and Moore (1946) originally held nearly all of the wild turkey population of Mexico. The south Mexican turkey occurred mainly in the Veracruz and Transverse Volcanic provinces, Gould's turkey in the Sierra Madre Occidental and Sinaloa provinces, and the Rio Grande turkey in the Tamaulipas and Sierra Madre Oriental provinces. The vegetation of the life zones is given in detail by Goldman (1951). An understanding of the turkey habitat in Mexico is simplified by taking the pine-oak zone of Leopold (1959:23). The annual rainfall varies from 18 to 70 inches. The pine-oak forests fall into four principal types:

Pine Forest.—The dominant trees are pines, and oaks, if present, are limited. In the northern Sierra Madre Oriental the principal pine is *Pinus chihuahuana,* and in central and southern Mexico and north to Durango, *Pinus montezumae.* In the Sierra Madre del Sur occurs *Pinus herrerai.* In appearance and ecological requirements these pines are similar to the ponderosa of the western United States.

Pine-Oak Woodland.—"Open, scattered stands are dominated by pines in some places, by oaks in others. Usually these woodlands occur between the oak scrub of low elevations and the high pine forest of the upper ridges. So many different species grow in this association that it is nearly impossible to call any particular combination typical. Between Chilpancingo and Omilteme, Guerrero, for example, the oak woodland is composed of three species of oak (*Quercus acutifolia, Q. lanigera,* and *Q. candicans*) with scattered yellow pines (*Pinus herrerai*) on the moist sites."

Piñon-Juniper Woodland.—In northern Mexico there are scattered stands of Mexican piñon (*Pinus cembroides*) on the arid foothills. Intermixed in some places are junipers, scrub oaks, and manzanita (*Arctostaphylos*).

Oak-Scrub.—A belt of stunted oaks, like shrubs, forms the lower edge of the pine-oak zone.

In southeastern Sonora, according to Moore (1938:112), *M. g. onusta* breeds at 4,000 to 8,500 feet, descending in autumn as low as about 2,500 feet.

The south Mexican turkey (*M. g. gallopavo*), the progenitor of our domestic turkey, was as adaptable as any of the other races. It once occupied the low coastal plain—the Tierra Caliente—of Veracruz, part of which is humid and tropical, and part arid. The average annual rainfall of the state of Veracruz is 64 inches. This turkey formerly ranged westward from Veracruz through the state of Mexico in the elevated oak-pine zone.

The ranges of the United States races of the turkey fall rather neatly into regions having different precipitations as will be seen by comparing Fig. 6 with Fig. 11. The eastern and Florida turkeys are to be found in the humid region, the Rio Grande turkey in the subhumid region, and the Merriam's and Gould's turkeys in the semiarid region. It seems clear that it is precipitation and not habitat *per se* that controls the distribution

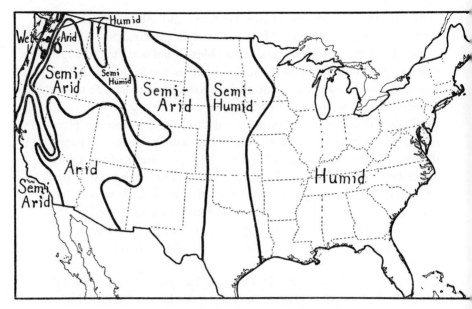

Fig. 11.—*Moisture belts of North America. (After McDougal* [1927].*)*

of races of the turkey. In Texas, the Rio Grande Plain, Edwards Plateau, and the Rolling Plains offer sharp ecological and topographical contrasts, yet all are occupied by the Rio Grande turkey. The one thing in common is the same precipitation. Within the three types of terrain, the several races find varied but suitable habitats.

10

Breeding and Nesting

Contemplation makes a rare turkey-cock of him:
How he jets under his advanced plumes!
SHAKESPEARE.

THERE IS A DIFFERENCE of opinion on whether wild turkeys breed or not when one year old. It is generally assumed that the hens of this age do breed and that the gobblers, though physiologically capable of doing so, are prevented by a psychological barrier raised by the presence of the mature males. Audubon (1831:4) has described the courting of a young hen: "If a cock meets a young hen, he alters his mode of procedure. He struts in a different manner, less pompously and more energetically, moves with rapidity, sometimes rises from the ground, taking a short flight around the hen ... and on alighting, runs with all his might, at the same time rubbing his tail and wings along the ground, for the space of perhaps ten yards. He then draws near the timorous female, allays her fears by purring, and when she at length assents, caresses her." I do not believe that the turkey ever drags its tail on the ground.

BREEDING AGE

The wild birds kept by Caton (1887.1:371) on a forty-acre tract at Ottawa, Illinois, did not breed until two years old. Some birds from the first generation bred when a year old, while the second and third generations generally reproduced at this age. Male and female Merriam's turkeys, according to Ligon (1946:6), usually do not show an inclination to breed until nearly two years of age. He adds that birds breeding at a younger age may be considered as containing some domestic blood. Based on three years of observations, Wheeler (1946.1:141) believed that few hens nest when one year of age. On the other hand, Leopold (1944:160) states that young hens of the eastern turkey breed and nest freely. Burget (1946:19) mentions a case where ten hens, seven of which were juveniles, produced seventy-five poults. If only the three mature hens had bred, it would have been necessary for each of them to produce twenty-five poults.

Each spring there are numerous hens that do not appear to have nested and are considered barren. Jordan (1898:330) denied that there are barren hens, the apparent condition being brought about by the loss of either eggs or young. In view of the high nest losses, he is possibly correct. Mosby and Handley (1943:170) state that "barren or unsuccessful" hens form flocks by themselves in summer. It is conceivable that under certain conditions breeding activity will be decreased. Barnes (1886) mentions that during one season in Arkansas, most of the food was destroyed because of the burning of the woods, and the turkeys came through the winter half-starved. In the spring there were few signs of breeding activity.

Under normal conditions, a yearling gobbler cowed by the mature gobblers will not copulate with the hens. Domestic gobblers one year old breed freely. Observations on young wild males raised at the National Agricultural Center showed that they were perfectly capable of breeding during their first year. Sperm was produced when they were thirty-eight to forty weeks old (Marsden and Martin, 1945:55). Wild males one year of age, in contrast to comparable domestic males, show only slight development of the secondary sex characters. Leopold (1944:182) states: "The initial development of the testes, however, is induced by gona-dotropic hormones released from the pituitary. The slow sexual develop-ment of young male wild turkeys is therefore probably attributable to lack of secretion of the gonadotropic hormone in the hypophysis and subsequent lack of growth and secretion of the testes."

Reports differ on the breeding of year-old gobblers when there is no competition from mature males. Two hens and fourteen poults were released on Bull Island, South Carolina. No young were produced until two years later (Davis, 1949:96). When yearling toms, obtained by mating captive wild hens with wild gobblers, were released with yearling hens, poults were produced, proving that they were sexually mature; however, when the young gobblers were confined with hens, no interest in breeding was shown (Mosby and Handley, 1943:107). Interesting observations on the breeding of young gobblers have been made by

Burget (1957:17). In one instance, the mature gobblers were so engrossed in displaying that a hen left the strutting ground and was served by one of the young gobblers which had previously dispersed. Burget describes three cases where hens and juvenile gobblers were released in areas remote from other turkeys. The spring following the release, poults were produced.

Pertinent information on the ability of year-old males to breed has been furnished by A. S. Leopold. Under date August 25, 1959, he wrote to me: "I have recently returned from two months in Mexico where we had a most pleasant and profitable stay in the Sierra del Nido, about 60 miles north and a little west of Chihuahua City. The turkey population there, which had been at very low ebb in 1957 following a 10-year drought, jumped up after the rains of 1958 and is now quite high. Additional rains this year should result in another big crop of young and a further increase in the total population. We ran into one curious situation that might interest you. A good many of the yearling gobblers born in 1958 are fully developed sexually, with heavy wattles and caruncles on the head, and with very large testes. And they are actively gobbling and acting in every way like fully adult birds. I strongly suspect that they bred this spring. I recall a similar situation in Missouri when I established a new refuge in the Ozarks which led to a sudden and dramatic increase in turkeys. In each of these two cases the population made up almost entirely of young birds, with very few adult gobblers, seems to produce breeding or at least sexually well-developed young gobblers when, as you know, sexual development in yearling gobblers is usually completely retarded in a normal population which contains an adequate quota of old toms. To me this looks like a case of social suppression by adult gobblers which form of suppression is released when the old toms are very scarce, and the young toms then blossom forth physiologically and physically to take over the responsibilities of mating."

The age for maximum sexual potency in males is unknown. Randall (1930) states that the wild gobblers should be two years old as they will not breed during the first year. Some of his gobblers were ten years old and still breeding strongly. Old males were the preferred breeders. Davis (1949:102), in early fall, has found the intact carcasses of males that had been dead for some months. He believes that old gobblers sometimes succumb under the stresses of the breeding season.

There is little information regarding the number of eggs laid by the hen according to her age. Sandys and Van Dyke (1904:259) were informed by an old woodsman that the young hen first lays seven to eight eggs, two more the next season, still more the third, then the number decreases. The difficulty of distinguishing the age of a hen after the first year renders this statement questionable. Under artificial light the number of eggs laid by domestic hens declined from fifty eggs the first laying season to fourteen eggs the fifth season (Marsden and Martin, 1945:195). Game farm hens one year of age laid eggs slightly smaller than did older hens (Gerstell and Long, 1939:5). W. W. Bailey (1941) found that first-year hens began laying fifteen to twenty days later than the older hens, and did not lay as regularly.

GOBBLING

The flocks of gobblers disintegrate in late winter, the males then associating with the hens. The beginning of the breeding season is announced by the gobbling of the males. Initiation of gobbling and its regularity are controlled largely by weather conditions. Brandt (1951:623) wrote: "On the morning of April 24, 1947, the temperature at Rustler Park had dropped to 24°, which with a strong wind made the blind uncomfortably cold. At dawn the turkeys on that day did not break loose with their gobbling, and were about two hours late for breakfast." In South Carolina, according to Davis (1949:98), a few old males will begin gobbling the latter half of February. If the weather is cold and cloudy, not a sound is to be heard. Towards the end of March each gobbler has a trysting place and the hens go to him.

The middle of April is the height of the gobbling season. Rutledge (1941.1:106) heard the "love challenge" of the gobblers the first of March. At Gulf Hammock, Florida, the first gobbling was heard by Fields (1953) in 1953 on January 22, but it did not become common until March 15 to April 15. Calling and strutting in Florida lasts from January to March but are most prominent in February (Anon., 1950:5). Gobbling in Virginia is normally heard on warm mornings the latter part of March. It may be heard several weeks earlier if there is an open winter followed by an early spring (Mosby and Handley, 1943:104). In Pennsylvania breeding activities begin in March and early April (Latham, 1956:28).

Regarding the mating season in Alabama, Wheeler (1948:31) wrote:

"The time of the mating season is influenced considerably by the weather conditions. During springs when the weather is consistently mild, breeding commences earlier than when the climatic conditions are changeable. A few consecutive mild days during the latter portion of winter quite frequently stimulate the sexual urge of both the male and female as is evidenced by spasmodic out-of-season gobbling and yelping. This urge is abruptly quelled at the return of cool weather." During the period 1943 through 1946, mating began on March 15, March 7, and March 21 respectively. It may be stated to begin about the middle of March and reach its peak the first week in April.

Gobbling on the Beaver Creek area, Kentucky, occurred from March 24 to June 1, 1949. Ridgetops were preferred sites for gobbling, during which time the males remained in relatively small areas. In 1950 the first gobbling was heard on March 25 but hens were seen in flocks as late as March 28. The first gobbling in 1952 took place on March 10 (Hardy, 1949–52). Groups of two to five birds are encountered in Missouri from late March to early April. Complete disintegration of the flocks does not take place until gobbling is well advanced. The gobbling period runs from March 15 to June 5; however, the main period of gobbling which results in mating is from April 15 to April 30 (Dalke et al., 1946:39).

The first mating activity in 1944 in southern Texas was observed by Glazener (1944.1) on February 5 when nine gobblers were strutting and gobbling around three hens. He estimated that 90 per cent of the hens that wintered on the Tepeguaje Ranch, located nineteen miles south of Falfurrias, left the area for nesting in preferred cover elsewhere. In 1945 on the Clear Fork of the Brazos in Texas, the first strutting by a gobbler was noted on February 8 (Jackson, 1945). Gobbling took place occasionally after this date and reached its peak the latter half of March. Strutting in Oklahoma occurred from February 7 to May 25, reaching a peak between March 8 and 14 (Thomas, 1954.1:8). According to Jordan (1898:371), from 30° to 33° north latitude, gobbling begins about the first of March and ends the last of May, the length of the period depending upon the weather. The gobbling season is shorter during a mild spring than when the weather is rainy and chilly.

The gobbling begins at dawn though the turkeys usually do not leave the roost until daylight. Kennard (1915.1:160) heard the first gobbling in the Big Cypress Swamp, Florida, at 5:03 A.M. on March 20, 1914. In

Virginia most of the gobbling is heard in early spring during the first
hour after sunrise, but as the season advances it may be heard up to
8 o'clock or later: "If a gobbler has not succeeded in attracting a hen to
him he may gobble frequently, often every five minutes or less, particularly during the first hour following sunrise. However, there appears
to be considerable individuality in the amount of calling indulged in by
the various males. Records of the gobbling of one tom, kept from 6:28 to
6:45 A.M. on April 27, 1939, showed that this particular male gobbled on
the average once a minute for the seventeen-minute period. After one
or more hens have joined an old tom, he will spend his time strutting
and seldom gobbles, except in answer to the call of neighboring toms or
to other similar noises" (Mosby and Handley, 1943:105). A Merriam's
male shows no uniformity in the number of gobbles, but at the height of
the season the call may be repeated two or three times a minute (Burget,
1957:13). Near Sinton, Texas, on March 19, 1959, I recorded the gobbles
of one turkey as follows: 9:27, 9:32, 9:40, 9:43, 9:51, 9:55, 9:57, 9:58, 10:00,
10:03, and 10:05 A.M. In the early morning, gobbles were heard from
6:05 to 6:45, and in the evening from 5:10 to 7:10.

The gobbling of Merriam's turkeys, stocked in California, was often
heard by Burger (1954:201) morning and evening during the middle of
April. Gobbling was noted until the last week in July and copulation was
observed on July 13, but there was a steady diminution of this act after
early May. In 1951 breeding activity lasted from February until late in
July, the peak being reached in April.

It has been stated that when a male is fat the gobble is clear and shrill,
but when in poor flesh it is "coarse and cracked" ("Pious Jeems," 1881).
The same opinion was expressed by J. Gordon (1883:761). On the other
hand, Baines (1890:345) states that for fat males the gobble is the
"heaviest and most muffled." Perhaps the quality of the sound is dependent more on age than physical condition. Burget (1957:13) writes:
"There is not enough tonal difference in the voice pitch of older gobblers
to distinguish between individuals but young gobblers can be distinguished by tone from the adults." The gobble of the turkeys of the
Brazos River bottoms was described by Jordan (1898:246) as a hoarse,
guttural rumble, quite different from the clear, loud, rolling gobble of
the cousins in the Trinity River country. I defer to his experience, but

the gobbles of the Rio Grande turkey and the eastern turkey sound alike to me.

I am not aware of a detailed description of the trachea, or windpipe, of the turkey. Stockwell (1888:133) states: "The most elaborate and complex form of gular apparatus undoubtedly is that of *Meleagris gallopavo*—the wild turkey—and its domesticated congener; this though single, is yet appartmental [*sic*] by virtue of being repeatedly flexed upon itself." This statement has no basis in fact. E. Coues has stated that this author is entirely unreliable.

THE TURKEY'S VOICE

There are numerous renditions of the vocal sounds made by turkeys. Before leaving the roosting tree during the mating season, according to Jordan (1914:174), the gobble is *gil-obble, obble, obble, quit, quit cut.* After alighting on the ground, the bird will gobble, then raise his head to scan the surroundings, then utter a "put-put." The *gil-obble-obble-obble* in the spring is more shrill than that of the domesticated bird, but becomes hoarser as the season advances (Simmons, 1925:84). If the gobbler thinks that he has heard the answering call of a hen, *cluck, cluck, keow, keow, keow,* he indulges in the booming strut, *vut-v-r-r-o-o-o-m-m-i,* followed by a thundering *gil-obble-obble-obble.* If the hen responds with a low, quavering, *keow, keow, keow,* he will call in a fierce, prolonged rattle. Following a *keow, keow, kee, kee* or *cluck, keow, ku-ku* from the hen, the gobbler responds with *gil-obble-obble-obble* and *cluck-v-r-r-o-o-mi.* With a *cut-o-r-r-r, cut-cut-keow,* the hen goes to him for mating. The young male is indifferent to the female at this season and her calls do not affect him. He is interested only in the calls of other young males, *croc-croc* or *cong-cong-croc-croc,* or *croc-croc-kee-kee* (Jordan, 1914:203).

A turkey when suspicious or in danger has an alarm note that has been rendered *put, purt,* or *quit.* The alarm note of the female Florida turkey, according to McLauren (1957:22), is *kwa-a-ah* and the danger signal *purt.* The assembly call is *heoh-heoh-heoh,* and when feeding undisturbed, *yedle-yedle-yedle.* The feeding note of Merriam's turkey is given as a soft *kew! kew!* (Burget, 1957:10). There is mention of the *chow-chow-chow* of the turkey hen (Lowndes, 1883); and a *yunk-yunk-yunk* that can be imitated by sucking air interruptedly through a clay pipe

(Sandys and Van Dyke, 1904:274). The leader of a flock of Merriam's gobblers on going to roost uttered "tremulous signal notes—quir-r-r-rt, quir-r-r-rt, quir-r-r-rt" (Goldman, 1902:126). One hunter ("Nick," 1885) mentions an Arkansas gobbler that called *goo-goo-goo* and *putttt-putttt-putttt*. Everitt (1928:30) gives the following renditions for the eastern turkey: hen, *queet, queet, cuick, cuick*; hen with brood, *cluck, cluck, cluck*; young gobbler, *cuionk, cuionk, cuionk*; before leaving roost in the morning, *keok, keok, keok*; and young separated from the flock, *k-ee, k-ee, k-ee*. It is impossible to coin a combination of letters that will imitate the calls satisfactorily. It would be interesting to determine if the gobble and other calls are distinguishable as to race.

The gobble of the turkey carries to great distances. Nowlin (1882:529) mentions that on quiet mornings in Wayne County, Michigan, turkeys could be heard gobbling a mile or two away. These distances are also given by Jordan (1914). Gerhardt (1853:379) makes the peculiar statement that, while gobbling, the turkey closes or contracts its eyes and appears to be so blind and dumb that even a missed shot does not frighten it. During this performance the hunter can advance towards the bird but must stop when gobbling ceases.

BEHAVIOR OF MALES

Audubon (1831:3) gives an interesting description of the behavior of the sexes during the breeding season. The fatal combats between the males, and the breaking of eggs, if they occur at all, are very rare. He writes: "As early as the middle of February, they begin to experience the impulse of propagation. The females separate, and fly from the males. The latter strenuously pursue, and begin to gobble or to utter the notes of exultation. The sexes roost apart, but at no great distance from each other. When a female utters a call-note, all the gobblers within hearing return the sound, rolling note after note with as much rapidity as if they intended to emit the last and first together, not with spread tail, as when fluttering round the females on the ground, or practising on the branches of the trees on which they have roosted for the night, but much in the manner of the domestic turkey, when an unusual or unexpected noise elicits its singular hubbub. If the call of the female comes from the ground, all the males immediately fly towards the spot, and the moment they reach it, whether the hen be in sight or not, spread out and erect their tail, draw the head back on the shoulders, depress their wings with a quivering motion, and strut pompously about, emitting at the same time a succession of puffs from the lungs, and stopping now and then to listen and look. But whether they spy the female or not, they continue to puff and strut, moving with as much celerity as their ideas of ceremony seem to admit. While thus occupied, the males often encounter each other, in which case desperate battles take place, ending in bloodshed, and often in the loss of many lives, the weaker falling under the repeated blows inflicted upon their head by the stronger."

He states that when two males are fighting fiercely, if one bird loses its hold, he is killed by the rival, which uses its wings and spurs. The winner then tramps upon the dead bird, but without manifestation of malice.

When a male meets a female, if she is more than one year of age, she also struts and gobbles, walks around him, then suddenly opens her wings, and throws herself towards him to receive his "caresses." The harem acquired by the gobbler roosts near the male, if not in his tree, until laying begins. The hens then separate and secrete their nests to prevent the male from breaking the eggs. He is then avoided except for brief periods daily. At this time the males begin to lose interest in the females who then make all the advances.

The gobblers sometimes strut and gobble on the roost. This activity is continued for hours at a time on clear or moonlight nights. During the performance the tail is raised and spread, the pulmonic puff issues, and the tail and other feathers are lowered.

At the close of the mating season, the males are emaciated, gobbling ceases, and the breast-sponge virtually disappears. They then separate from the hens and appear to have deserted the vicinity. However, they can be found lying beside a log in dense cover. At this time, covered with ticks, they will not fly, but will run swiftly. As soon as sufficient flesh is regained, they form wandering flocks. Audubon's original manuscript on the habits of the turkey has been published verbatim (Schorger, 1962). Some of his statements must be based on Gallic imagination.

The male frequently displays on the roost. Packard (1910:229) has described the behavior of a large gobbler after he had gone to roost in a big pine tree that was surrounded by hardwoods: "He looked this way and that for those missing hens that surely ought to be lured. . . . He gobbled to right and he gobbled to left in mingled defiance and entreaty, but there was no reply. Then he strutted and displayed all his magnificance. He spread the wide fan of his copper-red tail, drooped his wings till they hung below the limb and puffed out all his feathers. . . . Then he said 'Pouf'! once or twice in a half-hissing, sudden grunt that sounded as if it came from the bunghole of an empty barrel." Jordan (1914:126) often saw gobblers strut on the roost and shot them while in the act.

The best description of the strut that I have seen is that of Jordan (1914:128): "In the early morning, during the spring, a gobbler will fly from his roost to the ground, strutting and gobbling, whether a hen is in sight or not; this is done to attract the hens, and it is then you will hear the puffs to which Audubon refers. This sound is produced by the gobbler in expelling the air from its lungs, at the beginning of the strut, the sounds and motions of which have never been satisfactorily described. While going through the strut the gobbler produces a number of notes and motions that are of interest; first the wings are dropped until the first six or eight feathers at the end of the wings touch the ground; at the same time the tail is spread until like an open fan and erected at right angles to the body; the neck is drawn down and back until the head rests against the shoulder feathers, and the body feathers are all thrown forward until they stand about at right angles to their normal place. At the same time the body is inflated with air, which, with the drooping wings, spread tail, and ruffled feathers, gives the bird the appearance of a big ball. Having blown himself up to the full capacity of his skin, the gobbler suddenly releases the air, making a puff exactly as if a person, having inflated the cheeks to their full capacity, suddenly opens the mouth. As the puff is given, the bird steps quickly forward four or five paces, dragging the ends of the stiff wing feathers along the ground, making a rasping sound; he throws forward his chest, and, gradually contracting the muscles, forces the air from his body with a low, rumbling boom, the feathers resuming their normal position as the air is expelled. Three distinct sounds are produced: 'Puff, cluck, b-o-o-r-r-r-mi.' At the termination of the gobbling season the primaries of the wings [sic], which are used to produce the cluck, are badly worn by the continued dragging on the ground."

The Pulmonic Puff

It is generally accepted that the "pulmonic puff" of Audubon is the chief sound produced during the strut. Many laymen have thought that the scraping of the wings on the ground was the principal sound. Jones (1888) believed that the "roaring or buzzing sound" was produced by intense quivering of the tail feathers. Everitt (1928:22) states that at the height of the strut air is released from the body, thus producing a distinct *shuff*, followed by a rumble: "The whole performance is climaxed by the '*shuff-v-o-o-r-r-m*' of the escaping air and the loud scrape of the wings upon the ground." Baines (1890:344) wrote: "How the gobbler makes that thunder-like sound when he struts, I do not know, but am certain that it is not by scraping his wings on the ground, since he struts as loudly in a tree, where his wings touch nothing, and where he can not walk at all, as when on the ground. I am sure that his crop, puffed full of air, is an important factor, since no turkey ever struts without this."

The exact reservoirs from which the turkey draws air have not been established. Sandys and Van Dyke (1904:112) state: "If any one will pass his hand over a tame gobbler engaged in strutting, he will at once notice that the bird feels as though he were full of air. Parts of him are. In the region of the crop, and along the sides under the wings, he feels like a big, feathery bladder. Startle him, or slap him smartly, and he may let the air out through his mouth with a rush. If he be sufficiently tame to stand it, pat him smartly in rapid succession with the open hands, and the sound will be muffled beating, not at all unlike the drumming of the grouse."

Female domestic turkeys, especially those over a year old, sometimes show virilism, a term used for male behavior. Occasionally they will strut persistently and mount other females. Virilism in the female chicken is associated with a tumor on the adrenal glands which appears to cause secretion of a male hormone (Marsden and Martin, 1945:686).

Strutting Grounds

A strutting ground is usually open. It may be occupied by one or several males, and a male may use more than one place for strutting. Burget (1957:13) observed as many as sixteen gobblers on a strutting ground. Usually there were two or three mature gobblers, the others approximately a year old. Males approximately two years old were rare. A strutting ground in Colorado is usually a small open park or glade, or a sandy area in heavy timber. When an area is occupied by fifty or more birds, the strutting grounds may be 500 yards to one-half mile apart. Strutting grounds in Oklahoma are usually in flat, open woodland. A male may move 150 to 600 yards to defend another strutting area, or a male may challenge other males on a territory measuring 100 by 200 yards. The territory actually defended appears to comprise four to eight acres (Thomas, 1954.1:8).

It was found difficult in Missouri to note a definite boundary between the adjacent territories occupied by two gobblers. The average gobbling and strutting areas comprised one to three hundred acres. The distances between gobbling males varied from one-quarter mile to three-fourths of a mile, the average being four-tenths of a mile. Distribution of the gobblers was very irregular (Dalke *et al.*, 1946:43). Gobblers in Virginia show a preference for open areas for strutting. These may be openings in a forest, edges of fields, or roads in woods (Mosby and Handley, 1943:109).

COPULATION

The hen always comes to the gobbler for the purpose of copulation. The eagerness of the hen to copulate impressed Fabricius (1942:147), who wrote in 1621: "I keep at home a turkey hen which has a passion for the cock; even when we stand by and touch her back with our hands, she squats down under the cock, raises her tail, and exposes the vulva; at the same time this opening is so directed that the penis and semen may reach it." He thought erroneously that the semen was held in the bursa.

The behavior of Merriam's turkeys during copulation has been described by Brandt (1951:631). The trysting place is a well-wooded slope of a mountain, seemingly selected for protection during the sexual act, which is all-engrossing. The female makes the advance: "When the female is in the mood, she squats before her lord in abject enticement, with feathers loosely fluffed and head down, an object of complete supplication. It takes considerable coaxing on her part to bring the male out of his strut into sex recognition, and even as he starts his treading action some of his strutting feathers may be still partly erect.

". . . As she lies prone on the ground, the big tom hops on top and stamps on her, raising each foot forward with a treading action, literally walking and jumping all over her back in the roughest kind of manner. With a weight ratio of 2 to 1 against her, fantastic indeed is the indignity suffered by our major feminine fowl, yet she actually courts this treatment. In this preliminary nuptial action the male vigorously stamps on his mate from 20 to 40 times or even more and usually continues for at least five minutes. After this the hen tilts forward on her wishbone, raises her tail, and the actual caress then takes place. One act which I witnessed lasted many minutes, and when the hen finally arose, she seemed dazed as though from a severe beating, to which evidently she had been subjected."

It is assumed by Brandt that during treading the sharp claws of the male injure the back of the female as in the case of the domestic turkey, hence that the statement of Audubon that the female copulates daily is probably erroneous. Jordan (1898:226) states that during the sexual act the female domestic hen emits a cry that sounds distressing but the wild hen does not.

The observations of Heinroth (1941:331) on the copulation of domestic turkeys are as follows: "In fact the gobbler displays when alone, but especially if females are in the vicinity. Suddenly a hen separates from her companions, dances around the displaying gobbler with characteristic leaps and also with wing-spreading until she rests finally a short distance from him. The male with tail spread, feathers puffed, the tips of the primaries dragging on the ground, and the caruncles of the neck colored light blue, comes up to her with the known '*tuckuh*,' mounts her back in an upright position, and tramples around in the region of her rump for a considerable time, so that one may believe that she is undergoing severe injury. It often happens that interested males eject such a gobbler from the back of the female; then the hen moves a couple of steps and sits down again. During the trampling the tail of the hen gradually rises and that of the gobbler lowers, the male in the meantime settling on its tarsi and the sexual union takes place, whereupon the animals separate. The cloaca of the gobbler then swells and contracts for a time. Females uninterested in mating avoid the gobblers and it appears that a single copulation suffices to fertilize the entire clutch. Receptive hens at a distance are enticed by the gobbling of the male.

"If a gobbler is enraged, he does not indulge in display, but spreads the tail only moderately, becomes quite slender in front, and approaches the opponent with peculiar sounds which can be imitated with difficulty. Fighting gobblers and hens mutually seek to seize the frontal caruncle, and then struggle with one another until at length one gives way and assumes a submissive attitude by its crouching position. Then he is careful not to be further annoyed by the victor."

As an example of imprinting, a domestic gobbler, given special care on account of sickness, displayed and showed sexual reactions towards his mistress; however, though not displaying before the hen, he did copulate with her (Räber, 1948:239).

The important observation was made by Schein and Hale (1957) that the head of the female was the part of her anatomy that induced copulation. Taxidermic skins with detachable head and neck were used in the experiments. When a female dummy had her head in a normal position, males with sexual experience would display and mount the dummy as readily as receptive live females. If the head was missing, the males would display but not mount the dummy. When only the detached head was offered to eight males for a test period of five minutes, seven displayed and waltzed within one-half to three minutes. Only one bird displayed fully. A male, after mounting a live female, obtained proper anterior-posterior orientation by placing his head directly over that of the female. The same maneuver was made by the males reacting to the detached head, the floor being trod immediately back of the head.

The hen visits the gobbler until her clutch of eggs is almost complete and she begins to incubate. Audubon (1831:4) states that her visits are daily, and Jordan (1914:105) that they are daily or on alternate days. The hens usually join the gobblers soon after leaving the roost. The visits may be short or occupy most of the day (Mosby and Handley, 1943:110). According to Wheeler (1948:32), the hens remain until about 9:00 A.M. Burget (1957:16) has noted that the hen does not visit the same strutting ground daily unless only one is available. When several strut grounds are available, she may make irregular visits to one or more of them. He adds: "The nesting hen comes to a strut ground some time each day during the egg laying period. She may remain in the area from a few minutes to a few hours. She comes into the area with seeming indifference to the gobbler." Bailey *et al.* (1951:9) state that the hen visits the strutting ground usually daily for copulation and is served by the gobbler even far into the incubation period. A hen may, however, come to a strutting ground and avoid copulation.

NUMBER OF HENS IN THE HAREM

The number of hens in a harem in the wild in Virginia seldom exceeds four to six. Although one copulation is sufficient to fertilize all the eggs, the hens usually visit the gobbler almost daily until incubation commences (Mosby and Handley, 1943:107). The sex ratio on the Salt Springs Game Sanctuary, Alabama, was equal, but the average harem consisted of five hens (Wheeler, 1948:32). Thomas (1954.1) found that in Oklahoma the average harem comprised 5.5 females, the extreme being one to fourteen hens.

NESTING SITES

The hen usually selects a nesting site near the strutting ground and close to water. Normally the nest is well concealed by overhanging vegetation (Plate 24). Audubon (1831:5) wrote: "About the middle of April, when the season is dry, the hens begin to look for a place in which to deposit their eggs. . . . The nest, which consists of a few withered leaves, is placed on the ground, in a hollow scooped out, by the side of a log, or in the fallen top of a dry leafy tree, under a thicket of sumach or briars, or a few feet within the edge of a crane-brake, but always in a dry place." He mentions that islands are often chosen for nesting. Piles of driftwood are usually present and in these the birds hide when alarmed.

The nest of the Florida turkey, according to the information furnished Bendire (1892:114) by William L. Ralph, "is a slight depression in the ground, either at the foot of a tree or under a thick bush or saw palmetto. It is lined sparingly with dead leaves and grass, etc., but I could never find out whether this material was placed there by the birds or was there originally." A more recent publication (Anon., 1950:5) places the nest near an opening such as a trail or old road in the woods, and near water.

The preferred nesting areas of the eastern turkey in Alabama are in fairly open woodland (Wheeler, 1948:36). H. L. Stoddard, in a manuscript furnished Burleigh (1958:208) states that, as a rule, the nests are placed in patches of comparatively heavy ground cover which has escaped the general burning for two or three years. Shrubs and the sprouts of hardwood usually conceal the eggs well from any angle. The preference for nesting near open sites in Virginia (Mosby and Handley, 1943:110) is shown by the following: "The hens often choose nesting sites near the locality in which they consort with the gobblers. They show a decided preference for locating their nests near openings in the forest, usually choosing sites near trails, roads, or small abandoned fields. Some nests are located within five or ten feet of such openings, while others are situated greater distances from the clearings. Wild turkey nests are frequently located beneath small trees in abandoned fields, in honeysuckle tangles around old house sites, in thickets beside roads in the woods, or beneath tree laps (tops left by logging) of small pulpwood operations. Occasionally a hen will locate her nest at the base of a large tree. With rare exception, nests are at least partially concealed by low-growing vegetation of some kind, such as forest reproduction or shrubby ground cover, honeysuckle or smilax thickets, blackberry tangles, or beneath tree laps. Restocked wild turkeys show a tendency to locate their nests in more exposed situations than do native wild hens."

Nests in Missouri were so situated as to provide visibility overhead and in two or more lateral directions as well as an avenue for ready escape. Flat areas approachable from all directions were avoided. Nests on low ground protected by thick, high weeds, were atypical (Blakey, 1937:6). On Brown Ridge, Missouri, preferred nesting cover was in open stands of oak containing dense clumps of oak sprouts that provided concealment (Dalke et al., 1946:50).

On the Clear Fork of the Brazos and its tributaries, dispersion of Rio Grande turkeys to the nesting grounds takes place during the last half of March. The birds are thinly spread over upland mesquite pastures and high divides in Shackelford County (Jackson, 1945). In Wilbarger County most of the nests were in the open, often near well-traveled highways, and located in grain fields (Brandt, 1940:140). Glazener (1944.1) observed in southern Texas that the flocks began to break up between January 14 and 20, and move to the open mesquite country. The important nesting cover consisted of mesquite, lantana, prickly pear, and wild peach. Most of the wintering grounds were abandoned by March 7. The presence of little bluestem (*Andropogon scoparius*) and muhlygrass (*Muhlenbergia lindheimeri*), according to Walker (1948.1:10), is important for nesting purposes on the oak erosion area of the Edwards Plateau. In the mineral region of the plateau, in the spring of 1941, 60 per cent of the ten nests found in southern Mason County were under tasajillo cacti where there were tall grasses, and 10 per cent in tall grasses protected from livestock by prickly pear (*Opuntia*) (Walker, 1949.1:14).

Merriam's turkey generally places its nest in open situations on northern slopes at altitudes of 7,000 to 9,500 feet. Ligon (1946:33) examined many nests in New Mexico and Arizona, all above 7,000 feet. Only three had any cover, and these were only partially concealed by the dead branches of fallen pines. The remainder were in places sufficiently open to afford the hen a clear view for a considerable distance around the nest and permit rapid escape by flight.

The nests are sometimes located in odd places. A wild turkey captured in Ontario adapted herself to Scotch topography. As described by Gilmour (1876:13): "A high precipitous rock, standing peculiarly on the level grounds beside the house, crowned on the summit with a dense growth of ivy and overshadowed by a tree, attracted the attention of one of the hens; and in the summer of 1868, the hens having been let out of confinement for a change, one of them nested in the very centre of this bunch of ivy. Her mode of getting upstairs was original, and displayed her wild cunning, for she first of all got into the tree, and going along a branch that overhung the rock, let herself drop on to her nest; when on her nest not a vestige of her could be seen, and it was some time before her hiding-place was discovered." The keeper had to bring down the young after hatching.

Nests in equally hazardous situations were found in Missouri (Blakey, 1937:5). One was placed on so confined a space at the edge of a sinkhole about thirty feet deep that it could be reached only by flying. By pitching off the nest towards the eroded opposite side of the sinkhole, the hen could escape easily. Insofar as known, the brood was brought off without difficulty. Another nest was found within six inches of the edge of a sheer cliff one hundred feet high.

Manner of Leaving the Nest

The hen may leave the nest by flying or walking. It has been recommended that on approaching a nest the observer be as casual as possible, whistling or talking aloud, and not looking directly at the sitting hen (Mosby and Handley, 1943:117). If she realizes that she has been discovered, she will fly from the nest a short distance giving the *put* alarm note. A hasty departure may cause some of the eggs to be thrown out of the nest. In order to avoid desertion, it is preferable not to replace the scattered eggs. Audubon (1931:6) states that the hen runs from the nest. She does not move as long as she believes herself undiscovered. If the observer acts as though he did not see her, it is possible to approach within five or six paces before she runs away with her tail spread to one side.

Four of the hens of five nests found in Alabama flew from the nest on being disturbed. One hen ran approximately 150 feet before flying (Wheeler, 1948:38). Merriam's turkey is said to fly invariably to and from the nest (Ligon, 1946:34). Because of the difficulties in making observations, little is known about how the hens of other races approach and leave the nest.

Rutledge (1936:533) states that the female always flies to and from it. Information provided Bendire (1892:115) shows that the hen at times at least does walk to the nest. J. A. Singley wrote: "The hen leaves and approaches the nest invariably by the same route, and remembering this I trailed one to its nest." Captain B. F. Goss wrote to Bendire that while camped in southern Texas, he watched for three mornings a turkey stealing through the bushes. The nest was almost at his feet when the hen ran from it.

Date of Laying

The date of the beginning of laying depends upon the latitude, or altitude, and the state of the weather. The little information available on oviposition for the various states is given below.

Alabama.—Deposition begins soon after the first week in April, the majority of the clutches being completed by May 7 (Wheeler, 1948:34). In 1940 the earliest nest with eggs was found on February 15, and the first poults were seen on April 10 (Barkalow, 1942).

Arizona.—F. Stephens took an incomplete set of nine fresh eggs from a nest near Craterville (Greaterville), Pima County, on June 15, 1884, at an elevation of about 5,000 feet (Bendire, 1892:118). Howard (1900) described a nest found near Fort Huachuca, Cochise County, on July 1, 1899, containing nine addled eggs. He thought that they had been incubated for about six weeks.

Arkansas.—There are six eggs in the U. S. National Museum taken at Fort Smith on April 3, 1866.

California.—The nesting of stocked Merriam's turkeys began the latter part of March and reached a peak shortly after the first of April (Burger, 1954:201).

Florida.—W. L. Ralph found fresh eggs from the middle of March to May 1 (Bendire, 1892:114). Bent (1932:326, 341) gives the following dates for eggs: fifteen records covering from March 25 to May 22, of which eight were from April 10 to May 3. He had a set of ten eggs taken near Everglades, Collier County, March 28, 1908.

Georgia.—H. L. Stoddard (Burleigh, 1958:208) gives the following dates for Grady County: May 9, 1925, twelve eggs; April 13, 1940, fourteen eggs; April 6, 1944, two nests about seventy-five yards apart with nine and twenty-one eggs respectively. Nests mainly in April and May, but a brood of ten to twelve young only two to three days old was seen on July 15, 1946.

Iowa.—Peck (1921:115) states that he had eggs of the wild turkey taken in the state. No definite dates were found.

Kansas.—The hen begins laying early in April (Goss, 1891:230).

Kentucky.—Hens begin nesting in April, the average clutch being eleven eggs (Gale and Myers, 1954:41).

Louisiana.—Nesting usually begins in the early part of April (Kopman, 1921:86). Turkeys begin breeding early in April (Oberholser, 1938:193). On April 17, 1897, a set of fifteen eggs was taken at Hammond (Reed, 1904:146). A nest in which two hens deposited twenty-six eggs was found by G. E. Beyer on May 25, 1888 (Bendire, 1892:115).

Maryland.—Nest with two eggs was found in Montgomery County, June 4, 1859; a nest with seven eggs, in Allegany County, in May in the middle of the 1940's; and poults seen in June, July, and August (Stewart and Robbins, 1958:126).

Michigan.—There are three records for February 10 and May 5 and 6 (Bent, 1932:326). The February record is open to doubt.

259

THE WILD TURKEY

Mississippi.—Nests may be found from March to July, or later. Those found after May are believed to be second attempts (Cook, 1945:65).

Missouri.—The average season for oviposition in the southern part of the state runs from April 1 to May 15. The hatching date of May 12 for a clutch of sixteen eggs indicates laying began the end of March. The peak of egg deposition is in the last two weeks of April (Blakey, 1937:7). Estimated laying dates ran from April 1 to May 25 (Dalke *et al.*, 1946:46).

Nebraska.—Captain W. L. Carpenter found a nest with seven eggs at Fort Niobrara on May 1, 1880. There were eleven eggs when the nest was visited on May 20 (Bendire, 1892:115).

New Mexico.—Laying usually begins in April and generally all of the young are hatched by the middle of May (Ligon, 1927:113). Normally laying begins about the first of May (Ligon, 1946:33).

North Carolina.—The breeding season is from the first of May to the middle of June (Cairns, 1889:17).

Oklahoma.—The following eggs from the "Indian Territory" are in the U. S. National Museum:

Locality	Date	No. of Eggs
Washita River	May 16, 1860	3
Then Choctaw Nation	May 5, 1860	3
Then Choctaw Nation	May 5, 1860	4
Now Roger Mills County	June 7, 1860	3

The number of eggs is no indication of the size of the clutch. It was customary at this time to take "samples."

Pennsylvania.—A set of fourteen eggs in the Carnegie Museum was obtained near Hillside, Westmoreland County, on May 23, 1906 (Todd, 1940:181). Three nests were found by Harlow (1918:23): Vail, Blair County, May 17, 1912, six eggs; Greenwood Furnace, Huntingdon County, May 20, 1915, twelve eggs; and Bear Meadows, Centre County, June 22, 1916, twelve eggs. Sutton (1929) has described two nests: near Clearfield, Clearfield County, May 5, 1928, a set of eight fresh eggs, probably incomplete; and twelve miles from Lock Haven, Clinton County, a set of seventeen eggs advanced in incubation, on June 6, 1928. The latter nest contained eighteen eggs the previous day. There are five records for May 5 through June 30 (Bent, 1932:326).

South Carolina.—A nest with fifteen slightly incubated eggs on March

260

30, 1896, was exceptionally early. Laying begins usually the middle of April. Two nests with thirteen eggs each were found May 4 and 22, 1897 (Wayne, 1910:65). For this state and Georgia, there are fifteen records covering from March 30 to May 25, of which eight are from April 25 to May 22 (Bent, 1932:326).

Texas.—(*M. g. intermedia*) : a nest with eleven eggs was found by B. F. Goss on May 9, 1882 (Bendire, 1892:118). One with eleven eggs was found in Duval County on May 20, 1879 (T. Hughes, 1884:91). Lloyd (1887:187) found a nest with eight eggs on May 29, 1882, and he had heard of nests with ten to fourteen eggs to the southward. On the lower Río Grande, Sennett (1879:428) took a set with the chicks peeping in the shell on April 24, 1878, and a set of fifteen fresh eggs on April 26. Young just from the shell were seen by him near Hidalgo on May 8, 1877 (Sennett, 1878:53). Oviposition in Kerr County, according to Lacey (1911:206), usually begins in March. A nest found on June 4 represented a second attempt. Quite small young were seen in April. In 1944 in southern Texas, the first nest was found by Glazener (1944) on March 5. It contained five eggs and was located in a clump of prickly pear beneath an oak.

Based on twenty-three nests, including some from Mexico, Bent (1932:326) gives the dates March 4 to June 28, twelve nests being from May 1 to June 3. A hen taken in the Sierra del Carmen, Coahuila, Mexico, on April 2 was nearing oviposition, the largest ovum being 20 mm. (Miller, 1955:162). Most of the clutches in Shackelford County were assumed by A. S. Jackson (1945) to have been laid during the last half of May. There was evidence of renesting in June.

There are the following eggs in the U. S. National Museum:

Locality	Date	No. of Eggs
Archer County	May 7, 1874	4
Cameron County	June 7, 1892	9
Cameron County	May 26, 1894	6
Cameron County	May 29, 1894	5
Kerr County	June 4, 1893	2
Kerr County	May 2, 1913	15
Tyler County	May 12, 1914	14
Tyler County	May 13, 1905	10
Elk Creek (West Fork,* Red River)	July 15, 1874	6

*Catalogue states North Fork.

Virginia.—March 29 to April 12 is the peak period of laying between March 15 and May 5. Hens held in laying pens—the eggs being collected daily—showed three peaks in oviposition: the latter part of May, the latter part of June, and the middle of July (Mosby and Handley, 1943:187).

West Virginia.—Laying begins about the first of April and continues until a hen lays approximately twelve eggs (Legge, 1957:9).

The loss of eggs and young poults is so high it requires the laying of a large number of eggs in order to keep the population in balance. Davies (1898) stated that game birds lay a large number of eggs because the situation of the nests exposes them to many enemies. Fox (1899) broadened the suggestion to include all species subject to abnormal destruction.

Number of Eggs Laid

Determination of the number of eggs in a clutch is complicated by the laying of more than one hen in the same nest. When, for example, eighteen eggs are found, the nest must be watched to determine if one or more hens are in attendance. G. E. Beyer found a nest in Louisiana containing twenty-six eggs. One hen was sitting on the nest and another standing beside it (Bendire, 1892:115). Caton (1877:326) wrote: "It is not uncommon for two or three hens to lay in the same nest, and then set upon the eggs and raise the young together, though this I always look upon as a misfortune, for most likely they will not commence laying together, so that after one commences setting the other will keep on laying for a week or two before she begins. As neither will remain a day after the first chick is hatched, of course all the late-laid eggs are lost, unless they are taken out and put under a hen. . . ." Audubon (1831:6) once found three hens sitting on a nest containing forty-two eggs.

I know of no case in the wild where the eggs of a communal nest were divided for incubation. Two hens purported to have been hatched from wild eggs in South Carolina laid twenty eggs in the same nest. The day following the deposition of the twentieth egg, both hens were sitting on ten eggs each within a foot of each other ("Piseco," 1891).

The wild hen appears to be a determinate layer. Bouillod (1874:612) had four hens from which he removed the eggs every evening and replaced them with porcelain ones. They laid from fifteen to eighteen eggs each. Two hens raised by Avery (1886) from the eggs of wild birds laid ten and twelve eggs respectively.

The spring of 1937, 756 eggs were collected from sixty-six nests in enclosures in Pennsylvania (Wessell, 1937). This is an average of 11.5 eggs per nest. Unfortunately, the laying range is not given. Leon P. Keiser, superintendent of the Pennsylvania State Wild Turkey Farm, Williamsport, wrote to me as follows: "We have found that a normal hen will lay from 15 to 25 eggs in her first clutch and often from 10 to 15 in her second clutch if she is broken up immediately upon becoming broody. However, they do not always become broody but just stop laying. If given the opportunity they will usually mate again in about 10 days."

I have been informed (*in litt.*) by Dennis Hart, manager of the Virginia State Game Farm, Cumberland, that the average number of eggs per hen was thirty though some hens laid slightly over forty. He adds: "It appears that wild turkeys are physiologically adapted to making two trys, at about 15 eggs a try, at raising of a seasonal brood of young. Any few eggs over the approximate norm of 30 to 35 will be comparatively white, due to depleted physiological reserves of vitamin A, and will be very low in viability either as developing embryos or hatched poults. Any strain of turkeys that tends to produce over this approximately 30-egg average is likely to be tainted with the blood of a domestic strain where there has been some selection for egg production capability."

One or two eggs left in the nest are sufficient to induce the hen to continue to lay. A case is cited by Bement (1867:210) of a domestic hen that began to incubate two eggs left in the nest after sixteen other eggs had been removed from day to day. The range of clutch sizes of the wild turkey is shown in Table 20.

The productivity of the domestic female turkey, while quite large, is much below that of the chicken. In California the average annual egg production for bronze turkeys was 77, 50, 44, 45, and 28 eggs over a period of five years. The Oklahoma Experiment Station obtained an average of 86 eggs per hen from December 1 to July 1; however, by means of artificial illumination, the average was raised to 125 eggs with a maximum production of 205 eggs from one hen during a full calendar year. From the commencement of production to June 30, young bronze hens laid from 10 to 61 eggs in North Dakota (Marsden and Martin, 1945:198).

TABLE 20

CLUTCH SIZES OF WILD TURKEYS

State	Number of Nests	Range of Number of Eggs	Average Number	Reference
		M. g. osceola		
Florida	—	8–13	10	Bendire, 1892:114
		M. g. silvestris		
Alabama	—	8+	11	Wheeler, 1948:36
Alabama	20	—	12.45	Barkalow, 1942
Georgia	—	8–15	11–12	Burleigh, 1958:208
North Carolina	—	8–12	—	Cairns, 1889:17
South Carolina	3	13–15	13.7	Wayne, 1910:65
Virginia (1939)	17	7–16	10.8	Mosby and Handley, 1943:124
Virginia (1940)	10	9–17	12.2	Mosby and Handley
Virginia (1939)	8	7–21*	10.9	Mosby and Handley
Virginia (1940)	5	5–20*	10.4	Mosby and Handley
Virginia	34	7–18	12.3	McDowell, 1956:11
Pennsylvania	11	9–15	12.7	Kozicky, 1948.1
West Virginia	—	8–17	11–12	Bailey et al., 1951:11
Mississippi	23	7–16	12.1	Cook, 1945:66
Missouri	8	8–13	10.5	Leopold, 1944:163
Missouri	7	8–15**	12.9	Leopold
Missouri	25	8–15	11.1	Dalke et al., 1946:49

*Free ranging, captivity reared. Nests with twenty and twenty-one eggs probably "double."
**Hybrid.

		M. g. intermedia		
Texas	—	8–15	—	Simmons, 1925:84
Texas	10	8–21	11†	Glazener, 1945:159

†Due to one double nest of twenty-one eggs, the average number of eggs per hen was ten.

		M. g. merriami		
Arizona	5	—	10.5	Reeves, 1950
Colorado	5	9–19‡	13.4	Burget, 1949.1
New Mexico	—	9–12	—	F. M. Bailey, 1929:232
New Mexico	—	9–15‡‡	10	Ligon, 1946:35

‡ Probably a double nest.
‡‡Exceptional.

The laying cycle has been described by Blakey (1937:7) as follows: "The laying process begins irregularly, the hen often skipping a day. Study of the artificially propagated wild turkey shows that, when this function becomes regular, one egg is laid daily, approximately one hour later each day, beginning at about one hour after sunrise and continuing until sundown terminates the cycle. Then the hen may skip a day and begin over again at the early morning hour and repeat the cycle."

The rule-of-thumb estimate by Mosby and Handley (1943:113) of one and a half days per egg is considered by Dalke *et al.* (1946:44) to be a reliable approximation. Some other gallinaceous birds have a similar cycle. Pheasant hens held in enclosures deposited an egg every 1.3 days (Buss *et al.*, 1951:35). Since each female laid an average of thirty-six eggs, or twice the normal clutch, it is possible that the daily rate was prolonged because of the increase in the number of eggs. The rate of laying of the wild Hungarian partridge is 1.1 days per egg (McCabe and Hawkins, 1946:33), and for the sage grouse 1.3 days (Patterson, 1952:119). Domestic turkeys lay about 40 per cent of their eggs before noon and 60 per cent after noon (Stockton and Asmundson, 1950).

Covering the Eggs

The female, on leaving the nest, covers the eggs carefully with leaves as a protection against crows and other predators (Audubon, 1831:5). Accordingly, most of the nests are found by accident. Complete covering of the eggs is mentioned also by Jordan (1898:288), Davis (1949:103), Bailey *et al.* (1951:9), and others. Blakey (1937:8), Mosby and Handley (1943:113), Dalke *et al.* (1946:47), and Ligon (1946:35) state that the eggs are sometimes or usually covered. Regarding his wild turkeys, Caton (1877:324) wrote: "When the wild turkey in the forest voluntarily leaves her nest, she always covers it with leaves sufficient to hide the eggs and all evidence of the nest. This is less carefully done by the first descendents of the wild hen, and each succeeding generation becomes more careless in this regard, till now more than half the nests we find are not covered at all, and none are covered with the care always manifest in the wild state."

Persistence in Sitting on the Eggs

Prior to the start of incubation the hen will abandon her nest usually on slight provocation. When incubation is advanced, she will remain on the nest with great persistence. According to Audubon (1831:6): "They seldom abandon their nest, when it has been discovered by men; but I believe, never go near it again, when a snake or other animal has sucked any of the eggs. . . . The mother will not leave her eggs, when near hatching, under any circumstances, while life remains. She will even allow an enclosure to be made around her and thus suffer imprisonment, rather than abandon them."

Human intrusion, at present, is a frequent cause for abandonment of the nest. Ligon (1946:34) writes: "Even direct human disturbance is a serious factor. Hens with clutches in an advanced stage of incubation are more likely to remain on the eggs or, if flushed, to return to them without delay to cover the eggs, than are those with fresh eggs. One reason for nest abandonment as a result of disturbance is that laying or newly brooding hens scatter their eggs when suddenly flushed from the nest. Some hens are so wary and sensitive that any one of almost innumerable disturbances may result in abandonment of the nest." Five nests under the observation of Wheeler (1948:38) were abandoned after one or more flushings of the hen. Two of the nests were abandoned after the first flushing, two after the second flushing, and one after the third flushing. On two occasions Burget (1957:17) approached nests within two feet before the hens moved. On leaving a nest, the hen will sometimes act as though crippled, dragging a leg, wing, or both (Blakey, 1937:9).

The hen will sit on the eggs with great persistence. As early as 1577, Googe (1577:166v) mentioned that turkeys are such great incubators they will sit on a stone or an empty nest. If the eggs are addled, she may occupy the nest long after the normal period of incubation. Caton (1877:326) mentions a wild hen that sat on a nest for a week after the eggs had been scattered by a peafowl. A domestic turkey has been known to sit on a nest of eggs in the woods during a snowstorm in December (Lampman, 1925:325). Broodiness sometimes develops in domestic males, but the truly wild gobbler shows no interest in the nest. Herbert White sent to Sibley (1939) a photograph of a "wild" gobbler sitting on a nest of eggs. One or two young hatched but were crushed. The injection of prolactin might produce broodiness in males as it does in females. Crispens (1957) injected 18 mg. of prolactin into two wild hens daily for six days in March. They began to cluck after three injections and continued to brood poults and leghorn chicks for a period of four weeks.

INCUBATION BY DOMESTIC MALES

The first case of incubation by a domestic male turkey is described by Ödmann (1789), who mentioned that it was unusual for a polygamous male bird to incubate or to take care of young. A gobbler showed uneasiness at being separated from an incubating female and was allowed to join her. He sat beside her and eventually took some of her eggs to incubate. Finally he was given some chicken eggs which he hatched. A footnote by Jardine (Wilson and Bonaparte, 1832:362) states: "I have more than once known the domestic turkey-cock drive the hen from her nest, sit upon the eggs until hatched, and perform all the duties to the young incumbent on the female, and never during the time allow her to approach. I once knew it take place upon two addled eggs, which a hen had long persevered upon, and was at last succeeded by the male, who kept his place for nearly a fortnight." Two examples are given by Bement (1867:210) of gobblers taking over the nest and hatching the eggs, or confiscating the young after the hen had completed the incubation. Recently Taibell (1928) wrote that an old gobbler held by means of a sack fastened over its body on a nest containing artificial eggs became broody within four to five days. Two year-old gobblers began to incubate after being confined to the nest for only one day. They then hatched the eggs and took care of the poults.

The behavior of the wild hen during incubation has been described by Blakey (1937:8): "The incubation period begins irregularly. After laying an egg late in the afternoon, the hen may sit until nightfall, then leave and roost as usual. This action may continue a second day before she stays on the nest all night. Another hen may stay the first night, but leave the second. The third day generally begins regularity of incubation, interrupted only by regular periods for feeding and watering." As incubation progresses the hen leaves the nest daily for water, usually an hour before noon. The water is obtained always at the same spot. The trips become irregular towards the end of the incubation period and are discontinued entirely during the final two or more days. Copulation has never been observed after incubation has started.

The value of the turkey capon as a foster parent is quaintly explained by Markham (1623:140): "These Capons are of two uses: the one is, to lead chickens, ducklings, yong Turkies, Peahens, Phesants & Partriges, which he will doe altogether, both naturally and kindly, and through largenesse of his body will brood or cover easily thirty or thirty and five; he will lead them forth safely, and defend them against Kites or Buzzards, more better than the Hens: therefore the way to make him to take, is, with a small Brier, or else sharpe Nettles at night, to beate and sting all his breast and nether parts, and then in the darke to seate the Chickens under him, whose warmth taketh away his smart, hee will fall much in love with them, and whensoever hee proveth unkinde, you must sting, or beate him againe, and this will make him he will never forsake them."

Nesting Success

The nesting success[1] of the wild turkey is about 35 per cent. This is not unusually low. Data compiled by Kalmbach (1939:593) for several species of birds nesting on or near the ground showed an average success of 43 per cent. The eggs of only one nest out of nine under observation by Hargrave (1939.1:60c) in Arizona hatched. In 1940, in Alabama, nine of twenty nests were known to have hatched successfully (Barkalow, 1942:61). Four of the nests were destroyed and the fate of seven nests was unknown (Barkalow, 1949:51).

Wheeler (1944.1) reported in 1944 that less than 50 per cent of the hens incubate successfully. In August of the same year, only 27 per cent of the forty-one hens under observation had poults (Wheeler, 1948:42). Dalke et al. (1946:50) report that only eleven (38 per cent) of twenty-nine nests were successful. During the years 1939 and 1940, nine (33 per cent) of twenty-seven nests of native turkeys were successful in Virginia, and ten (77 per cent) of thirteen nests of pen-reared birds given free range (Mosby and Handley, 1943:125). It appears that pen-reared hens desert their nests less readily than the native wild hens. In 1953 in Virginia, thirteen (35 per cent) of thirty-seven nests were successful (McDowell, 1956:12).

Of 117 nests examined in Texas between 1937 and 1945, ten hatched,

[1] Nesting success of the per cent of nests in which one or more eggs hatch.

the fate of thirty-two was unknown, five were deserted, and seventy destroyed by predators or other agents (Taylor, 1948:225).

Normally, the wild turkey nests but once a year. Little is known about second nestings if the first nest is destroyed or abandoned because of disturbance. If the first eggs are destroyed when near the time of hatching, or the downy young are lost, it is doubtful if a second attempt is made. Caton (1877:325) wrote: "If the nest of a hen is broken up she immediately seeks the cocks and then returns to seclusion, and generally she will even make a third nest if the second is destroyed." Mosby and Handley (1943:129) state that there is every indication of a second attempt at nesting if the first clutch is destroyed. Broods of downy poults were observed by Wheeler (1948:39) on July 24, 1945, and August 3, 1943. Female poults, weighing approximately 2.5 pounds, were trapped on September 28 and October 3, hence the probable date of hatching was the last of July or the first of August. So many small groups of poultless hens were seen at all times during the day that it seemed that few attempts at a second nesting were made. Mature males were so rarely seen with females after the first of May that the probability of impotence in the males by this time was suggested.

11

Eggs, the Young, and Their Development to Maturity

THE EGGS OF THE SEVERAL RACES of the wild turkey and those of the domestic bird are so similar as to be indistinguishable with certainty. Caton (1877:324) informs us: "The eggs of the wild turkey vary much in coloring and somewhat in form, but in general are so like those of the tame turkey that no one can select one from the other. The ground color is white, over which are scattered reddish-brown specks. These differ in shades of color but much more in numbers. I have seen some on which scarcely any specks could be detected, while others were profusely covered with specks,—all laid by the same hen in the same nest." Shufeldt (1912) is in agreement with this statement.

DESCRIPTION OF EGGS

There are some pertinent comments by Blakey (1937:10) on the eggs: "Innumerable variations from the typical egg standard may be found. Some eggs are chalky white, some without or only partially covered by, the protective membrane. Others are coarsely marked with large brown spots on a rough shell. Some are extremely pointed at one end, others show no difference between the ends or are nearly round. Sometimes the eggs are soft-shelled or double-yolked. The percentage of such eggs is small however, and they are relatively unimportant in their effect on the sum total of turkey welfare." He states that strong, healthy poults frequently hatch, however, from the abnormal eggs. The smallest eggs are usually from young or very old hens. Each hen deposits eggs of a fairly uniform color pattern. A variation in the latter is an indication that more than one hen has laid in the same nest.

Descriptions of the eggs, so far as known, of the recognized races of the wild turkey are given below.

Eastern Turkey (*M. g. silvestris*).—Bendire (1892:116) has the following description: "In shape, the eggs of the Wild Turkey are usually ovate, occasionally they are elongate ovate. The ground color varies from pale creamy white to creamy buff. They are more or less heavily marked with well-defined spots and dots of pale chocolate and reddish brown. In an occasional set these spots are pale lavender. Generally the markings are all small, ranging in size from a No. 6 shot to that of dust shot, but an exceptional set is sometimes heavily covered with both spots and blotches of the size of buckshot, and even larger." Bent (1932:331) adds that the shell is smooth with little or no gloss. The markings are colored light vinaceous drab, pale purple drab, clay color, or pinkish buff.

Measurement of thirty-eight eggs in the U. S. National Museum showed: range, 59 x 45 to 68.5 x 46 to 68.5 x 46 mm.; average, 61.5 x 46.5 mm. (Bendire, 1892:116). Bent (1932:332) gives for fifty-six eggs: range, 68.5 x 46, 64.5 x 48.5, 59 x 45, and 64.7 x 42.4 mm.; average, 62.6 x 44.6 mm. The five hundred eggs from pen-reared wild hens measured by Blakey (1937:10) gave an average of 59.74 x 45.69 mm.; and fifty from native wild hens, 58.2 x 46.1 mm.

The average weight of the eggs of the pen-reared wild hen in Missouri was 69.19 gr., and for the native wild bird 66.55 gr. (Blakey, 1937:10). In Pennsylvania the average weight of one hundred eggs from game farm hens was 0.146 pound (66.22 gr.) in comparison with 0.141 pound (63.96 gr.) for the same number of eggs from game farm hens mated with wild gobblers (Gerstell and Long, 1939:5). It is evident that the eggs of wild hens containing domestic blood are heavier than those of the native wild hens.

The average weight of 196 eggs of the domestic turkey (breed not stated) was 81.76 gr. (Asmundson *et al.*, 1943:36). Bronze hens classified by the size of the eggs laid by them showed average weights of 67.00 gr. for the smallest eggs and 101.50 gr. for the largest. The over-all average was 83.68 gr. (Marsden and Martin, 1945:201).

The earliest plate of the egg of a turkey which I have seen was published by Zinanni (1737). The egg is uncolored and contains dark dots. A faintly spotted egg of the eastern turkey is shown in color by Bendire

(1892). A good photograph of four eggs showing a variation in color from light to dark is due to Shufeldt (1912). The reproduction in Mc-Ilhenny (1914:Pl. VI) is less satisfactory. The plate by Maynard (1890:Pl. VIII) is poor.

Florida Turkey (M. g. osceola).—The following description is by Shufeldt (1912): "I examined a number of eggs and sets of eggs of *M. g. osceola*, or Florida Turkey. In no. 25787, the eggs are short and broad, the ground color being pale whitish, slightly tinged with brown. Some of the spots on these eggs are unusually large in a few places, three or four running together, or are more or less confluent; others are isolated and of medium size; many are minute, all being of an earth-brown, varying in shades. In the case of no. 25787 of this set, the dark brown spots are more or less of a size and fewer in number; while one of them (no. 25787) is exactly like the eggs of number 3; finally, there is a pale one (no. 75787) with *fine* spots, few in number in middle third, very numerous at the ends. There are *scattered large spots* of a dark brown, the surface of which latter are raised with a kind of incrustation. Another egg (no. 27869) in the same tray (*M. g. osceola*) is *small*, pointed; pale ground color with very few spots of light brown (Coll. W. L. Ralph). Still another in this set (27868) is markedly *roundish*, with minute brown speckling, uniformly distributed. There are nine eggs in this clutch (no. 27868), and, apart from the differences in form, they all closely resemble each other, and this is by no means always the case, as the same hen may lay any of the various styles enumerated above, either as belonging to the same clutch, or at different seasons." Bent (1932:341) solves the problem by stating that the eggs are similar to those of other wild turkeys.

Measurements of the four extremes of fifty-six eggs were 66 x 46.7, 62.5 x 48.8, 56.3 x 46.4, and 65.2 x 41 mm. The average was 61 x 46.3 mm. (Bent, 1932:341). There is no appreciable difference in size from the egg of the eastern turkey.

Rio Grande Turkey (M. g. intermedia).—According to Sennett (1879:428): "The eggs have a cream ground-color. On the set of twelve the markings are numerous and consist of light-brown specks covering the whole surface, to which are added larger spots of darker brown at intervals. On the set of fifteen, one of which is of abnormal size, the markings are fainter, giving a decided light color to the eggs. The single egg of the third set is still lighter and has but few markings." Simmons (1925:84) states that the eggs are rich buff or cream color, the entire surface being speckled and dotted with brownish red.

The average size of twenty-eight eggs measured by Sennett (1879:428) was 2.43 (61.72) x 1.86 in. (47.24 mm.). An abnormally small egg measured 1.80 (45.72) x 1.50 in. (38.10 mm.). Simmons (1925:84) gives 2.46 (62.48) x 1.86 in. (47.24 mm.). Measurements of the four extremes of forty-nine eggs were 64.8 x 43.2, 64 x 48.6, 57.2 x 43.6, and 61.7 x 43.2 mm. The average was 62.4 x 46.5 mm. (Bent, 1932:344).

Merriam's Turkey (*M. g. merriami*).—Eggs from Arizona are described by Bendire (1892:119) as "ovate in shape, their ground color is creamy white, and they are profusely dotted with fine spots of reddish brown, pretty evenly distributed over the entire egg." According to Brandt (1951:635): "The multitudinous spots are originally of various shades of red or brown, some being considerably heavier than others; they rub paler as the bird continues to incubate, and often when the eggs are near hatching these markings become difficult to detect or fade out entirely. The style, shade, and density of the markings vary with different birds, but eggs of the same set are remarkably similar in both size and appearance."

The average measurements given by Bendire (1892:119) are 69 x 49 mm. Seven eggs found in a nest in the White Mountains, Arizona, by London L. Hargrave averaged 2.63 (66.80) x 1.92 in. (48.77 mm.) (Brandt, 1951:636). Measurements of the four extremes of sixteen eggs were: 70.5 x 49, 61.7 x 46.7, 64.5 x 46 mm., and one missing. The average was 65.8 x 47.3 mm. (Bent, 1932:324). The eggs average larger than those of the eastward races. An egg in color appears in Bendire (1892:Fig. 14, Pl. III).

South Mexican Turkey (*M. g. gallopavo*).—Published information on the nesting of the races of turkeys in Mexico is almost a blank. Sartorius, writing from the state of Veracruz to Baird (1867), contributed the following: "Its breeding season is in March or April, when the hens separate from the males to reunite into families again in September. . . . The female lays three to twelve brownish red, spotted eggs in the high grain, and hatches them out in thirty days, as is the case with the tame turkey."

It was stated by T. Flint (1832:340) that petrified eggs of the wild turkey were unearthed in Tennessee. This is improbable.

FORMATION OF THE EGG

The formation of the egg is described by Asmundson (1939). The protein in the albumen of the egg is secreted in the magnum; however, the albumen increases slightly in weight in the isthmus and by 35 to 40 per cent in the uterus. The shell membrane is secreted in the isthmus, and the secretion begins immediately when the egg enters the uterus. Before entering the uterus, the shape of the egg is determined. Usually when the egg enters the uterus, layering of the albumen begins. The shell membrane and shell begin forming at once after entry of the egg into the uterus. Pigment is deposited in the eggs of chickens during the entire period of formation of the shell; from 50 to 74 per cent is deposited during the five hours preceding laying of the egg. The markings on turkey eggs are not made until very near the time of oviposition, or approximately thirteen to fourteen hours after the shell is detectable. When the eggs were removed from the uterus shortly before normal oviposition, the markings smeared from handling, showing how recently the pigment had been deposited (Warren and Conrad, 1942).

The pigments in colored eggs have their source in the hemoglobin of the red corpuscles. On rupture of the red corpuscles, the released hemoglobin is changed to hematin, which through further chemical changes produces pigments of various colors. All the pigments are deposited while the egg is in the uterus.

SPECIFIC GRAVITY

The specific gravity of the egg is slightly greater than that of water. The average specific gravity of domestic turkey eggs was 1.085 based on 1,559 fertile eggs. Only four eggs had a specific gravity of 1.065 and only three of 1.10 (Asmundson and Lloyd, 1935). The specific gravity of the egg is controlled largely by the thickness of the shell (Phillips and Williams, 1944). Based on 196 eggs having an average specific gravity of 1.075 and a shell thickness of 0.35 mm., the specific gravity of the shell was 2.174 (Asmundson et al., 1943:36).

Plate 25.—Eastern wild turkeys on nest. (Courtesy Jack Dermid, North Carolina Wildlife Resources Commission.)

Plate 26.—Eastern wild turkey poult. (Courtesy Jack Dermid, North Carolina Wildlife Resources Commission.)

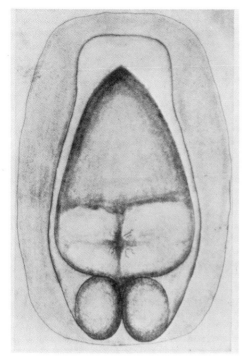 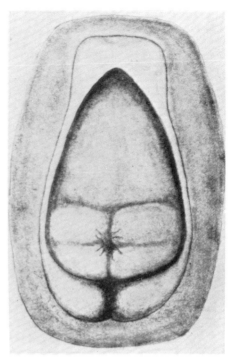

Plate 27a.   Plate 27b.

Plate 27a.—Diagram of sex organs of male poult one day old. The two spherical papillae are characteristic of the male. (U. S. Department of Agriculture.)

Plate 27b.—Diagram of sex organs of female poult one day old. (U. S. Department of Agriculture.)

Plate 28.—Female Pennsylvania game farm wild turkey with fully feathered neck. (From the Vilas Park Zoo, Madison, Wisconsin; photograph by R. A. McCabe.)

Plate 29a.—Semiplume from neck of ancient male Pueblo turkey, New Mexico.

Plate 29b.—Normal feather from neck of male *M. g. merriami*.

Plate 30.—Minnetaree warrior, Periska-Ruhpa, with headdress of turkey feathers, painted by Charles Bodmer. (From Maximilian's *Travels* [1839–41].)

Plate 31.—A "primitive" artist's conception of the Hinckley circular hunt by settlers in northern Ohio in 1818. (*American Field* [1890].)

Plate 32.—Pioneer hunter. (*Harper's Weekly* [1884].)

AVERAGE SPECIFIC GRAVITY	RANGE OF THICKNESS OF THE SHELL
Egg	*Millimeter*
1.070	0.28–0.30
1.080	0.33–0.36
1.090	0.38–0.41

COMPOSITION OF THE EGG

The composition of domestic turkey eggs as given by Asmundson *et al.* (1943:36) is:

	Grams	*Per cent*
Whole egg	81.76	100.00
Yolk	25.99	31.79
Albumen	47.21	57.74
Shell membrane	1.32	1.61
Shell	7.25	8.87

The composition of the eggs of the domestic turkey as given by Langworthy (1901) and by Hepburn and Miraglia (1937) is shown in Table 21. The variations are possibly due to differences in the thickness of the shell.

TABLE 21
COMPOSITION OF TURKEY EGGS

Constituent	Langworthy *Per cent*	Hepburn and Miraglia *Per cent*
Shell	13.8	9.88*
Water	63.5	64.31
Protein	12.2	11.69
Fat	9.7	11.08
Ash	.8	.59
Dextrose	—	.33

*Original figures have been recalculated to the whole egg.

The percentages of lysozyme and conalbumin in turkey and other eggs as determined by MacDonnell *et al.* (1954) are given in Table 22. The shells of eggs are porous and penetrable by bacteria. Lysozyme is a crystallizable, water soluble protein with very high antiseptic properties.

TABLE 22
PROTEINS IN CHICKEN, TURKEY, AND DUCK EGGS

	Lysozyme Per cent	Conalbumin Per cent
Chicken	3.40	12
Turkey	1.84	11
Mallard	0.86	15

Analyses of the eggs, exclusive of the shells, of two strains of wild turkeys are given by Gerstell and Long (1939:5) in Table 23. The WM eggs were from game farm hens mated with wild gobblers, and the GF eggs were from the tenth generation of game farm stock.

TABLE 23
COMPOSITION OF WILD TURKEY EGGS

Substances	WM Eggs Per cent	GF Eggs Per cent
Water	72.18	74.53
Protein	13.42	12.55
Fat	11.81	10.47
Carbohydrates	1.64	1.53
Ash	.95	.92
Phosphorus	.25	.23
Calcium	.11	.06

There is no explanation for the higher calcium content of the WM eggs. The ratio of calcium to phosphorus in the turkey embryo is close to that for monocalcium phosphate ($CaH_4P_2O_8$) up to the nineteenth day of incubation and subsequently, close to dicalcium phosphate ($CaHPO_4$) (Insko and Lyons, 1933).

INCUBATION PERIOD

The incubation period is close to twenty-eight days (Burns, 1915:282; Bergtold, 1917:87). Nearly all the data have been obtained from the domestic turkey, but there is no reason to believe that the period for the wild bird differs essentially. Tiedemann (1814:139), following Bechstein (1807:1,127), gave the period for the domestic turkey as from twenty-six to twenty-eight days. Evans (1891:78), from personal observations, obtained twenty-eight days. For wild turkeys raised in Europe, Bouillod

(1874:614) gives twenty-nine to thirty days, and Ghigi and Delacour (1931), twenty-seven to twenty-eight days. The period for the wild turkey is twenty-eight days according to Mosby and Handley (1943:187).

Few observers have defined the incubation period. According to Nice (1954:173), the period should be the time from the beginning of un-interrupted incubation starting from the laying of the last egg until all the eggs have hatched. Marsden and Martin (1945:257) state that twenty-eight full days are required and that the beginning of incubation should be the day following the one on which the eggs are set. The first hours are consumed in warming the egg throughout.

The temperature of the atmosphere at the time of oviposition influences the time of hatching. Development of the embryo begins before the egg is laid and may continue to develop in unusually warm weather. Merriam's turkey has about three and one-half months—between the disappearance of most of the snow and the start of the cold, early summer rains—in which to lay its eggs, incubate, and raise the young to the hardiness necessary for survival.

Ligon (1946:35) writes: "Turkeys appear to be aware of these limitations and are prompt and persistent in utilizing the available period. With so short and strictly limited a season for nesting and rearing the young to a comparatively safe age to withstand summer rains, laying is often under way while snow banks yet remain in shaded places and heavy frosts occur at night. Just how low the temperature must fall in order to kill the germ or freeze the egg of the adjusted stock is not known, but it is certain that the eggs are highly resistant to cold. Nevertheless, when undisturbed on leaving the eggs, an experienced hen usually covers them sufficiently with bark or other material gleaned near by, to provide some protection against cold. Further, nesting sites are probably selected with a view to getting the benefit of higher and more uniform temperatures, being generally on slopes favored by the tempering effect of forest trees and stones which store heat by day, these locations being rarely as cold as damp valleys or open table lands."

Concerning the effect of low temperatures, Reeves (1950.1:13) believed that the main cause of loss among wild turkeys during the summer of 1950 was the freezing of the eggs in the nest during the laying period. The prolonged cold period during the laying of eggs caused the loss of nests of the majority of the young hens and a reduction in the number of poults hatched from the nests of many of the older hens. A nest with twelve eggs was under observation from May 11 to May 25. The temperature was below 30° F. eighteen times in April and thirteen times in May. The hen left the nest with nine young before incubation was completed. Embryos in two of the abandoned eggs appeared to be completely developed. It was believed that the only way in which the eggs could have been saved from freezing was by the hen starting incubation before the clutch was completed. The temperature of the nest after the hen had departed with her young, taken at intervals during a twenty-four hour period, was only 2° warmer than the surrounding atmosphere.

Reeves adds that turkey eggs will freeze at 29°. Marsden and Martin (1945:260) state that the eggs begin to freeze at 28° F. According to Moran (1925), the white of the chicken egg freezes at -0.45° C. and the yolk at -0.65° C. (30.83° F.). Occasionally, he was able to supercool the whole egg to -11° C. (12.2° F.) without cracking the shell. It is doubtful if any turkey eggs are lost by freezing except when the shell cracks, which seems unlikely. Jull et. al. (1948) report that the eggs can be held for some time at 20° F. without cracking the shell. Holding the eggs for two days at this temperature reduced the hatchability somewhat, but if they were held for four days or longer the hatchability was zero.

Hatchability and Fertility

The hatchability of the eggs of the domestic turkey are markedly affected by temperature and the length of time the eggs are held prior to incubation (Table 24) (Scott, 1933). The high hatchability of the eggs of Merriam's turkey shows they are less susceptible to cold than those of the domestic bird. Ligon (1946:36) states that 100 per cent "fertility" is the rule.

TABLE 24
Effect of Holding Time and Temperature on Hatchability of Eggs

Lot Number	Holding Temperature F.	Days Held	Hatchability Per cent	Days Held	Hatchability Per cent
26	36.3°	0–6	65.63	28–34	0.00
28	54.2°	0–6	70.97	28–34	61.11

Fertility is sometimes used as synonymous with hatchability. Whenever the embryo shows development, the egg is fertile whether there is hatching or not. It has been stated frequently that one service by a gobbler is sufficient to fertilize all the eggs laid by a hen, but the desired result is not always accomplished. During five seasons of the wild turkey propagation program in Virginia, the fertility of the eggs varied from 48.4 to 77.9 per cent (Mosby and Handley, 1943:188). Fertilization in the wild appears to be very successful, but there are few actual data to support this assumption. The fertility is ordinarily 100 per cent or zero (Latham, 1956:33; Edminster, 1954:65). The eggs in second, or late nestings, are frequently infertile due, presumably, to the inability of the hen to secure the attentions of a male. The nest found by Howard (1900) in Arizona on July 1, 1899, contained addled eggs. Davis (1949:104) mentions a nest containing fifteen infertile eggs from which the hen was flushed the middle of June. In Virginia the infertility of the eggs from first nestings in the wild was 4.3 per cent, and 80 per cent for a deserted second nest found July 6 (Mosby and Handley, 1943:129).

The hatchability of the eggs varies with conditions. It appears to be much lower for hens that are confined than for those that are free ranging. During a five-year period the hatchability of the fertile eggs from game farm turkeys in Virginia ran from 65.6 to 95.0 per cent (Mosby and Handley, 1943:188). Based on the number of eggs set, the hatchability was very low, 38.9 to 62.6 per cent, the average for all of the eggs being 46.0 per cent. Wild hens restocked in large enclosures in Missouri incubated 997 eggs, of which only 12.4 per cent failed to hatch. Of this number, 3.8 per cent were infertile, 1.1 per cent failed to break out of the shell, and 7.3 per cent were lost to predators and other causes (Blakey, 1937:11). The hatchability of the eggs of native turkeys in the wild is high. According to McDowell (1956:12): "At least 153 of 158 eggs (96.8 per cent) were fertile in 13 nests reported to have hatched successfully in 1953."

It is not known how frequently the hen in the wild turns her eggs. In artificial incubation it is recommended that they be turned five times daily over a period of sixteen hours in order to prevent malformation of the embryo (Marsden and Martin, 1945:270; Greenberg, 1949:167).

Once incubation has started, no further mating has been observed (Blakey, 1937:8). At the beginning of incubation the hen leaves the nest between one-half hour before and one-half hour after sunrise for food and water. The gobbler calls at this time, and she joins him for a brief period. As incubation progresses, the hen remains on her nest except to obtain water at about 11.00 A.M. During the last two or three days of incubation, she does not leave the nest at all. Black caecal droppings at watering places show that a hen is nesting in the neighborhood (Mosby and Handley, 1943:117).

The behavior of the hen when the eggs are hatching has been described by Audubon (1831:6) as follows: "I once witnessed the hatching of a brood of Turkeys, which I watched for the purpose of securing them together with the parent. I concealed myself on the ground within a very few feet, and saw her raise herself half the length of her legs, look anxiously upon the eggs, cluck with a sound peculiar to the mother on such occasions, carefully remove each half-empty shell, and with her bill caress and dry the young birds, that already stood tottering and attempting to make their way out of the nest.... I have seen them all emerge from the shell, and, in a few moments after, tumble, roll, and push each other forward, with astonishing and inscrutable instinct.

"Before leaving the nest with her young brood, the mother shakes herself in a violent manner, picks and adjusts the feathers about her belly, and assumes quite a different aspect. She alternately inclines her eyes obliquely upwards and sideways, stretching out her neck, to discover hawks or other enemies, spreads her wings a little as she walks, and softly clucks to keep her innocent offspring close to her. They move slowly along, and as the hatching generally takes place in the afternoon, they frequently return to the nest to spend the first night there. After this, they remove to some distance, keeping on the highest undulated grounds, the mother dreading rainy weather, which is extremely dangerous to the young, in this tender state, when they are only covered by a kind of soft hairy down, of surprising delicacy. In very rainy seasons, Turkeys, are scarce, for if once completely wetted, the young seldom recover."

The poults demonstrate different degrees of vigor in freeing themselves from the shell when hatching (Blakey, 1937:11). Pipping among restocked birds usually occurs during a twelve- to eighteen-hour period under normal ground nesting conditions. Early in the morning following an average of one day and two nights continuously on the nest, the mother hen becomes restless as early-hatched poults start wandering around the nest (Plate 25). If the weather is favorable, particularly not

EGGS, YOUNG, AND THEIR DEVELOPMENT

too wet, the mother will begin wandering with her brood. According to the observation of Caton (1877:326), the hen will never remain on the nest longer than the morning after the first poult is hatched. If at this time only one poult has hatched, she will depart with it abandoning all the other eggs. Ligon (1946:39) states that the hen does not move from the nest until all of the eggs have hatched. Mosby and Handley (1943:118, 120) found that the eggs usually hatch within twenty-four hours, and that the hen leaves the nest with her brood when the hatch is completed.

MATERNAL CARE OF POULTS

The hen with young, when surprised, may "freeze" to escape detection or pretend to be crippled. The "cripple ruse" is mentioned by Beyers (1939) and Mosby and Handley (1943:121). The feigning habit is described by Samuel Clemens (1906) in his characteristic style: "I followed an ostensibly lame turkey over a considerable part of the United States one morning, because I believed in her and could not think she would deceive a mere boy, and one who was trusting her and considering her honest." In Florida, a hen with young showed no concern when first surprised; however, as soon as the poults reached the opposite side of a fence, she uttered a note of alarm and flew away (Palmer, 1909:27).

When danger threatens, the hen utters an ominous note that sends the poults into concealment under leaves or other vegetation with astonishing speed and effectiveness. She then draws attention to herself (Crane, 1897:431). Goebel (1889:128) wrote from long experience with the turkey in Missouri: "One, who will accidentally chance to come onto a hen which has just hatched her young, is in danger of being attacked by her; but these assaults are not very serious. This pugnacity, however, is of very short duration, and even if it has swarmed with young turkeys all around the old hen, not one of them can be seen one minute afterward, because they have tracelessly squatted and have hidden themselves in the leaves; the old hen will stay close around and whenever the disturber has left, she will call her little ones together again." While thus "frozen," the young can be walked or driven over without causing them to move (Caton, 1881:91).

The hiding ability of the young wild turkeys raised in the park of the New York Zoological Society has been described by Beebe (1901:191): "On June 14, of this year [1901], a turkey mother brought off eight chicks

281

from her nest of leaves near the center of the range, and they were allowed to remain in the enclosure a day before being removed to the
pheasant-breeding coops away from rats and other vermin. In catching
the young birds no precautions were taken except to drive the hen
Turkey and chicks to an opening in the undergrowth and then separate
the mother from her brood. Two of the young birds were picked up, but
ten minutes' search failed to discover a trace of the remaining six, although it was certain that they were within a radius of five feet. It was
necessary to allow the two captured chicks to go, and then drive the
mother to the spot, whereupon, at her low cluck, the entire six appeared
as if by magic."

The very young poults are brooded for long periods, especially in
inclement weather. There is practically unanimous agreement in the
literature on the lethal effect of cold, prolonged rains. Some writers believe that a thorough wetting by any means will prove fatal. Thorpe
(1846:60) wrote that the hunter bases his hopes on the plentifulness of
turkeys according to the dryness of the season. Jordan (1898:331) believed that the weather controlled the turkey population more than any
other cause. He had often observed that if May and June were dry,
turkeys and quail were plentiful the following fall. Arizona is considered to have an ideal climate for turkeys since the young are several
weeks old before the July rains come (Guthrie, 1926). Rutledge (1941:93)
was informed that turkeys were not increasing in the Pisgah National
Forest because of prolonged rain during the hatching period. Several
broods were found drowned. Ligon (1927:115) wrote: "I have observed
that during down-pours of rain, turkeys will seek the shelter of dense
spruce or fir trees. While the young are generally safe in such places,
continued rain will wet and chill the young birds, often causing practically all of a brood to perish."

The susceptibility of the poults to fatalities from wetting is mentioned
by Sandys and Van Dyke (1904:259): "An old farmer once told me that
he had seen a hen cover her chicks before a shower which began shortly
after he had finished his breakfast. He was working in a bit of woods,
and when he went to the house for his dinner the hen had not moved,
although the rain had entirely ceased some three hours before. After
the young have attained the size of grouse they appear to shake off

all infantile weaknesses, and once matured, they are as hardy as so many deer."

The first ten to fourteen days in the life of the poult (Plate 26) are critical insofar as wetting and chilling are concerned. Blakey (1937:11) found a restocked hen brooding nine dead poults, one week old, after a short spring shower. In order to protect the poults from wetting, the hen seeks the best overhead cover available, fluffs out her feathers, and stands in a crouched position so that the poults are visible.

A less pessimistic view of the effect of wetting on the wild poult was held by Caton (1877:326): "When a day old the chick can follow the hen, though it may tumble down on every foot of the ground it runs over. When two or three days old it will follow the hen with astonishing vigor, and will trail through the grass in a cold rain storm without injury, when similar exposure would have been fatal to the domestic turkey. I have had repeated opportunities to test this, and I do not believe that I ever lost a young bird by reason of its getting wet. Even the hybrids, when but a few days old, are capable of enduring exposure from which we should despair of the domestic bird."

The young are taught by the mother to hunt and catch insects, which form the major part of their diet. She will catch insects in her beak and with a few sharp clucks bring the poults running to her. A large insect is torn into pieces for them (Blakey, 1937:12).

A charming description of the wandering of the brood is given by "Clip" (1886:409): "They hurry along as if on a march to some particular point, sometimes tripping along in single file, one behind the other, and at other times scattered through the woods for fifty yards or more. When on these scattered marches it is pleasant to note some straggling youngster as he wanders out of sight of the main flock in an attempt to catch a fickle-winged butterfly, or delays by the wayside scratching amid the remains of a decayed log in search of a rich morsel in the shape of a grubworm. It is interesting to note his movements when he discovers that he is alone; that his 'mammy' and his mates are gone. He raises himself up, looks with his keen eyes in every direction for the flock, and, failing to discover them, gives the well-known coarse cluck. Then he raises his head high in the air, and listens intently for his mother's call. As soon as it is discovered that one is missing the whole flock stops, and the young turkeys raise their heads and await the signal from their mother. When she hears the note of the lost youngster, she gives a few anxious 'yelps,' which he answers, and then, opening his wings, he gives them a joyous flap or two and with a few sharp, quick 'yelps,' he goes on a run to join his companions. The march then continues with all busy picking a morsel here and there, and scratching away as busy as bees among the leaves and brush in search of bugs and worms. They continue their march through the day and generally wind up in the evening some-where in the vicinity of their roost of the preceeding night; very fre-quently at the same place, when not disturbed."

The hen may move some distance with the poults, but having selected a suitable "nursery" usually remains in its vicinity until the young are well-developed. It was thought by Rutledge (1936:533) that the hen did not range over an acre or two until the young could fly. In Virginia one hen moved with her sixteen poults, in less than two days, to a field one-quarter of a mile from the nest (Mosby and Handley, 1943:120). The brood usually can be seen in the same area until the poults are two to three weeks of age.

Age When Poults Can Fly

The poults are brooded on the ground at night until they are able to fly well. An attempt is made to brood the young even after they are capable of roosting in trees. Thoreau (1949:83) noticed a tame turkey roosting on a fence with wings outspread although the young were on a rail a foot or more below her. According to Latham (1956:34), the young spend the night on the ground under the protection of the hen for the first four to five weeks and, when roosting in trees has begun, may sit close to her on the limb.

The age at which poults can fly sufficiently to escape ground enemies is important, but it has not been determined with precision. Audubon (1831:7) wrote: "In about a fortnight, the young birds, which had previously rested on the ground, leave it and fly, at night, to some very large low branch, where they place themselves under the deeply curved wings of their kind and careful parent, dividing themselves for that purpose into two nearly equal parties." Knopp (1959:9) states that the first poults were seen in Arizona on June 20, 1958, when they were three days old. By July 10, when approximately three weeks of age, they could

284

fly sufficiently to escape enemies. Other writers have given two weeks (Portmann, 1938:294), and two to three weeks (Everitt, 1928:24).

According to Mosby and Handley (1943:122), they can fly distances of twenty-five to fifty feet when about four weeks of age and rise into low vegetation for roosting. We are informed by Wheeler (1948:41) that the poult cannot fly until somewhat more than two weeks of age, and becomes a strong flyer within six weeks. On May 3, Nicholson (1928) flushed a hen with five or six young not quite as large as a bobwhite. All the young arose with a strong flight and alighted on the lower limbs of a pine thirty feet tall. Ligon (1946:39) wrote: "At ten days to two weeks, the wings serve them well, particularly in getting into trees on sloping ground that permits a running start and level flight into the branches."

Two or more hens with broods may join company and wander together. As a rule, families remain united until the following breeding season. Though the young remain with the mother over so long a period, they are quite self-reliant when four to five weeks of age. On June 29, 1953, a hen with nine young the size of the bobwhite was flushed from a meadow in Pocahontas County, West Virginia. A week later the hen was found dead, apparently killed by a fox. On July 30, eight poults, evidently of the same brood, were observed within four hundred yards of the place where the hen was killed. They were seen regularly afterwards up to the opening of the hunting season. The normal fear of man was not shown. Another brood was observed on several occasions in Tucker County during the same year, and in no case was it seen with an adult (Bailey, 1955).

A day-old male domestic poult will sometimes strut (Marsden and Martin, 1945:685). Jordan (1898:330) never knew a young wild male to either gobble or strut up to November although domestic birds sometimes do. According to Mosby and Handley (1943:93), both male and female captive wild turkey poults will strut; hence, up to this age strutting is not a sex character. W. C. Glazener has informed me that a male among the Rio Grande poults which he had under observation began to strut and display when five days of age.

Sex Ratio of Poults

The ratio of male to female in the poults at the time of hatching is close to one to one. Of 19,446 domestic turkey embryos and poults examined, 50.17 per cent were males (Asmundson, 1941). There is no satisfactory method for determining the sex of live young poults except by examining the genital papillae (Plate 27) exposed by everting the anus (Hammond and Marsden, 1937). After about twelve weeks of age, the color of the tips of the breast feathers is diagnostic.

PRODUCTIVITY

Losses of members of a brood are due to a variety of causes, the principal ones being chilling and wetting, drought and flood, and predation. Some poults become lost by straying; others fall into depressions from which they cannot extricate themselves or become entangled in vegetation. Paul Wilhelm, Duke of Württemberg (1828:137), stated that during the months of May through July turkeys are scarce in the hilly regions along the Missouri. At this time the hens take their young to the bottoms covered with nettles and remain there until the young can fly. This would appear to be a poor habitat in which to keep the poults dry. Wheeler (1948:43) thought that exposure and exhaustion were the chief sources of mortality. The greatest loss occurred during the first six weeks of the life of the poult and particularly during the first two weeks. A poult that survived until the first of July had an excellent chance of becoming an adult.

The average size of the broods observed in 1944 was 4.5 poults in July and 4.9 in August (Wheeler, 1945.1). The increase in August was probably due to a better count. The decrease in the size of the broods in Missouri was as follows: June, 9.6; July, 8.8; August, 8.1; and September, 7.7 (Dalke *et al.*, 1946:51). This represents a decrease of two poults per brood over a period of three months. The years 1952 and 1953 were drought years in Missouri and the average brood size dropped decidedly as shown below. During the post-nesting season of 1953, of 235 hens observed, 165 (70.1 per cent) were without young.

BROOD SIZE BY MONTHS

Year	May	June	July	August	September	Reference
1952	11.3	9.6	7.8	7.8	7.1	Sadler (1953)
1953	10.0	8.3	7.0	6.7	5.0	Sadler (1954)

The average sizes of the broods in West Virginia in 1949 were: May,

9.7; June, 11.6; and July, 7.7 (Breiding, 1950). The number for June, 1950, was 8.8 poults (Uhlig and Dahl, 1950). During the four-year period 1947–50, the average loss of young for June was 31.3 per cent and for July, 3.5 per cent (Uhlig, 1951). The average size of the broods in September during the years 1953–59 ran from 5.3 to 7.3 in oak areas, and from 6.5 to 8.3 in northern hardwoods. The average for the seven years was 6.36 poults for the oak areas and 8.44 for the northern hardwoods (Bailey and Rinell, 1960:6). The average brood sizes in Virginia in 1953 for broods accompanied by a single hen were: May, 10.9; June, 10.8; July, 9.2; August, 8.5; September, 8.5 (McDowell, 1956:17).

In October, November, and December, 1949, thirty-five turkeys were released in the Peace River Swamp in Florida. Approximately 30 per cent of the hens hatched young, with an average of eight poults per brood (Stanberry and Gainey, 1950). In spite of the favorable weather in the Gulf Hammock in 1950, only about one hen in four or five raised a brood successfully. There was an average of five poults per brood in late July and August (Swindell and Jennings, 1951).

Based on 860 turkeys observed on the Edwards Plateau, Texas, in 1945, Hahn (1946.1) found one adult female to 1.7 poults. In early August, 1946, poultless hens were observed in flocks of two to fifteen. Of the eighty-nine hens observed, only fourteen (15.7 per cent) had broods. Since eighty-seven young were seen, the breeding hens had an average of 6.2 poults (Walker, 1947). The Menard area in 1948 had, counting all hens, 0.8 poult to one hen, and the San Saba Basin had 2.4 poults to one hen. A census made in mid-July, 1957, showed the following (Thomas and Green, 1957:24):

	COUNTY			
	Edwards	Medina	Kerr	Bandera
Adult male to adult female	1:2.22	1:8.00	1:4.40	1:17.6
Per cent females with young	19.9	3.75	39.3	83.8
Average brood size	6.48	10.7	6.3	7.6
Per cent increase in population	84.9	35.9	203.7	378.3

Merriam's turkey appears to raise fewer young than the eastern races. The brood sizes on the Gila National Forest, New Mexico, during a period of three years were:

Years	June and July Poults	September and October Poults
1951	6.1	5.4
1952	5.9	5.0
1953	7.2	6.7

The legal kill during the period consisted of 54 per cent young of the year (Gordon and McClellan, 1954). Spicer (1954) had forty-two hens under observation in 1954. Of this number, fifteen (35.7 per cent) attempted to nest and eleven (73.3 per cent) were successful. Of the total number of hens, only 26.2 per cent produced young. The average size of the broods was 6.27 poults. The month in which the brood count is made is important, and this is not given.

The hatch in Arizona in 1947 was good since of the 747 turkeys observed in July and August, 68.4 per cent were poults. Each breeding hen had an average of 5.5 poults (Hall, 1948.2). During the three succeeding years, the number of poults per hen was as follows (Reeves, 1951.2:3; Jantzen, 1956:4):

				Year Poults per Hen				
National Forest	1948	1949	1950	1951	1952	1953	1954	1955
Apache	6.0	5.1	2.4	4.6	4.2	1.3	4.5	1.26
Tonto	—	—	2.5	3.8	—	4.0	—	5.2
Coconino	4.5	4.4	2.4	4.6	4.6	2.0	3.3	0.8
Sitgreaves	6.8	7.1	0.6	3.2	4.2	2.4	2.3	0.8

The size of the broods in summer in Colorado, excluding hens without poults, as given by Burget and Hoffman (1954) was:

	Eastern Slope				Western Slope			
Year	1950	1951	1952	1953	1950	1951	1952	1953
Poults per hen	6.2	6.7	7.4	6.9	8.51	5.2	6.13	8.5

The productivity of Merriam's turkey introduced into California was studied by Burger (1954:204). By winter each successful hen had a brood of 3.7 young. Approximately 30 per cent of the females did not breed.

It is safe to count on 50 per cent of the young being lost by October. This factor, combined with the large number of hens that either do not nest or are unsuccessful in the attempt, gives an annual increase considerably below the potential. Wheeler (1944.1, 1946.1) has stated that less than 20 per cent of the poults arrive at maturity. Under the favorable conditions at the Salt Springs Game Sanctuary, the annual increase was less than 11.5 per cent of the breeding potential. In Virginia, Mosby (1956) thought that only one hen in six or seven was successful in raising a brood to autumn. Bailey (1957:5) concluded from an adult female to immature ratio of 1:1.8 that only one hen in three or four was successful in rearing a brood to the hunting season.

Natal and Juvenal Plumages

The natal plumage of the eastern turkey and its molt are described by Bent (1932:333) as follows: "In the wild-turkey chick the crown is 'pinkish cinnamon' and the back a somewhat lighter shade of the same, fading off to still lighter shades on the breast and flanks; the crown and upper parts are heavily spotted or blotched with dark, rich browns, 'bister' to 'Vandyke brown'; the sides of the head and underparts are 'pale pinkish buff' to 'ivory yellow,' nearly white on the chin and throat and almost 'straw yellow' on the belly.

"As with the quail and grouse, the young turkey starts to grow its wings when a small chick; these are soon followed by the plumage of the back, breast and flanks; the tail comes later, followed by the head and belly. The juvenal feathers of the back are 'walnut brown' edged with 'russet,' with a broad median 'russet' stripe, a whitish tip and large black areas near the tip; the wing coverts are similar, but in duller colors and with less black; the scapulars are 'sayal brown,' peppered with black and spotted or barred with black along the outer edge and at the tip; the tertials and secondaries are 'hair brown,' marked like the scapulars on the outer edge; the primaries are 'hair brown,' mottled and peppered with buffy white; the underparts are 'fuscous,' with whitish tips and shaft streaks; the tail is barred with dusky and 'pinkish cinnamon.'"

There is appreciable development of the wing feathers of the young turkey prior to hatching. Pycraft (1895:363) mentions that in the nestling domestic turkey the proximal remiges (one–seven) are developed considerably while the distal remiges (eight–ten) are represented by neossoptiles. This is confirmed by Leopold (1943:134) in the day-old poults of the eastern wild turkey. The primaries one–seven project 6 to 12 mm. from their sheaths while most of the secondaries are beginning to emerge.

289

In eleven days the longest primaries exceed 50 mm. and the longest secondaries 35 mm. Most of the rectrices are now protruding from the down.

POSTNATAL MOLT

The progress of the postnatal molt, according to Leopold (1943:134), is as follows: "The greater tail coverts, tertiaries, and some of the lesser wing coverts emerge in the second week. Growth of the juvenal body plumage becomes evident in the third week, in the anterolateral parts of the breast . . . and in the interscapular region of the back. The long feathers of the femoral tract soon appear. Molt spreads rapidly over the sternal and dorsal regions, thence posteriorly to the abdominal and pelvic regions. By the sixth week the full juvenal plumage has developed except on head and neck. . . . The anterior spread of the molt is much slower, particularly on the ventral side. At five weeks the head and neck still retain the natal down, but since the bird has increased considerably in size (body weight has increased approximately six times), the plumage of these areas looks thinned and skin shows between the feathers. In the sixth week juvenal feathers begin to appear in the ear tuft and middorsal cervical region, and thereafter molt progresses slowly over the top of the head to the crown and forehead, up the throat to the chin, and lastly takes in the cheeks, lores and areas around the eye."

OTHER PRE-ADULT STAGES

The postjuvenal molt begins early in the fourth week as shown by replacement of the central pair of tail feathers. All the rectrices are replaced by the seventh week except the two outer pairs which are retained until the fourteenth week. The first primary is shed in the sixth week and a new primary appears weekly until the fifth is reached. Replacement and growth of the feathers is then slower. The distal primaries (nine and ten) are not molted but retained through the first winter. These primaries have pointed rather than rounded ends and show with certainty that they belong to a bird of less than one year of age. The retention of the two distal primaries was mentioned by Bent (1932:333). No exceptions were mentioned by Petrides (1942:324) in his paper published in 1942. Subsequently, he (1945:225) noted that the Florida turkey (*M. g. osceola*) shows a tendency to retain only the outermost primary. The domestic turkey retains only the tenth primary. Hybrids between the domestic and the wild turkey may retain the tenth postjuvenal primary only, or both the ninth and tenth. There appears to be no regularity in the retention of the outermost postjuvenal primaries in the eastern turkey. Williams (1961) found that thirty-three of thirty-seven juveniles from the southeastern United States retained only the tenth primary. I have examined four specimens of the Rio Grande turkey taken in southern Texas between November 16 and December 31. All had the ninth primary replaced. In two cases this feather was not fully grown.

Continuing the description of the molt (Leopold, 1943:137): "Several days after the primary molt has started, the greater upper secondary coverts begin to molt, starting with no. 3, the sequence of replacement proceeding proximally. . . . In the seventh week the third secondary drops, and replacement of the secondaries follows that of the coverts in a proximal direction. . . . It is in the fourteenth or fifteenth week, when the molt of the other secondaries is largely completed, that the second and first greater secondary coverts are replaced, followed shortly by the two secondaries in that order. These late coverts become the largest of the series."

It was observed by Warren and Gordon (1935) that in the domestic turkey the "axial" and no. 1 secondary appeared much later than the adjacent secondaries. The above sequence of replacement of the secondaries appears to be characteristic of gallinaceous birds. The molt of the body feathers begins in the seventh week and follows practically the same order as in the postnatal molt.

The postnatal molt of the head is not completed until the tenth or eleventh week, and there is a delay in the replacement of the feathers. In the fourteenth week new feathers appear on the back of the neck, crown, forehead, and chin, and in the loral and cheek regions somewhat later. Leopold (1943:138) adds: "Whereas the juvenal head feathers were small (3–7 mm.) and buff colored, bearing widely spaced barbs to the tip of the rachis, the new feathers are usually black or dark brown, up to 16 mm. long, and barbs are borne no more than a third of the way up the rachis, the tips being hair-like. This gives an appearance of dark pubescence to the heads of young turkeys, most noticeable in *M. g. silvestris*, least so in domestic strains. The postjuvenal head plumage is retained through the first winter. In subsequent molts the heavy pubescence is lost, the feathers of the head being reduced both in size and number. In the native range of *silvestris* the legend of the little 'moss-head' turkeys, supposedly a distinct strain, may have arisen from failure to recognize the age classes, the 'moss-heads' actually being immature individuals."

The belief of hunters in the existence of strains of the wild turkey is of long standing. Waite (1882) hunted in southeastern Virginia where there occurred the "redlegged," and the "mossy-head" or "branch" turkey. He explains that the latter is one-third smaller and has many small feathers on the head giving it a "moss-grown" appearance. The existence of the "moss-head" is confirmed by a Tennessee hunter ("Davy," 1882) who described it as small, wary, and difficult to shoot. The "moss-heads" of Oklahoma were smaller in size and lighter in color than the "bronze" turkey and recognizable by "a fuzz on their heads" (Doolin, 1913). There is no question but that Leopold is correct in calling a "moss-head" an immature bird. Some Virginia hunters persist in the opinion that the "moss-head" differs from the normal wild turkey. Mosby and Handley (1943:103) take the philosophical position that if a hunter gets an extra thrill from killing one, nothing is to be gained by attempting to destroy his belief.

It was discovered by Leopold (1943:138) that the turkey undergoes a partial molt during the first winter. The postjuvenal plumage is worn through the first winter by most of the gallinaceous birds. Except for the region of the head, the postjuvenal plumage is almost fully developed at an age of approximately fourteen weeks. The two central pairs of rectrices are now fully grown but are exceeded in length and width by the adjacent tail feathers. In another week the two central pairs are shed, the replacements sometimes exceeding considerably the length of the other rectrices. During the winter molt, the remaining seven pairs of postjuvenal rectrices are usually retained by the eastern turkey and some of the hybrids. Molting, however, continues in the domestic bird in varying degree up to complete replacement of the remaining post-juvenal rectrices.

The body molt follows the usual pattern. After an age of twelve to fourteen weeks, the feathers of the back and breast begin to show sexual dimorphism (Mosby and Handley, 1943:95). The tips of these feathers are somewhat rounded and colored buff in the female, and truncated and colored black in the male. These are infallible marks for sexing. The light tips are controlled by female hormones. When the female hormone oestrin is injected into a male bronze turkey, the breast feathers on replacement have the light colored tips (Asmundson, 1934). The new body feathers of the female resemble closely those of the adult female, but those of the male lack the brilliance of the mature male.

The tail coverts, and the lesser and middle wing coverts are replaced; however, the remiges, greater primary coverts, alula, parts of the tail, and feathers of the head do not undergo this additional molt. The greater secondary coverts are not renewed in the eastern turkey, but are replaced in the domestic bird. The body molt is complete, or nearly so.

MOLT OF ADULTS

Adults have two molts annually. A complete molt occurs during late summer and early autumn. Yearling males, i.e. males entering their second year, are the first to begin molting and hens with late broods the last. An old gobbler requires about four months to complete the molt. Molt begins by the shedding of the first primary. All the primaries are replaced proceeding from the first to the tenth. In the secondaries the third feather is dropped first, the molt then proceeding proximally. The two distal feathers are dropped later and generally at the time the sixth and seventh are replaced. At this time, the eleventh secondary is shed, the molt spreading proximally until numbers eleven to sixteen are renewed. Accordingly, the molt is taking place simultaneously in three places for a short time.

The molt on the body usually begins after three or four primaries are shed. Molt starts on the sides of the breast and on the thighs, then spreads over the breast and abdomen, and down the legs, then to the rump and up the back. The feathers on the dorsal surface of the neck are the last to be replaced.

There is no regularity in renewal of the rectrices.[1] The replacement is centripetal. Molt normally starts in feathers eight–eight and proceeds inwardly. When the molt has reached nearly the center of the tail feathers, one–one and nine–nine are dropped simultaneously.

The prenuptial molt of adults has not been examined in detail. About

[1] The rectrices are usually in pairs and are numbered from the center of the tail outwards.

all that is known is that it begins in February and that a considerable part of the plumage is replaced.

The first secondary of the domestic bronze turkey is called the "axial" by Warren and Gordon (1935) because of its small size and distinctive behavior in time of appearance and molt. It appears when the poult is 5 weeks of age while the first secondary (the second of ornithologists) appears after 4 weeks. Primaries nine and ten appear in 5.9 and 7.7 weeks respectively.

The rate of growth of the postjuvenal primaries of the pheasant was used by Buss (1946:66) to determine the time of hatching. Refinements were introduced by Trautman (1950). The method has been used by Knoder (1959.1), who followed the growth of the juvenal and postjuvenal primaries of the wild turkey. His data were obtained from fifty game farm turkeys and five juvenile wild turkeys hatched from eggs collected in the wild. The rate of growth of the primaries during their early stages was quite uniform for both sexes. The average daily growth was 7.5 mm. A sufficient difference in the rate of growth of the juvenal primaries three and four appeared between the age of thirty and forty days to determine

TABLE 25

MEAN LENGTH IN MILLIMETERS OF THE EIGHTH POSTJUVENAL
PRIMARY OF MALE AND FEMALE WILD TURKEYS

Age in Days	Lengths	
	Males	Females
128	37	67
132	52	95
139	87	137
146	150	179
160	206	228
167	237	248
174	261	261
181	277	267
188	293	272
195	311	274
202	314	273
T.L.*	315	271

*T.L. = Terminal length.

the sex. These primaries were approximately 10 mm. longer in the male than in the female.

The eighth primary (Table 25) is the most useful for determining the hatching date of a turkey shot during a late fall hunting season. This primary on a bird hatched June 1 would not attain full growth until the middle of December. Knoder states that the mean age of juvenile wild turkeys between the ages of 7 and 190 days can be estimated within an accuracy of plus or minus three or four days. Measurements of the primaries of birds shot in the fall will permit fixing the hatching dates within periods of ten days. Bailey and Rinell (1960:2) found that the terminal lengths of West Virginia specimens were 10–20 mm. greater than those of the wild, but pen-reared birds used by Knoder.

The time of emergence of the postnatal primaries and the weights of the poults were determined by Gustafson (1961), using thirteen birds hatched from the eggs of a nest of Merriam's turkey taken in the wild. The approximate times of emergence of postnatal primaries from the skin were:

Primary No. 1	27–33 days	Primary No. 5	70–76 days
Primary No. 2	38–42 days	Primary No. 6	84–87 days
Primary No. 3	49–53 days	Primary No. 7	99–103 days
Primary No. 4	57–63 days	Primary No. 8	115–122 days

The poults were not sexed at the start of the investigation and it was assumed that the heaviest birds were males. The weights were:

Age in Days	Weight in Pounds	Age in Days	Weight in Pounds
30	0.58–0.78	78	2.68–3.94
37	0.82–1.18	86	3.46–4.78
46	1.20–1.74	144	6.5 female
55	1.56–2.24		9.5–10.5 males
62	1.80–2.66	173	7.5 female
69	2.15–2.99		11.3–11.7 males

The average weights of two strains of game farm poults twenty hours old were .113 (51.3) and .116 lb. (52.7 gr.) (Gerstell and Long, 1939:6). The rate of growth of game farm poults during the first forty weeks after birth was determined by Mosby and Handley (1943:98). The greatest increase in weight occurred between six and twenty-four weeks of age,

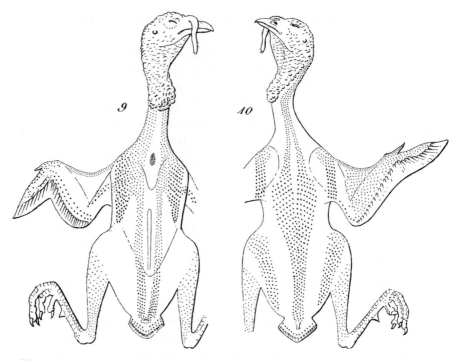

Fig. 12.—*Feather tracts of the turkey. (After Nitzsch [1867].)*

both sexes gaining approximately a pound during this period. After the fortieth week, the weights of both males and females remain quite stable for some months.

PTERYLOGRAPHY

The arrangement of the feather tracts on the turkey was examined by Nitzsch (1867:114). The two main ventral tracts remain separated to the anus (Fig. 12). This is not the case for *Gallus* and *Pavo*. He states: "The dorsal tract is rather sparsely feathered in the middle, and encloses a lanceolate space between the shoulder-blades, which also extends into the widened portion. The lumbar tracts are entirely free, and the axillary tracts on the whole not so strong as usual. The naked carunculated portions of the anterior part of the neck cause the two bands of the inferior tract to commence only on the middle of the latter, where they are separated from each other; but the dorsal tract reaches nearly to the occiput. In the wings I counted twenty-eight remiges of which the eleventh [first secondary] is very small; the tail contains eighteen rectrices. The after-shaft of the contour-feathers is minute, but is of considerable size on the down-feathers which form the borders of the tracts. The commencement of each band of the inferior tract near the branch also consists only of such down-feathers. The oil-gland has seven large umbellate plumes on its mamilla." Although Bonaparte (1825:99) and Nitzsch (1867:114) give the number of remiges as twenty-eight, Leopold (1943:135) has twenty-six, which is correct. There are two well-developed tertials that might be mistaken for secondaries.

TYPES OF FEATHERS

The frontal caruncle appears as a small knob prior to hatching. It is never covered with down feathers like the later naked parts of the head and neck. This caruncle is sparsely covered with filoplumes, the tip being rather thickly covered. Two types of feathers from the tip of the caruncle, presumably from a domestic bird, are shown by Schneider (1931). In Fig. 13 the barbs are stumpy due to wearing away at the ends, so that there is a tendency for them to end at the same height. Fig. 14 shows a new feather with branches projecting from the follicle. They are pointed and bristle-shaped like the shaft. New rami appear in whorls from the follicle and the growth of the feathers is continuous. The feathers show various shapes but those figured, especially, occur frequently. He considers it inadmissable to call them filoplumes or bristles since they occur as eyelashes and vibrissae, and introduces instead the term *bristle-feathers* (*Borstenfedern*). All of the feathers on the tip of the caruncle of wild turkeys which I have examined are unbranched filoplumes. An occasional one is forked.

Meckel (1815) published a paper on the development of the feathers of the turkey and goose from emergence to maturity. I am unable to understand the meaning of many of his terms.

The filoplumes of the spinal tract, according to Meijere (1895:584), are few and short. The shafts at the end bear a few barbs (*Strahlen*) with a few side branches. In addition to the down of the lateral apteria, some short filoplumes may be present. The barbules of the down feathers are not nodular and are briefly ciliated. The feathers of the almost naked neck are considered to be degenerate contour feathers. They have a long

297

shaft and some branches on the lower end only. On both sides of these feathers there often occur many small, colorless, branching feathers which are held to be filoplumes.

The barbules of the feathers of the turkey have been examined by Chandler (1916:340). The distal barbules of the remiges have the ventral teeth greatly developed as broad thin sheets, and the hooklets are very long and slender. The barbules of the down of gallinaceous birds differ considerably on different parts of the barbs and even on different barbs. They are most abundant at the base of the barb, sometimes as many as fifty per millimeter on each side of the barb, and gradually thin down toward the tip. They are exceptionally long and attain a length of 5 mm. in turkeys. The pennulum (the part of the barbule bearing nodes) in the down feather of the turkey has poorly developed nodes in the proximal part. They increase in size, however, and form typical rings which break

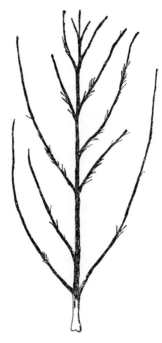

Fig. 13.—*Old feather from the tip of the frontal caruncle of the domestic turkey. The side rays are blunt and broken off, so that there is a tendency for them to end at an equal height. (After Schneider [1931].)*

Fig. 14.—*Freshly emerged feather from the tip of frontal caruncle. The side branches are pointed and bristly like the shaft. (After Schneider [1931].)*

loose from the nodes and sometimes assemble in groups of five or six. The ring structure is lost towards the tip of the barbules, the nodes being merely swollen. The outside diameter of the rings in the eastern wild turkey is about 0.012 mm., while that of the internodes is only 0.004 to 0.005 mm. The ring structure does not appear on the down at the base of the remiges and rectrices and in the aftershafts.

The neck and head of the male is bare except for filoplumes or "bristles." The dorsal-cervical region of the female is feathered. Occasionally, the neck of a wild female is fully covered with normal contour feathers. This phenomenon is more prevalent among game-farm females (Plate 28). An ancient male Pueblo turkey examined by Schorger (1961) was unique in that the neck was covered completely with *semiplumes* (Plate 29a). This bird was found in Tularosa Cave near Reserve, New Mexico, and dates from about 1100 A.D. Normal neck feathers are shown in Plate 29b.

COLOR VARIANTS

Color variants of the turkey are rare. Bonaparte (1825:104) mentioned the occurrence of white and immaculate black domestic turkeys and added: "In the wild state, a white, or even a speckled Turkey, is unknown; and we may venture to say, that a plain black one has hardly ever occurred." There is no reason why melanistic wild turkeys should not be found, but it would be difficult to prove the absence of crossing with domestic birds.

There are some careless observations in the early literature. Loskiel (1794:91) stated that in winter the color of the wild turkey is a shining black changing to light brown in summer. The wild bird, according to Schöpf (1911:218), was to be distinguished from the tame one only in being more uniformly black, brown, or dirty white. Several dozens of wild turkeys were shot by Schultz (1810: II, 19) in descending the Ohio River. He could not distinguish the slightest difference between them and the domestic turkeys.

Melanistic turkeys, reputed to have been a cross between the black domestic turkey and the wild bird, have been reported for North Carolina and Halifax County, Virginia (Mosby and Handley, 1943:93). Asmundson (1939.1) found black-winged, non-barred birds in flocks of domestic bronze turkeys and in a flock of supposedly pure Virginia wild turkeys; however, non-barred primaries have not been found in turkeys taken in the wild. The domestic bronze turkey resembles most closely the eastern wild turkey. As far as the principal color factors are concerned, the genetic composition of the two is identical (Robertson *et al.*, 1943).

The existence of white, or albino, wild turkeys is well authenticated. While below Fort Orange, Missouri, on April 24, 1811, Brackenridge (1814:216) wrote: "While Castor was out, he saw a *white turkey*, but not so fortunate as to kill it. I am told that they have sometimes been seen of this color." There is little probability of domestic turkeys having occurred in the area at this time. In 1825 one of Sibley's hunters shot a nearly white turkey in northeastern New Mexico (Gregg, 1952:99).

In 1882 the following note appeared: "E. Gray Pendleton sent us last week a white wild turkey which he shot near Berkeley Springs, Morgan County, West Virginia. It was beautifully marked with stripes of black, and is considered very rare. This week he sent us an old gobbler, weighing 20 lbs. which was as singularly marked as the white one. It was the most brilliant bronze, shaded down to blue green, and here and there on the breast and wings were pure white feathers, giving the bird a most peculiar appearance. The tail, which is very large, has a white feather on each side of it. The beard is about six inches in length" ("Victor," 1882).

Recently, Bailey (1955.1) reported the occurrence of eight specimens of albinistic turkeys in Pocahontas County, West Virginia. No domestic white turkeys were known to occur in the areas where the birds were found. A white gobbler was shot along the Allegheny River at some unspecified time (Myrick, 1897:6). The winter of 1878–79, Deane (1880:29) saw, presumably in the Boston market, an entirely white specimen said to have come from the West.

A resident of Mississippi mentions killing several white female turkeys perfectly wild in behavior ("Clip," 1886). The only male that he ever saw that was abnormal in color had the build of a tame turkey. The tail feathers had a white terminal band an inch wide. A hunter in Tennessee killed a young gobbler that was grayish white in color without a single dark feather. For several years, a large, very wild white gobbler was seen in the area where the young one was killed ("Davy," 1882).

Several instances of the occurrence of white turkeys in Virginia are given by Mosby and Handley (1943:92). P. T. Birdsong observed a white turkey in Prince George County in 1937. Guy Wright and Tom Putnam both killed white hens in Fluvanna County in 1935. A group of five white poults was observed in Bedford County in July, 1937, and white turkeys were reported in Nottoway and Sussex counties in 1939. In 1908, John H. Matthews killed a white turkey in Henry County. This bird was an albino since it had pink eyes, and is the only one so identified in the literature. Whether the other specimens were whites or albinos must remain unknown. A type of albinism exists in the domestic bronze turkey in which the plumage is almost devoid of pigment. Serious physiological defects exist. There is little melanin in the eye, and the poults are blind. Most of them die within six weeks after hatching (Hutt and Mueller, 1942). Three white turkeys were seen in northern Arizona by a district biologist in 1956 (Jantzen, 1957.1:10).

12

Mortality from Predators

THE MORTALITY OF TURKEYS due to natural causes derives from predators, weather, accidents, diseases, and endoparasites. Only predation will be discussed in this chapter.

The turkey, like the majority of wild animals, has numerous enemies. It was not until it declined drastically from hunting and destruction of its habitat that predators were seriously blamed. One kill by a fox is sufficient to condemn every member of the species. The number of proven cases of predation is so small that it is now difficult to find a field biologist who believes that predators have an important effect on the turkey population. Certainly no quantitative data are available. The victim is frequently sick or injured, or a game farm bird lacking sufficient wariness. The destruction of predators has been advocated from the belief that their former food supplies are now available in only limited quantity so that turkeys are taken in compensation. This has not been proved.

EXTENT OF PREDATION

Formerly there were large numbers of turkeys where the predator population was proportionally high. Recently, Ramsey (1958:16) wrote: "Presence of a heavy furbearer population on any turkey range does not always account for the low population or the total absence of wild turkeys there. Old-timers in the Hill Country tell us that the greatest numbers of wild turkeys existed at a time when the hills and valleys of Kerr County (Texas), for example, were literally infested with grey wolves, bobcats, foxes, coons, ringtails, opossums, great horned owls, hawks of many species, snakes, and skunks."

It is now generally conceded by game managers that the control of predators is not worth the effort. If the turkeys do not survive on a given area, it is unsuitable or the stock does not possess sufficient wild blood to insure self-preservation. The real wild turkey is very alert to danger and responds with astonishing speed. Having seen turkeys escape from cannon nets with unbelievable celerity, I am prone to believe that they suffer little from four-footed predators. Tooker (1933) reported that with the use of a turkey call he had killed cougars, timber wolves, and "lynx cats" in Arizona. Any predator, if sufficiently hungry, will respond to the call of a turkey, but this is no measure of destructiveness.

Predation may be a serious problem where turkeys are raised in enclosures. Randall (1934.1:117) has stated that turkeys, no matter how wild, cannot be raised unless crows, owls, and foxes are eliminated. One of the early methods of destroying predators on preserves was the use of poison by the Woodmont Rod and Gun Club, Washington County, Maryland. Strychnine was placed in the mouths of pigeons and house sparrows which, five hundred to one thousand at a time, were scattered along trails in January and February. Job (1915:70; cf. Bridges, 1953:150) on the authority of C. C. Worthington, states that thirty-four deer died from eating the poisoned sparrows, the birds having been found in their stomachs. This seems most unusual. There are a few records of deer eating fish.

The efforts of E. A. Schilling to increase the turkey population on an area of 100,000 acres in the Chattahoochee National Forest, northern Georgia, have been described by Riter (1941). The finding of wild turkey bones at the dens of bobcats, and evidence of kills by foxes led to the trapping of 126 bobcats and 116 gray foxes the winter of 1936–37. In the fall of 1937 a great increase in the turkey population was observed. The following winter, ninety-one bobcats and eighty-three foxes were trapped. There was an increase in the population in the fall of 1938, but it was not as great as in 1937. Trapping was believed to have been decidedly beneficial. According to Maher (1935:265), turkeys declined in Arizona with the decrease in the trapping of predators resulting from a drop in the price of furs.

Most investigators find it difficult to assign population fluctuations to any one cause. Cox (1947–48) found that on the Tepeguaje Ranch, southern Texas, predators made little inroad on adults and control did not lead to an increase in survival of young turkeys. Control during the nesting season could be of importance, especially in the absence of adequate cover. Examination of the stomachs of seventy-two bobcats, forty-three coyotes, ninety-five foxes, five cougars, four badgers, five skunks, and four raccoons in Arizona failed to reveal the remains of turkeys (Reeves, 1954). There was little difference in the survival of poults between an area where predators were abundant and another where they had been extensively controlled. Reeves thought that control might be advisable to protect released turkeys and remnant flocks.

Predation by carnivores in Missouri was considered to be "decidedly subordinate to persistent poaching by man" (Dalke et al., 1946:57). Red and gray foxes, coyotes, and dogs were believed to have a minimum effect on the turkey population (Dalke and Spencer, 1946:285). Control in Colorado was discontinued about 1945 since no adequate benefit could be perceived. Development of the turkey population in most of the stocked areas showed little difference whether there was pre-elimination of predators or not (Burget, 1946:4, 21). Studies of predation in Maryland as well as in other states have shown that it has no important effect on the turkey population (Kerns, 1959). Feral hogs and raccoons were removed from the Francis Marion Preserve, South Carolina, to protect the food patches. According to Holbrook (1958:2), bobcats, although numerous, provided little sign of predation. Destruction by bald eagles, golden eagles, and great horned owls was insufficient to justify a campaign of eradication.

The great majority of the cases of predation observed has been with released pen-reared birds. The fate of 440 turkeys released in Virginia in the fall of 1940 was followed by Phelps (1942). Of this number, 209 were located in the late spring of 1941. Insofar as could be determined, thirty-four were killed by foxes, three by bobcats, and thirty died from unknown causes. Some turkeys are so unwary that, following release, they will roost on the ground or so close to it that they fall an easy prey. Costly experience has shown that there is little hope in restoration unless captured wild stock is used for release. Where this is done, predation is a minor problem. Elimination of a clever predator which concentrates on turkeys may at times be necessary, but a general campaign of extermination is inadvisable. The elimination of predators may do more harm than good (Anon., 1950:17).

Predation on nests was investigated by J. R. Davis (1959) by constructing 107 dummy nests in which were placed turkey eggs containing an injection of strychnine sulphate (Table 26). Most of the predators died near the nests. If a nest remained undisturbed for forty-three days, it was considered successful.

TABLE 26

FATE OF DUMMY TURKEY NESTS

Predators	Nests Destroyed	
	Number	Per cent
Raccoons	31	29
Skunks	23	21
Opossums	15	14
Snakes	9	8
Crows	6	6
Foxes	2	2
Unknown	2	2
Cattle	1	1
Hogs	1	1
Dogs	1	1

The number of successful nests was fifteen. I have been informed by Davis that where the nests were placed under a thin overstory, the eggs were covered completely. The eggs under a heavy overstory were partially covered so that the outline of the eggs was not visible from a distance.

FIRE ANTS AS POTENTIAL PREDATORS

Insects and arachnids, such as ticks, which are frequently present in large numbers on the wild turkey, rarely cause the death of the host. In the South are two native species of fire ants (*Solonopsis geminata* and *S. xyloni*) and the imported fire ant (*S. saevissima richteri*). These ants are known to have entered the punctured egg of the bobwhite and devour the chick before it emerged (Stoddard, 1946:193). They are a potential danger to hatching turkeys, but I am unaware of a case of actual destruction of the young. Since the inauguration of the campaign to control the ants by the use of pesticides, several writers have claimed that these insects are not harmful to wildlife (George, 1958; Peters, 1958). Baker (1958) states that during the forty years that the Argentine ant has been present, game populations have shown a steady increase. Spray-

305

ing with heptachlor and dieldrin to remove the Argentine ant has been shown to produce sterility in turkeys. Clawson (1958) followed the fate of a population of eighty wild turkeys in Wilcox County, Alabama. Following spraying, there was a steady decline in numbers during the first breeding season. The first winter after treatment, only five gobblers, six hens, and one young were observed from baited blinds. The population remained depressed during the second season after spraying. Normal numbers of birds were found on untreated areas. Domestic turkeys were likewise affected. Of the fifty eggs laid by three hens, only seven hatched. The young survived only a short time.

Reptiles as Predators

There is the singular case of a turkey falling victim to an alligator (*Alligator mississippiensis*). Roemer (1849:172), a German naturalist, was at New Braunfels, Texas, in 1846. On March 18 there was brought to him an eleven-foot alligator caught in Comal Creek. Dissection of the stomach revealed the bones and hoofs of a deer and a partly digested wild turkey. Since the turkey will wade into water to drink, it was probably caught in this situation.

The effect of reptiles on the turkey population seems to be minor. Examination of 418 snakes, representing fifteen species, from the George Washington National Forest, Virginia, failed to reveal either the eggs or young of the wild turkey (Uhler *et al.*, 1939).

The behavior of wild turkeys in the presence of a snake has been described by Rutledge (1924:260): "I know not if the wild turkey suffers from snake-bite; but at sight of a large snake—too large, presumably, for the turkey to swallow—the bird will show extreme excitement. If a flock be present, a slow dance will be begun about the reptile, the birds lowering their wings, raising and spreading their tails, and making a continuous querulous calling. Single birds will detach themselves from the revolving circle to make frantic dashes at the snake. This dervish-like performance will continue for an hour or more. If the snake is not too formidable he will likely be killed; but a serpent of the proportions of a great diamondback rattler will be left unmolested." He once observed for half an hour a flock of twenty-six turkeys dance around a large king snake in the mountains of southern Pennsylvania. The description by Beyers (1939) of the behavior of wild turkeys in the presence of a snake is remarkably similar. This trait in turkeys has been utilized for the detection and capture of snakes (Smith, 1946). Rutledge (1935:521) thinks that the Hopi snake dance was derived from the behavior of turkeys in the presence of a snake.

The chicken snake (*Elaphe obsoleta*) was considered by Newman (1945:287) as one of the chief predators on eggs in eastern Texas. One cut open in Kerr County contained the remains of two turkey eggs (Sanders, 1939). No domestic turkeys were known to range in the vicinity. H. E. Davis (1949:280, 283) thought that a large snake of this species could be highly destructive. Eggs of both wild and domestic turkeys were known to have been swallowed. One snake was gorged with young chickens.

The copperhead (*Agkistrodon mokasen*), while numerous in Missouri, was known in only one instance to have swallowed a turkey egg (Blakey, 1937:13). The related water moccasin (*Agkistrodon piscivorus*) killed a domestic hen turkey in Florida and swallowed the entire clutch of ten eggs. The latter were crosswise in the snake, which measured five feet and eight inches, an exceptional length (Browne, 1938).

A black snake (*Coluber constrictor*), six feet in length, found on the Hercules Refuge, Missouri, had swallowed four turkey eggs. Of two other snakes of this species found in turkey nests, one had swallowed an egg while the other had not disturbed the eggs (Bennitt and Nagel, 1937:64). Blakey (1937:13) records that nine eggs removed from a black snake hatched normally under artificial conditions. This snake will return to a nest until all the eggs have been devoured. A large snake of this species was reported to have eaten six or seven turkey eggs in Buckingham County, Virginia (Mosby and Handley, 1943:128). Kozicky and Metz (1948:31) reported this snake destructive on propagating areas in Pennsylvania.

A large coachwhip (*Coluber flagellum*) had partially swallowed one of the poults held in confinement in Alabama (Wheeler, 1948:43). A specimen five feet in length, killed in a nesting area in Missouri, showed no evidence of having eaten eggs (Bennitt and Nagel, 1937:65). Maher (1935:265) states that in Arizona a cowboy cut open a bulging "cow" snake and found that it contained turkey eggs.

Wild turkeys do not hesitate to attack a rattlesnake (*Crotalus*) and will frequently kill it. According to Santleben (1910:48): "I was travel-

307

ing the road near Uvalde [Texas] when I saw a large flock of wild turkeys in an open glade near the highway. I stopped when I saw the gobblers had congregated in a circle where they seemed to be fighting, but I soon perceived that they were killing a large rattlesnake. One after the other would spring into the air in rapid succession and come down on the reptile, which they struck a hard blow with one wing that might have been heard quite a distance. Apparently all the gobblers took part in the fracas, and they appeared to be greatly excited, but the hens fed quietly in the vicinity and seemed to be indifferent to what was going on.

"I watched them about ten minutes before they observed my presence and became alarmed. After they disappeared in the brush I approached the place and found the snake coiled up and almost dead. Evidently the gobblers had been engaged in killing him for some time before I appeared on the scene, and if they had not been disturbed the victim would have provided a feast for the whole flock, because it was their custom to eat the snakes killed in this way."

A lone female wild turkey was observed by Jennings (1956) in Brooks County, Texas, dancing cautiously about a rattlesnake three feet in length and striking it with its left wing. The snake had no fight left in it and probably would have been killed but for the interruption. Similar attacks on rattlesnakes have been mentioned by Jackson (1942) and by Duncan (1945). The rattlesnake is not the only venomous snake that has been killed by turkeys. According to a newspaper article, two domestic turkeys killed a black-ringed cobra that entered their pen at Kestell, South Africa (Anon., 1960.1).

An account of the predation of the rattlesnake (*Crotalus*) on poults appeared in 1765. A family in Maryland missed fifteen young turkeys from a brood. The following day a rattlesnake was killed one-half mile distant. When the snake was cut open, many parts of young turkeys were found (J. B., 1765). Captain H. L. Harllee, according to H. E. Davis (1949:283), killed a large diamondback rattlesnake that had eaten a young wild turkey several weeks of age; and Rutledge (1946:77) mentions one which had swallowed a poult about two weeks old. In Pennsylvania, according to Erickson (1950), a rattlesnake 35 inches in length contained a poult. A rattlesnake killed a poult in the Carson National Forest, New Mexico. Hubbard (1948) gives a detailed description of the killing of this snake by a gobbler with its spurs. A similar case in Texas is mentioned by Dobie (1947).

Flack (1866:332) wrote that in Texas the rattlesnake "does not despise turkey's eggs." The timber rattlesnake (*Crotalus horridus*), according to Blakey (1937:13), is fond of the eggs of the wild turkey. One snake was found to have swallowed four of them.

Birds as Predators

The crow (*Corvus brachyrhynchos*) is a confirmed egger. A hole is pecked in the side of the egg through which the contents are eaten. Audubon (1834:321) wrote: "The most remarkable feat of the Crow, is the nicety with which it, like the Jay, pierces an egg with its bill in order to carry it off, and eat it with security. In this manner I have seen it steal, one after another, all the eggs of a wild Turkey's nest." The crow was considered to be one of the chief destroyers of eggs in Texas (Newman, 1945:287), as well as in Florida (Anon., 1950:17). The common crow and fish crow (*Corvus ossifragus*) were believed by Davis (1949:280) to be important destroyers of nests. His conclusion was based on the known destruction by both species of the eggs and young of the domestic turkey.

Depredation is much greater on the nests of domestic turkeys and pen-reared wild turkeys than on those of native birds. Cole (1909) reported that the nests of domestic turkeys, at liberty, placed remotely from farm buildings were particularly vulnerable to predation by crows. Johnson (1930) asserted that in raising wild turkeys the crow was the worst enemy because "They destroy annually for us over a hundred eggs. One pair of crows got over 50 eggs from us in one week." H. J. Brown (1953) likewise complained of the theft of eggs. In Pennsylvania crows were listed second only to racoons as enemies. They were especially harmful in spring before vegetation had developed sufficiently to protect the nests (Kozicky and Metz, 1948:31).

It is significant that in Virginia thirteen nests of free-ranging, pen-reared wild turkeys were destroyed by crows in 1939 and 1940, but none of native birds (Mosby and Handley, 1943:128). This indicates that the wild birds are more adept at secreting their nests. The wild turkeys raised by Mrs. Beyers (1939), on leaving the nest, covered the eggs so

309

carefully that they were safe from crows. In the Ozarks of Missouri crows were observed to follow turkey hens persistently, but no depredation on eggs was discovered (Blakey, 1937:14).

The killing of poults by crows appears to be very rare. A case of this nature was reported by H. H. Brimley (Pearson *et al.*, 1919:215) for White Lake, North Carolina.

The destruction of a nest of the wild turkey in Missouri is attributed to that lowly raptor, the turkey buzzard (*Cathartes aura*) (Leopold, 1944:163).

The deft accipiters can be especially destructive to poults. Brown (1953) had goshawks (*Accipiter gentilis*) swoop at his domestic turkeys, but they did not grapple. In France, Sacc (1863) observed his domestic turkeys attack and repulse birds of prey. In only one case did a turkey have a fatal encounter, and that was with an uncommonly large goshawk. Brooks (1934) wrote that in the winter of 1926–27 a goshawk attacked a fully grown wild turkey at the West Virginia State Game Farm at French Creek. By the time invading goshawks arrive, even the young turkeys of the year are so large that they are rarely killed.

Among the enemies of wild poults, Davis (1949:284) places the Cooper's hawk (*Accipiter cooperi*) and the sharp-shinned hawk (*Accipiter striatus*). Brown (1953) occasionally had domestic poults killed by the Cooper's hawk.

Some of the buteos have received a black mark. The red-shouldered hawk (*Buteo lineatus*) is branded by Hebard (1949) as an arch-enemy of young wild turkeys in southern Georgia. The red-tailed hawk (*Buteo jamaicensis*) occasionally captures poults and, although it attacks adults, is seldom able to kill them. In Missouri, Bennitt and Nagel (1937:65) had only four reports of this hawk attacking fully grown birds. On one of the game farms in Pennsylvania, an adult red-tailed hawk was promptly shot after it had knocked a turkey hen from a limb (Latham, 1956:64). Davis (1949:284) considered this hawk to be a serious enemy of wild poults. It responded to his turkey call, and he had even seen it attack fully grown birds. In one case the turkey, sitting in a pine tree, escaped; in another, a young gobbler was caught while in a tree, both victim and hawk falling into the water and drowning.

An interesting incident is described by Johnson (1961). In Gila County, Arizona, what was believed to be a zone-tailed hawk (*Buteo albonotatus*) attacked some poults about one-third grown. The hen rose into the air and knocked some wing and tail feathers from the hawk. A ranger informed Johnson of seeing a hen fly at a red-tailed hawk that was endangering her poults.

Flooding in Mississippi forced the turkeys into trees. According to Polk (1890), the birds were harassed by hawks and put to flight. This behavior was so consistent that the presence of hawks was used as an indication of where turkeys were to be found. The hawks were not identified but in view of the region they were probably buteos.

The golden eagle (*Aquila chrysaëtos*) experiences little difficulty in killing an adult wild turkey. Like Merriam's turkey, it prefers mountainous country and, in the opinion of Ligon (1946:9, 37), must be a formidable enemy. He mentions a case of this eagle that, on failing to strike one of a flock from the air, tried to capture a bird from the ground. Some old gobblers raised such a fuss that the eagle departed. An observer in the Lincoln National Forest in 1933 noted that a pair was preying on turkey eggs. One eagle was seen carrying an egg in its beak to its nest. H. J. Cook (1929) has described the killing of a turkey by this species at Cimarron, New Mexico. The distribution of the feathers showed that the struggle occupied a distance of thirty to forty yards. The turkey was still alive after suffering the following injuries: "His head and neck were uninjured but practically all the flesh was torn off his back and from between his wings and far down his sides! His backbone was exposed with all meat stripped off for more than six inches and his ribs stripped bare...."

On March 4, 1816, De Mun (1928:312) saw an eagle, presumably of this species, attack a flock of turkeys in the sandhills of southwestern Kansas. One bird was so wounded that he was able to run it down with ease. A golden eagle in Colorado was observed making several attempts to capture a turkey from a feeding flock (Burget, 1957:54). In another instance an eagle struck a gobbler that had separated from the flock and immediately began to feed from its breast. In Arizona, Hargrave (1939.1) found a female turkey, with an egg in the oviduct, killed by an eagle presumably of this species. During a freshet in South Carolina, a golden eagle was shot after it had knocked a young male turkey from a pine tree into the shallow water (Davis, 1949:290).

Three cases of the killing of turkeys by the golden eagle are given by

Arnold (1954:23). In January, 1945, W. C. Glazener flushed an eagle from a live-oak mott in Brooks County, Texas. In the mott were found the remains of a hen turkey. B. Wilson, in April, 1948, found one feeding on a large gobbler at Cerrososo Canyon, New Mexico. The turkey was still alive. The third account covers the killing of a fully grown turkey in 1945 on the Mescalero Indian Reservation, New Mexico. By the time the observers reached the spot where the eagle was seen to dive, nearly all the edible portion of the carcass had been devoured.

The behaviour of Merriam's turkeys in Wyoming in the presence of potential aerial enemies has been described as follows: "Whenever golden eagles flew over flocks of feeding turkeys, the latter immediately uttered a warning signal sounding like a 'put-put' and, arising as a group and continuing to make their excited danger calls, flew to nearby stands of heavy timber. Any larger birds of another species flying over the trapping site caused the turkeys' dispersal to the timber. On one occasion, an Army Air Force plane, flying low over the area during a search mission, aroused the birds to flight" (Crump and Sanderson, 1951:36).

The eating of fish by the bald eagle has not resulted in a completely benign disposition. It frequently pursues wild turkeys but does not often make a kill. While in Missouri in 1818, Evans (1819:205) observed a bald eagle perched on a tall oak. While he was admiring the bird, a wild turkey flying to the ground from a neighboring tree was pounced upon by the eagle. Before it could make a capture, the turkey was shot. While at Devils River, Texas, in February, 1853, Fröbel (1859:454) observed: "Eagles, with white bodies and black wings, and of an extraordinary size, are seen hovering over the bushes in which the turkeys lie." The attempt of an eagle to capture a turkey along the same stream was witnessed by another writer ("Rio Diablo," 1892).

This eagle was observed attacking a flock of fifteen to twenty old gobblers in Oklahoma ("Occident," 1882). Eifrig (1904:250) states that on September 17, 1902, a young bald eagle was captured while attacking a wild turkey on Knobly Mountain, West Virginia. The domestic turkeys kept by Brown were never molested by this eagle.

In the refuse beneath an eagle's nest in Hillsborough County, Florida, in 1913, A. Wetmore found the remains of one wild turkey (Howell, 1932:183; Imler and Kalmbach, 1955:34, 41). When a bald eagle is seen feeding on a turkey, it should be determined if it is a direct kill or carrion. Davis (1959:290) in one instance observed a bald eagle feeding on a domestic turkey that had been killed by a predator, and in another case on a wild turkey that a hunter had killed the day before and not found.

A quaint description of the method of attack by a pair of "grey eagles" in Missouri was given by Fate Jones to Turnbo (1904:123) : "I was hunting on horseback on Trimble's Creek and while I was riding along near a mile west of the main stream I heard a great noise among a flock of wild turkeys, and turning my horse's head in the direction the noise came from, I rode [with]in a few hundred yards of them and dismounted and hitched my horse and went on slowly toward them until I could see them.... At the time I caught sight of the turkeys I saw two grey eagles attacking them. The turkeys, which were nine in number, were all big gobblers, and when I saw them they were under a tree that the limbs put out close to the ground. The two eagles were skillful, for one would get down in the snow and drive the turkeys from under the limbs of the tree and the other, which would be sitting on a limb of the tree, would dart down and strike at one, then the turkeys would dodge back under the limbs. The eagle that struck at one would stay down and drive the turkeys out in the open again while the other would fly up into the tree and when the flock exposed themselves it would dart at one as the other did. In this manner the eagles would swap positions. Every now and then the eagle that would dart from the limb would hit one with its talons and cripple it but it never failed to break the eagle's hold and get back under the tree. Occasionally the eagle that was engaged in driving the turkeys from under the boughs of the tree apparently would grow very angry and would strike at a turkey and snatch out a bunch of feathers, but the gobbler appeared to be too smart for the eagle and would pull loose. I lay in the snow on my belly watching them until I was very cold. At this stage both eagles flew up into the tree, seemingly as though to council together how to make it a success to capture one of those tempting baits, as their work so far was a failure." Jones shot at the turkeys at this point and ended the contest. Turnbo states that it was common for eagles to kill and eat wild turkeys. This is doubtful.

The one freebooter without a friend is the great horned owl (*Bubo virginianus*). Direct proof of its destructiveness is easily obtained. It will return frequently to a carcass and is readily trapped. No hesitation is

313

shown in attacking and killing a fully grown domestic turkey. Instances of killing the wild bird are less frequent. The habit of the wild turkey of roosting in the topmost branches of trees, often dead ones, renders it particularly susceptible to attack; however, if there was unusual danger from this predilection, the turkey would certainly have changed its habits.

Audubon's (1831:8) description of the method of attack is: "As Turkeys usually roost in flocks, on naked branches of trees, they are easily discovered by their enemies, the owls, which, on silent wing, approach and hover around them, for the purpose of reconnoitring. This, however, is rarely done without being discovered, and a single *cluck* from one of the Turkeys announces to the whole party the approach of the murderer. They instantly start upon their legs, and watch the motions of the Owl, which, selecting one as its victim, comes down upon it like an arrow, and would invariably secure the Turkey, did not the latter at that moment lower its head, stoop, and spread its tail in an inverted manner over its back, by which action the aggressor is met by a smooth inclined plane, along which it glances without hurting the Turkey; immediately after which the latter drops to the ground, and thus escapes, merely with the loss of a few feathers."

The procedure described to McIlhenny (1914:240) by John Hamilton, who had witnessed the performance while hunting before daylight in the Brazos bottoms, Texas, is entirely different from the above. The owl alighted on a limb between the hen and the trunk of a tree. Uttering a low *who, who,* the owl moved gradually towards the turkey, eventually forcing it from the end of the limb. As soon as the turkey was in flight, it was pursued and killed. McIlhenny added that from his own observations he had known this owl to push chickens from their perches and catch them when in flight. I cannot conceive of a turkey remaining one instant on a perch to entertain a great horned owl.

It is the opinion of Davis (1949:84) that the owl forces the turkey from its roost and when it is in flight strikes at a vulnerable spot, usually the middle of the back. The kill is completed on the ground. He states that the owl cannot kill a turkey over water since the entangled birds would fall into it and the owl would drown. The inability of the owl to kill a turkey over water may be a reason for the turkey's preference for roosts in swamps. The difficulties in the way of actually observing the technique of an attack are enormous. Awaiting further knowledge, I prefer to believe that the owl grapples with the turkey on the roost and rides with it to earth for the denouement.

The paper by Brown (1953) is worth reading in its entirety for the descriptions of the havoc created by the great horned owl during his experience of fourteen years in raising domestic turkeys in Burnett County, Wisconsin. The owl appears to kill its victim by grasping its outstretched neck. He writes in part: "The horned owl was prompt in turning from his native prey to the turkeys, and I well remember the initial raid. My first flock, a small one of three hundred and fifty birds, had been out in the clearings for a few weeks without incident. The July night was fine and still, the full moon rising and the owls in full voice up and down the valley. Like the wolves, they seem to have a ceremonial howl before the hunt begins. An hour or so after nightfall, while I was in the cabin reading, there came a loud rushing roar that lifted me right out of the chair. I thought of falling trees, explosions, wind squalls and other things, and it was some time before I realized that the sound must have come from the turkeys. Taking the gun I hurried out to them. The moon shone on almost empty roosts, but I could see turkeys, like black hummocks, scattered over the clearing. As I passed these, each hissed like a snake and ran aimlessly a few feet. All had assumed what might be called the turkey position of fright—tail spread and depressed, feathers expanded and neck stretched out along the ground. I had never met such an expression of terror, and I grew a little nervous myself as I poked about in the shadows and the brush trying to find the cause and only starting up more terrorized birds. Most of the remainder of the night was spent driving what I could find of the flock back to the roosts. Another search in daylight failed to throw any light on the disturbance. I thought it was all probably due to a fox until a similar incident occurred two nights later and I found in the morning the body of a turkey with the head missing and some of the breast eaten. Traps set around the remains caught a horned owl the same night."

It was thought by Jordan (1898:330) that the great horned owl was the worst offender among the birds of prey, and that hawks killed very few turkeys. W. H. Fisher (1894) considered it the greatest enemy of the wild turkey in Maryland. It was known to have killed half-grown wild turkeys at Kerrville, Texas (Lacey, 1911:208). Adult wild turkeys were killed in Missouri. In one case a hen was attacked in full daylight (Blakey, 1937:15). One of the turkeys released in Sabine Parish, Louisiana, was killed by this owl (Collins, 1952).

There is no serious damage to wild turkeys by the great horned owl except at game farms. In Virginia it proved to be the worst predator of the pen-reared birds. In one case a nest of the raiders was found a mile distant (Mosby and Handley, 1943:135). Steinhart (1936:53) trapped four great horned owls after they had killed three fully grown wild gobblers which he had raised. The free-ranging wild turkeys raised by Randall (1933:60) in the Adirondacks roosted on poles in an old orchard. One night he heard a thump against the house. The following morning he found nine dead turkeys around his buildings and along the highway. Later, a great horned owl was trapped beside a half-plucked turkey.

Examination of 792 stomachs of great horned owls in Pennsylvania revealed the remains of turkeys in only one case. Whether the bird was wild or tame could not be determined. Most of the owls were taken in counties where turkeys were few or absent (Langenbach and McDowell, 1939).

Nothing is known of the snowy owl (*Nyctea scandica*) as a predator. It is merely mentioned as an enemy of turkeys (Audubon, 1831:8; Randall, 1933:60).

Poults about eight weeks of age, reared artificially in Missouri, were killed on the roost by both the short-eared owl (*Asio flammeus*) and the long-eared owl (*Asio otus*) (Blakey, 1937:15). Brown (1953) lost domestic poults occasionally to the barred owl (*Strix varia*).

MAMMALS AS PREDATORS

The opossum (*Didelphis virginiana*) is usually satisfied with eggs or poults. In Virginia two opossums attacked the recently hatched young in the nest of a free-ranging wild turkey that had been pen-reared. Nine of the young were eaten before the opossums were driven off (Mosby and Handley, 1943:134). Incidents of the kind must be rare with native turkeys. Blakey (1937:15) wrote: "The opossum has been caught red-handed taking restocked birds from a roost. The animal carefully approaches the roost, seizes a bird about the neck and body in a death grapple, and clings on until its victim is dead and falls from the roost." He mentions that an opossum has been observed, prior to eating an egg, to carry it 150 yards from the nest by breaking a hole in one end. On one occasion the egg was carried in the crook of the tail. In Alabama, Wheeler (1945) found opossum hairs attached to the egg shells of a nest which had been broken up. The destruction by this predator of a nest of the domestic turkey is mentioned by Davis (1949:280). It was found to be injurious in propagating areas in Pennsylvania (Kozicky and Metz, 1948:31).

Predation by the black bear (*Ursus americanus*) is insignificant, owing to sparse distribution. In Virginia in 1932 a bear killed a released turkey that was roosting on a low limb (Mosby and Handley, 1943:134). One bear shot on the Carson National Forest, New Mexico, had in its stomach the shells of several turkey eggs (Pooler, 1922). Several of the bears killed on the White River Indian Reservation in Arizona in 1939 had eaten the eggs. Evidence was also obtained in Arizona of a bear eating incubated eggs after the hen had been killed by a bobcat. Hugh Harris, in New Mexico, found that of the stomachs of six bears killed in spring, four contained remains of turkey eggs (Ligon, 1946:38).

The raccoon (*Procyon lotor*) has the reputation of being highly destructive. Mosby and Handley (1943:132) were informed by L. P. Keizer that in Pennsylvania the animal was very destructive to incubating hens and eggs in the propagating areas. This is to be expected under artificial conditions. Kozicky and Metz (1948:31) wrote: "Wild turkeys in propagating areas have suffered loss mainly from the raccoon . . . which is destructive to both wing-clipped hens and eggs." The small number of young turkeys produced in the Pocono Mountains, Pennsylvania, as Street (1954:23) was informed, was due to the ravages of raccoons. They are stated to prey on turkey eggs on the Francis Marion National Forest, South Carolina (Holbrook, 1952).

A flock of twenty-four artificially reared turkeys liberated in the San Catalina Mountains, Arizona, was reduced to eleven, ostensibly by raccoons. One raccoon was killed while climbing a tree where the birds were accustomed to roost (Anon., 1925). Predation on the Edwards Plateau, Texas, took place mainly at the roosts. The kills were attributed to raccoons since the bodies were dragged some distance before being eaten (Hahn, 1946). Bedichek (1950:53) did not believe that the raccoon was especially harmful on the Aransas Refuge, Texas, but owing to the poor success in re-establishing turkeys on the area, it was trapped vigorously on suspicion.

317

The mustelids have received surprisingly little blame. Kozicky and Metz (1948:31) state that weasels and mink are destructive where turkeys are being raised.

The activity of the skunk (*Mephitis mephitis*) appears to be limited to devouring the eggs. These are opened at the small end. Sutton (1929) mentions a nest that was deserted after most of the eggs had been eaten by a skunk. It is also mentioned as a predator in Pennsylvania (Kozicky and Metz, 1948:31). In Virginia, 4.3 per cent of the egg losses was attributed to skunks (Mosby and Handley, 1943:126). Predation on nests was also observed in Alabama (Barkalow, 1942). Henry Bridges informed Rutledge (1946:183) that skunks were very troublesome in raising turkeys at the Woodmont Club. In Texas skunks will sometimes roll eggs from the nest (Lacey, 1911:206).

The coyote (*Canis latrans*) is highly destructive to the unwary domestic turkey. Gier (1957:28) estimated that in 1949 coyotes caused a loss of $78,550 to the turkey industry in Kansas. In Nebraska, Mrs. Joana Hickenbottom (Purcell, 1936:142) was given a gobbler that was subsequently devoured by some animal. Then she knew "what had got him because a coyote always leaves the gizzard." Mrs. Beyers (1943) considered the coyote the worst enemy of the domestic bird in South Dakota. The progeny of a wild gobbler and domestic females was much more alert to this enemy than the domestic turkeys. The winter of 1882–83, in Major County, Oklahoma, the coyotes "finished" the white turkeys that Nelson (1953:85, 135) had been raising. Hunters going to market with wild turkeys had to discard many from spoilage when the weather turned warm. Coyotes lined the trail awaiting the discards.

The number of cases of definite predation on native turkeys are few in comparison with the numbers of these mammals. Sennett (1879:428), having found the debris of shells and feathers at a nest in Texas, concluded that it was plainly the work of a coyote. Glazener (1944) reported that at least four turkeys were killed and one nest destroyed within a period of three months in southern Texas. The great increase in turkeys in the Laureles and Santa Gertrudis divisions of the King Ranch was attributed by Lehman (1948:237) to the intensive control of coyotes inaugurated in 1946.

The first morning that game farm turkeys released in Fresno County, California, descended from the roost, two coyotes pounced upon them and killed three. Subsequently, the birds did not roost two nights in the same place (Thomas, 1915). The stomach contents of a coyote shot in 1946 near a flock of wild turkeys in the Mescalero Indian Reservation, New Mexico, consisted of 67 per cent bones and feathers, and some flesh, presumed to be of a wild bird. Opinion differed as to whether the fragments of egg shells were those of a duck or a turkey (Young and Jackson, 1951:149).

The coyote is believed to be a relatively new arrival in the habitat of the wild turkey in New Mexico, where it has become more numerous than the turkey. Ligon (1929:48) gave it first place among the enemies of the turkey as it has the ability to capture both poults and adults. He gives several examples. A coyote crippled one of three gobblers and probably would have killed it if it had not been prevented by the observers. A. L. Johnson of Lakeside, Arizona, observed a coyote attempting to catch poults. After the poults had taken to the trees, the coyote remained beneath them, apparently waiting until they flew, when they could be caught easily at the time of landing. The coyote was driven away when it appeared that the poults were about to fly to the ground. A trapped coyote had in its stomach three small poults that had been swallowed practically whole. Burget (1957:54) disagrees with Ligon. During fourteen years of observations in Colorado, only four kills could be attributed definitely to coyotes.

The wild turkey is not mentioned by Sperry (1941:48) in his extensive study of the food habits of the coyote. He concludes: "Sweeping charges that the coyote is responsible for wholesale and widespread destruction of game birds are not borne out by the stomach analyses, as remains of game birds were found in but 3 per cent of the stomachs and contributed less than 1 per cent of the total food."

Sometimes the tables are turned. Gage (1952) mentions that a flock of about fifty Merriam's turkeys in South Dakota flew into trees when molested by a coyote. One old gobbler, however, stood its ground and the coyote soon ran away. In conversation with W. S. Jennings, I was informed that he had seen a wild turkey give battle to a coyote in Texas. There does not appear to be a deep-seated fear of the coyote. Mrs. Headlee (1928), who raised wild turkeys in the Dakotas, wrote: "I have seen them play with a coyote and when tired of him would fly to some tree top some distance away and 'pert,' 'pert' at him."

There is a hoary tale from the southwest that a coyote finding a turkey up a tree would walk around and around it. The turkey, in attempting to follow the movements of the coyote, eventually became dizzy and fell from its perch!

No case is known to me where a wolf (*Canis lupus*) has caught a turkey. The small turkey population in southwestern New Mexico in 1876 was attributed to predation by wolves and cougars (Stephens, 1876). A hunter in Trumbull County, Ohio, noticing a place where turkeys had been scratching, proceeded to call them. Soon a wolf appeared, sniffing the air, and apparently looking for turkeys (Williams and Bro., 1882:338). An unsuccessful attempt of a wolf to catch a turkey in the Missouri Ozarks is mentioned by Turnbo (1904:89).

Severe predation by foxes is generally accepted as a fact. Usually, it is impossible to determine if a kill was made by a red fox (*Vulpes fulva*) or a gray one (*Urocyon cinereoargenteus*). Audubon and Bachman (1849–51: I, 164) stated that they had often seen feathers and egg shells at a nest where a sitting turkey had had a violent struggle with a gray fox. While hunting in North Carolina, Shay (1911) found a recently killed turkey and placed the blame on a red fox. In Pennsylvania, Sutton (1929:327) found that an incubating turkey had been killed and devoured. A trap set near the broken eggs caught a female gray fox. One reliable report of the destruction of poults by a gray fox was obtained by Barkalow (1942) in Alabama. Collins (1952) reported that four of twenty-one turkeys released in Louisiana were killed by foxes. During the winter of 1951–52, a flock of eleven turkeys west of Durango, Colorado, was reduced to eight within a week. The losses ceased after three gray foxes had been trapped (Burget, 1957:54).

It has been pointed out (Bailey *et al.*, 1951:24) that a healthy turkey is rarely caught by a fox or a bobcat, but the situation is quite different if the bird is in a weakened condition. During the severe winter of 1946–47, when turkeys approached starvation, several were caught by red foxes. During the late winter of 1959–60, while the snow was deep, two turkeys were killed by red foxes in West Virginia (Bailey and Rinell, 1960:14). When the snow is two feet or more in depth, the turkeys feed habitually in spring runs. Since these are usually below the top of the snow, a red fox can creep within a few feet of a feeding bird without giving warning.

Most of the food studies absolve foxes from predation on turkeys. None of the stomachs of red and gray foxes examined by Handley (1935:19) in Virginia during the years 1932 and 1933 showed remains of the turkey. No signs of predation on turkeys was found by Kozicky (1943) by the examination of 186 fox scats collected in Pennsylvania in late summer and early fall. K. A. Wilson (1947:205) in Maryland, examined 105 stomachs and 142 scats of foxes without finding turkey remains. The absence of remains of game farm turkeys was puzzling in view of the annual reports of hunters of finding the carcasses of banded birds.

In Missouri no direct proof of the destruction of turkeys and their eggs by foxes was obtained (Bennitt and Nagel, 1937:65). The scattered feathers around some nests merely showed that the hens had been attacked by some predator.

The method by which a gray fox captured a turkey feeding in a small opening has been described (Mosby and Handley, 1943:132). After approaching within twenty feet under cover of the vegetation, the fox made a sudden dash and caught the bird, apparently while its back was turned. Owing to the wariness of the turkey, occurrences of this kind are considered rare. In the case of the domestic birds, P. Flint (1905) wrote: "I have seen a fox annoy turkeys in a meadow, when they would form in battle array; with the old ones outside and the young inside the circle, at the same time making loud cries and showing fighting spirit in abundance."

A charge of mistaken identity has been placed against the fox. In 1702, Rev. Andreas Sandel (1906:290) wrote: "Heard a funny story. A person at his brother's was about to shoot a wild turkey, which a fox was trying to catch, while seeing the man hid among the bushes, and supposing him to be the turkey, rushed headlong on the man who caught the fox by the ears." Foxes will occasionally respond to a turkey call. Audubon and Bachman (1849–51: II, 270) tell of a man calling turkeys near Augusta, Georgia, just before sunrise. Two red foxes came to his call and both were killed by a single shot. A recent case of a fox responding to the yelping of a hunter is given by Mosby and Handley (1943:133).

The first condemnation of the cougar (*Felis concolor*) as a predator was by Henshaw (1874:435): "Apparently, the only danger they [turkeys] have to fear in these regions is from birds of prey, and especially the panthers. In certain portions of the Gila Cañon, the tracks of these animals are very numerous; these sections always appeared to have been depopulated of turkeys, an occasional pile of feathers marking the spot where one had fallen a victim to a panther." Hinton's (1878:336) account paraphrases Henshaw. Coues and Yarrow (1875:40) accused the cougars of killing hundreds of turkeys and thought that unless preventive measures were taken, the race would become nearly extinct in some localities in New Mexico and Arizona. The cougar hunts mainly at night so that about the only chance that it has to catch a turkey is at dusk when it goes to roost. Writing of the early history of Columbus, Ohio, A. E. Lee (1892:292) said that the wild turkey was the favorite prey of the cougar, which made such havoc in their ranks as to border on extermination; yet he does not fail to mention the former abundance of this bird.

Hunters in Texas, shooting at a roost in early morning, saw a "panther" seize a turkey and make off with it. Pursued on horseback, the cat dropped the bird, which had the breast and one leg torn off ("Almo," 1885). Clement (1901:93) mentions that a turkey was stalked by a cougar in Oklahoma.

In his study of the cougar in New Mexico, Hibben (1937:52) examined scats and stomachs. He failed to find that a bird of any kind had been eaten. The cougar, like many other predators, will respond to the notes of a turkey. J. Gordon (1885) mentions a case in Mississippi of a turkey, called to a blind, being seized by a cougar. One morning on the Indian River, Florida, Henshall (1883) entered a thicket, surrounded with bare white sand, where he had seen turkeys the day previously. As his "keouking" lured no birds, he left his ambush and was surprised to note from the tracks in the sand that a cougar had approached within six feet of his place of concealment. Viewing with modesty his ability as a caller, he thought that the cougar expected to find a turkey in distress.

The bobcat (*Lynx rufus*) is believed by many people to be the worst of the enemies of the turkey. As William Bartram (1791:110), in 1774, was about to fire at a large gobbler, some young males gave an alarm. He observed a bobcat stalking the flock. The discharge of a gun at a distance by a companion put both turkeys and bobcat to flight. Near Fort Capron, Florida, in 1883, a hunter found two bobcats on the top of a pen-trap containing several turkeys. One of the birds had been decapitated and another torn to shreds (G. F. W., 1883). Hunters informed Seton (1920) that the high price of furs had so stimulated trapping of bobcats in northeastern Arkansas that they were becoming scarce. As a result, turkeys were increasing steadily. Two bobcats which were stalking a flock in Clarke County, Alabama, were shot by J. H. Davis (Anon., 1938).

According to Ligon (1946:71), the bobcat is second only to the coyote as an enemy of turkeys, especially because of destroying the females on the nest. He cites five instances in Arizona in which bobcats were caught and a dead turkey found in each case. They were known to climb tall pines to capture domestic turkeys. Burget (1957:53) has reported that during a period of four years, 1950–54, eighty-one turkeys were killed by bobcats on the eastern slope in Colorado. Six kills are mentioned for the western slope. In one case the bird was intact and seemed to have been killed from sheer instinct. In his opinion, the bobcat is the most destructive of all predators. Predation on domestic turkeys may be severe. Moore (1946:55) reported that approximately ten bobcats were trapped on the Mount Royal estate, Putnam County, Florida, in order to reduce the heavy losses of these birds.

Some writers have believed that the loss by these cats is insignificant. Jordan (1898:330) in all his experience never knew a bobcat to kill a turkey. He cites instances where his brother and others had had one appear in response to their turkey calls. Hebard (1941:41) attributed the disappearance of the turkey from the Okefenokee Swamp to hunters, not to bobcats. There is little evidence of substantial predation in Arkansas. Holder (1951:87) wrote: "Hardin Point Island, which supports a heavy concentration of turkeys, is heavily infested with bobcats."

The stomach analyses which have been made do not show that turkeys are important prey. Generally, it is not possible to determine if turkey remains are from a wild or domestic bird. Burget (1948.1:19) mentions that the stomach of a bobcat trapped beside a turkey kill in Colorado did not contain turkey remains. He (1952:304) also reported that seven bobcats trapped in turkey territory the winter of 1951–52 were found blameless. The scats of bobcats in Arizona "invariably contained hair and bones of small mammals" (Galliziolli, 1953:12). According to Young (1958:76), turkeys formed 8.6 per cent of the stomach contents of thirty-eight bobcats taken in Missouri. The examination of thirty-eight scats of bobcats in Alabama by Wheeler (1945) gave negative results. A more extensive examination in this state was made by Davis (1955), who found turkey remains in only 1 of 239 stomachs. Progulske (1955:250) stated that three bobcats were trapped at the carcass of one wild turkey; however, examination of 57 stomachs, 50 intestines, and 124 scats of bobcats from Virginia and North Carolina showed that destruction of this game bird was insignificant.

The procedure by which the bobcat captures turkeys is described by Audubon and Bachman (1849–51: I, 12; II, 295): "When this animal discovers a flock of wild turkeys, he will generally follow them at a little distance for some time, and having ascertained the direction in which they are proceeding, make a rapid detour, and concealing himself behind a fallen tree, or in the lower branches of some leafy maple, patiently waits in ambush until the birds approach, when he suddenly springs on one of them, if near enough, and with one bound secures it." These authors state that the Texas bobcat will lurk in a thicket near a hunter, then seize and carry off the turkey which he shoots. All the eggs in a nest are devoured. Young (1958:96) gives a circumstantial account by E. M. Mercer of the capture of a Merriam's turkey by a bobcat on the Fort Apache Indian Reservation, Arizona, on November 17, 1950. The flock was feeding down a canyon bottom when the cat was encountered. It overhauled a running turkey and "killed it by severing the neck vertebrae just above the crop and then biting it through the head."

In the South, when I inquired about this cat as an enemy of the turkey, I was immediately told of cases where a bobcat had responded to the turkey call of a hunter and had even jumped upon him in error. Sass (1929:210) mentions that a bobcat came to the call of a hunter on the Pee Dee River. A flock of turkeys lured by Rutledge's (1941.1:142) call was awaited by a bobcat. He (1946:174) knew a man who had a "forty-pound" bobcat spring on his back while he was calling a turkey. In Arizona, Maher (1935:265) had one of these cats come out of the brush in response to his turkey call.

There is no definite information on the lynx (*Lynx canadensis*) as a predator on the wild turkey. The ranges of the bobcat and lynx overlap but little in wild turkey territory. The lynx that Audubon (1831:8) saw kill a gobbler along the lower Wabash was probably a bobcat.

Fresh tracks of a woodchuck (*Marmota monax*) were found in Missouri at nests that had been broken up and the eggs partially eaten (Blakey, 1937:14). Direct proof of predation by this mammal is lacking.

Two wild poults, about two weeks of age, attracted rock squirrels (*Citellus grammurus*) by their peeping in Texas. They were observed to be caught and eaten (Cook and Henry, 1940). Most of the species of rodents are potential eaters of meat.

Only one reference to the porcupine (*Erethizon dorsatum*) as a predator was found. Ligon (1946:73) wrote: "The residents of the Sacramento Mountains [New Mexico] contend that porcupines are serious enemies of nesting turkeys, wrecking the nests, and, it is claimed, eating the eggs." This is doubtful since, so far as known, the food of this animal is confined to vegetation.

The blame placed on the armadillo (*Dasypus novemcinctus*) as a destroyer of turkey nests is excessive. According to Lacey (1911:206), it will sometimes roll eggs from the nest. Smith (1916:188) attributed the increase in turkeys in Kerr County, Texas, in part to the reduction in numbers of the armadillo from hunting for commercial purposes. According to Fuller (1927:30), this mammal was positively harmful. He stated that in 1906 southwestern Texas was invaded by large numbers of armadillos from Mexico. Turkeys suffered severely from destruction of their eggs until about 1916 when hunting them for their armor began.

The careful examination of scats of the armadillo by V. Bailey (1905:56) failed to reveal animal food other than insects. Two cases of destruction of eggs of the wild turkey were reported to Kalmbach (1943:49); however, the examination of 281 stomachs did not show eggs or remains of the turkey. He concluded: "The fact that armadillos can and do on occasion destroy the nests of wild turkeys should not be made the basis of far-reaching conclusions as to the amount of harm done. The true relationship between predator and prey cannot be determined on the basis of fragmentary evidence, while contrary or negative data are ignored." Destruction of turkey eggs must be rare. Taber (1945:222) found that captive armadillos ignored chicken eggs unless they were first broken. Five armadillos in a pen left untouched for twenty-one days a dummy nest containing five bantam eggs.

There is limited information on the extent of predation by hogs and dogs. Destruction of nests by hogs has been reported from Alabama (Barkalow, 1942), Missouri (Blakey, 1937:14), and Florida (Anon.,

1950:17). According to Stegeman (1938:288), turkeys are most numerous in areas occupied by wild boars in the Cherokee National Forest. The feeding habits of the boars are definitely favorable to turkeys because they find tubers and insects by reworking the soil which the boars have upturned. It has been estimated by Hanson and Karstad (1959:73) that 1,500,000 feral swine inhabit 145,000 square miles of the Coastal Plain in southeastern United States. Aside from possible destruction of turkey nests, competition between turkeys and hogs for food may become severe as the latter have been known to die from starvation.

13

Mortality from Weather, Accidents, Diseases, and Parasites

THE TURKEY IS A VERY HARDY BIRD but some kinds of weather, irrespective of habitat, are destructive even to adults. In general, the turkey survives unusually low temperatures and deep snows. There are early accounts of high mortality of wild turkeys from sleet and snows of excessive depths. Poults cannot survive prolonged cool, rainy weather.

WIND

A hurricane and flood on August 27, 1893, exterminated a large flock of turkeys on the Heyward plantation on the Combahee River, Colleton County, South Carolina (Heyward, 1937:122). None was found afterwards. During a windstorm in Crawford County, Ohio, about 1821, deer and turkeys were mangled and killed by falling trees (Baskin and Battey, 1881:422). The behavior of turkeys on the Welder Wildlife Refuge, San Patricio County, Texas, during hurricane "Carla" on September 10, 1961, has been described by Cottam (1961) as follows: "Probably the most amusing incident we observed during the storm was eleven young toms of this year's production that tried to roost in their accustomed spot in one of the oaks in front of the Administration Building. They came to their roosting site quite early where they remained much later than usual before going to roost. Finally they decided to fly up and get settled for the night. In the course of an hour, five of the eleven had been blown out and the others were frantically weaving back and forth with the wind, trying to hang on to their roost. By morning only three of the more sturdy souls were able to survive the height and the winds and these were perched where they received some protection from the trunk of the tree. The next night the entire flock deserted this area and roosted in the denser shrubbery near our wooded area." None of the birds was injured, but many partially developed tail and wing feathers were lost.

FLOODS

Floods are usually destructive to the eggs and young only. Concerning eastern Florida, we have the following: "Many have been drowned in the heavy spring floods of the last two or three years and the nests have been broken up by the same cause" (S. C. C., 1878). Because of a break in the Mississippi levee near Laconia Circle, Arkansas, the spring of 1927, it was predicted that hunting would be materially affected by the destruction of the nests (H. P. Davis, 1927). In fact, as a result of the floods of this year, the hunting of turkeys in several parishes in Louisiana was not permitted (Arthur, 1928). The floods at Gayoso, Pemiscot County, Missouri, in 1882, are reputed to have destroyed most of the turkeys and other game (W. J. H., 1882). A hunting party taking advantage of the high water on the Little River, Dunklin County, Missouri, killed nineteen turkeys (Hall, 1899).

It would appear that floods can cause an emigration of turkeys to a considerable distance. Regarding floods along the Mississippi, Barnes (1897) wrote from White County, Arkansas: "Turkeys are wide rangers, usually know the lay of the land, and can stand a lot of starvation. Flying from tree to tree and subsisting meanwhile on the tender buds of the forest growth and upon the insect life swarming on the floating logs, they could easily distance the spreading waters.... Around Bald Knob, nearly fifty miles west of the flood limits, turkeys are more plentiful to-day than for many years past, and they are evidently strangers to the range, for the hunters stumble upon them in all sorts of unexpected places."

FREEZING RAIN

The worst condition is a freezing rain. There is not only the immediate effect on the turkey, but the prospect of starvation, and decimation by predators. Three weeks of freezing rain in December, 1848, nearly exterminated the wild turkeys in Moniteau County, Missouri (Ford, 1936:64). There was the same effect in Iowa the winter of 1856–57 when there was deep snow with sleet and rain (Babbitt, 1918). Regarding an exceptionally severe winter in Wisconsin, Hoy (1882:257) wrote: "I am told, by Dr. E. B. Wolcott, that turkeys were abundant in Wisconsin previous to the hard winter of 1842–43, when snow was yet two feet deep in March, with a firm crust, so that the turkeys could not get to the ground; they hence became so poor and weak that they could not fly and so were an easy prey for wolves, wildcats, foxes and minks. The Doctor further stated that he saw but one single turkey the next winter, and none since."

On rare occasions the wings of the turkeys became so coated with sleet that they could not fly and fell a ready prey to the hunter (J. L. Russell, 1947:79). The effect of a sleet storm in Arkansas is mentioned by Holder (1951:87): "Several reports indicate that a severe ice storm in the winter of 1901–02 was primarily responsible for the extermination of turkeys in some of our northern counties. These reports came from Izard, Newton, and Jackson counties. According to the local people, this sleet storm left a heavy coating of ice, covering the ground to a depth of several inches, and all the trees and other vegetation were coated. The ice stayed for weeks. Afterward, game of all kinds, especially turkeys, was very scarce."

Yorke (1890:73) states that balls of ice sometimes form on the wings and tail when a cold snap follows a thaw or rain. The birds are then run down easily. He adds that, in the fall, hunters on horseback slowly drove the turkeys, especially the young, through wet weeds in wet weather. Their feathers became so saturated with water that they could not fly far. Apparently, turkeys can be captured quite readily after a thorough wetting for Duis (1874:549) records that H. Crumbaugh, in McLean County, Illinois, caught eleven turkeys with his hands in about twenty minutes on a wet winter's day. Turkeys in Pennsylvania will feed in winter in spring seeps and wet the ends of their beards; then, in walking through cold, soft snow, ice balls up to 2.5 inches in diameter will form. Eventually the ball breaks off, shortening the beard (Wunz, 1963).

Large numbers of domestic turkeys have been killed at times by a freezing rain. Brandt (1951:623) writes that one of the worst disasters that can happen to domestic turkeys is a winter rain that freezes on their backs. Large numbers or entire flocks may perish if the freezing is accompanied by high wind. In 1916 thousands perished during a late fall blizzard in the Mississippi Valley.

The unusual storm on Armistice Day, November 11, 1940, caused the death of many domestic turkeys in Wisconsin. Concerning the loss on his father's farm near Black River Falls, George Knudsen of the Wisconsin Conservation Department has written me: "The late morning and most of the afternoon of this Armistice Day was warm and wet. The temperatures were well above freezing and there was a steady precipitation varying from a drizzle to a steady deluge. The turkeys were on a *coverless*, fenced-in range, and hence were soaked to the skin. Then, in the late afternoon the weather changed very rapidly to icy winds, sleet and snow. Trees and grasses rapidly glazed and started to crack and snap.

"The turkeys having nowhere to take cover did as turkeys often do when cold and 'piled up' to keep warm. We couldn't allow this or the ones in the middle of the pile would have smothered so we kept breaking up the piles, and dispersing the turkeys, hoping also that by moving them we'd keep their circulation going well. We drove as many as possible into our outbuildings, but had no room for the majority of the flock. These birds had to ride out the storm.

"In spite of my staying up all night and trying to keep the birds on the move, hundreds froze to death. Many were frozen while sitting huddled against the fence. The birds just seemed to get slower and slower as they cooled down until finally they were so cold they could not walk at which time they fell and froze to death, many completely glazed with ice. The insulating 'fluff' of their soaked feathers was non-existent. By morning we had approximately 1,000 dead turkeys on our range. The ones living through this ordeal were in bad shape and we lost many of them in subsequent days."

Turkeys cannot endure a strong, direct wind during a snowstorm, according to G. F. Johnson (1930). The snow drives into the feathers so that there is no protection for the head. The snow striking the head, melts, runs down the bill and freezes. The ice gradually gets thicker until it covers the nostrils and the bird actually smothers to death.

Having food available does not prevent turkeys from dying under certain weather conditions. Five wild turkeys found dead in southern Pennsylvania in February and March, 1936, were examined by Gerstell (1942:19). Two were found coated with ice immediately after a severe ice storm. The remainder died during periods of high winds and low temperatures. Since the crops contained corn and green food, the birds must have died of exposure.

Severe Cold

Peter Thacher, living near Boston, wrote in his diary on November 19, 1679: "Extremely cold I lost two turkeys" (Teele, 1888:644). Blaisdell (1890) in October sent to a brother in Hancock County, Maine, a pair of wild turkeys "domesticated" at Macomb, Illinois. They roosted on a beam in the barn. In January, when the temperature dropped to 33° below zero, both birds were found frozen on the beam. On the other hand, two wild turkeys roosted in a tree on the game farm of D. H. Bendick at Leduc, Alberta, when the temperature was 24° below zero (Corsan, 1926).

The severe winter of 1779–80, when so much game perished, left a deep impression on the settlers in Kentucky. Fleming (1916:636) wrote in his journal at Harrodsburg on March 20, 1780: "Last night it was cold and froze hard, the effects of the severe winter was now sensibly felt, the earth for so long a time being covered with snow and the water entirely froze, the Cane almost all kiled, the Hogs in the Country suffered greatly being frozen to death in their beds, the deer likewise not being able to get either water or food, were found in great numbers, tirkies dropt dead of[f] their roosts and even the Buffalos died starved to death. . . ." Most of the cattle and thousands of turkeys, deer, and other animals are stated to have perished (James, 1912). Many turkeys were found frozen to death also at McAfee's Station, Mercer County (Collins, 1848:456). They died during the severe weather that lasted from the end of November to February 15 or 20 (McAfee, 1927:29). Clinkenbeard (1928:112) described the status of the turkey at Strode's Station: "A great country for turkeys, and they had like to have starved to death; a heap! of them died. Greatest country for turkeys I ever saw." Muhlenberg (1849:432) killed some turkeys on the upper Ohio in April, 1784. All game was in poor condition because of the hard winter.

The winter of 1779–80 was reputed to have been the most severe ever known in America. The snow was four feet deep on the Allegheny and Laurel hills, Pennsylvania, and deer and turkeys died by the hundreds (Darlington, 1891:115; Hassler, 1900:104). This winter at French Lick, near Nashville, Tennessee, cattle would lie down and "put their heads to their sides, as is their way, and thus would be found frozen stiff—and turkies were known to freeze upon their roosts and tumble off"

331

(Donelson, 1844). The deep snow in western Indiana in 1834 caused a heavy loss of deer and turkeys (Beckwith, 1881:290). Holabird (1875), during a snowstorm in Porter County, Indiana, in November, 1834, killed with a club a flock of nine wild turkeys that went into an abandoned cabin to roost. During the very cold winter of 1840–41, raccoons froze in the snow, and a frozen turkey was found along a creek (Blanchard, 1883:213). Vast numbers of turkeys died of starvation in Morrow County, Ohio, the winter of 1824–25, when a crust formed on the snow that was twenty inches deep (Braughman and Bartlett, 1911:315; Baskin & Co., 1880:324).

Marquette (1903:261) and his party spent the winter of 1674–75—one of intense cold and deep snow—on the present site of Chicago. As early as December 12, he wrote in his diary: "We contented ourselves with killing three or four turkeys, out of many that came around our cabin because they were almost dying of hunger."

The winter of 1830–31 was known as that of the big snow in Illinois. Most of the turkeys and other game in Pike County died of starvation (Chapman and Co., 1880:215). In McDonough County, turkeys fell from the limbs of the trees (Clarke, 1878:24). According to Beckwith (1880:431), there was a crust on the snow. All the turkeys died in Iroquois County, for none was seen afterwards. They perished also in great numbers in Champaign (Stewart, 1918:127), Morgan (J. M. Rutledge, 1936:82), Sangamon (Power, 1876:64), and Tazewell (Allensworth, 1905:700) counties. In McLean County, J. G. Reyburn fed the wild turkeys from his window (Duis, 1874:463). So many turkeys died in Marshall County that they were not abundant again until 1840 (Ellsworth, 1880:400). They were common again and easily obtainable in Fulton County during the severe winter of 1842–43 (Chapman and Co., 1879:228).

The winter of 1848–49 was severe in Iowa. Many turkeys were found dead in the spring in Dallas Township, Marion County (Donnel, 1872:341). Weaver (1912:62) stated that the snow was so deep and so light that the turkeys could not fly to their roosts. One morning Hugh Patterson rode down as many turkeys as he could carry away. Mueller (1915:177), on the authority of A. J. Hoisington, reported that many turkeys perished in the cold winter of 1847–48, but that they rapidly increased again. Probably the winter of 1848–49 was the actual one.

Between shooting and the again severe winter of 1855–56, turkeys were practically exterminated. They were plentiful in Muscatine County up to this winter (Fultz, 1899–1901:221).

Many turkeys are reported to have frozen to death in Saline County, Missouri, during the winter of 1827–28, when the snow was very deep (Missouri Hist. Co., 1881.1:443). The memorable winter was that of 1830–31 when large numbers of turkeys died in Clay (National Hist. Co., 1885:122), Chariton (National Hist. Co., 1883:455), and Pike (Mills and Co., 1883:880) counties. A pioneer of Macon County stated: "The skeletons of turkeys . . . lay all over the bottom so plentiful that I supposed the last turkey was dead; but while we were hunting our hogs we saw three live ones, while I have no doubt we came across the bones of five hundred dead ones" (National Hist. Co., 1884:737). The deep snow and cold of the winter of 1878–79 are said to have destroyed quail and turkeys "by the cart loads" in Daviess County (L., 1879).

Prior to 1857, a dressed wild turkey sold for seventy-five cents at Nebraska City, Otoe County, Nebraska (Morton, 1876:18). The winter of 1856–57 was so severe that many turkeys died in this county and in Washington County (Selden, 1887:285).

Turkeys are reluctant to leave their roosts during a storm. Audubon (1831:9) mentions that after a heavy snowstorm they will remain on their roosts for three or four days or longer, demonstrating their ability to fast. Domestic turkeys have the same trait. Susan Cooper (1856:224) wrote at Cooperstown, New York, on January 12, 1849: "Severely cold. Thermometer 17° below zero at sunrise. . . . Such severe weather as this the turkeys can hardly be coaxed down from their roost even to feed; they sometimes sit thirty-six hours perched in a tree, or in the fowl-house, without touching the ground." The winter of "1896" there was a 24-inch snowfall in Texas. The turkeys must have remained in the trees until the snow had nearly all melted for no tracks could be seen until the ground was almost bare (Wright, 1942:77). Sylvester and Lane (1946:334) think that turkeys in winter may sense the approach of a storm which will limit their cruising range and will feed avidly the day previous. Perception of this nature requires confirmation.

The method of reaching the feeding ground after snowstorms has been described by Ligon (1946:57): "Mazon Calentine, manager of the Harvey Wildlife Preserve in the Sacramento Mountains, New Mexico, told

333

the author of observing, during continued snowstorms, a progressive movement of turkeys through trees from their main winter roosting place in Three L Canyon to feeding grounds in Eight-Mile Canyon. At times when the snow became too deep for travel on foot, they flew from one tree to another, over a distance of almost a mile, and descended to the ground at the regular feeding place, where snow had been removed or tramped down. Turkeys often remain in trees at high altitudes two or three days during continued snowstorms, when dependent only on natural foods, or until the weather clears and the snow begins to settle and thaw on exposed south slopes. No ill effects result if the turkeys are strong and nourishing food is available at the end of the storm."

The ability of turkeys to survive storms depends upon their physical condition and the extent of the severe winter weather. There was heavy mortality in some parts of West Virginia the winter of 1946–47 (Glover and Bailey, 1947). Following a snowstorm lasting three days in southwestern Colorado in October, 1932, turkeys remained on their roost for three days and nights, many dying of starvation (Beise, 1943:523). The turkey is so hardy a bird that the weather is seldom lethal. Game farm turkeys from Pennsylvania that had been released in Michigan survived the winter of 1957–58 without discoverable loss. The snow, 26 inches in depth, and the temperature of –17° F. did not prevent the turkeys from obtaining food (Wilson and Lewis, 1959). While the blizzard of March 22–24, 1957, in Texas County, Oklahoma, was very destructive to small wildlife, the wild turkeys survived. Four flocks at Hooker, numbering sixty-nine birds, had no losses (Steele, 1957). Randall (1929, 1933:71) advises that wild turkeys not be pampered. In the Adirondacks, the colder the weather, the higher they roosted in the trees. During a storm lasting three days, with the temperature 30° below zero and a wind of forty miles per hour, his birds simply swayed up and down and refused to come down to feed.

Resistance to Starvation

The length of time that game farm wild turkeys can survive without food was studied by Gerstell (1942:39–42) under artificial and natural weather conditions: (1) Two birds at 0° F. and with a wind of 5.8 miles per hour survived almost seven and nine days; average eight days; loss in weight 25.7 per cent; (2) two birds at 0° F. and no air movement survived eleven and sixteen days; average thirteen and a half days; loss in weight 67.8 per cent; (3) two birds, one killed accidentally, at 34 to 50° F. and no air movement; female survived approximately twenty-four days; loss in weight 57.7 per cent; (4) pair in unsheltered pen out of doors survived nine and nineteen days; average fourteen days; loss in weight 42.4 per cent. The data show that a turkey can endure a week of severe weather without food without endangering survival.

Among the game birds tested, only the ring-necked pheasant was more hardy. Latham (1947) found that under the above experimental conditions, three male turkeys lived only an average of 11.3 days while four females survived 15.2 days. Accordingly, the male has only 74 per cent of the hardiness of the female. He concludes that the female is the hardier among polygamous species while the reverse is true among monogamous species of game birds. Bailey et al., (1951:42) state that, in periods of deep snow, turkeys can endure for four to five weeks but not beyond this period. During this time they would be able to obtain some food.

The tame turkey is similar to the wild one in its resistance to starvation. Jesse (1838:176) wrote: "This latter bird is of a very torpid nature, and will continue to sit for many months together, on a very scanty supply of food." Some rather remarkable cases of survival have been recorded. Regarding the great snow at Boston in February, 1717, Cotton Mather (1856:447) stated: "Turkeys were found alive after five and twenty days, buried in ye Snow, and at a distance from ye ground, and altogether destitute of any thing to feed them." A pig survived burial for six weeks in the deep snow in Illinois the winter of 1830–31. A turkey also survived and presumably was buried a similar length of time (Duis, 1874:835). In Germany a turkey was found alive after being buried in straw for thirty-eight days (Bechstein, 1807:1126). A turkey hen, missing for four weeks, was found in January, 1868, in a well covered with snow and ice. Though reduced to nearly a ball of feathers, it subsequently recovered completely with food and warmth (Hoyningen-Huene, 1868). The external temperature was very cold, but that within the well must have been above freezing. A game dealer in Norwich, England, kept some turkeys in a basement overnight. One became imprisoned behind a couple of barrels where it remained without food for thirty-eight to forty days. It survived but two days after being found (Gunn, 1869).

ACCIDENTS

The wild turkey is subject to but few accidents under natural conditions. A turkey in southwestern Texas was found hanging by the head in the fork of a live oak, its feet being about a foot from the ground ("Rio Diablo," 1892.1). Presumably it was caught while jumping upwards to get an acorn. A similar accident occurred on a farm north of Indianapolis, Indiana, where a jungle of limbs was created by several oaks having been blown down. Here a wild turkey was found hanging by the neck, evidently having been caught during a sudden flight (Anon., 1880). Scoville (1920:36) wrote of an incident in Pennsylvania: "There too we found a magnificent wild turkey hanging dead in a little apple tree; it had come to a miserable end by catching the toes of one foot between two twigs in such a way that it could not release itself. The bright red color of its legs distinguished it from a tame turkey."

The turkey impales itself in flight less frequently than might be expected from so heavy a bird. A South Carolinian is stated to have flushed a turkey that flew into a snag and dropped dead (Anon., 1925.1). A Pennsylvania turkey, reported in November as having been shot with an arrow, was killed on December 26 by Neely (1961) who wrote: "The bird had a maple stick that had entered its body along its leg and came out of its back [extending 20 inches]. This stick was approximately three-quarters of an inch in diameter. The turkey had evidently flown into this stick driving it completely through its body but had managed to survive almost two months. This was a large gobbler and shows the amazing vitality that these large birds have."

Artificial obstructions have been hit more frequently. In the early days of Columbus, Ohio, a flock of turkeys alighted in a cornfield on the edge of town. When fired at by sportsmen, several birds became confused and flew into the town. One struck a building and was so injured by the impact as to be captured easily (Lee, 1892:296). In 1902, about 10:00 P.M., a wild turkey flew over Asheville, North Carolina, became bewildered, and dashed through a window. It weighed eighteen pounds (C. P. A., 1902). A game farm gobbler crashed through the window of a Mobil service station, Winslow, Illinois, early in the morning of May 30, 1961 (Anon., 1961.2). The evening of November 1, 1875, the headlight of an engine of the Wabash Railroad, west of Fort Wayne, was broken when the train struck a flock of turkeys flying across the track (Anon., 1876.1). A similar incident occurred near Charlotte, Michigan. In this case one of the birds struck the smokestack of the engine and was captured by the crew (Michigan Hist. Publ. Ass., n.d.:11). A flock of wild turkeys in South Dakota was harassed by an eagle. Although two of the birds struck telephone wires in their flight, they were retarded only momentarily (Elley, 1957).

The most frequent accidents at present are from automobiles. This applies especially to game farm turkeys. Dickerson (1939:105), in driving 12,228 miles across the continent, found only four dead turkeys over a period of three years. Two birds from a flock were killed by a driver near Laporte, Pennsylvania, in May, 1950 (Benscoter, 1950). One motorist killed at least one turkey from a flock into which he drove deliberately (De Long, 1950). A wild turkey, after being hit by a car at Bloomfield, Missouri, had a torn breast. The bird was released after the wound was stitched (Anon., 1961.3). Wilson and Lewis (1959:212) stated that during the period 1954–58 in Michigan, six turkeys were killed by automobiles and five by trains.

Diseases

The domestic turkey is afflicted with many diseases and parasites, few of which have been recorded as having a serious effect upon the wild bird. The widely ranging wild turkey seldom faces the problem of sanitation which arises when large numbers of domestic turkeys are confined in a limited space. There is nothing to indicate that the wild turkey was afflicted with any disease prior to the introduction of the domestic turkey. Practically no concerted effort has been made to determine the presence of diseases and parasites in wild turkeys under modern conditions. There is always the possibility that the wild turkey will have the same afflictions as the domestic bird since it is probable that temporary association will increase in the future. Only those diseases and parasites which have been recorded for the wild bird will be mentioned.

Fowl Cholera.—This disease is caused by *Pasteurella avicida*. It is not of common occurrence. It was first observed in Maryland where 17 per cent of a flock of about 175 turkeys died (De Volt and Davis, 1932). Apparently the disease is carried by the common housefly (Skidmore, 1932). Nelson (1953:132) stated that in the summer of 1883 the wild turkeys in Major County, Oklahoma, were almost exterminated by "cholera." It is impossible to determine if his diagnosis was correct. The disease has been reported among wild turkeys at large in Colorado (Burget, 1957:55). Cholera is considered by Blakey (1932:343) to be one of the three diseases most fatal to wild turkeys reared in confinement. It can be controlled by feeding lightly and placing a disinfectant in the water.

Fowl Pox (Avian Diptheria).—Fowl pox is caused by a filtrable virus. Pustules and scabs are formed on the naked skin of the head and neck, and cheesy patches in the mouth. There are several strains of the toxin, and there are varying reports of their effect on the hosts. Turkeys appear to be particularly susceptible to one type. Brandly and Dunlap (1938) found that the virus from poults was more severe with turkeys than with chickens. The strain from pigeon pox used by Tietz (1933) did not affect turkeys. Coronel (1934), working with turkey virus, concluded that it was distinct from the viruses found in chicken and pigeon pox. Beaudette and Hudson (1941), starting with a scab obtained from a wild turkey reared at the Game Conservation Institute, Clinton, New Jersey, found that the turkey strain produced the severest lesions. When turkeys were given turkey virus vaccine, they became immune to subsequent inoculations with turkey or chicken virus (Brunett, 1934). No immunity against turkey or chicken pox viruses was obtained when the turkeys were inoculated with pigeon pox virus. The type of pox found in the White Hollands with which he worked was indistinguishable from that in chickens.

Several investigators have found that the pox can be transmitted by mosquitoes. Kligler *et al.* (1929) used the mosquitoes *Culex pipiens* and *Aëdes aegypti*, and Matheson *et al.* (1931), *Aëdes vexans*, on chickens. The pox could be transmitted with *Culex pipiens* as late as fifty-eight days after this mosquito had fed on the infected birds (Blanc and Caminopetros, 1930). The pox can be spread by contact, by mosquitoes, and by mites (*Liponyssus sylviarum*) (Brody, 1936). On inanimate objects the virus remained viable for at least forty-two days. Subcutaneous vaccination with fowl pox vaccine has been used for several years (Hall and Wehr, 1949:18). The success has been variable. Dunn and Sherwood (1933) obtained good results by vaccinating day-old poults.

A weak, blind wild turkey found in Georgia died within two days.

Plate 33a.—Hunting turkeys. (*Chicago Field* [1876].)

Plate 33b.—Wild turkey trap. (After Peter Rindisbacher [1833].)

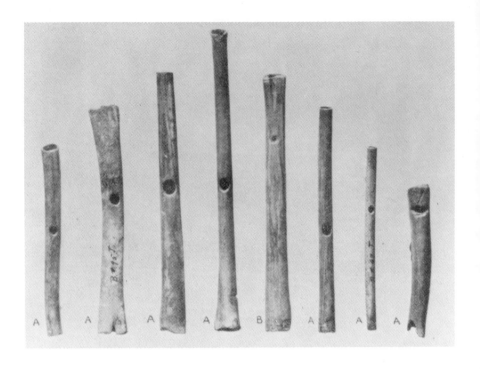

Plate 34a.—Bone tubes supposedly used by the early Pueblo Indians for calling turkeys. (After Jeançon [1923].)

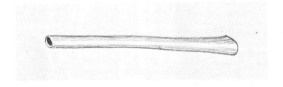

Plate 34b.—Wing bone caller.

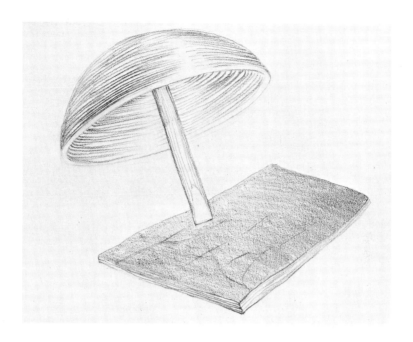

Plate 35a.—Coconut and slate caller.

Plate 35b.—Corncob
and slate caller.

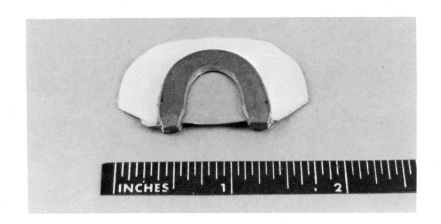

Plate 36a.—Diaphragm caller.

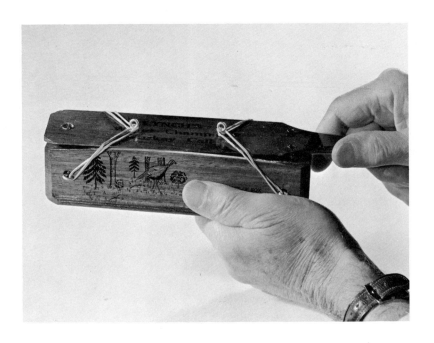

Plate 36b.—Lynch box caller.

Plate 37.—Drop net used in Texas. (Texas Parks and Wildlife Commission.)

Plate 38.—Loading one of the cannons which propel the net. (Colorado Fish and Game Department.)

Plate 39.—Turkeys under a cannon-net. A canvas is being drawn over them to keep them quiet. (Colorado Fish and Game Department.)

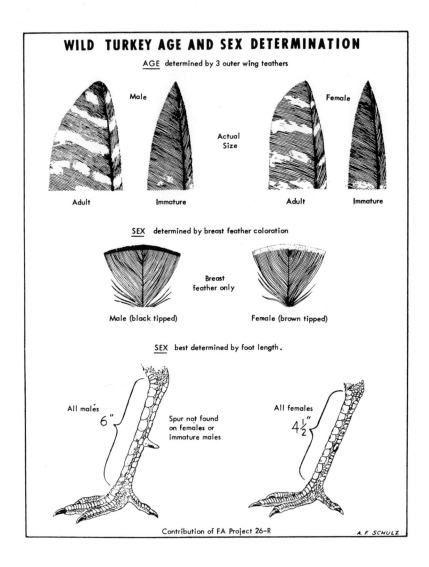

Plate 40.—Sex and age determination of the wild turkey by means of feathers and tarsi. (West Virginia Conservation Commission.)

This bird and another found dead in the woods had all the symptoms of pox (Webb, 1953). According to Shillinger and Morley (1937:12), pox is a common disease among wild turkeys, but this statement must refer to game farm birds.

Tuberculosis.—Tuberculosis is produced by *Mycobacterium tuberculosis avium*. More lesions are produced in turkeys than in chickens. The disease was reported in 1932 in domestic turkeys in California and Nevada (Hinshaw *et al.*, 1932). Van Roekel (1929:308) diagnosed as tuberculosis a disease among wild turkeys at the state game farm, Yountville, California. Wild turkeys of unknown origin were brought to the farm in 1925. There were some losses of turkeys from 1931 through 1936, but since blackhead occurred along with tuberculosis it was difficult to establish exactly the deaths from each disease (Rosen and Platt, 1949). The death of eastern wild turkeys in the New York Zoological Park in 1939 was attributed to tuberculosis (Goss, 1940:272). A young Merriam's turkey taken in the wild in 1947 was diagnosed as having tuberculosis (Burget, 1957:55).

PROTOZOAN DISEASES

Blackhead (Infectious Enterohepatitis).—Blackhead is produced by the flagellate *Histomonas meleagridis* and is one of the most destructive diseases of turkeys. The organism has an amoeboid stage, and many years elapsed before it was properly classified. In 1893, Cushman (1893.1:286) reported on a disease in turkeys in Rhode Island which he called "Black Head." T. Smith (1895) investigated the disease and determined the presence of an organism which he called *Amoeba meleagridis* and which became the *Hoemamoeba smithi* of Laveran and Lucet (1905). Hadley (1909), and later Cole *et al.* (1910), associated the disease with a species of *Coccidium*. It remained for Smith (1915) to show that blackhead and coccidiosis frequently occur together in individual turkeys and that blackhead could be found in turkeys free from coccidia. In 1911, Jowett (1911) reported the presence of flagellates (*Trichomonas*) in turkeys in South Africa but did not stress their presence as the cause of the disease as did Hadley (1916) a few years later. Tyzzer (1919) worked out the development stages of the organism. Typical is the "constant presence of an extranuclear body." The following year (1920) he named the parasite *Histomonas meleagridis* (Smith).

The dark head from which the disease derived the name "blackhead" may be found in other diseases also. Aside from discoloration of the head, there is droopiness, loss of weight and appetite, and yellow droppings. The organism is numerous in the caeca and, after apparently entering the walls, is carried by the bloodstream to the liver. Large numbers pass into the droppings. The caecal worm, *Heterakis gallinae*, is important in the spread of the disease. This nematode harbors *Histomonas* which pass into its eggs. *Histomonas* are abundant in the droppings. Turkeys appear to have acquired the disease from chickens, in which it is not as serious. There is no proof that the organism is transmitted through the eggs of the bird. The highest mortality rate (33 to 76 per cent), according to De Volt and Davis (1936:564), occurs during the second month of the life of the poults.

Blackhead may cause high mortality among pen-reared wild turkeys. In California the greatest mortality, approximately 10 per cent, occurred in birds four weeks to six months of age (Van Roekel, 1929:303). Loss of wild poults at the Kellogg bird sanctuary was not due to chilling but to blackhead (Pirnie, 1932:366). Fox (1938:27) reported the sudden appearance of this disease in a group of captive young wild turkeys, all of which died. The destruction of entire breeding groups of captive wild turkeys containing individuals suffering from blackhead failed to eradicate the disease in Virginia (Mosby and Handley, 1943:139).

Blackhead occurs among free-ranging wild turkeys. Stoddard (1940:24) wrote: "A two year old gobbler with a typical case of blackhead was captured in a very weakened condition by Sidney Stringer in late September in the heart of the great turkey range below Thomasville, Georgia. This is the sixth specimen of wild turkey with blackhead, contracted while living in the wild, we have encountered in this region of heavy turkey concentration during the past nine years. In the fall of 1933 three cases of this disease came to our attention in rapid succession, and we feared the possibility of heavy losses from this potentially dangerous malady, and, as a result, we have since urged that feed patches be rotated yearly, that no domestic turkeys or chickens (which are dangerous carriers of blackhead) be allowed in or near the heavily populated turkey range, and that no use be made of the manure of these birds in field fertilization. If these measures are continued here, and made a practice in other places where wild turkeys are especially numerous, losses from this disease can very likely be kept down."

The first cases of blackhead in turkeys in the wild in Virginia were found in 1940 and 1941 (Mosby and Handley, 1943:145). Involved were two adult males and one yearling male. Blackhead was determined to be the cause of death of a young wild hen from Halifax County, North Carolina (Craig and Barkalow, 1950). Kozicky (1948:265) mentioned that blackhead was diagnosed as the cause of death of four native wild turkeys in Pennsylvania. Losses of wild turkeys from blackhead in 1953 in Perry County, Pennsylvania, were traced to infection from domestic poultry or manure spread on the fields, and to the liberation of game farm birds that were carriers (Snyder, 1954). Several wild turkeys died in Cameron County in areas far removed from tilled land. The low survival of turkeys planted in Perry County may have been due to blackhead. All of the seven wild birds from this county examined for disease had blackhead (Roberts, 1954). In 1949 a flock of about fifty turkeys, mainly poults, in Archuleta County, Colorado, was reduced to twelve within a period of about two and one-half months (Burget, 1957:55). The decimation was attributed to blackhead.

Coccidiosis.—The species of coccidia found in game birds appear to be specific to the host. Tyzzer (1927) found it impossible to infect chickens with *Eimeria* oöcysts from turkeys and named the organism *E. meleagridis*. *E. meleagridis* and *E. meleagrimitis* (Tyzzer, 1929:320) have been found in domestic and wild turkeys. The disease is not readily recognizable except by examination of the droppings for the oöcysts by which it is spread.

Coccidiosis is most likely to affect pen-reared poults (Blakey, 1932:339). An outbreak among young poults in brooders was observed in Virginia in 1938 (Mosby and Handley, 1943:139). Two turkeys in the wild in Colorado were diagnosed as having coccidiosis in 1944 (Burget, 1957:55). It is usually spread from infected water holes. In Pennsylvania, Kozicky (1948:264) found oöcysts in thirty-eight of ninety-five droppings collected in nine counties. The use of sulfa drugs practically eliminated the disease at the game farm.

Leucocytozoon Infection.—While searching for the cause of blackhead, Smith (1895) found a protozoan parasite in the blood of turkeys. An organism was discovered by Laveran and Lucet (1905) in turkeys in France and named *Leucocytozoon smithi*. Stephan (1922) found the disease in both geese and turkeys in Germany, and Volkmar (1929) reported it in turkeys in North Dakota and Minnesota. Skidmore (1932.1) found that the death of some turkeys in Nebraska was due to *L. smithi* and that the vector was the black fly *Simulium occidentale* Townsend.

Losses of young turkeys in southwestern Virginia from a protozoan was traced by Johnson *et al.* (1938) to transmission by *Simulium nigroparvum* (Twinn), the larvae of which live in swift streams. Two species of the flies were found to be feeding on turkeys from the middle of May to the middle of October, the most numerous being *S. nigroparvum*. Poults up to twelve weeks of age are affected chiefly. The flies attach themselves to the head of the bird, usually to the throat wattle. Several wild turkeys raised in captivity were found to be carriers. Underhill (1940) reported *S. slossonae* Dyar and Shannon as also feeding on turkeys in Virginia. The turkey louse (*Goniodes meleagridis*) could not be established as a vector in Alabama (West and Starr, 1940). The first case of the disease in California was reported by Hinshaw and McNeil (1943). The vector was not established, but black flies were reported as feeding on turkeys. At this time the disease was prevalent among poults in central Texas (Banks, 1943). An outbreak of the disease in Manitoba resulted in severe mortality (Savage and Isa, 1945). No simulids were recognized, but present were innumerable mosquitoes and an abundance of flies belonging principally to the genus *Stomoxys*.

Sick birds lose their appetite, become droopy, and frequently lie down (Johnson *et al.*, 1938). The disease is accompanied by diarrhea, and when the bird is held by the feet, a cloudy, gray, vicous fluid runs from the mouth (Savage and Isa, 1945). The eyes are sunken and there is marked clouding of the cornea. Schizonts of *Leucocytozoon* were found by Newberne (1955) in the liver only. Twenty-five female black flies (*S. slossonae*) were collected by Rickey and Ware (1955) after they had fed on a turkey infected with *Leucocytozoon smithi*. The ten flies which survived for sixty hours were ground, mixed with saline solution, and injected intramuscularly into four noninfected turkeys which were subsequently killed and found to have the parasite. Disposal of carrier turkeys will not eradicate the disease. Johnson (1939) recommended that pens housing poults be proofed against simulids by enclosing them with very fine mesh wire or cheese cloth. Nothing can be done for ranging turkeys.

On account of the wide distribution of simulids and other insects serving as vectors, it is probable that there is a greater incidence of *Leucocytozoon* infection in wild turkeys than any other disease. *Simulium meridionale* is so widespread in the Mississippi Valley and so great a pest to sitting turkeys, it is known as the "turkey gnat" (Comstock, 1950:824). E. P. Johnson (1943) tested turkeys in Virginia for *Leucocytozoon* between the dates November, 1938, and December, 1940. Of 183 pen-reared birds, 80 (43.7 per cent) were infected, and of 45 native wild birds, 14 (31.1 per cent). The disease was common in domestic turkeys in South Carolina, Georgia, Florida, Alabama, and Missouri (Travis *et al.*, 1939). Five wild turkeys from Georgia and five from Florida were all infected. The protozoan was noted in small numbers in the blood of all of the game farm turkeys examined in Pennsylvania by Wehr and Coburn (1943:14). Further examinations were made by Kozicky (1948:264). All of the five native wild turkeys were infected, but only 19 (20.7 per cent) of 92 game farm birds. The degree of infection varied from zero to 100 per cent, depending on the locality.

The source of infection of domestic flocks in Florida was thought to be wild turkeys (Simpson *et al.*, 1956). The recent paper by Byrd (1959) leaves the vectors and pathogenicity of *Leucocytozoon* in a confused state. In his opinion, the real vector is *Prosimulium hirtipes* Fries. It is the earliest of the black flies to appear in spring and is present in the Cumberland National Forest, Virginia, until May 1. No infections were observed after May 15. This fly is commonly known as the Adirondack black fly in the northeast. It is believed that wild turkeys are carriers of the disease and that it is not pathogenetic.

Trichomoniasis.—Trichomoniasis is a disease of the digestive tract accompanied by chronic lesions. It is caused by protozoan flagellates, one being *Trichomonas gallinae*, supposedly limited to the upper tract including the proventriculus, and a second, *T. gallinarum*, confined to the lower tract. Allen and Olsen (1942) found acute and chronic phases of the disease in the lower tract. *T. gallinarum* was isolated from the liver of a turkey dying of blackhead (Kay, 1946). Infected birds have ruffled

343

feathers, drooping wings, and usually a greenish-yellow diarrhea. Jungherr (1927) found the disease in turkeys in Montana and thought that it was due to a fungus. Volkmar (1930) published the discovery of a supposedly new trichomonad, *T. diversa*, associated with the disease in turkeys in North Dakota and western Minnesota. That this organism was the causative agent was confirmed by Hawn (1937). Stabler (1938) showed that *T. diversa* was practically identical with *T. columbae*, which in turn was synonymous with *T. gallinae* Rivolta, 1878 (Stabler, 1938.1). Levine *et al.* (1941) obtained *T. gallinae* from the upper digestive tract of the chicken and was able to transmit the disease to turkeys and other birds. It was believed that all the trichomonads in the upper digestive tract of various species of birds belonged to a single species, *T. gallinae*.

Trichomoniasis is listed by Blakey (1937:16) as one of the diseases found in wild turkeys raised in captivity. An adult native wild gobbler in Pennsylvania was diagnosed as having died of this disease, but *Trichomonas* was not found (Kozicky, 1948:265). Stabler (1941:560) failed to find the parasite in any of the twelve domestic turkeys ranging a farm in Pennsylvania.

Haemoproteus Infection.—The protozoan *Haemoproteus* sp. produces a disease similar to malaria. Herman (1944), in his review of blood protozoa, lists a large number of species of birds that are hosts of *Haemoproteus*. Included are such gallinaceous birds as the ruffed grouse, bobwhite, and western quails but not the turkey. Kozicky (1948:265) stated that five (5.2 per cent) of ninety-seven blood smears collected in 1947 were positive for the organism. One adult native wild gobbler and four wild, pen-reared hens were infected.

MISCELLANEOUS DISEASES

Leukosis.—Frye (1958) has described a possible case of avian leukosis in a wild turkey found ten miles north of Tallahassee, Florida. The bones showed abnormal deposits of calcium.

Polyarthritis.—The death of a wild turkey in the Zoological Park, Vincennes, was diagnosed as due to chronic polyarthritis (Urbain *et al.*, 1951:167).

Bumblefoot.—A swelling of the pads of the feet is known as bumblefoot. Its cause is unknown. Recently, Bailey and Rinell (1960:13) reported the inspection of three wild turkeys from widely separated areas in West Virginia which showed symptoms of bumblefoot.

Carcinoma.—Leidy (1866) found a case of cancer of the liver in a turkey. The tumors ranged in size from that of a pea to a nutmeg. Adenocarcinoma of the ovary in captive wild turkeys has been reported by Fox (1912:224) and Ratcliffe (1933:126).

The young wild turkeys raised by Caton (1877.2) had a high death rate in September, 1877. He wrote: "The first symptom is a drooping attitude and disordered feathers, and then a staggering gait. After which they are sure to be found dead the next morning." More than one-half of his wild turkeys were lost by the same distemper in 1869. His tame and hybrid turkeys were not affected. The symptoms given are insufficient to determine the disease.

ECTOPARASITES

The lice found on turkeys belong to two orders. The Mallophaga are capable of chewing and live principally on feathers and dermal scales, while the Anoplura subsist by sucking blood. Over three thousand species have been described, many of which are specific to the host. I have followed the nomenclature of Hopkins and Clay (1952) on the Mallophaga in their recent revision of the order. Concerning the two species that may be considered peculiar to the turkey, Denny (1842) wrote that "Their mode of progression is rather singular as well as rapid. They slide as it were sideways extremely quick from one side of the fiber of a feather to the other, and move equally well in a forward or retrograde direction, which, together with their flat polished bodies, renders them extremely difficult to catch or hold. I have observed that where two or more genera infest one bird, they have each their favorite localities; for, while the *Goniodes stylifer* will be found on the breast and neck of the bird, the *Lipeurus polytrapezius* will be congregated in numbers on the webs and shafts of the primary wing feathers."

Biting Lice.—The *Chelopistes* (*Pediculus*) *meleagridis* of Linnaeus (1758:613) is commonly known as the large turkey louse. The *Goniodes stylifer* of Nitzsch (1818:294) is a synonym. It is recorded for North America by Kellogg (1900:67), Herrick (1916:723), Ewing (1929:119), and Hermes (1939:124), and for Java by Salm (1923:596). What Panzer (1793:51) believed to be *Pediculus meleagridis* Linnaeus, Nitzsch

(1818:300) named *Menopon* (*Menacanthus*) *stramineum*(*s*). *Menopon biseriatus* Piaget, 1880 = *Menacanthus stramineus*. Clay (1941) lists the wild turkey, *M. g. merriami*, of Texas as host for *Virgula* (*Chelopistes*) *meleagridis*. Without doubt, this should refer to the Rio Grande turkey (*M. g. intermedia*) if the state is correct. Emerson (1951) found this parasite on the eastern wild turkey from Pennsylvania, Virginia, and Oklahoma, and on Merriam's turkey from Arizona. It is also mentioned by Malcomson (1960). *Menacanthus stramineus* was found by him on the eastern wild turkey from Virginia and Oklahoma.

The domestic turkey, according to Nitzsch (1818:293) and Burmeister (1839:434), is host to *Oxylipeurus* (*Lipeurus*) *polytrapezius*. It is found on domestic turkeys in North America (Kellogg, 1900:63; Herrick, 1916:723). Clay (1941) reported it from domestic turkeys from Yorkshire, England, and from the skins of *M. g. merriami* (?) from Texas. It was found on the eastern wild turkey from North Carolina, Missouri, Oklahoma, and Texas, on Merriam's turkey from Arizona, and on the Florida turkey (*M. g. osceola*) by Emerson (1951). Salm (1923:596) reported it from Java. Osborn (1896:201) found it very common on domestic turkeys in the United States and stated that he had specimens from the wild turkey. A new species, *Oxylipeurus corpulentus*, was obtained from the skins of Merriam's turkey (?) from Texas (Clay, 1938:183).

According to Hopkins and Clay (1952:194), the *Lipeurus gallipavonis* of Geoffroy (1762:600) and Harrison (1916:83) is nonexistent. It is stated to occur on domestic turkeys in Oklahoma by Emerson (1940:105) and in Cuba by Zayas (1941). Backlund (1935), in Finland, found *Goniodes* (*Chelopistes*) *meleagridis* L. on all the turkeys examined, and *Eomenacanthus* (*Menacanthus*) *stramineus* Nitzsch more common on turkeys than chickens.

Hippoboscids (*Louse Flies*).—The hippoboscids live on the blood of the host. *Lynchia americana* is found on the eastern wild turkey according to Bequaert (1953:258, 259). *Olfersia coriacea* occurs chiefly on the ocellated turkey but is found occasionally on the domestic turkey in Brazil, where there is also a record of *Stilbometopa podopostyla*.

Ticks.—Ticks are the most important arachnids to be found on both the wild and domestic turkeys. There are several early statements that in summer the wild turkey was covered with ticks, especially about the head and neck. Banks (1908:34) reported the finding of *Haemaphysalis chordeilis* Packard on a domestic turkey from Taftsville, Vermont. Hadley (1909.1) found this tick so numerous at Norwich, Vermont, in June as to kill forty of a flock of forty-six young turkeys. The infested birds carried from seventy to eighty adult ticks as well as many immatures. Pettitt (1928:199) reported these ticks so abundant on turkeys in Michigan that they had to be removed by hand. Some young turkeys were killed by the tick. Ewing (1929:85) gives *H. chordeilis* as a synonym of *H. cinnabarina* Koch. The rabbit tick, *Haemaphysalis leporis-palustris* is widely distributed and occurs abundantly on wild gallinaceous birds in the northern states. It does not appear to have been found on turkeys.

The lone star tick, *Amblyomma americanum* L., is found throughout the southeast from New Jersey to southern Iowa, and south to Texas. According to Bishopp and Trembley (1945:3, 6), this species occurs abundantly on the wild turkey in the South but has not been found on the domestic bird. The decrease of turkeys on Bull Island, South Carolina, may have been due to the heavy infestation by the larvae and nymphs of this tick. The wild turkey has been the host of ticks over so long a time that it is doubtful if an appreciable mortality results from them. There is some parasitism of wild turkeys along the Gulf Coast by *Amblyomma cajennense*. A related species *A. hebraeum* Koch has been found on turkeys in the Belgian Congo (Ghesquière, 1921).

The fowl tick, *Argas persicus* (= *A. miniatus* Koch, 1844), is a common parasite of turkeys and chickens (Neveu-Lemaire, 1912:1,169). It has been found on the domestic turkey in the South and may be abundant at wild turkey roosts (Bishopp and Trembley, 1945:11). It was present on turkeys in the Sudan (King, 1921).

Mites.—A few species of mites occur on the feathers of turkeys. Rebrassier and Martin (1932) reported the quill mite, *Syringophilus bipectinatus* (Heller), on the golden pheasant, the chicken, and the turkey in Ohio. The following feather mites are listed by Neveu-Lemaire (1912:1,169) as occurring on turkeys: *Freyana chaneyi* Trouessart and Mégnin; *Dermoglyphus minor* (Nörner); and *Megninia cubitalis* (Mégnin). *F. (Microspalax) chaneyi* occurred in the thousands on turkeys in Maryland (Chapin, 1925). In some cases, the grooves of the remiges were filled completely with the shed skins and living mites. This mite was prevalent on turkeys in Louisiana but was not found in

Kansas (Bushnell and Twiehaus, 1939:87). *Megninia cubitalis* occurred on wild turkeys in Maryland (Gardiner and Wehr, 1949).

The mite, *Cytoleichnus* (*Cytoditis*) *nudus* (Vizoli), is actually an internal parasite living in the respiratory tract and other internal organs (Ewing, 1929:49). It has been found abundantly in turkeys (Banks, 1915:133). The red mite *Dermanyssus gallinae* (De Geer) sucks the blood of the host. Heavy infestations may cause the death of incubating turkeys (Cline, 1933:357). The depluming mite, *Cnemidocoptes gallinae* (Railliet) burrows into the feather follicles, producing such great irritation that the bird plucks its feathers. A member of the same genus, *C. mutans* (Robin and Lanquetin), produces scaly legs. A new mite, *Euschöngastia nunezi*, from a turkey from Tamaulipas, Mexico, has been described by Hoffman (1951). Burget (1957:56) states that mites have never been found on wild turkeys.

Endoparasites

Trematodes (Flukes).—*Collyriclum faba* (Bremser) is found encysted in the skin of turkeys and chickens. This "skin" fluke was found in turkeys and chickens at Vining, Minnesota, in 1923 (Riley and Kernkamp, 1924). Shortly thereafter, it was reported as a parasite of turkeys in Drôme Province, France (Marotel, 1926). Farner and Morgan (1944) gave but two areas for its occurrence in the United States: Maryland, New Jersey, and Massachusetts in the east; and Michigan, Wisconsin, and Minnesota in the north central. Harwood (1931) found in the intestines of turkeys in Texas a new variety of *Strigea falconis* (Szidat), which he named *S. f. meleagris. Echinoparyphium recurvatum* (Linstow) was found by Annereaux (1940) in turkeys in California. The parasite produces severe inflammation of the small intestine. This species and *Zygocotyle lunata* (Diesing) were found by Self and Bouchard (1950) in the Rio Grande wild turkey on the Wichita Mountains Wildlife Refuge.

The first occurrence of *Echinostoma revolutum* (Frölich) in a turkey was reported by Skrjabin (1915), who found it in a bird at Ekaterinburg, Russia. Its life history has been worked out by J. C. Johnson (1920) and Beaver (1937). Snails serve as the intermediate host. In Minnesota, Kitchell *et al.* (1947) found that about 6 per cent of a flock of 670 poults was ill with the parasite, of which about two hundred were recovered from four birds. Found on the grounds were snails, *Helisoma trivolvis,* with encysted flukes.

Brachylaemus commutatum occurs in the caeca of turkeys (Mönnig, 1950). This fluke was found in three of the twenty-three turkeys examined in Poland (Wadowski, 1939). A species of *Amphimerus* was found by Price (1931) in the liver of a turkey in North Dakota. *Tamerlanea bragai* occurred in large numbers in the kidneys of turkeys in Brazil (Barretto and Filho, 1945). Johnston (1943) found *Echinopary-phium recurvatum* in a turkey in Melbourne, Australia. *Prosthogonimus macrorchis* occurs in the oviduct of turkeys and prevents them from laying (Macy, 1939). The *Plagiorchis* (*Multiglandularis*) *megalorchis* found in dead poults in Wales and described as a new species by Rees (1952) may be identical with *Plagiorchis laricola* (Skrjabin) found by Foggie (1937) in turkeys in northern Ireland.

Cestodes (*Tapeworms*).—*Metroliasthes lucida,* discovered by Ransom (1900, 1909:88) in a turkey from Lincoln, Nebraska, is common in the small intestine of this bird. Fuhrmann (1908:104) mentions the turkey as a host for this parasite. It has been found in the eastern wild turkey in the Philadelphia Zoological Gardens (Williams, 1931), and in the Rio Grande turkey of the Wichita Mountains, Oklahoma (Self and Bouchard, 1950). Wardle and McLeod (1952:517) think that it was original in the American wild turkey.

Hymenolepis carioca (Magalhães) occurs in the chicken, quail, and turkey (Stafseth, 1939). The intermediate hosts are beetles. Polonio (1860) described *Taenia* (*Hymenolepis*) *cantaniana* from a turkey in northern Europe, and Railliet and Lucet (1899) reported it in the turkey in France. In 1909, Ransom (1909:36) mentioned its presence in turkeys in the United States. The *Drepanidotaenia* (*Hymenolepis*) *meleagris* and *D. musculosa* of Clerc (1902:574; 1903:248), and mentioned by Fuhrmann (1908:104) and Ransom (1909:94, 95) as found in turkeys, do not appear to be valid new species.

A new species of cestode, *Davainea meleagridis,* was found in the duodenum of a domestic turkey from the market in Washington, D. C. (Jones, 1936). This tapeworm was reported from two eastern wild turkeys from the Woodmont Rod and Gun Club, Hancock, Maryland (Gardiner and Wehr, 1949). Here the birds are pen-reared and would be expected to have more parasites than the native turkeys.

Several species of *Raillietina* have been reported to occur in turkeys. *Taenia* (*Raillietina*) *cesticillus* was described by Molin (1858:139) from a specimen found in a pheasant. Its occurrence in domestic turkeys is mentioned by Ransom (1909:67), Railliet (1921), and Stafseth (1939). The first report on its occurrence in the wild turkey was by Gardiner and Wehr (1949), who found it in Maryland birds. Williams (1931) described two new species, *Taenia* (*Raillietina*) *ransomi* and *Drepanidotaenia fuhrmanni* from the eastern wild turkey in the Philadelphia Zoological Gardens. *D. fuhrmanni* is a synonym of *Raillietina williamsi* Fuhrmann, 1932, which was found in wild turkeys in Maryland (Gardiner and Wehr, 1949). *R. ransomi* occurred in large numbers in wild turkeys at Honey Grove, Pennsylvania (Wehr and Coburn, 1943:15). *R. echinobothrida* Mégnin, 1881, has been reported in turkeys by Neveu-Lemaire (1912:1,169), Stafseth (1939), and Wardle and Mc-Cleod (1952:441). The intermediate hosts are ants and snails.

A new cestode, *R. magninumida*, was described by Jones (1930) from a guinea fowl from the market in Washington, D. C. The turkey is mentioned as a host (Wardle and McLeod, 1952:441). According to Hudson (1934), *R. magninumida* is a synonym for the variable *R. numida* Fuhrmann, 1912. *R. tetragona* (Molin, 1858), morphologically very similar to *R. echinobothrida*, is listed by Stafseth (1939) and Morgan and Hawkins (1949:373) as a parasite of turkeys. The intermediate hosts are house flies and ants.

A new species of cestode (*Raillietina georgiensis*) was found by Reid and Nugara (1961) to infect 90 per cent of a flock of 1,500 domestic turkeys near Winterville, Georgia. The parasite was introduced by pen-reared wild birds from Fitzgerald, Georgia.

Nematodes (*Roundworms*).—*Trichostrongylus tenuis* (Mehlis) occurs in the caeca and occasionally in the small intestine. In the United States it has been found in the turkey, pheasant, guinea fowl, chicken, bobwhite, and several species of geese. Cram and Wehr (1934) have shown that *T. pergracilis* is a synonym. It has been found in wild turkeys in Maryland (Gardiner and Wehr, 1949) and is a common parasite of domestic turkeys in Yugoslavia (Erlich and Mikacic, 1940).

Ascaridia galli (Schrank) is a large round worm, the female of which may attain a length of 11.6 cm. It is more common in chickens than in

350

turkeys. The habitat is the small intestine. Synonyms are: *Ascaris galli* Schrank, 1788: *Heterakis lineata* Schneider, 1866; and *Ascaris inflexa* Zeder, 1800. According to Ackert and Eisenbrandt (1935:203), bronze domestic turkeys are more resistant to the parasite than white leghorn chickens. It was the most common nematode in turkeys in Yugoslavia (Erlich and Mikacic, 1940). *Ascaridia dissimilis* was described by Vigueras (1931) as a new species from Cuban turkeys. It is smaller than *A. galli* but otherwise similar. Wehr (1942) and Wehr and Coburn (1943) have reported as host the wild turkey of Pennsylvania and Georgia. It has been found also in domestic turkeys in the United States (Harwood and Stunz, 1945).

Heterakis gallinae (Gmelin, 1790) is a common caecal nematode of chickens and turkeys in the United States (Cram, 1927:53). *H. peropicillum* (Rudolphi) and *H. versicularis* (Frölich), given by Neveu-Lemaire (1912:1,169) as parasites of turkeys in Europe, are synonyms. *H. gallinae* was the second most common parasite of turkeys in Yugoslavia (Erlich and Mikacic, 1940). Nine of the twenty-three turkeys examined in Poland were infected (Wadowski, 1939). Economically, this nematode is important since it is a vector of the blackhead-producing organism *Histomonas meleagridis*.

The cosmopolitan gizzard worm *Cheilospirura hamulosa* (Diesing) is more common in chickens than in turkeys in the United States. Cram (1927:226) states that it was found in a turkey by B. H. Ransom and M. C. Hall. This appears to be the first record in this country. *Cheilospirura* sp. was found in wild turkeys in Pennsylvania (Wehr and Coburn, 1943). Insects are vectors.

Ransom (1904) described a new crop worm, *Gongylonema ingluvicola*, found in chickens in Florida. Stoddard (1946:252) has reported this nematode in a wild turkey at Moultrie, Georgia. It is less frequent in turkeys than *Capillaria* (Wehr, 1937). *Capillaria annulata* (*Trichosomum annulatum*) was discovered in the chicken and pheasant by Molin (1858:156). Its occurrence in turkeys was reported for the first time by Cram (1926). All but about 50 of a flock of 175 to 200 turkeys in Maryland died of this parasite in the fall of 1925. Jungherr (1927) reported *Capillaria* sp. in the crop of turkeys in Montana. A wild turkey found in Perry County, Pennsylvania, was infested heavily with *Capillaria* sp.

(Roberts, 1954). According to Wehr (1937), *C. annulata* and *C. contorta* are the most common crop worms in turkeys. Wehr (1936) found that earthworms are essential vectors for *C. annulata*.

The crop worm *C. contorta* (Creplin) may occur in such great numbers as to be fatal to the host. Emmel (1939) examined three large flocks of turkeys infested with this parasite. Characteristic symptoms are weakness, droopiness, emaciation, frequent swallowing, and settling on the hocks in a penguin-like attitude. A satisfactory treatment was 5 per cent sulphur in the mash over a period of three weeks. The crops of turkeys at Manassas, Virginia, were infested with the parasite sufficiently to cause death (Wehr, 1948). Wehr and Coburn (1943) found the parasite in wild turkeys in Pennsylvania. No intermediate host is required as with *C. annulata*. In the opinion of Cram (1936:22), *C. perforans* Kotlán and Orosz, 1931, found in a single turkey in Hungary, may be a synonym of *C. contorta*. Madsen (1951) not only agrees with Cram but thinks that *C. annulata* is a synonym of *C. contorta*.

Some species of *Capillaria* are found in the small intestine of the turkey. The *Trichosomum meleagris-gallopavo* described by Barile (1912) from a turkey from Turin is a synonym of *Capillaria longicollis* Mehlis, 1831, according to Madsen (1945:79). Gardiner and Wehr (1949:17) reported *C. longicollis* (Rudolphi) from wild turkeys in Maryland. Graybill (1924) found *C. columbae* (Rudolphi) in chickens and turkeys in the United States. The same hosts harbored this parasite in Portugal (Ferreira, 1955). It has also been found in the turkey in Cuba (Vigueras, 1936). Wehr (1939:15) was successful in infecting turkeys and chickens by using the eggs of this parasite obtained from pigeons. According to Madsen (1951:260), *C. columbae* is a synonym of *C. caudinflata* (Molin, 1858).

Allen and Wehr (1942) reported the first occurrence of *C. caudinflata* in turkeys in the United States. They were able to infect turkeys by feeding them earthworms (*Allolobophora caliginosa*) harboring *C. caudinflata*. Morehouse (1944) concluded from his experiments that *Allolobophora caliginosa* was the true vector since he was unsuccessful in transmitting the parasite with the two earthworms, *Helodrilus (Eisenia) foetidus* and *Lumbricus terrestris*; however, Wehr and Allen (1945) subsequently found that *Eisenia foetida* would serve as a vector. In 1931, Cram (in Stoddard, 1946:273) mentioned the turkey as a host of

352

Capillaria retusa (Railliet). Two years later (1933), she reported the successful infection of turkeys with the eggs of *C. retusa* obtained from the droppings of turkeys located at the U. S. Soldiers Home, Washington, D. C. A nematode, *Capillaria combologiodes*, described as new by Erlich and Mikacic (1940), was obtained from turkeys in Yugoslavia.

Recently, Maxfield *et al.* (1963) published a comprehensive paper on the helminths found in the viscera of 390 wild turkeys, 76 pen-reared wild turkeys, and 68 domestic turkeys from ten southeastern states. The investigation revealed the presence of nineteen species of helminths in the wild turkeys. The largest infestations of these turkeys were: with *Moliasthes lucida*, 43.1 per cent; *Ascaridia dissimilis*, 66.2 per cent; and *Heterakis gallinae*, 62.3 per cent. The flukes *Brachylaema virginia* and *Cotylurus flabelliformis* were found in wild turkeys for the first time. Owing to the high parasitism in pen-reared wild turkeys, the danger in releasing them is obvious.

14

Utilization

THE UTILIZATION OF THE TURKEY by the Indians was much more complete than by the whites. It was a common item in the diet of the natives east of the Great Plains and its bones are found frequently at archaeological sites. The only Indian method of preservation of the flesh which I have found was smoking. On July 7, 1745, on the west branch of the Susquehanna, the provisions of Spangenberg's (1916:15) party were nearly exhausted: "In this strait an old Indian joined us, undid his pack, and took out a smoked turkey, and told us to boil it." A taboo existed on the method of cooking. Byrd (1929:194) wrote: "The Indian likewise Shot a Wild Turkey, but confest he wou'd not bring it to us, lest we shou'd continue to provoke the Guardian of the Forrest, by cooking the Beasts of the Fields and the Birds of the Air together in one vessel." The eggs of the wild turkey were sought diligently as they were considered a delicacy (Loskiel, 1794:91).

FOOD FOR THE INDIANS

The Cheyennes would not eat turkeys because they believed if they did, they would become cowardly (Keeling, 1910:308). The turkey's habit of running away at high speed, presumably, could become infectious. A party in the Southwest killed a turkey that was so old and tough that no amount of cooking would make it edible. When it was about to be thrown out, a party of Indians arrived and requested food: "The officer in command having little else, bethought him of the turkey, and ordered it to be set before the Indians. The old chief carefully examined the contents of the kettle, then gravely informed his followers that it was 'guacalote' [turkey], that to eat it would make them cowardly, that he was old, had not long to live, was not ambitious of further distinction, and would therefore risk it. After this exhortation he deliberately turned to the kettle, and in less than an hour emptied it completely, storing away, the officer declares, not less than two gallons, or sixteen pounds of solid and liquid food" (Dodge, 1883:275).

A Hopi Indian chief informed L. W. Simmons (1942:55) that the turkey was not eaten, but its feathers were pulled out to make prayer sticks. The Kiowas and Comanches would not eat the flesh of the turkey but did use the feathers for making arrows (Battey, 1876:323). The Papago Indians shot turkeys from the roost for their feathers for ceremonial purposes. The flesh was not eaten, nor were the feathers used generally on arrows because the turkey was a timid bird (Castetter and Underhill, 1935:41, 71). Another reason given by the Chiricahua Apaches for not eating the turkey was that it ate insects; however, the Indians at Hot Springs, Sierra County, New Mexico, did eat the bird (Opler, 1941:328).

The Chiracahua and Mescalero Apaches did not favor birds for food. Within memory, many Apache would not eat turkey, quail, or dove (Castetter and Opler, 1936:25). Wallace (1911:40) wrote that the Apaches do not kill turkeys, because of superstition. The related Navahos, however, did eat wild turkeys and used the feathers for arrows (Franciscan Fathers, 1910:213, 318). The bird was eaten after skinning and roasting and was never boiled. The tail feathers were used for making arrows and headdresses. If the feathers were to be used for ceremonial purposes, the turkey must be trapped and not shot (Hill, 1938:174). Buckelew (1925:90) stated that the Lipans ate no other fowl than the wild turkey. The Tonkawas of Texas caught turkeys for food and had a turkey dance (Sjoberg, 1953:286, 297). In the distant Malay Peninsula, some of the natives will not eat the turkey, Argus pheasant, or peafowl because of their belief that any bird spreading its tail fanwise and strutting is unclean (Beebe, 1922:125).

There has been much discussion whether the early Pueblos ate turkeys or kept them mainly or solely for their feathers. Coronado (1896:559) doubted that the bird was not eaten. While at Hawikuh, he wrote: "The Indians tell me that they do not eat these in any of the seven villages, but that they keep them merely for the sake of procuring the feathers. I do not believe this, because they are very good, and better than those of Mexico."

I have not seen the Spanish of Winship's translation, but it is probable that *better* should read *larger* as in Hakluyt (Coronado, 1904:156). Lange (1950:204) has suggested that the prevailing opinion that the turkey was kept for its feathers only is due to a poor translation by Bandelier (1892:48) of a passage in the *Relación del Suceso*. The passage, *"estas las tienen mas para la pluma que para comer,"* is translated "the latter they keep for the feathers rather than to eat" while the correct reading should be, "they are kept more for their feathers than for eating." Bandelier (1890:159), however, had expressed his views as follows: "The turkey, which was kept around the houses of the pueblo, was domesticated, not so much for its meat as for its feathers." There is no doubt that some of the New Mexican Indians were eating turkeys at the time of the conquest. Gallegos (1927:26, 44), who was attached to the Spanish expedition of 1581, wrote that the Piros "support themselves by means of corn, beans and calabashes. They make *tortillas* and *catoles* with buffalo meat and turkeys because they have large numbers of the latter." Following a Pueblo wedding there was plenty of food consisting of turkeys, buffalo, tamales, *tortillas*, and other items.

It is possible that in some areas and periods the turkey was not used for food. E. H. Morris (1939) wrote: "While at least as far back as middle Basket Maker III the turkey had been domesticated, it would seem to have been kept for the sole purpose of providing feathers for the manufacture of blankets. I have seen nothing to indicate that it was eaten, or dismembered for the use of any of its parts. In remains from the early horizons, if one comes upon the bone of a turkey, almost always it will be found to be in position in the skeleton or the remainder of the bones will be nearby, indicating definite interment. In contrast, scattered turkey bones are to be expected in Pueblo III refuse deposits, and it is from this period that most of the bird-bone awls emanate." Turkey bones were so abundant at the Pindi Pueblo, Santa Fe County, New Mexico, that no doubt was held that the bird was used for food (Stubbs and Stallings, 1953:126). Because of the broken turkey bones found in the ancient homes, Hendron (1946:73) believed that the opinion that the bird was not eaten must be discarded. Information given Jeançon (1929:2) renders it probable that some of the Río Grande people utilized both the meat and feathers.

Opinions differ on the present extent of the utilization of the turkey for food. Bartlett (1931:4) states that the Indians of the present time consider the turkey good food. Parsons (1936:23) found that contrary to practices elsewhere, except at Isleta, both the wild and domestic turkey were eaten at Taos. This was surprising to her since south of Taos the turkey was a ritual bird and the people claimed that it would not be eaten even in a time of famine (Parsons, 1939:22).

The Mexicans, when it came to eating the turkey, had no inhibitions. A feast given by an Aztec merchant included the following dish: "And then he provided turkeys, perhaps eight or a hundred of them. Then bought dogs to provide the people, as food, perhaps twenty or forty. When they died, they put them with the turkeys which they served; at the bottom of the sauce dish they placed the dog meat, on top they placed the turkey as required" (Dibble and Anderson, 1959:48).

FEATHERS FOR MAKING COVERINGS

Turkey feathers were used by the Indians from Maine to Arizona to make articles of clothing. Attachment of the feathers to cords was an art practiced only by the Indians north of Mexico (Wissler, 1926:56). The Indians of the eastern United States attached the feathers to cords made from wild hemp (*Apocynum*) so that they overlapped like shingles (Johnson, 1917:280), a custom not followed in the Southwest. In 1643, Roger Williams (1810:225) wrote: "Neyhommauashunck; a coat or mantle, curiously made of the fairest feathers of their ... turkies, which commonly their old men make, and is with them as velvet with us." Almost identical wording appears in a letter written in 1686 (Dunton, 1867). W. Wood (1865:108) stated that the squaws "weave coates of Turkie feathers"; Josselyn (1865:78) that they are woven for their children; and Morton (1838:22) that "they make likewise some Coates of the Feathers of Turkies, which they weave together with twine of their owne makinge, very pretily."

Writing from Fort Orange (Albany) in 1639, De Vries (1853:135) mentioned that the Indians in winter wore a covering of turkey's feathers which they had made. In an undated fragment of a manuscript found at The Hague, it is stated (Anon., 1851:4) that the New York Indians "go almost naked except a lap which hangs before their nakedness, and on the shoulders a deer skin or a mantle, a fathom square of woven Turkies feathers . . . ." When an Indian girl in New Jersey reached

357

marriageable age, she made herself a dress of turkey feathers (Philhower, 1931:10). The Delaware women made blankets of turkey and other feathers (Ettwein, 1848:32). A quilt of turkey feathers was worth one ell of white sewan (wampum) (Lindeström, 1925:224).

Concerning mantles in Virginia, Strachey (1849:65) wrote: "We have seene some use mantells made both of Turkey feathers and other fowle, so prettily wrought and woven with threeds, that nothing could be discerned but the feathers, which were exceeding warme, and very handsome." About 1700 a Santee Indian medicine man was wearing a coat of turkey feathers resembling silk plush (Lawson, 1937:13). In Florida blankets and other coverings were made from the breast feathers (Romans, 1776:85).

The La Salle expedition to the lower Mississippi in 1682 found the Quinipissa, a Choctaw tribe, living in St. Charles Parish, near New Orleans. They had robes made from cords and turkey feathers (La Salle, 1876:564). They were being used by the Indians of Biloxi in 1701 (Villiers, 1922:132). In 1700 the Toumika (Tunica) living on the Yazoo River, and the Huma of Baton Rouge had robes of turkey feathers and muskrat skins (Gravier, 1900:131). Du Pratz (1758:125) wrote: "The native women weave the feathers of the body like the makers of wigs in France do hair. In weaving, the feathers are so fastened to an old covering made from bark that the down is found on both sides." An English translation has the feathers fastened to "an old covering of bark," which is most unlikely. The Indians made cords from the bast fibers of the mulberry and basswood, which were sometimes woven into cloth.

In the spring of 1811, a male and female Indian were found buried in a cave in Warren County, Tennessee (Haywood, 1823:163). The female was wrapped in a feather blanket and held in her hand a fan made from the tail feathers of a turkey. An Indian woman wrapped in blankets of turkey feathers was also found in a saltpeter cave in Kentucky (Withers, 1831:37). Bonaparte (1825:92) stated: "The Indians make much use of ... [turkey's] tails as fans; the women weave their feathers with much art on a loose web made of the rind of the Birch tree [?] arranging them so as to keep the down on the inside, and exhibit the brilliant surface to the eye. A specimen of this cloth is in the Philadelphia Museum; it was found enveloping the body of an Indian female, in the great Saltpetre cave of Kentucky." Loskiel (1794:48) prepared his manuscript in 1788 and wrote that the coverings of turkey feathers were then seldom seen among the Indians.

There is no clear early description of the method of making the feather coverings by the eastern Indians. Heckewelder (1876:203) says: "The blankets made from feathers were also warm and durable. . . . It requires great patience, being the most tedious kind of work I have ever seen them perform, yet they do it in a most ingenious manner. The feathers, generally those of the turkey and goose, are so curiously arranged and interwoven together with thread or twine, which they prepare from the rind or bark of the wild hemp and nettle, that ingenuity and skill cannot be denied them." Adair (1775:423) adds: "They [Choctaw] likewise make turkey feather blankets with the long feathers of the neck and breast of that large fowl—they twist the inner end of the feathers very fast into a strong double thread of hemp, or the inner bark of the mulberry tree, of the size and strength of coarse twine, as the fibers are sufficiently fine and they work it in the manner of fine netting. As the feathers are long and glittering, this sort of blankets is not only very warm, but pleasing to the eye."

The method by which a Mattapony Indian woman of Virginia produced the feather work, the fabric being made of homespun cotton, is described by Speck (1928:436): "The plain knitting stitch is employed. Four steel or bone needles are used. . . . As the knitting proceeds, at a third or fourth stitch a single feather is worked into the fabric, being caught fast by its base and sometimes the shank of the plume, which is, of course soft and pliable, the feathers being carefully selected with this in view, and is caught in several stitches to hold it tight. In the better executed specimens the feathers are quite firmly attached."

The art of featherworking was not limited to the Indians. In Kentucky the wives of the squatters and farmers used the double feathers of the turkey (Audubon, 1831:15). These could be attached to the network more firmly than the single feathers. A photograph of a recent cape made of turkey feathers is shown by Mosby and Handley (1943:11).

The Spanish discoverers of the Southwest found the Indians making extensive use of rabbit fur and turkey feathers for coverings. The inhabitants of Cibola had long robes made of feathers. The natives of Uraba (Taos) and Cicuique (Pecos) had maize, beans, melons, hides, and some robes made of feathers which were twisted upon cords. These were

359

then woven into a kind of plain cloth from which mantles were made (Jaramillo, 1857:157). Luxán (1929:72) recorded in 1583 that the inhabitants of the Piro village near San Marcial wore mantles and slept under blankets made from the feathers of turkeys which they raised in quantity.

In preparing the feather strands, one or two cords made of yucca fiber were used. The feathers were of various types. Guernsey (1931:102) and Judd (1954:72) state that only the vanes were used. According to Amsden (1949:128), the quills were split. When fine down was used, it was twisted between two cords to hold it firmly (Hough, 1914:71). Nordenskjöld (1893:103) while exploring Step House, Mesa Verde, found materials for making the cloth, "a quantity of down of varying length, pieces of down cut to suitable length and tied in bunches, and cords wrapped in down." The down varied in length from 4 to 6 cm. The feathers resemble closely those of the wild turkey found in the area (Burget, 1957:iv).

The method of making the fabric is illustrated clearly by Nordenskjöld (1893: Fig. 67) and by Hough (1914:71). The latter states: "The process of feathering was to strip the downy piles of the turkey and wind them spirally around a cord of fiber, crossing the larger end under the first one or two winds and securing the smaller end under the beginning of the next winding."

Through the courtesy of Frank H. H. Roberts, Jr., of the Bureau of American Ethnology, I can add the following additional information: "The feathers used generally were the large wing and tail feathers of the turkey, and the pile was stripped from them and wrapped around the cord. In some instances a two-ply twist of cord was used and the ends of each strip were inserted through loops of the twisted cord. In other cases a smaller cord was wrapped around the main cord. The feather cords thus obtained were woven into a robe or blanket. The weave was not tight and the feathers remained quite fluffy."

The feather fabrics were produced as far back as the days of the Basket Makers. Articles made by the Pueblos consisted of clothing, blankets, pouches, ornaments for parts of costumes and for necklaces. Unusual was a jacket taken from a mummy found seven feet deep in the debris of Tularosa Cave, western New Mexico (Hough, 1914:72). In northeastern Arizona, at Pueblo II and Pueblo III sites, Guernsey

360

(1931:102) found two feather blankets, one measuring 18 by 26 inches while the other was 46 inches in length. A feather blanket found by Moorehead (1906:34) at Pueblo Bonito was 4 feet 3 inches by 6 feet 7 inches.

Indians living beyond the range of the turkey on the Missouri prized turkey feathers for ornaments and for feathering arrows. In 1795, Tabeau (1939:171) recommended that traders dealing with the Sioux and Ricârâ (Arikara) should have a supply of turkey feathers. The turkey was a curiosity among the Mandan, who on leaving Washington took with them a stuffed one (Cabot, 1844:80). Henry (1897: I, 355) wrote that the Big Bellies (Gros Ventre) obtained large numbers of the tails of gobblers from the Cheyennes for use as fans. In attempting to buy a tail, he first offered five rounds of ammunition, but that was gradually raised to forty rounds without success. Maximilian (1858:431) mentions that the Indians of the Missouri prized the wing feathers for their arrows. They also wore them on their heads (Plate 30) as a mark of distinction, a split quill signifying an arrow wound by which each hero boasted of the different kinds of wounds which he had received. The entire tail of a gobbler was carried in the hand as a fan and as an indication of the different bands or societies. With the Mandan, e.g., when it was attached to the head, it was a sign of the Dog Clan. The best-dressed Indian seen by Morgan (1959:149) at the Yankton Agency in 1862 had a headdress of turkey feathers.

The Cheyennes preferred turkey feathers for their arrows. The tribal sign was made by drawing the right index finger several times across the left forefinger. The preferred interpretation is that this sign indicated "stripe people" or "striped-arrow" from this tribe's custom of using the striped feathers of the wild turkey in making arrows (Mooney, 1896:1,024; Hodge, 1912: I, 251). The best feathers were obtained from the wings, and these are striped. The feathers were soaked in warm water so that the quills would split easily. The vanes were stripped off and three of them laid equidistantly along the arrow shaft for a distance of 6 to 8 inches, glued, and wrapped with fine sinew (Belden, 1872:102). The Cheyennes preferred the feathers of turkeys and "buzzards" since blood did not affect them (Grinnell, 1923: I, 181, 187; II, 134). Turkey feathers hung from their lances, and the beard was sometimes used to stir medicine.

The earliest information on the use of the feathers for arrows was obtained by Champlain (1922:360) during his voyage along the New England coast in 1604. The Indians of Maryland (Calvert, 1899:42) and Virginia (Strachey, 1849:106) also used turkey feathers for this purpose. Beverley (1705: III, 60) wrote: "They fledged their arrows with Turkey Feathers, which they fastened with Glue made of the Velvet Horns of a Deer." It is probable that this was a general custom among the eastern Indians.

Use of the Feathers in Ceremonies

The turkey played a very important role in the religion of the Indians of the Southwest: "The turkey is mentioned in the Zuni cosmogenic legend, and its tail-feather markings are said to be caused by the slime of the earlier wet world. It is a sacred bird, probably never eaten but preserved for its feathers, which were used both for ceremonial and practical purposes in *pahos* and in preparing the feather cord from which garments were constructed" (Hough, 1919:238). The feathers were believed capable of bringing rain. There is also the legend that the turkey, in trying to raise the sun, had the feathers of its head burned off; hence, the head is red and bare (Parsons, 1939:241). Because of plucking, the turkeys in the Hopi villages have a ragged aspect (Hough, 1915:172).

There is a large literature on the ceremonial use of the feathers. Parsons (1939) gives an extensive account of the uses to which they are put. There are many references in Stephen (1936) on the use of the feathers in making prayer sticks, masks, and headdresses. Uniformity is lacking both in the use of certain turkey feathers and in the objects made with them. Among the Hopis: "Feathers from the short layer in the turkey tail are put on the backs of two prayer sticks tied together to represent male and female. These feathers are tied with them to keep them warm. Others of the same feathers can be made into *nakwakosi* (common prayer plumes)" (Nequatewa, 1946:16). Bristles from the beard of the turkey were added to certain Hopi prayer sticks as "heart hairs" (Parsons, 1939:277). Only the feathers of the wild turkey were used for ceremonial purposes at Taos, those of the domestic bird, handled by whites, being considered unclean (Parsons, 1936:23). Feathers of the wild bird were preferred at Pueblo Bonito, but in 1939 the Indians begged Judd (1954:262) to secure for them feathers of the domestic turkey. The Indians of Texas, when going on a journey, stuck turkey feathers into ant hills as offerings (Benavides, 1945:43).

Use of Turkeys in Burials

It has been suggested by Parsons (1939:29) that the turkey was a sacrificial bird as in Mexico. This opinion is supported by the findings of articulated skeletons with the head missing. Turkeys (Wormington, 1947:70) "have been found buried with mortuary offerings. Corn was provided for the turkeys and bones for the dogs which were buried." A turkey found by Brew (1946:121) in southeastern Utah was definitely interred. Roberts (1939:230; 1940:134) found several human burials, especially of children, in eastern Arizona with turkeys buried beside them.

Miscellaneous Uses

The spurs of the turkey were used to a limited extent for heading arrows since they were only effective against small game. Strachey (1849:106) mentions the use of stone, spurs, and the bills of certain birds. Heading the arrows with spurs is mentioned by Beverley (1705: III, 60). The Choctaws of Mississippi also used them (Adair, 1775:425). Byrd (1929:150) would have us believe that spurs had been supplanted by flint points. Until recently, at least, spurs were still in use for heading arrows by the Rappahannock Indians (Speck, 1925:55).

There were other miscellaneous uses. The Indians of Virginia pierced their ears and hung in them the legs of turkeys and other birds (Strachey, 1849:67). A witness of the installation of the "King of Estetowee" in South Carolina about 1771 noted that he was made comfortable by two savages wielding two large fans made of the tails of turkeys (Brahm, 1856:223). Turkey feathers ornamented the moccasins of the high priest of the Chickasaws (Adair, 1775:84). The Indians of the Loup nation in camp at Point Pleasant, Tennessee, had fans made of turkey feathers to brush away the annoying flies (Montule, 1821:74).

The wing of a turkey was used by the Delawares to sweep out the Big House (Speck, 1931:91). About fifty miles from the mouth of the Grand Saline River, Illinois, the prairie grass was encrusted with salt which the Indians collected by brushing it into a vessel with the wing of a turkey (Brown, 1817:174). At their feast following the first fall hunt, the sachem

363

of the Lenapi (Delaware), after removing the entrails of a turkey and replacing them with "their money," hung it up as a target. The man who shot it down received the money (Lindeström, 1925:215). At present the Nanticokes, related to the Delawares, shoot at a mark to win a turkey (Speck, 1915:27). A pipe in the possession of Chief Saginaw was reputed to have once belonged to Tecumseh. The stem was made of the quills of the wild turkey reinforced with hickory splints and wrapped with deer sinew (Cook, 1889:12).

While traveling among the Georgia Indians, Bartram (1791:455) observed in their houses paintings and sculptures of human beings having the head of a turkey or other animal. The turkey was a common design painted on the pottery of the Southwest. Good examples have been found in the Mimbres Valley, southwestern New Mexico (Fewkes, 1923:28, 36). Effigy heads of the common turkey and ocellated turkey have been found on pottery from southern Mexico to Costa Rica. The Maya manuscripts contain many representations of the ocellated turkey, but the common turkey is seldom shown with certainty.

The leg bones of the turkey were favored for making awls. They were also used in the manufacture of beads and other ornaments, and wind instruments.

Uses in Mexico

Crossing into Mexico there is less varied information on the uses made of turkeys. Prescott (1843: II, 133) quotes from the manuscript of the licentiate Zuazo as follows: "I saw many mantles ornamented on both sides with such soft feathers of turkeys that on rubbing the hand with and against the grain, it was just like a very well made zibelene manta."

Lumholtz (1902: I, 72) has described an Indian burial found in Cave Valley, five miles north of Pacheco, Chihuahua: "Between the legs was a large wad of cotton mixed with feathers of the turkey, the large woodpecker, and the bluejay." He learned that the Tarahumaras had a turkey dance and used wild turkeys for sacrificial feasts. The Coahuiltecan Indians of Tamaulipas applied a resinous substance to their long hair on which were laid the tail feathers of turkeys or parrots (Ruecking, 1955:359). The Indians at Tlaxcala used the beard of the turkey for a hyssop (Motolinia, 1914:83). Turkeys were essential for the rites of the natives of Chan-Kom, Yucatán, but being hard to raise were kept in only small numbers (Redfield and Villa, 1934:47; Redfield, 1941:390). Special vessels were used to hold cooked turkey. A gobbler was not castrated, but if it was to be offered to the gods, it was kept from other turkeys, especially the hens. If a turkey took a dust-bath, it was a sign of rain. The Maya *cutz-cal-tzo* means: "A ritual strangling of turkeys during the fiesta of the patron saint of Dzitas."

Food for the Whites

The turkey was important in the economy of the pioneers. Doddridge (1876:105) wrote: "The wild turkeys, which used to be so abundant as to supply no inconsiderable portion of provision for the first settlers, are now rarely seen." Many years later, Remington Kellogg told Carhart (1946:171) that had it not been for the supply of meat from deer and turkeys available to the settlers, the settlement of the country would have been long delayed. Turkeys were once so plentiful and so easily shot that they were an emergency ration. In 1773, Joseph and Samuel Martin settled in what is now West Virginia, opposite the mouth of the Muskingum River. They lived exclusively for two or three months on boiled turkeys, without salt, until their corn matured (Hildreth, 1842:345). Mrs. Thomas Cunningham was captured by the Indians in 1785. For ten days all that she had to eat were three pawpaws and the head of a wild turkey, a portion apparently discarded by the Indians (Withers, 1831:27).

The spring of 1773, because of an Indian scare, Simon Kenton guided a surveying party from Three Islands on the Ohio to Greenbrier County, West Virginia (Kenton, 1930:44). No game was met with and the men lived on wild onions and various roots. Kenton found a nest of the wild turkey with eggs on the point of hatching. These were roasted and eaten with avidity. The Indians considered this dish a delicacy. Major David Rogers' command was decimated by the Indians in a battle above the mouth of the Licking River on October 4, 1779. Captain R. Benham was shot through both hips and a companion had both arms broken. Turkeys were abundant in the woods and the companion would drive them towards Benham, who usually killed two or three from a flock. In this way they subsisted on turkeys for several weeks until their wounds healed sufficiently to travel (McClung, 1832:171).

Sons of the pioneers were taught early to imitate the notes of the turkey.

Kercheval (1833:372) wrote: "One important pastime of our boys was that of imitating the noise of every bird and beast in the woods. This faculty was not merely a pastime, but a very necessary part of education, on account of its utility in certain circumstances. The imitations of the gobbling and other sounds of wild turkeys, often brought those keen eyed and ever watchful tenants of the forest within reach of the rifle. . . . This imitative faculty was sometimes requisite as a measure of precaution in war. The Indians when scattered about in a neighborhood, often collected together by imitating turkeys by day, and wolves or owls by night. In similar situations our people did the same. I have often witnessed the consternation of a whole neighborhood in consequence of a few screeches of owls."

The popularity of the turkey as a game bird may be judged from the numerous accounts of the Indians imitating the gobble to decoy white hunters. In the spring of 1777 the Indians attempted to waylay the people at the Bluegrass Fort in Scott County, Virginia. During the night an Indian climbed a tall cedar near the fort and in the morning imitated the gobble of a turkey. Some of the young men desired to go out and kill the turkey but were persuaded not to attempt it by Matthew Gray, an old Indian fighter. Approaching the tree by a circuitous route, he shot and killed the Indian (Coale, 1878:172).

Jessie Hughes, according to Cist (1846:11), prevented a boy at Marietta, Ohio, in 1779, from attempting to shoot a gobbler which he heard. Hughes went into the woods and shot an Indian who was imitating a turkey. De Hass (1851:410) places the incident at Clarksburg, West Virginia. While corn was being hoed at Grey's Station, Greene County, Kentucky, in 1790, a note like that of a turkey was heard. An old hunter advised the people not to follow the sound, but he did and killed an Indian (Spears, 1853:273). On April 25, 1777, Indians appeared at Harrodsburg, Kentucky, and imitated the sounds made by turkeys and other game. The ruse was detected readily (Draper, n.d.:124). While on the Republican River, Morrison (1868:200) was decoyed into the hands of two Indians, one of whom had imitated a sound resembling the gobble of a wild turkey.

Turkeys afforded Daniel Boone an opportunity to escape from the Indians by whom he was held captive. While near Chillicothe, Ohio, on June 16, 1778, the Indians flushed a flock of turkeys and pursued them three-fourths of a mile. As soon as they flew into trees, the Indians began shooting. Boone took advantage of their absence from camp to start for Boonesborough, 160 miles distant, which he reached within the surprising time of four days (Draper, n.d.:188). During his escape, he killed game for the first time after crossing the Ohio. Some writers state that he shot a turkey, but Draper says that the animal was a buffalo.

About 1800, at Chillicothe, Ohio, it was customary at Christmas time to lay in a supply of turkeys for spring and summer use. They were abundant and fat. The birds were cleaned, cut in two, salted in troughs, and hung to dry (Finley, 1867:152). In the early days of Howard County, Missouri, turkeys caught in traps were salted down for winter use (Chick, 1921:97). The breast, both fresh and dried, was considered a substitute for bread. Atkinson (1876:75) wrote: "They were hunted especially to secure their breasts, which were eaten with bear's meat in place of bread. No other portion of the turkey was eaten as food." The family of J. H. Jenkins settled in Fayette County, Texas, in 1828. When corn was not available, the dried breast of turkey was used for bread (Jenkins, 1958:8). In Georgia, in the 1830's, "For bread, they strung up and dried out the 'white' meat of wild turkey breasts, after which they cut it up and beat it into a kind of flour, and kneaded it for bread" (Covington, 1937:63).

The fat of the turkey was highly regarded for culinary purposes: "The wild ones have commonly a finger's thickness of fat on their back, which one uses for cakes and garden cooking, because it is sweet and far better for this than the best butter, as I myself have discovered" (Byrd, 1940:71). Heckewelder (1886:138, 146) mentions the use of wild turkey fat as a substitute for butter, and of turkey eggs for making dumplings.

The eggs were used extensively by the settlers (Beers & Co., 1882:293). Donalson (1842:430) was captured by the Indians on the Ohio River in 1791 and later escaped. He found a turkey's nest with two eggs in it, each with a double yolk, which provided two delicious meals on separate days. Nourse (1925:127) recorded on May 12, 1775, that at the mouth of the Big Sandy River, Kentucky, his party had many turkey eggs for breakfast. In 1873 wild turkey eggs were so plentiful in Wichita County, Texas, as to furnish four men with all the eggs that they desired to eat (Babb, 1923:77). A pioneer lady in Iowa found the eggs more palatable than those of the wild goose or wild duck (Brewer-Bonebright, 1921:77).

Use of the Feathers by the Whites

The feathers in one form or another were utilized rather widely. In Massachusetts they were used for beds, the wings for sweeping and dusting, and the tails for fans (C. Johnson, 1932:167). The wings were used as dusters as far distant as Kansas (Meredith, 1938:371). When I was a youth in northern Ohio, the wings of domestic turkeys were still used for this purpose at some farm homes. The wing was sometimes used as a fan (Fowler, 1934:297), but the tail was ideal for this purpose. In 1775 this type of fan was to be found in the cabins at Boonesborough, Kentucky (Ranck, 1901:41). Maximilian (1906: I, 133) records that the fans made from the tails of wild turkeys at Bordentown, New Jersey, in 1832 were luxuries. This type of fan was a necessary female accessory at Kansas camp meetings (Greene, 1910:486). The French of Louisiana, with their flair for the artistic, joined the tails of four turkeys to make an umbrella (Du Pratz, 1758:124).

Use for Thanksgiving

There is a widespread popular belief that following the first Thanksgiving in New England in 1621 this celebration became an annual affair, and that turkey was always served. Thanksgiving was, however, at first an irregular event, the day being set aside by a proclamation of the governor of a colony or state. This duty was subsequently assumed by the President of the United States when Thanksgiving became annual. Bradford (1898:127) wrote: "They begane now to gather in ye small harvest they had ... And now begane to come in store of foule, as winter aproached, of which this place did abound when they came first (but afterwards decreased by degrees) and besids water foule ther was great store of wild Turkies of which they tooke many, besids venison, &c." Four men in one day killed sufficient "fowl" for this first Thanksgiving to last the company a week (Winslow, 1897:489; Austin, 1876:11). Chief Massasoit and his warriors were invited to the feast. Love (1895:74), in discussing the thanksgivings of New England, is silent as to their frequency. Hempstead (1901) mentioned Thanksgiving in his diary from 1711-1758. As far as his entries go, it was just another day.

There are divergent references on the availability of turkeys in New England. Harcourt (1910:993) writes: "But there were plenty of turkeys always—big, fat birds which had fallen victims to the famous fiat of Alexander Hamilton that 'No citizen of the United States should refrain from turkey on Thanksgiving Day.'" On the other hand, even the wealthiest inhabitant of Hampshire, Massachusetts, did not have a tame turkey for Thanksgiving until after the Revolution (C. Johnson, 1932:167). Sewall (1878–82), in his diary running from December, 1673, to October, 1729, does not mention serving turkey on either Thanksgiving or Christmas. Turkey must have been a rare treat for James Parker (1915:300) for after being invited to supper on February 28, 1786, he wrote: "at evening had a rosted TURKEY for sup." There is no further mention by him of eating this bird until Christmas of 1803 and 1809.

It is doubtful that a turkey became a common adjunct to a Thanksgiving dinner until about 1800. On November 26, 1806, Bentley (1905–14: III, 264) recorded in his diary that a Thanksgiving was not complete without a turkey. Stuart (1833: I, 197) was in Boston during Thanksgiving, 1828, and wrote: "The annual thanksgiving day in the state of Massachusetts was held while we remained at Boston. We were advised to see the market on the evening previously. It was handsomely lighted, and was filled with provisions of all kinds; but the quantity of turkeys in relation to other kinds of food, seemed to us most extraordinary, until we were told, that on thanksgiving days persons of every condition have a roasted turkey at dinner . . . and the turkeys were sold quickly at from three to five and six shillings sterling."

According to Fluke (1940:4), Andrew Jackson's Thanksgiving proclamation of November 29, 1835, reads in part: "We thank thee for the bountiful supply of wildlife with which Thou has blessed our land; for the turkeys that gobble in our forests."

Turkeys had become rather common Christmas fare in England by 1575. Martha Goosley wrote from York, Virginia, on August 8, 1770, to John Norton, London, that she had sent him two turkeys for Christmas (Mason, 1937:142). This seems like sending coals to Newcastle. Turkey was eaten in America on various holidays. Marshall (1877:151) recorded at Philadelphia on December 25, 1777: "No company dined with us to-day, except Dr. Phyle. . . . We had good roast turkey, plain pudding, and minced pies." He does not mention the serving of turkey on Thanksgiving or on another Christmas. At primitive Marietta, Ohio, on December 25, 1788, Drowne (1883:287) dined on roast turkey and turkey

369

pie. The day was one of public thanksgiving by proclamation of the governor. A wild turkey was served at a feast on New Year's Day in New York in 1663 (Van Buren, 1923:62). A recent German author (Dürigen, 1923:332) was confused on dates and stated that in the United States turkey is served in celebration of July 4. This custom, however, once prevailed on the frontier.

PALATABILITY AND METHODS OF COOKING

There were varying opinions on the relative merits of the wild and domestic turkey for the table. The method of cooking may have played a part. Van der Donck (1841:172) wrote in 1656: "When they are well cleaned and roasted on a spit, then they are excellent, and differ little in taste from the tame turkeys; but the epicures prefer the wild kind." Colonists in the Carolinas roasted turkeys without removing the intestines (Catesby, 1754:x), a procedure scarcely conducive to a delicate flavor. A nineteenth-century traveler (Candler, 1824:79) in Virginia and the Carolinas had scant praise for the method of cooking them.

The Indians of the Southwest appear to have solved the problem satisfactorily. A wild turkey was bled, drawn, slightly plucked, then cast upon red hot coals: "When one would suppose that there was nothing left of the bird, the burnt, black mass was raked out, left to partially cool, then with a dexterous movement of the knife the skin is peeled or stripped from the neck downwards taking the burned feathers, revealing a white and tempting morsel to a hungry man" (Carter, 1935:279). The whites followed this example, the turkey being roasted in a hole in the ground without removal of the feathers (Dobie, 1929:147).

The wild turkey was given high praise by Strachey (1849:125) in 1612: "and yt is an excellent fowle, and so passing good meat, as I maye well saie, yt is the best of any kind of flesh which I have ever yet eaten there." Josselyn (1865:78) thought that the meat of the New England wild turkey was excellent and added that turkey "eggs are very wholesome and restore decayed nature exceedingly." When Norwood (1844:42) was in Virginia in 1649, a supper consisted of a "very savoury mess" of wild turkey boiled with oysters. Few would question that this was a "mess." Captain Morris (1904:321) was in northeastern Indiana in 1764 and wrote: "We were forced from want of water to stew a turkey in the fat of a racoon; and I thought I had never eaten anything so delicious, though salt was wanting; but perhaps it was hunger which made me think so." Prior to roasting, the early hunters in Tennessee would make in the body of the turkey numerous small incisions into which were placed pieces of fat bear meat and condiments (Draper, 1843:262).

A large wild turkey could be purchased from the Indians for twenty-five cents at Harrisburg (Houston), Texas, in 1837. Cutlets were made from the breast and the remainder of the bird given to the Mexican servants (Harris, 1921:140). In 1875, at the foot of the High Plains, "The wild turkeys went in big droves, and we would often kill eight or ten with one shot from a shotgun and we would take their breasts only for meat, frying it in buffalo tallow, which we got from the buffaloes" (Connellee, 1930:93). One of the most delicious meals eaten by Tibbits (1876:404) was the sliced breast of a young turkey fried in butter. When turkeys were easily obtainable in Missouri, only the breasts were used (Ford, 1936:70). When fried in tallow, this dish was considered unsurpassable. Dixon's (1914:305) taste was otherwise: "When we camped on a creek where wild turkeys were plentiful, we would kill fifteen or twenty and stew a potful of gizzards, hearts and livers. This was best of all, a dish fit for a king."

The palatability of the wild turkey depended upon its age and the season. In summer the turkey was always poor in flesh, and an old bird was always tough. Frequently, the turkey was so covered with ticks as to be repulsive. On May 23, 1793, a companion of Joseph Bishop (Gray, 1858:93) shot in southern Illinois a poor turkey with "ten thousand ticks." It could not have been eaten without skinning and was thrown away. Although turkeys and deer in Missouri were covered with ticks in summer, they were still considered edible (Finckh, 1949:338). Mather (1717:64) found its flesh tough and hard; but since he also mentioned that it sometimes weighed fifty to sixty pounds, it is reasonable to assume that he did not have much familiarity with the wild bird. A young turkey, according to Ashe (1808:135), had delicate white meat of exquisite flavor, while the flesh of an old male was black and tough. The fat was remarkable in that it never offended the stomach. An old fat gobbler was shot in a cornfield by Perry (1899:38) in northeastern Ohio in November, 1842. Though well roasted, it tasted so rank and strong that none of his family would eat it.

The type of food eaten by the turkeys had a pronounced effect on the taste. The flesh of turkeys that fed on Chinaberries in western Texas was bitter and inedible (Cook, 1907:114). Turkeys in spring ate eagerly the shoots of the wild leek. O'Hanlon (1890:154) wrote: "In early summer, a strong but not repulsive flavour of wild onions, on which these birds are fond of feeding, communicates that peculiar Spanish cookery taste to flesh of naturally agreeable delicacy, succulence and nutrition." The flavor of a turkey that had eaten the leaves of the leek was extolled by Roemer (1849:288).

Turkeys which had been feeding on the fruit of the hackberry in Oklahoma had a special richness (Keim, 1870:108). When piñon nuts are available, Merriam's turkey feeds almost exclusively upon them and the meat acquires a delicate flavor: "Their flesh was so highly scented by this food that, when the Turkeys were over the fire, they perfumed the camp with a most appetizing odor, and I know no better dish than a roasted Mexican Turkey that has been fed on piñon nuts" (Elliot, 1897:182). Too frequent eating of the best of turkeys cloyed the appetite. An Indian with Lawson (1937:22) killed some turkeys, and two skunks which he preferred to the turkeys: "We cooked our Supper, but having neither Bread or Salt, our fat Turkeys began to be loathsome to us, although we were never wanting of a good Appetite, yet a Continuance of one Diet made us weary."

Many preferences have been expressed for the flesh of the domesticated turkey. When Carteret (1897:168) was in South Carolina, he wrote: "here is also wilde turke which ye Indian brought but is not soe pleasant to eate of as ye tame, but very fleshy & farr bigger." Stuart (1833: II, 116) thought that the flesh of a fat bird was excellent. In Alabama wild turkeys in poor condition were often brought to the table so that he preferred the domestic bird. Both McConnell (1889:115) and Ward (1930:194) thought the domestic bird superior. The superiority of the wild bird over the tame, according to Fay (1884:848), lies in the imagination. Wild turkeys raised on a modern game farm are reputed to have no better flavor than the tame ones (Camp, 1958:124). There is a French opinion to the contrary. Wild turkeys raised in France like domestic turkeys, after some years, showed no change in the flesh. The meat was less dry, whiter, much nicer, with much more delicate flavor than that of the black domestic turkey, and somewhat gamy. The wild turkey is to the domestic turkey like the pheasant is to a chicken (Le Fort, 1891:564).

One explanation for a distaste for the wild bird is given by Dodge (1877:237). "For some few years past a very considerable number of wild turkeys have been sent from the plains to the eastern markets alive. These are caught in pens by a process too old and well known to need description, and taken in coops to the nearest railroad station. By the time these birds reach their destination they are, through fright and starvation, the mere shadows of their former selves. I have, within the last few years, met several gentlemen, whose highest ambition was to be thought epicurean, whose verdict was unanimous that the western wild turkey was unfit for human food. They had evidently been dining upon some of these unfortunate anatomical specimens. If they will make a trip west and try the bird in its natural condition, I think I can guarantee an entire change of opinion."

Superstitions regarding the eating of the turkey and its eggs appear to have been absent among the whites north of Mexico. For France we find: "The huswife shall not make any great account of Turkeie eggs: at least he that loueth his health, shall not esteeme of them for to use them: for phisitions hold, that eggs of Turkeies ingender grauell, and minister cause to breede the leprosie" (Estienne, 1600:117). The flesh was believed to be an aphrodisiac. Some European travelers asserted that it was dangerous to eat wild turkeys in America as they feed on poisonous berries or fruits which might indirectly cause death (Blasquez, 1868:327). A person disliked by a Mexican was given the frontal caruncle to eat in the belief that it would produce impotence (Sahagún, 1938:316).

During the first half of the nineteenth century, domestic turkeys became so common in some of the eastern states that they were served regularly at dinner parties and almost daily at inns. Hamilton (1833:182) attended a dinner in Philadelphia given by Caspar Wistar and wrote: "No man can say a harsh thing with his mouth full of turkey, and disputants forget their differences in unity of enjoyment."

PRICES

The price of wild turkeys varied with availability. They sold in Hartford about 1711 at 1s. to 1s. 4d. apiece. Dressed turkeys, weighing from five to fifteen pounds, were priced at one and one-half penny a pound at Northampton, Massachusetts, from 1730 to 1735. The price rose to three pence by 1788, and to 10 to 12½ cents by about 1820 (Judd, 1863:358). In 1757 a wild turkey cost 2s. 8d. at Deerfield (Sheldon, 1895:591). A New England shilling was worth 16.1 cents in 1763. Turkeys sold in New York in 1817 at 3s. 4¼d. to 5s. 7¼d. apiece (Fearon, 1818:43). It is not certain that the prices refer to the wild turkey, but at this time wild and tame birds usually sold at nearly the same price. The winter of 1874–75, wild turkeys retailed in New York City at 25 cents a pound (Anon., 1875.1).

In 1683 in Pennsylvania a wild turkey could be purchased for two or three pounds of lead shot (Paskel, 1882:326). About 1650 the Delaware Indians would sell a turkey for 4 stivers, about 5 cents (Lindeström, 1925:225). In 1707 the South Carolina Indians would produce a "40 pound" wild turkey for two English pence (Archdale, 1836:94). The winter of 1836–37 a wild turkey cost 75 cents in Washington, D. C. Near Uniontown, Moore (1950:90) in 1826 paid 12½ cents for a dinner that included wild turkey and roast beef. The "wild" turkeys hanging in front of the restaurants in Philadelphia in 1881 had black legs and white tips to the tail feathers ("Keouk," 1881). Frauds of this nature were common.

In the early days west of the Alleghenies, wild turkeys were obtainable for a pittance. A buck could be purchased for 50 cents, while turkeys were given away during the early settlement of Henderson County, Kentucky (Starling, 1887:28). Stuart (1952:14) went ashore on the lower Kentucky River on April 23, 1806, and purchased a turkey for 17 cents. According to Audubon (1831:15): "At the time when I removed to Kentucky . . . Turkeys were so abundant, that the price of one in the market was not equal to that of a common barn-fowl now. I have seen them offered for the sum of three pence each, the birds weighing from ten to twelve pounds. A first-rate Turkey, weighing from 25 to 30 pounds avoirdupois was considered well sold when it brought a quarter of a dollar."

In June, 1795, John Brickell (1844:55) hunted for the men employed at Grant's saltworks on the Licking River in Ohio. He received 12.5 cents for a turkey. In 1811 at Granville, Ohio, Enoch Graves traded nine fat turkeys, which he had trapped, for three pounds of sole leather (Bushnell, 1889:63). The price at Finlay from 1826–30 was 10 cents apiece

(Warner, Beers & Co., 1886:218). At late as 1848 a turkey could be purchased in Cincinnati for 25 cents (Hall, 1848:197). Hunters at Detroit in 1749 received for a turkey the high price of 1½ livres, or 30 cents (Anon., 1900.1:43).

The winter of 1823–24 was spent by C. C. Trowbridge on the White River, eighteen miles from Indianapolis, Indiana. The Indians provided him with turkeys at six cents apiece (Campbell, 1883:486). Some of the hardships of pioneer life are shown by the following: "Solomon Teverbaugh killed in one day seventeen wild turkeys and carried them home, a distance of six miles. The next day, he carried them on foot to Vincennes, a distance of thirteen miles, and exchanged them for a bag of salt, with which he returned on the same day (Goodspeed Bros. & Co., 1885:252). They must have been young birds as otherwise he could not have carried this number.

In southeastern Illinois, Birkbeck (1818:63) had wild turkey for dinner every day for a month. Five could be purchased for a dollar. Flower (1819:30) stated that in 1819 in Edwards County the prevailing price of a wild turkey was 25 cents. The same price is given by Woods (1822:196) and Brush (1944:57). According to Kingston (1876:306), as late as 1833 a turkey could be purchased in central Illinois for a pound of lead or shot, or a paper of pins or needles. Hall (1838:124) wrote that a turkey could be bought from an Illinois hunter for 12.5 cents.

The variation in the price of turkeys in the lower Mississippi valley is difficult to understand. On December 14, 1810, Bradbury (1819:204) bought from the Choctaw three turkeys and two hind quarters of venison for 75 cents, the asking price. Fearon (1818:278) in 1817 found provisions in New Orleans "enormously dear," turkeys costing three to five dollars each. While at Natchez, Mississippi, in December, 1820, Audubon (1929:92) noted that the Indians received the high price of $1.00 for a small wild turkey. The price of a domestic turkey at Lebanon, Tennessee, in 1820 was 37.5 cents (Bell, 1957:319). This indicates that wild turkeys were scarce, for at this time Nuttall (1821:56) found that in Arkansas a large wild turkey could be purchased from the Chickasaws for 25 cents. In 1874 a team load of wild turkeys from Craighead County, Arkansas, was taken to Memphis, the birds being sold at 50 cents apiece (Williams, 1930:289).

Wild turkeys in Scott County, Iowa, in 1837 were sold at 25 to 50 cents

(Barrows, 1863:26). In 1854 a wild turkey could still be purchased for 50 cents at Muscatine (Usher, 1922:26). St. Louis had a large game market, and prices remained relatively stable for many years. When Featherstonhaugh (1847:53) was in the city in 1835, he saw at least two hundred large wild turkeys in the markets. The Shawnees in 1810 received 25 cents for a turkey brought to St. Louis (Bradbury, 1819:269). Graf (1920:218) in 1833 could obtain a wild turkey at prices ranging from 12 to 25 cents. Audubon was in the city ten years later when either a wild or domestic bird was available at 25 cents (Audubon, 1900: I, 452). Prices were much lower away from the city market. Duden (1834:82), in 1825 in Montgomery County, could purchase a wild turkey from hunters for 12.5 cents. By 1884 the wild birds were being sold in the Kansas City market at 50 cents to $1.00 each ("Crocus," 1884). A large number of turkeys trapped in Menard County, Texas, in 1891, was shipped alive to St. Louis. They were sold for 75 cents for a gobbler and 50 cents for a hen irrespective of weight (Reid, 1947:12).

A turkey could be purchased from an Indian at Fort Cobb, Oklahoma, in 1868 for a pound of flour (Jacob, 1924:17). At San Antonio, Texas, wild turkeys were sold in 1878 at 30 cents each (Buffham, 1878), and the following year at 25 cents ("Almo," 1879). Wild turkeys in January, 1860, sold in Denver, Colorado, at $1.00 to $2.00 apiece (Hafen, 1927:138). In the early 1880's, hunters sold turkeys at $3.00 each to contractors building the Atlantic and Pacific Railroad in Arizona (Hulsey, 1944:6).

There are few data showing the extent of the commerce in wild turkeys. Bolton and Ross (1925:26) state that in 1639 there was a great demand for turkeys to provision the Spanish packets which plied between St. Augustine, Florida, Havana, and San Marcos Bay. Apalacha (Tallahassee) became the center of a brisk trade in turkeys and deerskins. In December, 1873, it was estimated that the Chicago markets had received 2,400 wild turkeys weighing 24,000 pounds (Anon., 1873.1). The purchase price was 12½ cents per pound. A steamboat arrived in New Orleans early in 1850 with over 1,400 Arkansas wild turkeys (Anon., 1850). Elliot (1881) mentioned a newspaper account of the shipment of seven hundred dozen wild turkeys to London.

15

Hunting

THE TURKEY WAS HUNTED with equal zeal by the eastern Indians and whites. Considerable ingenuity was shown in taking advantage of the habits of the turkey in order to effect its capture. In some cases it is impossible to determine if the method employed by the Indians was original with them or the whites. For example, E. S. Dodge (1945) has described a pen trap 3 feet high and 6 feet square made by the Delawares by driving poles into the ground. The pen was covered and provided with a trench so that it was essentially like the trap used by the whites. The period when this pen was used by the Indians is not given. Of Virginia, wrote Beverley (1705: II, 39): "The Indians have many pretty Inventions, to discover and come up to the Deer, Turkeys and other Game undiscen'd." Turkeys were taken in New England in nets laid under the oaks where they came to feed upon acorns (Williams, 1810:219). When Evelin (1641:6) wrote that in New Jersey "five hundred Turkeys in a flock" were secured with nets, he was setting bait for immigrants. At Jamestown in 1608, the only domestic animals kept by the Indians were curs such as the keepers have in England (Wynne, 1937). They were used for hunting turkeys and other game.

CIRCULAR HUNTS

In New England, "When they [Indians] went a hunting for turkies: they spreade over such a greate scope of ground, that a Turkie could hardly escape them" (Morton, 1838:31). This was probably a circular hunt which was not always as successful as Morton indicates. L. C. Aldrich (1889:454) has described a hunt of this type in Erie County, Ohio, as follows: "To see about one hundred Indians surround the same number of wild turkeys, to see the turkeys fly without one of them being killed, and to hear the outlandish gutteral ejaculations of the exasperated redskins, wishing the turkeys were in a place decidedly remote from the happy hunting-grounds, was very funny to the spectators." Circular hunts were common in pioneer days (Plate 31). He mentions that the Indians also drove wild turkeys into pens, a custom adopted by the whites.

Use of Snares

Van der Donk (1841:172) has described the use of snares in New York: "The Indians take many in snares, when the weather changes in winter. Then they lay bulbous roots, which the turkeys are fond of, in the small rills and streams of water, which the birds take up, when they are ensnared and held until the artful Indian takes the turkey as his prize." Snares were used also by the Delaware Indians (Johnson, 1917:281). At the time that Iowa was being settled, the Indians generally used a snare rather than a gun to obtain a turkey (Mueller, 1915:177). De Vries (1853:160) wrote that turkeys could fly only one or two thousand paces, then were so exhausted that the Indians caught them with their hands. They also shot them with arrows. The New York Indians shot the turkeys or caught them with a bait placed on a hook (Montanus, 1851:79; Ogilby, 1671:175).

Driving into Trees

The method described by Campbell (1793:202) seems to have been used widely. The Iroquois, Captain Brant, told him that on encountering a flock of turkeys, they galloped after them as fast as possible. This caused the birds to take to the trees from which seventeen were shot. An English prisoner among the Miami, in Indiana, was allowed to accompany them on a hunt. On encountering a flock, the Indians ran after them at top speed, yelling and making as much noise as possible to force them into trees from which they were shot. On December 31, 1785, Denny (1860:270) went on a hunt on the Ohio River with two Indians. He stated: "I set out in company with two Shawanees to provide a few turkeys for the first of the year. . . . After we had rode the distance of four or five miles . . . we got amongst the turkeys; and the first thing done was to *charge* upon them, so as to cause them to fly up on the trees, and all the time the [worst] howlings and frightful screeches I ever

378

heard, were given to effect this purpose. As soon as the turkeys rose we alighted and commenced firing. In this manner we sported with two flocks, until we had as many as we could conveniently carry home."

USE OF BLOWGUN

The use of a blowgun for hunting turkeys was apparently limited to children. The Cherokee youths killed the birds by shooting them in the eye (Timberlake, 1765:45). The children of the Chickasaws were also said to often kill turkeys with this weapon. McKenney (1846:163) wrote that an arrow a foot in length was shot from a cane eight to ten feet long. Kills could be made at a distance of twenty to thirty feet. The missile would not be effective on a turkey unless it struck the head.

Alexander Wilson (Ord, 1825:*cli*) in 1810 met some Indian boys with blowguns and was not impressed by their marksmanship: "At Bear Creek . . . I first observed the Indian boys with their *blow-guns*. These are tubes of cane seven feet long, and perfectly straight, when well made. The arrows are made of slender slips of cane, twisted, and straightened before the fire, and covered for several inches at one end with the down of thistles, in a spiral form, so as just to enter the tube. By a puff they can send these with such violence as to enter the body of a partridge, twenty yards off. I set several of them a hunting birds by promises of reward, but not one of them could succeed. I also tried some of the blow-guns myself, but found them generally defective in straightness."

CALLING

The Indians of northern Ohio used the wing bone of the turkey as a caller (Baldwin, 1888:106). It is doubtful if a device was used commonly for the Indian was too skillful in imitating the notes of wild animals to require instrumental aid. In 1780, John Hinkston (Withers, 1831:216) was captured by the Indians at Ruddle's Station, Kentucky, and later escaped. While seeking his way home he heard the "tremulous bleating of the fawn, the hoarse gobbling of the turkey" made by the Indians in their hunt for game. Both Indians and whites imitated the call of the young to lure the adult turkeys (Flint, 1832:73).

DECOYS

Decoys were sometimes used. While in the Mississippi Valley in 1687, Joutel (1878:404) noted that the Indians in hunting turkeys used the

379

head of this bird as a decoy. Hunter (1823:290), while a captive among the Indians of Missouri and Arkansas, observed: "The turkey is not much valued, though when fat, the Indians frequently take them alive in the following manner. Having prepared from the skin an apt resemblance of the living bird, they follow the turkey trails or haunts, till they discover a flock, when they secrete themselves behind a log, in such a manner as to elude discovery; partially display their decoy; and imitate the gobbling noise of the cock. This management generally succeeds to draw off first one then another from their companions, which from their social and unsuspecting habits, thus successively place themselves literally in the hands of the hunters, who quickly despatch them, and wait for the arrival of more. This species of hunting with fishing is more practised by the boys than the older Indians, who seldom, in fact, undertake them, unless closely pressed by hunger." A white hunter is known to have called in a gobbler that jumped upon the log behind which he was concealed and he seized it by the leg (J. K. M., 1933).

There is the story that Daniel Boone protected a young hunter from an Indian who imitated the call of a turkey and used the skin of one as a decoy (Coomers, 1878). "Clip" (1886) hunted with an Indian skilled in turkey hunting. While they were hidden behind a log, the Indian called to induce the wise old gobbler to approach. It refused to come within range until the Indian, after imitating the strutting sound, raised the spread tail of a turkey above the log and moved it like a strutting bird.

Capture by Hand at Roost

The hunting methods of the Six Nations have been described by Dodge (1945). The end of a root, called *wutundá si* by the Cayuga, was burned and rubbed on various parts of the hunter's body. This "medicine" permitted close approach to the turkeys. A pole was also used to capture the turkeys when they were roosting at night: "As the birds slept on the limb of a tree, the hunter with the end of a pole kept poking their feet. The disturbed birds would eventually step onto the pole and they could then be lowered to the ground and caught." Ella F. Robinson (Foreman, 1929:369) lived near Muskogee, Oklahoma. Whenever her people wanted a turkey, an Indian boy was sent to a roost near the Arkansas River. He would return sometimes with one turkey but often one would be caught in each hand. Both of the latter methods of capture are within the realm of possibility but there is a tantalizing lack of details. The turkeys must have roosted much lower than usual.

Nolen (1947:136) was told by an old Negro that he used to ride horseback under a roost at night and grab a turkey roosting overhead. Texans never fear that any story emanating from their state will place their honor in jeopardy. Old residents also told him that the Indians used to take turkeys by circling the foot of the tree in which they were perched. The birds became so dizzy following the circular movement that they fell from the limbs. The same technique has also been ascribed to the coyote.

There is no novelty in the few descriptions of the methods used by modern Indians. A Rappahannock Indian told Speck (1925:55) that he once killed twelve turkeys at one shot at a baited trench. This method was probably borrowed from the whites. The Navahos take turkeys both by trapping and shooting (Hill, 1938:174). If the snow is deep, the birds are run down since they seldom fly more than twice. While at the Taos Pueblo, I was informed by an Indian there that wild turkeys were shot with a rifle and not trapped. The Chiricahua Apaches usually do not make a special hunt for turkeys, but kill them when the opportunity offers. One Apache procedure was to have a party flush the turkeys from one bank of a stream toward another party stationed about one-half mile distant from the opposite bank where the birds were expected to alight. They were then shot with arrows or clubbed (Opler, 1941:328).

SHOOTING AT ROOSTS

Shooting at the roosts was one of the earliest methods of hunting used by the whites. Morton (1838:48) wrote: "They are easily killed at roosts, because the one being killed, the other sit fast nevertheless, and this is no bad commodity." While at Wilmington, Delaware, Hesselius (1947:90) recorded in his journal on September 30, 1712, that when turkeys are fired at on their roost, they only fly to the nearest tree so that all of them can be shot. Van der Donck (1841:172) is more specific: "Sometimes the turkeys are caught with dogs in the snow; but the greatest number are shot at night from the trees. The turkeys sleep in trees and frequently in large flocks together. They also usually sleep in the same place every night. When a sleeping place is discovered, then two or three gunners go to the place together at night, when they shoot the fowls, and in such cases frequently bring in a dozen or more."

There is an early description of hunting at a roost in Pennsylvania. The hunter approaches the roost silently and, on firing his gun, four or five turkeys are usually brought down. This arouses the birds, but if they hear no further noise will return to sleep again. This pattern is followed until all the birds are killed or he has enough. A wounded bird should be allowed to escape as an attempt to capture it may so alarm the birds in the trees that they take flight (J. C. B., 1941:33). The most charitable view of the statement that 150 turkeys are sometimes found roosting in a single tree is that the visibility was poor.

One evening Ruxton (1848:180) and his companions built their camp-fire beneath some trees at Valverde, New Mexico, where a flock of thirty turkeys proceeded to go to roost. The difficulty in hitting a roosting turkey is described: "At length the moon rose, but, unfortunately, clouded: nevertheless we thought there was sufficient light for our purpose, and, rifle in hand, approached the trees where the unconscious birds were roosting. Creeping close along the ground, we stopped under the first tree we came to, and, looking up, on one of the topmost naked limbs was a round black object. The *pas* [precedence] was given to me, and raising my rifle, I endeavored to obtain a sight, but the light was too obscure to draw 'a bead,' although there appeared no difficulty in getting a level. I fired, expecting to hear the crash of the falling bird follow the report, but the black object on the tree never moved. My companions chuckled, and I fired my second barrel with similar result, the bird still remaining perfectly quiet. The Canadian then stepped forth, and taking a deliberate aim, bang he went.

" 'Sacré enfant de Gârce!' he exclaimed, finding he too had missed the bird; 'I am straight, mais light très bad, sacré!'

"Bang went the other's rifle, and bang-bang went my two barrels immediately after, cutting the branch in two on which the bird was sitting, who, thinking this a hint to be off, and that he had sufficiently amused us, flew screaming away. The same compliments were paid to every individual, one bird standing nine shots before it flew off: and, to end the story, we fired every ball in our pouches without as much as touching a feather; the fact of the matter being, that the light was not sufficient to see an object through the fine sight of the rifles."

It was difficult to hit a turkey at roost with a rifle even when there was a full moon. The technique of an Ohio hunter was to attach to the end of the ramrod a glove or mitten so that it hung down three or four inches from the end of the barrel when the rifle was sighted. In aiming, the rifle was raised so that the glove would be just below the form of the turkey outlined against the moon, then fired (Curry, 1913:15).

Campion (1878:235) and a companion within twenty-five minutes killed thirteen turkeys from a flock of about thirty at a roost in the Wet Mountains, Colorado. The birds that escaped flew away by ones and twos since they were startled by the birds killed above them falling through the branches. He thought it strange that the report of the rifle and the flash of the powder seemed to stupefy rather than frighten them. Sage (1860:223) had previously written regarding hunting in Colorado that the birds rarely left the roost on account of the firing. They appeared to be bewildered and the hunter could pick them off one after another. The experience of Messiter (1890:116) was similar. A roost at the fork of the Solomon River, Kansas, contained about two hundred turkeys. When two were killed only the nearest flew away. Many more could have been killed easily.

Broad experience in hunting turkeys in the West was had by Dodge (1877:235). He states that shooting at a roost is successful only when there are no leaves on the trees. A clear starlit night was preferable to brilliant moonlight as the birds were less apt to fly after one or two shots. Anywhere from two or three turkeys, up to hundreds, with forty or fifty in one tree, could be found at a roost. There should be no talking as the sound of the human voice was more startling than the shooting. Care should be taken to shoot the bird nearest the ground and to remain perfectly quiet after each shot. Each bird shot at should be killed for if wounded it will cause a great disturbance by fluttering in the branches. A bird shot high up in a tree, even though killed, may in falling frighten away those below it.

On the Cimarron River, in 1872, he shot twelve turkeys in one tree; and a soldier in Texas killed twenty-six in one tree without changing position. On one occasion in Texas, four or five cavalrymen from his party, armed only with the inefficient musketoon, went into a large roost and in a couple of hours killed eighty-two birds. At the time he wrote, this feat could no longer be duplicated because roosting turkeys had acquired too much experience of gunfire.

A variation in hunting at a roost was employed in Missouri. Having arrived under the trees where the birds were roosting, one person rang a hand bell continuously while another held a lantern as high as he could. The hunter was then able to shoot several before the remainder flew away (Hesse, 1838:85). Kennard (1915:5) shot roosting birds in the Big Cypress Swamp, Florida. A gobbler could be located by his gobble or made to respond by imitating his gobble or the hoot of an owl. The difficulty in locating a large gobbler sitting in perfectly plain sight on the limb of a large old pine was amazing to him.

Hunting in the Snow

Turkeys soon tire in deep, soft snow. Mershon (1923:26) states that when snow came, the hunter followed the tracks with no attempt to remain quiet or out of sight. After a time, one, two, or three turkeys would split off from the flock, and their tracks were followed. Eventually, one turkey would hide in a fallen treetop or in a bunch of weeds from which it would flush within range. The same tactics were employed in Ohio (Beers & Co., 1882:312). In Kansas the flock was first scattered, then one track was selected and the bird walked down: "A brisk walk of several miles will tire the stoutest old gobbler sufficiently to make him sit down and rest" (G. B. R., 1887). One hunter recommended wrapping yourself in a white sheet when hunting in the snow ("Aztec," 1889.1). The hunter in Canada wore a white blanket coat and covered his cap with a white handkerchief (Anon., 1858).

Hunting turkeys in the snow in Illinois was preferred by Bogardus (1879:227), who gives the following description: "Turkeys in snow, with a man following in their track, soon begin to tire a little, if the snow is damp and no crust on top of it. After some time the hunter, who must be a good walker and capable of standing much fatigue, will see where one of the turkeys has diverged from the route of the flock. Following the track of the single turkey, it will be found that after having gone a little way, commonly not more than two hundred yards, and often less, it has squatted under thick brush or in the top of a fallen tree. As he draws near, it will start to run or fly, and it must then be shot. . . . A turkey going to fly is compelled to run eight or ten feet in order to get headway before rising from the ground, and I have often shot them in the head before they would take wing. After having killed his turkey, the hunter must take up the track of the flock again, and go on after it until he sees that another has diverged."

During a snowstorm, turkeys sit in thick brush or the tops of fallen trees and can be approached readily. When a flock takes wing, the line of flight is generally straight so that it is not difficult to find the tracks again. Usually they can be found within three or four hundred yards of the place of flushing. On the ground the path is sometimes winding. In crossing ravines and streams, they usually select the same place.

USE OF DOGS AND HORSES

An effective method of hunting was with a well-trained dog. The animal should trail silently and not give tongue until in the midst of the flock. The turkeys then scatter and rise into the trees. Their entire attention is devoted to the dog so that the hunter can approach for an easy shot. Not all of the turkeys were cooperative. Baines (1890:353) found that some of the flock would dodge around the dog and backtrack without taking wing. A dog was also extremely useful in running down cripples, for a winged bird ran away with such rapidity that the hunter himself had no chance of finding it (Buckingham, 1842:169).

The use of a dog in conjunction with a blind has been described by Gosse (1859:300) as follows: "As a flock of turkeys is known to be very regular in habit, coming day after day to the same spot, at the same hour, the fowler who has surprised them feeding has nothing to do but to mark the place and to build up a 'blind', or screen of logs, bushes, and branches of trees. To this he resorts before day, and hides himself with his dog whom he has trained to lie as quiet as himself. Soon after it is light, the fowls come to their familiar spot, where the hunter, waiting until he gets several in line, fires, and does great execution. The dog at the same moment dashes in the midst of the flock, which rises on the wing, and takes to the nearest tree; here the birds sit gazing on the dog, with absorbed attention, unobservant of the sportsman, who thus picks them down at his leisure." Turkeys are reported to have a strong odor, and that a good dog can scent them farther than it can a flock of quail ("Old Man," 1889).

Palmer (1909:25) recorded what he considered a singular incident. A turkey flushed by hunters flew into an old field covered with broom sedge (*Andropogon*) and hid. After being pointed by the dogs, one of the men seized the turkey by its outstretched neck. It was common for turkeys on alighting from the first flight to hide if the ground cover afforded concealment. Woodward (1876) stated that after the first long flight—usually not over a quarter of a mile—the turkey will lie to a dog in heavy grass or weeds. The hunter could approach within twenty or thirty yards before the bird would break cover and sometimes would permit him to pass at that distance.

The habit of hiding was prevalent in the West where the woodlands were bordered by prairies. When a hunter succeeded in approaching a flock unobserved, the explosion of the gun sent them into a panic. Some would alight in the nearest trees, some would squat where they were if cover was available, while others would fly to a distance and hide. After shooting at the birds in the trees, those on the ground received attention. Turkeys caught on the open prairie and frightened would run to the nearest ravine where they would sit so closely that they could be almost stepped on before taking flight (Dodge, 1877:233). In October, 1873, he killed twenty-two birds from a flock discovered in a ravine and driven to the prairie. Most of them were killed when he fired into the massed running birds from his galloping horse. The remainder were birds which were kicked up from the high grass in which they had squatted. Birds flushed by a barking dog laid close after alighting and could be hunted like quail. One morning he bagged fourteen fine turkeys in a patch of grass not exceeding two acres in area.

Carter (1935:41) mentions that while in western Texas, some dogs accompanying the troops started many turkeys. They ran hard for a short time, then took wing and flew into a neighboring valley. Here, frightened and exhausted, they thrust their necks into the grass and were secured easily. Along the Colorado River in Texas, a flock of turkeys was flushed by greyhounds and a gobbler was caught after the second flight. The first flight was stated to be fully a mile (Seely, 1887).

The most spectacular method of hunting was pursuit on horseback with or without dogs. This method could be employed only in open woods or on the prairie. Adair wrote (1775:360): "The wild turkeys live on the small red acorns, and grow so fat in March that they cannot fly farther than three or four hundred yards; and not being able to take the wing again, we speedily run them down with our horses and hunting mastiffs." This type of hunting was continued in Georgia until at least 1883 (Anon., 1883). Grant (1911) has described the capture of a large gobbler on the grassy plains south of Fort Myers, Florida, with the aid of dogs, while he was on horseback. The gobbler when flushed flew one-half mile, then was too exhausted to do other than run. It proved to be very fat.

Some men crossing a wide prairie in Lake County, Indiana, noticed a flock of seven wild turkeys. Unhitching the four horses, they pursued the birds and captured five without a shot being fired (Goodspeed and Blanchard, 1882:553). Concerning a chase on an Illinois prairie in 1842, Oliver (1924:145) wrote: "I have known an instance of one being chased about three miles and then lost, although it was pursued by a man on horseback, attended by two very stout and active dogs, quite accustomed to the business. The chase commenced in the open prairie; the man having got between the bird and the woods." A favorite method of hunting in the White and Blue Mountains of Arizona was to go on horseback (Sizer, 1933:22). When a flock was flushed, it was followed until the birds tired, which did not take long in the fall when they are fat. They were then hunted on foot. On seeing a flock of six turkeys along the Nueces River, Texas, Chapman's (1933:99) guide unhitched a horse and, using it as a blind, shot one of them.

Some cowboys in Texas attempted to keep a turkey afoot as long as possible in order to tire it out. If the bird flew, the speed of the horse was increased (Anon., 1860:162). The first sign of exhaustion was drooping of the wings (Jordan, 1898). Some cowboys fastened a bullet to the end of a whip and wrapped it about the turkey's neck, while others used a lasso. Turkeys run down in this manner usually scattered widely and, hiding in the tall grass, were difficult to find. Dodge (1877:234) has described the chase in Texas. A flock having been discovered on the edge of a prairie two to three miles in extent, a detour was made so that the horsemen came upon the turkeys through a bordering woods. With a yell they dashed at the flock, so frightening some of the birds that they flew into the open prairie. Depending on the weight and fatness of the bird, the first flight was from 400 to 600 yards, at the end of which it would generally be 200 to 300 yards ahead of the horseman. As the latter approached, a second flight carried the bird scarcely more than 100 to 200 yards. Following a third flight, the turkey generally resorted to running and dodging. The rider, carrying a stick four feet long and the diameter of a finger, killed the bird by a blow on the head as it attempted to dodge the horse. On one occasion he and a companion killed five turkeys from a flock in a single chase.

The army officers on the frontier kept dogs for hunting. The coursing of turkeys in southwestern Texas in 1875 is described vividly by Elliott Roosevelt in a letter to his brother Theodore (1891:106). The party, "taking the eleven greyhounds, struck off six or eight miles into the plains, then spreading into line we alternated dogs and horses, and keeping a general direction, beat up the small oak clumps, grass clusters, or mesquite jungles as we went along. Soon, with a loud whirr of wings, three or four turkeys rose out of the grass ahead, started up by one of the greyhounds; the rest of the party closed in from all sides; dogs and men choosing each the bird they marked as theirs. The turkey, after towering a bit, with wings set struck off at a pace like a bullet, and with eyes fixed upwards the hounds coursed after them. It was whip and spur for a mile as hard as horse, man, and hound could make the pace. The turkey at last came down nearer and nearer the ground, its small wings refusing to bear the weight of the heavy body. Finally, down he came and began running; then the hounds closed in on him and forced him up again as is always the case. The second flight was not a strong one, and soon he was skimming ten or even a less number of feet from the ground. Now, came the sport of it all; the hounds were bunched and running like a pack behind him. Suddenly old 'Grimbeard,' in the heart of the pack, thought it was time for the supreme effort; with a rush he went to the front, and as a mighty spring carried him up in the air, he snapped his clean, cruel fangs, under the brave old gobbler, who by a great effort rose just out of reach. One after another in the next twenty-five yards each hound made his trial and failed. At last the old hound again made his rush, sprang up a wonderful height into the air, and cut the bird down as with a knife.

"The first flight of a turkey when being coursed is rarely more than a mile, and the second about half as long. After that, if it gets up at all again, it is for very short flights so near the ground that it is soon cut down by any hound. . . . A turkey, after coming down from his first flight . . . will run its head into a clump of bushes and stand motionless as if, since it cannot see its foes, it were itself equally invisible. During the day the turkeys are scattered all over the plains, and it is no unusual thing to get in one afternoon's ride eight or ten of them."

STILL HUNTING

Most of the turkeys in the early days were killed by still hunting (Plates 32 and 33a). A rifle was used almost exclusively because ammunition for a shotgun was too expensive. In Illinois (Oliver, 1924:159), bullets numbering 80 to 120 to the pound were used, and in Missouri (Goebel, 1877:88) 75 to 90 to the pound. Cuming (1810:30) states that at Carlisle, Pennsylvania, the inhabitants considered a man a poor shot with a rifle if he missed the head of a turkey perched on the top of the tallest forest tree. Concerning the skill of the Mississippi boatmen with a rifle, Thorpe (1855:30) wrote for the benefit of the credulous: "Cutting off a wild turkey's head with a rifleball at a hundred yards' distance, while the bird was in full flight, was not looked upon as an extraordinary feat." In pioneer days the rifle was usually rested so no bullet would be wasted. Training to shoot began at an early age. Edwards (1914:75) wrote: "When a boy was given a rifle, a certain number of bullets were [was] counted into his hand and he was expected to bring back as many deer or wild turkeys." An air gun was preferred to any other weapon by Schultz (1810: I, 123). If there were five or six turkeys in a tree, all could be secured as none was frightened by the sound.

At times a hunter regretted the size of his bag. On October 17, 1789, at Wheeling, West Virginia, May (1921:164) wrote in his journal: "Rose at day break, having been awake three hours, took my gun, & went into the woods. Kept a good lookout for Indians, but a better for turkeys. Killed four stout fellows, and wounded a fifth, which I chased till I was thoroughly blown; then turned & left him. Took the four dead ones, & came home, & found, by the time I got there, that I did not want the fifth, as I was well tired carrying the four." The method employed by Perry (1899:66) to carry a turkey was to tie together the feet and neck with basswood bark and sling the bird over his shoulder.

Numerous devices were employed to get within range of a turkey. An Illinois hunter advised sitting in front of a tree or stump when a turkey was approaching as it always expects a hunter to be behind something

(C. H. A., 1882). Some hunters would get behind a log and with a hat pound the leaves to imitate the fighting of two gobblers so naturally that a flock, especially when led by pugnacious gobblers, would come right up to them (Gilbert, 1910:8). At times a hunter could draw a turkey within range by scratching in the dry leaves in imitation of a feeding bird. It was suggested by Baines (1890:356) that when it is impossible to slip up on turkeys in a tree, "walk right ahead as though you were going to pass by them, always circling gradually nearer, and avoid getting behind them. If one hesitate or waver [sic], he is almost sure to scare his turkey when employing this method." No one stratagem was always successful. Henry C. Brockmeyer was so stimulated by the philosophy of Hegel that he was confident that it could be used in hunting turkeys and squirrels (Harris, 1890:xiii). The odds against securing a turkey under modern conditions are such that the hunter is philosophical of necessity.

A novice had to learn that a definite procedure must be followed in shooting when there was a flock in a tree. Collot (1826:128) described his experience hunting turkeys on the Ohio. The birds were in such numbers that the "trees were literally rendered grey." They were easily approached and killed, but to secure several it was necessary to shoot at first those on the lowest limbs. Having committed the error of firing at those in the top of the tree, he was severely censored by the hunter accompanying him. The latter was so skilful in imitating the voice of the gobblers that, standing under the same tree, within less than half an hour he had it covered with turkeys. Following his instructions, enough were soon obtained for the entire crew of the boat.

Turkeys usually entered and departed from a cornfield in single file. The hunter placing himself in line could do great execution. Theophilus Powers in one shot killed seven turkeys from a flock running from a cornfield (Williams & Bros., 1881:538). Baiting was common practice and was particularly effective if corn or other grain was placed in a trench. In Missouri, Abner Smith baited a flock of turkeys for several days then shot into them with an old musket loaded with slugs and killed fourteen (National Hist. Co., 1884.1:157). A number of turkeys have been killed with a single bullet, but this feat owes as much to luck as skill. Isaac Clay shot at a flock, the bullet passing through the heads of three birds (Evers, 1897:257). J. H. Graham shot at a flock of turkeys in line with their heads up. He aimed at the neck and killed five large birds in one discharge of his rifle (Turnbo, 1904:80).

According to Gilbert (1910:9), when turkeys were feeding in a baited trench, the hunter gave a low whistle to make the birds alert. The nearest turkey was shot in the head with the chance of hitting several more. As many as eight were killed in this way with one bullet. The Moniteau Hunting Club offered a prize to the person who could kill the greatest number of turkeys at one shot with a rifle. It was won by Milton Wood, who was so fortunate as to kill four, all shot through the head (Ford, 1936:68). It is common for turkeys to travel in single file when the sole objective is to move from one place to another. Strong (1960:35) in Oklahoma, encountered a flock of 250 to 300 turkeys in unbroken succession, following a trail in single file. A narrow, well-defined game trail through grassland in northwestern Texas, used chiefly by turkeys, is shown by Jackson (1959:17).

Use of Traps

Turkeys were also captured by means of pen traps. These were used as far west as Texas (Manning, 1919:183) and Colorado (Burget, 1957:36). The first use of what appears to have been a pen trap is mentioned by Beverley (1705: IV, 73): "They have many pretty devices besides the Gun, to take wild Turkeys; And among others a Friend of mine invented a great Trap, wherein he at times caught many Turkeys, and particularly seventeen at one time, but he could not contrive it so, as to let others in after he had entrapped the first flock, until they were taken out."

This trap was probably like those that Perry (1899:23, 24) had in operation in Lorain County, Ohio, in January, 1839. They were built of poles and provided with drop doors attached by a string to a trigger. A trail of straw, which undoubtedly retained some grain, was made to lure the turkeys into the pens. Tracks in the snow showed that at one trap fifteen turkeys had entered, but the covering poles were too light and the turkeys by constantly jumping against them had forced an opening through which all escaped. A companion found twelve turkeys in another trap. They commenced to break out and he killed five of them by shooting. In December, 1841, the turkeys would not enter pens because mast was too abundant. Whittlesey (1843:57) described operation of the trap as follows: "They entered at an open door in the side, which was suspended by a string that led to a catch within. This string and catch were covered with chaff, which induced them to enter, and while engaged in scratching about the chaff to get at the grain mingled with it, some unlucky companion would strike the catch and let the door down behind them all."

The most popular traps were the trench pens (Plate 33b). Audubon (1831:12) gives a full description of their construction and operation. They were built in the woods where the turkeys were accustomed to roost. Trees 4 to 5 inches in diameter, cut into lengths of 12 or 14 feet, were piled upon each other to form a square structure about 4 feet high. The top, closed with similar poles placed 3 or 4 inches apart, was made immovable by two heavy logs. At one interior side of the pen, a trench 18 inches deep and of the same width, with an abrupt rise, was continued for some distance on the exterior where the bottom rose gradually to the level ground. On the interior next to the wall, a bridge of sticks about a foot in width was laid over the trench. The bridge, when the turkeys were racing about in the interior, prevented the birds from falling into the trench and perceiving a means of escape. Corn was placed inside the pen, scattered in the trench and beyond, sometimes to the distance of a mile.

When a turkey discovered the corn, he gave a cluck to inform the flock, which followed the trail of grain and eventually entered the trap. Having satisfied their appetite, the turkeys try to force their way through the top of the pen and run around over the bridge seeking a means of escape. A turkey never looks downward so that the entrance passage remains unnoticed. The largest number that Audubon ever caught at one time was seven although he heard of a catch of eighteen. A trap that he had under observation one winter caught seventy-six turkeys within a period of about two months. There is doubt that one turkey, having found the food, would call the others. All the turkeys which I have seen feeding were silent and more inclined to drive others from the food than to share it. According to Gosse (1859:57), the pen was not used in summer as the turkeys were in too poor condition then to be edible.

The pens were frequently made of rails. The turkeys, as a last resort, would fly continuously against the covering poles until exhausted. One or two were usually found dead the morning following capture

(Anburey, 1791:304). Jones (1898:192) knew of fifteen to be taken in one haul. He stated that the pen should be made of old timber as axe marks were objectionable. The wariness of the turkeys varied. In northern Ohio, the fall of 1827, Lewis (1858:34) built a pen to save his wheat. The first catch was nine turkeys and the second twelve. Thereafter, no turkeys returned to the field. Antrim (1872:21) wrote that a dozen could be caught at a time; however, the pen was not effective very long in the same locality because the turkeys became too cautious to enter it.

The number of turkeys caught in a pen at one time varied greatly. Sometimes the entire flock would be caught and sometimes only a part. Six to ten was considered a fair catch, but in one instance more than twenty were trapped (Ford, 1936:68). Ann Dickens (1903) stated that in Clinton County, Iowa, her husband's trap once held twenty-four birds. In Arkansas as many as fifteen to twenty were caught at one time (Williams, 1930:281), and in Ontario, nineteen (Anon., 1858:34). In the latter case, the turkeys were tolled to the trap by scattering a sheaf of wheat in a line running from the pen. It is doubtful that as many as fifty were taken at one time as stated by Atkinson (1876:75). A pen built in Fairfield County, Ohio, caught over two hundred turkeys (Scott, 1877:222); however, the length of time that the pen was in operation is not stated. Blane (1824:279) wrote that he had known seven to eight turkeys to enter a trap in Kentucky within twenty-four hours. It is probable that this represents an average catch.

Some large catches were made without constructing a pen. A Maryland planter, using corn, enticed a flock into his tobacco shed and closed the door (Anon., 1906:331). Bushnell (1889:64) wrote: "Mrs. Samuel Everitt caught twenty-three turkeys at one time, trapping them in a corn crib, luring them to the spot by sprinkling a few kernels of corn around." Six were captured in an old log stable baited with corn and provided with a trap door. Seizing the penned birds was accompanied by physical punishment (Newby, 1916:37). He stated: "I have never seen such a beating and flapping of wings as when I went in the stable to catch them." A young man in Georgia was severely buffeted when he attempted to remove from a rail pen a catch consisting of two large gobblers, seven hens, and four young (Herring, 1918:71). Audubon (1831:33) expressed his respect for the power of the turkey as follows:

393

"The great strength of a full grown Turkey-cock renders it no easy matter to hold it when but slightly wounded; and once or twice I have thought myself in jeopardy, when on entering a pen in which six or seven large cocks had imprisoned themselves, their flutterings and struggles rendered it extremely difficult to secure them."

A square pen in the shape of a cone, baited with corn, has been described by Cory (1896:73). Construction took place gradually to permit the turkeys to become accustomed to the trap. On entering the 12- to 18-inch opening at the top, the birds could not escape by jumping with spread wings. He was unable to make a capture with a pen of this type but was assured by old residents and hunters in Florida that it was effective.

Shufeldt (1911) was informed by a friend that the decrease of the turkey was due to the use of fishhooks by the Negroes. One method was to suspend a hook baited with a piece of dough about the size of a small acorn. The line to which the hook was attached was looped over a limb above that on which the turkey roosted, the other end of the line being fastened to a peg in the ground. The bait was within easy reach of a turkey on the roosting limb. The other method was to bait the hook with a grain of corn soaked in water to render it sufficiently soft for the insertion of the hook. In this case the line to which the hook was attached was placed on the ground and fastened at one end. It is difficult to believe that an adult turkey struggling in mid-air would not break the "very small fishhook" on the cord. One of the early settlers of Warren County, Pennsylvania, caught a wild turkey in a steel trap baited with oats (Schenck and Rann, 1887:517). Savage (1934:219), who lived in Van Buren County, Iowa, wrote in his journal on January 27, 1861, that he loaned L. Wells two big steel traps which he set for turkeys. No extensive use of this promising instrument appears to have been made. An occasional turkey was taken by methods too unimportant to mention.

Drive Hunting

Drive hunting has become very popular in the Southeast. From three to twelve gunners are stationed 75 to 100 yards apart across a wooded creek valley or in a semicircle in the open woods. The drivers, six to twelve in number and placed 50 to 100 yards apart, advance whistling, tapping the trunks of trees, and making other noises. Stoddard (n.d.)

writes: "The most spectacular effect is when the great birds come over in their beautiful glide with rigidly bowed wings. Anyone who has seen a flight composed mostly of old gobblers, with lighting effects right to bring out all their gorgeous coloration, has witnessed one of the most beautiful and spectacular sights of the sporting world. They may well be excused if they become so absorbed in the spectacle that guns are forgotten and the birds pass by without a shot being fired. The great birds come with deceptive speed, and the tyro usually shoots well behind his selected bird unless carefully coached by an experienced person."

Use of Live Decoys

Live decoys were sometimes used, but it does not appear to have been a general custom. Dr. R. Percy Sargent of Natchez, Mississippi, informed Lewis (1863:130) that he placed a tame turkey in an advantageous place, with a long cord attached to a leg. On pulling the cord the turkey would "cluck," and any gobbler within hearing would come to meet it. The use of a tethered tame gobbler is mentioned by "Southern" (1896), and by B. T. Jones (1922). A hunter in Alabama shot a wild gobbler that attacked a tame one which he was using as a decoy ("Edisto," 1888). A certain Sipe, in New York County, Pennsylvania, carried a tame turkey on his back, and when he used his turkey-bone caller, the turkey would answer. While crawling on his hands and knees, he was shot by another hunter (Gibson, 1886:682). A dead turkey propped into a natural position was used with success by Baines (1899).

Turkey Callers

It is probable that no method of hunting the turkey has had as long popularity as calling the bird within range by a hunter concealed in a blind. Bone tubes (Plate 34a) with one or more holes in the side have been found at archeological sites from the Atlantic to the Pacific. It is generally assumed that they were used to imitate the calls of birds, especially that of the turkey. They have been found, however, in regions where the turkey never existed. Regarding the instruments found in the Chama Valley, New Mexico, Jeançon (1923:27) wrote: "The manner in which they were used is as follows: The opening at the top of the bone is placed tightly against the lower lip, a little below the opening of the mouth; then drawing the upper lip down with a slight puckering of the whole

395

mouth, and sucking in with a short, chirping breath, the tone produced will resemble that of a mother turkey calling its young. By careful practice in covering and uncovering, more or less, the hole in the side, and a slight difference in the forming of the lips, it is an easy matter to imitate all of the calls of the wild turkey. These turkey calls are still in use in some of the pueblos and are especially used by the older men, who imitate the different calls in a remarkable manner."

Many tubes with from one to five lateral perforations, made from the femur, ulna, or radius of the turkey, were found at the Zuñi pueblo of Hawikuh (Hodge, 1920:121). Archaeologists usually call them flutes or bird callers. F. H. H. Roberts, Jr. (1932:138, Pl. 47) states that they are known as turkey callers. The tubes with a single perforation were said by the modern Pueblo Indians to have been used in decoying wild turkeys (Kidder, 1932:253, Fig. 211). Many of the same type of perforated bones have been found during archaeological excavations east of the Mississippi. Concerning "yelpers" made from a wing bone, Speck (1925:55) says: "Specimens of these interesting and aboriginal callers, uniformly similar, have been obtained from practically all the tribal bodies in Virginia." His illustrations of callers made from the secondary wing bone (radius) of the turkey, used by the Pamunkey and Mattapony Indians, are not perforated (Speck, 1928:356). In 1904 the Yuchi Indians, Creek Nation, Indian Territory, were calling turkeys with the wing bone of a turkey; also by grating a piece of stone on the end of a nail driven into a piece of wood (Speck, 1909:22).

The method and frequency of calling are subject to individual opinion. One hunter (M., 1881) writes: "The call which is superior to all others, when in experienced hands, is the larger bone of the second joint of a turkey's wing. The bone is first trimmed at each end, and then cleaned of all particles of flesh and marrow. One end is then inserted into a tube of cedar or elder, about as long and but little larger than a man's middle finger. The other end, to make the call, is placed between the lips and the air drawn in.

"With any but young turkeys you should never make more than three notes at a time, and at intervals of from thirty minutes to an hour. Old gobblers are more successfully brought within range by a *cluck* than any other note, except in the spring, when they will come to the yelp of the hen. The *cluck* is never made by the hen, but only by the gobblers, two or more of whom generally go together. It is a note that cannot be made by the hunter, except after careful observation and practice."

The advice of Jordan (1881) is to be near a roost at daybreak when the turkeys will utter occasional clucks, and then yelp before flying down. A hunter skilled in clucking will command their attention, and if he clucks and yelps more frequently than they do, they will alight near him on leaving the roost. He had no faith in limiting the number of clucks and yelps. They could be made as frequently as desired provided that they were exact imitations of the calls of a turkey.

Turkeys, especially the gobbler, are most easily called in during the spring mating season. Regarding his experience in the Big Cypress Swamp, Kennard (1915:5) wrote that the small wing bone of a turkey hen was used for a "yelper," but his guide could make most enticing calls with a leaf, blade of grass, and many other objects. In February little coaxing was necessary, the old gobblers coming on the run with slight inducement.

A turkey is quick to detect a false note on the part of the caller. Latrobe (1835:268) gives us the result of calling by a novice: "The practised hunter will induce them to approach him as he steals through the grass, by a skilful imitation of their gobble and piping. But, often as, buried in the thick cane brake, and watching one of those little openings where the birds sun themselves, I heard the tread, rustle, and voices of the turkeys around me, and have attempted to allure them to me by an imitation of their notes, I never succeeded in a single instance. I set up, for example, a weak, amorous, sentimental piping like the female—it was in vain! no broad-backed, round-tailed, burly turkey-cock made his appearance. I gobbled in the most seducing fashion, throwing as much devotion into my tones as I could contrive; I essayed to compress a thousand blandishments into the few gutteral sounds that were permissible, but these, far from eliciting any sympathetic response, seemed to put the whole gang to instant though cautious flight; for I invariably observed that very briefly after an attempt of the latter kind, every sound became hushed, but the beating of my own impatient and disappointed heart. It was evident that there was no mistaking me for a turkey, and all the birds that I ever brought to the mess, were the fruits of a less guileful, more straight-forward and summary mode of proceeding."

I have tried several types of callers, some of which produced notes which I thought would be effective. Occasionally the turkeys were in sight, but always they remained disgustingly indifferent. The calls of the hen and young can be imitated quite readily with instruments, but the gobble is another matter. Davis (1937.1) states that the best sounds are made with the throat. Proficiency results only from innate skill or long practice. Aside from detecting a false note, the turkey has the ability to locate the exact direction and distance from which a "perfect" call issues. Experienced hunters have told me that a gobbler will fly in and alight within a few feet of the blind. Browning (1928:143) and a companion were hunting turkeys in Garrett County, Maryland, in the spring of 1804. After he had started calling, "A gobbler heard me, and answered by a continued gobble after gobble. I told Sam that he would fly over us if he had no hen with him; and directly over he came, alighting within a rod or two of us." According to Geombeck (1890), it is unusual for a gobbler to respond to calls when rain is falling.

Just how early the whites began the use of an instrument to call turkeys is difficult to determine. In 1787, Beale Bosley was calling turkeys with a "turkey-bone" (Plate 34b) on the site of Nashville, Tennessee. He was nearly shot by an Indian in following up what he thought was an answering turkey (Putnam, 1859:274). Audubon (1831:12) states that hunters use the "second joint" wing bone. And: "In managing this, however, no fault must be committed, for Turkeys are quick in distinguishing counterfeit sounds, and when *half civilized* are very wary and cunning." In Alabama a reed or the "thigh-bone" of a turkey was used to imitate the call of the hen (Gosse, 1859:301).

The number of types of callers that have been used is large. Kit Carson called up turkeys with a quill (Drannan, 1900:35). The caller used by Jordan (1881) consisted of the radius from the wing bone of a turkey, and two pieces of reed each 1.5 to 2.0 inches in length (Fig. 15). The ends of the bone were removed by filing notches. The tube was cleaned and the ends smoothed with a file. One end of the bone was inserted into a small reed and the latter in turn into a larger reed. The joints were

Fig. 15.—*Jordan wing bone and cane caller.*

398

beveled and wrapped with waxed thread. The "cluck" was made by placing the end of the tongue on the end of the bone and giving with the tongue a "quick suck and jerk." His reluctance to give directions for making the other notes of the turkey is understandable.

Turpin (1927) runs the wing bone through a cork which is inserted in a walnut tube with an inner diameter of three-fourths of an inch. Another Turpin design is shown in Fig. 16. A caller much used formerly in the

Fig. 16.—*Turpin caller.*

south is made from a piece of fine-grained hardwood 6 to 8 inches long and hollowed with a tapered bit. The interior dimension of the large end is three-fourths of an inch. Into the small end is inserted a piece of cane for a mouthpiece ("Clip," 1886) (Fig. 17). Lowndes (1881) states that the tone depends on the size of the mouthpiece.

The "*yunk-yunk-yunk*" of the turkey can be imitated by sucking air through a new, common clay pipe: "A hand over . . . the pipe-bowl regulates the volume of sound, which is produced by an interrupted sucking between the compressed lips, difficult to describe in detail" (Sandys and Van Dyke, 1904:274). The bowl of a clay pipe can also be scraped on a piece of slate to imitate the call of a turkey (C. X., 1881).

Another type of caller consists of a cow horn with a flexible tube having

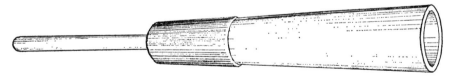

Fig. 17.—*Cane and wooden tube caller.*

a wing bone for a mouthpiece (Fig. 18). A highly recommended caller consists of a section 2.0 to 2.5 inches in length, cut from a cowhorn. The narrow end is closed with a thin piece of wood into the middle of which is inserted a wooden peg, round on the end and sufficiently long to project beyond the open end of the horn. The device is operated by holding the horn cup in one hand and rubbing the tip of the peg on a piece of slate held in the other hand ("Observer," 1873; Anon., 1894.1). A modification of this caller is one-half of the shell of a coconut into the bottom of which is fastened a peg made from the branch of a rhododendron bush (Plate 35a). The end of the peg has a knife edge. This device is also drawn across a piece of slate (Shiner, 1958). Sometimes the peg is attached to the exterior of the bottom. One of the simplest callers consists of a cedar peg inserted in the end of a small corncob. The cob is held at an angle and the end of the peg drawn across a piece of slate held in a cupped hand (Plate 35b). The top end of the cob is sometimes hollowed out.

The essential part of a diaphragm caller is a sheet of thin rubber. "Clip" (1886) wrote: "Some hunters prefer a thin piece of rubber—what the dentists call 'rubber dam'—with which to call an old gobbler, and

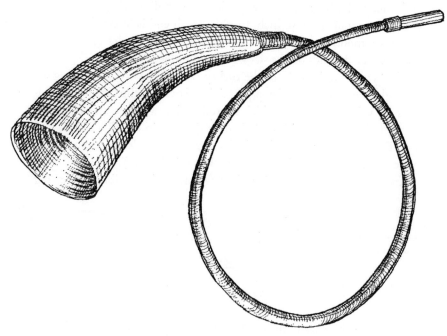

Fig. 18.—*Wing bone and cow horn caller.*

many good hunters contend that they can call more perfectly with this than any other device. The call is made with this by taking a small piece of the rubber dam, holding it between each forefinger and thumb and placing it flatways across the lips and blowing lightly over the top. I have heard some fine calling made in this way." Murphy (1882:24) states that the edge of the rubber sheet should be folded and the turkey calls "mouthed." Callers are also made by clamping the rubber diaphragm on a U-shaped piece of metal provided with lugs which are folded to hold the sheet. One device (Plate 36a) has a thin sheet of supple plastic in place of rubber. The caller is used by placing it in the roof of the mouth with the diaphragm forward and puffing. Manipulation is difficult and considerable practice is required to obtain the proper sounds. Some hunters can make successful calls with a leaf plucked from a tree.

There are several kinds of box callers. The following directions are given by A. J. W., (1890) for the making and use of one type: "Get a piece of white pine, or [but] poplar is better, 1 in. thick and 2 in. wide, and with a chisel and sharp knife make a mortise. . . . One side should be left about ⅛ in. wide and the other shaved down until it sounds exactly like a turkey. A slit should be cut in the middle of the thin side to give it a coarse kind of sound. A piece of slate ½ in. wide and 3 in. long is used on the thin side in about the same way as a bow is used on a violin, and by scraping in the middle the gobbler is imitated, and on near each end a hen is imitated. Great care should be taken to keep the slate scraped on the guard of your gun, so that it will not be too smooth, so as to squak. In a little while one gets very expert in the use of it, so that by one scrape with the slate flat on the edge of the caller, and two with the slate tilted on edge and three flat again you have the perfect call of a turkey, *keow, kee, kee, keow, keow, keow*." A hollowed block of black walnut that is rubbed on the gunstock has been illustrated and described although the author expressed a preference for calling with his mouth (H. L., 1890). The walnut caller was recommended by a sportsman (O. O. S., 1894). One of the box callers is simple to operate and even an amateur can produce with it calls which resemble closely those of a hen turkey. It consists of a cedar box with a cover held at one end by a screw. The lid is moved back and forth over the chalked edges of the box (Plate 36b).

A thorough exposition of calling and callers is given by Davis

(1949:149). Directions for making callers and their use are given by Latham (1956:176), Bruette (1923:62), and Shiner (1963). Turpin (1928.1) has illustrated and described two types of callers. Four types are shown by Cope (1932). He inclines to the belief that the box caller with a lid is the easiest to manipulate properly.

Vitality of Wounded Turkeys

The vitality of a wild turkey is astonishing. When a shotgun is used, the bird should be shot in the head if conditions permit. There is little hope of recovering a winged turkey except by the aid of a dog. Audubon (1831:10) wrote: "Turkeys are easily killed if shot in the head, the neck or the upper part of the breast; but if hit in the hind parts only, they often fly so far as to be lost to the hunter." Browning (1928:143) broke the wing of a turkey with his rifle. It floundered into Deep Creek, swam across, and escaped in an alder thicket. An old gobbler killed at Ogden's Landing, Kentucky, had five No. oo shot in its thighs and showed the scars of nine different rifle balls ("Ex.," 1887). Davis (1937) shot a turkey through the body with a rifle and it flew four hundred yards before falling. A bird shot in Mississippi flew the same distance before dropping dead (Wood, 1899). Sizer (1933) mentions that a BB shot passed through both eyes of a turkey without killing it.

A shot through the heart may not be fatal immediately. A hunter in Perry County, Pennsylvania, shot a turkey which his dog caught after a chase of two hundred yards. When the bird was served on the table, a No. 4 shot was found embedded in the heart (C. C. R., 1895). It is stated that Z. W. Pumphrey, while living in Webster County, Missouri, shot a turkey from a flock. It rose straight upward for about one hundred yards, then fell to the ground. The bullet had crushed the heart (Turnbo, 1904:73). A hunter in Louisiana shot with a rifle a gobbler sitting in a large oak. The bird circled upward to a great height before falling. It was found that the bullet had passed through the body within an inch of the heart (W. H. R., 1878).

Several examples are given by Everitt (1928:107) of turkeys which were shot through the body with one and two balls and which flew away to die at a distance, or remained on the perch for some time before falling. A good discussion of the use of rifles is given by Davis (1949:213), and he mentions cases of the escape of turkeys that were wounded mortally.

Waste of Turkeys by Hunters

There are conspicuous examples of waste of turkeys in the early days. Failure to visit the pens at regular intervals led to the death of many birds. Audubon (1831:13) wrote: "When these birds are abundant, the owners of the pens sometimes become satiated with their flesh, and neglect to visit the pens for several days, in some cases for weeks. The poor captives thus perish for want of food; . . . I have, more than once, found four or five, and even ten, dead in a pen, through inattention. Where Wolves or Lynxes are numerous, they are apt to secure the prize before the owner of the trap arrives." Smith (1936:176) expressed his indignation on finding on his land in Mississippi a pyramidal rail pen, with the usual trench, within which were five grown turkeys so starved that they could scarcely stand.

Where turkeys were abundant, settlers frequently removed the breasts for smoking and drying, and discarded the remainder. Hughes (1884:26) stated that at Concepcion, Duval County, Texas: "There are quantities of wild turkey in the woods; they run in flocks, and are so common that if a man shoots one he generally cooks the breast and throws away the rest." This was the usual practice when a turkey was looked upon as camp meat. Eight or ten turkeys would be killed and the breasts only utilized (Connellee, 1930:93). In Montgomery County, Missouri, in 1825, if a turkey shot by a hunter did not weigh at least fifteen pounds, he would not bother to take it home (Duden, 1834:82). Poults were considered choice food. Evans (1923:4) was informed by a Florida hunter that he killed seventy-seven young turkeys in the summer of 1921. This was waste; the birds should have been allowed to attain a respectable size. An unusual example of wildlife expenditure is given by Williams (1951:84). In 1882, two or three weeks prior to the arrival of his party at Lake Flirt, Florida, a band of Indians killed hundreds of turkeys and made no use of them. The ostensible purpose was to keep white hunters from the region.

The greatest waste occurred in the camps of sportsmen and market hunters from the spoilage of the turkeys in warm weather. One writer

("Almo," 1886) states that in southern Texas in the winter of 1885–86, he saw wagonloads of turkeys, holding sixty to one hundred birds each, sold at 25 cents apiece. They were half spoiled before purchasers were found. Another wrote from Jayton, Kent County, Texas: "Many of them [hunters] are hunting to supply the markets, and will load a wagon at the turkey roosts in a night or two. The continued warm weather spoiled load after load before reaching the markets, the railroad being eighty-five miles distant. It is not uncommon to see the game abandoned in camp because spoiled" ("Stockman," 1890). Because of a shortage of food, the men in Irving's (1944:144) party, while in Okfuskee County, Oklahoma, were alert for turkeys and eager for dinner. The entry of November 3, 1832, reads: "A few days since, they despised such small game & I have seen dead turkeys left behind on marching." In January, 1882, a party of hunters killed eighty-seven turkeys at Eagle Lake, Colorado County, Texas, of which number twenty-eight birds spoiled (Pratt, 1882). About 1886, Judge James R. Dougherty saw twenty-seven turkeys left to spoil in a hunting camp on the Nueces River, Texas (Anon., 1945:18). H. T. Bailey (1914:74), in Florida, saw thirteen wild turkeys, brought in by sportsmen, thrown on a garbage dump as they had spoiled from the heat. In Oklahoma, when the weather turned warm, sometimes an entire load of turkeys was thrown away by market hunters (Nelson, 1953:85). In the fall of 1880 a party of hunters camped on Skeleton Creek, Logan County, Oklahoma, and filled two wagons with turkeys. The weather turned warm and all the birds spoiled (Henderson, 1925:283). Many more were killed later. The large losses through hunting for the market are fortunately a thing of the past.

SHOOTING SEASONS

Differences of opinion exist as to the best time of the year for an open season. Some states permit the shooting of gobblers only during early spring when mating is taking place. The theory is that at this season there is a minimum of disturbance to the nesting hens, and that the harvesting of the surplus males is biologically sound (Allen, 1956–57). The ideal season in the Southeast, according to Davis (1949:308), is from January 1 to March 15, with hens protected. If the season is extended to April 15, there is the possibility that all the adult males will be destroyed.

It is easier to shoot a turkey in the spring than in the fall. The split season in Alabama resulted in the following kills (Allen, 1959):

	Turkeys		Turkeys
Fall of 1957	1,540	Fall of 1958	1,750
Spring of 1958	2,921	Spring of 1959	3,725

The first and last dates on which turkeys may be shot in states having an annual open season are given in Table 27. Many states have split seasons and varying lengths of open seasons within districts within the state so that the inclusive dates are not always statewide. Most of the southern states have a spring season in the belief that the shooting of gobblers at this time is not harmful to the breeding potential.

TABLE 27

HUNTING SEASONS IN VARIOUS STATES

State	Year	Length of season
Alabama	1959–60	November 10–January 1; March 20–April 20
Arizona	1960	October 15–18
Florida	1960–61	November 7–January 2; April 1–9
Georgia	1958–59	November 1–February 25
Louisiana	1960	April 2–8
Maryland	1960	October 5–31
Mississippi	1961	April 1–26
Missouri	1960	April 27–29
New Mexico	1960	September 24–November 27
North Carolina	1960–61	November 24–February 15
Pennsylvania	1960	October 29–November 26
South Carolina	1960–61	November 23–April 15
Texas	1960	November 16–December 5
Virginia	1960–61	November 21–January 31
West Virginia	1960–61	October 1–January 7

There is a limited amount of information available on the relative advantage of using a rifle or a shotgun in hunting. Jantzen (1956.3:7) found in Arizona that the crippling loss was 11.5 per cent with a shotgun and 7.5 per cent with a rifle. As a whole, the loss was 10 per cent. Hunters using a shotgun had a success of 41.4 per cent, and using a rifle 25.7 per cent. During the 1954 season, the crippling loss was 15.4 per cent. The average distance of shots with rifles was eighty-five yards (Jantzen,

1955.1:3). The loss in Virginia of cripples and dead birds not recovered was 10 per cent of the number bagged, or about 3 per cent of the total fall population (Mosby and Handley, 1943:42).

Hunting Success

Hunter success varies greatly. The fall of 1946 only 5 per cent of the hunters in West Virginia bagged a turkey (Glover, 1947.1). Not many hunters pursue the turkey in Colorado owing to the difficulties in hunting it; however, success is between 60 and 70 per cent (Kimball, 1958). During the 1954 season in Arizona, the number of turkeys shot by 410 hunters was 645, or 1.6 birds per hunter (Jantzen, 1955.1). Montana had an open season in 1958 with about 500 hunters participating (Woodgerd, 1959). Of the approximately 100 turkeys killed about 70 per cent were shot with shotguns and the remainder with rifles. There was no difference in crippling loss. About 70 per cent were juveniles. It required about fifty man-hours of hunting to secure a turkey. The first open season in South Dakota was held in 1954. Here fourteen man-days were required to kill a bird (Zieman, 1955). In 1958, 561 turkeys were killed in this state with a hunter success of 28.6 per cent. It required 2.6 days of hunting to bag a bird (Novak, 1960). Hunter success in Wyoming was 40.6 per cent in 1955, 60.4 per cent in 1956, 44.1 per cent in 1957 (Anon., 1958.1:18), and 37.0 per cent in 1959 (Anon., 1960.2). The successful sportsman hunted 1.77 days and the unsuccessful one 2.05 days.

In Alabama the average hunter spent 3.8 hours per hunting day, and 51 hours were required to kill a turkey (Younger, 1960). New York had an open season in Allegany and Cattaraugus counties running October 5–7, 1959. Over 2,000 permits were issued. Although only 125 turkeys were tallied, it was estimated that 250 to 300 were killed (Hyde, 1960). It cost $186.98 to kill a gobbler in Texas (Vessels, 1951) where almost all of the hunting is on the large ranches, and a fee is required.

Sex and Age of Turkeys Shot

Normally, 50 to 70 per cent of the turkeys killed are juveniles. During the hunting seasons 1947–54 in Arizona, an average of 59.6 per cent of the kill was juvenile (Jantzen, 1956.1). Only 20.5 per cent of the 1955 kill was juvenile, indicating a season of poor reproduction. Juveniles comprised at least 57 per cent of the kill in West Virginia in 1953 (Dahl,

TABLE 28
Approximate Annual Kill in the United States
Turkeys killed and estimated populations in various states in 1958
(Fish and Wildlife Service, 1959).

State	Kill	Population	State	Kill	Population
Alabama	5,711	54,310	New Mexico	2,200	25,000
Arizona	727	27,000	New York	—	3,000
Arkansas	389	—	North Carolina	2,500	15,000
California	—	1,500	North Dakota	88	—
Colorado	343	—	Ohio	—	300
Florida	20,200	74,500	Pennsylvania	13,000	40,000
Georgia	3,000	25,000	South Carolina	1,200	17,000
Indiana	—	25	South Dakota	640	5,000
Kansas	—	114	Tennessee	87	8,500
Kentucky	—	1,350	Texas	6,200	100,000
Louisiana	215	—	Utah	—	500
Maryland	575	7,500	Virginia	1,679	15,000
Michigan	—	600	West Virginia	1,499	12,000
Mississippi	1,425	20,000	Wyoming	1,638	—
Montana	100	—	Total	63,416	453,249

1954). In this state the kill in 1954 consisted of 71 per cent juveniles, and in 1956 of 50 per cent (Bailey, 1957.1). Immatures are more vulnerable to hunting than adults, and among adults, males more so than females. The limited data available do show clearly now that males of all age classes are less easily shot than females. The turkeys sexed during four hunting seasons in Virginia showed 57.7 per cent females. As pointed out by Mosby and Handley (1943:39), hunters frequently mistake a first-year gobbler for a female, so that the per cent of males may not be accurate. The kills in Wyoming during the seasons 1955, 1956, and 1957 showed 43.7, 54.1, and 49.9 per cent respectively of males (Anon., 1958.1:19). During the 1953–54 season in Virginia, 275 old females to 191 old males were shot (McDowell, 1956:24).

The largest kill is made during the first day of the season, then the number fades. In Pennsylvania, 50 per cent of the kill took place the first day and 88.88 per cent during the first week (H. A. Roberts, 1957:22). During the 1959 season in Wyoming, 45.0 per cent of the kill was made the opening day, and 16.7 per cent the following day (Gustafson, 1961.1).

Bailey (1959:4) found in West Virginia that 60 to 65 per cent of the kill in a normal season is made during the first seven days. The approximate annual kills in the United States are shown in Table 28.

In Table 28, some states reported kills and no population estimates while others did the opposite primarily because there was no open season. Assuming that the omissions cancel each other, the kill was 14 per cent of the population. Pennsylvania killed 33 per cent of the population. This state releases several thousand game farm turkeys prior to the opening of the hunting season so that the inroad on the wild population is not nearly as great as the figures indicate. For example, this state during the biennium 1958–59 released 13,321 turkeys while the kill for the period was 27,236 birds (Anon., 1960.3). Kerns (1959) reported that in Maryland 715 surplus gobblers were released prior to the 1958 season and that the total kill was 511 birds or 71 per cent.

16

Management

THE ESSENTIAL PRECURSOR OF MANAGEMENT is the passage of laws protecting game, for without them few species could persist. The earliest act to protect the wild turkey was passed in colonial New York on September 18, 1708. The killing of wild turkeys was prohibited "within the Countyes of Suffolk, Queens Count[y] and Kings County" except between August 1 and April 1 (Carroll et al., 1894:619). The early laws were concerned with protection in one or more counties where the need was greatest. Some states still have laws applicable to certain counties rather than to the state as a whole. In 1838, Pennsylvania passed her first law which protected turkeys in Dauphin and Adams counties from January 15 to September 1. Gradually other counties were added until 1873 when the birds were protected throughout the state from January 1 to October 1. Missouri in 1851 passed a law, applicable to St. Louis County only, protecting turkeys from February 1 to September 1. In 1854, Alabama prohibited the killing of turkeys or capturing them in pens, traps, or snares, in Baldwin, Mobile, and Washington counties between April 1 and October 1. Protection was extended to fourteen counties in 1877 and to nineteen in 1879. Sunflower County, Mississippi, went so far as to limit hunting to its residents. In 1856 any person not a citizen of the county was subject to a fine of $50 for camping within its boundaries for the purpose of hunting turkeys or other game. Maiming or killing a turkey between May 1 and September 1 brought a fine of $25.00 (Halsell, 1951:106). Turkeys had become so scarce in New Jersey by 1874 that hunting was prohibited for a period of six years.

Legal Protection

Baiting, building blinds, and trapping or snaring of wild turkeys was prohibited in Pennsylvania in 1869. The eggs were protected in Warren County, North Carolina, in 1883. An emergency act to protect the starving turkeys in Virginia until February 2, 1912, did not become effective until January 20. Late attention was given to daily and seasonal bag limits. Pennsylvania in 1897 permitted taking two turkeys daily but there was no season limit. In 1905 the limit was one per day and four per season. South Carolina in 1910 permitted two birds daily. A hunter in De Soto County, Florida, was allowed ten turkeys per year, and in Marion County one daily. A statewide act of 1913 stipulated two gobblers per day and five in a season. Kentucky in 1916 protected turkeys until November 15, 1920, when two per season could be taken. Because the number of turkeys failed to increase, protection was extended by several four-year periods. Texas in 1919 placed the season limit at three gobblers, and protected hens. The daily limit in Virginia in 1920 was two. In 1924 the daily limit was the same but the season limit was six. The dates for broad protection are given in Table 29.

Winter Feeding

When serious management of turkey populations was begun, it was assumed that supplemental winter feeding would be highly beneficial. As on several other phases of management, opinion has been reversed. Feeding has been practiced most extensively in Pennsylvania. Conlin and Morton (1935) have described the following types of feeders: hopper shelter and feeder, wire basket, suspended tray, crib-hopper, box, and rack. Feeding shelters can be protected by a fence which admits turkeys but excludes deer, the chief competitor for the food (Dittmar, 1942). Detailed drawings of gravity feeders are shown by Tiller and Springs (1960). The great increase in the turkey population of the Edwards Plateau from 1920 to 1948 was thought to have been due to supplemental feeding (Walker, 1948.1:12). Ligon (1946:64) thought that winter feeding was sometimes desirable. On the White River Indian Reservation, Arizona, 1,080 bushels of oats were fed to approximately 8,000 turkeys during the winter of 1939–40. Because of the more abundant mast, little feeding was required during the following three winters. Funds for

TABLE 29
STATEWIDE PROTECTION

State	Year	Closed Season
Alabama	1907	March 1–December 1
Arizona	1887	March 1–September 1
Arkansas	1885	May 1–September 1
Colorado	1867	January 15–August 15
Florida	1913	February 20–November 20
Georgia	1891	May 1–September 1
Illinois	1873	January 1–August 15
Indiana	1857	March 1–September 1
Iowa	1857	February 1–July 15
Kansas	1861	April 1–September 1
Kentucky	1916	Until November 15, 1920
Louisiana	1877	April 1–September 1
Maryland	1870	Washington County
		March 1–November 1
Michigan	1859	February 1–September 1
Mississippi	1876	May 1–September 15
Missouri	1877	March 1–September 15
Nebraska	1860	February 1–September 1
New Jersey	1874	To November 1, 1880
New Mexico	1880	May 1–September 1
North Carolina	1875	Eleven counties
		April 1–October 1
Ohio	1857	February 1–September 15
Oklahoma	1890	January 1–October 1
Pennsylvania	1873	January 1–October 1
South Carolina	1906	Various counties
		March 1–November 15
Tennessee	1905	Haywood County
		May 1–December 1
Texas	1917	Twelve counties
		May–February
Virginia	1924	January 31–November 15
West Virginia	1887	January 1–September 15

supplemental feeding were lacking for the winter of 1943–44 when there was practically no mast. It was estimated that, during the winter, 4,000 turkeys, or 25 per cent of the population, were lost because of starvation and predation. If this was the case, the population was nevertheless double that of the winter of 1939–40.

In Texas it was found that the feeding of turkeys in January and February accelerated reproduction since the hens laid earlier and had larger clutches. In 1943 the eggs in two nests hatched by March 25, an unusually early date (Anon., 1945:26). It would seem that hatching of the eggs at an abnormally early date would be a disadvantage to the young. Most of the turkeys killed on the Edwards Plateau are shot from baited blinds, and the feeding is usually discontinued at the end of the hunting season. Feeding alone is not a reliable procedure for holding turkeys on some areas. Artificial feeding is not recommended except under very adverse conditions. At best it cannot offset a deteriorated range.

After determining the resistance of the turkey to death by starvation, Gerstell (1942:98) concluded that there was no need to supplement natural foods in winter, and Latham (1958) labeled it a waste of money. Three flocks of turkeys in Maryland were fed corn during the severe winter of 1944–45 when acorns were scarce. Fifteen flocks received no help. None died of starvation and all appeared to be in good condition (Wilson, 1945:28). In spite of management measures and winter feeding in West Virginia, the number of turkeys found within the managed areas did not exceed in number those outside the areas (Uhlig and Bailey, 1952:30). The apparent lack of increase may have been due to greater hunting pressure at the managed areas. Bailey (1955.2:5) is one who believes supplementary feeding is seldom necessary.

Continuous winter feeding, regardless of need, is frowned upon by Mosby and Handley (1943:234) because of its "pauperizing" influence. If it is desired to feed the turkeys during severe weather, preparations should be made early in the winter by establishing feeding stations where grain is placed from time to time. Insufficient grain is used to make the birds dependent upon it. Preliminary feeding renders it easier to locate flocks during periods of deep snow. This practice allows the turkeys to become accustomed to the new food so that it will be accepted when the time arrives when feeding is desirable. Some flocks refuse to move to the feeding stations during severe weather so that it is necessary to establish new ones, especially near honeysuckle thickets which provide shelter. Feeding devices should not be used as turkeys are frequently suspicious of them. The best procedure is to place the food on the ground where the snow has been removed.

There is no winter feeding in New York, where the restoration of the turkey is being attempted although there is some mortality from starvation (Bailey and Rinell, 1960.1). Turkeys move off the Divide in Kerr County, Texas, in fall. Attempts to hold them by means of feeding stations were not an unqualified success (Ramsay and Taylor, 1942). Clearly, other factors than food entered the picture. Supplemental winter feeding in Arizona, according to Reeves (1954:8), was of no material benefit as most of the flocks moved to areas where adequate, natural foods were available. Burget (1954:29) stated that "winter feeding is one of the most dangerous things that can be done for the birds. First, it has a tendency to make the birds dependent and robs them of their stamina. Second, it lowers their alertness to natural hazards." Pennsylvania spends $50,000 to $90,000 annually on winter feeding. Latham (1961) has written that there is insufficient information available to decide definitely if winter feeding is desirable and necessary, or not.

Turkeys must learn to eat foods to which they are unaccustomed. Game farm turkeys released in Fresno County, California, did not recognize acorns as food until after they were crushed (Thomas, 1915). Following a snowstorm in Colorado, the birds refused to eat corn and wheat, apparently because they were not recognized as food (Beise, 1943). Glover and Bailey (1949:263) found that starved turkeys walked over corn and oats without eating them. By adding raisins, which resemble a natural food, the grains were eventually sampled and recognized as foods. On the other hand, pen-reared turkeys released in October in Maryland had no difficulty in recognizing natural foods (Wilson, 1945:33).

Food Plantings

The Woodmont Rod and Gun Club, at Woodmont, Maryland, established in 1870, pioneered in turkey management (Quarles, 1918). The 6,000 acres belonging to the club contained twenty-eight clearings of five acres each, spaced two miles apart. The openings were planted with wheat, millet, buckwheat, and corn. The breeding enclosures contained one gobbler to five hens, and each turkey had a space of three acres. The hens laid clutches of thirteen to eighteen eggs and were allowed to hatch

413

them. The first egg was rarely laid later than April 1. The hen with her young was given her liberty on the fourth or fifth day after hatching, but the family was driven into a vermin proof enclosure in the evening.

Food patches have proved valuable in some areas and not in others. Stoddard (1935:332) advised the planting of chufas, peanuts, challu and other sorghums, proso, cowpeas, and a panic grass known as brown-top millet (*Panicum fasciculatum*). Oats, wheat, and rye are planted for winter greens. Since turkeys strip the seed heads, bearded grasses and grains should be avoided. Plantings were studied extensively in Virginia, where it was found that localized distribution of turkeys could be obtained throughout an area (Mosby and Handley, 1943:221). The plantings should consist of areas of one to two acres, with good soil, in fairly extensive hardwood forests. Test plots of various seeds showed that chufa, millet, buckwheat, cowpeas, and soybeans could be raised satisfactorily and were acceptable turkey foods. Chufa (*Cyperus esculentus*) is a preferred food. The small spherical tubers are eaten eagerly by turkeys. The birds in Virginia soon learned to obtain the "nuts" by scratching, but in Georgia it was found necessary to pull up some of the plants to expose the tubers where chufas were planted for the first time. In some localities in the Southeast, deer compete with the turkeys for the tubers which they expose by pawing.

Food plots were believed by Wilson (1945:27) to be of doubtful value in Maryland. Planted foods were consumed in abundance in the spring, summer, and sometimes fall, but rarely in winter when the need was greatest. The green shoots of wheat were eaten in quantity in March but all of the grain that matured was consumed before winter. During the summer months, millet and buckwheat were also consumed, but by fall the turkeys were roaming the mountains in quest of fruits, acorns, and other mast. The food patches were scarcely used in fall and by early December were covered with deep snow. Subsequently, Arner (1954:4) concluded: "These seeded areas are of inestimable value to the wild turkey in that they provide a source of greens very early in the spring when the reserve of body fat has been depleted and the mating and nesting season is at hand. The vitamin A content in greens is very important in egg production. A one-acre plot seeded to Ladino clover and orchard grass will produce approximately 1,500 pounds of greens in comparison to an oak forest, which will produce between 100 and 150 pounds of acorns and

414

20 to 30 pounds of buds per acre. In addition, a pasture will produce approximately 200,000 more large insects such as grasshoppers and cicadas to the acre than will a forest area. Insects comprise approximately 80% of young turkey poult's diet."

On the food plots in Alabama, rye grass was eaten in the largest quantity followed by wheat and barley. A plot on the Bankhead National Forest was grazed so closely by the turkeys that no grain developed. Both deer and turkeys utilized clovers, all types of which appeared to be preferred foods, until the plants reached maturity (Holland, 1950). Younger (1960) found that the preference for various forage plants varied with the area. The preference ratings were: Blue Springs Management Area—Albruzzia rye, rye grass, crimson clover, rescue grass (*Bromus*); Salt Springs Sanctuary—rye grass, crimson clover, Albruzzia rye, rescue grass; Sipsey River Refuge—oats preferred; Oak Mountain—vetch ranked first; Choccolocco Management Area—wheat was consumed as rapidly as it grew.

Food patches, according to Bailey *et al.* (1951:33, 38), are of doubtful value in West Virginia since they receive severe competition from deer and are not utilizable during the critical winter months. Preferable to food patches is the planting of trees and shrubs that produce food. The native chestnut (*Castanea dentata*), except for small isolated plantings, has for practical purposes been exterminated by the imported fungus, *Endothia parasitica*. The small chestnuts were highly relished by all game animals. In the spring of 1949, 20,000 seedlings of the Nanking strain of the Asiatic chestnut were planted by the state of West Virginia. The following plants have been recommended for planting since they have the important property of holding their fruit:

Black haw (*Viburnum prunifolium*)
Mapleleaf viburnum (*V. acerifolium*)
Arrowwood (*V. dentatum*)
Sheepberry (*V. lentago*)
Possum haw (*V. nudum*)
High-bush cranberry (*V. opulus*)
Japanese honeysuckle (*Lonicera japonica*)
Virginia creeper (*Parthenocissus quinquefolia*)
Persimmon (*Diospyros virginiana*)

Wild grape (*Vitis*)
Fragrant sumac (*Rhus aromatica*)
Smooth sumac (*R. glabra*)
Greenbrier (*Smilax rotundifolia*)
Am. holly (*Ilex opaca*)
Deciduous holly (*I. monticola*)
Winterberry (*I. verticillata*)

Flowering dogwood (*Cornus florida*)
Hazelnut (*Corylus americana*)

The aggressive nature of the Japanese honeysuckle (*Lonicera japonica*) is a deterrent to its use as it soon exterminates the native low shrubs (Handley, 1945). The new growth and fruit, however, are comparable in nutritive value to corn. Although the lespedezas have proved to be valuable foods for quail and some other game animals (Davison, 1945), they do not appear to be used extensively by turkeys. None of the native species of lespedezas are as desirable as the foreign annuals, *Lespedeza striata*, and *L. stipulacea*. Blakey (1937:30) lists six species of lespedezas utilized by turkeys in Missouri, but in Virginia they were minor items in their diet (Mosby and Handley, 1943:162). I have long thought that one of the greatest boons to wildlife would be the development of strains of the native wild grapes that would retain their fruit into late winter. In Wisconsin an occasional vine of the frost grape (*Vitis riparia*) will hold its fruit until well into the winter.

Controlled Burning

Controlled burning of parts of the turkey range is recommended by Stoddard (1935:331) because it has several advantages. The areas should be burned every three or four years to produce in abundance such turkey foods as chinquapins, ground and runner oaks, huckleberry, blueberry, and similar shrubs. The shrubs do not fruit well the year of the burn, but much green vegetation attractive to turkeys is produced. Burning helps to control ticks, chiggers, and other parasites, and diseases of these birds. Equally important is the destruction of the dense undergrowth, which turkeys shun. In the management of the Francis Marion Preserve, the pine lands are burned every three years since a heavy understory makes a poor turkey range (Holbrook, 1958:2). It was doubted that controlled burning would prove to be as beneficial in Virginia as in Georgia owing to the difference in plant succession (Mosby and Handley, 1943:81). The "rough" is so extensive in the Piedmont National Wildlife Refuge, north central Georgia, that burning is necessary to maintain a suitable turkey habitat (Givens, 1962). It should be pointed out that fires intentionally set are very difficult to control in broken country.

Water Supply

The necessity for an ample supply of water is fully recognized by game managers. Spring-fed streams that remain open throughout the winter are a great asset. Turkeys with their broods left the coastal plains of Georgia entirely during seasons when there was no standing water, but remained in the season (1949) when the supply of water was ample (Webb, 1952). Many areas in the Southwest are suitable for turkeys except for lack of water. This has been shown especially in Texas (Anon., 1945:29): "It has been clearly demonstrated that water developments have helped to maintain and spread the wild turkey population.... Wild turkeys were seldom seen on the higher elevations or 'divide country' before windmills and other watering devices were installed for live-stock." When it was noticed on the King Ranch that turkeys were most numerous near leaking windmill storage tanks, thirty-three wells were adjusted to provide water for the birds. An increase in the turkey population in both oak areas and tall mesquite brushland generally followed an increase in the supply of water, along with protection and occasional emergency feeding (Lea, 1957:761). Lack of suitable distribution of water affects breeding. In the spring of 1939, turkeys on the Edwards Plateau, Texas, did not breed on account of the drought and moved about in flocks of five to fifteen individuals (Sanders, 1939).

REARING WILD TURKEYS IN CAPTIVITY

The earliest attempts to restore wild turkeys to areas in which they had been extirpated were made with stock of doubtful purity. Eventually, wild turkeys with some domestic blood were used for propagation since the increase from pure, captive wild birds was very unsatisfactory. The planting of game farm birds was attractive, but over a period of years has proved in most cases to be a costly failure. In the struggle for survival, no turkey tainted with domestic blood is a match for the native, wild bird.

There was early interest in Pennsylvania in restoring the turkey. In 1879 some of J. D. Caton's Illinois wild turkeys were released at Blooming Grove, Pennsylvania (Phillips, 1928:10). All of them vanished. It is very doubtful if they were of pure stock. The reply to an inquiry in 1874 whether wild turkeys would thrive in Pike County was that there was too much snow and the mountains were too high (J. V. S., 1874). Enty (1905) wrote from Templeton, Armstrong County, that in the "winter of 1888" eight fine wild turkeys came into the hills back of his home. They were part of a large flock raised from birds obtained from the mountains of central Pennsylvania. The greatest obstacle to their increase

417

was the impossibility of keeping people from killing them. The following fall the flock, numbering forty, was soon decimated. His solution was to obtain an exclusive right to shoot on the property of a tenant or owner who would be allowed two turkeys per year and payment for any excessive damage to crops. There was to be a liberal reward for apprehending violators. It was stated in 1911 that, three years previously, Dr. J. Kalbfus planted two wild hens in "the flats," Adams County, where there was a wild gobbler (Anon., 1911). They multiplied to the extent that six large birds were seen in the game preserve at Mount Alto, Franklin County, fifteen miles distant. The origin of the turkeys seen can be only conjecture.

In 1912, Kalbfus (1913) suggested the purchase of wild poults from Maryland and placing them in a suitable preserve of three or four acres enclosed with an eight foot fence. The increase was to be released in various sections of Pennsylvania. No records of releases in the state were kept prior to 1918 (Christy and Sutton, 1929:115). In 1919–20, ninety-six turkeys were imported from Hancock, Allegheny County, Maryland, and sixty-four from a game farm in North Dakota. Virginia began raising game farm turkeys in 1930 (Mosby and Handley, 1943:181). These birds were culled to conform to the standards set for the wild bird. Of the total, 1,328 were considered to be acceptable in coloration and in the shape of the body. These birds proved to be unsuitable for stocking areas from which the wild stock had been extirpated.

The Pennsylvania system of obtaining stock for release was described in 1936 (Luttringer, 1936; Fluke, 1936). Wild hens raised at the game farm were placed, after their wings were clipped, in a fenced area so situated that they could be mated with wild gobblers which flew in and out of the enclosure. In some cases the first clutch of eggs was collected and hatched in an incubator, and the hen allowed to hatch the second clutch. In others the hen was allowed to hatch the first clutch (Fluke, 1940.1).

The results obtained in hatching in the spring of 1937 were far better than during the previous seasons (Wessell, 1937.1). From 2,226 eggs from the State Game Farm, 1,619 poults were obtained. The 4,185 eggs supposedly fertilized by wild gobblers on the propagating areas produced 1,144 poults. The hatchability of 27.3 per cent indicates that fertilization by the wild gobblers was poor. The method of propagation was supposed to produce offspring very close to the native wild birds; however, the trace of domestic blood transmitted from the hen to the poults, coupled with raising them in captivity, did not produce completely wild birds.

Virginia in 1935 started the method of breeding the hens in enclosures with wild gobblers (Mosby and Handley, 1943:182). Blakey (1937:23) mentioned success with the method in Missouri. The great difficulty encountered in Virginia was getting the gobblers inside the enclosures (Bailey, 1941). The gobbler would pace up and down the fence, strut before the hens, but seldom try to fly into the enclosure. Driving the gobbler so that he would be forced to fly over the fence, ramps built to the top of the fence, and a drift fence leading to a funnel opening into the enclosure would work with some gobblers and not with others.

The Pennsylvania system was tried in Maryland with limited success (Arner, 1954). An improvement was the use of forest hardening pens, ten acres in area, in which the poults were placed at ages of eighteen to twenty weeks to accustom them to life in the woods. Two new methods of propagation were tried. In the first, a brooding hen was used to brood poults a day old in a small enclosure, the hen being taken away after about six weeks. The thought was that the hen would teach the poults awareness of enemies and when she was removed they would range the immediate area instead of wandering. Encouraging reports were obtained. The second method was to allow the hen to hatch her young in a wooded enclosure, then drive the hen and poults into the surrounding forest. This plan was defeated by predators. Skunks, raccoons, and opossums succeeded so many times in crossing the charged wire and squeezing through the five-inch meshes of the fence that nearly all the eggs, and twelve hens, were destroyed on the three propagating areas. When the eggs were gathered daily, predators seldom attempted to enter the enclosure.

Approximately twenty-six states have tried stocking with game farm turkeys and have found them unsatisfactory with the exception of Pennsylvania, and possibly Michigan. A good portion of the game farm turkeys released on the Red Dirt and Catahoula Preserves in Louisiana wandered off the refuges and failed to become wild. They refused to show alarm when approached closely and roosted at farm houses in the vicinity of the refugees (Moody, 1951). From 1949 through 1953, a total of 568 turkeys was released on six management areas in Louisiana. The 1953 census gave an estimated 95 birds, a survival of only 16.7 per cent including reproduction (Moody and Collins, 1954). From 1925 to 1942, 14,000 game farm turkeys were released in Missouri but the population continued to decline (Lewis, 1957.1). Recent releases were made of game farm turkeys to determine if a better strain had been obtained, but there was no improvement in results. A turkey raised in captivity, though considered to be 99 per cent wild, is still no match for the native bird.

The case against the game farm turkey has been well summarized (Bailey and Knoder, 1958). Pure eastern wild turkeys have seldom been raised, simply because they are too wild. Stocking with game farm birds has rarely accomplished its purpose, and when releases are made where a native population exists, more harm than good may be accomplished as a result of dilution. They add: "In connection with the CCC program of the 1930's, West Virginia produced and released game farm turkeys by the hundreds. The results were so discouraging that the entire project was terminated even before abandonment of the CCC program. In the late 40's and early 50's, more than 10 years after any substantial releases had been made, the state's turkey population began to expand in area and density. This expansion was undoubtedly due to improved quality of the range as a result of maturity forest." Successful management of wild turkeys is tied to good wild stock and a range of adequate size and quality.

Stocking should be made with captured wild birds (Gwynn, 1958). Thoroughly wild birds refuse to eat in captivity and cannot be raised. Physiologically, game farm turkeys are little suited for stocking because they are not sufficiently alert. Should it happen that a successful planting is made with game farm birds, no further additions should be made as this will reduce the acquired wildness of the original turkeys.

Where turkeys are raised for "put and take" shooting, as in Pennsylvania, it has become customary to release the birds shortly before the opening of the hunting season. At one time it was thought best to release the poults when they were fourteen to eighteen weeks of age (Blakey, 1937:5). Year-old turkeys could not adapt themselves readily to an open range. An age of about sixteen weeks for release has been recommended (Mosby and Handley, 1943:194; Jull, 1947:427). According to Roberts (1957), captivity-reared poults reach a definite peak of wildness at an age of eleven to twelve weeks. Banded birds of this age released in south-central Pennsylvania showed a return of only 4.2 per cent. When the turkeys were "hardened" by subjecting them to the rigors of the wild prior to release in mid-October, the return was 23 per cent. In the south-central area, banded birds constituted 54.0 per cent of the kill, while breeding stock released in spring gave a return of only 7.3 per cent. In 1948, based on the liberation of eighty-five turkeys (of which approximately 60 per cent were lost prior to the hunting season), Kozicky and Metz (1948:21) suggested that it would be more economical to liberate young gobblers during the hunting season.

Standards for Wild Turkeys

An early desire of the breeders of wild turkeys was a criterion for the purity of their stock. McIlhenney (1918) thought that the color of the head was more reliable as a mark of purity than that of the plumage. He said: "I wish to speak of the color of the head of the toms. There is a vast difference between the color of the head of the wild turkey and that of the domestic bird, or any bird that shows any domestic blood. I, too, have found a great many birds in the wild which show domestic blood, and it shows first, I think, in the color of the head of the gobblers. It does not show so strongly in the hens. You will never see a pure-bred wild turkey if, when the gobbler is in strut, he shows red on the ends of the caruncles. They will show blue almost always, or bluish-white. On the top of the head there will not be shown any blue at all, but a shining white. In the domestic bird, and any bird that has any domestic blood in him, although you get him in the woods, and he may be apparently a wild turkey, when he is in strut that spot on the top of his head, which in the wild bird is white, will show a streak of blue, although the balance of the head may be as blue as the wild turkey's head. Between the wattles of the wild bird you will see the red markings but not on the ends. There is very little red about the head of the wild bird when he is in strut. I have seen many birds in museums that had their heads painted but never painted right. They always put too much red in it, and from my investigation, and from studying the bird, I find more [wild] gobblers can be told by the color on their heads than on their feathers. I have bred birds from the southern branch of the eastern strain whose feathers were as dark as these ... and in three-fourths of the wild birds the color was just as high, but they would always show the cross by the color of the head.

"Of course there is considerable red in the wattles in the non-breeding season. The red in the breeding season extends only between the wattles, but when the gobbler goes in strut, it turns a brilliant blue or bluish-white."

It was thought in the 1930's that turkeys suitable for stocking could be obtained by holding to certain standards. In the last analysis the most desirable characteristic—and the one most difficult to obtain—was wildness. According to Davis (1931:228), a true wild turkey is "active, quick, wild, wary, ever alert, ever cautious, acute of hearing, keen in vision, and keyed up to run or fly on the instant." While admitting that wildness was highly desirable, Randall (1931.1:177) was unwilling to sacrifice type and color even if the birds were more domestic. Turkeys with chocolate-tipped tails could be bred quite readily, but the metallic sheen of the wild bird was difficult to obtain. Turkeys having truly wild characteristics, according to Randall (1933.1), will not lose their wildness in the first and second generations but will do so eventually when closely confined and fed heavily. The reversion can be prevented by securing native wild gobblers every two years.

The requirements for a pure bird given by Randall (1931:91) were a slim build, fairly long legs, powerful wings, a decidedly small head bare of feathers, but with stiff bristles in many specimens. He then proposed the following standard: "General plumage coppery bronze, with metallic reflections of copper color, green and purple, the feathers edged with rich black; the head small, snakelike, naked and of blue color, studded with excrescences of purplish red; tail dark chesnut, with bars and a sub-terminal band of black; upper tail coverts and tips of tail feathers chesnut; wings dusky, banded by dull white; general build slim and racy; legs long; wings powerful. Male with conspicuous tuft of bristles depending from the breast. Female, similar to male in color, but smaller, paler, and duller. May, or may not have tassel." Mature females should weigh seven to ten pounds and males twelve to seventeen pounds. Any male weighing over seventeen pounds probably has domestic blood. Johnson (1932) was not impressed by color as a standard. Body contour and flying ability were the important criteria. He had two rangy young gobblers that without difficulty could fly to the top of a smokestack one hundred feet high.

At the request of the North American Game Breeders' Association, Sibley (1933) headed a committee to submit standards for the eastern wild turkey. The standards published in 1933 were republished in 1940 (Sibley, 1940). The following is a condensation in part:

Head.—Small, slim, snaky, with some caruncles, the fewer the better.

Throat-wattle.—Small, almost wanting in the best specimens, having few or no caruncles.

Body.—Long and slim.

Legs.—Lower thighs (tibiae) long and muscular; shanks (tarsi) slim, long, and strong.

Carriage.—Upright, nervous, alert. Backline of body and tail carried at about 45° to the horizontal.

Weights.—Adult male (two years or over) sixteen to seventeen pounds; adult female seven to nine pounds.

Colors.—Serious defects are white feathers in any part of the plumage; absence of barring on flight feathers; presence of white tips to rump and tail feathers; absence of buff or brown edging on breast feathers of the female; shanks other than red or pink in adults.

COLOR OF MALE

Head.—Blue, changing to reddish purple, the bluer the better.

Wings.—Parallel black and white bars of primaries of about equal width.

Back.—"From neck to middle of back, rich coppery bronze, each feather terminating in a narrow black band; from middle of back to tail coverts, black, each feather having a broad, brilliant coppery band extending across it near the end, feathers ending in a distinct black band, gradually narrowing as the tail coverts are approached."

Tail.—"Main tail and greater coverts dull black, each feather distinctly marked transversely with parallel lines of brown, each feather having a wide band of brilliant iridescent coppery bronze across it near the end, a distinct black band bordering the bronze and terminating in a broad edging of deep coffee brown; the more distinct and brilliant the colors, the better."

Breast.—Feathers terminate in a black band.

COLOR OF FEMALE

Plumage.—"Similar to male, but less brilliant. Also a narrow edging of buff on feathers of back, wing-bows, wing coverts, breast and body.

This edging narrow in front, gradually widens as it approaches the rear of the bird, where it emerges into the deep brown terminal edging of tail coverts and main tail feathers."

Aside from differences due to age and sex, as Pirnie (1935) has noted, the shapes and colors of the soft parts vary with the season. Leopold (1944:172) found that the color of the plumage is not a reliable index of wildness.

Randall (1932) made a plea for propagating turkeys from the purest wild birds obtainable. He thought at the time that the native turkeys of South Carolina were the best of the eastern race. The release of game farm turkeys where there were a few remaining wild birds could be catastrophic. Leopold (1943.1), after long experience, advised concentrating effort on the wild stock that remained. At the same time, regarding the stocking of Merriam's turkey in Wyoming, Ligon (1943) wrote: "Only the streamlined, wild, adjusted birds can readily meet the challenge of winter storms, predacious animals, and poachers." It is now very generally recognized that restoration of turkeys must be made with native birds, races being selected to fit the habitat. Florida turkeys released in Michigan or Rio Grande turkeys liberated in Mississippi would have little chance of survival.

Capture of Wild Birds for Restocking

Much ingenuity has been expended in capturing the wild birds for transplanting. After years of experience, opinions still differ on the most suitable trap. The first trap used was the pole trap of pioneer days (Plate 33). This trap, about 10 feet square, had sides and top built of poles, and a ditch by which the turkeys could enter when lured by grain. Its efficiency was low for the wild turkey of today is more wary than formerly; however, Ligon (1946:79) considered it to be the best device for taking Merriam's turkeys. The trap used by him had internal measurements of 10 by 12 feet and 3 feet high. It was built of perfectly smooth peeled poles having a diameter of about 3.5 inches and so laid that the spaces between the poles did not exceed four inches. The cover poles were fastened to prevent displacement by rolling. The use of two trap doors at the ends of the structure, released by pulling wires from a blind, was considered less desirable because it meant tedious waiting for the manipulator and the possibility of frightening the birds, both within and without the trap, when the doors were released. An objection to the pole trap is its lack of portability. In Colorado a portable trap, with end gates, was built of 1- by 4-inch boards or slats (Burget, 1957:38). Most of the turkeys transplanted were taken in a trap of this type.

Attempts made in Florida to drive turkeys into a funnel trap were unsuccessful (Gainey, 1950). The birds would enter the area between the wings but not the funnel.

Various types of traps and their efficiency have been described by Sylvester and Lane (1946). Their most successful trap was made of chicken wire and provided with drop doors of the same size as the ends of the trap. The trap should be 10 to 16 feet wide and 6 feet high. W. P. Baldwin (1947:33) favored a trap of this type with a "roll-front," but thought that a drop-net trap had the greater possibilities. Ellis (1961) preferred the drop-net. He has described a nylon net, 60 feet by 60 feet, with 2-inch mesh, made of size 15 or larger cord. It is placed from one-fourth to one-half mile from the roost, preferably along travel-ways used by the turkeys. The site is baited with maize prior to the erection of the net. For future identification the legs of the captured birds were marked with plastic bands, notched and clamped with 14-gauge galvanized iron wire. Neck bands were also used. An entirely satisfactory method of marking turkeys has yet to be devised. A type of drop-net used in Texas is shown in Plate 37.

The trend in trapping in recent years has been towards the use of the cannon-net, originally devised for the capture of wildfowl. The nets vary in size from 30 by 60 to 40 by 80 feet. One edge of the net is fastened to the ground and the loose portion folded over this edge. Two cannons are set behind the net, one at each corner, at an angle of about 20° to the horizontal and outward about 45° to keep the net taut while in flight. One end of a short rope is tied to the corner of the net, the other end fastened to a projectile which is placed in the cannon. The propellant is black powder in a 12-gauge shell which is fired electrically from a blind (Plate 38). All parts of the equipment should be camouflaged as completely as possible with a covering of leaves and grass. The area in front of the net is baited until the turkeys become accustomed to feeding at the site. When it is decided to attempt capture, the food should be placed close to the net. The cannons are not fired until the birds are close to the folded net; otherwise, some will dash from under the net before it falls.

Holbrook (1958.1) recommended attaching webbing three feet in width to the free edges of the net, to act as a curtain to prevent the birds from escaping.

Turkeys are extremely suspicious of anything new in their customary haunts. It is easier, however, to camouflage a cannon-net than any other type of trap. Bailey (1959.1:6) writes: "By the fall of 1957, turkeys were sufficiently bait and trap shy as to be avoiding baited areas or areas where they had been trapped. Blinds had to be erected farther from the traps than formerly. Sometimes the birds would flush at sight of the blind. Nets had to be perfectly camouflaged, i.e. concealed beneath leaves, grass, etc. If a single wire or piece of net or metal were seen by the turkeys they would immediately run or flush. They were particularly responsive to the dark, hollow insides of a mortar. They often approached the bait with utmost caution and when they first began feeding were ready to flush at the slightest cause. Upon arriving at the bait, they would approach it, or the net, no more closely than necessary, stretching their necks as far forward as possible. Furtively pecking the grain, their bodies held low to the ground, their wings half-spread to enable instantaneous flight, as though prepared for sudden danger.

"Turkeys as alert as mentioned above were trapped only through close attention to details of procedure. Each time an observer visited a bait site during the baiting period, leaves and grass were added to a smooth row of such materials at the exact spot where the net would lie and heaped in a pile at the place where each mortar would be positioned. Turkeys were likely to abandon any baited area in which sudden changes were made."

The speed with which turkeys will outrace the net is incredible. Bailey used a movie camera while netting two gobblers and found that the 30-foot-wide net had an average speed of 30 feet in 5/34 of a second, or roughly 140 miles per hour. The first 15 feet of the net was propelled in 1/34 second, or 400 miles per hour. Young turkeys and hens frequently outraced the net, probably because it did not attain the above speed. Their capture was never assured. Adult males, on the other hand, never escaped.

Trapping is most successful where there is a high concentration of turkeys, but is always difficult when natural foods are abundant. The traps should be placed on bare areas that the birds frequent, or by paths by which they are accustomed to travel on account of the terrain. After one catch has been made with the cannon-net, it should be moved to a new location. Wheat was preferred by Sylvester and Lane (1946:335) to any other bait. Corn, vetch, oats, soybeans, chicken scratch feed, sunflower seeds, and Korean lespedeza were less successful. W. P. Baldwin (1947:25) found that the best baits were wheat, rough rice, and chicken scratch feed. In trapping Merriam's turkey, Burget (1957:35) found corn to be an excellent bait, but the turkeys filled their crops rapidly and left the area. Wheat, being a small grain, was preferable. Barley and millet were not preferred foods. Milo, buckwheat, and berries of the Russian olive were highly acceptable, but sunflower seeds were preferred to all other foods. Bailey (1959:3) commonly used a mixture of wheat and oats. He found it impossible to tell when the turkeys would arrive at the trap. Sometimes the arrival was before sunrise and as late as 5:30 A.M. Probably three-fourths of the catches were made before 11:00 A.M. Trapping in general is most successful in the fall and early winter; however, unless there is a shortage of natural foods, the best results may be obtained from January through March.

The cannon-net, though superior to other traps in making rapid catches, has two defects according to Holbrook (1951). The birds become more excited than when taken in other types of traps and lose more feathers in their struggles to escape from the net. In Missouri socks were placed over the heads of the birds to quiet them (Stanford, 1959:2). A common practice is to cover them with canvas of light weight (Plate 39). Crump and Sanderson (1951:8) state that a turkey will not struggle if both feet are held in one hand and the body supported by the other hand and arm. I was present when some hens were being removed from a cannon-net in Mississippi. When held suspended by the legs, they remained completely quiet. There does not appear to be a material difference in direct deaths and injuries between the cannon-net and dropdoor traps. An occasional turkey will die of shock immediately after being caught, irrespective of the type of trap.

Anesthetization has been suggested for ease of handling trapped turkeys but has not been put to practical use. Sadler (1954.1) experimented with chloral hydrate and sodium nembutal, a derivative of barbituric acid. It was recommended that 2.2 cc. of sodium nembutal per five pounds of weight of the turkey be injected intramuscularly immediately after removal from the trap. Total recovery from the anesthetic

should be allowed before release. Bait treated with Avertin (tribromoeth-
anol dissolved in amyl alcohol) was used by Mosby and Canter (1956)
for capturing wild turkeys. To produce narcosis, 0.06 to 0.09 cc. was required per pound of weight. The average dose, 0.75 cc., was distributed
over sixty grains of whole corn. Anesthetization followed in three to
seventeen minutes. The difficulty lay in preventing the turkeys from
taking an overdose. If insufficient grain was taken to produce anesthetization, the birds would not touch it again. After capture, the crop of the
turkey should be irrigated with water to remove the bait.

As soon as the turkeys are removed from the traps, they should be
placed in containers. When the distance to which the turkeys are to be
transported can be reached in a few hours by truck, they should be
placed in crates made of plywood or hardpanel board. When light is
reduced to a minimum, the birds will remain relatively quiet, and the
smooth interior of the crate prevents bodily injury. The only openings
should be holes bored near the top of the crate, or handholds. The
simplest procedure is to place the birds in sacks where they can be held
for eight to ten hours; however, there is some danger of abrasion and
breakage of the flight feathers (Ellis, 1961). Transportation to the place
of release should be as rapid as possible. If the distance is several hundred
miles, a plane should be used. Florida has been successful in stocking
places difficult to reach by tossing the turkeys from a low-flying plane
(Everett, 1956; Naggiar, 1958).

A number of turkeys should be released at one place and not scattered.
When all or part of a captured flock is released, the birds are much more
likely to remain together than if the release consists of turkeys taken in
several localities. Sommers (1958) recommends that the birds be released
at night as they usually fly into the nearest trees, and in the morning fly
down and begin feeding. If released in the daytime, they may fly completely out of the area. The best season for stocking is in the fall or early
winter, then normal nesting occurs in the spring (Gainey, 1950). This
does not happen if the release is made in late winter or spring.

Cost of Trapped Birds

The cost of trapping a turkey varies considerably depending on the
type of trap used, the experience of the operator, the wildness of the
birds and the number in the area, and so on. Also, it is unknown if

identical items were used in the cost accounting. De Lime (1948), in one season in Kentucky, trapped twenty-two turkeys of which nine escaped because of faulty construction of the trap, and four died after capture. The nine birds released cost $195.83 apiece. The following season he trapped forty-four turkeys of which ten died of shock. The thirty-four released cost $141.37 per bird (De Lime, 1949). The costs on two areas in Texas were much lower. Jackson (1950) trapped 133 turkeys at a cost of $10.97 per bird for trapping and releasing; and Colbath (1954), fifty at a cost of $14.70 each. Twenty turkeys released along the Tamiami Trail, Florida, cost $350.00, or $17.50 apiece (Hunn, 1960). In Mississippi, as a result of experience, the cost of $24.21 to trap a turkey in 1955–56 was reduced to $6.72 in 1957–58 (Johnson, 1959).

Drifting Following Release

An unsolved problem in turkey management is drifting from the place of release. Game managers select stocking areas which in their opinion are most suitable for turkeys. Frequently, the birds show little respect for their judgment and will move considerable distances. It is not certain that drifting is due to the unsuitability of the place of release. Nervousness from capture and strange surroundings may impel turkeys to move until calmness is restored and they can settle down. The drift in mountainous country in Virginia is often more than ten to fifteen miles (Mosby and Handley, 1943:195). Mosby (1941:90) reported that the normal distance traveled was three to five miles, the longest airline distance being thirteen miles. In September, 1956, a flock of twenty native turkeys was trapped, banded, and released near Neola, West Virginia. Some of the flock moved fifteen to twenty miles as shown by kills by hunters (Bailey, 1957.1:8). Subsequently, recoveries of banded birds were obtained up to twenty-five miles distant (Bailey, 1959:7).

Following the release of thirty-five turkeys in the Peace River Swamp, Florida, 43 per cent of the birds moved from five to twenty-five miles from the point of release, then settled down (Stanberry and Gainey, 1950). The remainder stayed within a radius of two miles. The greatest distance that any turkey was seen from the point of release in Texas was fifteen miles (Goodrum, 1941:195). Birds released on the Kaibab National Game Preserve, Arizona, moved to distances up to forty miles (Russo, 1959:175). Concerning a release in Colorado, Burget (1957:46) wrote: "In one case some birds moved over fifty miles and were found to be getting along quite nicely in the new location." Merriam's turkeys released in Hoover Canyon, Yakima County, Washington, moved from the area, some being seen sixty miles distant (Oliver and Barnett, 1961).

Population Densities Attainable

The density of turkeys attainable depends upon the habitat and other conditions. Stoddard (1932:97) stated: "Where large areas of suitable and continuous range can be protected from over-shooting, and plantings can be made of such well-known turkey feeds as peanuts, chufas . . . turkeys can be increased easier than any upland game bird known to the speaker, at least in half-forested areas of the Southeastern Coastal Plain." He doubted that turkeys have a definite saturation point like quail. A good population would be one bird to fifteen to twenty-five acres of high quality, well-managed habitat (Stoddard, 1935:327). The winter of 1944–45 the Salt Springs Game Sanctuary had one turkey to twenty-seven acres, which Wheeler (1948:48) believed might be the limit of its carrying capacity.

In three areas in West Virginia there was one turkey to 171, 208, and 304 acres respectively. Bailey *et al.* (1951:8) doubted if even in the better ranges the fall populations exceeded one turkey per 125 acres. In Virginia there was one turkey to 375 acres of occupied range in comparison with one to 755 acres in Florida in 1939. Mosby and Handley (1943:220) thought that with good management practices and by prevention of over-shooting, it should be possible to obtain one turkey per forty acres on management areas of 10,000 to 15,000 acres. A reasonable objective would be one bird to fifty acres. In Missouri where there were more than nine hundred acres of timber improvement, there were 9.3 turkeys per township; where less than nine hundred acres, 6.7 turkeys; and where there was no improvement, 5.7 turkeys (Crawford, 1952). The standard township has an area of thirty-six square miles.

The winter of 1950–51, there was one turkey to 95.5 acres on the Kerr Wildlife Management Area, Texas (Hahn, 1951). The highest densities of which I am aware have occurred on the King Ranch. The density on the Norias Division in 1945 was one turkey to about thirty acres. The peak densities were one bird to four acres of oak brush land and one to fifteen acres in mesquite areas. One study area of 140,000 acres, consisting predominantly of oak, had in 1949 a population of approximately 35,000, which is one to four acres (Lea, 1957:764). The White River Indian Reservation, Arizona, comprising 2,460 square miles held 15,000 to 18,000 turkeys in 1942, a population of six to seven turkeys per square mile (Ligon, 1946:56). This reservation is now the best area for Merriam's turkey within its range. Further data on present densities will be found in Table 3 (p. 56).

DETERMINATION OF SEX AND AGE

The sex of a turkey after it is three or four months of age can be determined from the breast feathers. Sibley (1933:49), in his standard for the wild turkey, mentioned that in the male these feathers are tipped with black and in the female with buff. Juveniles, up to the age of eight months, can be determined by the bursa of Fabricius. The bursa disappears when a bird nears sexual maturity. Its function is uncertain. A pointed tenth, or outer primary (Plate 40), shows that the bird is less than fifteen months of age. During the second summer this feather is replaced with one having a rounded tip and usually marked with white. The length of the beard and the spurs of males are indicative of age, but they show considerable variation between turkeys of the same age. The age of hens more than fifteen months old cannot be determined with certainty. Keiser and Kozicky (1943) state that the middle toe of old females never measures more than three inches. The length of the middle toe, without claw, of adult female eastern turkeys, according to Ridgway and Friedmann (1946:442), is 2.42 to 2.68 inches.

Gobblers shot by hunters in Texas were classified by age by Walker (1947.1) using the following criteria: juveniles have very short spurs, relatively short beards, and gray tarsi with moderately small scales; mature birds, two years or more of age, have longer beards and spurs, and reddish tarsi with relatively large scales.

Sex, according to Bailey (1956), can be determined by the shape of the droppings. Those of an adult gobbler are straighter, longer, and greater in diameter than those of the hen. A typical one has a curlicue on the large end. The droppings of juvenile gobblers in fall seldom exceed 10 mm. in diameter, while those of older males may be as much as 15 mm. in diameter. The droppings of a hen are 5 to 8 mm. in diameter, shorter than those of the males, and are spiral, looped, or bulbous in shape. Some

431

specialists in turkeys doubt the reliability of this method of determining sex.

POPULATION CENSUS

The status of a population is determinable only by making a census. The census is usually compiled from questionnaires, reports of wardens, and interviews with local residents. It is seldom feasible, except for small populations, to make as complete a census by direct count as was done by Burger (1954:205) (Table 30).

TABLE 30

SEX AND AGE COMPOSITION OF THE CASTRO VALLEY RANCH POPULATION
IN CALIFORNIA IN 1951

Sex and age groups	Actual number	Per cent of adult population	Per cent of fall population	Number per 100 females
Old males	14	20	7.4	32.5
Yearling males	13	18	6.9	30.2
Total—males	27	38	14.3	62.7
Females with young	31	44	16.5	—
Females without young	12	17	6.4	—
Total—females	43	61	22.9	100
Total—adults	70	100	37.2	—
5-month young	117	—	62.8	272
Total population	187	—	—	—

A hunting season should not be set without data on the number of turkeys present, and their sex and age. In a normal season about 60 per cent of the turkeys killed are young of the year. If the kill of young falls much below this figure, it is certain that there was a poor hatch. Of the 211 birds observed in early August, 1946, on the Edwards Plateau, only 87 (41.2 per cent) were young birds (Walker, 1947). The fall kill consisted of 52.6 per cent young and 47.4 per cent adults (Walker, 1947.1). The ratio of hens to poults in the Texas Panhandle, obtained by De Arment (1959:4) over a period of five years, is shown in Table 31. The low ratio in 1956 was due apparently to subnormal rainfall. With a ratio of one poult to one hen, a population could barely maintain itself.

The ratio of poults to adults determined prior to the hunting season in Arizona checked well with that of the kill (Table 32) (Jantzen, 1955.2:6). The percentages of adults and young in the reported kill, as

TABLE 31

FALL HEN-POULT RATIOS IN THE TEXAS PANHANDLE FOR FIVE YEARS

Year	Hens	Poults	Hen-Poult Ratio
1954	152	691	1:5
1955	205	556	1:3
1956	423	623	1:1
1957	284	511	1:2
1958	283	733	1:3
Totals	*1,347*	*3,114*	*1:2*

given by Jantzen (1956.1:5), over a period of years are shown in Table 33. Reproduction in 1955 was very poor as shown by the summer census and the kill which consisted of four adults to one young. Of the total kill, 69 per cent were hens. Between the high number of adults and high pro-

TABLE 32

POULT TO ADULT RATIOS BY SURVEY AND HUNTER KILL

Forest	1953		1954	
	Survey	Hunt	Survey	Hunt
Apache	0.6:1	0.9:1	2.5:1	1.4:1
Sitgreaves	1.4:1	1.2:1	1.3:1	1.3:1
Coconino	0.8:1	0.8:1	0.9:1	1.0:1

portion of females killed, the hunting season would appear to have been a severe drain on the population. This was not the case. When a 10 per cent crippling loss was added to the adjusted kill of 887, the total kill for 976. Jantzen (*l.c.*, 8) states: "Population estimates for the state would necessitate a removal of from 3,000 to 6,000 birds to include 20

TABLE 33

PERCENTAGES OF ADULTS AND YOUNG IN REPORTED HUNTER KILL

Year	Number killed		Percent of Total	
	Adult	Young	Adult	Young
1947	102	158	39.2	60.8
1948	65	198	24.7	75.3
1949	86	106	44.8	55.2
1951	82	149	35.8	64.2
1952	252	309	45.0	55.0
1953	459	464	49.8	50.2
1954	275	353	43.8	56.2
1955	601	155	79.5	20.5

per cent of the total." A total of 968 hunters reported seeing 19,689 turkeys (Jantzen, 1956.2:2). Even if this had been the total population, only 5 per cent would have been removed.

The ratio of adult males to adult females varies widely with the area and the year. Reliable data on adults are obtainable only in spring and summer, and even then the census usually includes yearlings. There are usually more gobblers than hens in a population which is not hunted, the lower number of hens being attributed to losses during the nesting season. In states where only gobblers may be shot, there is a preponderance of hens. Some ratios of males to females are given in Table 34. The number of gobblers surviving hunting is ample for the following breeding season. However, when the hens greatly outnumber the gobblers, there may be a clamor to shoot hens also. One of the arguments for shooting hens is that the inexperienced hunter is unable to distinguish a juvenile gobbler from a hen. It has yet to be shown that regulated shooting of males affects reproduction.

TABLE 34

RATIOS OF ADULT MALES TO ADULT FEMALES

Year	State	Area	Ratio of Males to Females	Reference
1952	Arizona		1:2.7**	Jantzen, 1955: Tab. I
1953	Arizona		1:1.2**	Jantzen
1954	Arizona		1:1.0**	Jantzen
—	Florida	—	1:0.62	Gainey, 1954.2: Tab. 3
1943–48	Texas	Edwards Plateau	1:2.7*	Walker, 1948.2: Tab. I
1945	Texas	Edwards Plateau	1:3.8	Hahn, 1946.1
1947	Texas	Menard	1:2.3	Becknell, 1948
1947	Texas	San Saba	1:2.1	Becknell
—	Texas	King Ranch	1:0.7	Lea, 1957:764
1957	Texas	Edwards County	1:2.2	Thomas and Green, 1957:24
1957	Texas	Medina County	1:8	Thomas and Green
1957	Texas	Kerr County	1:4.4	Thomas and Green
1957	Texas	Bandera County	1:17.6	Thomas and Green

* Average. The ratios ran from 1:1.1 to 1:8.
** Average of three national forests.

Nesting success is about 35 per cent (p. 268). In spite of this low success, a population is usually able to maintain itself with some hunting. Bailey

(1957:5) wrote: "An adult female:immature ratio of 1:1 during the hunting period theoretically enables a population to maintain itself with a total loss to hunting of about 25–30 per cent, assuming there are only slight natural losses." The kill for all states having an open season averages about 15 per cent of the estimated populations. Legitimate hunting, therefore, removes less of the surplus than is considered allowable.

The theoretical fate of a flock of one hundred turkeys over a period of one year, as given by Edminster (1954:98), implies a mortality of 73 per cent. Data on birds banded in West Virginia are given by Bailey (1959.1: Tab. 1). Based on the ninety-five bands recovered by Bailey, J. J. Hickey has calculated an annual loss of 74 to 75 per cent of the population. In making the calculations, it was assumed that there were no significant variations in recruitment from year to year, there was no loss of bands, and that the birds dying from natural phenomena did so in the same proportions as those killed by hunters. A larger sample taken under a variety of conditions is desirable.

The status of a turkey population cannot be determined except by an annual inventory. At least one census should be made, preferably in early fall, to determine the number of young to the total number of hens. Desirable additional information is the number of hens without broods and the number of adult gobblers. It is difficult to determine the number of non-productive hens since they frequently associate with hens having young. The number of turkeys must be determined by actual count and this presupposes an intimate knowledge of the areas used by individual flocks. Where roosting sites are limited on account of the scarcity of timber, a count close to the actual number of birds can be made at the roosts. It would seem advisable in a year when the production of young was poor to close the season or reduce the kill. Some of the states do not observe this precaution, the thought being that the reproductive capacity of the wild turkey is sufficiently high that the population can recover in a single good nesting season. Also, hunting pressure diminishes in a season when the birds are relatively scarce.

Reams have been written on the management of the wild turkey, yet the truly effective activities are limited to law enforcement, regulated hunting, and restocking. Except for burning, the usefulness of which is generally limited to the Southeast, any large scale modification of habitat is prohibitively expensive.

Factors governing the successful management of the wild turkey will vary with the locality. Following are the general requirements.

1. The habitat should consist of woods with open areas and in the main free of thick undergrowth, or open areas with some trees. The area should provide adequate natural foods and water. The minimum size of an area should be usually 15,000 acres, preferably much larger.

2. Sanctuaries of 800 to 1,000 acres.

3. Food patches.

4. Winter feeding is seldom desirable.

5. Human activity should be at a minimum. Logging and portable sawmills are to be avoided if possible.

6. The range should be free of livestock such as hogs, cattle, and sheep.

7. Predator control has little effect in maintaining a population and should be confined to local depredations.

8. Over-shooting should be avoided. The allowable kill should be predicated on the estimated fall population.

9. All transplants should be made with pure wild stock.

10. Enforcement of the game laws should be efficient.

17

Restorations and Introductions

M OST OF THE STATES which had turkeys originally have engaged in restocking. Detailed records of many of the early plantings were not kept or have been lost. Others have not been published. Attempts have also been made to establish wild turkeys in states where they had not occurred previously. Brief accounts of plantings in various states are given below.

ALABAMA

It was a common early mistake to plant domestic turkeys, but its repetition as late as 1940 seems paradoxical. Barkalow (1949:48) wrote: "During the summer questionnaire survey, it was discovered that numerous domestic turkeys were being liberated in some of the best turkey ranges of the State and that a serious dilution of the wild stock was occurring. This condition is viewed with considerable concern and recommendations were made to the Director to prohibit this practice."

Possibly as a result of this unwise introduction, a 30.5-pound gobbler was shot in the Talladega National Forest (Anon., 1942). In 1942 poults and adults were trapped and, after pinioning or wing-clipping, placed in an enclosure (Wheeler, 1948:77). The poults were to be released in depleted areas and the eggs from the adults incubated artificially. The project was abandoned after most of the birds had escaped in one way or another. Trapping the birds for immediate release was found to be the most satisfactory procedure. Up to 1948, little restocking had been done. Eight birds were liberated on the Ted Joy Preserve and thirty-nine on the Colbert Game Sanctuary. Recently a project was started to obtain turkeys for stocking purposes by artificially hatching the eggs obtained

437

from the nests of wild birds. During 1956 a total of 384 birds from this source was released (Kyle, 1957).

ARIZONA

According to the U. S. Forest Service records, twenty-six turkeys were planted in the Mt. Graham area, Graham County, in 1926. Sixteen were released in 1940, eleven in 1941, and eleven in 1944. The Forest Service in 1947 estimated the population at 1,200. Six years later, Galliziolli (1953:10) reported that there were very few signs of turkeys. Fourteen turkeys were released on December 18, 1943, two miles west of the Walnut Creek Ranger Station, Prescott, Yavapai County, where there was a remnant population. In 1947 the birds were found in eighteen different localities over an area eight by seventeen miles (Edwards, 1948). During the late summer and early autumn of 1917, ten pairs of wild turkeys were liberated where the Canelo Hills merge into the Huachuca Mountains, Cochise County (Pooler, 1922.1). A flock of about twenty birds was seen in June, 1921. It was estimated that there were perhaps fifty turkeys high in the Huachucas in an area about four miles square. A like number was liberated on the eastern slope of the Huachucas, but the birds were destroyed in a short time with the exception of a male which was killed by a predator a year later.

According to Jantzen (1957.1:10), the flocks on the Kaibab North and Santa Catalina mountains, Pima County, were established from transplants made in 1947 and 1948. In 1949, fourteen males and twenty-eight females were released on the western slope near the Pine Flat water catchment, Kaibab National Game Preserve (Russo, 1959:175). On July 27, 1950, a group of twenty-five turkeys was seen at Point Sublime, Grand Canyon National Park, twenty-five miles air line from the point of release. That this place would be selected by the turkeys as a favorable habitat could not have been foretold. On July 9, 1951, a flock of nine turkeys was seen at Cape Royal, forty air-line miles from the release site. By 1958 all the summer range in the Game Preserve and National Park on the north rim had been occupied. No birds moved to the eastern side of the mountains. But few turkeys wintered at the release site. Many wintered in the Grand Canyon proper, especially in the area of Bright Angel Creek. During the hunting season of 1956, ninety-one turkeys were killed, and fifty-nine in that of 1957. Prior to the spring hatch of 1953, it

438

was estimated that there were three to four hundred turkeys on Kaibab North (Schwank *et al.*, 1954). In February of 1961 and 1962, releases of Rio Grande turkeys were made in the oak–grass land area west of Pena Blanca Lake, Santa Cruz County, where plants of Merriam's turkeys had failed. Six poults were seen in July, 1962 (Reed, 1963).

ARKANSAS

Holder (1951:84) states: "The first recorded efforts to restock were in 1932. In that year the following number of turkey releases were made in the refuges: Howard County 10; Ouachita Co. 7 or 8; Grant Co. 8–10; Monroe Co. 2–3. These birds came from North Dakota and Mississippi." Data on releases in the Arkansas Ozarks are given by Preston (1959). The release of several hundred pen-reared turkeys in 1940 and 1941 ended in failure. In 1950–58 releases were made of 101 native birds trapped in the southern part of the state. Eighty pen-reared birds of the Pennsylvania strain were also released in 1958. The wild birds have been able to at least maintain their original numbers, but the ultimate fate of the game farm releases remains in doubt.

CALIFORNIA

Attempts to establish the wild turkey in California cover a long period. Caton (1877:328) sent about forty turkeys to California hoping that they would become established; and that last spring some were placed on Santa Clara (Cruz) Island where three broods were raised. The winter of 1886–87, he sent ten turkeys to Monterey. The nine that remained alive were liberated and several of the birds nested. According to Caton (1886), the twelve birds which he sent to Santa Cruz had increased to an estimated 40,000! This would be almost a bird per acre. The turkeys on the island degenerated so in size that is was impossible to find a gobbler weighing over six pounds (Caton, 1887.1:351). In 1883 it was reported that wild turkeys raised at Marin were selling in San Francisco at 30 cents a pound (Anon., 1883.1). The breeding stock, imported from the east, cost $40.00 per bird. About 1,240 Mexican wild turkeys were liberated in the state between 1888 and 1918 (Phillips, 1928:10).

The California Fish and Game Commission (1910) in March, 1908, sent W. E. Van Slyke to Sinaloa, Mexico, where he secured twenty-two wild turkeys that were liberated in the San Bernadino Mountains at an elevation of 4,000 feet on June 15, 1908. An additional shipment of twenty-six birds made from Mazatlán, Sinaloa, was held at the State Game Farm for breeding purposes. The turkeys cost $50.00 apiece. About 300 turkeys were raised in 1909 and 1910, and the following releases were made: 30 in the San Bernadino Mountains, 48 in the lower Yosemite Valley, 119 in the Sequoia National Park, and 10 in Tulare County.

In 1911 five wild turkeys from Virginia were obtained for breeding stock, but only a few young from this race were raised (Grinnell et al., 1918:36). Death of most of the breeding stock from blackhead led to discontinuance of the breeding program in 1913. One writer stated that in 1911 there were 650 young turkeys—the progeny of the Mexican turkeys—at the State Game Farm ("Golden Gate," 1911). According to W. J. De Long (1911), the breeding stock came from the mountains of Sonora, probably confused with Sinaloa. In color they were "entirely black." Some were light bronze shading almost to white. The dark birds were selected for breeding. They were taller and slimmer than the eastern wild turkeys at the farm. The colors show that the turkeys were not of a pure wild race. The U. S. National Museum has a small, entirely black female, No. 185280, collected at La Salada, a ranch forty miles south of Uruapan, Michoacán, in 1903. Though labeled *M. g. gallopavo*, I think it is a domestic bird. The tarsi are dark without a trace of pink.

The California Commission (1913) reported the liberation of wild turkeys in the lower Sierra Nevada region, and in the counties of San Diego, San Bernardino, Monterey, San Benito, Alameda, Sonoma, Shasta, and Humboldt. A total of 216 turkeys was distributed from July 1, 1912, to June 30, 1914 (Dirks, 1914). In 1928 wild turkeys from Arizona were brought in for liberation (Grinnell, 1928). The state in 1929 liberated "Mexican bronze" (Arizona) turkeys in the northwestern corner of Napa County; also, 125 at Eureka, Fort Seward, Kellog (Sonoma County), and Redding (Anon., 1929). The following year turkeys were released in Humboldt, Plumas, Mariposa, and San Diego counties (Anon., 1931). Grinnell and Miller (1944:565) wrote that they were unaware that any of the introductions had been successful.

A summary of introductions from 1928–1951, which extended nearly the length of the state, is given by Burger (1954.1:123). Since 1928, 3,062 turkeys and poults from 311 eggs were distributed in 118 separate plants. By 1951 only four of the release sites had apparently successful populations. They contained 90 per cent of the 1,410 to 1,665 turkeys estimated to occur in California. All the birds released up to 1949 were semi-domestic hybrids, and the failures were attributed to lack of sufficient inherent wildness. The successful plants arose from the release of trapped wild birds from Arizona in 1949 and 1950 on the western slope of the Sierra Nevada. A hybrid population (*M. g. merriami* x *M. g. domestica*) in the Castro Valley appeared to be faring well in 1951 (Burger, 1954:205). It resulted from the release of forty-nine turkeys in 1939 and 1946. The maximum range of fourteen square miles for this population was reduced to six square miles by 1951.

Information on recent stockings has been furnished by the California Department of Fish and Game. On November 15, 1959, fifty-seven Rio Grande turkeys trapped on the King Ranch, Texas, were liberated on the Rancho Corte Madera, three miles southwest of Pine Valley, San Diego County. Five months after the release, forty birds remained on the area. A year later the flock had increased to seventy-five to one hundred birds. Reproduction in 1961 was very poor. In February, 1960, twenty-six Merriam's turkeys were released in the Volcan Mountains, six miles northeast of Wynola, San Diego County. The two releases were thirty miles apart. Eleven birds were observed in the spring of 1961. No young were observed after the breeding season. The conclusion has been reached that there is very limited suitable habitat for turkeys in California. No further importations are contemplated.

COLORADO

The native population of turkeys reached a low of 250 in 1925. Attempts at restocking began in 1934 and continued through 1937 (Burget, 1954:27). The birds were obtained from game farms in Arkansas, Oklahoma, Texas, and New Mexico so that presumably three subspecies were represented. Also, some Florida turkeys held near Monument Lake Park, west of Trinidad, escaped. The first release was of about thirty birds on Grand Mesa, at Kahnah Creek, Mesa County (Burget, 1957:30). There is no reason to believe that any of the plantings of imported stock was successful. By 1940 turkeys were confined to three areas: (1) The Spanish Peaks, Huerfano and Las Animas counties; (2) Piedra River to the head of the San Juan River and south, Archuleta County; and (3) Pine River, north of Bayfield, La Plata County. The first release of native turkeys was made in March, 1942, when twelve birds trapped at the Devil Creek Ranch were liberated at Beaver Canyon, near McFee (McPhee), Montezuma County (Carhart, 1943:19). In February, 1943, birds were released at Chicken Creek, near Mancos, Montezuma County, and at Salters Canyon in Dolores County, north of McPhee; and in March at Lost Canyon Creek, near Glenco, Montezuma County.

Ten trapped turkeys were released on the eastern slope of the Rampart Range in March, 1954 (Burget and Hoffman, 1954.1). A record of the earlier plantings is given by Burget (1946). A map giving the present and past ranges of the turkey is shown by Burget (1954:26). Some plants have been made in areas in which the birds were never known to have occurred, as in the Glenwood Springs—Rifle district (Garfield County), the Grand Mesa (Mesa County), and Cedaredge (Delta County) area (Burget, 1957:49). The eastern slope of the Rocky Mountains offers slight opportunity for successful restocking because of human activities.

CONNECTICUT

The earliest attempt at stocking which I have found goes back to the seventeenth century. In 1682, Wait Winthrop (1882:433, 498), living in Boston, wrote to Fitz-John Winthrop that he had been unable so far to obtain any wild turkeys for him, but he had heard that some were to be found at Saybrook and Haddam, Connecticut. At the time, the Winthrops owned Fishers Island and considerable land near New London. Evidently, an attempt was being made to establish a game preserve on Fishers Island, for on October 31, 1691, Wait Winthrop wrote: ". . . and it may be best to have an improvement at that end of the island; there must be reservation for the deer and turkeyes coming freely there without disturbance."

The information on plantings given below has been furnished by Arroll L. Lamson, chief of the Game Division. All the releases were made in the towns of Norfolk, Colebrook, and Litchfield, Litchfield County, and the town of Hartland, Hartford County. Some thirty birds obtained from a game breeder in New York in 1957 disappeared soon after liberation. The following year forty-eight adults purchased from the Alleghany Game Farm were released in late summer. In 1959, five hundred eggs were obtained from the Alleghany Game Farm, hatched locally, and 225 poults liberated when they were sixteen weeks of age.

442

The same procedure was followed in 1960 when two hundred birds were liberated. The mortality of the released birds was high, but flocks of fifteen or more birds were seen recently.

FLORIDA

The initial attempts at restoration were with game farm turkeys. During the two-year period 1947–48, there were purchased and liberated 337 birds (Frye, 1949), and during the next two years, 525 birds of the same strain (Frye, 1951). During the 1949–50 period, 224 wild birds were trapped in Glades and Polk counties and released in understocked areas. The origin of the 416 turkeys released in 1951–52 is not clear (Chamberlain, 1953). Altogether 682 trapped wild turkeys were used for stocking in the period 1949–54 (Chamberlain, 1955). The use of game farm birds was discontinued in 1953. Not a single return was obtained from them.

The thirty-five turkeys planted in October, November, and December, 1949, in the Peace River swamp were wild birds apparently, for they became established (Stanberry and Gainey, 1950). From the beginning of the restoration program to 1958, 1,210 turkeys had been trapped, banded, and transplanted. The band return was approximately 8 per cent (Powell and Gainey, 1959:3). The stocking of 270 birds in De Soto, Hardee, Manatee, and Sarasota counties in 1949–50 proved so successful that a limited open season was held in 1955 (Powell, 1961:15). Since the program has been initiated, over 2,000 native birds have been trapped and banded with a band return of 12.6 per cent. A higher mortality, hence a lower band return, is to be expected from birds released in strange surroundings in comparison with those released at the trapping site. Gainey (1954.1) stated in 1954 that stocking varied from one bird to 46 acres to one to 171 acres, the average being 64 acres. The census of 1948 gave the state a population of 25,779 turkeys. A decade later the population had trebled, so the management program can be considered to have been very successful.

IDAHO

Turkeys were not native to the state. Seventeen Merriam's turkeys from Colorado were released in mid-January, 1961, above the lower Salmon River drainage. Pen-reared birds released in 1937 on the Middle Fork of the Salmon did not become established. Fifteen adults hatched

443

from eggs at the state hatchery were released on Hitt Mountain early in 1961 (Anon., 1961.4).

ILLINOIS

Hough (1890) wrote that John Wentworth of Summit, Cook County, had raised wild turkeys for a number of years. Some of them drifted to Wisconsin and Indiana. He still had two to three hundred birds left. About three hundred turkeys were raised and released by the state in each of the years 1955 and 1956. Altogether about seven hundred were released in the Shawnee National Forest, in Jackson, Union, Alexander, Saline, Gallatin, Pope, Hardin, Massac and Johnson counties (Casey, 1957). Four turkeys from a number released at Lake Le-Aqua-Na the summer of 1960 decided to take up residence at the village of Winslow, Stephenson County. The sole survivor now roams the village streets (Anon., 1961.5).

INDIANA

Perkins (1930:235) stated that thirty-eight young turkeys raised from wild North Dakota stock were liberated in Brown County in 1928 and 1929. The Indiana Department of Conservation in 1934 purchased forty wild turkeys for liberation. A year later, one hundred poults were being raised in Brown County for stocking in the southern part of the state (Anon., 1934, 1935).

IOWA

According to Leopold (1932), four turkeys were liberated in Monona County in 1928, five in Marion County in 1930, and twenty-four in Boone County in 1931. These liberations by the Iowa Fish and Game Commission were only temporarily successful (Scott and Hendrickson, 1936:23). Forty-two turkeys in 1927 and twenty in 1934 were planted in the Yellow River Forest area, Allamakee County, and sixty-eight in 1938 at the Amana colonies, Iowa County (Haugen, 1961). Twenty Rio Grande turkeys trapped at Sonora, Sutton County, Texas (Johnson, 1961), were released on the Yellow River Forest on November 18, 1960 (Anon., 1960.4), and nineteen on March 6, 1961. During the summer of 1961, about sixty young were sighted (Anon., 1962). It is questionable if a successful planting of Rio Grande turkeys can be made under the conditions in Iowa.

KANSAS

A small planting made in Linn County in 1937 resulted in failure (Hanzlick, 1960). In December, 1959, forty-three wild turkeys were trapped on the Albert Baird farm near Silverdale, Cowley County. They were part of a flock of about two hundred birds which entered the county from Oklahoma. I have been informed by David C. Coleman that the trapped birds were liberated in Cowley, Chautauqua, and Linn counties. William Peabody has written me that the Rio Grande turkeys from Oklahoma have spread into all the southern counties from Elk and Chautauqua west to Morton.

Some Rio Grande turkeys have appeared along Prairie Dog Creek, Norton County, from releases made in southwestern Nebraska. It is uncertain if report of their presence in Decatur County is correct. Some pen-reared eastern turkeys from Pennsylvania, liberated in eastern Oklahoma, have appeared in Labette and Cherokee counties. Game farm birds have also been released by sportsmen in Hamilton County.

KENTUCKY

The native population was finally confined to the Kentucky Woodlands National Wildlife Refuge, an area of 65,000 acres lying between the Cumberland River and the Kentucky Reservoir on the Tennessee River. By 1947 the population had increased to the point where a few birds could be taken for restocking (Baker and Sylvester, 1947). Records of plantings made in Kentucky are given by Hardy (1959). From 1948 through 1958, a total of 3,923 pen-reared birds was released on thirteen areas. With the possible exception of two, all the releases were failures. Most of the stock was released when the birds were twelve to eighteen weeks of age. Between 1946–1956, a total of 214 trapped wild birds was liberated on six areas. Turkeys became established on all of them. A release of eight to twelve wild birds is considered adequate to establish a colony. Further planting of game farm birds cannot be justified. The first open season in forty-one years was held in the Kentucky Woodlands between April 27–29, 1960 (Murphy, 1960). Twelve gobblers were killed from an estimated population of three to six hundred birds.

LOUISIANA

Arthur (1931:227) stated: "Attempts to breed good wild stock and

445

turn the young out in the depleted coverts has not, yet, proved entirely successful. Edward Butler, of West Feliciana Parish, is making consistent attempts to repopulate that area with birds, but it is too early to prognosticate the ultimate outcome of the venture." Fifty wild turkeys of a desirable strain were purchased in Mississippi. Birds six weeks of age were chosen so as to rear them under as wild conditions as possible. In October, 1945, they were placed in a fenced area at Chicot State Park, Evangeline Parish, where most of them survived the winter (Wells, 1946). Of all the releases of game farm turkeys made in the early 1950's, only one led to the establishment of a flock and that was in Vernon Parish (K. Smith *et al.*, 1959). The total population for the state in 1946 was 1,463, a decline of 15 per cent from the year 1942 (Hollis, 1950:12). The present population cannot be considered more than stable.

MAINE

The Department of Inland Fisheries and Game released twenty-four turkeys on Swan Island, Sagadahoc County, in 1942. The last bird disappeared from the island in 1946 (Anderson, 1963).

MARYLAND

The raising of wild turkeys was begun in 1899 by Henry P. Bridges on a farm at Hancock, Washington County (Martin, 1935). Up to 1953, about 50,000 wild turkeys were raised at the Woodmont Rod and Gun Club (Bridges, 1953:95). Le Compte (1930) stated that wild turkeys had been stocked in the three westernmost counties since 1925. The planting of 215 propagated turkeys in the fall of 1944 ended in failure (Wilson, 1945:36). Two days after the release, a large gobbler was run down and caught. The Pennsylvania method of enclosing pen-reared hens and allowing them to be mated by wild gobblers was introduced in 1941 and has been continued (Longwell and Kerns, 1959). Garrett, Allegany, and Washington counties in the west and Worcester, Somerset, and Dorchester counties on the coast were stocked with 3,610 turkeys in 1957. The following year the same counties received 1,582 birds from the state game farm. Turkey hunting is largely "put-and-take." Prior to the 1958 season, 715 gobblers were released (Kerns, 1958, 1959). The management plan calls for the release of 600 hens in spring and an equal number of gobblers in late September (Kerns, 1961).

446

MASSACHUSETTS

In 1911, J. H. Reader of Wilbraham obtained a setting of eggs of a pure strain of wild turkey from Virginia. Only two eggs hatched, and only one bird survived (Morris, 1911). Some wild turkeys were to be liberated in the western part of the state the following spring by N. D. Bill of Springfield. Turkeys from the Wilbraham state game farm were released near the farm in 1915 and 1918. The Division of Fisheries and Game also tried to establish turkeys in the Mount Tom Reservation by liberating wild birds from Maryland or Virginia. They disappeared within a year (Bagg and Eliot, 1937:176).

According to Pollack and Cowardin (1961:18), a total of 271 turkeys has been released in the state. The 1915 release at Wilbraham consisted of nineteen birds. Other releases have been: sixty-one birds in 1936 at the Beartown Wildlife Sanctuary, Berkshire County; twelve in 1937 in the Savoy Game Refuge; seventy-nine in 1946–47 in the Quabbin Reservoir area, Hampden County; and seventeen in 1960 in the latter area. Some of the released birds were trapped wild in the mountains of a southern state (Poole, 1961). The state of New York in January, 1961, planted eleven trapped turkeys in the extreme southwestern corner of Berkshire County. The ancestors of these birds, though of game farm origin, had sustained themselves in the wild for three or four generations.

MICHIGAN

The Cleveland Cliffs Mining Company released turkeys on Grand Island in Lake Superior in their experiment to introduce foreign birds (Phillips, 1928:10) about 1905 (Wood, 1951:144). The Sault Ste. Marie (Michigan) *Evening News* of January 17, 1958, states that Alton F. Woods released twenty-four wild turkeys on Drummond Island on December 6, 1956. The Michigan Department of Conservation in 1954 purchased fifty turkeys and four hundred eggs from the Allegheny Wild Turkey Farm, Julian, Pennsylvania, the original stock coming from the Woodmont Rod and Gun Club, Hancock, Maryland (Wilson and Lewis, 1959). The fifty turkeys were released in the Allegan Forest area, followed by the release in September of 152 poults fourteen weeks of age raised from the eggs. During the following winter some of the birds joined domestic flocks, and some were fed by farmers and local

447

residents. The summer population in 1958 was 430. From a release area of 26 square miles, the turkeys had spread over 233 square miles the approximate limit of habitable territory. By 1958 the birds were present in at least part of eight counties: Allegan, Lake, Newaygo, Ogemaw, Roscommon, Gladwin, Clare, and Alcona (Jansen, 1959). The winter loss has been approximately 50 per cent of the summer peak. Friley (1959) stated that during the past few years the fall population has been four to five hundred, the latter being probably the maximum attainable. Owing to the high winter loss, it is unlikely that there will ever be an open season.

MINNESOTA

An anonymous writer (1877.1) mentions seeing in New York, in a crate, wild turkeys which had been "domesticated" on the farm of C. H. Reed at Far Rockaway, and that "These birds came from stock procured in Minnesota, and are vouched for as being of the true type of wild turkey (*Meleagris gallopavo*)." The early accounts of the introduction of the wild turkey differ somewhat. Roberts (1932:427) stated that the breeding of the wild birds began in 1923. Twenty-four birds escaped in 1924, and 250 were released the following year. The stock came from Texas, Pennsylvania, and Maryland. It has also been said that approximately fifty birds obtained from Texas were pinioned and released in 1924 near the woods on the state game farm at Mound, Carver County (Anon., 1924).

A comprehensive account of the releases in Minnesota is given by Ledin (1959). Frank Blair, director of the Division of Game and Fish, received in 1923 at the game farm at Mound twenty-five turkeys from Texas and one hundred from Maryland and Pennsylvania. The birds were placed in a fenced wooded area where they bred. There were 350 turkeys at the close of the first year and 592 at the end of the second year. Approximately 250 turkeys were released February 26, 1926, in Hennepin, Ramsey, Carver, Dakota, Scott, Wright, Meeker, McLeod, Morrison, Pine, Rice, and Washington counties. Releases were also made in Winona and Houston counties. All of the turkeys eventually disappeared. In September, 1957, thirty-seven adult Pennsylvania game farm turkeys, costing $694.00, were released on the Whitewater Refuge and Public Hunting Grounds. Some, at least, were surviving the winter of 1958–59.

Various sportsmen's clubs from 1955–57 have liberated game farm turkeys in several counties. It is doubtful if any of the releases will produce a permanent population.

MISSISSIPPI

In 1934 the Mississippi Game and Fish Commission began the purchase of turkeys from game farms in the South (Johnson, 1959). Between 1934 and 1939 a total of 2,743 birds was released in eighty-one counties. It was found in the fall of 1941 that of the 576 individual plants made, only 179 were successful, 57 partly successful, 28 uncertain, and 374 failures. From 1951–52 through 1957–58, by the use of a cannon net, 303 turkeys were trapped for restocking (Anon., 1958.2). According to Johnson (*l.c.*), the trapping program was initiated on July 1, 1954.

MISSOURI

The state began the liberation of pen-reared turkeys in 1925. From this year to 1943, over 14,000 birds of this type were released (Dalke *et al.*, 1946:58). While hybrid populations were successfully established on several refuges, they no more than held their own in spite of good protection and management. Accordingly, stocking was discontinued in 1943 for a time and efforts concentrated on management of the native population. The population decreased from 4,340 in 1942 to 3,087 in 1957 (Lewis, 1958). It was known in 1942 that on the refuges the native birds had responded better than those from game farms (Leopold and Dalke, 1943:435). A program for trapping and transplanting was initiated in 1954 (Lewis, 1961). Approximately 250 turkeys have been trapped. The use of native birds is a big step in advance. While the program of transplanting was developing, recourse was again had to the release of Pennsylvania game farm turkeys of supposedly high quality. Two promising areas received 237 birds in 1954 and 1955. These releases eventually failed. During the open season in April, 1960, the first in twenty-three years, ninety-four gobblers were killed (Lewis, 1961.1).

MONTANA

Turkeys were not native to the state. Kurz (1937:329, 333) spent the winter of 1851–52 at Fort Union, Roosevelt County. He is supposed to have said that turkeys were to be found in the vicinity. This is obviously an error since, on returning down the Missouri River, he mentions that the first turkeys were seen on May 6, 1852, in South Dakota. According to Robinson (1958), who examined a photostatic copy of the original journal, Kurz on arriving at Fort Union wrote that turkeys were no longer to be found. He had ascended the Missouri River.

On November 13, 1954, five male and eight female Merriam's turkeys from Colorado were released in the Lime Kiln area of the Judith Mountains northeast of Lewistown (Bergeson, 1954). Plants that failed had been made previously by sportsmen's clubs at Billings, Forsyth, and Kalispell. Five toms and thirteen hens from Wyoming were released in the Longpine Hills near Ekalaka, Carter County, in January, 1955 (Woodgerd, 1959). There was an incredible increase to 1,000 by the fall of 1958 when an open season of three days resulted in the killing of about 100 birds. The approximate populations at Longpine were 65 in 1955, 175 in 1956, and 700 in 1957 (Eng, 1959). The winter of 1956–57, releases were made in the Beaver Creek area near Ashland, Rosebud County, the Sarpy Creek Hills south of Hysham, Treasure County, and the Fort Peck Game Range south of Malta, Phillips County (Rose, 1958). In October and November, 1957, transplants were also made on Indian Creek, northwest of Jordan, Garfield County, and at Knowlton, eastern Custer County. Releases have been made at eleven different sites (Anon., 1959.1).

Nebraska

I have been informed by D. H. Schaffer of the Nebraska Game, Forestation and Parks Commission that the original plantings of Merriam's turkeys were: seventeen hens and three toms at Cottonwood Creek, January 16 and February 10, 1959; and five hens and three toms at Deadhorse Creek, February 28 and March 11, 1959. Both localities are in Dawes County. After two breeding seasons, the population was estimated at 300 to 350 birds (Brashier, 1960). According to the Mathisens (1960), the lot of eight birds was trapped in South Dakota and that of twenty in Wyoming. Fifteen releases of Merriam's turkeys have been made. Numerous attempts have been made by the state and by sportsmen to restore the eastern race using game farm birds. Five turkeys released by sportsmen in 1954 along the Niobrara River south of Gordon, Sheridan County, have produced a population of about one hundred. Other similar populations occur along the Dismal River, Hooker County, along the Platte River, Lincoln County, and at Reddington, Banner County.

In 1961 and 1962 a total of 487 Rio Grande turkeys, obtained from Texas, was liberated by the state in twenty-three localities, principally in the central and southwestern parts of the state. Reproduction has been promising.

NEVADA

Two plantings of Merriam's turkeys, totaling nine males and thirty-five females, were made in the Spring Mountains, western Clark County, on February 8, 1960, and March 6, 1962 (Anon., 1962.1). One brood was seen the summer of 1960.

NEW JERSEY

The U. S. National Museum has eight juveniles from Bergen County taken in 1912 and 1913 and one from Leonia, near Hackensack, taken in 1926. These certainly are not from native stock. In 1914 at the state game farm in Ocean County, eleven wild turkeys produced thirty-five young (Anon., 1914). Persistent attempts have been made in recent years to establish the wild turkey. In the fall of 1956 eight young and several adults were seen at the edge of the Millville tract, Cumberland County (McCormick, 1956). They came apparently from a release made about two miles from the point of observation. Turkeys released on the Wharton tract, in February, 1959, were thought to have disappeared by the following September; however, six birds were seen by Robert Mattson on December 7 (McCormick, 1960). The division of game management advised that the $200 appropriated for further experimentation should be spent on wild trapped birds. Owing to the difficulty in finding any eastern state that could furnish them, twenty-six game farm turkeys were obtained from the Pennsylvania Game Commission for liberation on the Wharton tract (Underhill, 1961).

NEW MEXICO

In 1929 the game department released twelve locally reared eastern "wild" turkeys in the Sandia State Game Refuge east of Albuquerque (Ligon, 1946:77). They were soon annihilated by predators. Another planting in east central New Mexico met the same fate. In the 1920's, Colonel J. C. Jackling planted three to four hundred "genuine Eastern" turkeys near the headwaters of the Mimbres River and on the three branches of the Gila. These became mixed with domestic birds. Between 1928 and 1932 the state pioneered in trapping and transplanting native turkeys. Ligon thought that any hybridization between Merriam's and domestic turkeys will disappear in the wild in a relatively short time. By 1955, Lee (1955) could report that, by transplanting, practically all of the original range in the state was again occupied. I have been informed by A. S. Jackson (1959.1) that on October 28, 1951, he and Levon Lee liberated twenty-three Rio Grande turkeys along the Canadian near Tucumcari, Quay County. The birds had been trapped in northwestern Oldham County, Texas. This appears to be the origin of the Rio Grande turkey in New Mexico. Over five hundred turkeys had been trapped for stocking in New Mexico and other states (Lee, 1959). The population is between 25,000 and 30,000, and the annual kill about 2,000.

New York

The fall of 1949, turkeys from Pennsylvania began drifting into the border counties of south central New York (English and Bramble, 1950). The first release, about two hundred birds, by the state of New York was made in 1952 in Cattaraugus County (Robeson, 1955–56). Summer and fall releases in 1953 were almost complete failures so that spring releases were finally decided upon. In the spring of 1956, approximately 550 turkeys were released in Allegany, Steuben, Delaware, and Broome counties. Post-release losses were heaviest during the first two weeks (R. H. Smith, 1954). Up to 1958 about 2,700 birds had been released, there being populations in 118 townships in twenty counties (Mason, 1958). A colony in the Catskills appears to be established (Anon., 1959.2). About 4,000 turkeys raised from pen-reared poults obtained from Pennsylvania had been released by 1961 (Anon., 1961.6). No plantings of native wild birds have been made. Turkeys have been the most successful in Cattaraugus County. There was an open season in Allegany and Cattaraugus counties in the fall of 1959. Though only 125 birds were tallied, the estimated kill was 250 to 300 (Hyde, 1960).

North Carolina

England (1930) wrote that the state would raise approximately two hundred turkeys from "pure wild stock," and that some success had been obtained by releasing domestic turkeys on several of the large refuges. The inadvisability of having any admixture of domestic blood was not yet understood. From 1928 until abandonment in 1946, the state raised and released 9,321 turkeys (Thornton, 1953). Hundreds of others were released by sportsmen. In addition to the release of about 10,000 birds, approximately 2,000 eggs were distributed among cooperators (Amundson, 1957). No benefit was obtained from the game farm birds. In fact, the population continued to decrease until the passage of a law in 1948 permitting the shooting of gobblers only. Wild birds trapped on the Sandhills area and released on the Flat Top, Little Grandfather, and South Mountains areas have become established (Kennett, 1957; Connelly, 1959).

NORTH DAKOTA

Turkeys are not known with certainty to have been indigenous. Reid (1955) was informed by a Mr. Jones of Bismarck that when he was a boy wild turkeys occurred along the Red River in Walsh County. Keeney (1875) had written that the turkey did not occur in the state and that he had never seen one in the Red River Valley. Three races of turkeys have been planted, the history of which is given by Reid (1955). In 1951 a few adult turkeys and 150 eggs of the eastern turkey were obtained from game farms. As a result of the breeding program, 75 birds were released in 1952, 120 in 1953, 175 in 1954, and 120 in 1955. The releases, generally made about the middle of September, took place in wooded areas along the Missouri and Heart rivers. On January 18, 1953, six hens and two gobblers (*M. g. merriami*) obtained from New Mexico were released along the Little Missouri River in "Western Slope County." A population of forty to sixty birds of this race was estimated to exist in 1955. In February, 1955, fifty-three Rio Grande turkeys from Texas were released when the temperature was 31° below zero. Approximately one-half was released in the Badlands on the Little Missouri River north of Medora, Billings County, and the remainder along the Missouri in McLean County. The shipment of Rio Grande turkeys amounted to fifty-four so that the loss was slight (Dodgen, 1956). Both Merriam's and Rio Grande turkeys were released in the Western Badlands (Wheeler, 1958). There was an open season November 14-23, 1958, and sixty-three turkeys were reported killed (Anon., 1958.3:14).

Ohio

On April 15, 1959, I received from Milton B. Trautman information on wild turkeys introduced on Rattlesnake Island between 1935 and 1945 by Hubert D. Bennett, president of the Toledo Scales Company. The island has an area of seventy to ninety acres and when the population attained about 175, most of the turkeys flew from the island one October day. Some drowned birds were found on the south shore of South Bass Island. Others reached Middle Bass Island and Sugar Island and were shot by the inhabitants. When Trautman left South Bass Island in September, 1955, there were still a few turkeys on Rattlesnake Island.

Restoration was officially initiated in October, 1952, when fifty-three game farm turkeys from Maryland and Pennsylvania were released in the Zaleski State Forest, Vinton County (Chapman, 1953). By 1955, 204 turkeys had been released over a three-year period, but the population was estimated at only 50–70 birds (Knoder, 1955). It was recognized that the results were due to the use of game farm birds, and in 1956 the practice was discontinued (Knoder, 1957). A complete history of the releases is given by Sickels (1959). In all, since 1952, 1,400 game farm turkeys were released. A census in 1958 indicated 232 birds remaining, a decrease of 84 per cent. The first night after release many of the turkeys roosted on the ground or in shrubs four to five feet from the ground and became an easy prey for predators. During 1956 and 1957, eighteen wild trapped eastern turkeys from West Virginia were released on the Vinton Furnace Forest; in 1957, twenty-four Rio Grande birds were planted in the Shawnee State Forest; and in the same year, six Florida turkeys in the Wayne National Forest. As a result of the release of the 48 wild birds, the fall population in 1958 was estimated at 78 to 138 birds.

Oklahoma

The farsighted and knowledgeable George Bird Grinnell (1909) pointed out that the turkey was a bird of the wilderness and that pure wild stock should be planted in the Wichita Preserve and elsewhere. About 1910 a gobbler and several hens were secured from a trapper in southwestern Missouri and released in the Wichita Preserve (Barde, 1914:29). The flock increased to forty. According to J. E. Scott (1924), the U. S. Biological Survey in 1921 shipped thirteen wild turkeys from

Atoka, Oklahoma, to the Wichita National Forest. Kept in an enclosure, all died of disease except a gobbler and two hens. These hatched twenty-five young of which twenty-two were raised. They were liberated about June 15, 1921, and formed the nucleus of the then Wichita flock of over three hundred birds. The last native birds in the Wichita group disappeared two years previously. During the biennium 1934-36, 501 half-grown turkeys from game farms were released. All died of disease (Duck and Fletcher, 1945:87). The outcome of the release of two hundred young 'travel-worn' birds from a breeder in Missouri was unknown.

In 1947 the turkey was considered to be practically extinct in western Oklahoma (Temple, 1947). Within a year, turkeys were present in about a dozen counties. From all indications these birds drifted into the state, principally along the Canadian and Washita rivers, as a result of the plantings by the state of Texas of Rio Grande turkeys in nearby places in the Texas Panhandle (Ellis, 1948; Walker, 1949:338).

Restoration has been spasmodic and the subspecies of the liberated birds seldom is given. In 1958 it was stated that four hens and two toms from western Oklahoma, presumably of the Rio Grande race, were being held on a ranch in Pontotoc County (Anon., 1958.4). After the birds bred, the young were to be released. Two years later, twenty-one hens and four gobblers of unstated origin, from the state hatchery near El Reno, were liberated in Caddo County (Anon., 1960.5). During the first open season, in the fall of 1960, about two hundred turkeys were killed (Anon., 1961.7). The area most intensively hunted was at Tonkawa, Kay County.

OREGON

Simpson (1927:96) wrote that Oregon was successfully stocking its southernmost counties with eastern wild turkeys from the state game farm at Pendleton. In 1930, fifty-two turkeys were released in the timber along the southern Willamette Valley (Gullion, 1951:137). There are no subsequent records of them. During February and March, 1961, fifty-eight wild Merriam's turkeys from Colorado, Arizona, and New Mexico were released near Troy, Wallowa County (Anon., 1961.8).

PENNSYLVANIA

The early efforts at restoration will be found on p. 417. About 1,771

455

birds were released between 1915 and 1925. The Commission established the State Wild Turkey Farm in Juniata County in 1929. During the following decade, over 11,000 turkeys were raised and released (Gerstell and Long, 1939:2). In 1936 a new method of propagation was begun. The game farm hens, with wings clipped, were placed in enclosures where they could be mated by wild gobblers that flew over the fence (Luttringer, 1936). For breeding purposes, the hens were selected by characters to be found in the native wild bird (Wessell, 1937). The eggs were collected and hatched in an incubator. Subsequently some of the hens were allowed to hatch the first clutch of eggs laid by them (Fluke, 1940.1). The "saturation" of Perry County with game farm poults in 1952 did not result in a higher breeding population in the following spring (Snyder, 1953). Hunting and the fact that too few poults reached maturity were responsible for elimination of about one-half of the fall population. The winter of 1957–58, there were liberated in Perry County seventeen hens and eleven gobblers that had been trapped in the north central counties (Anon., 1958.5). During the biennium 1958–59, there were released 13,321 turkeys, while the kill during the same period was 27,236 (Anon., 1960.3). It has been the practice to liberate game farm turkeys shortly before the opening of the hunting season.

South Carolina

The first important attempt to improve the status of the turkey in South Carolina was on Bull Island which had been acquired by the federal government (Blakey, 1941). The hybrid local population was trapped and removed, and replaced with sixteen wild birds from the Waterhorn Peninsula (Davis, 1949:96). A population of one hundred was never exceeded. Rutledge (1941:95) was not optimistic over the project on account of the scarcity of natural foods on the island and its infestation with ticks and chiggers. An act was passed in 1947 creating the Francis Marion National Forest Wildlife Management Area of 60,000 acres. The following year an agreement was reached between the state and federal governments for management of the area. The Waterhorn tract of 17,000 acres on the lower Santee River has received intense management for turkeys. Webb (1958:11) expressed the opinion that the turkey population on this preserve was the purest to be found. Live trapping of turkeys for transplanting was begun in 1951 (Holbrook,

1958, 1958.1). The aim is to stock all suitable localities in the state. Of the eleven areas stocked, four have been successful, six uncertain, and one a failure.

South Dakota

Eighty-five eastern game farm turkeys from Virginia were released in the Custer State Park in 1930. Owing to a lack of sufficient wildness, they did not prosper. Prior to 1937, an unknown number of supposed game farm turkeys from the east were released on American Island in the Missouri River. About fifty birds remained in 1947 when they were taken to the Custer Park (Walker, 1949:340). On March 21, 1948, eight Merriam's turkeys—six hens and two toms—from New Mexico were released four miles southwest of Spearfish in the Black Hills of Lawrence County (Gage, 1952). A great increase was noted a year later (Kimball, 1949). By the spring of 1951 the population at Spearfish was estimated at 350 birds (Anon., 1952). In February, 1950, eight Merriam's turkeys from Colorado were released near Custer and in March six were planted in Hells Canyon, Custer County. A contemporary statement has ten birds in the February release (Anon., 1950.1). According to Burget (1950), fifteen turkeys in all were sent from Colorado. On March 14, 1951, four hens and one tom from New Mexico were released near Hot Springs, Fall River County.

Transplanting of local birds began in March, 1951, when ten hens and two toms trapped near Spearfish were released on Victoria Creek near Pactola, Pennington County. A year later, twenty-four turkeys trapped near Spearfish were liberated in the vicinity of Sturgis, Meade County (Anon., 1952). In the spring of 1952 the population in the Black Hills was estimated at 600, in the fall of this year at 1,000, and in the fall of 1953 at 3,000 (Gage, 1954). During an open season in the fall of 1954, approximately 135 birds were shot (Podoll, 1955:2). Hybridization between Merriam's and domestic turkeys had become rather common. A map published in 1954 shows the locations of the original plants, transplants, and observations (Zieman, 1954:3). The Lincoln County Wildlife Club hatched and released fifty-four turkeys in the Newton Hills area in 1954 (Anon., 1954). At least six turkeys were present in the area in the spring of 1957 (Sundling, 1957). Turkey hunting in the vicinity of Custer in the fall of 1957 was only fair.

TENNESSEE

A game farm established on the Cheatham area produced several hundred turkeys which were used for stocking. The project was abandoned since the birds refused to go wild (Anon., 1958.6). The releases from 1941–50 have been itemized by Schultz (1955). The original breeding stock came from the Woodmont Rod and Gun Club, Maryland, and from a Mr. Strickland, Kosciusko, Mississippi. Beginning in 1953, only trapped wild birds have been used for stocking. The highest turkey populations in 1958 were on the Central Peninsula, Cheatham, and Anderson–Tully Wildlife Management Areas (Grelan, 1958). Wild trapped birds consisting of five males, fourteen females, and three poults were released in 1960 on the grounds of the Arnold Engineering Development Center, an area of 42,000 acres (Anon., 1961.9).

TEXAS

All the releases of Rio Grande turkeys in eastern Texas between 1924 and 1941 were unsuccessful (Newman, 1945:284). Owing to the failure with Rio Grande turkeys, resort was had in 1941 to raising turkeys from pen-reared birds obtained from Mississippi and Alabama. The releases made with these turkeys also ended in failure. In 1945 it was estimated that about one hundred native eastern turkeys remained in eastern Texas (Anon., 1945:22). Through protection, the remnant populations in the Devil's Pocket area, Newton County, and in the Big Thicket area in Hardin County were able to show small increases. The Aransas Wildlife Refuge of 47,261 acres, established in 1937, is situated in parts of Aransas, Refugio, and Calhoun counties. While his place was still a ranch, L. G. Denham, Sr., between May 14, 1931, and December 16, 1933, released Rio Grande turkeys on the area (Halloran and Howard, 1956). The stock came from the King Ranch. This introduction was temporarily successful. Walker (1953) recommended that only eastern turkeys be stocked in the east. Stocking with Rio Grande turkeys failed in twenty-one counties where the average rainfall was 30.18 inches, but it succeeded where the rainfall was 24.78 inches.

On March 8, 1932, twelve Merriam's turkeys were released by J. S. Ligon in the Davis Mountains, Jeff Davis County (Anon., 1945:15). Plantings have also been made in Reeves and Brewster counties. Both

458

Merriam's and Rio Grande turkeys were released in the Davis Mountains area (Walker, 1949:338). Three Merriam's turkeys were seen in
1960 at Guadalupe Pass, Culberson County (Anon., 1960.6:5). These
birds may have come from the Guadalupe Mountains, New Mexico, or
from a planting made in the Guadalupe Mountains, Texas, in 1951. Rio
Grande turkeys have been liberated in northwestern Texas. Plantings
were made on Horse Creek; at two places on the Canadian, Oldham
County; on Mustang Creek, Hartley County; on the South Palo Duro,
northeastern Moore County; and along the Canadian in Potter County
(Jackson, 1959). Turkeys trapped in Florida have been released recently
in Jasper County, and birds from South Carolina released in the Davy
Crocket National Forest, Trinity County (Carpenter, 1959). On December 13, 1961, A. J. Springs wrote to me that since the publication of the
distribution map in 1945, there have been transplants in eighty-five
counties. A very good summary of releases in Texas through the spring
of 1961 has been published recently by Glazener (1963).

UTAH

Between 1925 and 1948, approximately 185 turkeys, most of them pen-
reared, were released without success. On October 15, 1952, sixteen Merriam's turkeys were liberated at the head of Castle Creek Canyon in the
La Sal Mountains in extreme southeastern Grand County (Greenhalgh
and Nielson, 1953). This was followed by a release of fifteen birds in the
Abajo Mountains, central San Juan County, in February, 1957 (Reynolds,
1957). The release in the La Sal Mountains was considered successful.
Eleven Merriam's turkeys trapped on the north rim of the Kaibab were
released in Lydias Canyon, Kane County in 1958 (Reynolds, 1959). This
plant was supplemented with fifteen birds from the same source the
following year.

VIRGINIA

Prior to 1930, the Virginia Commission of Game and Inland Fisheries
purchased game farm turkeys for stocking (Mosby and Handley,
1943:181). In this year it began raising turkeys for liberation. Between
1930 and 1935, a total of 1,328 "acceptable" birds were produced. With
these turkeys it was found impossible to effect a restoration in areas where
native turkeys were absent. Accordingly, in 1936 the experiment was

459

tried of mating the best of the pen-reared hens with wild gobblers. As the poults increased in wildness, the losses in rearing increased and attained 29 per cent in 1939. Of 440 pen-reared birds released in the fall of 1940, 209 were definitely located in the late spring of 1941 (Phelps, 1942). In the fall of 1949, 746 birds of the same type were released in ten counties (Phelps, 1950). By 1961 the birds had been restored in sixty-six of Virginia's ninety-eight counties (Anon., 1961.10). The annual kill rose from 2,082 during the season 1954–55 to 4,597 during 1960–61 (Cross, 1961).

WASHINGTON

Six wild turkeys of unknown origin were stocked in Yakima County between June 12, 1913, and February 28, 1914, and twelve the following year (Taylor, 1923:10; Hurley, 1921:15). They did not become established. In 1929 it was stated that a shipment of wild turkeys was received at the state game farm in Thurston County where they would probably be held for breeding purposes (Anon., 1929.1). Wild turkeys had been reared at the time at several of the state game farms and liberated in various parts of the state.

Seventeen Merriam's turkeys, consisting of sixteen yearling hens and one yearling tom, trapped at Flagstaff, Arizona, were released March 7, 1960, in the oak–pine thickets of Hoover Canyon (Oliver and Barnett, 1961). The latter drains into Oak Creek, Yakima County. Four mature males were released in mid-March. The birds moved out, some being later seen sixty miles distant. On February 23, 1960, eight hens and four toms trapped in New Mexico were released on the Klickitat Game Refuge near Wahkiacus, Klickitat County. A brood of six young was reported in mid-July. The outcome of the plants remains in doubt.

WEST VIRGINIA

During the Civilian Conservation Corps program of the 1930's, the state produced and released several hundred game farm turkeys (Bailey and Knoder, 1958). The discouraging results led to abandonment of the project prior to termination of the CCC program. Trapping and transplanting of native wild birds, initiated in 1950, has been successful. A history of the transplants is given by Lane (1961). Between 1950 and 1960, 101 turkeys have been trapped and shifted to eleven areas. Various sportsmen's clubs released approximately 150 Pennsylvania game farm turkeys in the period 1956–58 (Gilpin, 1959). As an additional experiment, the state in 1958 stocked twenty-nine pen-reared turkeys on the Lewis Wetzel Public Hunting Area, Wetzel County, where no wild birds occurred. The kills in the state were 1,511 birds in 1959 and 1,259 in 1960 (Bailey, 1961).

Wisconsin

A Mr. Gordon of Janesville is said to have obtained two pairs of wild turkeys from the Indian Territory and released them in the woods on his place in 1887 (Schorger, 1942:180). By 1890 there was a considerable increase apparently due to mating with domestic turkeys. Hough (1891) stated that the Peck brothers of Janesville had a flock of wild turkeys which originated from half a dozen birds brought from Mexico. The state stocked about 3,000 pen-reared turkeys between 1929 and 1939 (Hopkins, 1940). The birds went to farms and were insufficiently wary of predators and hunters. During a bow season in 1939, fifty-four birds were killed by archers, a proof of lack of wildness. Human predation has been continuous. A few hours after some turkeys from the State Game Farm at Poynette had been released in the Baraboo Hills on July 8, 1938, four of them were killed by poachers (Anon., 1938.1). During the three years 1937–39, 507 birds were released in Sauk County. In 1937 five of these turkeys appeared at a farm at Hickory Bluff near Grand Marsh, Adams County, and associated with domestic turkeys. The last one died February 1, 1958 (Schorger, 1958).

The state, after consultation with Roger M. Latham, in 1954 purchased sixty-nine turkeys of an "improved" strain from a game breeder in Pennsylvania (Wagner, 1954). They were released on the Central Wisconsin Conservation Area and on the Necedah National Wildlife Refuge, Juneau County. Additional releases of 217 birds were made in 1956 and 460 in 1957 (Plis and Hartman, 1958). In 1958 a minimum of thirty-four broods numbering 240 poults was observed. Some birds were reported thirty miles from previous release sites (Hartman, 1959). Turkeys have been observed in Juneau, Adams, Wood, Monroe, and Jackson counties. The winter of 1958–59 was severe and the spring of 1960 exceptionally wet during the nesting season. As a result only ten broods, containing forty-eight young, were observed during the summer of 1960 (Plis, 1960).

461

WYOMING

Nine female and six male Merriam's turkeys from New Mexico were liberated on March 6, 1935, on Cottonwood Creek, near Laramie Peak, Platte County (Ligon, 1943). The failure of a planting in the Black Hills was attributed to impure Merriam stock. The original plant of fifteen birds at Laramie Peak increased to six hundred by 1942 and the range was extended to sixteen townships (Coughlin, 1943). Most of the birds ranged between the elevation of 6,000 to 7,000 feet. Some domestic birds joined the Laramie flock. A planting in Sheridan Valley was absorbed by domestic turkeys, and introduction into the northern Big Horn Basin failed (Anon., 1943). In 1947 it was estimated that the Laramie population was 1,100 (Anon., 1947). The following year it was thought that the birds were disappearing from the Laramie Peak area because the snow was too deep and remained too long on the ground (McDowell, 1948).

Of seventy-three turkeys trapped in February, 1952, on the Clifford Peterson Ranch, Converse County, thirty-two were planted in the Bearlodge Mountains, Crook County, eight on Pat O'Hara Creek, Park County, and ten in the Haystack Mountains, Goshen County. The remaining twenty-three birds were banded and released at the trap site for further study. In February, 1950, twenty-one turkeys trapped at the McLeod Ranch on Sybille Creek, Platte County, were released at Pat O'Hara Creek, Park County, and Ferris Mountain, Carbon County. Forty-seven birds were trapped in Converse County in January, 1951, of which ten were planted on Redwater Creek, Bearlodge Mountains, eleven on Red Fork of Middle Fork, Powder River, Johnson County, and twenty-six released at the trap site. Twenty-six turkeys received from New Mexico in February, 1951, were added to previous plants in Crook, Natrona, and Carbon counties (Anon., 1952.1).

In 1955, successful or apparently successful plants existed in Park, Johnson, Crook, Natrona, Converse, Carbon, Albany, and Platte counties (Anon., 1955). The most successful plant has been in the Bearlodge area of Crook County. Here is a yellow pine–oak forest similar to the natural habitat of Merriam's turkey (Gustafson, 1959). A history of the thirty-two plants made between 1935 and 1959 is given by Gustafson (1961.2). About 50 per cent of them were successful. During the open season of 1959, 686 turkeys were killed (Anon., 1960.2).

18

Introduction of the Turkey Abroad and At Home

THE YEARS GIVEN BY WRITERS as the dates when the turkey was first introduced into the various countries after the discovery of America are frequently unsupported by personal observation or contemporary documents. The first European country to receive the turkey was Spain. Armas (1888:101) states that Pedro Alonso Niño discovered the turkey in 1499 on the coast of Cumaná, Tierra Firme, and in 1500 took it to Europe. These dates are given by Purvis (1918). According to Barton (1939:5), Francisco Fernández carried turkeys to Spain in 1519. The time given by McGraw (1904:3) was between 1518 and 1526. Michaux (1805:218) assumes that it was after 1525. Then there is the statement of Robinson (1924:279) that, until recently, it was thought that turkeys were first brought to Europe about 1524; however, old Spanish records were recently found showing that they were introduced into Spain in 1498. The source for the assertion is unknown to me. Devoe (1953:222) has the birds firmly established on the poultry farms in Spain by 1530.

Montezuma in 1519 gave to Cortés some magnificent presents, including the famous sun of gold and moon of silver. In July of that year, Cortés sent Francisco de Montejo and Alonzo Hernández de Puerto Carrero to Spain to present these gifts to the Emperor Charles V. The latter was in the Low Countries at the time and the treasures were sent on to him. Dürer (1913:47, 50) was in Brussels in August, 1520, and after viewing the Aztec gifts wrote that in "all my life I have seen nothing that reaches my heart so much as these. . . ." Then follows a September entry made in Antwerp: "I breakfasted with the Portuguese factor, who gave me three porcelain dishes, and Rodrigo gave me some Calicut feathers." It would be unsafe to assume that these were turkey feathers; however, one of the earliest German names for the turkey was *Kalecuter*.

The Spanish literature is indefinite on the date of introduction. All that is to be obtained from a recent Spanish encyclopedia (*Enciclopedia*, n.d.) is that the turkey was brought to Spain in 1524. A very important contribution to the subject has been made recently by Cárcer y Disdier (1960) who discovered in the Archives of the Indias, documents showing that turkeys were brought to Spain by at least 1511. These follow:

> To Miguel de Passamonte in order that he have brought in each ship 10 turkeys [*pabos*]. Dated in Burgos 24 October, 1511.
>
> Miguel de Passamonte, our chief treasurer of the Islands and Tierra Firme of the ocean sea, because I desire that there be bred here some cocks and hens, of those which you have there and were brought from Tierra Firme, so that they start a breed here. Therefore I order you that in each of those ships that come here from the above mentioned islands, you bring us well guarded ten turkeys, half males and the other half females, and have them given to our officials of the Casa de la Contrataçion, who reside in the city of Seville, that they keep them for whatever purpose we order. Dated in Burgos 24 October, 1511, I the King. By order of his highness Lope Conchillos, signed by the Bishop of Valencia.
>
> So to the officials of Seville that they hand over the turkeys to whomever the Bishop says. Dated in Logroño 30 September, 1512.
>
> "The King. Our officials of the Casa de la Contrataçion de las Indias who reside in the city of Seville, I the King order you that the two turkeys which were brought from Ysla Española [Haiti] in those last ships which arrived, you give and hand over to the person that the reverend in Christ, Father Bishop of Palencia and of our council approves, and that there be put no obstacle in the way because in this manner it fulfills my service. Dated in Logroño 30 September, 1512. I the King."

The turkey arrived in Italy early in the sixteenth century. Geraldini (1631:253) wrote his *Itinerarium* in 1524. He was appointed Bishop of Haiti in 1520 and shortly thereafter sent a pair of turkeys to Rome. The female was white. Gyllius (Aelianus, 1533:456) states that he had seen turkeys and that the hen was white. He lived in Albi, department of Tarn, southern France. In preparation for his work on animals, he visited the French Mediterranean coast, then went to Venice and Naples. Since many of the first novelties from the New World which were received in Spain were sent on to Rome, it is probable that he saw the turkeys in Italy. In his edition of Claudius Aelianus, he made the important statement that this fowl (*Gallo peregrino*) was brought from the New World. Among the early descriptions of the turkey, his is one of the most complete.

The male seen by Gyllius apparently had considerable white in its plumage and, in comparing it with a falcon, he may have had the gyrfalcon in mind. Aldrovandi (1599, Part II[XIII]:41) criticized the description as failing to mention that the male has a beard and that spurs are lacking. In turn, Willughby (1678:160) pointed out that it does have spurs, but that they are short and blunt.

The magistrates of Venice in 1557 passed an ordinance repressing luxury, such as the eating of the rare turkey along with a second luxury such as the partridge (Zanon, 1763:32). Jacopo Bassano (1510–92) painted a pair of white turkeys among the animals entering the Ark. In 1570, Bartolomeo Scappi (1570, *Cap.* 141:47, *Cap.* 148:49) printed his book on cookery in which several recipes were given for preparing this bird for the table. No date for the appearance of the turkey in Italy is given by Bettoni (1868). He states merely that the date of introduction into Europe is uncertain.

The turkey was definitely present in France in 1538 (Ruble, 1877:7). Odolant-Desnos (1787:562, 567), in his history of Alençon, Normandy, mentions that in this year Jeanne D'Albrecht purchased six gobblers and six hens of which she became very fond. On leaving Alençon, she provided an annuity of three livres, eight sols, and six deniers for their care with the stipulation that a part of the increase in birds be sent to the convent of Ave-Maria. Since, according to the author, this was the first appearance of the turkey in France, credit for their introduction cannot go to the Jesuits. Feuilloy (1884) cites a poem read at the *Banquet des Palinods de Rouen* in 1546 which mentions the serving of turkeys. Gouberville (1892:541; Anon., 1875.2), who lived in the Cotentin Peninsula, entered in his journal on December 27, 1549: "A servant of Martin Lucas, of Sainte Croye à la Hague, brought me a cock and hen turkey (*coq et une poule d'Inde*), I gave him 4 sols." It is to be inferred that he was familiar with turkeys since there is no comment on novelty.

The birds were well known in France by 1552 for Rabelais (1533:144v) wrote that turkey cocks, hens, and poults (*Coqs, poulles et poulletz*

465

d'Inde) were served at the feast of the Gastrolaters. These names at an earlier date were applied to another bird. Maulde (1879:333) quotes a letter written prior to 1491 showing that the terms *Coqs* and *poulles d'Inde* were in use before the discovery of America. The birds mentioned by him as received at Marseilles for Anne de Beaujeu must have been of African or Asiatic origin.

The turkey was described by Belon (1555:248) without comment on its status in France. Five years later, Bruyerin (1560:831) published an adequate description of the turkey. He mentions that the *gallina Indica* was introduced by the Portuguese and Spaniards from the Indian Islands and had been known in France for some years. His work is said by Lhuys (1877:292) to have been written thirty years earlier. He calls attention to the tradition that Admiral Phillipe de Chabot, who died in 1543, introduced the turkey during the reign of Francis I. The magistrates of Amiens presented twelve turkeys to Charles IX when he passed through that city in 1566 (Aussy, 1782:290). When this monarch was married in 1570, turkeys were served at the wedding feast (Anderson, 1790:177). The bird had so increased during the latter half of the sixteenth century that it was no longer a curiosity. Estienne (1600:116), who died in 1564, commented in some detail on raising the bird. Judging from the translation of the edition of 1570, he thought it a gluttonous animal of dirty habits and only fair meat for the table. Cardinal Perron (1691:71) commented: "The turkey is a bird which has increased wonderfully in a short time. It has been a very good asset, people driving them from Languedoc to Spain in flocks like sheep."

In August, 1603, while Henry IV was passing through Mantes, he met some poulterers whom he wished to make prisoners. The reason was that they had taken all the turkeys from the villages, without payment, with the excuse that they were for the Queen (L'Éstoile, 1958:112). Some of the statements of Brillat-Savarin (1926:48) must be taken with reservations. He assumes that the turkey did not appear in Europe until the end of the seventeenth century and that it was brought to France by the Jesuits, who raised large numbers at Bruges; hence, the turkey was called a Jesuit. A turkey in Paris cost twenty francs. About 1840 in this city alone, during the four winter months, three hundred turkeys were consumed daily, giving a total of 36,000 birds.

I have been unable to find authority for the statements that the first

Plate 41.—Bronze turkey, by Giovanni da Bologna, *ca.* 1560.

Plate 42.—Turkey-head handle on a pre-Columbian pottery jar from Costa Rica. (After Lothrop [1926].)

Plate 43.—Domestic Mexican turkeys. (After Sahagún [*ca.* 1570].)

Plate 44a.—Turkeys. (After Bellonius [1555].)

Plate 44b.—Turkey, painted
by Ustād Mansūr for the
Emperor Jahangir (1612).

Plate 45.—Turkeys in scene of Port Royal, South Carolina, *ca.* 1565, drawn by Jacques Le Moyne. (After De Bry [1590]; courtesy Hans Reese.)

Plate 46a.—Painting of battle between gobbler and rooster by Paul de
Vos (1596–1678). (Hamburg Art Museum.)

Plate 46b.—Merriam's
turkeys, painted by
Roger Tory Peterson.
(From H. Brandt [1951].)

Plate 47.—Copy made by Audubon in 1826 of his painting of the wild turkey. (Royal Institution, Liverpool; courtesy Desmond S. Bland, University of Liverpool.)

Plate 48.—Another copy made by Audubon of his painting of the wild turkey. (Thomas Gilcrease Institute of American History and Art, Tulsa, Oklahoma.)

turkeys received in France came from Canada (Watson, 1846:101), and that the French in Georgia sent turkeys to the King of France, presumably from the abortive settlement at Port Royal in 1562 (Lovell, 1932:9). During Lafayette's visit to the United States in 1824–25, a gentleman living near Baltimore gave him some wild turkeys for the purpose of improving the domestic breed in France. These birds were placed on Lafayette's estate at La Grange (Levasseur, 1829:10, 120). Some wild turkeys were liberated about 1830 by Superintendent Recope in the forest of Marly (Cherville, 1892). The experiences, beginning in 1866, in raising wild turkeys from eggs obtained from a Mr. Lambert in England have been described (Roger, 1870).

Some of the early dates for the introduction of the turkey into England cannot be verified. Dixon (1853:361) gives about the year 1524. He was told by one of the Stricklands that an ancestor of Sir George Strickland, Bart., brought the first turkey to England, hence the presence of a "Turkey Cock in his pride" for the family crest. Doyle (n.d.:207) cites "Norfolk Archaeology" for this information and adds that the grant of arms was given to William Strickland by Edward VI about 1550. Burke (1938:2349) states that William Strickland of Boynton is said to have accompanied Sebastian Cabot on some of his voyages to the New World. This tradition is the basis for the supposition that the turkey was brought to England during one of Cabot's voyages. The design of the turkey in the 1939 edition of Burke's *Peerage* is quite changed. The crest in J. P. Elven (1856:Pl. 72) is again different. C. N. Elvin (1889:Pl. 34) shows a strutting turkey without giving a family connection.

The supposition that the turkey was introduced in 1524 has no basis other than the popular rhyme:

> *Turkeys, Carps, Hoppes, Piccarel, and Beer,*
> *Came into England all in one year.*

It is quoted by Baker (1674:298) in his *Chronicle*. Newton (1893–96:995) points out that there is no reason to believe in the novelty of some of the imports. Aubrey (1626–97) wrote that various items were introduced into England during the fifteenth year (1524) of the reign of Henry VIII (Aubrey, 1949: *xliii*). This gave rise to:

> *Greeke, Heresie, Turkey-cocks, and Beer,*
> *Came into England all in a year.*

The statement that it was introduced into England in 1523 by the Levant or Turkey merchants (Clark, 1938:58) needs verification. It is much more probable that the bird was brought from Spain. That the turkey was not seen in England prior to 1530, as stated by Googe (1577:166v), arises from his translation of the work of the German writer Heresbach (1570:290v).

The first concrete date for the turkey in England is 1541. In the constitution of Archbishop Cranmer, dated 1541, it is stated: "It was also provided, that of the greatest fyshes or fowles, there should be but one in a dishe, as Crane, Swan, Turkeycocke . . ." (Leland, 1770:38). Dugdale (1671:135) gives the cost of the turkeys served at the Sarjeants-at-law dinner in 1555: two "turkies" at 4s. each and four "turky-chicks" at 4s. each. Whatever the difference, if any, between the turkeys, the price was the same. The first sale of turkeys recorded by Rogers (1882–87, III:195, 198; IV:344; V:367) was in 1560 when the city of Oxford purchased two turkey cocks at 5s. each. The subsequent decline in prices was gradual. Owing to the comparative rarity of sales of turkeys, he concludes that they were not raised commonly at the beginning of the reign of Queen Elizabeth in 1558. The proclamation of 1633, fixing the prices of poultry, indicates that turkeys sold according to sex, age, and condition (Rymer, 1743:53). The prices of a prime turkey cock was 4s. 6d., and of a hen 3s. Since the best cock pheasant brought 6s., the inference is that the pheasant was rarer than the turkey or considered much more desirable for the table.

The turkey was to become a common and popular bird in England. Concerning the outlandish birds called "Ginny Cocks," or "Turky Cocks," Googe (1577:167v) says: "But because this kind of Foule, both for their rareness, and also the greatnesse of their body, is at this day kept in great flockes, it shall not be much amisse to speake of them." Their colors were usually white, black, or mixed white and black, occasionally blue and black. Anderson (1790:60) stated that, though a delicate species, it had multiplied exceedingly. It is mentioned by Latham (1823:126) that the color tends to black. A fine male would weigh fourteen or fifteen pounds, twenty-five pounds being exceeded rarely. The birds were raised in large numbers in the northern counties of England and usually driven to the London market in autumn. He adds that in 1793 there were sent by coach "between one Saturday morning and

Sunday night, 1700 Turkies, weighing 9 tons, 2 cwt., 1 quarter and 2 pounds—value supposed £680 sterling, and two days after half as many more."

Many attempts have been made to establish the wild turkey in Great Britain. When Captain Christopher Newport returned to England from Virginia in the spring of 1608, Chief Powhatan presented him with twenty turkeys in return for as many swords (Smith, 1910:106; Percy, 1705:833). Fiske (1897:122) stretched the incident to: "On that same voyage he carried home a coop of plump turkeys the first that ever graced an English bill of fare." Nothing has been found to indicate that the turkeys were alive. They were probably dead and eaten on the voyage home. According to Buckingham (1842:286), Virginia was first in sending turkeys to England. This is possible if he had the wild bird in mind.

On December 14, 1681, C. Rousby (1887) wrote from England to a friend in Pocomoke, Maryland, begging that there be sent to him a cock and a hen of the wild kind. Hockley (1904:39), on November 1, 1742, wrote from Philadelphia to Thomas Penn, London, that he was sending the wild turkeys requested as "I have had the good luck to gett four of the wild breed which Capt Elvis Master of the Constantine has promised to take particular care of."

Dates of introduction are usually lacking. Jesse (1838:136) was informed that during the reign of George II (1727–60) not less than 3,000 wild turkeys were kept regularly at Richmond Park. In autumn and winter they fed on acorns and stacks of barley which were provided. They were hunted with dogs and shot from trees in which they had taken refuge. All the turkeys were destroyed at the end of his reign because of the danger from poachers to which the keepers were exposed. At the time of writing, Jesse knew of but two places where wild turkeys were still kept. There were about five hundred birds in the park of Sir Watkin Williams Wynne, at Wynnstay, and some in the park of Lord Ducie in Gloucestershire.

An attempt to keep them in Windsor Park failed. Gilpin (1808:334), however, states that while the Duke of Cumberland was alive (he died in 1765), there were many wild turkeys in this park. In form and color, Gilpin thought the turkey superior to the peafowl. Doubt on the purity of the birds is cast by the statement of Pennant (1781:68) that the closest color to the wild turkey which he had seen in Richmond and other parks was black. Gilmour (1876:15) was informed by Lord Ducie that the wild turkeys drove away his pheasants. In 1866, Gilmour, living in Argyllshire, Scotland, received a male and two female wild turkeys that had been caught at Sarnia, Ontario. They bred well. There is an undocumented quotation by Huntington (1908:736) on the raising of wild turkeys on an estate in Oxfordshire. When there was a shooting day, the turkeys took to the tops of trees and refused to be dislodged.

Considerable information on introductions is given by Darwin (1868: I, 293): "Wild turkeys, believed in every instance to have been imported from the United States, have been kept in the parks of Lords Powis, Leicester, Hill, and Derby. The Rev. W. D. Fox procured birds from the two first-named parks, and he informs me that they certainly differed a little from each other in shape of their bodies and in the barred plumage on their wings. These birds likewise differed from Lord Hill's stock. Some of the latter kept at Oulton by Sir P. Egerton, though precluded from crossing with common turkeys, occasionally produced much paler-coloured birds, and one that was almost white, but not an albino. . . . We must suppose that the differences have resulted from the prevention of free intercrossing between birds ranging over a wide area, and from the changed conditions to which they have been exposed in England."

Bones of the turkey have been found in several places in Ireland: Lough Gûr (Glennon, 1847; Fisher, 1848), caves of Kesh, Siglo County (Scharff and Ussher, 1903), caves of Clare County (Scharff and Newton, 1906), and at Castlepook Cave, Cork County (Ussher, 1909). All the bones are from the domestic turkey.

Little is known about the introduction of the turkey into Norway. Pontoppidan (1755: 78), writing in the middle of the eighteenth century, mentions that turkeys thrive in Norway but do not grow as large as in other countries. It is generally stated that turkeys were brought to Norway and Denmark the middle of the sixteenth century.

The early history of the turkey in Sweden is given by Möller (1881:112). The turkey had arrived in Sweden by 1556 since it is listed in the inventory of the king's farm, Kroneberg. John III (1568–92) supplied the royal table with turkeys raised on his farm, Ulvasund, now called Kungsör. From this time on, they occur quite frequently in the accounts of the royal estates. Turkeys must have been raised quite generally on private farms from 1600 on, since in 1622 parliament introduced a small duty on all farm products brought into the cities. The tax on a gobbler was one penny, and one-half that amount for a hen. In 1623 the King was served turkey on February 7 and 8 (Gjörwell, 1762:102). During the stay of Charles XI on Ekholmssund, December 6–10, 1688, three turkeys were served daily. The following year, twenty-three were consumed.

In March, 1938, three male and four female wild turkeys from Pennsylvania were released by Major Herbert Jacobsson (1939) on his estate of Storeberg. The offspring were mainly males.

The German humanist Heresbach (1496–1576) stated that the turkey was not known in Germany prior to 1530 (1570:290v). He is said to have had turkeys, peafowl, and other poultry on his estate (Wolters, 1867:139). Longolius (1544), who was professor of medicine at Cologne and died in 1543, described the turkey, but I failed to find any mention of its occurrence in Germany. The date 1530 is given by Bechstein (1807:1,124) and by Colerus (1620:523), who stated that it came "aus India." One hundred and fifty turkeys were served at a wedding feast in Arnstadt in 1560. There were served in 1561 at the House of Fugger, Augsburg, two large turkeys and four young cocks costing respectively 3½ and 2 guilders apiece (Dürigen, 1923:327).

Reichenow (1913:305) states that the American wild turkey has been introduced into Germany and Hungary and naturalized. According to Kauffman (1962), ten game farm wild turkeys and four hundred eggs were sent to Germany in 1957 and 1958. R. Bolts in 1957 obtained one hundred eggs from the Allegheny Wild Turkey Farm, Julian, Pennsylvania. After arrival in Germany, 65 per cent of them hatched. In 1958 he raised over six hundred turkeys from the stock of the previous year. Some of the best specimens were released near Oldenburg. There was some reproduction.

Considerable excitement was created in Germany in 1940 by the discovery of turkeys painted on the frieze of a mural in the cathedral in Schleswig (Anon., 1940.1). There were eight small paintings of turkeys on the mural, supposedly painted in 1280. This prompted the suggestion that the Norse voyagers may have brought turkeys to northern Europe from North America (Hennig and Strechow, 1940). Two papers by

Stresemann (1940, 1941) were devoted to the subject. He pronounced the paintings a fraud. They were evidently painted by the artist August Olbers while he was engaged in restoring the mural in 1890 or 1891.

In 1884, Dürigen (1906:284) had a letter from Herr August Graf Bruenner stating that he had obtained wild turkeys from America. When kept in confinement the eggs were infertile. In 1881 he released the remaining birds on his estate in Lower Austria. He had about two hundred birds in 1884. Guérard (1888) adds that within a few years they increased to 580, not counting 150 strays shot on adjacent grounds. Crown Prince Rudolph, during his last stay with the Count, shot forty in one day. Some of them weighed twenty-one pounds.

A recent paper by Bökönyi and Jánossy (1958) attempts to show that the turkey occurred in Europe prior to the discovery of America. A supposed tarsometatarsus of a turkey was found during the excavation of the Royal Castle of Buda, Hungary, in a layer dating from the fourteenth century. Alexander Wetmore has made a critical examination of the drawing of the bone and informs me that it is from a peacock. Without doubt, the bone mentioned as found in Switzerland and reported in 1939 is likewise from a peacock.

No early dates for the turkey in Russia have been found. Pallas (1812: I, 52; II, 459), who traveled in southern Russia in 1793 and 1794, noted turkeys at Klyoutshik and in the Crimea. Clarke (1816:11) mentions wild turkeys among the game seen near the Black Sea. These turkeys may have been wandering or feral.

Turkeys were known in India by at least the beginning of the seventeenth century. In 1612 the Mogul Emperor Jahangir (1909:215) sent his agent to Goa to buy curiosities. Knowing his master's great interest in natural history, the envoy did not hesitate to pay handsomely for two turkeys in the hands of the Portuguese. The Emperor wrote a detailed description of the turkeys and had them painted. Goa was conquered by the Portuguese in 1510, but when they introduced the turkey is unknown. The Indian name for the turkey, pīrū, is identical with the Portuguese.

The inhabitants of the small village of Kalourie were engaged largely in raising turkeys (Haafner, 1811:284). The flocks were attended by men with dogs. Blyth (1847) reported that the turkey in India had degenerated in size, was incapable of flight, was black in color, and had the frontal caruncle enormously developed. Darwin (1868: II, 161) was informed by Dr. Falconer that in the hot and arid province of Delhi, the eggs, even though placed under a hen, were not very likely to hatch.

While traveling through Persia in 1607, Coverte (1631:57) noted that turkeys, hens, and other fowls were plentiful. Writing in 1676, Tavernier (1712: I, 426) stated that originally there were no turkeys in all of Asia and that the first were brought to Europe from the West Indies. Armenian traders brought some turkeys to Ispahan (Isfahan), Iran. When the King had eaten some, he ordered that the eggs be distributed among the rich Armenians of Zulpha to raise young and give him a certain number annually. The Armenians, seeing in this order another tribute, allowed the young to die. The officials of the Persian king, perceiving a fraud, obliged the Armenians to keep watch over the dead birds to teach them a lesson. He was surprised, when in Zulpha, to find the story as related to him corroborated by a notice attached to the wall of a house. Tavernier mentions that the Dutch brought turkeys from Holland to Batavia where there was a good increase. One of his plates shows the animals to be served to the people attending the funeral of the King of Tunquin (Tonkin). At the extreme right of the picture is undoubtedly a turkey, judging from the frontal caruncle and the tail, although the latter has spots near the end.

While Sir John Malcolm was at the Persian court (*ca.* 1800), some members of his staff rode twenty miles from Teheran to see a wonderful bird which proved to be a turkey cock (Crawfurd, 1863:454). Turkey eggs were flown from America in 1952 to Al Kharj, Arabia, where they were hatched successfully (Meulen, 1957:208).

The last visit of Barbot (1732:217) to Africa was in 1682. He wrote that the heads of the European forts of North and South Guinea had a few turkeys that in edibility were far below those of the European birds. The blacks had none because they were too troublesome to raise. In Nigeria the Yoruba name for the turkey is *tolótoló* (Bowen, 1858:130).

The turkey was brought to St. Helena by the Portuguese who discovered the island in 1502 and subsequently occupied it irregularly. Thomas Cavendish (1890:53) stopped at the island on June 9, 1588, which at the time was inhabited. He wrote: "Wee found moreover in this place great store of Guinie cocks, which we call Turkies, of colour blacke and white, with red heads; they are much about the same bignesse which ours be of in England: their eggs be white and as bigge as a

Turkies egge." When John Davis (1880:184) arrived in 1606, the island was uninhabited. He found "Turkie Cockes and Ginnie Hennes" plentiful. Evidently, the introduced fowls had become feral.

The turkey received early distribution throughout the West Indies. Oviedo's (1950:173) book on the natural history of the islands was published in 1526. Regarding turkeys, he wrote that many had been brought to the islands and to Castilla del Oro (Darien, Panama), and were kept in domestication by the Christians. The assumption of Humboldt (1836:153) that the first domestic turkeys in the Antilles were obtained from Florida has no support in the literature. When they were brought to Cuba is uncertain. Armas (1888:101) assumes that it was between 1511 and 1517. They do very well in Cuba when allowed to range freely (W. F. Johnson, 1920:279). George, Earl of Cumberland (1906:93), writing of Puerto Rico in 1596, stated that they have "excellent Poultrie, Cocks and Hens and Capons, some Turkies and Ginny-hens." Tomson (1890:141) was on San Domingo in 1555 when "Guinycocks and Guinyhens" were plentiful.

Turkeys, according to Tertre (1667:266), were to be found in all the islands of the Antilles, where they hatched three or four times a year. The young should not be allowed to run before the sun has dispersed the dew. They are so delicate that if the dew wets the head ever so little, they will die. They are also subject to a vertigo that kills them, apparently due to the heat of the sun on the head. Those who have establishments for raising the birds find it very profitable, and some of the best families on Saint Christopher are enriched by them. Sloane (1725:301) informs us that turkeys thrive wonderfully in all parts of the West Indies.

These birds, according to Browne (1789:470), throve well in some parts of Jamaica, but, when young, required a moderate climate and considerable care. Gosse (1847:329) was told by Richard Hill that the turkey was found domesticated in the Greater Antilles by the Spanish discoverers. This statement awaits verification. Turkeys had so increased in the Bermudas within a span of three or four years that by 1624 many of them had become feral from neglect. In 1621 a bark from Virginia landed at the islands and traded for turkeys and other commodities. A "desperate fellow" was arrested on the islands for stealing a turkey (Smith, 1910:627, 682, 683). The Bermudas were colonized in 1612. In

1634 the inhabitants of the Barbados asked 50s. for a turkey (White, 1899:32).

It is not known how early the turkey was domesticated in Mexico. Bones of the domestic bird from the Palo Blanco period, 200 B.C. to 700 A.D., have been found in the valley of Tehuacán (MacNeish, 1964:537).

Specific dates for the introduction of the turkey into South America are wanting. The bird was unknown in Peru prior to introduction by the Spaniards (Vega, 1871:485). Cobo (1890–91: II, 237) adds that they were brought from Nicaragua for which reason they were called *Gallinas de Nicaragua*. Garcia (1945:363) is mistaken in placing the range of the turkey from Canada to Peru at the time of the discovery of the western hemisphere; however, the Portuguese names *pirú* and *perúa* are said to have originated in the belief that this bird was found in Peru. It is called *pisco* in Colombia (Suarez, 1940:118). Ovalle (1703:37), writing in 1646, stated that the Chilians had all of the European domestic fowls, including the turkey.

Leon (1864:21, 95, 237), writing mainly of Peru, confuses the issue by mentioning both wild and tame turkeys. There certainly were no turkeys on the uninhabited island of Gorona off the southwest coast of Colombia. He may have been correct that the Indians of the town of Neyva were well supplied with turkeys. Thomas Cavendish (1890:28) was on Puná Island in the Gulf of Guayaquil, Ecuador, in 1587. He stated that the inhabitants had pigeons, turkeys, and ducks remarkably large.

The English navigators, beginning with Captain Cook, established the custom of carrying domestic animals for distribution among the inhabitants of the Pacific Islands. Capt. Portlock (1789:45) was southwest of the Falkland Islands on January 24, 1786, when he wrote: "About seven o'clock the only hen turkey I had flew overboard. . . . I was sorry for the accident, as I had reserved her and a cock, together with some other poultry, to leave as breeders at any place where I thought there was a possibility of their breeding and being taken care of." In the *Hawaiian Almanac and Annual* for 1906, it is stated that turkeys were first introduced into the Hawaiian Islands in 1815. They were brought to Kailua from Coquimbo, Chili, by Captain John Meek of the *Enterprise* (Bice, 1947:2). This date, given also by other writers, is incorrect for the first introduction.

475

Captain William Barkley came to Hawaii in 1787 on the ship *Imperial Eagle*. On a return voyage in 1792, Mrs. Barkley (Howay, 1930:26; Kuykendall, 1938:28) wrote: "We were afterwards highly gratified to find turkeys on the island which are the produce of a turkey cock and hen we left or rather gave a chief five years ago.

"They did not, however, bring any for sale. They are too highly prized and principally handed from one chief to another as a peace offering upon great occasions.—Originals having caused a desperate war."

In 1788 two ships, the *Felice* and *Iphigenia*, sailed from India for America. Each ship contained turkeys and other animals to be placed on islands for the comfort of the inhabitants. It is unknown if any distribution was made. Support for the date 1787 is found in the remarks of Captain Douglas (Meares, 1790:356) of the *Iphigenia* who visited Kawaihae, Hawaii, on March 8, 1789: "It may be a matter of curiosity to mention that at the same time a boat came into the bay with a cock and hen turkey. These animals were going round to breed at the village of Wipeeo (Waipio). The hen, we were told, had already sat twice in different parts of the island and reared her broods to the number of twenty, so that in a few years there will be a great abundance of that species of fowl in these islands." When Bloxam (1925:30) was at Honoruru in 1824, he noted that ducks, turkeys, and geese were abundant. In 1840, Wilkes (1845:53, 205) attended a dinner in Honolulu at which ham, turkey, and chicken were served. The asking price for a turkey at Puahai (Puhi) was one dollar.

Eventually, some of the turkeys in the various islands became feral as a result of many generations living in the wild state in the mountain forests (Bryan, 1915:295, 308). Caton (1882:391; 1887:623) was on the islands in 1878 and was impressed by the assumption by these birds of some of the characters of the wild turkey. There was a decided tendency to revert to the original colors. The tips of the tail feathers had acquired a tawny shade and the legs a light color with a pink shade. The tail-tips should have remained white since the original stock must have been from the nominal Mexican race.

The feral turkeys afforded sport for a long period (J. J. W., 1899). Those on the island of Molokai were very wary. Here Savary (1901) and a companion saw twenty-one birds and shot two of them. The Honolulu

Advertiser mentioned that although wild turkeys were sometimes taken on all the islands, they had become very scarce (Anon., 1906.1). Where the numbers were large, they were decimated by disease. Many were caught on the roosts at night by the aid of a torch and a long bamboo pole on the end of which was a noose that was slipped over the extended neck of the turkey. The Hawaiian name is *palahu* or *pelehu*, referring to the red skin on the head and neck expanded during display (Munro, 1960:155).

In 1947 a few were seen on the volcanic peak, Puu Waawaa, on the western side of Hawaii (P. H. Baldwin, 1947:118). Schwartz (1949:117) estimated that less than two hundred wild turkeys remained on the island. They were located at elevations of 2,000 to 5,000 feet on the western side. Turkeys were plentiful prior to 1938 but between this year and 1941, their numbers were reduced greatly by some disease, presumably blackhead (*Histomonas*). Bryan (1958:12) stated in 1958 that feral turkeys were common on Hawaii and occurred also on other main islands.

The present stronghold of the turkey is Niihau Island, located about 150 miles northwest of Honolulu. It is an arid island seventeen miles long and five miles wide. According to Fisher (1951:33, 38), turkeys occur in the thousands on the entire area but are most abundant on the lowlands where they feed on the beans of the kiawe trees (*Prosopis chilensis*). Their only enemy of importance is the feral cat. On three areas there were consistently a ratio of eight bronze turkeys to three white ones. One of the owners of the island, Aylmer E. Robinson, wrote to me on May 12, 1959, that he did not know just when turkeys were brought to the island: "The birds may not unlikely have been brought in by our family when they bought the island in the early sixties of last century, or may possibly have been there already. I do know that they were reasonably plentiful a short time after that.

"The original stock appears to have been a domestic type Bronze Turkey. About forty or fifty years ago some white birds were brought in, but their influence on the present bird population is negligible. The same applies to an importation of black Mexican wild turkeys one or two decades later. They did fairly well but were soon absorbed by the much greater numbers of the old type.

477

"The turkeys on the island have adapted themselves to a dry, hot, area, and are relatively small, compared to present day domestic types, but active and of good quality."

Rio Grande turkeys (*M. g. intermedia*), numbering ninety-eight, from the King Ranch, Texas, were released in the Hawaiian Islands in February, 1961. Joseph S. Medeiros, Wildlife Biologist, has informed me that twenty-two birds were released on each of the islands Kauai, Molokai, Lanai, and Maui, and ten on Hawaii.

Domestic turkeys have become feral in several localities in New Zealand since the unknown date of their introduction. They occurred formerly near the Kaimanawa Range and Hawke's Bay, North Island; also along the Waimakariri River and in Nelson province, South Island. Their disappearance has been attributed to lack of sufficient insect food to raise young, the shortage arising from competition with starlings and other introduced birds (Thomson, 1922:108). In 1890 turkeys occurred on the Chatham Islands (44° S, 176° 30′ W) but have now disappeared. At the present time they are to be found in a few localities in the provinces of Wellington, Hawke's Bay, and Marlborough, North Island (Oliver, 1955:619). There appeared in 1876 a statement that ten pairs of wild turkeys trapped in Iowa would be shipped from San Francisco to Auckland, New Zealand, for planting (Anon., 1876).

The wild turkey was on the list of protected birds in the Fiji Islands. If ever introduced, it is no longer a part of the fauna (Wood and Wetmore, 1926:99).

The early documentary history of the Philippines by Blair and Robertson (1903–1909) mentions about every other domestic fowl except the turkey. Gemelli-Careri (1719: V, 95) was in the Philippines in 1693. He states that the Spaniards brought in turkeys from New Spain. They did not thrive, supposedly because of the dampness of the soil. When the turkey was introduced is unknown. The islands were discovered by Magellan in 1521. The early commerce with them was conducted from the west coast of America, goods from the islands being transported across the Isthmus of Panama for shipment to Spain. At present a considerable number of turkeys are raised in the islands, especially in the province of Rizal (Fonda, 1925).

Domestic turkeys arrived in the United States by a circuitous route. Taken from Central America to Spain, then to England, they finally

478

arrived in Virginia and Massachusetts. In 1584, long before any English settlements were established, a document was drawn up listing the supplies to be furnished the future colonies in the New World. In the list were "turkies, male and female" for increase (Hakluyt, 1889:271).

Turkeys arrived at Jamestown, Virginia, at the time of settlement, 1607, or shortly thereafter. The twenty-first law of the code of Governor Sir Thomas Dale (1844:15) of the year 1611 commands the death penalty for killing any domestic animal, including the turkey. By 1614, Hamor (1860:23) could write that the colonists have "Poultry great store besides tame Turkies, Peacockes and Pigeons plentifully increasing." Francis Bacon (1890:800), about 1620, wrote this advice for settlers: "For beasts or birds take chiefly such as are least subject to diseases, and multiply fastest; as swine, goats, cocks, hens, turkeys, geese, house-dogs and the like." A proclamation of 1623 imposed the death penalty for the theft of a turkey or other domestic animal whose value exceeded 12d. (Wyatt, 1935:284).

There was no shortage of turkeys for the upper class after 1630. On July 13, 1634, Captain Young (1856:37) wrote from Jamestown that in the homes of good planters the tables were furnished with chickens, turkeys, and other domestic animals. Act LXXIII of the year 1643 stipulated that the Governor shall be supplied with geese, turkeys, and kids at 5s. apiece (Hening, 1823:281). Some of the Indians appear to have kept domestic turkeys. Durand (1687:107) mentions that, at an Indian village in Virginia in 1686, his companion was given two wild turkeys and a domestic one.

By the beginning of the eighteenth century, turkeys were being raised in large numbers. Michel (1916:37) wrote: "Turkeys . . . [and] chickens are very common." In 1705 the colonists sold a hen turkey for 15 to 18d., and a cock for 2s. or half a crown (Beverley, 1705: IV, 55). In 1737 everyone raised turkeys and they were to be had in great abundance (Byrd, 1940:71). They were usually fed acorns. In October, 1783, Washington (1888:171) bought four turkeys costing 4s. each. An English traveler wrote: "At dinner, there are frequently four or five turkies on the table. . . . I will mention that I do not recollect to have dined a single day from my arrival in America, till I left Virginia, without a turkey on the table" (Hodgson, 1824:31).

The first turkeys for Massachusetts were sent from England apparently in 1629. A London letter reads: "Tame Turkyes shalbe now sent you if may bee, if not pr other Shipps" (Massachusetts Bay Co., 1857:87; Shurtleff, 1853:25). Winthrop (1863:515) went to the mouth of the Connecticut River to found the town of Saybrook. On April 7, 1636, he wrote: "I have but one turky, which as they say proves to be a cocke." Shortly afterwards, he was supplied with a cock and hen obtained at Mystic, near Boston (Winthrop, 1943:283). Bentley (1905-14: II, 408) recorded in his diary on January 11, 1802, the "singular circumstance" that several hundred turkeys were driven to the Salem market.

At a meeting of the Governor and Council of Safety at Hartford on January 9, 1783, Gamaliel Bayley was permitted to return to Long Island with his possessions, which included six turkeys (Labaree, 1943:83). In February, 1782, Hazard (1930:30) recorded in his diary at Kingston, Rhode Island, that he killed a turkey for his cousin and helped search for another that had strayed. While at Newport in 1781, a French officer (Du Bourg, 1880:210) wrote that there were numbers of geese and turkeys like those in France.

Domestic turkeys in New Hampshire had so degenerated that they were only about one-half of the size of the wild birds. They could not be fattened until the snow stopped their wanderings (Belknap, 1792:170). As to the thousands of turkeys driven to market over the Londonderry Turnpike: "But for them no established halting places had charms to offer for their consideration. When the shades of evening had reached a certain degree of density, suddenly the whole drove with one accord rose from the road and sought a perch in the neighboring trees. The drover was prepared for such a halt and drew up his wagon beside the road, where he passed the night" (Gilbert, 1907:325). Van der Donck (1841:167), writing of New Netherlands, in 1656 reported the presence of all of the domestic fowls of Holland, including the turkey. In 1661, Mesaack Martenzen was interrogated in New Amsterdam about how many fowls, turkeys, and other eatables he had stolen (Fernow, 1897:409). During the American Revolution, Crèvecoeur (1925:131) was living a few miles from New York City. Some wives, he stated, were famous for raising turkeys which abounded in autumn.

Domestic turkeys were plentiful in Pennsylvania in 1698 (Thomas, 1848:23). By 1750, according to Mittelberger (1898), almost everybody raised the birds. The price was 24 to 30 kronen. Turkeys were also plentiful in New Jersey in 1698 (Thomas, *l.c.*). Presumably this was true for Maryland at this date. At the close of the eighteenth century, Parkinson (1805:299) observed that a great many turkeys were being raised near Baltimore. They were somewhat smaller than the wild birds but scarcely distinguishable from them in color.

Early dates for the domestic turkey in the southeastern states appear to be lacking. In 1670, Brayne (1897:215, 248) put on shipboard at Bermuda eight turkeys for a settlement on the Cape Fear River. They were held for a time at Charleston. Lawson (1937:156) mentioned in 1714 that the wild birds sometimes bred with the tame ones. While at Wilmington in 1775, a gentleman assured Janet Schaw (1923:166) that more turkeys were raised there than at any other place in the world. Turkeys are not listed among the domestic fowls at the Moravian settlement at Salem in 1764. On February 10, 1785, it was recorded that the turkeys belonging to people living in the heart of the town were doing damage; and on May 20, 1788, the turkeys of Brother Yarrell were injuring fields and gardens. It was an old law that turkeys must be confined (Fries, 1941:2,091, 2,235).

While in South Carolina in 1682, an unknown writer (Anon., 1682:2) was informed that Lady Yeomans had a drove of five hundred turkeys. The Indians plundered the English homes at Pamlico in 1711 and, among other things, carried away the turkeys (Barnwell, 1898:401). Small numbers of turkeys were exported from Georgia from 1763-70 (Gray, 1941:104). Formerly, hundreds of turkeys, raised in Union County, Georgia, and adjoining counties, were driven to the markets in the southern part of the state. The regular camping places had to be reached by nightfall or the birds would go to roost in the trees wherever night overtook them. If the turkeys were not brought under control in the morning on leaving the roost, they would scatter in the fields and woods and could not be assembled again (Cain, 1932:54).

Turkeys are listed among the domestic animals of the inhabitants of Biloxi, Mississippi, in 1699 (D'Iberville, 1875:110). About 1857, thousands of turkeys collected from the hills of Tennessee and Kentucky were driven up the French Broad to Spartanburg, South Carolina, the nearest rail center (Dykeman, 1955).

The spread of the domestic turkey westward of the Alleghenies must have been more rapid and earlier than most of the dates in the literature indicate. While Audubon (1831:14) was living at Henderson, Kentucky, in the period 1810–19, he had a wild turkey that would not roost with the domestic birds. Concerning the flatboats assembled at New Madrid, Missouri, in 1816, Flint (1826: 104) wrote: "There are boats fitted on purpose, and loaded entirely with turkeys, that, having little else to do, gobble most furiously." Many turkeys were raised at this time on the upper Ohio and sent to New Orleans. The price of a domestic turkey in the Cincinnati market in 1828 was 50 cents (Trollope, 1832:86). In 1837 one could be purchased at Circleville as low as 25 to 30 cents (Van Cleaf, 1906:96). Prior to the construction of railroads in Ohio, turkeys were sometimes driven as far west as Missouri (King, 1908:248).

Woods (1822:188), while on the lower Ohio about 1820, saw but few domestic turkeys and guinea fowls. In 1823, while his steamer was at Fever River, Illinois, Beltrami (1828:161) saw on board an emigrating Kentucky family with baggage, including chickens and turkeys. An Englishwoman (Burlend, 1936:60) who came to Pike County, Illinois, in 1831 remarked that it was not uncommon for an old settler to have a turkey or other domestic fowl for dinner.

An attempt was made as early as 1819 to bring turkeys to Wisconsin. In that year, Bostwick (1911) wrote from Detroit to John Lawe of Green Bay that it would be almost impossible to procure the sheep, turkeys, and pigeons requested. In 1830, Hollman (1922:29) had turkeys on his farm near Platteville. Thure Kumlien butchered a large gobbler at his farm at Lake Koshkonong on January 5, 1847 (Main, 1943:200). The winter of 1848–49, the farmers at Mequon, Ozaukee County, had chickens, turkeys, and guinea fowls (Ficker, 1942:346). The Englishman Greening (1942:214) wrote from Mazomanie in 1847 that it was amusing to hear the Yankees call a turkey cock a gobbler. Equally amusing to them would have been the English name "bubbly-jock."

The early settlers of Madison County, Iowa, are said to have obtained their tame turkeys by hatching the eggs of wild ones (Mueller, 1915:178). Turkeys and geese were supposedly absent in Minneapolis when the first Thanksgiving for the Minnesota Territory was celebrated in December, 1850 (Atwater, 1893:67, 68); however, on January 2, 1851, turkeys were available in St. Paul at $1.00 to $3.00 each (Saint Paul, 1851). Turkeys were served at a ladies' fair in St. Paul in December of this year.

The market price was $1.50 to $2.00 a turkey. The greater number, at least, of the birds came from Iowa and Illinois (Burris, 1933:391).

At the lower Delaware crossing of the Kansas River, Kansas, a Delaware woman had a large flock of turkeys which was being fed when Parkman (1916:21) passed through in 1846. Mrs. Roe (1909:85), while at Fort Dodge, Kansas, in 1873, expressed gratitude that her dog did not catch a gobbler, since in this area a turkey was rare and valuable. The firm of Beason and Bunker of Beloit, Mitchell County, was accustomed in fall to buying up to 5,000 turkeys and driving them as a single flock to the railroad at Waterville, about eighty miles distant. After a breakfast of corn, the birds offered no resistance to continuing the journey (Bertram, 1902:201).

The first turkeys kept in Colorado, aside from those of the early Pueblos, were at Bent's Fort (Dick, 1941:16). William Bent completed the fort in 1832. It is not known if the birds were obtained from the East or from the Indians of New Mexico. Smiley (1903:341) mentions that on the afternoon of January 30, 1860, the "Bummers" robbed a ranchman of a wagonload of turkeys which he had brought to Auraria (Denver).

An interesting account of the driving of turkeys to Denver in 1863 is given by Bruffey (1925:27): "We were now about one hundred and twenty-five miles from Denver. We were much interested by a man who had a drove of turkeys of over five hundred driven by two boys. The owner had bought them in Iowa and Missouri. His wagon, drawn by six horses and mules, was loaded with shelled corn. The birds foraged on grasshoppers. At night they roosted all over his wagon, and many of them lay limp on the sand. At early dawn they were all up chasing the first grasshopper. When the wind was favorable the boys had an easy time driving them, and they could make as much as twenty-five miles in a day. But when the wind was from the west, you may be sure the two boys had their hands full. They wore out a good many pairs of moccasins on that trip. I met the owner after he got to Denver and he told me that he had done well and lost but few." There is another account of the same incident stating that, between Julesburg and Denver, the turkeys escaped and many were not recovered (Root and Connelley, 1901:184).

Judge A. P, McCormick in 1840 had domestic turkeys at his home in Fort Bend County, Texas (Wharton, 1939:66). They were scarce in the vicinity of Galveston in 1843 and sold at $1.00 apiece (Houston, 1845:130, 138).

I have no information on the first raising of turkeys by ranchers in Arizona. Ives (1861:126) wrote on May 15, 1858, that both turkeys and chickens had been seen at the Moqui (Hopi) pueblos. Regarding these pueblos, Fewkes (1900:690) later wrote, somewhat at variance: "When our people first visited these villages, fifty years ago, the Hopi had no tame turkeys; indeed as late as 1890 there were none of these birds and but few chickens at Hopi villages. The turkeys now owned on the East Mesa of Tusayan are descendents of those introduced about 1894 and later. There are many of these domesticated birds on all three mesas, and they appear to thrive notwithstanding the rather harsh way in which they are sometimes treated."

Turkeys were available on the west coast in the early part of the nineteenth century. On September 1, 1836, Mrs. Marcus Whitman (Elliott, 1936:99, 181) recorded seeing hens, turkeys, and pigeons at Fort Walla Walla, Washington. Two weeks later, turkeys were observed at Fort Vancouver.

Alexander Henry (1897: II, 771), nephew of Henry the elder, on December 13, 1813, obtained from the British ship *Raccoon*, two cock turkeys and a gamecock. These were taken to Astoria, renamed Fort George, located in Oregon on the southern bank of the Columbia, about twelve miles from its mouth. The unabridged Coventry transcription contains the additional entry for February 27, 1814: "The Turkey Cock killed a Cock." In 1846 they were being raised successfully in Oregon (Howison, 1913:49). Turkeys in 1854 were still quite rare in California. Gobblers sold in Sacramento at $7.00 each, while a breeding pair cost $20.00 to $30.00 (Flagg, 1946). They must have been plentiful in California by 1866 for in this year Henry C. Hooker bought five hundred from ranchers around Placerville at $1.50 apiece. They were driven to Carson City and Victory, Nevada, where they were sold at $5.00 each (Lockwood, 1928:142).

The Jesuit Relations show that the French at Quebec had turkeys as early as 1647: "At epiphany, Monsieur the governor sent 2 Turkeys (*Poule d'Inde*) and four Capons" (Anon., 1898:69). For New Year, 1649, the governor gave two bottles of Spanish wine and a turkey (*coq d'Inde*) (Anon., 1898.1:39). Boucher (1883:42, 43) wrote in 1664 that turkeys had been brought from France, and that at Quebec they frequently roosted in trees during the severest weather. Lambert (1810:143, 437) mentions the hardiness of the turkey in Quebec, and that great numbers were raised in Canada.

The vernacular names for the turkey that have been used in Mexico are given in Chapter I. Names for the bird in other countries are given below.

Argentina:—Male, *pavo*; female, *pava*.

Brazil:—Male, *perú*; female, *perúa*.

China:—*Huo-chi* or *ho-chi*; Hakka dialect (*fò-kiē*).

Egypt:—Male, *deek roumy*; female, *farkha roumy*.

England:—Turkey, "bubbly-jock."

France:—Male, *dindon, coq d'Inde*; female, *dinde*; young turkey, *dindonneau*.

Germany:—Male, *Truthahn*; female, *Truthenne* or *Truthuhn*. Old names: *gemeiner Kalecut, indianischer Hahn, Kalekuter, kalekuti-scher Hahn, Kalkun, Kuhnhahn, Knurre, Pipe, Puder, Puter, Puterhuhn, Puthe, Putchen, türkischer Hahn, wälscher Hahn* (Bechstein, 1807:1,112); *indianisches* or *welsches Huen* (Byrd, 1737:195); *Guller* or *Gullerie*. (*Kalecut* refers to Calicut on the Malabar Coast, not to Calcutta, and shows the former belief in the oriental origin of the turkey. The Portuguese, who brought the turkey to India, established a trading post at Calicut in 1511).

Hawaii:—*Palahu, pelehu* (Munro, 1944:155).

Holland:—*Kalkoen*.

Hungary:—*Póka, pulyka*; male, *kanpulyka*; female, *nösténypulyka*.

India:—*Pērú* or *pīrū, filmurg*.

Israel:—*Tarnegól hódu* (cock of India).

Italy:—*Tachini*; male, *gallo d'India*; female, *gallina d'India*; *gallina Indiana* (Zinanni, 1737:27).

Japan:—*Shichimenchō* (seven-faced), *choseicho*.

Morocco:—*Bibi*.

Norway:—*Kalkun*.

Poland:—*Indyk*.

Portugal:—Male, *perú*; female, *perúa*.

Russia:—*Indyuk, indeiskii petukh*.

Spain:—*Pavo, pavo vulgar, pavon de las Indias*.

Sweden:—*Kalkon*; male, *kalkontupp.*

Syria:—*Deek hindy, djage hindy* (Russell, 1794:192, 202).

Turkey:—*Hindi*; male, *babahindi.*

United States:—Turkey; male, gobbler; juvenile male, jasper, jake, button, moss-head; juvenile female, ginny. Mountain turkey and peep in North and South Carolina (McAtee, 1954:90). Early New York Dutch, *kalkoen, calicoon*; Pennsylvania German, *wilte Welsh-hinkel* (Beck, 1924:292). Southwest, *gallina*, usually *gallina de la tierra*; New Mexico, *gallo* and *gallina*, usually *gallina de la tierra* (Gregg, 1844:108).

There is no consistency in the orthography of the American Indian names for the turkey. Correct interpretation of the Indian languages is highly technical.

Abnaki:—Singular, *nahame*; plural, *nahamak* (Rasles, 1833:383); *nahamá* (Duponceau, 1825:105; Speck, 1921:357).

Acoma and Laguna Pueblos (Keresan family):—*Tsi-na* (Gatschet, 1879:449).

Adayes, Adai (Caddoan):—*Owachuk* (Duponceau, *l.c.*).

Apache:—*Arivaípa, kă-ji, tio-i-sho*; Jicarilla, *a-shee-tah-tche-shit-teh* (Gatschet, *l.c.*).

Atakapa, Attacapa (Attacapan):—*Skillig* (Duponceau, *l.c.*); *ai, anian, nohámc* (Gatschet and Swanton, 1932:179).

Biloxi (Siouan):—*Ma*; plural *mani*; wild turkey, *ma yoká*; feathers, *mahi^n* (Dorsey and Swanton, 1912).

Caddo:—*Noe* (Duponceau, *l.c.*).

Capote (Ute):—*Qua-nàts-see* (Gatschet, *l.c.*).

Cherokee:—*Kainna, oocoocoo* (Duponeau, *l.c.*).

Cheyenne:—*Ma-ka-in* (Abert, 1848:429).

Chickasaw:—*Fukit* (Duponceau, *l.c.*).

Chippewa, Ojibway:—*Weenecobbo* (Long, 1791:233); *mississa* (Maximilian, 1858:431); *mezissa* (Ruttenber, 1872:360); *mesesá* (Wilson, 1874:390); *misisse*; young turkey, *misissens* (Baraga, 1878:270); *mi-siś-si* (Cooke, 1884:247).

Choctaw, Chetimachas:—*Tsante hatiseche hase, oopuh* (Duponceau, *l.c.*); *fá-kit* (Whipple, 1856: III, 63); little turkey, *fakitchipunta* (Read, 1937:32); *fakit, aka^nk chaha*; male, *fakit nakni*; young male, *fakit kucha^nkah*; cock, *fakit homatti, fakit nakni*; female, *fakit ishke, faƙit teƙ*; young, *faƙit ushi*; very young, *bibli[n] sbili*; spur, *faƙit inchahe* (Byington, 1915:589).

Cochiti Pueblo (Keresan):—*Tséna* (Henderson and Harrington, 1914:34).

Comanche (Shoshonean):—*Pí-apth-e-cú-yo-nis-te* (Whipple, *l.c.*, 73).

Cree, Kristinaux:—*Ktschipinäh* (Maximilian, 1858:431).

Creek:—*Pinewau* (Duponceau, *l.c.*); *pinnua* (Pope, 1888:66); turkey dance, *pin-e-bun-gau* (Hawkins, 1848:76); *pinwalgi*; Hitchiti division, *faitāli*; Alabama division, *fito ayeƙsa* (Swanton, 1928:115).

Delaware, Lenape, Leni-Lenape:—*Chicƙenum* (Lindeström, 1925:313); *sicƙenem* (Holm, 1834:149); *tshìƙenum, bloeu*; cock, *gulúƙochsün*; hen, *ochquehelleu* (Zeisberger, 1887:206); *chiƙenum* (Heckewelder, 1848); *chí-ƙe-no* (Whipple, *l.c.*, 58); *pullaeu* (Brinton, 1885:39); *plaeu* (Ettwein, 1848:43); *ploeu* (Brinton and Anthony, 1888:26); Unalachtigo division, *pol-lo-uƙ* (Philhower, 1931:5); Munsee division, *peléu* (Dodge, 1945:342).

Fox (Algonquian):—*Mässessá, messesá* (Maximilian, 1906: III, 276); *penah* (Lockwood, 1856:131).

Hopi, Moki (Shoshonean):—*Koyona* (Fewkes, 1903:80); *koyonya* (Hodge, 1912: I, 562); *coi-yungŏ*; beard, *coi-yung-work-sē* (Mearns, 1896:397).

Huron (Iroquoian):—*Ondetontaque* (Sagard-Theodat, 1632).

Illinois (Algonquian):—*Pireouah* (Duponceau, *l.c.*).

Isleta Pueblo (Tiguan):—*To-ti-ron* (Gatschet, 1879:449).

Keres Pueblo (Keresan):—*'Tsi-na* (Whipple, *l.c.*, 88).

Kiowa:—*Cú-pe-sa* (Whipple, *l.c.*, 79); *pẹi'* (Harrington, 1928:233).

Kristinaux, Cree:—*Mes-sei-thew* (Mackenzie, 1801:cix).

Malecite, Etchimin:—*Nah-mh-napmneh*; plural, *nehmeyuƙ* (Barratt, 1851:13); *ne[c]p*; plural, *ne[c]mi' iƙ* (Speck, 1921:357).

Mandan (Siouan):—*Máhnu* (Maximilian, 1906; III, 248).

Menominee (Algonquian):—*Massénä* (Hoffman, 1896:327).

Miami (Algonquian):—*Pilauoh* (Duponceau, *l.c.*); wild turkey, *nalauƙƙi piläwa*; gobbler, *mayočiƙa* (Voegelin, 1938–40:373, 383).

Micmac (Algonquian):—*Ap-tah-ƙe-ƙeetajeet*; plural, *ah-put-tah-he-cheet* (Barratt, *l.c.*); *abootăbĕgeĕjit* (Rand, 1888:270).

Minnetaree, Gros Ventre:—*Sihs-ƙichtia* (Maximilian, 1906: III, 275).

Mohave (Yuman):—*Oŏrōwtă* (Gatschet, *l.c.*).

487

Mohawk (Iroquoian):—*Netachrochwa* (Ettwein, 1848:43); *skahwur-lowurnee* (Ruttenber, *l.c.*); *schawariwane* (Van Curler, 1896:100).

Nanticoke (related to Delaware):—*Pah! quun* (Murray, 1792; Speck, 1927:51); *paquun* (Duponceau, *l.c.*).

Narragansett, Natick:—*Neyhom*; plural *neyhommauog* (Williams, 1810:219, 225); *nahenan* (Wood, 1865:app.; Trumbull, 1903:337).

Navaho (Athapascan):—*Tqåzhi*; beard, *tqåzhi baeězhō'*; tail feathers, *tqåzhi bitzě*; track, *tqåzhi bikhě* (Franciscan Fathers, 1910:159).

Nottoway (Iroquoian):—*Kunum* (Duponceau, *l.c.*).

Ofo (Siouan:—*Ama^n*; male, *ama^n'*; *ama^n itó ķi*; female, *ama^n' iyáñķi* (Dorsey and Swanton, 1912).

Omaha (Siouan):—*Ze-ze-ķah* (Duponceau, *l.c.*); *sihsiķah* (Maximilian, 1906: III, 285).

Onondaga (Iroquoian):—Cock, *netachróchwa gatschínak*; hen, *neta-chróchwa gonhechtá* (Zeisberger, 1887:206).

Osage (Siouan):—*Súhķa* (Maximilian, 1906: III, 300); male, *su-ķa ton-ga*; female, *su-ķa* (Bradbury, 1819:223); male, *suķah tingah*; female, *inchuga suķah* (Duponceau, *l.c.*); *çiu-ķa, çiu-ķa ţo^n-ga* (La Flesche, 1932:348).

Oto (Siouan):—*Wa-eķ-ķung-ja* (Duponceau, *l.c.*); *wåe-ink-chontjeh* (Maximilian, 1906: III, 293).

Penobscot (Abnaki confederacy):—*Néheme* (Speck, *l.c.*).

Powhatan (related to Delaware):—*Monanaw*; cock, *ospanno* (Strachey, 1849:195); *mon-y-naugh*; cock, *os-pan-no* (Sams, 1916:304).

San Felipe Pueblo (Keresan):—*Tsina* (Hodge, 1912: II, 433).

Santa Ana Pueblo (Keresan):—*Tsinha* (Hodge, 1912: II, 454).

Sauk (Algonquian):—*Pänáh* (Maximilian, 1906: III, 295); Turkey River, *pe-na-ķun-sebo* (Price, 1866:710); *penaon* (Say, 1824:455).

Seminole:—*Penwaw* (Anon., 1822:100); *pen-na-waw*; gobbler, *pen-ni-chaw*; hen, *pen-nit-ķee*; beard, *pen-na-waw-en-to-wee*; cry, *pen-cha-ho-gaw* (Willoughby, 1910:180).

Seneca (Iroquoian):—*Osoon* (Parker, 1923); place of turkeys, *o-só-ont-geh* (Beauchamp, 1907:83).

Shawnee (Algonquian):—*Pelewa* (Atwater, 1820:288); *pellewaa* (Jones, 1865:20); female, *pealeywaw*; male, *awķitsee* (Ridout, 1890:377); *be-la-wa* (Spencer, 1908:387); wild turkey, *nälauķķi-piläwa* (Voegelin, 1938–40:91); *pe-lé-o* (Whipple, *l.c.*, 58).

488

Shoshoni (Shoshonean):—*Kó-io-nit* (Hoffman, 1885:10).

Sia, Silla Pueblo (Keresan):—*Tsi* (Hodge, 1912: II, 563); *tchi-i-na* (Gatschet, *l.c.*).

Sioux:—Dakota division, *zichatanka* (Say, *l.c.*); *zícá tanka*; (Riggs, 1852:334); *zezeha, zezecha tunka* (Atwater, 1831:166); *wah-gay'-leck-shahn* (Hyer, 1866:30); Teton division, *waglekśuntanka* (Riggs, 1890:649). Yankton division, *sisitscha-kanka* (Maximilian, 1906: III, 226).

Taos Pueblo (Tiguan):—*Tchu-u-lah-pah-bo* (Gatschet, *l.c.*).

Tehua, Tewa, Los Luceros Pueblo (Tanoan):—*Indee* (Gatschet, *l.c.*); *di* (Henderson and Harrington, 1914:34); *ndi* (Hewett and Dutton, 1945:112).

Tonto, Gohun, Mohave Apache:—*Mal-ya* (Gatschet, *l.c.*).

Tuscarora (Iroquoian):—*Keuhnuh* (Schoolcraft, 1846:255).

Uchee, Yuchi (Uchean):—*Witch-pshah* (Duponceau, *l.c.*).

Unquachoag, Patchoag (on Long Island):—*Nahiam* (Duponceau, *l.c.*; Ruttenber, *l.c.*).

Wichita (Caddoan):—*Naa* (Dorsey, 1904:289).

Winnebago (Siouan:—*Ce-ce-carrah* (Price, 1866:711).

Wyandotts, Huron (Iroquoian):—*Daigh-ton-tah* (Atwater, 1820:293).

Zuñi Pueblo (Zuñian):—*Tó-na* (Whipple, *l.c.*, 92); turkey folk, *to-na-kwe* (Hodge, 1912: II, 1018).

19

The Turkey in Art

THE EARLIEST MENTION OF THE TURKEY in art dates back to 1519. While Cortés was at Cholula, the ambassadors of Montezuma brought him valuable presents including six gold turkeys richly worked (Ixtlilxochitl, 1840:211). There was found at Tepic, Nayarit, Mexico, a terra cotta jar with a handle representing the head and neck of an ocellated turkey, the caruncles being covered with gold leaf. Lumholtz (1902: Op. 296, 298) thought that the jar was made in the Tierra Caliente of Guatemala, or in southernmost Mexico, and reached Nayarit through commerce. One of the salt cellars of Queen Elizabeth was a turkey cock carved in agate and adorned with gold, pearls, and other stones (Burton, 1958:109). On October 2, 1826, Audubon drew for Lady Rathbone a turkey the size of his thumb nail. Shortly afterwards, she presented him with a seal having the turkey and the motto "America, My Country" (M. R. Audubon, 1900: I, 131, 160). A poor reproduction of the seal appears in a note by Tyler (1899), who stated that it was cut in topaz and worn by Audubon on his watch chain as long as he lived.

The Museo Nazionale, Florence, has a bronze turkey (Plate 41) by Giovanni da Bologna (1524–1608). A turkey is represented on a silver caudle cup in the Henry Francis du Pont Winterthur Museum, Winterthur, Delaware. It was made by Robert Sanderson (1608–93) of Boston. De Jonge (1956–57) mentions a turkey on a Nuremberg pewter platter (*ca.* 1590), and on German faïence and porcelain from the latter half of the eighteenth century. A dinner set of birds was painted for President Hayes by Theodore R. Davis and made by Haviland. The turkey on one of the plates was engraved by Felix Draquemond.

The turkey is relatively infrequent in the art of the American Indian north of Mexico. There is a colored plate by Simpson (1850: Pl. 8) show-ing turkeys painted on the walls of an estufa at Jemez, New Mexico (Fig. 19). Conventional designs of the turkey were used on pottery during the Mimbres Phase (*ca*. 950 or 1000 A.D.). An example (Fig. 20) is from a bowl found at the Swarts ruin, near Silver City, New Mexico (Cosgrove and Cosgrove, 1932: Pl. 216). Fewkes (1923: Figs. 11 and 58) gives two examples. One of the turkeys has three heads. Two Mimbres bowls with turkey designs are shown by Kelemen (1943: Pl. 107). One bowl shows four turkeys with square tails, the other, a single turkey with greatly enlarged frontal caruncle. A fine example of the head of a turkey on a pottery jar (Plate 42) from Bolsón, Costa Rica, is figured by Lothrop (1926:116, 117, Pl. XIII). He states: "The turkey head and neck marked by raised dots, especially in the form of a handle, is frequently found in the pottery of Mexico and shows unbroken distribution as far south as Costa Rica." The crude but interesting illustrations of Mexican domestic turkeys from Sahagún (1938: Pl. 3) are shown in Plate 43.

The first European illustrations of the turkey appeared in 1555. The bird shown by Gesner (1555:464) has a feather for the beard. The wood-cut of Bellonius (1555:249) contains three turkeys, none with a beard (Plate 44a). Jaques Le Moyne was at French Fort Caroline on the St.

Fig. 19.—*Turkeys painted on the walls of an estufa at Jemez, New Mexico. (After J. H. Simpson [1850].)*

491

Johns River, Florida, in 1564–65 in the capacity of artist. Elsie G. Allen (1951:440; 1938) suggests that he made the first illustration (Plate 45) of the North American wild turkey. When the fort was captured by the Spaniards, he and a few other Frenchmen escaped and spent the night wading in a swamp with water over their waists. Under the circumstances, it is doubtful if he got away with more than the clothes on his

Fig. 20.—*Design on Mimbres bowl, New Mexico (ca. A.D. 800). (After Cosgrove and Cosgrove [1932].)*

back. His *Brevis Narratio* was published by De Bry (1950). Plate V, accompanying the text and showing four turkeys, is supposed to represent life at Port Royal (Charleston, South Carolina). No evidence exists that Le Moyne was ever at Port Royal. There is every indication that the drawing was made in England after his escape. The enormous frontal caruncle and thick legs of his turkeys are typical of the domestic bird. Furthermore, the horns of the deer are those of the European red deer, not those of the white-tailed deer which would have been seen at either

Port Royal or Fort Caroline. The plate from De Bry was reproduced by Gottfriedt (1655:325).

There is a crude cut of a gobbler with a long frontal caruncle in Aldrovandi (1599:39). The title page in Herrera (1944), taken from the edition of 1726–30, shows two men fighting in Mexico and a turkey with its tail spread. Turkeys appear among the decorations by Simon Vouet (1590–1649) of Paris on the wall panels in the royal chambers at Versailles (Félibien, 1676). It was customary to adorn the early maps with native plants and animals. Ogilby (1671: Op. 168) has one of the few maps with a turkey.

A good engraving of a turkey displaying is shown in Willughby (1678: Pl. 27). There is a fairly good figure of a turkey in Brickell (1911: Op. 171), without assurance that it was made from the wild bird. The frontispiece to Fleming's book (1719) on hunting shows several species of animals in pairs, including turkeys. The two plates by Johnstone (1756: Pl. 24 and 29) are indifferent. A large woodcut of a strutting turkey, good for the period, was published by Brisson (1760: Pl. 16). Two quite good birds are illustrated by Bewick (1797:286). The cut of a wild turkey in Bonnaterre and Vieillot (1823: Pl. 83) is poor. A much better illustration occurs in Bennett (1831:209). It was made from an immature wild male brought to England by Audubon.

A small woodcut in Nuttall (1832:639) shows a gobbler standing erect and a hen feeding. A good drawing of a gobbler, hen, and several poults, by L. Palmer, appears in an article by Crane (1897: Op. 432). A very poor illustration of four turkeys, drawn by Jean L. Pray, is in Cory (1909:443). There are good figures of the domesticated turkey, of several wild races, and of the ocellated turkey by Neave (1958:865). The quality of the illustrations in American publications has increased greatly in recent years. The gravures by E. Stanley Smith in Davis (1949) are exceptionally attractive. Hines (1955) has great skill with game birds. A good drawing of three turkeys and the head of a female was made for Leopold (1959: Fig. 102) by Charles Schwartz.

Some illustrations deserve mention for their quaintness. In Flint (1833: Op. 43) is a crude woodcut of "Boone's first view of Kentucky." In the foreground are Daniel Boone and three companions, and in the background, buffalo, deer, bear, and two turkeys. The frontispiece in Lewis (1863:126, 135, 142) depicts hunting turkeys in the Far West. He has also illustrations of a pair of wild turkeys and a turkey trap in operation. A drawing by J. M. Tracy in Leffingwell (1890:367) shows a hunter sitting behind a bush and aiming at a turkey on the edge of a wood.

Good drawings of the head of the turkey are to be found in Gray (1849: Pl. 128), Elliot (1872: Pl. I), and Pearson (1919:155). The drawings in Leopold (1944:181) of the heads of first-year and adult males of native, hybrid, and domestic turkeys are particularly valuable in showing the size of the throat wattle in winter. There is a good photograph of the head of a yearling gobbler by Mosby and Handley (1943:90).

The turkey has not appeared very often in engravings. Peter Bruegel (1525–69) has a strutting bird in his "Seven Deadly Sins: Envy" in the Metropolitan Museum of Art. An entire family of turkeys was engraved by Simon de Vlieger (1600–40) of Rotterdam. A small engraving of a gobbler by E. Sheppard appears in Turnbull (1869:34). Bishop's etching (1936: Pl. 68) of gobblers in flight is not equal to his usual quality.

There are several good early paintings in which the domestic turkey is shown. The Venetian, Jacopo Bassano (1510–92) painted two white turkeys in his "Animals Entering the Ark," which is in the Royal Galleries of the Academy of Venice. The copy in the Louvre is not identical. Turkeys also appear in "Animals Leaving the Ark," in the Bordeaux Museum. In "The Cookmaid," by Sir Nathaniel Bacon (1585–1627), the maid, surrounded by dead birds, is stroking a live turkey in her lap. In the Doria Gallery, Rome, is a painting by Paul Bril (1554–1626) of Flanders. The landscape is filled with birds, including a turkey in display. S. Dillon Ripley, of the Smithsonian Institution, has a painting attributed to Jan van Kessel (1626–79). In the foreground at the base of a tree are a bustard and a turkey. The Flemish painter, Melchior d'Hondecoeter (1636–95), in "The Barnyard," has an excellent figure of a turkey. The painting is in the Detroit Institute of Art. The "Battle Between Gobbler and Cock," by Paul de Vos, in the Hamburg Art Museum, does not show the turkey in a normal fighting pose (Plate 46a).

In 1612, Ustād Mansūr painted a gobbler for Jahangir, Emperor of Hindustan. The bird was obtained from the Portuguese colony at Goa. The original is in the Victoria and Albert Museum, South Kensington (Plate 44b). Another painting of a turkey from the same court is in the Fitzwilliam Museum, Cambridge. The turkey also appears in the "Landscape with Birds" (ca. 1626) by Roelandt Savery. This painting is in the Kunsthistorisches Museum, Vienna. The Musee Royal des Beaux-arts, Antwerp, has the painting, "Oiseaux," by the same artist. Two turkeys are perched on a limb on the right-hand side of a tree.

The early colored figures of the turkey which appeared in technical books are wretched. The turkey cock of Albin (1738: Pl. 35) does not have a beard. Gerini (1769: Pl. CCXXII, CCXXVI) has two crudely colored plates. The male has a pronounced crest of feathers. The strutting male of Buffon (1772: Pl. 97) has red feet, head, and neck. The upper tail coverts are brown. The red feet and tail coverts indicate the wild bird, but the color of the body plumage has little resemblance to this race. In the reproduction of 1808, the only color is red on the frontal caruncle and back of the head (Buffon, 1808:179). The turkey in Schaeffer (1774: Pl. 37) is rather well drawn but poorly colored. The head and neck are brick red, the back and tail greenish yellow, and the body almost colorless. In a book published subsequently, only the head of the turkey is colored. A colored figure of the tongue is included (Schaeffer, 1779: Pl. 37). The colored plate in Bechstein (1807: Pl. 41) is indifferent. The skin of the head and neck is blue, the caruncles, red. The turkey in Frisch (1817: Pl. 122) has little color.

The first unquestionable plates of the wild turkey appeared in 1825. The *dindon sauvage* of Vieillot and Outart (1825: Pl. 201) is well colored, but the rump is distorted. The head is blue except for a few red caruncles. A triple beard is shown. In this same year, Bonaparte (1825: Pl. 9) published a plate of a pair of turkeys that, in draftsmanship and color excelled all previous delineations. The drawing was from nature by Titian R. Peale, who used as a model for the male one of several fine specimens collected in April near Engineer Cantonment, which was on the Missouri five miles below Council Bluffs, Iowa. Peale was attached to Long's expedition in 1819 and shot several turkeys along the Missouri. The female is of the Florida race and is too gray.

No paintings of the turkey have received as much publicity as those of Audubon. The originals for Plates I and VI of the elephant folio were purchased from Mrs. Audubon by the New York Historical Society in 1863. A history of the two plates is given by Stone (1906) and Herrick (1917:355, 363). The plates were published in 1827. Audubon engaged W. H. Lizars of Edinburgh to make the plates. His color work was unsatisfactory, so Robert Havell of London was employed. This resulted

495

in two editions of the plates. Under Havell, the plates were retouched and the titles changed. The set at the University of Wisconsin has the plates of the first edition. The legends are:

> Plate I. "Great American Cock Male—Vulgo (Wild Turkey) Meleagris Gallopavo. Drawn by J. J. Audubon, M.W.S. Engraved by W. H. Lizars Edin^r."
>
> Plate VI. "Great American Hen & Young, Vulgo, Female Wild Turkey —Meleagris Gallopavo. Drawn from nature by John J. Audubon F.R.S.E. M.W.S. Engraved by W. H. Lizars. Edinb^r."

The hen in Plate VI has a beard. Plate I was offered for sale by R. H. Macy, New York, in 1931 for $374 (Fries, 1958:245). The prints issued in full size by Lockwood by chromolithography in 1860 are inferior to the engravings. The octavo edition (1840) of *The Birds of America* has reduced plates. There have been many subsequent reproductions of Audubon's turkeys.

While Audubon was in Edinburgh in 1826, he painted in sixteen days a "Turkey Cock, a hen, and nine young, all of the size of life." A dealer had offered one hundred guineas for it. Audubon was proud of his turkeys and was taken aback when the Lizars expressed a preference for the painting of the otter. The picture was intended as a gift to the Royal Society of Edinburgh. It remained, however, in possession of the family and was subsequently sold to John E. Thayer, who eventually donated it to the Museum of Comparative Zoology, Cambridge, Massachusetts. This institution has also a small watercolor of a hen and seven chicks that may have been done by J. J. Audubon or by John W. Audubon. It has been reproduced by Peattie (1940: Op. 198). A third painting of the female turkey has recently been found at Harvard University. It is without a signature and there is no assurance that it is the work of Audubon. It may have been painted by Audubon's youthful assistant, J. B. Kidd.

In August, 1826, while residing at Liverpool, Audubon copied his large original of the cock turkey for the Royal Institution of that city. According to Bland (1962), the background of the painting (Plate 47) has been restored recently. The vegetation is not the same as in Plate I. R. R. Rathbone wrote to Maria R. Audubon on May 14, 1897, that Audubon painted for his father "a full-length, life-sized portrait of the American Turkey, striding through the forest," and that it went to a public collection in Liverpool. Under date August 10, 1962, Miss Mary Walker of the Walker Art Gallery, Liverpool, informed me that the painting mentioned by Rathbone has never been traced and that he may have confused it with the one in the Royal Institution.

An entry in Audubon's journal for October 10, 1826, mentions that he dined at the home of Mr. Dockray, Manchester, and that he sketched a wild turkey for a member of the family. It is unknown if this drawing is extant.

The Thomas Gilcrease Institute of American History and Art, Tulsa, Oklahoma, has a painting of a wild turkey by Audubon (Plate 48). Through the courtesy of Bruce Wear, Curator of Art of this institution, I am able to quote the following letter:

June 9, 1945.

To Whom it may concern:

Here is the story of the original oil painting of "The Turkey Cock" done by John James Audubon, my great grandfather.

It was painted about 1845 at "Minnie's Land," Audubon Park, New York, where Audubon built his home. When his elder son's widow, Mrs. Victor G. Audubon, moved from the park in 1881 she sent this painting to New Haven to my mother, her daughter Delia Talman Audubon (Mrs. Morris F. Tyler), who gave it to me in 1910. It has never been out of the family.

Sincerely yours,
Signed: VICTOR MORRIS TYLER.

Edward H. Dwight, who has specialized in Audubon's paintings, thinks that the above was painted about 1827 (*in litt.*). After 1830, Audubon did little or no painting in oil.

Audubon had a flair for the dramatic so that the pose of some of his birds is decidedly unusual. The turkey suffered less in this respect than some other species. Maximilian (1858:461) thought that the heads in Audubon's turkeys are too small, and that Bonaparte's male is far better and quite beautiful, but fails completely in coloration. Rutledge (1941:94) thought that Audubon's turkeys are too heavy in the body and that their neck and legs are too short and thick. On comparing Plate 47 with Plate 7, it will be seen that the neck in Audubon's bird is too short and that the tibiae are barely visible.

A colored plate of a male turkey was published by Doughty (1833:

497

Pl. II, Op. 13). A small black turkey with red head and neck is shown by Comte (1839: Pl. 18). Oken (1843: Pl. 85) has a good colored plate in his atlas. A water color of a gobbler by J. W. Hill appears in De Kay (1844: Pl. 76) as a figure 9.5 cm. in height; the pose is good. There is much white in the flight feathers, especially in the secondaries. The figures in Jardine (1853: Pl. 1 and 2) are poorly drawn and colored. A chromolithograph of a pair of wild turkeys is a frontispiece in King (1866). While pleasing to the eye, the tarsi are too large, and there is no white at all in the secondaries. A colored plate of a domestic male was published by Tegetmeier (1867: Op. 272).

Following Audubon, the most pretentious plates of the turkey are those of Elliot (1869: Pl. 38). In 1869 he published the drawing, made by J. Wolf, of Gould's specimen of "*Meleagris mexicana.*" There are good metallic reflections in the plumage, but the tips of the rectrices and upper tail coverts are bluish gray. Three years later there appeared a plate of the eastern turkey and a new one of *M. mexicana* (Elliot, 1872: Pl. 30 and 31). The colors are unexceptional. The necks are marred by the appearance of being telescoped.

There is a chromolithographic illustration by Edwin Sheppard in Gentry (1882: Pl. XXXVII) of a pair of turkeys with a nest of eggs. The coloring and draftsmanship of the birds are superior to those of most of the previous illustrations. The eggs are packed between two fallen limbs. The plate in Warren (1890: Pl. 74) is an incorrectly colored reproduction of Audubon's gobbler. Nothing favorable can be said of the colored illustration of a pair of Rio Grande turkeys drawn by Ernest E. Thompson for the paper by Sennett (1892: Pl. III, Op. 209). It was reproduced in black and white by Knowlton and Ridgway (1909: Fig. 91). A poorly colored pair is to be found in Studer (1903: Pl. CXV). The mediocre illustration of a male, "Copyright 1900, by A. W. Mumford, Chicago," was used by Dawson (1903: Pl. 50). Chapman (1909) has a good colored frontispiece of a gobbler, hen and chicks in the mountains of West Virginia.

The skill of Louis A. Fuertes as an artist fell short when a wild turkey was the subject. The male, by Fuertes, shown by Sandys and Van Dyke (1904: Op. 252) in black and white, is too stocky and the fleshy appendages much too large. In his painting of a turkey standing in the snow on a fallen log, the fore-neck and throat wattle are colored bright red, and the wattle is of a size scarcely attained even during the mating season

(Fuertes, 1955–56). This was one of thirteen paintings, forming a calendar of game birds, photoengraved by the Beck Engraving Company, Philadelphia, in 1907. There are two reprintings of the calendar plates. In 1915 the original painting of the turkey was in the possession of F. F. Brewster (Chapman, 1915: Pl. 3).

A painting by Lynn Bogue Hunt of a turkey strutting and gobbling simultaneously appeared in *Outing* (Foster, 1907: Op. 272). This is a feat of which I believe the turkey is incapable. Another of his paintings is a winter scene with a male in the foreground and two females in the background (Hunt and Forbush, 1917). The turkeys painted by E. L. Poole for Bailey (1913: Op. 91), at least in the plate, are of a general bronze color, with little white in the flight feathers. In the plate of two Florida wild turkeys by G. M. Sutton, the coloring is poor (Bailey, 1925: Pl. 32).

A good colored frontispiece of a gobbler by E. J. Sawyer appears in Skinner and Achorn (1928). A painting of a pair of turkeys by Allan Brooks is in a paper by Wetmore (1936.1: Op. 468). Ghigi's illustration (1936: Pl. VII) of a pair is mediocre. The frontispiece to Mosby and Handley (1943) is an exceptionally good painting by Frederick Everett, from life, of a female and a male in display. A male was also figured by this artist for the Pennsylvania Game Commission (Luttringer and Gerstell, 1952:10). The illustrations are notable for their coppery sheen. There is a good painting by Philip Rickman of a female and a displaying male (Pollard and Barclay-Smith, 1945: Op. 23).

Judgment on the color of a plate must be tempered by the probability that it falls short of that of the original. The artist is at the mercy of the printer. The frontispiece by Walter A. Weber in Davis (1949) shows a gobbler in downward flight. A pleasing painting of a pair of Merriam's turkeys, the male in display (Plate 46b), was made by Roger Tory Peterson for Brandt (1951: Op. 624). The coloring is poor on the pair of Florida turkeys by Francis L. Jacques (Howell, 1932: Pl. 31). An alert gobbler, painted by George M. Sutton, appears in Burleigh (1958: Op. 114). The bird is well drawn except for the tail. The coloring is fair. A well-drawn and colored figure of a male turkey by Arthur Singer illustrates a paper by Martin (1958). This artist has very good colored figures of the ocellated and eastern turkey in Austin (1961:99).

Many good colored illustrations of turkeys have appeared in recent years in conservation journals and sportsmen's magazines. Some paintings have not been published. Owen J. Gromme, of the Milwaukee Public Museum, has been particularly successful with turkeys. A list of his oils follows:

1. A strutting male, immature male and three females, 25 x 34.5 inches. Richard Mellon Collection.

2. A strutting male, a female, and five birds in the background, 16 x 20 inches. Owned by Jock Whitney, Greenwood Plantation, Thomasville, Georgia.

3. Male in flight, 12 x 16 inches. Owned by H. L. Stoddard, Jr. Thomasville, Georgia.

4. Two gobblers and two hens in grass, 24 x 34 inches. Richard Mellon Collection.

5. Two gobblers (1954). Owned by H. L. Stoddard, Sherwood Plantation, Thomasville, Georgia.

6. Gobbler with two hens in the foreground and three birds in the background in pine woods. Owned by Mrs. Jean H. Gallien, Cleveland, Ohio.

7. Two gobblers in flight, 24 x 36 inches. Museum of Art, Atlanta.

8. Lone gobbler in full strut on bank of the Flint River, Georgia, 24 x 30 inches. Owned by Richard Tift, Albany, New York.

9. Three gobblers beside a live oak, 24 x 30 inches. Owned by Mrs. Royal Firman, Jr. Cleveland, Ohio.

10. Two gobblers in flight among Georgia pines with a mixture of fog and smoke from spring burning, 30 x 40 inches. In possession of the artist.

A very attractive water color of three wild turkeys in pines is owned by Francis Bowman, Madison, Wisconsin. It was painted in 1940 by Aiden Lassell Ripley. I have a water color, 21 x 27.5 inches of three turkeys in the oak openings of southwestern Wisconsin, painted by Jens Von Sivers in 1959.

Plates of the eggs of the turkey by Zinanni (1737: Pl. 2), Klein (1766: Pl. 13), and Maynard (1890: Pl. VIII) are poor. Colored figures of the eggs of two races of the turkey are shown by Bendire (1892: Pl. III).

So far as I have been able to learn, C. L. Jordan pioneered in photographing the wild turkey. He began to use the camera in Alabama in November, 1899, and continued the work for six months. In fact, he was active in this field until his death in 1909. Good examples of his photographs will be found in McIlhenny (1914). A female photographed by Brownell (1904:161) is reproduced in Bent (1932:Pl. 75). An attractive photograph of two turkeys, in the snow and near an open brook, was taken by Norman McClintock near Ligonier, Pennsylvania. It appeared in a paper by Christy and Sutton (1929: Op. 112), also in Bent (*l.c.*: Pl. 76). Allan D. Cruickshank has been particularly successful in photographing the wild turkey. A male looking backward is shown in Lowery (1955:219). Another is to be found in Sprunt and Chamberlain (1949:307). Noteworthy photographs of turkeys in flight appear in Mosby and Handley (1942:172) and in Burget (1957: Fig. 22).

Superb photographs of the hen on the nest and of the young (Plates 24 and 25) have been taken by Jack Dermid and printed in *Wildlife in North Carolina*, August, 1957. The colored cover shows three poults appearing from beneath the mother.

A photograph of a turkey's nest with nine eggs was taken in the Santa Rita Mountains, Santa Cruz County, Arizona, by Frank Stephens, June 15, 1884. It will be found in Bent (1932: Pl. 77). Only a few good photographs of nests have appeared. Howard (1900: Figs. 1 and 2) published a cut of a nest with nine eggs taken in the Huachuca Mountains, Arizona, July 1, 1900. Bent (*l.c.*: Pl. 74) shows a nest of the eastern turkey with nine eggs photographed by Paul Bartsch near Falls Church, Virginia, May 10, 1903. Two photographs of nests were taken in Pennsylvania in 1928 by Sutton (1929: Pl. XVIII). A female is sitting on a nest which originally contained eighteen eggs, some of which are visible. The other nest shows eight eggs. Sprunt and Chamberlain (1949:274) have a figure of a partially concealed hen on a nest. Two exposed nests with eggs of Merriam's turkey are shown in Ligon (1946: Pl. IX). In two photographs of nests, taken in Colorado, there is good concealment by vegetation (Burget, 1957: Figs. 3 and 4). Scoville (1919: Op. 14) published a photograph by A. D. McGrew of a nest with eleven eggs in a brush heap taken near State College, Pennsylvania. The photograph by Shufeldt (1912: Fig. 82) of four eggs of the eastern turkey shows the great variation that occurs in the markings.

The turkey has not been forgotten in modern art. Two turkeys of welded steel have been exhibited at the University of Wisconsin, one by Edward Ayers in 1959, the other by W. Wartmann in 1960.

BIBLIOGRAPHY

A., C. H.
   1882. "Wild Turkey Hunting," *Forest and Stream*, 18:211.

A., C. P.
   1902. "A Wild Turkey Invades Asheville," *Forest and Stream*, 58:48.

A., J.
   1877. "Middleburg (Ind.) Notes," *Chicago Field*, 8:299.

Abert, J. W.
   1848. In W. H. Emory, *Notes of a Military Reconnaissance from Fort Leavenworth . . .*, 30 Cong., 1 sess., *House Ex. Doc. 41:* 386–546.

Ackert, J. E., and L. Eisenbrandt.
   1935. "Comparative Resistance of Bronze Turkeys and White Leghorn Chickens to the Intestinal Nematode, *Ascaridia lineata* (Schneider)," *Jour. Parasit.*, 21:200–204.

Adair, J.
   1775. *The History of the American Indians*. London.

Adams, A. L.
   1873. *Field and Forest Rambles*. London.

Aelianus, Claudius.
   1533. *Ex Aeliani historia per P. Gyllium . . . .* Lugduni.

Albin, E.
   1738. *A Natural History of Birds.* Vol. III. London.

Albrecht, W. A.
   1944. *Soil Fertility and Wildlife—Cause and Effect; Trans.* 9th N. Am. Wildl. Conf., 19–28; *Wildlife and the Soil*, Mo. Consv. Comm. *Circ. 134.*

Albright, W. P.
   1930–32. "Turkey Egg Fertility Declines Soon after Mating," *Bien. Rept. Okla. Ag. Exp. Sta. for 1930–32*, 107–108.

Aldrich, J. W., and A. J. Duvall.
   1955. *Distribution of American Gallinaceous Game Birds*, Fish and Wildl. Serv. *Circ. 34.*

Aldrich, L. C.
   1889. *History of Erie County, Ohio.* Syracuse.

Aldrovandi, U.
   1599. *Ornithologiae hoc est, de avibus historiae.* Part II (XIII). Bononiae.

Alexander, Col. G. D.
   1888. "A Turkey Hunt on Platt River," *Am. Field*, 29:508.

Alexander, H. G., and P. Reiter.
  1935. "Report on the Excavation of Jemez Cave, New Mexico," Univ. N.M. and School Am. Res. *Monog. 1*(3).

Alford, I. B.
  1940. "Old Ramon," *South. Sportsm.*, 4(6):10, 27–29.

Allen, E. A., and M. W. Olsen.
  1942. "Clinical Pathology of Trichomoniasis of the Lower Digestive Tract of Turkeys," *Poultry Sci.*, 21:464.

Allen, Elsie G.
  1938. "Jaques Le Moyne, First Zoological Artist in America," *Auk*, 55:106–11.

———.
  1951. "The History of American Ornithology before Audubon," *Trans. Am. Phil. Soc.*, 41(3): 387–591.

Allen, J. A.
  1871. "On the Mammals and Winter Birds of East Florida," *Bull. Mus. Comp. Zool.* 2(3):161–450.

———.
  1893. "The Geographical Origin and Distribution of North American Birds, Considered in Relation to Faunal Areas of North America," *Auk*, 10:97–150.

Allen, J. T.
  1918. *Early Pioneer Days in Texas*. Dallas.

Allen, R., and W. T. Neill.
  1955. "The Wild Turkey," *Fla. Wildl.*, 9(7):7, 38.

Allen, Ralph H.
  1956–57. "Is a Spring Gobbling Season Biologically Sound?" *Ala. Cons.*, 28(3):22–23; *Proc.* 10th Ann. Conf. Southeast. Ass.

Game and Fish Comm. (1956), 124–26.

———.
  1959. "Turkey Hunting Best Ever," *Ala. Cons.*, 31(1):17.

Allen, R. W., and E. E. Wehr.
  1942. "Earthworms as Possible Intermediate Hosts of *Capillaria caudinflata* of the Chicken and Turkey," *Proc.* Helminth. Soc. Washington, 9:72–73.

Allensworth, B. C.
  1905. *Historical Encyclopedia of Illinois and History of Tazewell County.* Vol. II, 503–1103. Chicago.

"Almo."
  1879. "San Antonio, Texas," *Chicago Field*, 10:338.

———.
  1885. "Shooting Turkeys in Texas," *Am. Field*, 23:52–53.

———.
  1886. "When Turkeys Should Not Be Hunted," *Am. Field*, 26:507.

Alsop, G.
  1880. *A Character of the Province of Maryland (1666)*, Md. Hist. Soc. Fund *Publ. 15.*

Altshelter, B.
  1931. The Long Hunters and James Knox, Their Leader," *Filson Club Hist. Quart.*, 5:169–85.

Alvarado, Hernando de.
  1857. "*Relación de lo que Hernando de Alvarado y Fray Juan de Padilla descubrieron en demanda de la mar del sur.*" In B. Smith, *Colección de Varios Documentos para la Historia de la Florida* (London), 65–66; *Col. Doc. Ineditos*, 3:511–13.

American Ornithologists' Union.
  1903. "Twelfth Supplement to the

American Ornithologists' Union Check-List of North American Birds," *Auk*, 20:331–68.

——.
1957. *Check-list of North American Birds*. 5th ed.

Ammann, G. A.
1957. *The Prairie Grouse of Michigan*. Lansing, Mich. Dept. Cons.

Amsden, C. A.
1949. *Prehistoric Southwesterners from Basket-Maker to Pueblo*. Los Angeles.

Amundson, R.
1957. "The Wild Turkey," *Wildl. in N. Carolina*, 21(8):6–10.

Anburey, T.
1791. *Travels Through the Interior Parts of America in a Series of Letters*. New ed., Vol. II. London.

Anderson, A.
1790. *Historical and Chronological Deduction of the Origin of Commerce* (1764). Vol. II. Dublin.

Anderson, K. H.
1963. "What about Wild Turkeys for Maine?" *Maine Fish and Game*, 5(2):10–12.

Anderson, R. J.
1900. "The Crookedness in the Sterna of Certain Breeds of Domestic Fowls," *Irish Nat.*, 9:150–52.

Anderson, T. G.
1882. "Narrative," *Wis. Hist. Colls.*, 9:137–206.

Annereaux, R. F.
1940. "A Note on *Echinoparyphium recurvatum* (von Linstow) Parasitic in California Turkeys," *Jour. Am. Vet. Med. Ass.*, 96:62–64.

Anon.
1682. *True Description of Carolina* (Photostat). London.

Anon.
1822. *Notices of East Florida*. Charleston.

Anon.
1832. "Turkeys Eat Caterpillars Which Feed on Tobacco," *Mag. Nat. Hist.* London, 5:472.

Anon.
1836. *A Visit to Texas*. 2nd ed. New York.

Anon.
1876. [Wild turkeys for New Zealand], *Rod and Gun*, 8:103.

Anon.
1850. Milwaukee (d) *Sentinel*, Feb. 22.

Anon.
1851. "Journal of New Netherland," *Doc. Hist. N.Y.*, 4:1–17.

Anon.
1857. "*Relación del Suceso de la Jornada que Francisco Vásquez hizo en el descubrimiento de Civola.*" In B. Smith, *Colección de Varios Documentos para la Historia de la Florida* (London), 147–54.

Anon.
1858. "Sporting Scenes in Canada," *Leslie's Ill. Newsp.*, 7 (Dec. 18):34.

Anon.
1860. *Western Texas, the Australia of America*. Cincinnati.

Anon.
1870. "*Relación del Suceso de la Jornada que Francisco Vásquez hizo en el descubrimiento de Cibola,*" *Col. Doc. Ineditos*, 14:318–29.

Anon.

1873. *"Traslado de la nuevas y noticias que dieron sobre el descubrimiento . . . Cibola, situada en la Tierra Nueva,"* Col. Doc. Ineditos, 19:529–32.

Anon.

1873.1. "Chicago's Trade in Wild Game," *Am. Sportsm.*, 3:204.

Anon.

1875. [Turkeys Fly the Susquehanna], *Forest and Stream*, 5:252.

Anon.

1875.1. "Game in Market," *Forest and Stream*, 3:346.

Anon.

1875.2. *"Époque de l'introduction du dindon en France,"* Bull. soc. zool. acclim., (3)2:359–60.

Anon.

1876. *Historical Collections of the Mahoning Valley.* Mahoning Valley Hist. Soc. Youngstown.

Anon.

1876.1. "Wild Turkeys," *Chicago Field*, 6:210.

Anon.

1877. "Wild Turkeys," *Forest and Stream*, 9:22.

Anon.

1877.1. "Domesticated Wild Turkeys," *Forest and Stream*, 9:366.

Anon.

1880. "Hunting the Wild Turkey," *Forest and Stream*, 13:973.

Anon.

1882. "Shooting Turkeys Over Points," *Forest and Stream*, 18:25.

Anon.

1883. "Turkey Hunting in Georgia," *Am. Field*, 19:8.

Anon.

1883.1. "Wild Turkeys in California," *Forest and Stream*, 20:228.

Anon.

1894. *"Rudo ensayo (1763)"* (E. Guiteras, transl.), *Records Am. Cath. Hist. Soc. Philadelphia*, 5:109–264.

Anon.

1894.1. "An Indian Turkey Call," *Forest and Stream*, 42.357.

Anon.

1896. *"Traslado de las Nuevas y Noticias . . . Cibola, situada en la Tierra Nueva."* In G. P. Winship, *The Coronado Expedition, 1540–1542. 14th Ann. Rept.* Bur. Am. Ethn., Part I:564–68; 1873. *Col. Doc. Ineditos* 19:529–32.

Anon.

1898. *Relations for 1647–48.* Cleveland. *Jesuit Relations*, 32.

Anon.

1898.1 *Relation for 1649.* Cleveland. *Jesuit Relations*, 34.

Anon.

1900. "Wild Turkey Weights," *Forest and Stream*, 54:365.

Anon.

1900.1 *Account-Book of the Huron Mission of Detroit.* Cleveland. *Jesuit Relations*, 70.

Anon.

1903. *Relación de las Ceremonias y Ritos y Población y Gobernación de los Indios de la Provincia de Mehuacan.* Morelia.

Anon.

1905, 1906. *Relaciónes Geográficas de la Diócesis de Mexico.* Pap. Nueva España. Madrid. (2)6; 1906.(2)7.

Anon.
 1906. "Narrative of a Voyage to Maryland, 1705–1706," *Am. Hist. Rev.*, 12:330–31.

Anon.
 1906.1 "Game in Hawaii," *Forest and Stream*, 67:296.

Anon.
 1911. "Wild Turkeys in Pennsylvania," *Mag. Hist.*, 13:43.

Anon.
 1913. [Turkeys Cross the Mississippi]. *Am. Field*, 80:423.

Anon.
 1914. [Wild Turkeys in New Jersey], *Am. Field*, 81:384.

Anon.
 1916. *Collection of Nebraska Pioneer Reminiscences.* Cedar Rapids, Daughters of the American Revolution.

Anon.
 1924. "Re-introducing the Wild Turkey," *Fins, Feathers and Fur* No. 37 (March), 152, 164; cf. W. Stone (1924), *Auk*, 41:513.

Anon.
 1925. "Coons Kill Turkeys," *U. S. Forest Service Daily Bull.*, Southw. District. Oct. 9.

Anon.
 1925.1 "True Turkey Tales," *Sat. Eve. Post*, 198 (Aug. 29):48.

Anon.
 1929. [Transplanting Turkeys], *Cal. Fish and Game*, 15:70, 185.

Anon.
 1929.1 "Introducing Wild Turkeys," *Mont. Wild Life*, 1(11):9.

Anon.
 1931. [Transplanting Turkeys], *Cal. Fish and Game*, 17:101, 102, 454, 485.

Anon.
 1934, 1935. [Turkeys for Indiana], *Am. Field*, 121:509; 1935. 123:-604.

Anon.
 1938. [Alabama Notes], *Am. Field*, 129:92.

Anon.
 1938.1. "Turkey Troubles," Wis. Cons. *Bull.*, 3(8):27.

Anon.
 1940. "Four-bearded Gobbler," *Va. Wildl.* 3(7):4.

Anon.
 1940.1. *"Die verräterischen Truthähne," Deutsche Rundsch.*, 263:119–20.

Anon.
 1942. [Large Gobbler Shot], *Ala. Consv.*, 14(5):5.

Anon.
 1943. "The Wild Turkey," *Wyo. Wild Life*, 8(6):6, 19–20.

Anon.
 1945. *Principal Game Birds and Mammals of Texas.* Austin, Tex. Game, Fish and Oyster Comm.

Anon.
 1947. "How Have Turkeys Fared?" *Wyo. Wild Life*, 11 (10):4–12, 39.

Anon.
 1950. *The Florida Wild Turkey.* Tallahassee, Florida Game and Fresh Water Fish Comm.

Anon.
 1950.1. "Wild Turkeys Released at Custer," *S.D. Consv. Digest*, 17(4):3.

Anon.
 1952. "Increase in Turkey Population Stirs Talk of Season," *S.D. Consv. Digest*, 19(12):6–7.

Anon.

1952.1. "More Turkeys Trapped in Restoration Program," *Wyo. Wild Life*, 16(2):33.

Anon.

1954. "Large Number Turkeys Planted," *S.D. Consv. Digest*, 21(11):15.

Anon.

1955. "Turkeys in Wyoming," *Wyo. Wild Life*, 19(3):24–28.

Anon.

1956. "One Gobbler — Four Beards," *Texas Game and Fish*, 14(3):28.

Anon.

1958. "Big Game with Feathers," *S.D. Consv. Digest*, 25(2):10–13, 27.

Anon.

1958.1. *Game Bird Survey*. Wyo. Game and Fish Comm., April 1.

Anon.

1958.2. "The Live-trapping and Restocking Program," *Miss. Game and Fish*, 22(2):4–5.

Anon.

1958.3. "Thanksgiving Turkey— The Hard Way," *N.D. Outdoors*, 21(6):8, 14.

Anon.

1958.4 "Wild Turkey Project Started in Pontotoc," *Okla. Wildl.*, 14(4):11.

Anon.

1958.5. "Wild Turkeys Are Wary of Traps," *Pa. Game News*, 29(7):29.

Anon.

1958.6. "Turkey," *Tenn. Consv.*, 24(9):7.

Anon.

1959. "Fatherless Fowl Produces Brood of Normal Offspring," Milwaukee (Wis.) *Journal*, March 7.

Anon.

1959.1. "Merriam's Wild Turkey," *Mont. Wildlife*, Nov.:28–30.

Anon.

1959.2. "Talking Turkey," *N.Y. Consv.*, 14(1):35.

Anon.

1960. "Gobblers Park Aloft," *Okla. Wildlife*, 16(1):5.

Anon.

1960.1. "Turkeys Find Cobra in Their Pen, Kill It," Milwaukee (Wis.) *Journal*, Dec. 15.

Anon.

1960.2. "Wildlife Windup," *Wyo. Wildl.*, 26(4):39.

Anon.

1960.3. "Figures and Facts," *Pa. Game News*, 31(11):37.

Anon.

1960.4. "Turkeys Launched Successfully in Iowa," *Modern Game Breeding*, 30(12):5.

Anon.

1960.5. "Caddo County Receives Turkeys for Propagation," *Okla. Wildl.* 16(11):9.

Anon.

1960.6. "Elk Census," *Texas Game and Fish*, 18(11):4–5, 30.

Anon.

1961. "Nine-bearded Gobbler," *Texas Game and Fish*, 19 (11):21.

Anon.

1961.2. "Wild Turkey Hits Window in Winslow," Freeport (Ill.) *Journal-Standard*, June 1.

Anon.

1961.3. Press Release, Nat. Wildl. Fed., July 12.

507

Anon.
1961.4. "The Merriam's Wild Turkey in Idaho," *Idaho Wildl. Rev.*, 13(5):3–5.

Anon.
1961.5. "Four Wild Turkeys Move to Winslow for the Winter," Freeport (Ill.) *Journal-Standard*, Jan. 24; 1962, Jan. 17.

Anon.
1961.6. "Turkey Transfer," *N.Y. Consv.*, 16(1):40.

Anon.
1961.7. "Gobblers and Feathers to Bald Knobs," *Okla. Wildl.*, 17 (1):10–11.

Anon.
1961.8. "New Home for Turkeys," Oregon Game Comm. *Bull.*, 16 (4):6–7.

Anon.
1961.9. "Wildlife and Wind Tunnels," *Tenn. Consv.*, 27(8):15–16.

Anon.
1961.10. "Virginia's Game Birds," *Va. Wildlife*, 21(5):6–9.

Anon.
1962. "Sixty Young Turkeys Sighted at Yellow River State Forest," *Iowa Consv.*, 21(1):2.

Anon.
1962.1. "Second Plant of Turkeys Made in Spring Mountains," *Nev. Wildl.*, 2(10):3–4.

Anonymous Conqueror.
1917. *Narrative of Some Things of New Spain*. Cortés Soc., New York.

Antonius, O.
1933. "*Bemerkungen über Bastarde und Bastardzucht*," *Biol. Gen.*, 9:39–47.

Antrim, J.
1872. *The History of Champaign and Logan Counties*. Bellefontaine.

Aranda, Joan de.
1871. *Testimonio dado en Méjico sobre el descubrimiento de doscientas leguas adelante, de las minas de Santa Bárbola . . .* (Años de 1582 y 1583). *Col. Doc. Ineditos*, 15:80–150.

Archdale, J.
1836. A New Description of that Fertile and Pleasant Province of Carolina. 1707. In B. R. Carroll, *Hist. Colls. S. Carolina*. Vol. II, 85–120. New York. 2:85–120.

Aristotle.
1862. *History of Animals*. London.

Armas, Juan I. de.
1888. *La zoologica de Colón y los primos exploradores de América*. Habana.

Arner, D. H.
1954. The Wild Turkey in Maryland, Its Ecology and Management. *Md. Consv.*, 31(4):3–8.

Arnold, L. W.
1954. *The Golden Eagle and Its Economic Status*. Fish and Wildl. Serv. *Circ. 27*.

Arthur, S. C.
1928. *Report of the Division of Wild Life. 8th Bien. Rept.* La. Dept. Consv. for 1926–28.

———.
1931. *The Birds of Louisiana*. La. Consv. Dept. *Bull. 20*.

Ashe, T.
1808. *Travels in America, Performed in 1806*. London.

Askins, C.
1931. *Game Bird Shooting*. New York.

Asmundson, V. S.

1934. "The Turkey as an Experimental Animal," *Am. Nat.*, 68:466–67.

———.

1939. "The Formation of the Egg in the Oviduct of the Turkey," *Jour. Exp. Zool.*, 82:287–304.

———.

1939.1. "Inherited Non-barring of the Flight Feathers in Turkeys," *Jour. Hered.*, 30:343–48.

———.

1941. "Note on the Sex Ratio and Mortality in Turkeys," *Am. Nat.*, 75:389–93.

———.

1957. "The Turkey's Origin and Transformation," *Zoonooz*, 30 (11):3–7.

———, G. A. Baker, and J. T. Emlen.

1943. "Certain Relations Between the Parts of Birds' Egg," *Auk*, 60:34–44.

———, and W. E. Lloyd.

1935. "The Effect of Age on Reproduction of the Turkey Hen," *Poultry Sci.*, 14:259–66.

———, and F. W. Lorenz.

1955. "Pheasant–Turkey Hybrids," *Science*, 121:307–308.

———, and F. W. Lorenz.

1957. "Hybrids of Ring-Necked Pheasants, Turkeys, and Domestic Fowl," *Poultry Science*, 36:1,-323–34.

Athias, M.

1928. "*Influence de la castration chez le dindon*," *Compt. rend. soc. biol.*, 98:1606–1608.

———.

1929. "*Les effets de la castration chez le dindon*," *Compt. rend. soc. biol.*, 100:513–14.

———.

1931. "*Les caractères sexuels somatiques et leur conditionnement physiologique*," *Proc.* 2nd Int. Congress Sex Research 145–49. London.

———.

1931.1. "*La regéneration du testicule chez le dindon incomplètement chatré*," *Compt. rend. soc. biol.*, 107:1177–1180.

———.

1947. *Os perus . . . Bull. soc. Portug. cienc. nat.*, 15:169–80.

Atkinson, G. W.

1876. *History of Kanawha County* [West Virginia]. Charleston.

Atwater, C.

1820. "Description of the Antiquities . . . Ohio." *Trans. and Colls. Am. Antiq. Soc.*, 1:109–299.

———.

1831. *Remarks Made on a Tour to Prairie du Chien . . . in 1829.* Columbus.

Atwater, I.

1893. *History of the City of Minneapolis, Minnesota.* Vol. I. New York.

Aubrey, John.

1949. *Aubrey's Brief Lives.* O. L. Dick, ed. London.

Audubon, J. J.

1831. *Ornithological Biography.* Vol. I. Edinburgh.

———.

1834. *Ornithological Biography.* Vol. II. Edinburgh.

———.

1839. *A Synopsis of the Birds of North America.* Edinburgh.

———.

1839.1. *Ornithological Biography.* Vol. V. Edinburgh.

——.
1929. *Journal of John James Audubon Made During his Trip to New Orleans in 1820–1821.* H. Corning, ed. Club of Odd Volumes, Boston.

——.
1942. "Journey up the Mississippi," *Jour. Ill. State Hist. Soc.*, 35:148–73.

——, and J. Bachman.
1849–51. *The Quadrupeds of North America.* Vols. I & II. New York.

Audubon, Maria R.
1900. *Audubon and His Journals.* Vols. I & II. New York.

Aughey, S.
1878. "Notes on the Nature of the Food of the Birds of Nebraska," In *First Ann. Rept.* U. S. Entom. Comm. for 1877, App. II:13–62.

Aussy, Pierre J. B. d'
1782. *Histoire de la vie privée des Français.* Vol. I. Paris.

Austin, G. L.
1876. *The History of Massachusetts.* Boston.

Austin, O. L., Jr.
1961. *Birds of the World.* New York.

A[very], W. C.
1886. "Domestication of the Wild Turkey," *Am. Field*, 26:343.

"Aztec."
1889. "The Mexican Wild Turkey," *Forest and Stream*, 33:123.

——.
1889.1. "The Ozark Mountains," *Forest and Stream*, 33:5.

B., J.
1765. "Remarkable and Authentic Instances of the Fascinating Power of the Rattlesnake . . ."

Gentleman's Mag. (London), 35:511–14.

B., J. C.
1941. *Travels in New France* (1751–61). Harrisburg.

Babb, T. A.
1923. *In the Bosom of the Comanches.* Dallas.

Babbitt, C. H.
1918. "The Missouri Slope Fifty Years Ago," *Forest and Stream*, 88:523.

Babcock, Rufus.
1864. *Forty Years of Pioneer Life: Memoir of John Mason Peck D.D.* Philadelphia.

Bachman, J.
1855. *Examination of the characteristics of Genera and Species* . . . Charleston.

Backlund, H. O.
1935. "A Contribution to the Knowledge of the Poultry-lice in Finland," *Mem. soc. fauna flor. fenn.*, 10:42–46.

Bacon, Francis.
1670. *Sylva sylvarum; or a Natural History in Ten Centuries.* London.

——.
1890. "Of Plantations, 1620–24." In A. Brown, *Genesis of the United States.* Vol. II, 525–1157. Boston.

Bagg, A. C., and S. A. Eliot, Jr.
1937. *Birds of the Connecticut Valley in Massachusetts.* Northampton.

Bailey, A. M., and H. B. Conover.
1935. "Notes from the State of Durango, Mexico," *Auk*, 52:421–24.

Bailey, F. M.
1904. "Additional Notes on the

Birds of the Upper Pecos," *Auk*, 21:349–63.

———.

1928. *Birds of New Mexico*. Santa Fe.

Bailey, H. H.

1913. *The Birds of Virginia*. Lynchburg.

———.

1925. *The Birds of Florida*. Baltimore.

Bailey, H. T.

1914. [Egg Collecting], *Oologist*, 31:74.

Bailey, R. W.

1950. "Live-trapping of Wild Turkeys," *W. Va. Consv.*, 14(5):6–8, 33–35.

———.

1955. "Two Records of Turkey Brood Survival after Death of Hen," *Jour. Wildl. Manag.*, 19:408–409.

———.

1955.1. "Notes on Albinism in the Eastern Wild Turkey," *Jour. Wildl. Manag.*, 19:408.

———.

1955.2. "Wild Turkeys Are 'Tough,'" *W. Va. Consv.*, 19 (5):2–5.

———.

1956. "Sex Determination of Adult Wild Turkeys by Means of Dropping Configuration," *Jour. Wildl. Manag.*, 20:220.

———.

1957. "Population Characteristics of the Wild Turkey in West Virginia," *Northeast Sec. Wildl. Soc.* New Haven (Jan. 8. Mimeo. 12p.).

———.

1957.1. "The 1956 Wild Turkey Kill," W. Va. Consv. Comm. Proj. 26–R–8 ([29p.] Mimeo).

———.

1959. "The 1958 Wild Turkey Kill," W. Va. Consv. Comm. Proj. W–33–R–6, Work Plan II, Job A (8p.).

———.

1959.1. *Preliminary Report on Wild Turkey Banding Studies as Applicable to Management in West Virginia*. Wild turkey symposium. Memphis. Feb. 13–14.

———.

1961. "Highlights of the Reported Turkey Kill," *W. Va. Consv.*, 25(4):16–17, 26.

———, *et al.*

1951. "Wild Turkey Management in West Virginia," W. Va. Cons. Comm., Game Manag. *Bull* 2.

———, and C. E. Knoder.

1958. "Who Wants a Game Farm Turkey?" *W. Va. Consv.*, 22 (8): 20–23.

———, and K. Rinell.

1960. "Forest Game Research," W. Va. Consv. Comm. Proj. 39–R–1 ([37p.] Mimeo).

———, and K. Rinell.

1960.1. "Summation of Observations and Conclusions Therefrom During Recent Trip to Allegheny State Park, New York," W. Va. Consv. Comm. (Memo Oct. 19 [3p.] Mimeo).

Bailey, V.

1905. "Biological Survey of Texas," *N. Am. Fauna*, No. 25.

———.

1913. "Life Zones and Crop Zones of New Mexico," *N. Am. Fauna*, No. 35.

Bailey, W. W.
    1941. "A Method of Producing Genuine Wild Turkeys for Restocking Purposes," Thesis, Va. Polyt. Inst.
Bain, J. A., and H. F. Deutsch.
    1947. "An Electrophoretic Study of the Egg White Proteins of Various Birds," *Jour. Biol. Chem.*, 171:531–41.
Baines, G. W. ("Fusil").
    1888. "Remarkable Shots," *Am. Field*, 29:601.

——.
    1890. In W. B. Leffingwell, *Shooting on Upland, Marsh, and Stream*. Chicago.

——.
    1899. "That Turkey Decoy Again," *Shooting and Fishing*, 25:249.
Baird, S. F.
    1850. "On the Bone Caves of Pennsylvania," *Proc. Am. Ass. Adv. Sci.*, Cambridge, 1849, 352–55.

——.
    1858. *Birds Rept.* Pacific Ry. Survey, 9:1,005p.

——.
    1867. "The Origin of the Domestic Turkey," U. S. Agr. *Rept. for 1866*, 288–90.
Baird, S. F., T. M. Brewer, and R. Ridgway.
    1874. *A History of North American Birds: Land Birds*. Vol. III. Boston.
Baker, G. F.
    1943. "Notes on the Wild Turkey in Western Kentucky," *Ky. Warbler*, 19:25–27.

——.
    1943.1. "Notes from Woodlands," *Ky. Warbler*, 19:2.

——, and W. Sylvester.
    1947. "Kentucky's National Wild Life Refuge," *Ky. Warbler*, 23:17–21.
Baker, M. F.
    1958. "Fire Ant a Wildlife Menace?" *Va. Wildl.*, 19(11):27.
Baker, Richard.
    1674. *A Chronicle of the Kings of England*. London.
Baldwin, C. C.
    1888. "Indian Narrative of Judge Hugh Welch. . . ." Western Reserve Hist. Soc. *Tracts*, 2:105–10.
Baldwin, P. H.
    1947. "Foods of the Hawaiian Goose," *Condor*, 49:108–20.
Baldwin, W. P.
    1947. "Trapping Wild Turkeys in South Carolina," *Jour. Wildl. Manag.*, 11:24–36.
Ballowitz, E.
    1888. *"Untersuchungen über die Struktur der Spermatozoën,"* Archiv f. mikrosp. Anat. u. Entwichlungsmech., 32:401–73.
Bandelier, A. F.
    1890. *Final Report of Investigations among the Indians of the Southwestern United States.* Pap. Arch. Inst. Am., 3(1).

——.
    1892. "An Outline of the Documentary History of the Zuñi Tribe," *Jour. Am. Ethn. and Arch.*, 3.
——, and E. L. Hewett.
    1937. *Indians of the Río Grande Valley*. Albuquerque.
Banks, N.
    1908. *A Revision of the Ixodoides, or Ticks, of the United States.* U. S. Dept. Agr., Bur. Entom. *Tech. Bull. 15*.

———.
1915. *The Acarina or Mites.* U. S. Dept. Agr. *Rept. 108.*

Banks, W. C.
1943. *"Leucocytozoon smithi* Infection and Other Diseases of Turkey Poults in Central Texas," *Jour. Am. Vet. Med. Ass.,* 102:467–68.

Banta, D. D.
1881. *A Historical Sketch of Johnson County, Indiana.* Chicago.

Baraga, Bishop.
1878. *A Dictionary of the Otchipwe Language.* Montreal.

Barbot, J.
1732. *A Description of the Coasts of North and South-Guinea . . . Churchill's Collection of Voyages and Travels.* Vol. V. London.

Barde, F. S.
1914. *Outdoor Oklahoma. Ann. Rept.* State Game and Fish Warden, Guthrie.

Barile, C.
1912. *Sur une espèce de trichosome signalée chez de dindon* (Meleagris gallopavo domestica [L.]). *Bull. soc. zool. France,* 37:126–33.

Barkalow, F. S., Jr.
1942. *Turkey Nest and Brood Reports. Ann. Rept.* Ala. Dept. Consv. 1939–40.

———.
1949. *A Game Inventory of Alabama.* Ala. Dept. Consv.

Barnard, C. M.
1958. *Wild Turkey Propagation Practices at Brookmount Farm.* Fairfield.

Barnes, S. D.
1886. "Arkansas Game Notes," *Am. Field,* 26:75.

———.
1897. "Swampland Whisperings," *Shooting and Fishing,* 22:48.

Barnes, W.
1936. "Our Thanksgiving Turkey: An American Bird and an American Festal Day," *Cattleman,* 23 (Nov.):19, 22.

Barnett, R. D.
1956. "Phoenicia and the Ivory Trade," *Archaeology,* 9:87–97.

Barnwell, J.
1898. "Journal of John Barnwell," *Va. Mag. Hist. and Biog.,* 5:391–402.

Barratt, J.
1851. *The Indian of New England.* Middletown.

Barreiro, A.
1832. *Ojeada Sobre Nuevo-México.* Puebla.

Barrère, P.
1745. *Ornithologiae specimen novum.* Perpiniani.

Barretto, J. F., and Antonio Mies Filho.
1945. "First Observations on *Tamerlanea bragai* in Kidneys of the Turkey," *Biol. Abstr.,* 19:5653.

Barrington, D.
1781. *Miscellanies.* London.

Barrows, W.
1863. "History of Scott County, Iowa," *Ann. Iowa,* 1:8–47.

Bartlett, A. E.
1898. *Wild Animals in Captivity.* London.

Bartlett, K.
1931. "Prehistoric Pueblo Food,"

Mus. North. Ariz. *Notes*, 4(4): 1–4.

——.

1934. *The Material Culture of Pueblo II in the San Francisco Mountains, Arizona.* Mus. North Ariz. *Bull. 7.*

[Barton, B. S.].

1805. "On the Food of the Common Wild Turkey of the United States, *Meleagris palawa,*" *Barton's Med. and Phys. Jour.*, 2(1): 163–64.

Barton, O. A.

1939. *Turkeys: Origin, History, and Distribution.* N.D. Agr. Coll., *Extens. Serv. Circ. 167.*

Bartram, J.

1751. *Observations on the Inhabitants, . . . Animals, and Other Matters Worthy of Notice.* London.

Bartram, W.

1791. *Travels through North and South Carolina, Georgia, and East and West Florida.* Philadelphia.

——.

1799. *Voyage dans les parties suds de l'Amerique septentrionale.* Vol. I. Paris.

Baskin and Battey.

1881. *History of Crawford County, Ohio.* Chicago.

Baskin & Co., O. L.

1880. *History of Morrow County and Ohio.* Chicago.

——.

1883. *History of Effingham County, Illinois.* Part I. Chicago.

"Basso."

1874. "A Little Turkey Story," *Forest and Stream*, 2:59.

Bates, E. F.

1918. *History and Reminiscences of Denton County (Texas).* Denton.

Battey & Co., F. A.

1883. *Counties of White and Pulaski, Indiana.* Chicago.

Battey, Thomas C.

1876. *The Life and Adventures of a Quaker among the Indians.* Boston.

Beal, W. J.

1903. "Pioneer Life in Southern Michigan in the Thirties," Mich. Hist. *Colls.*, 32:236–46.

Beals, R. L.

1943. *The Aboriginal Culture of the Cáhita Indians.* Ibero-Am., No. 19.

——, et al.

1945. *Archaeological Studies in Northeast Arizona.* Univ. Cal. Publ. Arch. Ethn. *44.*

Beauchamp, W. M.

1907. *Aboriginal Place Names of New York.* N.Y. State Mus. *Bull. 108, Archeol. 12.*

Beaudette, F. R., and C. B. Hudson.

1941. "Egg Propagation of Turkey Pox Virus," *Poultry Sci.*, 20:79–82.

Beaver, P. C.

1937. "Experimental Studies on *Echinostoma revolutum* (Froelich), a Fluke from Birds and Mammals," *Ill. Biol. Monogr.*, 15:1–96.

Bechstein, J. M.

1807. *Gemeinnützige Naturgeschichte der Vögel Deutschlands.* Vol. III. Leipzig.

Beck, H. H.

1924. "The Pennsylvania German

Names of Birds," *Auk*, 41:288–95.

Beck, J. R., and D. O. Beck.
1955. "A Method for Nutritional Evaluation of Wildlife Foods," *Jour. Wildl. Manag.*, 19:198–205.

Becknell, W. F.
1948. "San Saba River Basin Wildlife Development: Texas," *P-R Quart.*, 8(4):489.

Beckwith, H. W.
1880. *History of Iroquois County* [Illinois]. Part I. Chicago.

———.
1881. *History of Fountain County* [Indiana]. Part I. Chicago.

Beddard, F. E.
1898. *The Structure and Classification of Birds*. London.

Bedichek, R.
1950. *Karankaway Country*. Garden City.

Beebe, C. W.
1901. "A Bird of the Season," *Bird-Lore*, 3:190–92.

Beebe, W.
1918. *A Monograph of the Pheasants*. Vol. I. London.

———.
1922. *A Monograph of the Pheasants*. Vol. IV. London.

———.
1939. "Gobble and Turk," *Harper's Mag.*, 179:647–57.

Beers & Co., W. H.
1880. *The History of Miami County, Ohio*. Chicago.

———.
1882. *The History of Montgomery County, Ohio*. Part I. Chicago.

Beise, C. J.
1943. "Piedra Turkeys," *Nat. Mag.*, 36:523–26.

Belden, G. P.
1872. *Belden, the White Chief*. Cincinnati.

Belknap, J.
1792. *The History of New-Hampshire*. Vol. III. Boston.

Bell, Capt. J. R.
1957. *The Journal of Captain John R. Bell ... 1820*. Glendale.

Belon (Bellonius), P.
1555. *L'histoire de la Nature des Oyseaux*. Paris.

Beltrami, J. (G.) C.
1828. *A Pilgrimage in Europe and America*. Vol. II. London.

Bement, C. N.
1867. *The American Poulterer's Companion*. New York.

Benavides, A. de.
1945. *Revised Memorial of 1634*. Albuquerque.

Bendire, C. E.
1892. *Life Histories of North American Birds*. Vol. I. U. S. Nat. Mus.

Bennett, E. T.
1831. *The Gardens and Menagerie of the Zoological Society Delineated: Birds*. Vol. II. London.

Bennett, J. A.
1947. "A Dragoon in New Mexico, 1850–1856," *N.M. Hist. Rev.*, 22:51–97.

Bennett, L. J., and P. F. English.
1941. "November Foods of the Wild Turkey," *Pa. Game News*, 11(10):8.

Bennett, W. C., and R. M. Zingg.
1935. *The Tarahumara, an Indian Tribe of Northern Mexico*. Chicago.

Bennitt, R., and W. O. Nagel.
1937. *A Survey of the Resident*

Game and Furbearers of Missouri. Univ. Mo. *Studies 12*(2).

Benscoter, R.
1950. [Turkeys Killed by Car].
Pa. Game News, 21(4):21.

Bent, A. C.
1932. *Life Histories of North American Gallinaceous Birds*. U. S. Nat. Mus. *Bull. 162*.

Bentley.
1883. [Turkeys in Indian Territory]. *Am. Field*, 19:8.

Bentley, W.
1905–14. *The Diary of William Bentley*. Vols. III & IV. Salem.

Bequaert, J. C.
1953. "The Hippoboscidae or Louse-Flies (Diptera) of Mammals and Birds," *Entom. Am.*, n.s. 33:211–442.

Beretta, A. B.
1945. *Cristóbal Colón y el descubrimiento de América*. Vol. II. Barcelona & Buenos Aires.

Bergeson, W. R.
1954. "Turkey Talk," *Mont. Wildlife*, 4(3):20–21.

Bergtold, W. H.
1917. *A Study of the Incubation Periods of Birds*. Denver.

Berlioz, J.
1950. In "*Les Oiseaux,*" *Traite de zoologie*. Paris, 15:1,164p.

Bertram, G. W.
1902. "Reminiscences of Northwest Kansas," *Trans.* Kansas State Hist. Soc. for 1901–1902, 7:198–202.

Bettoni, Eugenio.
1868. *Storia naturale degli uccelli che nidificano in Lombardia*. Vol. II. Milano.

Beverley, R.
1705. *The History and Present State of Virginia*. Books II, III, & IV. London.

Bewick, T.
1797. *History of British Birds*. Vol. I. Newcastle.

Beyers, Lillian E.
1939. "Rearing Wild Turkeys in the Wild," *Game Breeder and Sportsm.*, 43(1):2, 3, 14.

Beyers, Mrs. O. P.
1943. "Raises Wild Turkeys," *Dakota Farmer*, 43:195.

Bice, C. M.
1947. *Poultry Production in Hawaii*. Honolulu.

Bick, G. H.
1947. "The Wild Turkey in Louisiana," *Jour. Wildl. Manag.*, 11:126–39.

Billberg, G. J.
1828. "*Synopsis faunae scandinaviae,*" Vol. I (2). *Aves.* Holmiae.

Bingham, H. L.
1878. "A Thousand Wild Turkeys," *Forest and Stream*, 11:410–11.

Birdsall & Dean.
1882. *The History of Daviess County, Missouri*. Kansas City.

Birkbeck, M.
1818. *Letters from Illinois*. Philadelphia.

Bishop, R. E.
1936. *Birds: Etchings of Waterfowl and Upland Game Birds.* 73 plates. Philadelphia.

Bishop, W. H.
1927. *History of Roane County, West Virginia*. Spencer.

Bishopp, F. C., and H. L. Trembley.
1945. "Distribution and Hosts of Certain North American Ticks," *Jour. Parasit.*, 31:1–54.

Blair, E.
1915. *History of Johnson County, Kansas.* Lawrence.
Blair, E. H., and J. A. Robertson.
1903–1909. *The Philippine Islands.* 55 vols. Cleveland.
Blaisdell, W. O.
1890. "Wild Turkeys in New England," *Forest and Stream,* 35:352.
Blakey, H. L.
1932. "Biological Problems Confronting the Artificial Propagation of Wild Turkeys in Missouri," *Trans.* 19th N. Am. Game Conf., 337–43.

———.
1937. *The Wild Turkey on the Missouri Ozark Range.* U.S.D.A., Biol. Surv., *Wildl. Res. and Manag. Leafl.* BS-77.

———.
1941. "A Vanishing American," *Fla. Game and Fish,* 2(5):3–5, 11.
Blanc, G., and J. Caminopetros.
1930. *"La transmission des varioles aviaires par les moustiques,"* *Comp. rend. acad. sci. Paris,* 190:954–56.
Blanchard, C.
1883. *Counties of Howard and Tipton, Indiana.* Part I. Chicago.

———.
1884. *Counties of Morgan, Monroe, and Brown, Indiana.* Chicago.
Bland, Desmond S.
1962. "Audubon in Liverpool," *Outlook,* Univ. Liverpool, *Bull. Dept. Extra-Mural Studies No. 4* (Spring):2–6.
Bland-Sutton, J.
[1920]. *Selected Lectures and Essays.* London.

Blane, W. N.
1824. *An Excursion Through the United States and Canada during the Years 1822–23.* London.
Blasquez, P.
1868. *El Cazador Mexicano.* Puebla.
Blood, H. A.
1860. *The History of Temple, N.H.* Boston.
Blount, W. P.
1947. *Diseases of Poultry.* Baltimore.
Bloxam, A.
1925. *Diary of Andrew Bloxam . . . Hawaiian Islands, 1824–25.* Bishop Mus. *Sp. Publ. 10.*
Bluhm, E. A.
1957. *The Sawmill Site, a Reserve Phase Village, Pine Lawn Valley, Western New Mexico.* Fieldiana: Anth. 47(1).
Blyth, E.
1847. "A Few Critical Remarks on M. Carl J. Sundevall's Paper on the Birds of Calcutta," *Ann. and Mag. Nat. Hist.,* 20:391.
Bogardus, A. H.
1879. *Field, Cover, and Trap Shooting.* New York.
Bohl, W. H., and S. P. Gordon.
1958. "A Range Extension of *Meleagris gallopavo mexicana* into Southwestern New Mexico," *Condor,* 60:338–39.
Bökönyi, S., and D. Jánossy.
1958. "Data about the Occurrence of the Turkey in Europe before the time of Columbus," *Aquila,* 65:265–69.
Bolton, H. E.
1916. *Spanish Exploration in the Southwest, 1542–1706.* New York.

————, and M. Ross.
1925. *The Debatable Land*. Berkeley.

Bonaparte, C. L.
1825. *American Ornithology; or, The Natural History of Birds Inhabiting the United States, Not Given by Wilson*. Vol. I. Philadelphia.

Boone, Capt. N.
1929. "Journal," *Chron. Okla.*, 7:58–105.

Bonnaterre, J. P., and L. J. P. Vieillot.
1823. *Tableau encyclopédique et methodique . . . Ornithologie*. Paris.

Borelli, G. A.
1681. *De motu animalium*. Vol. II. Rome.

Bostwick, O. N.
1911. Letter, September 10, 1819, Detroit, to John Lawe, Green Bay. *Wis. Hist. Colls.* 20:125.

Boucher, P.
1883. *Canada in the Seventeenth Century*. Montreal.

Bouillod, E.
1874. *Sur l'élevage des dindons sauvages*. *Bull. soc. zool. acclim.* Paris. (3)1:612–17.

Bowen, T. J.
1858. *A Grammar and Dictionary of the Yoruba Language*. Smith. *Contr. Knowl.*, 10(4):71 + 136p.

Bowers, G. L.
1958. "Grouse Grumblings and Turkey Tallies — 1957," *Pa. Game News*, 29(4):50–51.

Boyer, S. P.
1930. "A Nation-wide Survey of the Wild Turkey," *Am. Field*, 113:59–61; W. T. Hornaday.

1931. *Thirty Years War for Wild Life*. New York.

Bracht, V.
1849. *Texas im Jahre 1848*. Elberfeld.

Brackenridge, H. M.
1814. *Views of Louisiana; Together with a Journal of a Voyage Up the Missouri River, in 1811*. Pittsburgh.

————.
1834. *Recollections of Persons and Places in the West*. Philadelphia.

Bradbury, J.
1819. *Travels in the Interior of America in the Years 1809, 1810, and 1811*. 2d ed. London.

Bradfield, W.
1931. *Cameron Creek Village*. *Monogr. School Am. Res. 1*.

Bradford, W.
1898. *History "Of Plimoth Plantation."* Boston.

Brahm, W. G. de.
1856. Philosophico-Historico-Hydrogeography of South Carolina, Georgia, and East Florida. In P. C. J. Weston, *Documents Connected with the History of South Carolina*. London.

Brand, D. D., *et al.*
1937. *Tseh So, a Small House Ruin, Chaco Canyon, New Mexico*. Univ. N. M. *Anth. Ser.* 2(2).

Brandly, C. A., and G. L. Dunlap.
1938. "An Outbreak of Pox in Turkeys, with Notes on Diagnosis and Immunization," *Poultry Sci.*, 17:511–15.

Brandt, H.
1940. *Texas Bird Adventures in the Chicos Mountains and on the North Plains*. Cleveland.

———.

1951. *Arizona and Its Bird Life.* Cleveland.

Brashier, Mary.

1960. "Merriam's Turkey," *Outdoor Nebraska* 38(2):26–27.

Braughman, A. J., and R. F. Bartlett.

1911. *History of Morrow County, Ohio.* Vol. I. Chicago–New York.

Brayne, H.

1897. "Letters from Carolina," S.C. Hist. Soc. *Colls.* 5:181–275.

Breiding, G. H.

1946. "Moonseed Fruits as Bird Food," *Auk*, 63:589.

Breiding, G.

1950. "Turkey Brood Counts: West Virginia," *P-R Quart.*, 10(1):101.

Brew, J. O.

1946. *Archaeology of Alkali Ridge, Southeastern Utah.* Peabody Mus. *Pap. 21.*

Brewer-Bonebright, Sarah.

1921. *Reminiscences of Newcastle, Iowa, 1848.* Des Moines.

Brewster, W.

1886. An Ornithological Reconnaissance in Western North Carolina," *Auk*, 3:94–112.

Brewster, W.

1950. "St. Mary's, Georgia: 1877." From the journal of William Brewster. F. V. Hebard, ed. *Oriole*, 15(2):15–21.

Brickell, J.

1911. *The Natural History of North Carolina* (1737). Raleigh.

Brickell, John.

1844. "Narrative of John Brickell's Captivity among the Delaware Indians," *Am. Pioneer*, I:43–56.

Bridges, H. P.

1953. *The Woodmont Story.* New York.

Brillat-Savarin, J. A.

1926. *The Physiology of Taste* (1843). New York.

Brinton, D. G.

1885. *The Lenape and Their Legends.* Philadelphia.

———, and A. S. Anthony.

1888. *A Lenape-English Dictionary.* Philadelphia.

Brisson, M. J.

1760. *Ornithologie.* Vol. I. Paris.

Broderip, W. J.

1849. *Zoological Recreations.* London.

Brodkorb, P.

1964. "Catalogue of Fossil Birds, Part 2," *Bull.* Florida State Mus. 8(3):195–335.

———.

1964.1. "Notes on Fossil Turkeys," *Quart. Jour. Florida Acad. Sci.*, 27:223–29.

Brody, A. L.

1936. "The Transmission of Fowlpox." N.Y. State Agr. Exp. Sta. *Mem. 195:1–37.*

Brooks, F. D.

1933. "Influence of Sex on Utilization of Feed in Turkeys," *Poultry Sci.*, 12:299–304.

Brooks, M.

1934. "Eastern Goshawk Flights in West Virginia," Wilson *Bull.* 46:259.

———.

1943. "*Ilex collina* Fruits as Bird Food," Wilson *Bull.* 55:246.

———.

1943.1. "Birds of the Cheat Mountains," *Cardinal*, 6(2):22–45.

Brown, B.
   1909. "The Conard Fissure, a Pleis-
   tocene Bone Deposit in Northern
   Arkansas," *Mem.* Am. Mus.
   Nat. Hist. 9(4):157–208.
Brown, C. E.
   1928. "Longevity of Birds in Captivity," *Auk*, 45:345–48.
Brown, H. J.
   1953. "Bandits of the Pine Barrens," *Minn. Nat.* 3(3):33–38.
Brown, S. R.
   1817. *The Western Gazetteer.*
   Auburn.
Brown, Tarleton.
   1924. "Memoirs (1843)," *Mag.
   Hist.*, Extra No. 101:1–36.
Browne, P.
   1789. *The Civil and Natural History of Jamaica (1756).* 2d ed.
   London.
Browne, W. E.
   1938. "Wild Turkeys at Many-
   wings," *Fla. Nat.*, 11:57–61.
Brownell, L. W.
   1904. *Photography for the Sportsman Naturalist.* New York.
Browning, M.
   1928. *Forty-four Years of the Life
   of a Hunter (1859).* Philadelphia.
Bruette, W. A.
   [*ca.* 1923]. *Sportsmen's Encyclopedia.* Vol. I. New York.
Bruffey, G. A.
   1925. *Eighty-one Years in the West.*
   Butte.
Brunett, E. L.
   1934. "Some Observations on Pox
   Virus Obtained from a Turkey,"
   Ann. Rept. N.Y. State Vet. Coll.
   for 1932–33, p.69–70.

Brush, D. H.
   1944. *Growing Up in Southern
   Illinois, 1820–1861.* Chicago.
Bruyerin (Bruyerinus Campegius),
Jean B.
   1560. *De re cibaria.* Lugduni.
Bryan, E. H., Jr.
   1958. *Check list and Summary of
   Hawaiian Birds.* Honolulu.
Bryan, W. A.
   1915. *Natural History of Hawaii.*
   Honolulu.
Bryant, H.
   1859. [Supposedly new species of
   turkey described by Gould].
   Proc. Boston Soc. Nat. Hist. for
   1856–59. 6:158–59.
Buckelew, F. M.
   1925. *The Life of F. M. Buckelew,
   the Indian Captive.* Bandera.
Buckingham, J. S.
   1842. *The Slave States of America.*
   Vol. II. London.
Buckton, T. J.
   1866. "The Algum-tree and Peacocks," *Notes and Queries*, (3)
   9:68.
Buechner, H. K.
   1944. "The Range Vegetation of
   Kerr County, Texas, in Relation
   to Livestock and White-tailed
   Deer," *Am. Midl. Nat.*, 31:697–
   743.
Buffham, B. R.
   1878. "San Antonio, Bexar Co.,
   Texas," *Chicago Field*, 10:241.
Buffon, G. L. L. de.
   1771. *Histoire Naturelle . . . avec
   la description du Cabinet du Roi.*
   Vol. XVII. Paris.
   ———.
   1772. *Histoire naturelle des oiseaux.*
   Vol. II. Paris.

——.
1808. *Natural History of Birds, Fish, Insects and Reptiles.* Vol. I. London.

Bulliard, H.
1926. *"La brosse du dindon (Meleagris gallopavo L.),"* Comp. rend. ass. anat. Nancy, 21:132–45.

Burger, G. V.
1954. "Wild Turkeys in Central Coastal California," *Condor*, 56:198–206.

——.
1954.1. "The Status of Introduced Wild Turkeys in California," *Cal. Fish and Game*, 40:123–45.

Burget, M. L.
[1946]. *Colorado Wild Turkey* (1943–46). Vol. II. Colo. Game and Fish Dept.

——.
1948. "Wild Turkey Investigations: Colorado," *P-R Quart.*, 8(2):170–71.

——.
1948.1. "Wild Turkey Investigations: Colorado," *P-R Quart.*, 8(1):18–20.

——.
1949. "Wild Turkey Investigations," *P-R Quart.*, 9(4):467.

——.
1949.1. "Wild Turkey Investigations: Colorado," *P-R Quart.*, 9(1):18; 9(4):467.

——.
1950. "Upland Game Bird Development: Colorado," *P-R Quart.*, 10(3):272.

——.
1952. "Wild Turkey Investigations," *P-R Quart.*, 12(4):304.

——.
1954. "Turkey Comeback," *Colo. Consv.*, 3(5):25–30.

——.
1957. *The Wild Turkey in Colorado.* Federal Aid in Wildl. Rest., Project W–39–R.

——, and D. M. Hoffman.
1954. "Wild Turkey Investigations," *P-R Quart.*, 14(1):18–19.

——.
1954.1. "Wild Turkey Investigations," *P-R Quart.*, 14(3):243.

Burke, Sir Bernard.
1938. *Burke's Peerage.* London.

Burleigh, T. D.
1931. "Notes on the Breeding Birds of State College, Center County, Pennsylvania," *Wilson Bull.*, 43:37–54.

——.
1958. *Georgia Birds.* Norman.

Burlend, Rebecca.
1936. *A True Picture of Emigration (ca. 1848).* Chicago.

Burmeister, H.
1939. *Handbuch der Entomologie.* Vol. II. Berlin.

Burns, F. L.
1915. "Comparative Periods of Deposition and Incubation of Some North American Birds," *Wilson Bull.*, 27:275–86.

Burris, E. A.
1933. "Frontier Food," *Minn. Hist.*, 14:378–92.

Burrows, W. H., and J. S. Marsden.
1938. "Artificial Breeding of Turkeys," *Poultry Sci.*, 17:408–11.

Burt, Edward.
1818. *Letters from a Gentleman in the North of Scotland to His Friend in London (1754).* 5th ed. Vol. II. London.

521

Burton, E.
1958: *The Pageant of Elizabethan England*. New York.
Burtt, T. H.
1876. "Jefferson City Notes," *Chicago Field*, 6:274.
Bushnell, Rev. Henry.
1889. *The History of Granville, Licking County, Ohio*. Columbus.
Bushnell, L. D., and M. J. Twiehaus.
1939. *Poultry Diseases, Their Prevention and Control*. Rev. ed. Kan. Agr. Exp. Sta. *Bull. 284*.
Buss, I. O.
1946. *Wisconsin Pheasant Populations*. Wis. Consv. Dept. *Publ. 326, A–46*.
———, et al.
1951. "Wisconsin Pheasant Reproduction Studies Based on Ovulated Follicle Technique," *Jour. Wildl. Manag.*, 15:32–46.
Bustamente, Piedro de.
1871. "*Testimonio Dado en Méjico Sobre el Descubrimiento . . . de las Minas de Santa Barbola* (1582–1583)," *Col. Doc. Ineditos*, 15:80–88.
Butler, A. W.
1913. "Further Notes on Indiana Birds," *Proc*. Ind. Acad. Sci. for 1912, 59–65.
Butler, R.
1848. "Journal of General Butler," *The Olden Time*, 2:433–64.
Byington, C.
1915. *A Dictionary of the Choctaw Language*. Bur. Am. Ethn. *Bull. 46*.
Byrd, M. A.
1959. "Observations on *Leucocytozoon* in Pen-raised and Free-ranging Wild Turkeys," *Jour.*

Wildl. Manag., 23:145–56.
Byrd, W.
1737. *Neu-gefundenes Eden*. Bern.
———.
1929. *Histories of the Dividing Line betwixt Virginia and North Carolina*. Raleigh.
———.
1940. *Natural History of Virginia (1737)*. Richmond.
C., D.
1880. "Quaint Old Winchester," *Forest and Stream*, 14:193.
C., S. C.
1878. "Notes on the Birds of Halifax Inlet, East Florida," No. 1. *Forest and Stream*, 10:255.
Cabot, S., Jr.
1844. "Remarks on Meleagris and Other Gallinae of North America," *Proc*. Boston Soc. Nat. Hist. for 1842, 1:80–81.
Cahn, A. R.
1921. "Summer birds in the Vicinity of Lake Caddo, Harrison County, Texas," Wilson *Bull.*, 33:165–76.
Cain, A. W.
1932. *History of Lumpkin County*. Atlanta.
Cairns, J. S.
1889. "The Summer Birds of Buncombe County, North Carolina," *Orn. and Oolog.*, 14:17–23.
California Board of Fish and Game Commissioners.
1913. Introduced Game Birds. *22d Bien. Rept. . . . 1910–12*. pp. 23–24.
California Fish and Game Commission.
1910. *21st Bien. Rept. . . . 1909–10*, pp. 57–60. *Cf.* T. S. Palmer and H. Oldys. 1911. "Progress of

Game Protection in 1910," Biol. Surv. *Circ. 80:22.*

Calvert, L.
1899. "A Briefe Relation of the Voyage unto Maryland (1633)," Md. Hist. Soc. Fund *Publ. No. 35:26–45.*

Cambrensis, Giraldus.
1602. *Topographia Hiberniae.* n.p. Lib. iii:47; 1863. *The Historical Works of Giraldus Cambrensis: The Topography of Ireland.* London.

Camp, R. R.
1958. *Game Cookery in America and Europe.* New York.

Campbell, J. V.
1883. "Biographical Sketch of Charles Christopher Trowbridge," Mich. Pion. and Hist. *Colls. 6:478–91.*

Campbell, L. W.
1940. *Birds of Lucas County. Bull.* Toledo Mus. Sci. 1.

Campbell, P.
1793. *Travels in the Interior Inhabited Parts of North America in the Years 1791 and 1792.* Edinburgh.

Camper, P.
1773. "*Mémoire sur la structure des os dans les oiseaux et de leurs diversites dans les différentes espèces," Mém.* math. phys. inst. fr. 7:328–35.

Campion, J. S.
1878. *On the Frontier.* 2d ed. London.

[Candler, I.].
1824. *A Summary View of America.* London.

Cárcer y Disdier, M. de.
1960. *Los Pavos: In Homenaje a Rafael Garcia Granados.* Mexico.

Carhart, A. H.
1943. "Wild Turkey Program," Colo. Game and Fish Comm. (Typed).

———.
1946. "Long Rifles and Raw Meat," In 1945 Denver *Westerners Brand Book,* 171–94.

Carpenter, C.
1959. "Return of an Exile," *Tex. Game and Fish,* 17(4):24–25.

Carroll, E. A., *et al.*
1894. *The Colonial Laws of New York.* Vol. I, 619. Albany.

Carroll, H. B., and J. V. Haggard.
1942. *Three New Mexico Chronicles.* Vol. XI. Quivira Soc. Albuquerque.

Carroll, J. J.
1900. "Notes on the Birds of Refugio County, Texas," *Auk,* 17:337–48.

Carter, R. G.
1935. *On the Border with MacKenzie.* Washington.

Carter, W. T.
1931. *The Soils of Texas.* Tex. Agr. Exp. Sta. *Bull. 431.*

Carteret, N.
1897. "Relation, 1670," S. C. Hist. Soc. *Colls.* 5, 165–68.

Cary, M.
1911. *A Biological Survey of Colorado. N. Am. Fauna,* 33.

Casey, W. H.
1957. "Turkey Talk," *Outdoors in Ill.,* 4(2):24–27.

Castetter, E. F., and M. E. Opler.
1936. Ethnobiological Studies in the American Southwest. III. *The Ethnobiology of the Chiricahua and Mescalero Apache.* Univ. N.M. Biol. Ser. 4(5).

———, and R. M. Underhill.
1935. *Ethnobiological Studies in the American Southwest. II. The Ethnobiology of the Papago Indians.* Univ. N.M. Biol. Ser. *Bull. 4.*

Catchings, C. E.
1898. "Comments on Mr. Jordan's Articles," *Shooting and Fishing,* 24:288.

Catesby, M.
1754. *The Natural History of Carolina, Florida, and the Bahama Islands.* Rev. ed. Vol. II. London.

Caton, J. D.
1873. "The Senses of Sight and Hearing in the Wild Turkey and Common Deer," *Am. Nat.,* 7:431.

———.
1877. "The Wild Turkey and Its Domestication," *Am. Nat.,* 11:321–30.

———.
1877.1. *The Antelope and Deer of America.* New York.

———.
1877.2. The Domestication of the Wild Turkey," *Chicago Field,* 8:209.

Caton, J. D.
1881. "The Wild Turkey in Domestication," *Am. Field,* 16:90–91.

———.
1882. "Effects of Reversion in the Wild State in Our Domestic Animals," *Am. Field,* 18:391.

———.
1886. "The Wild Turkey—Its Domestication and Hybridization," *Am. Field,* 26:247.

———.
1887. "Effects of Reversion to the Wild State in Our Domestic Animals," *Am. Field,* 27:623.

———.
1887.1. "The Origin of a Small Race of Turkeys," *Am. Nat.,* 21:350–54.

Cavendish, Thomas.
1890. "Voyage of Thomas Candish (Cavendish) in 1586–88," Vol. XVI of Hakluyt's *The Principal Navigations . . . of the English Nation.*

Caywood, L. R., and E. H. Spicer.
1935. *Tuzigoot: The Excavation and Repair of a Ruin on the Verde River near Clarkdale, Arizona.* Berkeley.

Cervantes, G. Gómez de.
1944. *La Vida económica y Social de Nueva España, al Finalizar el Siglo XVI.* Mexico.

Chamberlain, E. B.
1953. *Game Management. Bien Rept.* Fla. Game and Fresh Water Fish Comm. 1951–52.

———.
1953. *Game Management. Bien. Rept.* Fla. Game and Fresh Water Fish Comm. 1953–54.

Chambers, O. L.
1945. "Nimrod on the Loose in Pioneer Oklahoma," *Chron. Okla.,* 23:399–405.

Champlain, S. de.
1922. *The Works of Samuel de Champlain.* Vol. I. H. P. Biggar, ed. Toronto.

Champy, C.
1924. *Les caractères sexuels.* Paris.
———, and N. Kritch.
1926. *"Etude histologique de la crête des gallinacés et de ses variations sous l'influence des fac-*

teurs sexuels," *Arch. morph. gen. éxp. No. 25,* 1–31.

——, and M. Demay.

1930. *Structure et homologie des papilles charnues des régions denudées de la tête des gallinacés. Bull.* soc. zool. France, 55:410–18.

——, N. Kritch, and A. Llombart.

1929. *"Etude de quelques structures communes a des variants sexuels divers," Compt. rend. ass. anat.* 24:120–38.

Chandler, A. C.

1916. "A Study of the Structure of Feathers, with Reference to Their Taxonomic Significance," Univ. Cal. *Pub. Zool.* 13(11): 243–446.

Chapin, E. A.

1925. *"Freyana (Microspalax) chaneyi* from a turkey, *Meleagris gallopavo," Jour. Parasit.,* 12:-113.

Chapin, F. H.

1892. *The Land of Cliff-dwellers.* Boston.

Chapman and Co., C. C.

1879. *History of Fulton County, Illinois.* Peoria.

——.

1880. *History of Pike County, Illinois.* Chicago.

Chapman, F. B.

1953. "Ohio Tackles Turkey Restoration," Ohio Consv. *Bull. 17* (1):20–21.

Chapman, F. M.

1891. "On the Birds Observed near Corpus Christi, Texas, during Parts of March and April, 1891," *Bull.* Am. Mus. Nat. Hist., 3(2):315–28.

——.

1896. "Notes on Birds Observed in Yucatan," *Bull.* Am. Mus. Nat. Hist., 8(18):271–90.

——.

1909. *The Habitat Groups of North American Birds in the American Museum of Natural History. Guide Leaflet No. 28.*

——.

1915. "Louis Agassiz Fuertes—Painter of Birds," *Am. Mus. Jour.,* 15:221–24.

——.

1933. *Autobiography of a Bird Lover.* New York.

Charleton, G.

1677. *Exercitationes de diffentiis et nominibus animalium.* Oxoniae. (First published, 1668, as *Onomasticon zoicon.* Londini. This I have not seen).

Cherville, M. G. de.

1892. *"Le dindon sauvage dans la fôret de Marly," Bull.* soc. zool. acclim. 39(2):236–37.

[Chew, J.]

1890. "The Diary of an Officer in the Indian country in 1794," *Mag. West. Hist.,* 11:383–88.

Chick, W. H.

1921. "A Journey to Missouri in 1822," Mo. Valley Hist. Soc. *Publ. 1:*97–103.

Christy, B. H., and G. M. Sutton.

1929. "The Turkey in Pennsylvania," *Cardinal,* 2:109–16.

Cist, C.

1846. "Jessie and Elias Hughes," *Cincinnati Miscellany,* 2:9–12.

Clark, J. C.

1938. *Codex Mendoza.* Vol. I. London.

Clarke, Edward D.
1816. *Travels in Various Countries of Europe, Asia and Africa*. Vol. II. London.

Clarke, S. J.
1878. *History of McDonough County, Illinois*. Springfield.

Clavigero, F. S.
1787. *The History of Mexico*. Vol. I. London.

Clay, T.
1938. "A Revision of the Genera and Species of Mallophaga Occurring on Gallinaceous Hosts. —Part I. *Lipeurus* and related genera," *Proc.* Zool. Soc. London, 108B:109–204.

———.
1941. "A New Genus and Species of Mallophaga," *Parasit.*, 33:119–29.

Clawson, S. G.
1958. "Wild Turkey Populations on an Area Treated with Heptachlor and Dieldrin," *Ala. Birdlife*, 6(3–4):4–8.

Clayton, J.
1844. "A Letter . . . Giving an Account of Several Observables in Virginia (1688)," Washington. *Force's Tracts*, 3(12):1–45.

Clemens, Samuel (Mark Twain).
1906. "Hunting the Deceitful Turkey," *Harper's Mag.*, 114:57–58.

Clement, P.
1901. "A Turkey Hunt in the Southwest," *Outing*, 39:90–93.

Clerc, W.
1902. "*Contribution a l'étude de la faune helminthologique de l'Oural*," *Zool. Anz.*, 25:569–75.

———.
1903. "*Contribution a l'étude de la faune helminthologique de l'Oural*," *Rev. suisse zool.*, 11:243–68.

Clifton.
1883. "A Turkey Hunt by Moonlight," *Forest and Stream*, 20:9.

Cline, L. E.
1933. *Turkey Production*. Rev. ed. New York.

Clinkenbeard, W.
1928. "Reverend John D. Shane's Interview with Pioneer William Clinkenbeard," *Filson Club. Hist. Quart.*, 2:95–128. MS in Wis. Hist. Soc. Lib.

Clinton, Dewitt.
1815. "An Introductory Discourse Delivered on the 4th of May, 1814," *Trans*. Lit. and Phil. Soc. N.Y., 1:21–184.

"Clip."
1886. "Hunting the Wild Turkey," *Am. Field*, 26:409–10, 433–34.

Clodfelter, F.
1943. "Wild Turkey Blitz," *Nat. Mag.*, 36:480.

Coale, C. B.
1878. *Life and Adventures of Wilburn Waters*. Richmond.

Cobo, Bernabé.
1890–91. *Historia del Nuevo Mundo*. Vols. I & II. Seville.

Cockrum, W. M.
1907. *Pioneer History of Indiana*. Oakland City.

Codex Borgia.
1904–1909. E. Seler, ed. Vol. I. Berlin.

Codex "Troano."
1939. Mexico.

Cogolludo, Diego López de.
1867. *Historia de Yucatán (1688)*. 3d ed. Vol. I. Mérida.

Colbath, G. E.
1951. "Deer and Turkey Census," *P-R Quart.*, 11(2):221.

———.
1954. "Trapping and Transplanting: Texas," *P-R Quart.*, 14(4): 479.

Cole, L. J.
1909. "The Crow as a Menace to Poultry Raising," *Rept.* Rhode Island Exp. Sta. for 1908, 312–16.

———, P. B. Hadley, and W. F. Kirkpatrick.
1910. *Blackhead in Turkeys: A Study in Avian Coccidiosis.* R.I. Agr. Exp. Sta. *Bull. 141.*

Colerus, J.
1620. *Calendarium perpetuum, et libri oconomici.* Wittenberg.

Collins, J. O.
1952. "Evaluation of Wildlife Management Practices in Louisiana," *P-R Quart.*, 12(2):136.

Collins, L.
1848. *Historical Sketches of Kentucky.* Cincinnati.

Collot, G. H. V.
1826. *A Journey in North America.* Vol. I. Paris.

Colón, Hernando.
1947. *Vida del Almirante Don Cristóbal Colón.* Mexico.

Comstock, J. H.
1950. *An Introduction to Entomology.* 9th ed. rev. Ithaca.

Comte, J. A.
1839. *Keepsake d'histoire naturelle.* Paris; 1841. *The Book of Birds.* London.

Conkling, R. P.
1932. "Conkling Cavern: the discoveries in the bone cave at Bishop's Cap, New Mexico," West Texas Hist. and Sci. Soc. *Bull.* 44:7–23.

Conlin, W. G., and J. N. Morton.
1935. *More Food for Upland Game.* 4th ed. Pa. Game Comm. *Bull. 11.*

Connellee, C. U.
1930. "Some Experiences of a Pioneer Surveyor," West Texas Hist. Ass. *Year Book* 6, 80–93.

Connelly, J. A.
1959. *Wild Turkey Restoration and Management. 6th Bien. Rept.* N.C. Wildl. Res. Comm. July 1, 1956–June 30, 1958.

Cook, A. H., and W. H. Henry.
1940. "Texas Rock Squirrels Catch and Eat Young Wild Turkeys," *Jour. Mam.*, 21:92.

Cook, D. B.
1889. *Six Months among Indians . . . in the Forests of Allegan County, Mich., in the Winter of 1839 and 1840.* Niles.

Cook, F. A.
1945. *Game Birds of Mississippi.* Miss. Game and Fish Comm.

Cook, H. J.
1929. "The Eagle as a Killer of the Vanishing Wild Turkey," *Outdoor Life*, 63(4):37, 87.

Cook, J. R.
1907. *The Border and the Buffalo.* Topeka.

Cook, S. F.
1949. *The Historical Demography and Ecology of Teotlalpan.* Ibero-Am., 33.

Cooke, W. W.
1884. "Bird Nomenclature of the Chippewa Indians," *Auk*, 1:242–50.

———.
1888. *Report on Bird Migration in*

the Mississippi Valley. U. S. Dept. Agr., Div. Econ. Ornith. *Bull. 2.*

———.
1909. "The birds of Colorado—third supplement," *Auk,* 26: 400–22.

———.
1913. "The Wild Turkeys of Colorado," *Condor,* 15:104–105.

Coomers, A.
1878. "A Turkey Hunt," *Chicago Field,* 10:241.

Cooper, J. G.
1870. *Ornithology of California.* Cambridge.

Cooper, Susan F.
1856. *Journal of a Naturalist in the United States.* Vol. II. London.

Cooper, Thomas.
1584. *Thesavrvs lingvae Romanae & Brittannicae (1565).* London.

Cope, E. B.
1932. "The Wild Turkey, Its Hunting and Future in Louisiana," *La. Consv. Rev.,* 2(10):4–7, 32–33.

Cope, E. D.
1871. "Synopsis of the Extinct Batrachia, Reptilia, and Aves of North America," *Trans.* Am. Phil. Soc., 14(1):238–40.

Coronado, Francisco Vásquez.
1896. Letter to Mendoza, August 3, 1540. In G. P. Winship, *The Coronado Expedition, 1540–1542. 14th Ann. Rept.* Bur. Ethn., Part I:329–613.

———.
1904. *The relation . . . Countrey of Cibola . . . 1540. Hakluyt's Voyages.* Glasgow. 9:145–204.

Coronel, A. B.
1934. "Fowl-pox Vaccine from Virus of Turkey Origin," *Philippine Jour. Anim. Ind.,* 1:85–90.

Corsan, G. H.
1926. "Breeding of Game Birds in America," *Am. Field,* 105:629.

Cortés, F.
1852. *"Cartas de relación sobre el descubrimiento y conquista de Nueva España,"* In E. de Vedia, *Bibl. autores españoles* (Madrid), 22:1–153.

Cortés, Hernando.
1932. *Cartas de Relación de la Conquista de Méjico.* Vol. I. Madrid.

Cory, C. B.
1896. *Hunting and Fishing in Florida.* Boston.

———.
1909. *The Birds of Illinois and Wisconsin.* Chicago.

Cosgrove, C. B.
1947. "Caves of the Upper Gila and Hueco Areas in New Mexico and Texas," *Pap.* Peabody Mus. Am. Arch. and Ethn., 24(2):1–181.

Cosgrove, H. S. and C. B.
1932. *The Swarts Ruin, a Typical Mimbres Site in Southwestern New Mexico. Pap.* Peabody Mus. Am. Arch. and Ethn., 15.

Cottam, C.
1961. "The Cottams and 'Carla.'" (Mimeo.).

Coues, E.
1866. "List of the Birds of Fort Whipple, Arizona," *Proc.* Acad. Nat. Sci. Philadelphia, 18:39–100.

———.
1872. *Key to North American Birds.* Boston.

———.
1873. *Check-list of North American Birds.* Salem.

———.
1873.1. "Some United States Birds New to Science, and Other Things Ornithological," *Am. Nat.*, 7:321–31.

———.
1874. *Field Ornithology.* Part II. Salem.

———.
1875. "*Fasti ornithologiae redivivi. —No. 1. Bartram's 'Travels,' "Proc.* Acad. Nat. Sci. Philadelphia, 338–58.

———.
1880. "Notes and Queries Concerning the Nomenclature of North American Birds," *Bull.* Nutt. Orn. Club 5:95–102.

———.
1897. "The Turkey Question," *Auk,* 14:272–75.

———.
1899. "Note on *Meleagris gallopavo fera," Auk,* 16:77.

———, and H. C. Yarrow.
1875. "Report upon the Collection of Mammals Made in Nevada . . . Arizona . . .," *Rept.* U. S. Geol. Surv. West of 100th Meridian, 5, Chap. 2:35–129.

Coughlin, L. E.
1943. "Wild Turkeys on Laramie Peak," *Wyo. Wild Life* 8(10):1–6. Map.

Coujard, R.
1941. "*Innervation sympathique de la crête et des barbillons du coq," Compt. rend. soc. biol.* 135: 1149–52.

Covarrubias, M.
1946. *Mexico South: The Isthmus of Tehuantepec.* New York.

Coverte, R.
1631. *A True and Almost Incredible Report of an Englishman . . . in Cambaya . . .* London.

Covington, W. A.
1937. *History of Colquitt County.* Atlanta.

Cox, M. L.
1947–48. "Investigation of Río Grande Turkey in Lower South Texas," *P-R Quart.,* 7(4):258–59; 8(2):217; 8(3):337–38.

———.
1948. "Investigation of Río Grande Turkey in Lower South Texas," *P-R Quart.,* 8(4):488.

Craig, F. R., and F. S. Barkalow, Jr.
1950. "Blackhead in Wild Turkeys on Free Range in North Carolina," *Wildl. in N.C.,* 14(2):18–19.

Cram, E. B.
1926. "A Parasitic Disease of the Esophagus of Turkeys," *N. Am. Vet.,* 7(10):46–48.

———.
1927. *Bird Parasites of the Nematode Suborders Strongylata, Ascaridata, and Spirurata.* U. S. Nat. Mus. *Bull. 140.*

Cram, E. B.
1933. "New Records of Nematodes of Birds," *Jour Parasit.,* 19:93–94.

———.
1936. *Species of* Capillaria *Parasitic in the Upper Digestive Tract of Birds.* U. S. Dept. Agr. *Tech. Bull. 516.*

———, and E. E. Wehr.
1934. "The Status of Species of

Trichostrongylus of Birds," *Parasit.*, 26:335–39.

Crane, C. J.
1886. "Fort Sill, I. T., notes," *Forest and Stream*, 26:68.

———.
1897. "Wild Turkey Shooting," *Recreation*, 6:431–33.

Crawford, B. T.
1952. "Turkey studies," *P-R Quart.*, 12(4):331.

Crawfurd, John.
1863. "On the Relation of the Domesticated Animals to Civilization," *Trans.* Ethn. Soc. London, (2)2:387–468.

Crèvecoeur, F. F.
1902. *Old Settlers' Tales . . . Pottawatomie and Nemaha Counties.* Onaga.

Crèvecoeur, S. de.
1925. *Sketches of Eighteenth-Century America* (1782). New Haven.

Crispens, C. G., Jr.
1957. "The Use of Prolactin to Induce Broodiness in Two Wild Turkeys," *Jour. Wildl. Manag.*, 21:462.

"Crocus."
1881. "Kansas Notes," *Chicago Field*, 15:282.

———.
1884. "Kansas City Notes," *Am. Field*, 21:131.

Cross, R. H., Jr.
1961. "Virginia's Deer, Bear and Turkey Kill for 1960–61," *Va. Wildlife*, 22(5):22.

Crump, W. I., and H. B. Sanderson.
1951. "Wild Turkey Trapping and Transplanting," *Wyo. Wild Life*, 5(4):4–11, 36–37.

Cubas, A. Garcia.
1884. *Cuadro Geográfico, Estadístico . . . Estados Unidos Mexicanos.* Mexico.

Cuenot, L. C.
1911. *La genèse des espèces animales.* Paris.

Culbertson, A. B.
1948. "Annual Variation of the Winter Foods Taken by Wild Turkeys on the Virginia State Forests," *Va. Wildl.*, 9(9):14–16; 1948. "Annual Variations in the Early Winter Foods of the Wild Turkey and Their Management Implications Principally on the Virginia State Forests," MS Thesis. Va, Polyt. Inst.

Cullen, E. K.
1903. "A Morphological Study of the Blood of Certain Fishes and Birds with Special Reference to the Leucocytes of Birds," *Bull.* Johns Hopkins Hosp., 14:352–56.

Cuming, F.
1810. *Sketches of a Tour of the Western Country, through the States of Ohio and Kentucky.* Pittsburgh.

Cummings, B.
1940. *Kinishba: A Prehistoric Pueblo of the Great Pueblo Period.* Univ. Ariz., Tucson.

Curry, W. L.
1913. *History of Jerome Township, Union County, Ohio.* Columbus.

Curtis, J. D., and D. W. Lynch.
1957. *Silvics of Ponderosa Pine.* Intermount. Forest and Range Exp. Sta., Ogden, *Misc. Publ. 12.*

Cushman, S.
1893. "Turkeys," R.I. Exp. Sta. *Bull. 25*, 89–123.

———.
1893.1. "Experiments with Turkeys (two seasons)," *Rept.* R.I. Agr. Exp. Sta., 281–310.

Custer, Elizabeth B.
1890. *Following the Guidon.* New York.

D., W. J.
1882. "Antelope and Turkeys," *Forest and Stream*, 18:408.

Dahl, H. C.
1954. "1953 Wild Turkey Kill," *P-R Quart.*, 14(4):499–500.

Dale, Sir Thomas.
1844. *"Articles, Lawes, and Orders ..." Force's Tracts.*, III(2).

Dalke, P. D.
1953. "Yields of Seeds and Mast in Second Growth Hardwood Forest, South Central Missouri," *Jour. Wildl. Manag.*, 17:378–80.

———, W. K. Clark, Jr., and L. J. Korschgen.
1942. "Food Habits Trends of the Wild Turkey in Missouri as Determined by Dropping Analysis," *Jour. Wildl. Manag.*, 6:237–42.

———, A. S. Leopold, and D. L. Spencer.
1946. *The Ecology and Management of the Wild Turkey in Missouri.* Mo. Consv. Comm. Tech. Bull. 1.

———, and D. L. Spencer.
1946. "Some Ecological Aspects of the Missouri Wild Turkey Studies," *Trans.* 11th N. Am. Wildl. Conf., 280–85.

Dall, W. H.
1915. *Spencer Fullerton Baird: A Biography.* Philadelphia.

Dalrymple, B. W.
1957. "Spring Turkey Hunt," *Outdoor Life*, 119(3):106.

Darlington, W. M.
1891. "Pennsylvania Weather Records, 1644–1835," *Pa. Mag. Hist. Biog.*, 15:109–21.

Darwin, C.
1868. *The Variation of Animals and Plants Under Domestication.* Vols. I & II. London.

———.
1896. *The Origin of Species.* Vol. I. New York.

Darwin, Erasmus.
1809. *Zoonomia; or, The Laws of Organic Life (1796).* Vol. I. Boston.

Daudin, F. M.
1800. *Traité élémentaire et complet d'ornithologie.* Vol. I. Paris.

Davies, B.
1898. "Varying Fecundity in Birds," *Zoologist*, (4)2:495–99.

Davis, H. E.
1931. "The Wild Turkey in South Carolina," *Game Breeder*, 35:243.

———.
1937. "Hunting the Wild Turkey," *Am. Rifleman*, 85(8):17–20.

———.
1937.1. "More about Hunting the Wild Turkey," *Am. Rifleman*, 85(9):14–15, 18.

———.
1949. *The American Wild Turkey.* Georgetown.

Davis, H. P.
1927. "The Mississippi Flood and the Game," *Am. Field*, 107:495–96.

Davis (Davys), John.
1880. *The Voyages and Works of*

John Davis. Hakluyt Soc. London, (1)59.

Davis, J. R.
1955. "Food Habits of the Bobcat in Alabama." M. A. thesis, Ala. Polyt. Inst.

———.
1959. "A Preliminary Report on Nest Predation as a Limiting Factor in Wild Turkey Populations," Nat. Wild Turkey Symposium. Memphis. (Mimeo).

Davis, W. T.
1912. "Tame Wild Turkeys," *Bird-Lore*, 14:342–44.

Davison, J. L.
1894. "The Last Wild Turkey of Niagara," *Forest and Stream*, 42:93.

Davison, V. E.
1945. "Wildlife Values of Lespedezas," *Jour. Wildl. Manag.*, 9:1–9.

———, and W. R. Van Dersal.
1941. "Broomsedge as a Food for Wildlife," *Jour. Wildl. Manag.*, 5:180.

"Davy."
1882. "Wild Turkey Notes," *Forest and Stream*, 18:67.

Davy, J.
1839. *Researches: Physiological and Anatomical*. Vol. II. London.

Dawson, W. L.
1903. *The Birds of Ohio*. Columbus.

Dayhart, D.
1963. "Wild Turkeys," *N.Y. Conserv.*, 17(6):46.

Deane, R.
1880. "Additional Cases of Albinism and Melanism in North American Birds," *Bull.* Nutt. Orn. Club, 5:25–30.

De Arment, R.
1959. *Turkey Hen-Poult Ratios as an Index to Reproductive Trends*. Wild Turkey Symposium. Memphis.

De Bry, J. T.
1590. *Americae*. Part II: Plate V. Frankfort.

De Hass, W.
1851. *History of the Early Settlement and Indian Wars of Western Virginia*. Wheeling.

De Jonge, Eric.
1956–57. "The American Turkey as a European Motif," *Antiques*, 70:450–51; 72: 450–51.

De Kay, J. E.
1844. *Zoology of New York; Birds*. Part 2. Albany.

De Laguna, F.
1942. "The Bryn Mawr Dig at Cinder Park, Ariz.," *Mus. North. Ariz. Plateau*, 14(4):53–56.

De Land, C. V.
1903. *History of Jackson County, Michigan* [Logansport, Ind.?].

De Lime, J. L.
1948. "Live-trapping and Restocking: Kentucky," *P-R Quart.*, 8(4):438.

———.
1949. "Live-trapping and Restocking: Kentucky," *P-R Quart.*, 9(4):483.

De Long, J.
1950. " 'Careful' driver: Cause for Regret," *Pa. Game News*, 21(7): 44.

De Long, W. J.
1911. "Mexican Wild Turkeys in

California," *Forest and Stream*, 77:646.

De Mun, Jules.
1928. "Journal," Mo. Hist. Soc. *Colls.* 5, 167–208, 311–26.

Denny, Major E.
1860. "Military Journal," *Mem. Hist. Soc. Pa.* 7, 237–409.

Denny, H.
1842. *Monographia anoplurorum Brittaniae; or, An Essay on the British Species of Parasite Insects.* London.

Denton, J. F., and D. Neal.
1951. "The Abundance and Distribution of Some Summer Birds of Tray Mountain, Georgia," *Oriole*, 16(3):25–30.

Deutsch, H. F. and M. B. Goodloe.
1945. "An Electrophoretic Survey of Various Animal Plasmas," *Jour. Biol. Chem.*, 161:1–20.

Devoe, A.
1953. "A Fowl To Give Thanks For," *Aud. Mag.*, 55:222–24.

De Volt, H. M., and C. R. Davis.
1932. "A Cholera-like Disease in Turkeys," *Cornell Vet.*, 22:78–80.

———.
1936. "Blackhead (infectious enterohepatitis) in Turkeys, with Notes on Other Intestinal Protozoa," Md. Agr. Exp. Sta. *Bull.* 392, 493–567.

De Vries, D. P.
1853. *Voyages from Holland to America, A.D. 1632 to 1644.* New York.

Díaz del Castillo, Bernal.
1933–34. *Verdadera y notable Relación del Descubrimiento y Conquista de la Nueva España y Guatemala.* Vols. I & II. Guatemala.

Díaz, E.
1901. "*Hybridismo en las Aves,*" *An. Acad. Cien. Méd.*, Habana, 38:231–33.

Díaz, Juan.
1939. *Itinerario de la Armada del Rey Católico a la Isla de Yucatán . . . año de 1518 . . . Juan de Grijalva.* In A. Yañez, *Crónicas de la Conquista de México.* Mexico.

Dibble, C. E., and A. J. O. Anderson.
1959. *Florentine Codex.* Book IX. Santa Fe.

D'Iberville, F. L.
1875. "Historical Journal; or, Narrative of the Expeditions . . . To Colonize Louisiana." In B. F. French, *Hist. Colls. La. and Fla.* n.s. 2:29–142.

Dick, E. N.
1941. *Vanguards of the Frontier.* New York.

Dickens, Ann.
1903. "Tales of the Frontier," Old Settler's Edition, McGregor *North Iowa Times*, Feb. 19.

Dickerson, L. M.
1939. "The Problem of Wildlife Destruction by Automobile Traffic, *Jour. Wildl. Manag.*, 3:104–16.

Dictionnaire Universal.
1752. *Coq d'Inde.* Paris.

Dimock, A. W.
1926. *Florida Enchantments.* Rev. ed. New York.

Di Peso (Dipeso), C. C.
1951. *The Babocomari Village Site on the Babocomari River, Southeastern Arizona.* Dragoon. Amerind Found.

533

————.
1958. *The Reeve Ruin of South-eastern Arizona.* Amerind Found., *Publ. 8.*

Dirks, W. N.
1914. "Report of Superintendent of Game Farm." *23d Bien. Rept.* Cal. Fish and Game Comm. for 1912–1914, 102–106.

Dittmar, J. S.
1942. "Protecting Feeding Shelters," *Pa. Game News,* 12(11): 11, 24.

Dixon, B.
[1914]. *Life and Adventures of Billy Dixon.* Guthrie.

Dixon, E. S.
1853. *A Treatise on the Management of Ornamental and Domestic Poultry.* 3d ed. Philadelphia.

Dobie, J. F.
1929. *A Vaquero of the Brush Country.* Dallas.

————.
1947. "Gobbler–Rattler Fight," *Dallas Morning News,* Dec. 14.

Doddridge, J.
1876. *Notes on the Settlement and Indian Wars of the Western Parts of Virginia and Pennsylvania from 1763 to 1783, Inclusive* (1824). Albany.

Dodge, E. S.
1945. "Notes from the Six Nations on the Hunting and Trapping of Wild Turkeys and Passenger Pigeons," *Jour. Wash. Acad. Sci.,* 35:342–43.

Dodge, R. I.
1877. *The Plains of the Great West and Their Inhabitants.* New York.

————.
1883. *Our Wild Indians.* Hartford.

Dodgen, H. D.
1956. *Ann. Rept.* Texas Game and Fish Comm. for 1954–55.

Donalson, I.
1842. "Captivity of Israel Donalson," *Am. Pioneer,* I:425–33.

Donelson, Mrs. John.
1844. "Recollections," Wis. Hist. Soc. Lib., Draper MS, 32KS:306.

Donnel, W. M.
1872. *Pioneers of Marion County.* Des Moines.

Doolin, John B.
1913. "When Wild Turkeys Were Numerous in Oklahoma," *Am. Field,* 80:184.

Dorman ("Herbert"), G. W.
1873. "Wild Turkey Shooting," *Forest and Stream,* 1:242.

Dorsey, G. A.
1904. *The Mythology of the Wichita.* Carnegie Inst. Washington *Publ. 21.*

Dorsey, J. O., and J. R. Swanton.
1912. A Dictionary of the Biloxi and Ofo Languages. Bur. Am. Ethn. *Bull. 47.*

Doughty, J., and T.
1833. *Cabinet of Natural History and American Rural Sports.* Vol. III, Plate II, Op. 13. Philadelphia.

Douthit, E.
1942. "Some Experiences of a West Texas Lawyer," West Texas Hist. Ass. *Year Book,* 18:33–46.

Doyle, M.
N.d. *The Illustrated Book of Domestic Poultry.* New ed. Philadelphia.

Drake, Daniel.
1820. *Pioneer Life in Kentucky.* Cincinnati.

Drane, J. W.
 1899. "The Wild Turkey's Sharp Eye," *Forest and Stream*, 53:510.

Drannan, W. F.
 1900. *Thirty-one Years on the Plains and in the Mountains.* Chicago.

Draper, L. C.
 N.d. "Life of Boone," Wis. Hist. Soc., MS 4B.

———.
 1843. "Hunter's Life and Customs," Wis. Hist. Soc., MS 30S:262–64.

———.
 1851. "Interview in 1851 with Col. Nathan Boone," Wis. Hist. Soc., MS 6S.

Dresser, H. E.
 1866. "Notes on the Birds of Southern Texas," *Ibis*, 23–46.

Drew, F. M.
 1885. "On the Vertical Range of Birds in Colorado," *Auk*, 2:11–18.

Drowne, S.
 1883. "Journal and Letters of Solomon Drowne on the Treaty of Fort Harmer," *Mag. Am. Hist.*, 9:287–88.

Du Bourg, Baron C.
 1880. "Diary of a French Officer, 1781," *Mag. Am. Hist.*, 4:205–14.

Duck, L. G., and J. B. Fletcher.
 1945. "A Survey of the Game and Furbearing Animals of Oklahoma," Okla. Game and Fish Comm. *Bull. 3.*

Duden, G.
 1834. *Bericht über eine Reise nach den westlichen Staaten Nordamerika's . . . 1824, 1825, 1826, und 1827.* 2d ed. Bonn.

Dugdale, W.
 1671. *Origines juridiciales.* 2d ed. London.

Duis, E.
 1874. *The Good Old Times in McLean County, Illinois.* Bloomington.

Duncan, V.
 1945. "The Snake without a Friend," *Southwest. Rev.*, 30:167.

Dunn, R. D., and R. M. Sherwood.
 1933. "Immunization of Day-old Chicks and Poults against Fowl Pox," *Poultry Sci.*, 12:323–24.

Dunton, J.
 1867. "Letters from New England," Prince Soc. *Publ. 4,* 224–25.

Du Petit, F.
 1738. *"Description anatomique de l'oeil du coq d'inde," Mem.* acad. roy. sci. for 1735, Paris, 123–53.

Duponceau, P. S.
 1825. In C. L. Bonaparte, *American Ornithology.* Vol. I. Philadelphia.

Dupont.
 1888. "Aquatic Turkeys," *Forest and Stream*, 30:223.

Du Pratz, Le Page.
 1758. *Histoire de la Louisiane.* Vol. II. Paris.

Durand, of Dauphiné.
 1687. *Voyages d'un Francois, exile pour la religion.* Haye.

Durant, S. W., and F. A. Durant.
 1877. *History of Lawrence County, Pennsylvania.* Philadelphia.

Dürer, Albrecht.
 1913. *Records of Journeys to Venice and the Low Countries.* R. Fry, ed. Boston.

535

Dürigen, Bruno.
 1906. *Die Geflügelzucht nach ihren jetzigen rationellen Standpunkt*. 2d ed. Berlin.

———.
 1923. *Die Geflügelzucht*. 4th and 5th ed. Vol. I. Berlin.

Dutton, B. P.
 1938. *Leyit Kin, a Small House Ruin, Chaco Canyon, New Mexico*. Univ. N. M. and School Am. Res. *Monog*. 7.

Dwight, T.
 1821. *Travels in New England and New York*. Vol. I. New Haven.

Dykeman, W.
 1955. *The French Broad*. New York.

Eden, R.
 1885. *The First Three English Books on America*. Birmingham.

"Edisto."
 1888. "A Turkey Hunt," *Am. Field*, 29:410.

Edminister, F. C.
 1954. *American Game Birds of Field and Forest*. New York.

Edwards, A. C.
 1948. "Turkey Management Research: Arizona," *P-R Quart*., 8(1):8–9.

Edwards, G.
 1761. "An Account of a Bird Supposed to be Bred between a Turkey and a Pheasant," *Phil. Trans*., London, 51(2):833–37.

———.
 1806. *Gleanings of Natural History*. Part III. London: 217–347.

Edwards, W. W.
 1914. "Morgan and his Riflemen," William and Mary Coll., *Quart. Hist. Mag*., 23:73–105.

Edwords, C. E.
 1894. *Camp-fires of a Naturalist . . . from the Field Notes of Lewis Lindsay Dyche*. New York.

Eifrig, G.
 1904. "Birds of Allegany and Garrett Counties, Western Maryland," *Auk*, 21:234–50.

Elgin, J.
 1938. "Christmas Dinner on the Upper Brazos in 1872," West Texas Hist. Ass. *Year Book*, 14:83–91.

Elley, W. B.
 1957. "Eagles Harrass [*sic*] Turkeys," *S.D. Consv. Digest*, 24(1–2):13.

Elliot, D. G.
 1869. *The New and Heretofore Unfigured Species of the Birds of North America*. Vol. II, 38 pl. New York.

———.
 1872. A Monograph of the Phasianidae or Family of the Pheasants. Vol. I, 33 pl. New York.

———.
 1881. "What Becomes of the Game," *Forest and Stream*, 16:128.

———.
 1897. *The Gallinaceous Game Birds of North America*. New York.

———.
 1899. "On Some Genera and Species," *Auk*, 16:227–32.

Elliott, T. C.
 1936. "The Coming of the White Woman, 1836," *Oregon Hist. Soc. Quart*., 37:87–101.

Ellis, J. B.
1917. "Forty Years Ago and Now," *Oologist* 34:3–4.

Ellis, R. J.
1948. "Welfare Status and Outlook for the Wild Turkey in Western Oklahoma," Okl. Coop. Wildl. Res. Unit, Quart. Prog. *Rept.*, 11(1):15–16.

———.
1961. "Trapping and Marking Río Grande Wild Turkeys," *Proc. Okla. Acad. Sci.*, 41:202–12.

Ellsworth, S.
1880. *Records of the Olden Time.* Lacon.

[Elven, J. P.].
1856. *The Book of Family Crests.* 8th ed. I:Pl. 72, Fig. 30.

Elvin, C. N.
1889. *A Dictionary of Heraldry.* Pl. 34, Fig. 3. London.

Elyot, Sir Thomas.
1552. *Bibliotheca Eliotes.* London.

Emerson, K. C.
1940. "Records of Mallophaga from Oklahoma Hosts," *Can. Entom.*, 72:104–108.

———.
1951. "A List of Mallophaga from Gallinaceous Birds of North America," *Jour. Wildl. Manag.*, 15:193–95.

Emmel, M. W.
1939. "Observations on *Capillaria contorta* in Turkeys," *Jour. Am. Vet. Med. Ass.*, 94:612–15.

Enciclopedia universal ilustrada.
N.d. Barcelona, 42:1,026.

Enciso, M. Fernández de.
1897. *Descripción de las Indias Occidentalis.* Santiago.

Eng, R. L.
1959. *Status of Turkey in Montana.* Nat. Wild Turkey Symposium. Memphis.

England, C. H.
1930. "Game Conservation in North Carolina," *Trans.* 17th Am. Game Conf., 194–97.

English, P. F., and W. C. Bramble.
1950. "Humans and Deer Combine in Keeping Turkey Populations at Low Level," Pa. State College, Sci. for Farmer. June: 7–8. *Cf.* Ralph H. Smith. 1953. "The Wild Turkey in New York," Univ. State N.Y. *Bull. to Schools* 39:228–31.

Enty, G.
1905. "Growing Wild Turkeys," *Forest and Stream,* 64:68.

Erickson, N.
1950. "Strike Out," *Pa. Game News,* 21(7):43.

Erlich, I., and D. Mikacic.
1940. *Parazitoloske pretrage purana* (Meleagris gallopavo). *Veterinarski Arhiv,* 10:115–29.

Escalante, Phelipe de.
1871. *"Nuevo Méjico," Col. Doc. Ineditos,* 15:148.

Espejo, Antonio de.
1871. *"Relación del Viaje, que yo, Antonio Espejo . . . á las Provincias y Poblaciónes de la Nueva Mexico . . . (1582–83)," Col. Doc. Ineditos,* 15:101–26.

Espinoza, A. Vázquez de.
1948. *Compendio y Descripción de las Indias Occidentales.* Smith. Misc. Colls., 108.

Estienne, C.
1600. *Maison Rustique: or The Countrie Farme* (1580). London.

Ettwein, J.
1848. "Remarks upon the Tradi-

tions, &c. of the Indians of North America," *Bull*. Hist. Soc. Pa. for 1845, I(3):29–44.

Evans, E.
1819. *A Pedestrious Tour* . . . Concord.

Evans, L. I.
1923. "An Annotated List of Birds Observed in South Florida," *Oologist*, 40:2–8.

Evans, W.
1891. "On the Periods Occupied by Birds in the Incubation of Their Eggs," *Ibis*, 52–93.

Evelin, R.
1641. *A Direction for Adventurers* . . . London (?).

Everett, F.
1956. "Airborne Turkeys," *Fla. Wildl.*, 9(12):8–9, 29.

Everitt, S. W.
1928. *Tales of Wild Turkey Hunting*. Chicago.

Evermann, B. W., and H. W. Clark.
1920. *Lake Maxinkuckee*. Vol. I. Indianapolis.

Evers, C. W.
1897. *Commemorative Historical and Biographical Record of Wood County, Ohio*. Chicago.

Ewing, H. E.
1929. *A Manual of External Parasites*. Springfield.

"Ex."
1887. "Paducah, Ky., Notes," *Am. Field*, 27:149.

Eyton, T. C.
1867. *Osteologia avium*. Wellington, Salop.

Fabricius, H.
1942. *The Embryological Treatises of Hieronymus Fabricius of Aquapendente*. H. B. Adelmann, transl. Ithaca.

Farner, D. S.
1942. "The Hydrogen Ion Concentration in Avian Digestive Tracts," *Poultry Sci.*, 21:445–50.

Farner, D. S., and B. B. Morgan.
1944. "Occurrence and Distribution of the Trematode *Collyriclum faba* (Bremser) in Birds," *Auk*, 61:421–26.

Faux, W.
1823. *Memorable Days in America*. London.

Fay, G.
1884. "The Wild Turkey," *Harper's Weekly*, 28:848.

Fearon, H. B.
1818. *Sketches of America*. 2d ed. London.

Featherstonhaugh, G. W.
1844. *Excursions through the Slave States*. Vol. II. London.

———.
1847. *A Canoe Voyage up the Minnay Sotor*. Vol. II. London.

Federal Writers' Project.
1941. *Alabama, a Guide to the Deep South*. New York.

Félibien, André.
1676. *Description de la grotte de Versailles*. 12p., Engr. Pl. Paris.

Fernow, B.
1897. *The Records of New Amsterdam from 1653 to 1674 Anno Domini*. Vol. III. New York.

Ferreira, L. D. B. Borges.
1955. "A *Capillaria columbae* (Rudolphi, 1819) Travassos, 1915," *Bol. Pecuario*, Lisbon, 23:19–29.

Feuilloy.
1884. "L'introduction des dindons en France," *La nature*, 12:286–87.

Fewkes, J. W.

1898. "Archaeological Expedition to Arizona in 1895," *17th Ann. Rept.* Bur. Am. Ethn., Part II:519–744.

———. 1900. "Property-right in Eagles among the Hopi," *Am. Anth.*, (2)2:690–707.

———. 1903. "Hopi Katcinas," *21st Ann. Rept.* Am. Bur. Ethn. for 1899–1900, 3–126.

———. 1904. "Two Summers' Work in Pueblo Ruins," *22d Ann. Rept.* Bur. Am. Ethn. for 1900–1901, Part I:3–195.

———. 1909. "Antiquities of the Mesa Verde National Park," Bur. Am. Ethn. *Bull. 41.*

———. 1912. Casa Grande, Arizona. *28th Ann. Rept.* Bur. Am. Ethn., 25–179.

———. 1923. "Designs of Prehistoric Pottery from the Mimbres Valley, New Mexico," Smith. *Misc. Colls.*, 74(6):1–47.

Ficalbi, E.

1891. "*Sulla architettura istologica di alcuni peli degli uccelli con considerazioni sulla filogenia,*" *Mem.* soc. tosc. sci. nat., 11:227–66.

Ficker, C. T.

1942. "Advice to Emigrants," *Wis. Mag. Hist.*, 25:331–55.

Fields, H. M.

1953. "Turkeys," *P-R Quart.*, 13 (4):350.

Finckh, Alice H.

1949. "Gottfried Duden Views Missouri, 1824–27," *Mo. Hist. Rev.*, 43:334–43.

Finley, J. B.

1867. *Autobiography.* Cincinnati.

Fish and Wildlife Service.

1959. "Big Game Inventory for 1958," *Wildl. Leaflet*, 411.

Fisher, Harvey I.

1951. "The Avifauna of Niihau Island, Hawaiian Archipelago," *Condor*, 53:31–42.

Fisher, O. C.

1937. *It Occurred in Kimble.* Houston.

Fisher, W. H.

1894. "Maryland Birds That Interest the Sportsman," *Oologist*, 11:138–39.

Fisher, W. R.

1848. "On the Supposed Occurrence of Turkeys' Bones at Lough Gûr," *Zoologist*, 6:2064–65.

Fiske, J.

1897. *Old Virginia and Her Neighbors.* Vol. I. Boston.

Flack, Capt.

1866. *A Hunter's Experience in the Southern States of America.* London.

Flagg, J. F.

1946. "A Philadelphia Forty-niner," *Pa. Mag. Hist. Biog.*, 70:390–422.

Fleming, H. F. von.

1719. *Der vollkommene teutsche Jägers.* Vol. I. Leipzig.

Fleming, Col. W.

1916. *Journal of Travels in Kentucky, 1779–1780.* In N. D. Mereness, *Travels in the Ameri-*

can Colonies. New York. MS in Wis. Hist. Soc. Lib.

Flint, P.
1905. "Tom, Turkey and Fox," *Forest and Stream,* 64:70.

Flint, T.
1826. *Recollections of the Last Ten Years.* Boston.

———.
1832. *The History and Geography of the Mississippi Valley.* 2d ed. Vol. I. Cincinnati.

———.
1833. *Biographical Memoir of Daniel Boone.* Cincinnati.

Flower, R.
1819. *Letters from Lexington and the Illinois.* London.

Flower, S. S.
1925. "Contributions to our Knowledge of the Duration of Life in Vertebrate Animals.—IV. Birds." *Proc.* Zool. Soc. London, pp. 1365–1422.

———.
1938. "Further Notes on the Duration of Life in Animals.—IV. Birds," *Proc.* Zool. Soc. London, 108A:195–235.

Fluke, W. G.
1936. "A New Wild Turkey Program," *Pa. Game News,* 7(7):5, 23.

———.
1940. "The Wild Turkey, Noblest of Game Birds," *Pa. Game News,* 11(7):4–5, 26. (I have been unable to locate Jackson's proclamation.)
1940.1. "Propagating Wild Turkeys in the Wild," *Pa. Game News,* 11(1):4, 32.

Foggie, A.
1937. "An Outbreak of Parasitic

Necrosis in Turkeys Caused by *Plagiorchis laricola* (Skrjabin)," *Jour. Helminth.,* 15:35–36.

Fonda, F. M.
1925. "The Turkey Industry of Añgona, Rizal," *Philip. Agr.,* 14:283–88.

Foote, J. S.
1921. *The Circulatory System in Bone.* Smith. *Mis. Colls.,* 72(10).

Forbes, S. E., and J. E. Harney, Jr.
1952. *The Bulldozer, a Tool of Wildlife Management.* Pa. Game Comm. *Final Rept.* P-R Proj. 31–R.

Ford, J. E.
1936. *A History of Moniteau County, Missouri.* California.

Foreman, C. T.
1929. "A Cherokee Pioneer— Ella Floora Coodey Robinson," *Chron. Okla.,* 7:364–74.

Foster, M.
1907. "In Quiet Covers: The Story of a North Carolina Turkey Hunt," *Outing,* 51:271–74.

Fowler, I. E.
1934. "The Tradewater River Country in Western Kentucky," *Ky. State Hist. Soc. Reg.,* 32:278–300.

Fox, H.
1912. "Observations upon Neoplasms in Wild Animals in the Philadelphia Zoological Gardens, *Jour. Path. Bact.,* 17:217–31.

———.
1923. *Disease in Captive Wild Mammals and Birds.* Philadelphia.

———.
1938. "*Infectious Diseases,*" *Rept.* Penrose Res. Lab., 27.

Fox, W. S.
 1899. "Varying Fecundity in Birds," *Zoologist*, (4)3:23–26.

Franciscan Fathers.
 1910. *An Ethnologic Dictionary of the Navaho Language*. Saint Michaels.

Friedmann, H.
 1927. "Testicular Asymmetry and Sex Ratios in Birds," *Biol. Bull.*, 52:197–207.

Fries, A. L.
 1941. *Records of the Moravians in North Carolina*. Vol. V, 1963–2450. Raleigh.

Fries, W. H.
 1958. "The Elephant Hunter," *Aud. Mag.*, 60:245.

Friley, C. E., Jr.
 1959. "Turkey Talk from Swan Creek," *Mich. Consv.*, 28(5): 22–24.

Frisch, J. L.
 1817. *Vorstellung der Vögel Deutschlandes*. Vol. I, Pl 122. Berlin.

Fröbel, J.
 1859. *Seven Years' Travel in . . . Far West of the United States*. London.

Frye, Jr., O. E.
 1949. *Game Management Division. Bien. Rept.* Fla. Game and Fresh Water Fish Comm. 1947–48.

——.
 1951. *Game Management Division. Bien Rept.* Fla. Game and Fresh Water Fish Comm. 1949–50.

——.
 1958. "A Possible Occurrence of Avian Leukosis in the Wild Turkey," *Jour. Wildl. Manag.*, 22:94.

Fuertes, L. A.
 1955–56. "Turkey," reproduced on inner cover of *N.Y. Conservationist*, 10(3).

Fuhrman, O.
 1908. *"Die Cestoden der Vögel,"* *Zool. Jahrb. Suppl.*, 10:1–232.

Fuller, H. E.
 1927. "The Ways of the Wild Turkey," *Outdoor Life and Rec.*, 60(6):28–30, 76.

Fultz, W. S.
 1899–1901. "Life of the Pioneer Farmer," *Ann. Iowa*, (3)4:219–22.

Gage, R.
 1952. "Wild Turkey Progress," *S.D. Consv. Digest*, 19(3):4–6.

——.
 1954. "Merriam Turkey Restoration," *P-R Quart.*, 14(2):193.

Gainey, L. F.
 1950. "Trapping Wild Turkeys in South Florida," Paper read at October meeting, Richmond, Southeast. Game Comm. Ass. 7p. (Mimeo.).

——.
 1954. "Management Area Research," *P-R Quart.*, 14(4):372.

——.
 1954.1. "Florida Deer and Turkey Restoration," *P-R Quart.*, 14(4): 369.

——.
 1954.2. *The Composition of Turkey Populations in Florida*, 8th Ann. Meeting Southeast. Ass. Game and Fish Comm. New Orleans. 9p. (Mimeo.).

Galbreath, E. C.
 1938. "Post-glacial Fossil Vertebrates from East-central Illinois," Field Mus. Nat. Hist., *Geol. Ser.*, 6:303–13.

Gale, L. R., and R. H. Myers.
1954. *Kentucky Wildlife.* Ky. Dept. Fish and Wildl. Resources.

Gallegos, H.
1927. *The Gallegos Relation of the Rodríguez Expedition to New Mexico.* Hist. Soc. N.M., *Publ. Hist.* 4, 1–69.

Galliziolli, S.
1953. *Investigation of the Mt. Graham Area.* Ariz. Game and Fish Comm., *Compl. Repts.* Proj. W–53–R–3, W–P–5, Job 1.

Garcia, Juan C.
1945. *Examen de algunas locuciones.* Bol. Inst. Caro y Cuerro (Thesaurus) 11.

Gardiner, J. L., and E. E. Wehr.
1949. "Some Parasites of the Wild Turkey (*Meleagris gallopavo silvestris*) in Maryland," *Proc. Helminth. Soc. Washington,* 16:16–19.

Garrison, R. C.
1954. "Collier Wildlife Investigation," *P-R Quart.,* 14(3):247; (4):370–71.

Garrod, A. H.
1873. On the Carotid Arteries of Birds. *Proc. Zool. Soc. London,* 457–72.

Gatschet, A. S.
1879. "Classification into Seven Linguistic Stocks of Western Indian Dialects Contained in Forty Vocabularies," In *Rept.* U. S. Geogr. Sur. West of 100th Meridian. Vol. VII, 403–85. Washington.
———, and J. R. Swanton.
1932. *A Dictionary of the Atakapa Language.* Bur. Am. Ethn. *Bull. 108.*

Gaumer, F. Cited by W. R. Ogilvie-Grant.
1897. *Game Birds.* Vol. II. London.

Gemelli-Careri, G. F.
1719. *Giro del mondo (1699–1700).* Vols. V & VI. Venice; 1704. *Churchill's Voyages.* Vol. IV, 1–607. London.

Gentry, T. G.
1882. *Nests and Eggs of Birds of the United States.* Philadelphia.

Geoffroy, E. L.
1762. Vol. II. *Histoire abrégée des insectes que se trouvent aux environs de Paris.*

Geombeck.
1890. "Arkansas Wild Turkeys," *Forest and Stream,* 34:169.

George, Earl of Cumberland.
1906. *A Briefe Relation of the Severall* Voyages . . . Purchas His Pilgrimes. Vol. XVI, 5–106. Glasgow.

George, John L.
1958. *The Program to Eradicate the Imported Fire Ant.* Preliminary observations. Cons. Found., New York.

Geraldini, Alexander.
1631. *Itinerarium ad regiones* . . . Rome.

Gerhardt, A.
1853. "*Die jagdbaren Vögel der Vereinigten Staaten von Nord-Amerika,*" *Naumania,* 3:378–391.

Gerini, G.
1769. *Storia naturale degli uccelli.* Vol. II, ccxxii, ccxxvi. Florence.

Gerstell, R.
1942. *The Place of Winter Feeding in Practical Wildlife Manage-*

ment. Pa. Game Comm., *Res. Bull. No. 3.*

———, and W. H. Long.
1939. *Physiological Variations in Wild Turkeys, and Their Significance in Management.* Pa. Game Comm., *Res. Bull. No. 2.*

Gesner, C.
1555. *Historia Animalium, Liber III.* Zurich.

Ghesquière, J.
1921. *Note sur quelques parasites des oiseaux au Congo Belge,"* Ann. Gembloux Brussels, 27: 239–42.

Ghigi, A.
1936. *Gallini di faraone e tacchini.* Milan.

———, and J. Delacour.
1931. "Aviculture," *Hertford,* Vol. III: 750–52; *Avicult. Mag.,* (4)9:11–13.

Gibson, J.
1886. *History of York County, Pennsylvania.* Chicago.

Gier, H. T.
1957. *Coyotes in Kansas.* Kansas Agr. Exp. Sta. *Bull. 393.*

Gilbert, E.
1907. *History of Salem, N.H.* Concord.

Gilbert, F. M.
1910. *History of the City of Evansville and Vanderburg County, Indiana.* Vol. I. Chicago.

Gilliard, E. T.
1958. *Living Birds of the World.* Garden City.

Gillin, J.
1955. *Archeological Investigation in Nine Mile Canyon, Utah.* Univ. Utah *Anth. Pap. 21.*

Gillmore, Parker.
1872. *Prairie Farms and Prairie Folk.* Vol. I. London.

———.
1874. *Prairie and Forest.* New York.

Gilmour, John.
1876. "On the Introduction of the Wild Turkey (*Meleagris gallopavo*) into Argyllshire," *Proc. Nat. Hist. Soc. Glasgow,* 2:11–16.

Gilpin, D. D.
1959. *Recent Results of Wild Turkey Restocking Efforts in West Virginia.* Nat. Wild Turkey Symposium. Memphis. (Mimeo.).

Gilpin, W.
1808. *Remarks on Forest Scenery* (1791). 3d ed. Vol. I. London.

Givens, L. S.
1962. "Use of Fire on Southeastern Wildlife Refuges," *Proc.* 1st Tall Timbers Fire Ecol. Conf. Tallahassee, 121–26.

Gjörwell, C. C.
1762. *Nya svenska biblioteket.* Vol. I. Stockholm.

Gladwin, H. S., *et al.*
1937. *Excavations at Snaketown.* Medallion Papers, 25.

Glazener, W. C.
1944. "Management of the Wild Turkey in Lower South Texas," *P-R Quart.,* 4(3):121–22.

———.
1944.1. "Management of the Wild Turkey in Lower South Texas," *P-R Quart.,* 4(3):121–22; 4(4): 169–70.

———.
1945. "Management of Turkeys

in Lower South Texas," *P-R Quart.*, 5(4):158–60.

———.

Letter of February 26, 1962.

———.

1963. "The Wild Turkey in Texas, Restoration Progress," *Tex. Game and Fish*, 21(1):8–10, 27.

Glennon, R.

1847. "On the Discovery of the Bones of Extinct Deer, &c. at Lough Gûr," *Zoologist*, 5:1589–93.

Gloger, C. W. L.

1834. *Vollständiges Handbuch der Naturgeschichte der Vögel Europa's, mit besonderer Rücksicht auf Deutschland.* Breslau.

Glover, F. A.

1947. "Flight Speed of Wild Turkeys," *Auk*, 64:623–24.

———.

1947.1. *Wild Turkey Investigation: Final Report and Management Plan.* P-R Project 12–R. Cons. Comm. W. Va. (Mimeo.).

———.

1948. "Winter Activities of Wild Turkey in West Virginia," *Jour. Wildl. Manag.*, 12:416–27.

———, and R. W. Bailey.

1947. "Wild Turkey Investigation," *P-R Quart.*, 7(4):273.

———, and R. W. Bailey.

1949. "Wild Turkey Foods in West Virginia," *Jour. Wildl. Manag.*, 13:255–65.

Godsey, T.

1930. "Missouri Note," *Am. Field*, 113:85.

Goebel, Gert.

1877. *Länger als ein Menschenleben in Missouri.* St. Louis.

———.

1889. "The Nature of the Wild Turkey and Turkey-hunting," *Am. Field*, 31:128–30.

"Golden Gate."

1911. "Game Bird Farm," *Forest and Stream*, 77:14.

Goldman, E. A.

1902. "In Search of a New Turkey in Arizona," *Auk*, 19:121–27.

———.

1951. *Biological Investigations in Mexico.* Smith. *Misc. Colls.* 115.

———, and R. T. Moore.

1946. "The Biotic Provinces of Mexico," *Jour. Mam.*, 26:347–60.

Goldsmith, Oliver.

1855. *A History of the Earth and Animated Nature.* Vol. II. Edinburgh and London.

Golson, J. P.

1950. *Bailey's Light.* San Antonio.

Gómara, F. López de.

1554. *La Historia General de las Indias.* Anvers.

———.

1943. *Historia de la Conquista de México.* Mexico.

Good, H. G., and L. G. Webb.

1940. "Spring Foods of the Wild Turkey in Alabama," *Ala. Game and Fish News*, 12(3):3–4, 13; *Am. Wildl.*, 29:288–90.

Goodrum, P. D.

1941. "Capture of Wild Turkeys in Texas for Restocking, *P-R Quart.*, 1(4):191–96.

Goodspeed Bros. and Co.

1884. *History of Greene and Sullivan Counties, State of Indiana.* Chicago.

———.
1885. *History of Pike and Dubois Counties, Indiana.* Chicago.

Goodspeed, W. A., and C. Blanchard.
1882. *Counties of Porter and Lake, Indiana.* Chicago.

Goodspeed Publishing Co.
1887. *History of Lewis, Clark, Knox and Scotland Counties, Missouri.* St. Louis.

Googe, Barnaby.
1577. *Foure bookes of husbandry.* London.

Gordon, C. G.
1885. *The Journals of Major-Gen. C. G. Gordon, C. B. at Kartoum.* Boston.

Gordon, J.
1883. In A. M. Mayer, *Sport with Gun and Rod in American Woods and Waters.* New York.

———.
1885. "A Camp Hunt in Mississippi," *Outing,* 7:65.

Gordon, L. S., and J. McClellan.
1952. "Investigation of Game Species in the Gila National Forest," *P-R Quart.,* 12(2):154.

———.
1954. "Investigations of Game Species in the Gila National Forest, *P-R Quart.,* 14(4):445.

Goss, L. J.
1940. "Report of the Hospital and Laboratory of the New York Zoological Park, 1939. Mortality Statistics of the Society's Collection," *Zoologica,* 25:269–79.

Goss, N. S.
1891. *History of the Birds of Kansas.* Topeka.

Gosse, P. H.
1847. *The Birds of Jamaica.* London.

———.
1859. *Letters from Alabama (U. S.), Chiefly Relating to Natural History.* London.

Gottfriedt, J. L.
1655. *Newe Welt und Americanische Historien.* Frankfort.

Gouberville, Sire de.
1892. *Le journal du Sire de Gouberville* (1553–62). *Copie par A. Tollemer. Mem. soc. antiq. de Normandie* (4)1.

Gould, J.
1856. "On a New Turkey, *Meleagris mexicana,*" *Proc. Zool. Soc.* London, 61–63.

Graf, A.
1920. Letter. St. Louis, December 16, 1833. *Mo. Hist. Rev.,* 14:218.

Grafe, W.
1948. "*Vergleichende Untersuchungen am Lauf der Haushühner,*" *Anat. Anz.,* 96:361–64.

Grahame, A.
1953. "Pennsylvania Talks Turkey," *Outdoor Life,* 112:104.

Grant, C.
1911. "Running Down Turkeys," *Forest and Stream,* 76:532.

Gravier, J.
1900. "Voyage in 1700 from the Country of the Illinois to the Mouth of the Mississippi River," *Jesuit Relations,* 65.

Gray, G. R.
1849. *The Genera of Birds.* Vol. III, 484–669. London.

———.
1870. *Hand-list of the Genera and Species of Birds, Distinguishing Those Contained in the British Museum.* Part II. London.

Gray, John W.
    1858. *The Life of Joseph Bishop.*
    Nashville.
Gray, L. C.
    1941. *History of Agriculture in the
    Southern United States to 1860.*
    Vol. I. New York.
Graybill, H. W.
    1924. *"Capillaria columbae* (Rud.)
    from the Chicken and Turkey,"
    Jour. Parasit., 10:205–207.
Greenberg, D. B.
    1949. *Raising Game Birds in Cap-
    tivity.* New York.
Greene, A. R.
    1910. *In Remembrance.* Kansas
    State Hist. Soc. *Colls. for 1909–
    10*, 11:480–88.
Greenhalgh, C. M., and L. Nielson.
    1953. "Turkey Releases," *P-R
    Quart.*, 13(2):195.
Greening, J.
    1942. "A Mazomanie Pioneer of
    1847," *Wis. Mag. Hist.*, 26:208–
    18.
Gregg, J.
    1844. *Commerce of the Prairies.*
    Vol. I. New York.
Gregg, Kate L.
    1952. *The Road to Santa Fe.* Albu-
    querque.
Grelan, T.
    1958. "The Deer and Turkey Re-
    storation Project," *Tenn. Consv.*,
    24(12):14–15, 18.
Griffiths, D., Jr.
    1835. *Two Years' Residence in the
    New Settlements of Ohio, North
    America.* London.
[Grinnell, G. B.]
    1909. "The Wild Turkey in Pre-
    serves," *Forest and Stream*, 73:
    847.

———.
    1909.1. "The Wild Turkey: Amer-
    ica's Greatest Game Bird," *For-
    est and Stream*, 73:852–54, 891–
    92.
———.
    1923. *The Cheyenne Indians.* Vols.
    I & II. New Haven.
Grinnell, J.
    1928. [Introduction of Wild Tur-
    key into California]. *Condor*,
    30:195.
———, H. C. Bryant, and T. I.
Storer.
    1918. *The Game Birds of Cali-
    fornia.* Berkeley.
———, and A. H. Miller.
    1944. *The Distribution of the Birds
    of California. Pacific Coast Avif.*,
    27.
Griscom, L.
    1932. *The Distribution of Bird-life
    in Guatemala. Bull. Am. Mus.
    Nat. Hist.*, 64.
Griswold, Gillett.
    1958. "Old Fort Sill: The First
    Seven Years," *Chron. Okla.*,
    36:2–14.
Guérard, G. de.
    1888. *"Les dindons sauvages,"
    Bull.* soc. zool. acclim. Paris,
    (4)5:762–63.
Guernsey, S. J.
    1931. *Explorations in Northeastern
    Arizona. Pap.* Peabody Mus.
    Am. Arch. Ethn., 12(1).
———, and A. V. Kidder.
    1921. *Basket-Maker Caves of
    Northeastern Arizona. Pap.* Pea-
    body Mus. Am. Arch. and Ethn.
    8(2).
Gullion, G. W.
    1951. "Birds of the Southern Wil-

lamette Valley, Oregon," *Condor*, 53:129–49.

Gulliver, G.
1875. "Observations on the Sizes and Shapes of the Red Corpuscles of the Blood of Vertebrates," *Proc. Zool. Soc. London*, 474–95.

Gunn, J. M.
1917. *Schat-Chen: History, Traditions and Narratives of the Queres Indians of Laguna and Acoma.* Albuquerque.

Gunn, T. E.
1869. "Vitality of a Turkey," *Zoologist*, (2)4:1,722.

Gustafson, R.
1959. "The Big Bird," *Wyo. Wild Life*, 23(8):14–17.

————.
1961. *Investigation into Physical Development and Wing Molt Progression in Merriam's Wild Turkey.* Wyo. Game and Fish Comm. Proj. W–50–R–9. Plan 5, Job 3.

————.
1961.1. *Wild Turkey Hunter Questionnaire.* Wyo. Game and Fish Comm. Proj. W–50–R–9, Plan 7, Job 2.

————.
1961.2. *Evaluation of Wild Turkey Restoration Program.* Wyo. Game and Fish Comm. Proj. W–50–R–9, Plan 5, Job 2.

Guthrie, J. D.
1926. "Notes on the Wild Turkey," MS. Library Dept. Wildl. Manag., Univ. Wisconsin.

Guyon.
1879. "The Wild Turkey," *Chicago Field*, 11:209–11.

Gwynn, J. V.
1958. "The Conflict between Wild and Domestic Turkeys," *Va. Wildl.*, 19(12):20–21.

H., I. N. de.
1905. "Tamed Wild Turkeys," *Forest and Stream*, 64:354.

H., J. D.
1879. "Kentucky Turkey Shooting," *Forest and Stream*, 13:893.

H., W. J.
1882. "The Mississippi Floods," *Forest and Stream*, 18:150.

Haafner, J. G.
1811. *Voyages dans la péninsula occidentale de l'Inde et dans l'isle de Ceilan.* Vol. II. Paris.

Hachisuka, M.
1928. *Variations among Birds* (chiefly game birds), *Suppl. Publ. Orn. Soc. Japan No. 12.*

Hadley, P. B.
1909. "Studies in Avian Coccidiosis. . . ." Centralbl. f. Bact., Abt. I, Orig., 50:348–53.

————.
1909.1. "Notes on the parasitism of *Cytodites nudus* and *Haemaphysalis chordeilis*," *Science*, 30:605–606.

————.
1916. *The Role of the Flagellated Protozoa in Infective Processes of the Intestines and Liver.* R.I. Agr. Exp. Sta. *Bull. 166.*

Hafen, L. R.
1927. "Supplies and Market Prices in Pioneer Denver," *Colo. Mag.*, 4(4):136–42.

Hahn, H. C.
1946. "Deer and Turkey Investigations in the Edwards Plateau Region," *P-R Quart.*, 6(3):122; E. A. Walker. 1951.1.

———.
1946.1. [Turkey Census in the Edwards Plateau Region, Texas], *P-R Quart.*, 6(1):24.

———.
1951. *Inventory of Wildlife on Kerr Wildlife Management Area* [Texas]. Proj. W–53–R, Job V. (Mimeo.).

Hahn, H. C., Jr.
1951.1. *Inventory of the Vegetation of Kerr Wildlife Management Area.* Proj. W–53–R, Job IV. (Mimeo.).

H[akluyt], R.
1889. "A Discourse of Western Planting, 1584," *Hakluyt's Voyages*, 13(2):175–282.

Hale, E. B., and M. W. Schein.
1962. "The Behaviour of Turkeys." In E. S. E. Hafez, *The Behaviour of Domestic Animals*, 531–64. London.

Hall, E. T., Jr.
1944. *Early Stockaded Settlements in the Governador, New Mexico: A Marginal Anasazi Development from Basket Maker III to Pueblo I Times.* Columbia Studies Arch. and Ethn., 2(1).

Hall, James.
1838. *Notes on the Western States.* Philadelphia.

———.
1848. *The West: Commerce and Navigation.* Cincinnati.

Hall, J. M.
1948. "Turkey Management Research: Arizona," *P-R Quart.*, 8(1):7.

———.
1948.1. "Elk, Deer, and Turkey Management Research: Arizona," *P-R Quart.*, 8(2):162.

———.
1948.2. "Turkey Management Research: Arizona," *P-R Quart.*, 8(1):7; (3):266.

———.
1949. "Elk, Deer, and Turkey Management Research, Arizona," *P-R Quart.*, 9(1):3–4.

———.
1949.1. "Elk, Deer, and Turkey Management Research," *P-R Quart.*, 9(3):303–304.

———.
1950. "Elk, Deer, and Turkey Management Research, Arizona," *P-R Quart.*, 10(3):262.

———.
1952. *Turkey Hunt Information,* Ariz. Game and Fish Comm. *Compl. Rept.*, 53R2–WP2–J7.

Hall, J. N.
1899. "A Missouri Outing," *Forest and Stream*, 52:29.

Hall, W. J., and E. E. Wehr.
1949. *Diseases and Parasites of Poultry.* U. S. Dept. Agr. *Farmers' Bull. 1652.*

Hallock, C.
1876. *Camp Life in Florida.* New York.

———.
1905. "Wild Domestic Turkeys as Game," *Forest and Stream*, 65:436.

Halloran, A. F., and J. A. Howard.
1956. "Aransas Refuge Wildlife Introductions," *Jour. Wildl. Manag.*, 20:460–61.

Halsell, H. H.
1948. *My Autobiography.* Dallas.

Halsell, W. D.
1951. "Protection of Game in Sunflower County One Hundred

Years Ago," *Jour. Miss. Hist.*, 13:105–107.

Hamilton, Capt. Thomas.
1833. *Men and Manners in America.* Philadelphia.

Hammond, G. P.
1926. "The Founding of New Mexico," *N.M. Hist. Rev.*, 1:445–77.

Hammond, J. C., and S. J. Marsden.
1937. "Sexing Turkeys from Hatching to Maturity," *Poultry Sci.*, 16:287–88.

Hamor, R.
[1860]. *A True Discourse of the Present Estate of Virginia . . . 1614.* Albany.

Hampton, O. H.
1900. "Stock the Preserve with Turkeys," *Forest and Stream*, 54:349.

Hancock, J. L.
1887. "Notes and Observations on the Ornithology of Corpus Christi and Vicinity, Texas," Ridgway Ornith. Club *Bull.*, 2: 11–23.

Handley, C. O.
1935. "Game Propagation Report," *Ann. Rept.* Va. Comm. Game and Inland Fisheries for 1934, 19–22.

———.
1945. "Japanese Honeysuckle in Wildlife Management," *Jour. Wildl. Manag.*, 9:261–64.

Hanson, R. P., and L. Karstad.
1959. "Feral Swine in the Southeastern United States," *Jour. Wildl. Manag.*, 23:64–74.

Hanzlick, B.
1960. "Wild Turkeys in Kansas," *Kan. Fish and Game*, 17(4):7–9.

Harcourt, Helen.
1910. "How Our Ancestors Observed Thanksgiving Day," *Americana*, 5:992–96.

Hardy, F. C.
1949, 1950, 1952. "Forest Wildlife Management Investigations," *P-R Quart.*, 9(4):485; 10(3):- 298; 12(3):216.

———.
1959. *Results of Stocking Wild-trapped and Game Farm Turkeys in Kentucky.* Nat. Wild Turkey Symposium. Memphis. 1958. (Mimeo.).

Hargrave, L. L.
1929. "Elden Pueblo," Mus. North. Ariz. *Notes 2(5):*1–3.

———.
1939. "Bird Bones from Abandoned Indian Dwellings in Arizona and Utah," *Condor*, 41: 208.

———.
1939.1. "Investigations of Controlling Factors of Wild Turkey Populations in Arizona," Bur. Biol. Survey Abstr. *Quart. Rept.* for 1939–40. (Mimeo.).

Harlow, R. C.
1918. "Notes on the Breeding Birds of Pennsylvania and New Jersey," *Auk*, 35:18–29.

Harper, F.
1942. "William Bartram's Names of Birds," *Proc.* Rochester Acad. Sci. 8:208–21.

Harrington, J. P.
1928. *Vocabulary of the Kiowa Language.* Bur. Am. Ethn. *Bull. 84.*

Harrington, M. R.
1927. "A Primitive Pueblo in Ne-

vada," *Am. Anth.*, (2)29:262–77.

———.
1930. "Archeological Explorations in Southern Nevada," Southw. Mus. *Pap. 4*, 5–25.

Harris, F. G.
1897. "A Brace of Wild Turkeys," *Forest and Stream*, 49:385.

Harris, L. B.
1921. "Journal, 1836–1842," *Southw. Hist. Quart.*, 25:140.

Harris, W. T.
1890. *Hegel's Logic*. Chicago.

Harrison, L.
1916. "The Genera and Species of Mallophaga," *Parasit.*, 9:1–156.

Hartman, F. A.
1955. "Heart Weight in Birds," *Condor*, 57:221–38.

Hartman, G. F.
1959. "Wisconsin's Wild Turkey Project," Nat. Wild Turkey Symposium. Memphis. (Mimeo.).

Harwood, P. D.
1931. [*Strigea falconis meleagris* n. var.], *Jour. Parasit.*, 18:51.

———, and D. I. Stunz.
1945. "Phenothiazine and Nicotine-Bentonite as an Anthelmitic in Turkeys," *Proc. Helminth. Soc. Washington*, 12:1–2.

Hassler, E. W.
1900. *Old Westmoreland* [County, Pennsylvania]. Cleveland.

Hatt, R. T., *et al.*
1953. "Faunal and Archaeological Researches in Yucatan Caves," Cranbrook Inst. Sci. *Bull. 33*.

Haugen, A. O.
1961. "Turkey Talk for Paint Creek," *Iowa Consv.*, 20(1): 100–101.

Haury, E. W.
1936. *The Mogollon Culture of Southwestern New Mexico*. Medallion Pap., 20.

———.
1941. "Excavations in the Forestdale Valley, East-Central Arizona," Univ. Ariz. Soc. Sci. *Bull. 12*.

———.
1945. *The Excavation of Los Muertos and Neighboring Ruins in the Salt River Valley, Southern Arizona. Pap.* Peabody Mus. Am. Arch. Ethn., 24(1).

———.
1945.1. *Painted Cave, Northeastern Arizona.* Amerind Found. *Publ.* 3.

———.
1950. *The Stratigraphy and Archaeology of Ventana Cave, Arizona.* Tucson and Albuquerque.

Havard, C.
1953. "Wild Turkey Survey and Inventory," *P-R Quart.*, 23(2): 157.

Hawkins, B.
1848. "A Sketch of the Creek Country Written in the Years 1798 and 1799," *Ga. Hist. Soc. Colls.*, 3(1):19–88.

Hawn, M. C.
1937. "Trichomoniasis of Turkeys," *Jour. Infect. Dis.*, 61:184–97.

Hay, O. P.
1892. "The Batracians and Reptiles of the State of Indiana," *Rept.* Ind. Dept. Geol and Nat. Resources for 1891, pp. 409–602.

———.
1924. *The Pleistocene of the Mid-*

dle Region of North America and Its Vertebrated Animals. Carnegie Inst. Washington, *Publ. 322A.*

Hayden, A. H.
  1961. *Range Analysis and Habitat Requirements of the Wild Turkey in Cameron County, Pennsylvania.* Penn. Coop. Wildl. Res. Unit *Quart. Rept.* 23(3): 3–7.

Hayes, Mrs. A. M.
  1896. "Reminiscences of Pioneer Days in Hastings," Mich. Hist. *Colls.* 26, 235–41.

Haywood, J.
  1823. *The Natural and Aboriginal History of Tennessee.* Nashville.

Hazard, C.
  1930. *Nailor Tom's Diary.* Boston.

Headlee, Mrs. F. D.
  1928. "My Experience in Raising Wild Turkeys," *Dakota Farmer,* 48:92.

Hebard, F. V.
  1941. *Winter Birds of the Okefenokee and Coleraine.* Ga. Soc. Nat. *Bull. 3.*

————.
  1949. "Glaucous Gull Records and Other Notes," *Fla. Natur.,* 22:36.

Heckewelder, J.
  1848. "Memorandum of the names . . . 'Delawares' had given to rivers, streams, places . . ." Presented by Maurice C. Jones. *Bull.* Hist. Soc. Pa., 1:139–54.

————.
  1876. *History, Manners, and Customs of the Indian Nations.* Mem. Hist. Soc. Pa., 12.

————.
  1886. "Notes of Travel . . . to

Gnadenhuetten . . . 1797," *Pa. Mag. Hist. Biog.,* 10:125–57.

Heilborn, A.
  1930. *Liebesspiele der Tiere.* Berlin-Charlottenburg.

Heinroth, O.
  1941. "Pfauen-und Truthahnbalz," *Zeits. Tierpsych.,* 4:330–32.

Hellmayr, C. E., and B. Conover.
  1942. *Catalogue of Birds of the Americas.* Part I(1). Field Mus. Chicago.

Hempstead, J.
  1901. *Diary.* New London.

Henderson, J., and J. P. Harrington.
  1914. *Ethnozoology of the Tewa Indians.* Bur. Am. Ethn. *Bull. 56.*

Henderson, J. H.
  1925. "Reminiscences of a Range Rider," *Chron. Okla.,* 3:253–88.

Hendron, J. W.
  1946. *Frijoles: A Hidden Valley in the New World.* Santa Fe.

Hening, W. W.
  1823. *The statutes at large; . . . laws of Virginia, from . . . the Year 1619.* Vol. I. New York.

Hennig, R., and E. Strechow.
  1940. "Vorcolumbische Darstellung von amerikanischen Truthähnen im Dom zu Schleswig," *Petermanns Geog. Mitteil.,* 86: 90–92.

Henry, A.
  1897. In E. Coues, *New Light on the Early History of the Greater Northwest: The Manuscript Journals of Alexander Henry and of David Thompson, 1799–1814.* Vols. I & II. New York.

Henshall, J. A.
  1883. "Around the Coast of Florida," *Forest and Stream,* 20:4.

Henshaw, H. W.
1874. "Report upon the Ornithological Collections made in Portions of Nevada, Utah, California, Colorado, New Mexico, and Arizona," Chap. 3. *Wheeler Surv. West of 100th Meridian.*

Hepburn, J. S. and P. R. Miraglia.
1937. "A Contribution to the Chemistry of Turkey Eggs," *Jour. Frankl. Inst.,* 223:375–77.

Heresbach, Conrad.
1570. *Rei rustica libri quatuor.* Coloniae.

Herman, C. M.
1944. "The Blood Protozoa of North American Birds," *Bird-Band.,* 15:89–112.

Hermes, W. B.
1939. *Medical Entomology.* 3d ed. New York.

Hernández, Francisco.
1651. *"Rerum medicarvm Novae Hispaniae thesavrvs sev plantarvm animalivn," Historiae animalium.* Rome.

Herrera, Antonio de.
1944. "*Historia General de los Hechos de los Castellanos. . . .*" (1601). Vol. III. Asunción.

Herrick, F. H.
1917. *Audubon the Naturalist.* Vol. I. New York.

Herrick, G. W.
1916. "Some External Parasites of Poultry with Special Reference to Mallophaga . . ." Cornell Univ. Agr. Exp. Sta. *Bull. 359:* 230–68.

Herring, J. L.
1918. *Saturday Night Sketches.* Boston.

Hesse, Nicholas.
1838. *Das westliche Nordamerika.* Paderborn.

Hesselius, A.
1947. "Journal, 1711–1724," *Del. Hist.,* 2:69–118.

Hewett, E. L., and B. P. Dutton.
1945. *The Pueblo World.* Albuquerque.

Heyward, D. C.
1937. *Seed from Madagascar.* Chapel Hill.

Hibben, F. C.
1937. *A Preliminary Study of the Mountain Lion (Felis oregonensis* sp.). Univ. N.M. Biol. Ser., *Bull. 5(3).*

Hildreth, S. P.
1836. [Wild Turkeys in the Kanawha valley], *Am. Jour. Sci.,* 29:85.

———.
1842. "Biographical Sketch of Isaac Williams," *Am. Pioneer,* I:343–51.

———.
1843. "Early Emigration . . . 1788," *Am. Pioneer,* II:112–34.

———.
1848. *Pioneer History: . . . Ohio Valley.* Cincinnati.

Hill, A.
1905. "Can Birds Smell?" *Nature,* 71:318–19.

Hill, R. T., and A. S. Parkes.
1934. "Hypophysectomy. III. Effect on Gonads, Accessory Organs, and Head Furnishings," *Proc. Roy. Soc. London,* 116B:221–36.

Hill, W. W.
1938. *The Agricultural and Hunting Methods of the Navaho Indians.* Yale Univ. *Publ. Anth. 18.*

Hines, Robert. In J. W. Aldrich and A. J. Duvall.
 1955. *Distribution of American Gallinaceous Game Birds*. Fish and Wildl. Service *Circ. 34.*

Hinshaw, W. R., and E. McNeil.
 1943. "*Leucocytozoon* sp. from turkeys in California," *Poultry Sci.*, 22:268–69.

———, K. W. Niemann, and W. H. Busic.
 1932. "Studies of Tuberculosis of Turkeys," *Jour. Am. Vet. Med. Ass.*, 80:765–77.

Hinton, R. J.
 1878. *The Handbook to Arizona.* San Francisco.

Historical Publishing Co.
 1901. *Franklin County*. Columbus.

Hockley, R.
 1904. "Selected Letters from the Letter-book of Richard Hockley, of Philadelphia, 1739–1742," *Pa. Mag. Hist. Biog.*, 28:26–44.

Hodge, F. W.
 1912. *Handbook of American Indians North of Mexico*. Vols. I & II. Washington.

———.
 1920. *Hawikuh Bonework*. Ind. Notes and Monog., 3(3).

———.
 1923. *Circular Kivas near Hawikuh, New Mexico. Contr.* Mus. Am. Indian 7(1).

Hodgson, A.
 1824. *Letters from North America, Written during a Tour in the United States and Canada.* Vol. I. London.

Hoffman, A.
 1951. "*Contribuciones al conocimiento de los trombiculidos*

mexicanos," *Ciencia*, 11(1, 2): 29–36.

Hoffman, W. J.
 1885. "Bird Names of the Selish, Pah-Uta, and Shoshoni Indians," *Auk*, 2:7–10.

———.
 1896. *The Memomini Indians. 14th Ann. Rept.* Bur. Am. Ethn. Part I.

Holabird, W. H.
 1875. "An Unvarnished Tale of 1834," *Forest and Stream*, 3:394.

Holbrook, H. L.
 1951. "Turkey Trapping," *P-R Quart.*, 11(4):452.

———.
 1952. *The Francis Marion Turkey Project.* Sixth Ann. Conf. Southeast. Ass. Game and Fish Comm. Savannah.

———.
 1958. "Francis Marion Preserve Objectives Are Achieved," *S.C. Wildl.*, 5(1):2–3, 16–17.

———.
 1958.1. "The Francis Marion Turkey Project," *Proc.* 11th Ann. Conf. Southeast. Ass. Game and Fish Comms. 1957, pp. 355–63.

Holden, W. C.
 1931. "Texas Tech Archeological Expedition Summer of 1930," *Bull.* Texas Arch. and Pal. Soc., 3:43–52.

———.
 1932. *Rollie Burns: or An Account of the Ranching Industry on the South Plains.* Dallas.

Holder, T. H.
 1951. *A Survey of Arkansas Game.* Ark. Game and Fish Comm.

Holland, W. J.
 1908. "A Preliminary Account of

the Pleistocene Fauna Discovered in a Cave Opened at Frankstown, Pennsylvania, in April and May, 1907," *Ann.* Carnegie Mus. 4:228–233; 1912. *Proc.* 7th Int. Zool. Cong. Boston, 1907, pp. 748–52.

Holland, W. L.
1950. "State-wide Turkey Management: Alabama," *P-R Quart.*, 10(4):396.

Hollibaugh, Mrs. E. F.
1902. *Biographical History of Cloud County, Kansas.* N.p.

Hollis, F. D.
[*ca.* 1950]. *The Present Status of the Wild Turkey in Louisiana.* La. Dept. Wild Life and Fisheries.

Hollman, F. G.
[1922]. *Auto-biography of Fredrick G. Hollman: Settled in Platteville, Wisconsin, in 1828.* Platteville.

Holm, T. Campanius.
1834. *A Short Description of the Province of New Sweden.* Pa. Hist. Soc. *Mem.* 3(1).

Home, E.
1796. "On Muscular Motion," *Trans.* Phil. Soc. London, 86:1–26.

———.
1807. "Observations on the Structure of the Stomachs of Different Animals . . ." *Trans.* Phil. Soc. London, 97(2):139–79.

Hopkins, F.
1940. "The Wild Turkey Problem in Wisconsin," Wis. Consv. *Bull.* 5(12): 47–48.

Hopkins, G. H. E., and T. Clay.
1952. *A Check List of the Genera and Species of Mallophaga.* London.

Hopkinson, E.
1934. "More Additions to Breeding Records," *Avicult. Mag.*, (4)12: 310–24.

Hough, E.
1890. "Chicago and the West," *Forest and Stream*, 34:308.

———.
1891. "Chicago and the West," *Forest and Stream*, 37:469.

———.
1898. "Chicago and the West," *Forest and Stream*, 51:349.

———.
1903. "Chicago and the West," *Forest and Stream*, 60:52

Hough, W.
1903. "Archaeological Work in Northeastern Arizona," *Rept.* U.S. Nat. Mus. for 1901, pp. 287–358.

———.
1914. *Culture of the Ancient Pueblos of the Upper Gila River Region, New Mexico and Arizona.* U. S. Nat. Mus. *Bull.* 87.

———.
1915. *The Hopi Indians.* Cedar Rapids.

———.
1919. "The Hopi Indian Collection in the United States National Museum," *Proc.* U. S. Nat. Mus., 54:235–96.

Houstoun, Mrs.
1845. *Texas and the Gulf of Mexico.* Philadelphia.

Howard, E. B.
1932. "Caves along the Slopes of the Guadalupe Mountains," *Bull.* Texas Arch. and Pal. Soc., 4:7–19.

554

Howard, H.

1927. "A Review of the Fossil Bird *Parapavo californicus* (Miller), from the Pleistocene Asphalt Beds of Rancho La Brea," Univ. Cal., *Bull.* Dept. Geol. Sci., 17:1–30.

———.

1928. "The Beak of *Parapavo californicus* (Miller)," *Bull.* South. Cal. Acad. Sci., 27:90–91.

———.

1929. "The Avifauna of Emeryville Shellmound," Univ. Cal. *Publ. Zool.* 32:301–94.

Howard, H.

1930. "A Census of the Pleistocene Birds of Rancho La Brea from the Collections of the Los Angeles Museum," *Condor*, 32:81–88.

———.

1936. "A New Record for *Parapavo californicus* (Miller)," *Condor*, 38:249–50.

———.

1945. "Observations on Young Tarsometatarsi of the Fossil Turkey *Parapavo californicus* (Miller)," *Auk*, 62:596–603.

———.

1950. "Fossil Evidence of Avian Evolution," *Ibis*, 92:1–21.

———.

1963. *Fossil Birds from the Anza-Borrego Desert*. Los Angeles Co. Mus., *Contrib. Sci. No. 73.*

———, and A. H. Miller.

1933. "Bird Remains from Cave Deposits in New Mexico," *Condor*, 35:15–18.

Howard, M. C.

1938. "The Use of Power in Making Small Clearings in Bear Oak Brush for Wildlife," *Jour. Wildl. Manag.*, 2:179–80.

Howard, O. W.

1900. "Nesting of the Mexican Wild Turkey in the Huachuca Mts., Arizona," *Condor*, 2:55–57.

Howay, F. W.

1930. "Early Relations between the Hawaiian Islands and the Northwest Coast." In A. P. Taylor and R. S. Kuykendall, *The Hawaiian Islands*. Honolulu.

Howell, A. H.

1921. "A List of the Birds of Royal Palm Hammock, Florida," *Auk*, 38:250–63.

———.

1932. *Florida Bird Life*. New York.

Howison, Lieut. N. M.

1913. "Report on Oregon, 1846," *Oregon Hist. Soc. Quart.*, 14:1–60.

Hoy, P. R.

1882. "The Larger Wild Animals That Have Become Extinct in Wisconsin," *Trans.* Wis. Acad. Sci., 5:255–57.

Hoyningen-Huene, A.

1868. "*Notiz über* Meleagris gallopavo," *Jour. für Ornith.*, 16:358.

Hubbard, J. H.

1875. "Wild Turkeys Playing Out," *Rod and Gun*, 6(4):58.

Hubbard, W. P.

1948. "Revenge in the Meadow," *Nat. Mag.*, 41:233–36.

Hudson, A. P.

1942. "An Attala Boyhood," *Jour. Miss. Hist.*, 4:127–55.

Hudson, G. E., P. J. Lanzillotti, and G. D. Edwards.

1959. "Muscles of the Pelvic Limb

in Galliform Birds," *Am. Mid. Nat.*, 61:1–67.

Hudson, J. R.
1934. "Notes on Some Avian Cestodes," *Ann. and Mag. Nat. Hist.*, (10)14:314–18.

Hughes, J.
1932. *Pioneer West Virginia.* Charleston.

Hughes, T.
1884. *Gone to Texas.* London.

Hulsey, S.
1944. "Wildlife in the White Mountains of Arizona in Pioneer Days," *Ariz. Wildlife*, 6(5):6, 10.

Humboldt, A. von.
1836. *Kritische Untersuchungen über die historische Entwicklung . . . Neuen Welt.* Vol. II. Berlin.

Hunn, M.
1960. "Turkey Money in the Big Cypress," *Fla. Wildl.*, 14(3):16–17.

Hunt, Alice.
1953. *Archeological Survey of the La Sal Mountain Area, Utah,* Univ. Utah *Anth. Pap. 14.*

Hunt, L. B., and E. H. Forbush.
1917. *Our American Game Birds.* Wilmington.

Hunter, John D.
1823. *Manners and Customs of Several Indian Tribes West of the Mississippi.* Philadelphia.

Huntington, D. W.
1908. "How To Save the Wild Turkey," *Independent*, 64:731–36.

Hurley, J. B.
1921. "Birds of Yakima County, Wash.," *Oologist*, 38:14–17.

Hutt, F. B., and C. D. Mueller.
1942. "Sex-linked Albinism in the

Turkey, *Meleagris gallopavo*," *Jour. Hered.*, 33:69–77.

Huxley, T. H.
1868. "On the Classification and Distribution of the Alectromorphae and Heteromorphae," *Proc.* Zool. Soc. London, 294–319.

Hyde, R. E.
1960. "Our First Wild Turkey Season," *N.Y. Consv.*, 14(4):7.

[Hyer, J. K.].
1866. *Dictionary of the Sioux (Lacotah) language.* Fort Laramie.

"Ignis Fatuus."
1885. "Southern Illinois as a Game Country Forty Years Ago," *Am. Field*, 23:30.

Imler, R. H., and E. R. Kalmbach.
1955. *The Bald Eagle and Its Economic Status.* Fish and Wildl. Serv. *Circ. 30.*

Inman, H.
1881. *Stories of the Old Santa Fe Trail.* Kansas City.

Insko, N. M. Jr., and M. Lyons.
1933. "Calcium and Phosphorus in the Development of the Turkey Embryo," *Jour. Nutrit.*, 6:507–13.

Inter-State Publishing Co.
1883. *History of White County, Illinois.* Chicago.

———.
1883.1. *History of Daviess County, Kentucky.* Chicago.

Irving, W.
1944. *The Western Journals of Washington Irving.* J. F. McDermott, ed. Norman.

Ives, J. C.
1861. *Report upon the Colorado*

River of the West. Part I. Washington.

Ixtlilxochitl, F. d'Alva.

1840. *Historia des Chichimègues: Ternaux-Compans' Voyages.* Vols. XII and XIII. Paris.

Izacke, R.

1681. "Remarkable Antiquities of the City of Exeter." App. *Catalogue of Sheriffs.* London.

Jackson, A. S.

1945. "Brazos Clear Fork Wildlife Development," *P-R Quart.,* 5 (4):157–58.

———.

1950. "Turkey Live-trapping and Transplanting: Texas," *P-R Quart.,* 10(3):362.

———.

1959. *Dynamics of Rodent-Quail Relationships in Northwest Texas.* Job Compl. Rept. No. 10, Proj. W–45–R–9. (Mimeo.).

———.

1959.1. Letter, September 21.

Jackson, E.

1942. "Handle with Care," *Ariz. Highways,* 18(2):42.

Jackson, J. B. S.

1875. [Malformed sternum of a turkey]. *Proc.* Boston Soc. Nat. Hist. for 1874–75, 17:454.

Jacob, R. T.

1924. "Military Reminiscences," *Chron. Okla.,* 2:11–36.

Jacobsson, H.

1939. "The Wild Turkey in Swedish Forests," *Pa. Game News,* 10(6):3, 27.

Jahangir, Emperor.

1909. *Memoirs.* Vol. I. A. Rogers, transl. London.

James, E.

1823. *Account of an expedition from Pittsburgh to the Rocky Mountains . . .* Vol. II. London.

James, J. A.

1912. *George Rogers Clark papers, 1771–1781.* Ill. Hist. *Colls.* 8.

Jansen, V.

1959. *Summary of 1958 Michigan Turkey Populations.* Nat. Wild Turkey Symposium. Memphis, 1958.

Jantzen, R. A.

1954. *Turkey Hunt Information.* Ariz. Game and Fish Dept., Compl. Rept. Proj. W–53–R–4, W–P2, Job 7.

———.

1955. *Turkey Survey.* Ariz. Game and Fish Dept., Comp. Rept. Proj. W–53–R–5, W–P3, Job 7.

———.

1955.1. *Report on Turkey Questionnaire Cards Concerning the 1954 Season.* Ariz. Game and Fish Dept. Compl. Rept. Proj. W–53–R–5, W–P2, Job 7.

———.

1955.2. *Turkey Hunt Information.* Ariz. Game and Fish Dept., Compl. Rept. Proj. W–53–R–5, W–P2, Job 7.

———.

1956. *Turkey Survey.* Ariz. Game and Fish Dept., Compl. Rept. Proj. W–53–R–6, W–P3, Job 7.

———.

1956.1. *Turkey Hunt Information.* Ariz. Game and Fish Dept., Compl. Rept. Proj. W–53–R–6, W–P2, Job 7.

———.

1956.2. *Report on Turkey Questionnaire Cards Concerning the 1955 Season.* Ariz. Game and

Fish Dept., Compl. Rept. Proj. W–53–R–6, W–P2, Job 7.

——.

1956.3. "Let's Talk Turkey," *Ariz. Wildl. News*, 3(2):6–7.

——.

1957. *Turkey Survey*. Ariz. Game and Fish Dept., Compl. Rept. Proj. W–53–R–7, W–P3, Job 7.

——.

1957.1. *Turkey Hunt Information*. Ariz. Game and Fish Dept., Compl. Rept. Proj. W–53–R–7, W–P2, Job 7.

——.

1957.2. *Turkey Survey*. Ariz. Game and Fish Dept., Compl. Rept., Proj. W–53–R–8, W–P3, Job 7.

——.

1958. *Turkey Hunt Information*. Ariz. Game and Fish Dept., Compl. Rept. Proj. W–53–R–8, W–P–2, Job 7.

——.

1959. *Research Needs for Merriam Turkey in Arizona*. Nat. Wild Turkey Symposium, Memphis. (Mimeo.).

——, L. E. Powell, T. Knipe, and S. Gallizioli.

1954.1. *Turkey Survey*. Ariz. Game and Fish Dept., Compl. Rept. Proj. W–53–R–4, W–P3, Job 7.

Jaramillo, Juan.

1857. "*Relación que dió el Capitán Juan Jaramillo, de la Jornado que hizo á la Tierra Neuva, de la que fué General Francisco Vásquez de Coronado.*" In B. Smith, *Colección de Varios Documentos para la Historia de la Florida.*

London, 1870. *Col. Doc. Ineditos*, 14:309.

Jardine, W.

1853. *Gallinaceous Birds*. Edinburgh and London.

Jeançon, J. A.

1923. *Excavations in the Chama Valley, New Mexico*. Bur. Am. Ethn. *Bull. 81.*

——.

1929. *Archeological Investigations in the Taos Valley, New Mexico, during 1920*. Smith. Mis. *Colls. 81(12).*

Jegorow, J.

1887. "*Über den Einfluss des Sympathicus auf die Vogelpupille,*" *Pflüger's Arch. f. ges. Phys.*, 41:326–48.

——.

1890. "*Über das Verhältnis des Sympahticus zur Kopfverzierung eineger Vögel,*" *Archiv. f. Anat. u. Phys. Suppl. Bd.*, 33–56.

Jenkins, J. H.

1958. *Recollections of Early Texas: The Memoirs of John Holland Jenkins*. J. H. Jenkins III, ed. Austin.

Jenks, R.

1931. *Ornithology of the Life Zones Summit of San Francisco Mts.* Nat. Park Serv., Grand Canyon Nat. Park, *Tech Bull. 5* (Mimeo.).

Jennings, W. S.

1956. "Wild Turkey Beats Rattler in Scrap," *Texas Game and Fish*, 14(8):3.

Jesse, E.

1838. *Gleanings in Natural History*. New ed. Vol. I. London.

Job, H. K.
1915. *Propagation of Wild Birds.* Garden City.

Johenning, L.
1940. "Double-bearded Gobbler," *Va. Wildlife,* 3(5):5, 7.

Johnson, A.
1917. "The Indians and Their Culture as Described in Swedish and Dutch Records from 1614 to 1664," *Proc.* 19th Int. Cong. Am. 1915, pp. 277–82.

Johnson, B.
1959. "History of Turkey Restoration in Mississippi and Its Effect on Present Management," *Miss. Game and Fish,* 22(7):4–5, 11; 1959. Nat. Wild Turkey Symposium, Memphis.

Johnson, C.
1932. *Historic Hampshire in the Connecticut Valley.* Springfield.

Johnson, Clifton.
1918. *Highways and Byways of Florida.* New York.

Johnson, E. P.
1939. *A Method of Raising Turkeys in Confinement to Prevent Parasitic Diseases.* Va. Agr. Exp. Sta. *Bull. 323.*

———.
1943. In H. S. Mosby and C. O. Handley, *The Wild Turkey in Virginia.* Richmond.

———, *et al.*
1938. "A Blood Protozoan of Turkeys Transmitted by *Simulium nigroparvum* (Twinn)," *Am. Jour. Hyg.,* 27:649–65.

Johnson, G. F.
[*ca.* 1930]. *The North American Wild Turkey.* Blabon.

———.
1932. "Build Is the Best Index to Wild Turkey Purity," *Game Breeder,* 36:54.

Johnson, J. C.
1920. "The Life Cycle of *Echinostoma revolutum* (Froelich)," Univ. Cal. *Publ. Zool.* 19:335–88.

Johnson, M. K.
1961. "Turkeys Stocked in Yellow River Forest," *Iowa Consv.,* 20(1):97, 104.

Johnson, R. R.
1961. "Aerial Pursuit of Hawks by Turkeys," *Auk,* 78:646.

Johnson, Samuel.
1755. *A Dictionary of the English Language.* London.

Johnson, W. F.
1920. *The History of Cuba.* Vol. V. New York.

Johnson, W. S.
1897. "A Turkey Swims," *Osprey,* 1:136.

Johnston, T. H.
1943. "Trematodes from Australian Birds. I. Cormorants and Darters," *Trans.* Roy. Soc. South Australia, 66:226–42.

Johnstone, J.
1756. *Theatrum universale de avibus.* Heilbronn.

Jones, B. T.
1922. "Decoying Wild Turkeys," *Outdoor Life,* 50(5):325–26.

Jones, D.
1865. *A Journal of Two Visits made to . . . Indians . . . in the Years 1772 and 1773.* New York.

Jones, H. E.
1887. "The Capture of the Boss Wild Gobbler of Pine Swamp," *Am. Field,* 27:218.

————.
1888. "Drumming of the Ruffed Grouse," *Am. Field*, 29:247.

Jones, M. F.
1930. [A New Tapeworm from a Guinea Fowl]. *Jour. Parasit.*, 16:158–59.

————.
1936. "A New Species of Cestode, *Davainea meleagridis* (Davaineidae) from the Turkey with a Key to Species of *Davainea* from Galliform Birds," *Proc.* Helminth. Soc. Washington, 3:49–52.

Jones, N. E.
1898. *The Squirrel Hunters of Ohio*. Cincinnati.

J[ordan], C. L.
1879. "When to Hunt Turkeys," *Forest and Stream*, 12:273–74.

————.
1881. "More About Turkey Calling," *Forest and Stream*, 17:389.

————.
1898. "The Wild Turkey: Its Habits and Directions for Hunting It," *Shooting and Fishing*, 24:206, 226–27, 246–47, 267, 288, 310–11, 330–31; 25:50.

————.
1914. In E. A. McIlhenny, *The Wild Turkey and Its Hunting*. New York.

Josselyn, J.
1860. *New England's Rarities Discovered* (1672). Worcester.

————.
1865. *An Account of Two Voyages to New-England, Made During the Years 1638, 1663* (1675). Boston.

Josserand, P.
1938. "Ozark Gobblers," *Field and Stream*, 43(7):7.

Joutel, H.
1878. "Relation." In P. Margry, *Découvertes et établissements des Français . . . l'Amerique Septentrionale* (1614–1754). Vol. III, 91–534. Paris.

Jowett, W.
1911. "Blackhead. Infectious entero-hepatitis or typhlo-hepatitis. A disease of young turkeys," *Jour. Comp. Path. and Therap.*, 24:289–302.

Joynes, T. R.
1902. "Memoranda Made by Thomas R. Joynes on a Journey to the States of Ohio and Kentucky, 1810," *William and Mary Coll. Quart. Hist. Mag.*, 10:145–58.

Judd, N. M.
1925. "Everyday life in Pueblo Bonito," *Nat. Geogr. Mag.*, 48:227–62.

————.
1930. "The Excavation and Repair of Betatakin," *Proc. U. S. Nat. Mus.*, 77(5).

————.
1954. *The Material Culture of Pueblo Bonito*. Smith. Mis. Colls., 124.

————.
1959. *Pueblo del Arroyo, Chaco Canyon, New Mexico*. Smith. Mis. Colls., 138(1).

Judd, S.
1863. *History of Hadley*. Northampton.

Judd, S. D.
1905. *The Grouse and Wild Tur-*

keys of the United States, and Their Economic Value. Biol. Surv. *Bull. 24.*

Jull, M. A.
1947. *Raising Turkeys, Ducks, Geese, Game Birds.* New York.
———, et al.
1948. "Hatchability of Chicken and Turkey Eggs Held in Freezing Temperatures," *Poultry Sci.,* 27:136–40.

Jungherr, E.
1927. "Two Interesting Turkey Diseases," *Jour. Am. Vet. Med. Ass.,* 71:636–40.

Kalbfus, J.
1913. *Annual Report* of the Game Commissioners of the State of Pennsylvania . . . for 1912, p. 10.

Kalm, P.
1772. *Travels into North America.* 2d ed. Vol. I. London.

Kalmbach, E. R.
1939. "Nesting Success: Its Significance in Waterfowl Reproduction," *Trans.* 4th N. Am. Wildl. Conf., p. 591–604.
———.
1943. *The Armadillo: Its Relation to Agriculture and Game.* Texas Game, Fish and Oyster Comm. Austin.

Kanoy, W. C.
1936. "How Fast Can a Wild Turkey Fly?" *Field and Stream,* 40(11):86–87.

Karns, H. J.
1954. *Unknown Arizona and Sonora. 1693–1721.* From F. F. del Castillo version of "*Luz de Tierra Incógnita,*" by Capt. J. M. Manje. Tucson.

Kauffman, H. H.
1962. "Pennsylvania Wild Turkeys

in Germany," *Pa. Game News,* 33(5):27–29.

Kay, M. W.
1946. "Studies on Flagellates from Domesticated Birds. The behavior of *Trichomonas gallinarum* in culture," *Jour. Exp. Zool.,* 101:407–24.

Keeler, C. A.
1893. *Evolution of Colors of North American Birds.* Cal. Acad. Sci., *Occ. Pap. 3.*

Keeling, H. C.
1910. "The Indians: My experience with the Cheyenne Indians," Kan. State Hist. Soc. *Colls. for 1909–10.* 11:306–15.

Keeney, G. J.
1875. [Turkeys Absent in North Dakota]. *Forest and Stream,* 5:220.

Keim, De B. R.
1870. *Sheridan's Troopers on the Borders.* Philadelphia.

Keiser, L. P., and E. L. Kozicky.
1943. "Sex and Age Determination of Wild Turkeys," *Pa. Game News,* 14(8):10–11, 26.

Kelemen, P.
1943. *Medieval American Art.* Vol. II. New York.

Kellogg, V. L.
1900. "A List of the Biting Lice (Mallophaga) Taken from Birds and Mammals of North America," *Proc.* U. S. Nat. Mus., 22:39–100.

Kelly, W.
1851. *An Excursion to California.* Vol. I. London.

Kennamer, E. F.
1959. "Longevity and Range of a Crippled Turkey Tom," *Jour. Wildl. Manag.,* 23:460.

Kennard, F. H.
  1915. "On the Trail of the Ivory-bill," *Auk*, 32:1–14.

——.
  1915.1. "The Okaloacoochee Slough," *Auk*, 32:154–66.
Kennerly, C. B. R.
  1856. *Field Notes and Explanations.* Pacific Ry. Surveys IV(vi).
Kennett, H. C.
  1957. *Game Division 5th Bien. Rept.* N.C. Wildl. Res. Comm., July 1, 1954–June 30, 1956.
Kenny, J.
  1938. "Journal, 1761–63." In J. W. Harpster, *Pen Pictures of Early Western Pennsylvania.* Pittsburgh.
Kenton, Edna.
  1930. *Simon Kenton.* Garden City.
Kenworthy, C. J. ("Al Fresco").
  1882. "Florida Game Abundant," *Forest and Stream*, 18:229.
"Keouk."
  1881. "About Wild Turkeys," *Forest and Stream*, 17:429.
Kercheval, S.
  1833. *A History of the Valley of Virginia.* Winchester.
Kerns, C.
  1958. "Maryland Wild Turkey Stocking," *Md. Consv.*, 35(4):26–27.

——.
  1959. "Maryland Wild Turkey Management — 1958" *Md. Consv.*, 36(1):5–6.
Kerns, C. M.
  1961. "Game Management," *Md. Consv.*, 38(6):10–11.
[Kester, J. Y.].
  1928. *The American Shooter's Manual* (1827). New York, pp. 126–27.

Ketchum, W.
  1865. *An Authentic and Comprehensive History of Buffalo.* Vol. II. Buffalo.
Kidder, A. V.
  1917. "Prehistoric Cultures of the San Juan Drainage," *Proc.* 19th Int. Cong. Am., pp. 108–13.

——.
  1932. *The Artifacts of Pecos.* New Haven.

——, and S. J. Guernsey.
  1919. *Archeological Explorations in Northeastern Arizona.* Bur. Am. Ethn. *Bull. 65.*
Kidder, F., and A. A. Gould.
  1852. *The History of New Ipswich* (New Hampshire). Boston.
Kimball, J.
  1949. "Progress Report on Our Wild Turkeys," *S. D. Consv. Digest*, 16(7):10.
Kimball, T. L.
  1958. "Turkey," *Ann. Rept.* Colo. Dept. Fish and Game for 1956–57, p. 30.
King, D. S.
  1949. *Nalakiku Excavations at a Pueblo III Site on Wupatki National Monument, Arizona.* Mus. North. Ariz. *Bull. 23.*
King, H. H.
  1921. "The Fowl Tick (*Argas persicus*, Oken)," Wellcome Trop. Res. Lab. Khartoum, *Ent. Bull. 16.*
King, I. F.
  1908. "The Coming and Going of Ohio Droving," Ohio Arch. Hist. Soc. *Publ.* 17:247–53.
King, W. R.
  1866. *The Sportsman and Naturalist in Canada.* London.

562

Kingston, J. T.
   1876. "Early Western Days," Wis. Hist. *Colls.* 7:297–344.
Kitchell, R. L., J. S. Cass, and J. H. Sauter.
   1947. "An Infestation in Domestic Turkeys with Intestinal Flukes," *Jour. Am. Vet. Med. Ass.*, 111: 379–81.
Klein, J. T.
   1750. *Historiae avium prodromus* . . . Lubeck.

————.
   1766. *Ova avium* . . . Leipzig.
Kligler, I. J., R. S. Muckenfuss, and T. M. Rivers.
   1929. "Transmission of Fowl-pox by Mosquitoes," *Jour. Exp. Med.*, 49:649–60.
Kluckhohn, C., *et al.*
   1939. "Preliminary Report on the 1937 Excavations Bc 50–51, Chaco Canyon, New Mexico." Univ. N.M. *Bull., Anthrop. Ser.* *3(2)*.
Knoder, E.
   1955. "Let's Talk Turkey," Ohio *Consv. Bull.* *19(4)*: 6–7.

————.
   1957. "Last of the Farm Turkeys," Ohio *Consv. Bull.* *21(3)*: 12–13.

————.
   1959. *Morphological Indicators of Heritable Wildness in Turkeys* (Meleagris gallopavo) *and Their Relation to Survival*. Nat. Wild Turkey Symp. Memphis.

————.
   1959.1. *An Aging Technique for Juvenal* [juvenile] *Wild Turkeys Based on the Rate of Primary Feather, Moult and Growth. Proc.* First Nat. Wild

Turkey Management Symposium. Memphis.
Knopp, T. B.
   1959. "Factors Affecting the Abundance and Distribution of Merriam's Turkey (*Meleagris gallopavo merriami*) in Southeastern Arizona." Univ. Ariz., M.Sc. Thesis.
Knott, A. A.
   1888. "Turkeys in the Nation," *Forest and Stream*, 31:45–46.
Knowlton, F. H., and R. Ridgway.
   1909. *Birds of the World*. New York.
Koch, A.
   1889. "*Wilde Truthühner in Pennsylvanien*," *Mitth. orn. Verein, Wien*, 13:129–34.
Kondo, D.
   1947. "On Turkey–Chicken Hybrids, with Special Reference to Their Abnormal Development," *Seibutu*, 2:110–14.
Kopman, H. H.
   1921. *Wildlife Resources of Louisiana*. La. Dept. Consv. *Bull. 10*.
Kosin, I. L., and H. Nagra.
   1956. *Frequency of Abortive Parthenogenesis in Domestic Turkey. Proc.* Soc. Exp. Biol. Med., 93:605–608.
————, and W. J. Wakely.
   1950. Persistency of the Functional Capacity of Breed-heterologous Turkey Semen. Poultry Sci. 29:258–63.
————, I. Sato, and H. Nagra.
   1962. *Estudios sobre partenogenésis en el guajolote domestico y en el pollo*. 11th World's Poultry Congress. Mexico City.
Kozicky, E. L.
   1942. "Pennsylvania Wild Turkey

Food Habits," *Pa. Game News*, 13(8):10–11, 28–29, 31.

———. 1943. "Food Habits of Foxes in Wild Turkey Territory," *Pa. Game News*, 4(4):8, 9, 28.

———. 1948. "Some Protozoan Parasites of the Eastern Wild Turkey in Pennsylvania," *Jour. Wildl. Manag.*, 12:263–66.

———. 1948.1. "Life history and management of the wild turkey (*Meleagris gallopavo silvestris*) in Pennsylvania," Pa. State College, Ph.D. Thesis.

———, and R. Metz. 1948. "The Management of the Wild Turkey in Pennsylvania," *Pa. Game News*, 19(4):3, 20–21, 26–27, 30–31.

Krukenberg, C. F. W. 1882–85. *Vergleichend-physiologische Vorträge*. Vol. III, 85–184. Heidelberg.

Kurz, R. F. 1937. *Journal of Rudolph Friederich Kurz*, Bur. Am. Eth. *Bull. 115.*

Kuykendall, R. S. 1938. *The Hawaiian Kingdom, 1778–1854*. Honolulu.

Kyle, G. 1957. "Turkeys for Every County," *Ala. Consv.*, 29(1):4–6.

L. 1879. "Gallatin (Mo.) Notes," *Chicago Field*, 10:338.

L., H. 1890. "A Turkey Call," *Forest and Stream*, 34:491.

Labaree, L. W. 1943. *Pub. Rec. State Conn.*, 5.

Lacey, H. 1911. "The Birds of Kerrville, Texas, and Vicinity," *Auk*, 28:200–19.

Lack, D. 1941. "Some Aspects of Instinctive Behaviour and Display in Birds," *Ibis*, 407–41.

La Flesche, F. 1932. *A Dictionary of the Osage Language*. Bur. Am. Ethn. *Bull. 109.*

La Farge, O. and D. Byers. 1931. *The Year Bearer's People*. Tulane Univ., Mid. Am. Res. Ser., *Publ. 3.*

Lambert, J. 1810. *Travels through Lower Canada and the United States*. Vol. I. London.

Lampman, B. H. 1925. "A Sultan in Bronze," *Nat. Mag.*, 6:332–35.

Landsteiner, K., L. G. Longworth, and J. Van der Scheer. 1938. "Electrophoresis Experiments with Egg Albumins and Hemoglobins," *Science*, 88:83–85.

Landa, Diego de. 1937. *Yucatán Before and After the Conquest*. W. Gates, trans. Baltimore.

Lane, H. H. 1926. *Oklahoma*. In V. E. Shelford, *Naturalist's Guide to the Americas*. Baltimore.

Lane, W. M. 1961. "Facts about the Live-Trapping and Transplanting Program," *W. Va. Consv.*, 25(3):1, 12–15.

Lange, C. H. 1950. "Notes on the Use of Turkeys by Pueblo Indians," *El Palicio*, 57(7):204–209.

Langenbach, J. R., and R. D. McDowell.
1939. "Report on the Food Habits Study of the Great Horned Owl," *Pa. Game News*, 9(10): 6–9.

Langworthy, C. F.
1901. *Eggs and Their Use as Food.* U. S. Dept. Agr., *Farmer's Bull. 128.*

Laruelle, L., J. Reumont [Reamont], and E. Legait.
1951. *"Recherches sur le mécanisme des changements de couleur des caroncules vasculaires du dindon (Meleagris gallopavo L.),"* Arch. anat. micros. et morph. exptl., 40:91–113.

————.
1952. *"Modification de structure des caroncules vasculaires de* Meleagris gallopavo *L. male après section de branches cutanées des nerfs rachidiens cervicaux ou après castration,"* Comp. rend. ass. anat., 38:637–39.

————.
1952.1. *"Structure des caroncules de* Meleagris gallopavo *L. male et femelle,"* Comp. rend. ass. anat., 38:640–42.

La Salle, Nicolas de.
1876. *"Relation de la découverte que M. de La Salle . . . 1682."* In P. Margry, *Découverte et établissements des Français,* I:547–70.

Las Casas, Bartolomé de.
1951. *Historia de las Indias.* Vol. III. Mexico.

Latham, J.
1823. *A General History of Birds.* Vol. VIII. Winchester.

Latham, R. M.
1947. "Differential Ability of Male and Female Game Birds To Withstand Starvation and Climatic Extremes," *Jour. Wildl. Manag.*, 11:139–49.

————.
1956. *Complete Book of the Wild Turkey.* Harrisburg.

————.
1958. "Factors Affecting Distribution and Abundance of Wild Turkeys in Pennsylvania." Pa. State Univ. Ph.D. Thesis.

————.
1961. "Some Considerations Concerning the Emergency Winter Feeding of Wild Turkeys in Northern States," *W. Va. Consv.*, 25(7):12–15, 30–31.

Latimer, H. B.
1927. "Correlations of the Weights and Lengths of the Body, Systems and Organs of the Turkey Hen," *Anat. Rec.*, 35:365–77.
————, and J. A. Rosenbaum.
1926. "A Quantitative Study of the Anatomy of the Turkey Hen," *Anat. Rec.*, 34:15–23.

Latrobe, C. J.
1835. *The Rambler in North America.* Vol. I. London.

Laveran, C. L. A., and A. Lucet.
1905. *"Deux hématozoaires nouveaux de la perdrix et du dindon,"* Comp. rend. acad. sci., Paris, 141:673–76.

Law, G. R. J., and I. L. Kosin.
1958. "Seasonal Reproductive Ability of Male Domestic Turkeys as

Observed under Two Ambient Temperatures," *Poultry Sci.*, 37:1,034–1,047.

Lawson, J.
1937. *The History of North Carolina* (1714). Richmond.

Lea, Tom.
1957. *The King Ranch*. Vol. II. Boston.

Leach, A. J.
1909. *A History of Antelope County, Nebraska*. Chicago.

Le Compte, E. L.
1930. "Maryland Game Refuges Successful," *Am. Field*, 114:4.

Le Conte, J.
1858. "Observations on the Wild Turkey, or *Gallopavo sylvestris* of Ray," *Proc.* Acad. Nat. Sci. Philadelphia for 1857, 9:179–81.

Ledin, D. H.
1959. "The Wild Turkey in Minnesota," *Consv. Volunteer*, 22 (130):26–31.

Lee, A. E.
1892. *History of the City of Columbus, Capitol of Ohio*. Vol. I. New York and Chicago.

Lee, L.
1955. "Wild Turkey Restoration and Range Expansion in New Mexico," *Proc.* 35th Ann. Conf. West. Assn. State Game and Fish Comms., 223–25.

———.
1959. *The Present Status of the Wild Turkey in New Mexico*. Proc. Nat. Wild Turkey Symposium. Memphis.

Leffingwell, W. B.
1890. *Shooting on Upland Marsh and Stream*. Chicago.

Le Fort, L.
1891. *De l'élevage des dindons*

sauvages américains. *Bull.* soc. zool. acclim 38: 561–65.

Legge, L. E.
1957. "Let's Talk Turkey," *W. Va. Consv.*, 21(9):8–11.

Lehmann, V. W.
1948. "Restocking on King Ranch," *Trans.* 13th N. Am. Wildl. Conf., 237.

Leidy, J.
1866. "Remarks on Cancer of the Liver in a Turkey," *Proc.* Acad. Nat. Sci. Philadelphia, 18:9.

———.
1880. "Bone Caves of Pennsylvania," *Proc.* Acad. Nat. Sci. Philadelphia, 32:346–49.

———.
1889. "Notice and Description of Fossils in Caves and Crevices of the Limestone Rocks of Pennsylvania," *Ann. Rept.* Geol. Surv. Pa. for 1887, 1–20.

Leland, J.
1770. *Joannis Lelandi antiquarii. De rebus Britannicis collectanea.* Vol. VI. London.

León, P. de Cieza de.
1864. *Travels* (1553). Hakluyt Soc. 33.

Leonard, L. W.
1855. *History of Dublin, N.H.* Boston.

Leopold, A.
1931. *Report on a Game Survey of the North Central States*. Madison.

———.
1932. "Game Survey of Iowa," MS. Chap. VII.

Leopold, A. S.
1941. *Report on the Management of the Caney Mountain Turkey*

Refuge, Ozark County, Missouri. (Mimeo.).

——.
1942. "Woven Wire and the Wild Turkey," *Mo. Cons.*, 3(7):2.

——.
1943. "The Moults of Young Wild and Domestic Turkeys," *Condor*, 45:133–45.

——.
1943.1. "Conservation of Game," *Trans.* Acad. Sci. St. Louis, 31 (3):63–67.

——.
1944. "The Nature of Heritable Wildness in Turkeys," *Condor*, 46:133–97.

——.
1948. *"The Wild Turkeys of Mexico," Trans.* 13th N. Am. Wildl. Conf., 393–400.

——.
1953. "Intestinal Morphology of Gallinaceous Birds in Relation to Food Habits," *Jour. Wildl. Manag.*, 17:197–203.

——.
1959. *Wildlife of Mexico.* Berkeley.
——, and P. D. Dalke.
1943. "The 1942 Status of Wild Turkeys in Missouri," *Jour. Forestry*, 41:428–35.

Lesson, R. P.
1831. *Traité d'ornithologie.* Paris.

——.
1836. *Histoire naturelle . . . mammifères et de oiseaux découverts depuis la mort de Buffon.* Vol. VII. Paris.

L'Éstoile, Pierre de.
1958. *Journal pour la regne de Henri IV.* Vol. II. Paris.

Levasseur, A.
1829. *Lafayette in America in 1824 and 1825.* Vol. II. Philadelphia.

Levine, N. D., L. E. Boley, and H. R. Hester.
1941. "Experimental transmission of *Trichomonas gallinae* from the Chicken to Other Birds," *Am. Jour. Hyg.*, 33(C):23–32.

Lewis.
1899. "The Adventures of the 'Lively' Immigrants," *Texas State Hist. Ass. Quart.*, 3:1–32.

Lewis, E. J.
1863. *The American Sportsman.* 3d ed. Philadelphia.

Lewis, J. B.
1957.1. "Tough to Trap," *Mo. Consv.*, 18(8):13.

——.
1958. "Trends in the Wild Turkey Population in the Missouri Ozarks," *Proc.* Soc. Am. For. for 1957, 92–94.

——.
1961. "Wild Turkeys in Missouri, 1940–1960." *Trans.* 26th N. Am. Wildl. Conf., 505–13.

——.
1961.1. "Turkey Hunt Dream Comes True," *Mo. Consv.*, 22 (3):17.

Lewis, L.
1885. "Turkey Shooting," *Am. Field*, 24:220.

Lewis, M.
1905. Letter, March 31, 1805. In R. G. Thwaites, *Original Journals of the Lewis and Clark Expedition.* Vol. VII. New York.

Lewis, S. B.
1858. "Memoirs of Townships. Norwalk." *Fire Lands Pion.*, 1(1):32–35.

Lhuys, D. de.
　1877. *"Origine et acclimation du dindon,"* *Bull.* soc. zool. acclim., (3)4:289–95.
Lieberkühn, N.
　1860 *"Die Ossification des Sehnengewebe,"* *Arch. Anat. Physiol.,* 824–46.
Ligon, J. S.
　1927. *Wild Life of New Mexico.* N.M. Dept. Game and Fish.

——.
　1929. "Restoring the Wild Turkey in New Mexico," *Southwest Wilds and Waters,* Dec.:10–12, 48.

——.
　1943. "Mountain Turkeys in Wyoming," *Wyo. Wild Life,* 8(10):1, 14–16.

——.
　1946. *History and Management of Merriam's Wild Turkey.* N.M. Game and Fish Comm.

——.
　1961. *New Mexican Birds.* Albuquerque.
Lindeström, P.
　1925. *Geographia Americae . . . 1654–1656.* Philadelphia.
Linnaeus, C.
　1746. *Fauna Suecica.* Stockholm.

——.
　1758. *Systema Naturae.* 10th ed. Holmiae.

——.
　1766. *Systema Naturae.* 12th ed. Holmiae.
Lint, K. C.
　1952. *Breeding Ocellated Turkeys in Captivity.* *Bull.* Zool. Soc., San Diego, No. 27.
Lloyd, W.
　1887. "Birds of Tom Green and Concho Counties, Texas," *Auk,* 4:181–93.
Lockett, H. C., and L. L. Hargrave.
　1953. *Woodchuck Cave, a Basketmaker II Site in Tsegi Canyon, Arizona.* Mus. North. Ariz. *Bull.* 26.
Lockwood, F. C.
　1928. *Arizona Characters.* Los Angeles.
Lockwood, J. H.
　1856. "Early Times and Events in Wisconsin," Wis. Hist. *Colls.* 2:- 98–196.
Löer.
　1911. *"Vergleichende Untersuchungen über die Maasse und Proportionalgewichte des Vogelherzens,"* *Pflüger's Arch. ges. Phys.,* 140:293–324.
Long, J.
　1791. *Voyages and Travels of an Indian Interpreter and Trader.* London.
Long, W. H.
　1939. "The Heat Production and Muscular Activity of Two Strains of Wild Turkeys," Pa. Game Comm. Res. *Bull.* 2, Part II:20–60.
Longfield, R.
　1868. *The Game Laws of Ireland.* 2d ed. Dublin.
Longolius, Gybertus.
　1544. *Dialogus de avibus.* Coloniae.
Longwell, J. R., and C. Kerns.
　1959. "Turkey Management Paying Dividends," *Md. Consv.,* 36(5):12–14.
López, C. M.
　1911. *Caza Mexicana.* Mexico.
Lorenz, F. W.
　1950. "Onset and Duration of Fer-

tility in Turkeys," *Poultry Sci.*, 29:20–26.

——, V. S. Asmundson, and N. E. Wilson.

1956. "Turkey Hybrids (*Meleagris ocellata* x *Meleagris gallopavo*)," *Jour. Heredity*, 47:143–46.

Lorenz, K. Z.

1939. *Vergleichende Verhaltensforschung*. Zool. Anz. Suppl., 12:69–102.

——.

1952. *King Solomon's Ring*. New York.

Lorenzana y Buitrón, F. A.

1770. *Historia de Neuva-España*. Mexico.

Loskiel, G. H.

1794. *History of the Mission of the United Brethren among the Indians in North America*. Part I. London.

Lothrop, S. K.

1926. *Pottery of Costa Rica and Nicaragua*. Contr. Mus. Am. Indian 8.

Love, W. D., Jr.

1895. *The Fast and Thanksgiving Days of New England*. Boston.

Loveless, C. M.

1951. "Wild Turkey Survey and Inventory," *P-R Quart.*, 11(1): 49–50.

——.

1951.1. "Wild Turkey Survey and Inventory," *P-R Quart.*, 11(4): 418–19.

——.

1951.2. "The Wild Turkey in Mississippi," *Miss. Game and Fish*, 14(11):10–11, 14.

Lovell, C. C.

1932. *The Golden Isles of Georgia*. Boston.

Lowe, P. R.

1926. "More Notes on the Quadrate as a Factor in Avian Classification," *Ibis*, 167–68.

——.

1933. "The Differential Characters in the Tarso-metatarsi of *Gallus* and *Phasianus* as They Bear on the Problem of the Introduction of the Pheasant into Europe and the British Isles," *Ibis*, 332–43.

Lowery, G. H.

1955. *Louisiana Birds*. Baton Rouge.

Lowndes.

1881. "Wild Turkey Calls," *Forest and Stream*, 17:271.

——.

1883. "A Mississippi Turkey Hunt," *Am. Field*, 19:296.

Lumholtz, C.

1902. *Unknown Mexico*. Vols. I & II. New York.

——.

1912. *New Trails in Mexico*. New York.

Luttringer, L. A., Jr.

1936. "Breeding Refuges for Wild Turkeys," *Pa. Game News*, 7(4):10.

——, and R. Gerstell.

1952. "Pennsylvania Wildlife," Rev. Pa. Game Comm., *Bull. 18*.

Luxán, D. P. de.

1929. *Expedition into New Mexico Made by Antonio de Espejo, 1582–1583*. Quivira Soc. Los Angeles.

Lyell, C.

1845. *Travels in North America in the Years 1841–42*. Vol. I. New York.

M.
1878. "Shooting Around Wooster, Ohio," *Chicago Field*, 10:249.

M.
1881. "Wild Turkey Hunting," *Forest and Stream*, 17:229.

M., J. K.
1933. "Battles Gobbler with Hands Only," *Am. Field*, 120:561.

MacDonald, D.
1961. "Turkeys Trap Themselves," *N.M. Game and Fish News*, July, 6:3.

MacDonnell, L. R., *et al.*
1954. "Proteins of Chicken, Duck, and Turkey Eggs," *Biochim. Biophys. Acta*, 13:140–41.

Mackenzie, A.
1801. *Voyages from Montreal . . . through the continent of North America . . .* London.

MacNeish, R. S.
1964. "Ancient Mesoamerican Civilization," *Science*, 143:531–37.

[MacQuin, A. D.].
1820. *Tabella Cibaria*. London.

Macy, R. W.
1939. "Disease in Turkeys due to *Prosthogonimus macrorchis*," *Jour. Am. Vet. Med. Ass.*, 94:-537–38.

Madsen, H.
1945. "The species of *Capillaria* (nematodes, Trichinelloidea) parasitic in the digestive tract of Danish gallinaceous and anatine game birds, with a revised list of species of *Capillaria* in birds," *Danish Rev. Game Biol.*, 1:1–112.

———.
1951. "Notes on the Species of *Capillaria* Zeder, 1880, Known from Gallinaceous Birds, *Jour. Parasit.*, 37:257–65.

Maher, R. E.
1935. "Wild Turkey Conservation in Arizona," *Game Breeder and Sportsm.*, 39:252, 264–65.

Main, A. K.
1943. "Thure Kumlien, Koshkonong Naturalist," *Wis Mag. Hist.*, 27:321–43.

Mainardi, D.
1958. "Immunology and Chromatography in Taxonomic Studies on Gallinaceous Birds," *Nature*, 182:1388–1389.

———.
1959. "Immunological Distances among Some Gallinaceous Birds,," *Nature*, 184:913–14.

Major, R. H.
1847. *Select Letters of Christopher Columbus*. Hakluyt Soc., Vol. 2.

Malassez, L.
1872. *"De la numération des globules rouges du sang chez les mammifères, les oiseaux et les poissons,"* *Comp. rend. acad. sci.*, 75:1528–1531.

Malcomson, R. O.
1960. "Mallophaga from Birds of North America," *Wilson Bull.* 72:182–97.

Mann, W.
1883. "Impregnation in the Turkey," *Science*, 2:105.

Mann, W. M.
1930. *Wild Animals In and Out of the Zoo*. New York. Smith. Sci. Ser., 6.

Manning, W.
1919. *Some History of Van Zandt County*. Des Moines.

Marcy, R. B.

1866. *Thirty Years of Army Life on the Border.* New York.

Margolf, P. H., J. A. Harper, and E. W. Callenbach.

1947. "Response of Turkeys to Artificial Illumination," Pa. Agr. Expt. Sta. *Bull. 486.*

Markham, G.

1623. *Cheap and Good Husbandry* (1614). 3d ed. London.

Marotel, G.

1926. "*Une nouvelle maladie parasitaire: La monostomidose cutanée du dindon,*" *Rev. vét.* 78:725–36.

Marquette, Jacques.

1903. In J. G. Shea, *Discovery and Exploration of the Mississippi Valley.* 2d ed. Albany.

Marsden, S. J., and J. H. Martin.

1945. *Turkey Management.* 3d ed. Danville.

Marsh, O. C.

1870. [Fossil Turkey]. *Proc.* Acad. Nat. Sci. Philadelphia.

———.

1871. "Notice of Some New Fossil Mammals and Birds from the Tertiary Formation of the West," *Am. Jour. Sci.,* 3(2):120–27.

———.

1871.1. "New Fossil Turkey," *Am. Nat.,* 4:317.

———.

1872. "Notice of Some New Tertiary and Post-tertiary Birds," *Am. Jour. Sci.,* (3)4:256–62.

Marshall, C.

1877. *Extracts from the Diary of Christópher Marshall.* Albany.

Marshall, William.

1895. *Der Bau der Vögel.* Leipzig.

Martin, A. C., F. H. May, and T. E. Clarke.

1939. "Early Winter Food Preferences of the Wild Turkey on the George Washington National Forest," *Trans.* 4th N. Am. Wildl. Conf., 570–78.

Martin, J. S.

1958. "The Wild Turkey Comes Back," *Reader's Digest,* 73:148–50.

Martin, L. M., and T. Z. Atkeson.

1954. *Swimming by Wild Turkey Poults. Wilson Bull.,* 66:271.

Martin, P. S.

1929. "The 1928 Archaeological Expedition of the State Historical Society of Colorado," *Colo. Mag.,* 6:1–35.

———.

1930. "The 1929 Archaeological Expedition of the State Historical Society of Colorado," *Colo. Mag.,* 7:1–40.

———.

1943. *The SU Site: Excavations at a Mogollon Village in Western New Mexico, Second Season, 1941.* Field Mus. Anth. Ser. 32(2).

Martin, P. S. *et al.*

1936. *Lowry Ruin in Southwestern Colorado.* Field Mus. Anth. Ser., 23(1).

——— *et al.*

1940. *The SU Site: Excavations at a Mogollon Village Western New Mexico, 1939.* Field Mus. Anth. Ser., 32(1).

——— *et al.*

1949. *Cochise and Mogollon Sites, Pine Lawn Valley, Western New Mexico.* Fieldiana: Anth., 38(1).

571

————.

1952. *Mogollon Cultural Continuity and Change: . . . Tularosa and Cordova Caves.* Fieldiana: Anth., 40.

———— *et al.*

1954. *Caves of the Reserve Area.* Fieldiana: Anth., 42.

————, G. I. Quimby, and D. Collier.

1947. *Indians before Columbus.* Chicago.

————, and J. Rinaldo.

1947. *The SU Site: Excavations at a Mogollon Village, Western New Mexico, Third Season, 1946.* Field Mus. Anth. Ser., 32(3):275–382.

————, and J. Rinaldo.

1950. *Turkey Foot Ridge Site, a Mogollon Village, Pine Lawn Valley, Western New Mexico.* Field Mus. Anth. Ser., 38(2): 237–396.

————, and J. Rinaldo.

1950.1. *Sites of the Reserve Phase, Pine Lawn Valley, Western New Mexico.* Fieldiana: Anth., 38(3): 403–577.

Martin, R. E.

1935. "Wild Turkey Paradise," *Pop. Sci.*, 126:22–23, 109–10.

Mártir de Anglería, Pedro.

1944. Decadas del Nuevo Mondo. Buenos Aires.

Martire d'Anghiera, Pietro.

1587. *De orbe novo.* Paris.

Mason, C.

1958. "The Return of a Native: The Wild Turkey Digs In To Stay," *N.Y. Consv.*, 13(2):32–33. Map.

Mason, F. N.

1937. *John Norton & Sons: Merchants of London and Virginia.* Richmond.

Massachusetts Bay Company.

1857. "Records," *Trans. Am. Antiq. Soc.*, 3.

Mather, Cotton.

1717. "An Extract of Several Letters from Cotton Mather, D.D.," *Phil. Trans.*, London, 29:64.

————.

1856. "An Horrid Snow." In J. W. Barber, *The History and Antiquities of New England.* 3d ed. Hartford.

Matheson, R., E. L. Brunett, and A. L. Brody.

1931. "The Transmission of Fowlpox by Mosquitoes: Preliminary Report," *Poultry Sci.*, 10:211–23.

Mathisen, John and Ann.

1960. "History and Status of Introduced Game Birds in Nebraska," *Nebr. Bird Rev.*, 28(2): 19–22.

Maulde, R. de.

1879. "*De l'origine des dindons,*" *Bibliot. l'ecole des chartes* (Paris), 40:332–34.

Maxfield, B. G., W. M. Reid, and F. A. Hayes.

1963. "Gastrointestinal Helminths from Turkeys in Southeastern United States," *Jour. Wildl. Manag.*, 27:261–71.

Maximilian, Prince of Wied.

1858. "*Verzeichniss der Vögel, welche auf einer Reise in Nord-America beobachtet wurden,*" *Jour. für Ornith.*, 6:417–44.

————.

1906. *Travels in the Interior of North America, 1832–1834.* Vols. I & III. Cleveland.

May, Col. J.
1873. *Journal and Letters of Col. John May, of Boston, Relative to Two Journeys to the Ohio Country in 1788 and '89.* Cincinnati.

———.
1921. "Journal . . . Relative to a Journey to the Ohio Country, 1789," *Pa. Mag. Hist. Biog.,* 45:101–79.

Maynard, C. J.
1881. *The Birds of Eastern North America.* Newtonville.

———.
1890. *Eggs of North American Birds.* Boston.

Mayr, E.
1946. "History of North American Bird Fauna," *Wilson Bull.,* 58:3–41.

———, and D. Amadon.
1951. "A Classification of Recent Birds." Am. Mus. Nat. Hist. *Novit. No. 1496,* 1–42.

McAfee, R. B.
1927. "The Life and Times of Robert B. McAfee and his Family Connections," Ky. State Hist. Soc. *Reg. 25,* 5–37.

McAtee, W. L.
1947. "Vieillot's Names for the Wild Turkey," *Auk,* 64:303.

———.
1947.1. "Wild Turkey Anting," *Auk,* 64:130.

———.
1954. "Carolina Bird Names," *Chat,* 18:87–94.

McCabe, R. A., and H. F. Deutsch.
1952. "The Relationships of Certain Birds as Indicated by Their Egg White Proteins," *Auk,* 69:1–18.

———, and A. S. Hawkins.
1946. "The Hungarian Partridge in Wisconsin," *Am. Midl. Nat.,* 36:1–75.

McClanahan, R. C.
1940. *Original and Present Breeding Range of Certain Game Birds in the United States,* Biol. Surv. Wildl. *Leafl. BS–158.*

McClung, J. A.
1832. *Sketches of Western Adventure.* Philadelphia.

McConnell, H. H.
1889. *Five Years a Cavalryman.* Jacksboro.

McCormick, F. L.
1956. "Council Highlights," *N. J. Outdoors,* 7(5):29.

———.
1960. "Council Highlights," *N.J. Outdoors,* 10(7):26; (8):28; (10):25.

McDougal, E.
1927. "Moisture belts of North America," *Geograph. Rev.,* 17:322–23.

McDowell, K.
1948. "Turkey Population Study—Laramie Peak," *P-R Quart.,* 8(3):358.

McDowell, R. D.
1954. "Productivity of the Wild Turkey in Virginia," Ph.D. Thesis, Va. Polyt. Inst., Blacksburg.

———.
1956. Productivity of the Wild Turkey in Virginia. Va. Comm. Game and Inland Fisheries, *Tech. Bull. I.*

McGraw, T. F.
1904. Turkeys: Standard Varieties and Management. U. S. Dept. Agr., *Farm. Bull. 200.*

McGregor, J. C.
  1941. *Southwestern Archaeology.*
  New York.

———.
  1941.1. *Winona and Ridge Ruin.*
  Mus. North. Ariz. *Bull. 18.*

McIlhenny, E. A.
  1914. *The Wild Turkey and Its
  Hunting.* Garden City.

———.
  1918. In E. A. Quarles, *Breeding
  the Wild Turkey. Bull. Am.
  Game Protect. Ass.,* 7(3):16–18.

McKenney, T. L.
  1846. *Memoirs Official and Personal.* Vol. I. New York.

McLaurin, E.
  1957. "You Gotta Out-smart 'Em,"
  Florida Wildl., 11(7):20–23, 35.

McNeale, D. M.
  1925. "Getting a Turkey Under
  Difficulties," *Forest and Stream,*
  95:558, 563.

McNight, W. J.
  1917. *Jefferson County, Pennsylvania.* Vol. I. Chicago.

McNitt, Frank.
  1957. *Richard Wetherill, Anasazi.*
  Albuquerque.

Meacham, J. L.
  1926. "The Second Spanish Expedition to New Mexico, *N.M.
  Hist. Rev.,* 1:265–91.

Meanley, B.
  1956. *Foods of the Wild Turkey in
  the White River Bottomlands of
  Southeastern Arkansas. Wilson
  Bull.,* 68:305–11.

Meares, John.
  1790. *Voyages Made in the Years
  1788 and 1789, from China to
  the Northwest Coast of America.*
  Topographia Press. London.

Mearns, E. A.
  1890. "Observations on the Avifauna of Portions of Arizona,"
  Auk, 7:45–55.

———.
  1896. "Ornithological Vocabulary
  of the Moki Indians," *Am.
  Anth.,* (1)9:391–403.

———.
  1907. "Mammals of the Mexican
  boundary of the United States,"
  U. S. Nat. Mus. *Bull. 56.*

Meckel, A.
  1815. *"Über die Federbildung,"*
  Arch. Physiol. Halle, 12:37–96.

Meijere, J. C. H. de.
  1895. *"Über die Federn der Vögel,
  insbesondere über ihre Anord-
  nung,"* Morph. Jahrb, 23:562–
  91.

"Meleagris."
  1889. "Our Turkey Hunt," *Forest
  and Stream,* 33:287.

Membré, Z.
  1852. "Narrative of La Salle's
  Voyage Down the Mississippi
  (1682)." In B. F. French, *Hist.
  Colls. La.,* 4:165–84.

Mercer, H. C.
  1896. *The Hill-caves of Yucatán.*
  Philadelphia.

———.
  1899. "The Bone Cave at Port
  Kennedy, Pennsylvania, and Its
  Partial Excavation in 1894, 1895,
  and 1896," *Jour. Acad. Nat.
  Sci.,* Philadelphia, (2)11:269–86.

Meredith, W. J.
  1938. "The Old Plum Grove
  Colony," *Kansas Hist. Quart.,*
  7:339–75.

Merriam, C. H.
  1890. "Results of a Biological Survey of San Francisco Mountain

Region and Desert of the Little
Colorado, Arizona," *N. Am.
Fauna,* 3.

Mershon, W. B.
1923. *Recollections of My Fifty
Years Hunting and Fishing.*
Boston.

Messiter, C. A.
1890. *Sport and Adventure among
the North-American Indians.*
London.

Mestier.
1877. "On Cash[e] River," *Chicago Field,* 7:129.

Meulen, D. Van der.
1957. *The Wells of Ibn Sa'ud.* New
York.

Michaux, F. A.
1805. *Travels to the Westward of
the Allegany Mountains . . .*
London.

Michel, F. L.
1916. "Report of the Journey of
Francis Louis Michel from
Berne, Switzerland, October 2,
1701–December 1, 1702," W. J.
Hinke, ed. *Va. Mag. Hist. and
Biog.,* 24:1–43.

Michigan Historical Publishing Assn.
n.d. *The Past and Present of
Eaton County, Michigan.* Lansing.

Milby, T. T., and R. Penquite.
1940. "Feeding Grasshoppers to
Turkeys," *Poultry Sci.,* 19:332–
36.

Milford, L. E.
1961. "Music Lovers," *Pa. Game
News,* 32(4):31.

Miller, A. H.
1932. "Bird Remains from Indian
Dwellings in Arizona," *Condor,*
34:138–39.

———.
1955. "The Avifauna of the Sierra
del Carmen of Coahuila, Mexico," *Condor,* 57:154–78.

———, and R. I. Bowman.
1956. "Fossil Birds of the Late
Pliocene of Cita Canyon, Texas,"
Wilson Bull. 68:38–46.

Miller, L. H.
1909. "*Pavo californicus,* a Fossil
Peacock from the Quaternary
Asphalt Beds of Rancho La
Brea," Univ. Cal., *Bull. Dept.
Geol.* 5(19), 285–89.

———.
1916. "A Review of the Species
Pavo californicus," Univ. Cal.,
Bull. Dept. Geol. 9(9), 89–96.

———.
1940. "A New Pleistocene Turkey
from Mexico," *Condor,* 42:154–
56.

1942. "A New Fossil Bird Locality," *Condor,* 44:283–84.

———, and C. S. Johnstone.
1937. "A Pliocene Record of *Parapavo* from Texas," *Condor,*
39:229.

Mills and Company.
1883. *The History of Pike County,
Missouri.* Des Moines.

Milman, J. B.
1931. "The Opening of the Cherokee Outlet," *Chron. Okl.,* 9:268–
86.

Missouri Historical Co.
1881. *History of Ray County, Mo.*
St. Louis.

———.
1881.1. *History of Saline County,
Missouri.* St. Louis.

Mitchell, W. A.
1928. *Linn County, Kansas: A
History.* Kansas City.

Mitchell, W. I.
    1898. "The Summer Birds of San
    Miguel County, New Mexico,"
    Auk, 15:306–11.
Mittelberger, G.
    1898. *Journey to Pennsylvania . . .
    1750*. Philadelphia.
Moehring, P. H. G.
    1752. *Avium genera*. Auricae.
Molin, R.
    1858. *"Prospectus helminthum,
    quae in prodromo faunae helm-
    inthologicae Venetiae contin-
    entur,"* *Sitzungsb. ḳ. Aḳad.
    Wiss. Wien, Math. Naturw*. Cl.,
    30:127–58.
Molina, A. de.
    1944. *Vocabulario en Lengua Cas-
    tellana y Mexicana* (1571).
    Madrid.
Möller, P. von.
    1881. *Strödda utḳast rörande
    svensḳa jordbruḳets historia.*
    Stockholm.
Möllhausen, B.
    1858. *Diary of a Journey from the
    Mississippi to the Coasts of the
    Pacific.* Vols. I & II. London.
Mönnig, H. O.
    1950. *Veterinary Helminthology
    and Entomology*. 3d ed. London.
Montanus, A.
    1851. "Description of New Nether-
    land, 1671," *Doc. Hist. N.Y.*,
    4:75–83.
Montule, E.
    1821. *A Voyage to North America
    and the West Indies, in 1817.*
    London.
Moody, R. D.
    1951. "Evaluation of Wildlife
    Practices," *P-R Quart.*, 11(2):
    172.

———, and J. O. Collins.
    1954. "Evaluation of Wildlife
    Management Practices in Louis-
    iana," *P-R Quart.*, 14(4):387.
Mooney, J.
    1896. "The Ghost-Dance Religion
    and the Sioux Outbreak of
    1890," *14th Ann. Rept.* Bur.
    Ethn. for 1892–93, Part II.
Moore, J. C.
    1946. "Mammals from Welaka,
    Putnam County, Florida," *Jour.
    Mam.*, 27:49–59.
Moore, J. V.
    1950. "Trip to the West, 1826–
    1828," *Del. Hist.*, 4:69–104.
Moore, R. T.
    1938. "A New Race of Wild Tur-
    key," *Auk*, 55:112–15.
Moorehead, W. K.
    1906. *A Narrative of Explorations
    in New Mexico, Arizona, In-
    diana, etc.* Phillips Acad., Dept.
    Arch. *Bull. 3.*
Moran, T.
    1925. "The effect of low tempera-
    ture on hens' eggs," *Proc.* Roy.
    Soc. London, 98B:436–56.
Morehouse, N. F.
    1944. "Life Cycle of *Capillaria
    caudinflata*, a Nematode Para-
    site of the Common Fowl," *Iowa
    State Coll. Jour. Sci.*, 18:217–53.
Morgan, B. B., and P. A. Hawkins.
    1949. *Veterinary Helminthology.*
    Minneapolis.
Morgan, Lewis H.
    1959. *The Indian Journals, 1859–
    62*. L. A. White, ed. Ann Arbor.
Morris, Ann A.
    1933. *Digging in the Southwest.*
    New York.
Morris, E. H.
    1939. "Archaeological Studies in

the La Plata District, South-western Colorado and North-western New Mexico," Carnegie Inst. *Publ. 519:298.*

Morris, R. O.

1911. "Turkeys for Massachusetts," *Forest and Stream*, 77:904.

Morris, T.

1904. *Journal of Captain Thomas Morris of his Majesty's XVII Regiment of Infantry; Detroit, September 25, 1764. Thwaites' Early Western Travels*, Vol. I. Cleveland.

Morrison, C. F.

1888. "A List of Some Birds of La Plata County, Col., with Annotations," *Orn. and Oolog.*, 13:70, 107, 115, 139.

Morrison, M. V. B.

1868. *The Orphan's Experience: or, The Hunter and Trapper.* Des Moines.

Morss, N.

1931. *The Ancient Culture of the Fremont River in Utah.* Pap. Peabody Mus. Am. Arch. and Ethn. 12(3).

Morton, J. S.

1876. *A Commemorative Pamphlet ... Nebraska City, Otoe County, Nebraska.* Chicago.

Morton, T.

1838. *New English Canaan (1632). Force's Tracts*, II(V).

Mosby, H. S.

1940. [Multiple Beards]. *Va. Wildl.*, 3(5):7.

———.

1941. "Restoration of the Wild Turkey: Virginia," *P.R Quart.*, 1(1):90, 92–93.

———.

1949. "The Present Status and the Future Outlook of the Eastern and Florida Wild Turkeys," *Trans.* 14th N. Am. Wildl. Conf., 346–58.

———.

1956. "Measurement of the Productivity of the Wild Turkey in Virginia," *Quart. Prog. Rept.* Va. Coop. Wildl. Res. Unit., 3–5.

———, and D. E. Canter.

1956. "The Use of Avertin in Capturing Wild Turkeys and as an Oral-basal Anaesthetic for Other Wild Animals," *Southw. Vet.*, 9(2):132–36.

[Mosby, H. S., and C. O. Handley].

1942. *The Wild Turkey in Virginia.* Va. Comm. Game and Inland Fisheries.

———, and C. O. Handley.

1943. *The Wild Turkey in Virginia.* Richmond.

Moser, E.

1906. *Die Haut des Vogels.* In W. Ellenberger, *Handbuch der vergleichenden mikroskopischen Anatomie.* Vol. I, 192–232. Berlin.

Motolinía, T. de.

1914. *Historia de los Indios de la Nueva España escrita a mediados del siglo XVI.* Barcelona.

Mowbray, L. L.

1922. "Another Pheasant Hybrid," *Forest and Stream*, 92:303.

Mueller, H. A.

1915. *History of Madison County, Iowa.* Vol. I. Chicago.

Muhlenberg, H. A.

1849. *The Life of Major-General Peter Muhlenberg.* Philadelphia.

Mulloy, W.

1942. *The Hagen Site: A Prehistoric Village on the Lower Yel-*

lowstone. Univ. Montana *Publ. Soc. Sci. 1.*

Munro, G. C.
1960. *Birds of Hawaii.* Rev. ed. Rutland and Tokyo.

Murie, A.
1946. "The Merriam Turkey on the San Carlos Indian Reservation," *Jour. Wildl. Manag.*, 10: 329–33.

Murphy, John.
1960. "12 Gobblers Fall to Kentuckians in Controlled Hunt," *Happy Hunt. Ground*, 16(4):16.

Murphy, J. M.
1882. *American Game Bird Shooting.* New York.

Murray, C. A.
1841. *Travels in North America during the years 1834, 1835, and 1836.* 2d ed. Vol. II. London.

Murray, W. V.
1792. "Nanticoke Vocabulary," Am. Phil. Soc. Lib. Philadelphia. MS.

Myrick, H.
1897. *Turkeys and How To Grow Them.* New York.

Naggiar, M.
1958. "Air Drop Turkeys," *Fla. Wildl.*, 11(12):18–20.

National Historical Co.
1882. *The History of Nodaway County, Missouri.* St. Joseph.

———.
1883. *History of Howard and Chariton Counties, Missouri.* St. Louis.

———.
1884. *History of Randolph and Macon Counties, Missouri.* St. Louis.

1884.1. *History of Audrain County, Missouri.* St. Louis.

———.
1885. *History of Clay and Platte Counties, Missouri.* St. Louis.

Nauman, E. D.
1924. "Birds of Early Iowa," *Palimpsest*, 5:134–35.

Neave, Parker.
1958. "King of the Christmas Table," *Illus. London News*, 233:865.

Needham, C. E.
1936. "Vertebrate Remains from Cenozoic Rocks," *Science*, 84: 537.

Neely, W. D.
1961. "Turkey on a Stick," *Pa. Game News*, 32(3):29.

Nehrling, H.
1882. "List of Birds Observed at Houston, Harris Co., Texas, and in the Counties Montgomery, Galveston and Ford(t) Bend," *Bull.* Nutt. Orn. Club, 7:166–75.

Nelson, A. L., and A. C. Martin.
1953. "Gamebird Weights," *Jour. Wildl. Manag.*, 17:36–42.

Nelson, E. W.
1891–1904. *Mexican Field Notebooks.* Fish and Wildlife Service, Washington.

———.
1900. "Description of a New Subspecies of *Meleagris gallopavo* and Proposed Changes in the Nomenclature of Certain North American Birds," *Auk*, 17:120–23.

Nelson, O.
1953. *The Cowman's Southwest, being the Reminiscences of Oliver Nelson.* Glendale.

Nequatewa, E.
1946. "The Place of Corn and Feathers in Hopi Ceremonies,"

Mus. North. Ariz., *Plateau* 19:-
15–16.

Nesbitt, P. H.
1931. "The Ancient Mimbreños,"
Beloit College, Logan Mus. *Bull.*
4.

Neugebauer, L. A.
1845. *"Systema venosum avium."*
Verhandl. d. kaiserl. leop.-carol.
Akad. d. Naturforscher, 13(2):
519–697.

Neveu-Lemaire, M.
1912. *Parasitologie des animaux*
domestiques maladies parasit-
aires non bactériennes. Paris.

Newberne, J. W.
1955. "The Pathology of *Leucocy-*
tozoon Infection in Turkeys
with a Note on Its Tissue
Stages," *Am. Jour. Vet. Res.,*
16:593–97.

Newby, T. T.
1916. *Reminiscences.* Carthage.

Newman, C. C.
1945. "Turkey Restocking Efforts
in East Texas," *Jour. Wildl.*
Manag. 9:279–89. Map.

————.
1950. *The Florida Wild Turkey.*
Fla. Game and Fresh Water Fish
Comm. Tallahassee.

————, and E. Griffin.
1950. *Deer and Turkey Habitats*
and Populations of Florida. Fla.
Game and Fresh Water Fish
Comm., *Tech. Bull. 1.*

Newton, A.
1868. *"Phasianidae,"* Zool. *Record,*
5:101–102.

————.
1881. "Brissel-cock: Turkey,"
Notes and Queries, (6)3:22–23.

————, and H. Gadow.
1893–96. *A Dictionary of Birds.*
London.

Nice, M. M.
1954. "Problems of Incubation
Periods in North American
Birds," *Condor,* 56:173–97.

Nicholson, D. J.
1928. "Actions of Baby Florida
Wild Turkeys," *Florida Nat.,*
2(1):32.

"Nick."
1885. "Shooting Turkeys in Arkansas," *Am. Field,* 23:338.

Nitzsch, C. L.
1818. *"Die Familien und Gattun-*
gen der Thierinsekten (insecta
epizoica)," *Germar's Mag. Ent.*
Halle, 3:261–316.

————.
1867. *Pterylography.* London.

Nolen, O. W.
1947. *Galloping Down the Texas*
Trail. Odem.

Nordenskiöld, G.
1893. *The Cliff Dwellers of the*
Mesa Verde. Chicago.

North, M. O.
1939. *Breastbones of Turkeys in*
Relation to Roosting. Wyo. Agr.
Exp. Sta. *Bull. 232.*

Norwood, H.
1844. *A Voyage to Virginia*
(1649). Force's Tracts 3.

Nourse, J.
1925. "Journey to Kentucky in
1775," *Jour. Am. Hist.,* 19:121–
38.

Novak, C. A.
1960. *An Analysis of the 1958*
Hunter Report Card Return.
S.D. Dept. Game, Fish, and
Parks. P-R Project 74–R–1, Job
Outline No. T–6. 1–1.

Nowlin, W.
1882. "The Bark-covered House, or Pioneer Life in Michigan," Mich. Hist. *Colls.* 4:480–541.

Nuttall, T.
1821. *A Journal of Travels into the Arkansas Territory, during the Year 1819.* Philadelphia.

――――.
1832. *A Manual of the Ornithology of the United States and of Canada: The Land Birds.* Vol. I. Cambridge.

Nuttall, Z.
1926. "Official Reports on the Towns of Tequizistlan, Tepechpan . . .," *Peabody Mus. Papers, Am. Arch. Ethn.,* 11(2).

Ober, F. A.
1874. "Birds of Lake Okeechobee," *Forest and Stream,* 2:162–63.

Oberholser, H. C.
1938. *The Bird Life of Louisiana.* La. Dept. Consv., *Bull.* 28.

Obregón, Balthazar de.
1924. *Historia de los Descubrimientos Antiguos . . . 1584.* M. Cuevas, ed. Mexico.

O'Bryan, D.
1950. *Excavations in Mesa Verde National Park.* Medallion Pap., 39.

"Observer."
1873. "Wild Turkeys," *Forest and Stream,* 1:290.

"Occident."
1882. "Shooting in the Indian Territory," *Am. Field,* 17:226.

Ödmann, S.
1789. *"Om en Kalkontupp, som utlegat honsägg,"* K. *Vet. Acad. Nya Handlgr.,* 10:236–38.

Odolant-Desnos, Pierre J.
1787. *Memoires historiques sur la ville d'Alençon et sur ses seigneurs.* Vol. II. Alençon.

Ogilby, J.
1671. *America.* London.

Ogilvie-Grant, W. R.
1893. *Catalogue of the Birds in the British Museum: Game Birds.* Vol. XXII. London.

――――.
1902. "Remarks on the Species of American Gallinae Recently Described and Notes on Their Nomenclature," *Ibis,* 235–37.

Ogorodny, U. M.
1935. "Success in Hybridization of Fowls." *Ascania-Nova Bull. Agr. Sci.,* 1:25.

Oken, L.
1843. *Allegemeine Naturgeschichte für alle Stände. Abbildungen.* Stuttgart.

[O'Hanlon, J.]
1890. *Life and Scenery in Missouri.* Dublin.

"Old Man."
1889. "Turkey Shooting in Surry County, Virginia," *Forest and Stream,* 32:394.

"Old Scout."
1874. "Game and Sporting in Texas," *Forest and Stream,* 2:371.

"Old Subscriber."
1893. "Turkey Hunting in Middle Georgia," *Forest and Stream,* 40:362.

Olds, F. A.
1905. "North Carolina People Are Happy," *Forest and Stream,* 65:453.

――――.
1909. "Turkey–Guinea Cross," *Forest and Stream,* 73:171.

Oliver, William.
1924. *Eight Months in Illinois* (1843). Chicago.

Oliver, W., and D. Barnett.
1961. "Turkey Talk," Wash. State Game *Bull. 13(1)*:5.

Oliver, W. R. B.
1955. *New Zeaalnd Birds*. 2d ed. Wellington.

Olsen, M. W.
1960. Performance Record of a Parthenogenetic Turkey Male. *Science*, 132:1,661.

———.
1961. "Surprising Development: The Chicken–Turkey Hybrid," *Agr. Research*, 9(7):10.

———, and S. J. Marsden.
1953. "Embryonic Development in Turkey Eggs Laid 60–224 Days Following Removal of Males," *Proc. Soc. Exptl. Biol. Med.* 82:638–41.

———, and S. J. Marsden.
1954. "Development of Unfertilized Turkey Eggs," *Jour. Exp. Zool.*, 126:337–48.

———, and S. J. Marsden.
1954.1. "Natural Parthenogenesis in Turkey Eggs," *Science*, 120:545.

———, and S. J. Marsden.
1956. "Parthenogenesis in Eggs of Beltsville Small White Turkeys," *Poult. Sci.*, 35:674–82.

Olson, E. C.
1958. "Report of the Fauna of Pictograph Cave," App. A. Univ. Wyo. *Publ.* 22:224–25.

Onstot, T. G.
1902. *Pioneers of Menard and Mason Counties*. Forest City.

Oordt, G. J. van.
1931. "The Relation between the Gonads and the Secondary Sexual Characters in Vertebrates, Especially in Birds," *Ibis*, 1–11.

———.
1931.1. "*Die hormonalen Beziehungen zwischen Gonade und sekundären Geschlechtsmerkmalen, insbesondere der Sporenentwicklung beim Truthahn*," *Verhandl. deutsch. zool. Ges.*, 34:322–23.

———.
1933. "*Weitere Untersuchungen über den Einfluss der Geschlectshormone auf die sekundären Geschlechtsmerkmale des Truthuhns, Ovariektomie der Truthenne.*" *Arch. Ent.-mech. Org.*, 131:11–18.

———.
1936. "The Effect of Gonadectomy on the Secondary Sexual Characters of the Turkey," *Arch. port. sci. biol.*, 5:205–11.

———, and C. J. J. van der Maas.
1929. "*Kastrationsversuche am Truthahn*," *Arch. Ent.-mech. Org.*, 115:651–67.

Opler, M. E.
1941. *An Apache Life-way*. Chicago.

Ord, G.
1825. *Supplement to the American Ornithology of Alexander Wilson*. Philadelphia. IX: *cli*.

Osborn, H.
1896. *Insects Affecting Domestic Animals*. U. S. Dept. Agr., Div. Entom., n.s., *Bull. 5*.

Osborn, H. F.
1925. "Mammals and Birds of the California Tar Pools," *Nat. Hist.*, 25:527–43.

"Osceola."
1924. "A Talk on Turkeys," *Forest and Stream*, 94:691.

———.
1924.1. "Roosting Turkeys," *Forest and Stream*, 94:121.

———.
1927. "The Ways of the Wild Turkey," *Forest and Stream*, 97:16–17, 59–61.

Osgood, W. H.
1921. "The Turkey as a Subject for Experiment," *Am. Nat.*, 55:84–88.

Oswald, G.
1924. "*Beitrag zur Kenntnis des normalen Baues und der Sklerodermie der Hautanhänge beim Hahn und Truthahn*," *Diss. München. Abstr. Münchener Tierärtzl. Wochensch.*, 75:133–35.

Oustalet, E.
1899. "*Notes sur la longévité des oiseaux*," *Ornis*, 10:62.

Ovalle, Alson de.
1703. "An Historical Relation of the Kingdom of Chile." In *Churchill's Voyages*, Vol. III. London.

Oviedo y Valdés, G. Fernández de.
1851. *Historia General y Natural de las Indias* Vols. I & III. Madrid.

———.
1950. *Sumario de la Natural Historia de las Indias* (1526). Mexico.

Owen, R.
1837. "Dissection of the Head of the Turkey Buzzard and That of the Common Turkey," *Proc. Zool. Soc. London*, 5:34–35.

Packard, W.
1910. *Florida Trails*. Boston.

Padoa, E.
1931. "*La gonadectomia nei tacchini*," *Boll. soc. di biol. sper.*, 6:689–92.

———.
1933. "*Il determinismo dei caratteri sessuali secondari*," *Attualitá zoologiche*, 1:251–53.

Paige, L. R.
1877. *History of Cambridge, Massachusetts, 1630–1877*. Boston.

Pallas, P. S.
1812. *Travels through the Southern Provinces of the Russian Empire in the Years 1793 and 1794*. 2d ed. Vols. I & II. London.

Palmer, John.
1818. *Journal of Travels in the United States of North America . . . in the Year 1817*. London.

Palmer, W.
1909. "Instinctive Stillness in Birds," *Auk*, 26:25–27.

Pangalo, I.
1906. "On the Structure of the Comb in Fowls," *Ann. inst. agron. Moscow*, 12(1):15–19. In Russian.

Panzer, G. W. F.
1793. *Faunae insectorum germanicae initia*. Nürnberg.

Parker, A. C.
1923. *Seneca Myths and Folk Tales*. Buffalo Hist. Soc. *Publ.* 27.

Parker, J.
1915, 1916. "Extracts from the Diary of James Parker of Shirley, Mass.," *New Engl. Hist. Gen. Reg.*, 69:294–308; 70:210–20, 294–308.

Parker, J. E.
　1946. "Semen Production in Broad-Breasted Bronze Turkeys," *Poultry Sci.*, 25:65–68.

―――.
　1947. "The Influence of Season on Reproduction in Turkeys," *Poultry Sci.*, 26:118–21.

Parker, W. K.
　1866. "On the Osteology of Gallinaceous Birds and Tinamous," *Trans. Zool. Soc. London*, 5:149–241.

Parkinson, R.
　1805. *A Tour in America, in 1798, 1799, and 1800.* Vol. I. London.

Parkman, F.
　1916. *The Oregon Trail.* Boston.

Parsons, E. C.
　1936. *Taos Pueblo.* Gen. Ser. Anth. 2.

―――.
　1939. *Pueblo Indian Religion.* Vol. I. Chicago.

Paskel, T.
　1882. "Extract from a letter written in Pennsylvania by Thomas Paskel . . . dated Feb. 10, 1683, new style," *Pa. Mag. Hist. and Biog.*, 6:323–28.

Paso y Troncoso, Francisco del.
　1905. *Relaciónes Geográphicas de la Diócesis de Oaxaca. Pap. de Neuva España.* Madrid. (2)4.

―――.
　1905.1. *Relaciónes Geográphicas de la Diócesis de México. Pap. de Neuva España,* Madrid. (2)6.

Passantino, G.
　1938. "*Note anatomiche sul tacchino, Meleagris gallopavo domestica, Apparecchio locomotre,*" *Arch. Ital. Anat. Embr.*, 39:439–84.

Patterson, E. H. N.
　1942. "Diary." In L. R. Hafen, *Overland Routes to the Gold Fields.* Glendale.

Patterson, R. L.
　1952. *The Sage Grouse in Wyoming.* Denver.

Paul Wilhelm, Herzog von Württemberg.
　1828. *Reise in Nord-amerika während den Jahren 1822, 1823 und 1824.* Vol. II. Mergentheim.

Paynter, R. A., Jr.
　1955. *The Ornithogeography of the Yucatán Peninsula.* Peabody Mus. Nat. Hist., *Bull. 9.*

Pearson, T. G., C. S. Brimley, and H. H. Brimley.
　1919. *Birds of North Carolina.* Raleigh.

Peattie, D. C.
　1940. *Audubon's America.* Boston.

Pech, Ah Nakuk.
　1939. *Crónica de Chac-Kulub-Chen.* In A. Yáñez, *Crónicas de la Conquista de México.* Mexico.

Peck, G. D.
　1921. "Memories," *Oologist,* 38:114–17.

[Peck, John M.].
　1853. "Birds of the Mississippi Valley," *West. Jour. and Civilian,* 10:29–39.

Pelouze, J.
　1865. "*Sur l'analyse volumétrique du fer contenu dans le sang.,*" *Comp. rend. acad. sci.* Paris, 60:880–84.

Penicaut, Sieur.
　1869. "Annals of Louisiana, from 1698 to 1722." In B. F. French, *Hist. Colls. La. and Fla.*, n.s., 1:35–162.

Pennant, T.
1781. "An Account of the Turkey," *Trans*. Roy. Soc. London, 71:67–81.

Pepper, G. H.
1909. "The Exploration of a Burial-Room in Pueblo Bonito, New Mexico." In Putnam anniversary volume: anthropological essays. New York, 196–252.

———.
1920. *Pueblo Bonito*. Am. Mus. Nat. Hist. *Anth. Pap.* 27.

Percy, G.
1705. "An Account of the Plantation of the Southern Colony in Virginia. A.D. 1606." In John Harris, *Navigantium atque itinerantium bibliotheca*. Vol. I. London.

Perkins, S. E. III.
1930. "Notes on the Wild Turkey in Indiana," *Wilson Bull.*, 42:233–35.

Perron, Jacques Davy du.
1691. *Perroniana et thuana* (1667). Coloniae.

Perry, O. H.
1899. *Hunting Expeditions of Oliver Hazard Perry of Cleveland, Verbatim from his Diaries*. Cleveland.

Peters, H.
1958. "Is It Possible That You Are Being Stung?" *Fla. Wildl.*, 12(6):4, 42.

Peterson, O. A.
1926. "The Fossils of the Frankstown Cave, Blair County, Pennsylvania." *Ann.* Carnegie Mus., 16(6):249–97.

Peterson, W. J.
1943. "Come to the Turkey Valley," *Palimpsest*, 24:358–59.

Petrides, G. A.
1942. "Age Determination in American Gallinaceous Game Birds," *Trans*. 7th N. Am. Wildl. Conf., 308–28.

———.
1945. "First-winter Plumages in the Galliformes," *Auk*, 62:223–27.

Pettitt, R. H.
1928. *Report of the Section of Entomology*. In *Ann. Rept.* State Bd. Agr. Mich. 1927–28.

Phelps, C. F.
1942. "Restoration of the Wild Turkey: Virginia," *P-R Quart.*, 2(1):46.

———.
1950. "Restoration of the Wild Turkey," *P-R Quart.*, 10(1):96–97.

Philhower, C. A.
1931. "South Jersey Indians on the Bay, the Cape and the Coast," *Proc.* N.J. Hist. Soc. n.s., 16:1–21.

Phillips, J. C.
1928. *Wild Birds Introduced or Transplanted in North America*. U. S. Dept. Agr., *Techn. Bull.* 61.

Phillips, R. E. and C. S. Williams.
1944. "The Relationship of Specific Gravity and Shell Appearance to the Hatchability of Fertile Turkey Eggs," *Poultry Sci.*, 23:110–13.

"Pious Jeems."
1881. "Tilley's River," *Am. Field*, 16:97.

Pirnie, M. D.
1932. "Game Bird Research at the W. K. Kellogg Bird Sanctuary,"

Trans. 19th Am. Game Conf., 362–68.

———. 1935. "Wild Turkey Standards," *Trans.* 21st Am. Game Conf. 260–62.

"Piseco."
1891. "Can Turkeys Count?" *Forest and Stream*, 36:347.

Platt, F. L.
1925. *All Breeds of Poultry.* Chicago.

Plinii Secundi, C.
1826. *Historia Naturalis libri XXXVII*, 4:1679–2250. Londini.

Plis, S.
1960. "How Are Our Turkeys Doing?" Wis. Consv. Dept. MS.
———, and G. Hartman.
1958. "Are the Turkeys Taking?" Wis. Consv. *Bull. 23(2)*:11–14.

Podoll, E.
1955. *The 1954 Merriam's Wild Turkey Hunting Season.* S.D. Dept. Game, Fish and Parks. (Mimeo.).

Polk, W. L.
1890. "Wild Turkeys in the Overflow," *Forest and Stream*, 35:432.

Poll, H.
1920. *"Mischlingsstudien. VIII. Pfaumischlinge,"* Arch. mikr. anat., 94:365–458.

Pollack, B., and L. Cowardin.
1961. "Wild Turkeys in Massachusetts?" *Mass. Wildlife*, 12 (3):15–20.

Pollard, H. B. C., and P. Barclay-Smith.
1945. *British and American Game Birds.* London.

Pollock, H. E. D., and C. E. Ray.
1957. "Notes on vertebrate animal remains from Mayapan," Carnegie Inst., Washington, D.C., Dept. Arch. *Current Repts.*, XLI:636–56.

Polonio, A. F.
1860. *"Novae helminthum species,"* Lotos, Prague, 10:21–23.

Ponce, Alonso.
1932. *Fray Alonso Ponce in Yucatán, 1588.* E. Noyes, ed. Tulane Univ., Dept. Mid. Am. Res. IV:297–372.

Pontoppidan, E. L.
1755. *The Natural History of Norway.* Vol. II. London.

Poole, D. A.
1961. "Turkeys in Massachusetts," Wildl. Manag. Inst., *Outd. News Bull. 15(22)*, 5.

Poole, E. L.
1938. "Weights and Wing Areas in North American Birds," *Auk*, 55:511–17.

Pooler, F. C. W.
1922. "Bears on the Carson," U. S. Forest Service *Daily Bull.*, Southw. District. June 27.

———.
1922.1. "Wild Turkeys in the Huachuca Mountains," Forest Service *Daily Bull.*, Southw. District. Jan. 18.

Pope, J.
1888. *A Tour through the Southern and Western Territories of the United States* (1792). New York.

Portlock, Capt. N.
1789. *A Voyage Round the World . . . to the North-west Coast of America: Performed in 1785 . . . 1788.* London.

Portmann, A.
1938. *"Beiträge zur Kenntnis der*

postembryonalen Entwicklung der Vögel," Rev. Suisse Zool., 45:273–348.

Powell, J. A.
1961. "Facts about Florida Wild Turkey," *Fla. Wildl.,* 15(6):12–17.

——, and L. F. Gainey.
1959. *The Aerial Drop Method of Releasing Wild Trapped Turkeys for Restocking Purposes.* Nat. Wild Turkey Symposium. Memphis. (Mimeo.).

Power, J. C.
1876. *History of the Early Settlers of Sangamon County, Illinois.* Springfield.

Pratt, C. J.
1882. "Wild Turkey Shooting in Texas," *Am. Field,* 17:161.

Prescott, W. H.
1843. *History of the Conquest of Mexico.* Vols. I, II, & III. Chicago.

Preston, J. R.
1959. *Turkey Restoration Efforts in the Ozark Region of Arkansas.* Nat. Wild Turkey Symposium. Memphis.

Price, E.
1866. "The Origin and Interpretation of the Names of the Rivers and Streams of Clayton County (Iowa)," *Ann. Iowa,* 4:710–11.

Price, E. W.
1931. "Trematode of Genus *Amphimerus* in Liver of Domestic Turkey, *Jour. Parasit.,* 18:51.

Priest, W.
1802. *Travels in the United States of America: Commencing in the Year 1793 and Ending in 1797.* London.

Progulske, D. R.
1955. "Game Animals Utilized as Food by the Bobcat in the Southern Appalachians," *Jour. Wildl. Manag.,* 19:249–53.

Przibram, H.
1910. "*Experimental-Zoologie, Artbastarde der Vögel (Aves).*" Leipzig. 3(IVh):84.

Pugh, E. A.
1954. "The Status of Birds in the Mount Elden Area," *Mus. North. Arizona Plateau,* 26:117–23.

Purcell, E. R.
1936. *Pioneer Stories of Custer County, Nebraska.* Broken Bow.

Purvis, M.
1918. "How the Turkey Was Named," *Breeder's Gaz.,* 73:1034.

Putnam, A. W.
1859. *History of Middle Tennessee.* Nashville.

Pycraft, W. P.
1895. "On the Pterylography of the Hoatzin," *Ibis,* 345–73.

Quarles, E. A.
1918. "The Wild Turkey at Woodmont," *Bull. Am. Game Protect. Ass.,* 7(3):13–15.

Quinn, J. P., W. H. Burrows, and T. C. Byerly.
1937. "Turkey–Chicken Hybrids," *Jour. Heredity,* 28:169–73.

R., C. C.
1895. "Wild Turkey Vitality," *Forest and Stream,* 45:470.

R., G. B.
1887. "Still Hunting the Wild Turkey," *Am. Field,* 27:75.

R., J. E.
1881. "An Arkansas Turkey

Hunt," *Forest and Stream*, 17: 47–48.

R., W.
1901. "A Christmas Turkey," *Forest and Stream*, 56:7–8.

R., W. H.
1878. "Birds Towering," *Forest and Stream*, 10:235.

Rabelais, F.
1552. *Le quart livre des faicts et dicts heroiques du bon Pantagruel*. Paris.

Räber, H.
1948. "*Analyse des Balzverhaltes eines domestizierten Truthahnes (Meleagris)*." *Behaviour*, 1:237–66.

Railliet, A.
1921. "*Les cestodes des oiseaux domestiques: détermination pratique*," *Rec. med. vét.*, 97:185–205.
———, and A. Lucet.
1899. "*Sur l'identite du* Davainea oligophora *Magalhães, 1898, et du* Taenia cantaniana *Polonio, 1860*," *Arch. Parasit.*, Paris, 2:144–46.

Rale, S.
1900. "Letter . . . 12th of October, 1723," *Jesuit Relations*, Vol. LXVII, 133–229. Cleveland.

Ramsay, A. O.
1951. "Familial Recognition in Domestic Birds," *Auk*, 68:1–16.

Ramsey, R. R.
1958. "Turkeys for Tomorrow," *Texas Game and Fish*, 16(11): 16–17, 28.
———, and W. P. Taylor.
1942. "A Winter Feeding Program for the Wild Turkey in Texas." Agr. Exp. Sta., A. and

M. Coll. Texas, *Prog. Rept. 808*. (Mimeo.).

Ramusio, G. B.
1606. *Delle Navigazioni e Viaggi*. Vol. III. Venecia.

Ranck, G. W.
1901. *Boonesborough*. Filson Club *Publ. 16*.

Rand, S. T.
1888. *Dictionary of the Language of the Micmac Indians*. Halifax.

Randall, W.
1929. "On Raising Wild Turkeys," *Game Breeder*, 33:7–8.
———.
1930. "Wild Turkeys," *Game Breeder*, 34:105–106.
———.
1931. "Our Wild Turkey Problem," *Game Breeder*, 35:72–73, 91–93.
———.
1931.1. "More about the Wild Turkey," *Game Breeder*, 35:177–87.
———.
1932. "The Wild Turkey—Today and Tomorrow," *Game Breeder*, 36:35, 50–51, 71, 90–91.
———.
1933. "Wild Turkeys and Northern Winters," *Game Breeder*, 37:60, 67, 71.
———.
1933.1. "Building the Wild Turkey Flock," *Game Breeder*, 37:172, 181, 185.
———.
1934. "Hybrids," *Game Breeder and Sportsm.*, 38(1):4.
———.
1934.1. "Breeding and Stocking Wild Turkeys," *Game Breeder and Sportsm.*, 38:103, 117, 132, 148–49, 151.

Ransom, B. H.
   1900. "A New Avian Cestode—
      Metroliasthes lucida," *Trans.*
      Am. Micr. Soc., 21:213–26.

———.
   1904. *A New Nematode* (Gongyl-
      onema ingluvicola) *Parasitic in*
      the Crop of Chickens. U. S.
      Dept. Agr., Bur. An. Ind. *Circ.*
      64.

———.
   1909. The Taenioid Cestodes of
      North American Birds. U. S.
      Nat. Mus. *Bull.* 69.

Rasieres, I. de.
   1849. "New Netherland in 1627,"
      N.Y. Hist. Soc. *Colls.* n.s. 2(2):
      339–54.

Rasles, S.
   1833. "A Dictionary of the Abnaki
      Language in North America..."
      Mem. Am. Acad. Sci. n.s.,
      1:375–574.

Ratcliffe, H. L.
   1933. "Incidence and Nature of
      Tumors in Captive Wild Mam-
      mals and Birds," *Jour. Cancer*
      Res. 17:116–35.

Ray, J. (Joannis Raii).
   1713. *Synopsis methodica avium &*
      piscium. Avium. London.

Read, W. A.
   1937. *Indian Place-Names in Ala-*
      bama. Baton Rouge.

Réaumur, R. A. F. de.
   1756. "*Sur la digestion des*
      oiseaux," *Mem. acad. sci. Paris,*
      for 1752, p. 266–307.

Rebrassier, R. E., and E. D. Martin.
   1932. "*Syringophilus bipectinatus,*
      a Quill Mite of Poultry," *Science,*
      76:128.

Redfield, R.
   1941. *The Folk Culture of Yuca-*
      tan. Chicago.
———, and A. Villa R.
   1934. *Chan-Kom, a Maya Village.*
      Carnegie Inst., Washington.

Reed, C. A.
   1904. *North American Birds' Eggs.*
      New York.

Reed, J.
   1963. "A Report on Those Río
      Grande Turkeys," *Wildl. Views,*
      10(4):16–17.

Rees, G.
   1952. "The structure of the adult
      and larval stages of *Plagiorchis*
      (*Multiglandularis*) *megalorchis,*
      n. nom. from the turkey and an
      experimental demonstration of
      the life history," *Parasit.,* 42:92–
      113.

Reeves, R. H.
   1950. *Turkey Winter Range In-*
      vestigation. Ariz. Game and
      Fish Comm., *Compl. Rept.,*
      Proj. 49–R–1, Job 1.

———.
   1950.1. *Turkey Summer Range*
      Investigation. Ariz. Game and
      Fish Comm., *Compl. Rept.,*
      49R, Job 2.

———.
   1950.2. *Turkey Population Trend*
      and Age and Sex Ratio Survey
      Development. Ariz. Game and
      Fish Comm., *Compl. Rept.,*
      Proj. 49–R, Job 3.
———.
   1950.3. "Merriam's Turkey Man-
      agement Research," *P-R Quart.,*
      10(4):402.
———.
   1951. *Turkey Winter Range In-*

vestigation. Ariz. Game and Fish Comm., *Compl. Rept.,* Proj. 49–R–2, Job 1.

1951.1. *Turkey Summer Range Investigation.* Ariz. Game and Fish Comm., *Compl. Rept.,* Proj. 49–R–2. Job 2.

————. 1951.2. *Turkey Population Trend and Age and Sex Ratio Survey Development.* Ariz. Game and Fish Comm., *Compl. Rept.,* Proj. 49–R–2, Job 3.

————. 1951.3. "Merriam's Turkey Management Research," *P-R Quart.,* 11(1):7.

————. 1951.4. "Merriam's Turkey Management Research," *P-R Quart.,* 11(2):135.

————. 1952. "Merriam's Turkey Management Research," *P-R Quart.,* 12(1):7.

————. 1952.1. "Merriam's Turkey Management Research," *P-R Quart.,* 12(2):111.

————. 1952.2. "Merriam's Turkey Management Research," *P-R Quart.,* 12(3):195.

————. 1954. "Merriam's Turkey Management Research," *P-R Quart.,* 14(1):7–9.

Reichenow, A. 1913. *Die Vögel; Handbuch der systematischen Ornithologie.* Vol. I. Stuttgart.

Reichert, E. T., and A. P. Brown. 1909. *The Differentiation and Specificity of Corresponding Proteins . . .: the Crystallography of Hemoglobins.* Carnegie Inst. Washington, *Publ. 116.*

Reid, D. H. 1947. "The Texas Turkey Industry," *Tex. Geogr. Mag.,* 11(2): 12–16.

Reid, R. 1955. *1955 North Dakota Wild Turkey Story.* Mo. Slope Chapter Izaak Walton League of America. Bismarck.

Reid, V. H. and P. D. Goodrum. 1957. *Factors Influencing the Yield and Wildlife Use of Acorns.* 6th Ann. La. State Univ. Forest. Symposium. Baton Rouge. April 4.

Reid, W. M., and D. Nugara. 1961. "Description and Life Cycle of *Raillietina georgiensis* n. sp., a Tapeworm from Wild and Domestic Turkeys," *Jour. Parasit.,* 47:885–89.

Retterer, E., and A. Lelièvre. 1911. "Phénomènes cytologiques des tendons en voie d'ossification," *Comp. rend. soc. biol.,* Paris, 71:596–99.

Révoil, B. 1875. *The Hunter and Trapper in North America.* London.

Reynolds, T. 1957. "Turkey Talk," *Utah Fish and Game Mag.,* 13(11):5.

Reynolds, T. A., Jr. 1959. "Hunting Turkeys with Cannons," *Utah Fish and Game,* 15(2):12–15.

Rhian, M., W. O. Wilson, and A. L. Moxon. 1944. "Composition of Blood of Normal Turkeys," *Poult. Sci.,* 23:224–29.

Ribaut, J.
1927. *The Whole & True Discouverye of Terra Florida*. Reprint, London ed. 1563. Deland.

Rickey, D. J., and R. E. Ware.
1955. "Schizonts of *Leucocytozoon smithi* in Artificially Infected Turkeys," *Cornell Vet.*, 45:642–43.

Ridgway, R., and H. Friedmann.
1946. *The Birds of North and Middle America*. U. S. Nat. Mus. *Bull. 50(X)*.

Ridout, T.
1890. "Narrative of the Captivity among the Shawanese Indians." In M. Edgar, *Ten Years of Upper Canada*. Toronto.

Riggs, S. R.
1852. *Grammar and Dictionary of the Dakota Language*. Smith. Contr. Knowl. 4.

———.
1890. *A Dakota-English Dictionary*. U. S. Geogr. and Geol. Surv. Contr. N. Am. Ethn. 7.

Riley, W., and H. Kernkamp.
1924. "Flukes of the Genus *Collyriclum* as Parasites of Turkeys and Chickens," *Jour. Am. Vet. Med. Ass.*, 64:1–9.

"Rio Diablo."
1892. "Texas Wild Turkeys," *Forest and Stream*, 38:610.

———.
1892.1. "A Wild Turkey's Fate," *Forest and Stream*, 38:611.

Riter, W. E.
1941. "Predator Control and Wildlife Management," *Trans. 6th N. Am. Wildl. Conf.*, 295–96.

Rivers, D. G.
1940. "Food Habits of the Wild Turkey in Virginia." M.S.

Thesis, Va. Polyt. Inst. Blacksburg.

Roberts, F. H. H., Jr.
1930. *Early Pueblo Ruins in the Piedra District, Southwestern Colorado*. Bur. Am. Eth. *Bull. 96*.

———.
1932. *The Village of the Great Kivas on the Zuñi Reservation, New Mexico*. Bur. Am. Ethn. *Bull. 111*.

———.
1939. *Archeological Remains in the Whitewater District, Eastern Arizona*. I. Bur. Am. Ethn. *Bull. 121* (I), 1940. *126*(II).

Roberts, H. A.
1954. "Wild Turkey Study," *P-R Quart.*, 14(4):469–70.

———.
1957. "Factors Affecting the Wild Turkey Population in Pennsylvania," *Pa. Game News*, 28(6): 15–24.

Roberts, T. S.
1932. *The Birds of Minnesota*. Vol. I. Minneapolis.

Roberts, W. H.
1901. "The Wild Turkey, Its Habitat and Habits," *Am. Field*, 55:41–42.

Robertson, C.
1886. *History of Morgan County, Ohio*. Chicago.

Robertson, W. R. B., B. B. Bohren, and D. C. Warren.
1943. "The Inheritance of Plumage Color in the Turkey," *Jour. Hered.*, 34:246–56.

Robeson, S.
1955–56. "More about Wild Turkeys," *N.Y. Consv.*, 10(3):12–13.

Robinson, H.
1921. "The Haunts of the Wild Turkey," *Forest and Stream*, 91:101–104, 137–38.

Robinson, J. H.
[1924]. *Popular Breeds of Domestic Poultry, American and Foreign*. Dayton.

Robinson, K. W., and D. H. K. Lee.
1946. *Animal Behavior and Heat Regulation in Hot Atmospheres*. Univ. Queensland *Pap*., Dept. Phys. 1(9).

Robinson, T.
1958. "An Erroneous Record of the Carolina Parakeet and Other Animals in Montana," *Auk*, 75:91–93.

Roe, F. M. A.
1909. *Army Letters from an Officer's Wife, 1871–1888*. New York.

Roemer, F.
1849. *Texas, mit besonderer Rücksicht auf deutsche Auswanderung*. Bonn.

Roger, E.
1870. "*Reproduction des dindons sauvages d'Amerique en liberté*," *Bull. soc. zool. acclim.*, (2)7: 264–66.

Rogers, J. E. T.
1882–87. *A History of Agriculture and Prices in England*. Vols. III, IV, V. Oxford.

Romans, B.
1776. *A Concise Natural History of East and West Florida*. New York.

Roosevelt, T.
1891. *Hunting Trips of a Ranchman*. New York.

Root, F. A., and W. E. Connelley.
1901. *The Overland Stage to California*. Topeka.

Rose, B. J.
1958. "A Turkey Season in Montana," *Mont. Wildlife*, Jan.:5–8.

Rosen, M. N., and E. D. Platt.
1949. "The Control of Avian Tuberculosis in a State Game Farm," *Cal. Fish and Game*, 35:323–27.

Ross, R., and J. Race.
1911. "Constants of Chicken and Turkey Fats," *Analyst*, 36:213.

Rousby, C.
1887. Letter, December 14, 1681. *Arch. Md.*, 5:307.

Ruble, Alphonse de.
1877. *Le mariage de Jeanne D'Albert*. Paris.

Ruecking, F. Jr.
1955. "The Social Organization of the Coahuiltecan Indians of Southern Texas and Northeastern Mexico," *Texas Jour. Sci.*, 7:357–88.

Ruha, N. M.
1958. "Jet Age Gobbler," *Pa. Game News*, 29(7):39.

Russell, Alexander.
1794. *The Natural History of Aleppo*. Vol. II. London.

Russell, J. L.
1947. *Behind These Ozark Hills*. New York.

Russell, M. B.
1951. *Lowndes Court House*. Montgomery.

Russo, J. P.
1959. *Kaibab Turkey Transplant*. Proc. 38th Ann. Conf. West. Assn. State Game and Fish Comm., Sun Valley, Idaho, June 23–25, 1958.

591

Rutledge, A. H.
1919. "That Twenty-five Pound Gobbler," *Outing*, 73:305–307, 342.

———. 1923. "Make Room for the Turkey," *Outlook*, 134:25–27.

———. 1923.1. "The Wild Turkey Stages a Comeback," *Independent*, 111:246–47.

———. 1924. *Days Off in Dixie*. New York; *cf.* Rutledge. 1941.1:104.

———. 1930. "Wildlife in a Drought," *Outdoor Life*, 66(5):12–13, 82.

———. 1935. "The Great King," *Va. Quart. Rev.*, 11:518–28.

———. 1936. "Wildwood Majesty," *Am. Forests*, 42:491–93, 532–33.

———. 1941. "Can the Wild Turkey Survive?" *Fauna* 3:93–95.

———. 1941.1. *Home by the River*. Indianapolis.

———. 1946. *Hunter's Choice*. New York.

———. 1959. "Their Baffling Maneuvers," *Florida Wildl.*, 13(7):16.

Rutledge, J. M.
1936. "The memoirs of . . . 1814–1899," *Jour. Ill. State Hist. Soc.*, 29:76–88.

Ruttenber, E. M.
1872. *History of the Indian Tribes of Hudson's River*. Albany.

Ruxton, G. F.
1848. *Adventures in Mexico and the Rocky Mountains*. New York.

Ryan, P.
1958. "Facts, Figures, and Forecasts on the Wild Turkey," *Miss. Game and Fish*, 21(8):5.

Ryle, M.
1957. "Studies on Possible Serological Blocks to Species Hybridization in Poultry," *Jour Exp. Biol.*, 34:365–77.

———, and M. Simonsen. 1956. "Attempts at Hybridization of Chickens and Turkeys Which Are Tolerant to Each Others' Antigens," *Nature*, 177:437–38.

Rymer, Thomas.
1743. *Foedera*. 3d ed. VIII(IV). Hagal Comitis.

Rzaczynski, G.
1721. *Historia naturalis curiosa regni Poloniae*. Sandomiriae.

S., G. W.
1880. [Turkeys at Fort Sill], *Forest and Stream*, 13:953.

S., J. G.
1882. "A Turkey Beard," *Forest and Stream*, 18:226.

S., J. V.
1874. [Stocking in Pennsylvania], *Forest and Stream*, 3:343.

S., O. O.
1894. "A Turkey Call that Calls," *Forest and Stream*, 43:511.

S., P. M.
1882. "A Texas Turkey Hunt," *Forest and Stream*, 19:106.

S., T. J.
1890. "A Well-Bearded Turkey," *Forest and Stream*, 34:269.

Sacc, Dr.
1863. "*Sur le dindon* (Meleagris gallopavo)," *Bull. soc. zool. acclim.*, 10:663–67.

Sadler, K. C.
  1953. "Wild Turkey Hatch and Subsequent Poult Loss," *P-R Quart.*, 13(2):159.
———.
  1954. "Turkey Brood Survey: Missouri," *P-R Quart.*, 14(1):45.
———.
  1954.1. "Methods of Anesthetizing Wild Turkeys," *P-R Quart.*, 14(4):417–18.
Sagard-Theodat, G.
  1632. *Dictionaire de la langve hvronne.* Paris.
Sage, R. B.
  1860. *Rocky Mountain Life.* Boston.
Sahagún, B. de.
  1938. *Historia General de la Cosas de Neuva España (c. 1570).* Vol. III. Mexico.
Saint Paul.
  1851. *Minnesota Pioneer*, January 2, December 25:2, 3.
Salazar, F. Cervantes de.
  1914–36. *Crónica de Neuva España.* Vol. I & II. Madrid.
Salgues, R.
  1934. "*La nature des matières inertes du gésier des granivores,*" *L'Ois. Rev. franc. d'ornith.*, 4:534.
Salm, A. J.
  1923. "*Sur quelque parasites du dindon dans les isles de la Sonde,*" *Bull. soc. path. exot.*, 16:594–98.
Sams, C. W.
  1916. *The Conquest of Virginia.* New York.
Sandel, A.
  1906. "Extracts from the Journal of Rev. Andreas Sandel," *Penn. Mag. Hist. Biog.*, 30:287–99.

Sanders, E.
  1939. "Wildlife Survey, Region No. 8. Texas Game, Fish and Oyster Comm.," *Activ. Rept.*, P-R Proj. 1–R. May 1, p. 7–8.
Sandoz, O. N., and J. W. Stovall.
  1936. "A New Species of Fossil Turkey-Peacock of Oklahoma," *Proc. Okla. Acad. Sci.*, 16:77.
Sandys, E., and T. S. Van Dyke.
  1904. *Upland Game Birds.* New York.
Santa Cruz, Alonso de.
  1920. *Crónica del emperador Carlos V.* Vol. I. Madrid.
Santleben, A.
  1910. *A Texas Pioneer.* New York; cf. M. L. Crimmins. 1931. "Rattlesnakes and Their Enemies in the Southwest," *Bull. Antiv. Inst. of Am.* 5(2):46; R. Phares. 1954. *Texas Tradition.* New York.
Sass, H. R.
  1929. *On the Wings of a Bird.* Garden City.
Savage, A., and J. M. Isa.
  1945. "An Outbreak of *Leucocytozoon* Disease in Turkeys," *Cornell Vet.*, 35:270–72.
Savage, W.
  1934. "Iowa Pioneer Diarist, and Painter of Birds," *Ann. Iowa*, (3)19:189–220.
Savary, P.
  1901. "Hawaiian wild turkeys," *Forest and Stream*, 56:84.
"Saxet."
  1884. "Wild Turkey Stories," *Forest and Stream*, 22:84–85.
Say, T.
  1824. "Vocabularies of Indian Languages," In W. H. Keating, *Narrative of an Expedition to*

593

*the Source of the St. Peter's River
. . . Vol. II.*

Scappi, Bartolomeo.
1570. *Opera. . . . Nel secundo si
tratta di diverse vivande di
carne, si di quadrupedí, come di
volatili.* Venice.

Schaeffer, J. C.
1774. *Elementa ornithologica iconi-
bus vivis coloribus expressis illustrata.* Ratisbonae.

———.
1779. *Elementa ornithologica.* Ratisbonae.

Schaff, Gen. Morris.
1905. *Etna and Kirkersville.* Boston.

Scharff, R. F., and E. T. Newton.
1906. "The Exploration of the
Caves of County Clare," *Trans.
Roy. Irish Acad.*, 33:57.

———, and R. J. Ussher.
1903. "The Explorations of the
Caves of Kesh, County Siglo,"
Trans. Roy. Irish Acad., 32:187.

Schaw, Janet.
1923. *Journal of a Lady of Quality
. . . 1774 to 1776.* E. W. and
C. M. Andrews, eds. New
Haven.

Schein, M. W., and E. B. Hale.
1957. "The Head as a Stimulus for
Orientation and Arousal of Sexual Behaviour of Male Turkeys,"
Bull. Ecol. Soc. Am. 38(3):74–
75.

Schemnitz, S. D.
1956. "Wild Turkey Food Habits
in Florida," *Jour. Wildl. Manag.*,
20:132–37.

Schenck, J. S., and W. S. Rann.
1887. *History of Warren County,
Pennsylvania.* Syracuse.

Schjelderup-Ebbe, T.
1924. "Instinctive Behaviour and
Reactions of Peacocks, Turkeys,
and Domestic Hens," *Scand. Sci.
Rev.*, 3(2):108–16.

———.
1931. "*Die Despotie im socialen
Leben der Vögel,*" *Forsch.
Völkerpsych. und Sociol.*, 10
(2):77–137.

———.
1932. "*Instinkte und Reaktionen
bei Pfauen und Truthühnern,*"
Kwart. Psychol., 3:205–207.

Schleidt, M.
1954. "*Untersuchungen des Kol-
lerns beim Truthahn (Meleagris
gallopavo),*" *Zeits. Thierpsych.*,
11:417–35.

Schleidt, W. M.
1961. "*Reaktionen von Truthühnern auf fliegende Raubvogel
und Versuche zur Analyse ihrer
AAM's,*" *Zeit. Tierpsych.*, 18:
534–60.

———, M. Schleidt, and M. Magg.
1960. "*Störung des Mutter-Kind-
Beziehung durch Gehörverlust,*"
Behaviour, 16:254–60.

Schmid, B.
1937. *Interviewing Animals.* Boston.

Schneider, A.
1931. *Über den Kopfanhang des
Truthuhns (Meleagris gallopavo
L.),*" *Jour. f. Ornith.*, 79:236–55.

Schoolcraft, H. R.
1819. *A View of the Lead Mines of
Missouri.* New York.

———.
1846. *Notes on the Iroquois.* New
York.

Schöpf, J. D.
1911. *Travels in the Confederation*

(*1783–1784*). Vol. I. Philadelphia.

Schorger, A. W.

1942. "The Wild Turkey in Early Wisconsin," *Wilson Bull. 54*, 173–82.

——. 1949. "Squirrels in Early Wisconsin," *Trans.* Wis. Acad. Sci., 39:95–247.

——. 1957. "The Beard of the Wild Turkey," *Auk*, 74:441–46.

——. 1958. "Extirpation of a Flock of Wild Turkeys in Adams County, Wisconsin," *Pass. Pigeon*, 20:170–71.

——. 1960. "The Crushing of *Carya* Nuts in the Gizzard of the Turkey," *Auk*, 77:337–40.

——. 1961. "An Ancient Pueblo Turkey," *Auk*, 78:138–44.

——. 1962. "Audubon's Original Notes on the Habits of the Wild Turkey Written for Charles Lucien Bonaparte," *Auk*, 79:444–52.

——. 1963. "The Domestic Turkey in Mexico and Central America in the Sixteenth Century," *Wis. Acad. Sci.*, 52:133–52.

Schroeder, A. H.

1955. *Archeology of Zion Park.* Univ. Utah Anth. *Pap.* 22.

Schultz, C.

1810. *Travels on an Inland Voyage* ... Vols. I & II. New York.

Schultz, C. B., and E. B. Howard.

1936. "The Fauna of Burnet Cave, Guadalupe Mountains, New Mexico," *Proc.* Acad. Nat. Sci. Phil. for 1935, 87:273–98.

Schultz, J. W.

1909. "In Arizona," *Forest and Stream*, 72:928–30.

Schultz, V.

1955. "Status of the Wild Turkey in Tennessee," *Migrant* 26(1): 1–8.

Schwank, W. G., *et al.*

1954. "Merriam's Turkey," *P-R Quart.*, 14(3):226.

Schwartz, C. W., and E. R. Schwartz.

1949. *A Reconnaissance of the Game Birds in Hawaii.* Hilo. Board Com. Agr. Forest.

Scott.

1883. [Turkeys in Iowa], *Am. Field*, 20:414.

Scott, H.

1877. *A Complete History of Fairfield County, Ohio.* Columbus.

Scott, H. M.

1933. "The Effect of Age and Holding Temperatures on Hatchability of Turkey and Chicken Eggs," *Poult. Sci.*, 12:49–54.

——. 1937. "Turkey Production in Kansas," Kan. Agr. Exp. Sta. *Bull.* 276.

——, and L. F. Payne.

1934. "The Effect of Gonadectomy on the Secondary Sexual Characters of the Bronze Turkey (*Meleagris gallopavo*)," *Jour. Exp. Zool.*, 69:123–31.

——, P. J. Serfontein, and D. H. Sieling.

1933. "Blood Analysis of Normal Bronze Turkeys," *Poult. Sci.*, 12:17–19.

595

Scott, J. E.
   1924. "What We Owe the Wild Turkey," *Am. Forests and Forest Life*, 30:661–62.
Scott, T. G., and G. O. Hendrickson.
   1936. *Upland Game Birds in Iowa*. Iowa State Coll., *Ext. Circ.* 228.
Scott, W. E. D.
   1886. "On the Avi-fauna of Pinal County, with Remarks on Some Birds of Pima and Gila Counties, Arizona," *Auk*, 3:383–89.

———.
   1890. "Description of a New Subspecies of Wild Turkey," *Auk*, 7:376–77.

———.
   1892. "Notes on the Birds of the Caloosahatchie Region of Florida," *Auk*, 9:209–18; Abstr. Proc. Linn. Soc. New York No. 5:6.
Scoville, S., Jr.
   1919. "The Pileated Woodpecker," *Cassinia No.* 23:14–22.

———.
   1920. "The Raven's Nest," *Atlantic Month.*, 126:32–37.
[Sears, G. W.]. "Nessmuk."
   1920. *Woodcraft*. 14th ed. New York.
Sedgwick, Mrs. W. T.
   1926. *Acoma, the Sky City*. Cambridge.
Seely, H.
   1887. "Coursing Wild Turkeys on the Colorado," *Outing*, 10:13–15.
Selden, P.
   1887. "History of Washington County," *Trans. and Repts.* Neb. State Hist. Soc., 2:274–92.
Seler, E.
   1909. "*Die Tierbilder der Mexi-*

kanischen und der Maya-Handschriften," *Zeit. Ethn.*, 41:817–26.
Self, J. T., and J. L. Bouchard.
   1950. "Parasites of the Wild Turkey, *Meleagris gallopavo intermedia* Sennett, from the Wichita Mountains Wildlife Refuge," *Jour. Parasit.*, 36:502–503.
Sennett, G. B.
   1878. "Notes on the Ornithology of the Lower Rio Grande of Texas . . . during the Season of 1877," U. S. Geol. and Geograph. Surv. *Bull. I(1)*:1–66.

———.
   1879. "Further Notes on the Ornithology of the Lower Río Grande of Texas from Observations Made During the Spring of 1878," U. S. Geol. and Geogr. Surv. *Bull. 5(3)*:371–440.

———.
   1892. "Description of a New Turkey," *Auk*, 9:167–69.
Serebrovsky, A. S.
   1929. "Observations on Interspecific Hybrids of the Fowl," *Jour. Genet.*, 21:327–40.

———.
   1935. "New Avian Hybrids," All-Union Lenin Acad. Agr. Sci. *Bull. 1(8)*:20. (In Russian).
Seton, E. T.
   1920. "Bobcats and Wild Turkeys," *Jour. Mam.*, 1:140.
Sewall, Samuel.
   1878–82. "Diary." Mass. Hist. Soc. *Colls.* (5)5:509p.; 6:462p.; 7:572p.
Sharp, D. L.
   1914. *Beyond the Pasture Bars*. New York.

Sharpe, E. L.
1889. "Game in Southern Texas," *Am. Field*, 31:550.

Sharpe, R. B.
1899. *A Hand-List of the Genera and Species of Birds.* Vol. I. London.

Shay, W. H.
1911. "Real Life," *Forest and Stream*, 76:454–55.

Sheldon, G.
1895. *A History of Deerfield, Massachusetts.* Vol. I. Deerfield.

Sheldon, H. H.
1919. "Hunting Merriam Wild Turkey," *Forest and Stream*, 89:91.

Shepard, E. M.
1883. "Impregnation in the Turkey," *Science*, 1:576.

Sherborn, C. D.
1902. "In re *Meleagris sylvestris* Vieillot," *Auk*, 19:419–20.

Sherman, A. R.
1913. "The Extermination of the Wild Turkey in Clayton County, Iowa," *Wilson Bull.*, 25:87–90.

Shillinger, J. E., and L. C. Morley.
1937. *Diseases of Upland Game Birds.* U. S. Dept. Agr., *Farmer's Bull. 1781.*

Shiner, Don.
1958. "Carve a Cocoanut Caller," *Fla. Wildl.*, 12(6):24–25.

———.
1963. "Let's Talk Turkey," *Pa. Game News*, 34(9):32–33.

Shiwago, P. L.
1929. "*Über den Chromosomenkomplex der Truthennen,*" *Zeit. f. Zellf. u. mikros. Anat.*, 9:106–15.

Shreve, F.
1926. In V. E. Shelford, *Naturalist's Guide to the Americas.* Baltimore.

Shufeldt, R. W.
1887. "A Critical Comparison of a Series of Skulls of the Wild and Domesticated Turkeys," *Jour. Comp. Med. and Surg.* New York. 8:207–22.

———.
1887.1. "The Turkey Skull," *Am. Nat.*, 21:777.

———.
1897. "On Fossil Bird-bones Obtained by Expeditions of the University of Pennsylvania from the Bone Caves of Tennessee," *Am. Nat.*, 31:648–49.

———.
1909. *Osteology of Birds.* N.Y. State Mus. *Bull. 130.*

———.
1911. "The Extermination of the Wild Turkey in Virginia," *Auk*, 28:144–46.

———.
1912. "Study of the Eggs of Meleagridae," *Condor*, 14:209–13.

———.
1913. "Further Studies of Fossil Birds with Descriptions of New and Extinct Species," *Bull. Am. Mus. Nat. Hist.*, 32(16):285–314.

———.
1913.1. "Contributions to Avian Paleontology," *Auk*, 30:29–36.

———.
1914. "On the Skeleton of the Ocellated Turkey (*Agriocharis ocellata*), with Notes on the Osteology of Other Meleagridae," *Aquila*, 21:1–52.

597

———.

1914.1. In E. A. McIlhenny, *The Wild Turkey and Its Hunting.* New York.

———.

1915. "Fossil Birds in the Marsh Collection of Yale University," *Trans.* Conn. Acad. Arts and Sci. 19:5–78.

———.

1917. "Report on Fossil Birds from Vero, Florida," *Jour. Geol.*, 25:18–20; *Ninth Ann. Rept.* Florida State Geol. Surv., 35–42.

———.

1918. "Notes on Some Bird Fossils from Florida," *Auk*, 35:357–58.

Shurtleff, N. B.

1853. *Records of the Governor and Company of the Massachusetts Bay in New England.* Vol. I. Boston.

Sibbald, R.

1684. *Scotia illustrata sive prodromus historiae naturalis . . . Pars secunde specialis.* Part II (III). Edinburgh.

Sibley, C. G.

1960. "The Electrophoretic Patterns of Avian Egg-white Proteins as Taxonomic Characters," *Ibis*, 102:215–84.

Sibley, C. L.

1933. "A Proposed Standard Ideal for the Wild Turkey," *Game Breeder*, 37(2):34, 49–50.

———.

1939. "On the Game Farm: The Personal Touch," *Game Breeder and Sportsm.*, 43(11):175.

———.

1940. "Standard for Northeastern Wild Turkey," *Modern Game Breeder*, 10(5):4–5; *Game Breeder and Sportsm.*, 44(4):55–56.

Sickels, A. C.

1959. *Comparative Results of Stocking Game Farm and Wild Trapped Turkeys in Ohio.* Nat. Wild Turkey Symposium. Memphis.

Sikkem, E. A.

1921. [Turkeys in Virginia], *Oologist*, 38:51.

Simmons, G. F.

1915. "On the Nesting of Certain Birds in Texas," *Auk*, 32:317–31.

———.

1925. *Birds of the Austin Region.* Austin.

Simmons, L. W.

1942. *Sun Chief, the Autobiography of a Hopi Indian.* New Haven.

Simpson, D. F., D. W. Anthony, and F. Young.

1956. "Parasitism of Adult Turkeys in Florida by *Leucocytozoon smithi* (Laveran and Lucet)," *Jour. Am. Vet. Med. Ass.*, 129:573–76.

Simpson, E. M.

1927. "We Must Produce If We Would Destroy," *Cal. Fish and Game*, 13:93, 95, 96.

Simpson, J. H.

1850. "The Report . . . of an Expedition into the Navajo Country in 1849," 31 Cong., 1 sess., *Sen. Ex. Doc. 64:* 55–250.

Singley, J. A.

1893. *Contributions to the Natural History of Texas.* Part II. "Texas Birds," *Ann. Rept.* Geol. Survey of Texas for 1892, 345–75.

Sippel, W.
  1908. *"Das Munddach der Vögel und Säuger,"* Geg. Morph. Jahrb., 37:490–524.
Sizer, E. R.
  1933. "As to Wild Turkeys, Well," *Am. Rifleman*, 81(2):22, 23.
Sjoberg, A. F.
  1953. "The Culture of the Tonkawa, a Texas Indian Tribe," *Texas Jour. Sci.*, 5:280–304.
Skidmore, L. V.
  1932. "The Transmission of Fowl Cholera to Turkeys by the Common Housefly (*Musca domestica* Linn.) with Brief Notes on the Viability of Fowl Cholera Microorganisms," *Cornell Vet.*, 22: 281–85.

———.
  1932.1. *"Leucocytozoon smithi* Infection in Turkeys and Its Transmission by *Simulium occidentale* Townsend," *Zentbl. Bakt., Parasitenk. u. Infektionskrank.*, Abt. 1, Orig., 125:329–35.
Skinner, M. P., and J. W. Achorn.
  1928. *A Guide to the Winter Birds of the North Carolina Sandhills.* Albany.
Skrjabin, K.
  1915. *"Trematodes des oiseaux de l'Oural,"* Ann. Mus. Zool. Acad. Sci. St. Petersburg, 20:395–417.
Sloane, H.
  1725. *A Voyage to the Islands of Madera, . . . Jamaica, . . .* Vol. II. London.
Smiley, J. C.
  1903. *History of Denver.* Denver.
Smith, A. P.
  1916. "Additions to the Avifauna of Kerr Co., Texas," *Auk*, 33: 187–93.
Smith, A. W.
  1894. "Deer and Turkey in West Virginia," *Forest and Stream*, 42:8.
Smith, B.
  1866. *Narratives of the Career of Hernando de Soto in the Conquest of Florida.* New York.
Smith, H. M.
  1946. "Snake Detection," *Chicago Nat.*, 9:63–67.
Smith, H. W.
  1936. *A Sporting Family of the Old South.* Albany.
Smith, Capt. John.
  1910. *Travels and Works.* Edinburgh.
Smith, J. O.
  1932. [Turkey Attacks Rabbit], *Pa. Game News*, 2(23):11.
Smith, K., J. L. Herring, and C. E. Harrison.
  1959. "Wild Turkey in Louisiana," *La. Consv.*, 11(11):23–24.
Smith, Ralph H.
  1954. "Upland Game Bird Studies," *P-R Quart.*, 14(4):452.
Smith, T.
  1895. "An Infectious Disease among Turkeys Caused by Protozoa (infectious entero-hepatitis)," U. S. Dept. Agr., Bur. Anim. Ind. *Bull. 8.*

———.
  1915. "Further Investigations into the Etiology of the Protozoan Disease of Turkeys Known as Blackhead, Entero-hepatitis, Typhlitis, etc.," *Jour. Med. Res.*, 33:243–70.
Smith, Watson.
  1952. "Kiva Mural Decorations at

Awatovi and Kawaika-a," *Pap. Peabody Mus. Am. Arch. and Ethn.*, 37:67–241.

———.
1952.1. "Excavations in Big Hawk Valley, Wupatki National Monument, Arizona," *Mus. North. Ariz. Bull. 24.*

Smithe, F. B., and R. A. Paynter, Jr.
1963. "Birds of Tykal, Guatemala," *Bull. Mus. Comp. Zool.*, 128:247–324.

Smyth, J. F. D.
1784. *A Tour in the United States of America.* Vol. I. London.

Smyth, J. R., Jr.
1955. "Selection for Different Levels of Sexual Receptivity in the Female Turkey," *Genetics*, 40:596.

———, and A. T. Leighton, Jr.
1953. "A Study of Certain Factors Affecting Fertility in the Turkey," *Poultry Sci.*, 32:1004–1013.

Snyder, R. L.
1953. "Wild Turkey Study," *P-R Quart.*, 13(4):428.

———.
1954. "Wild Turkey Study," *P-R Quart.*, 14(1):77–78; 14(2):189.

Sokolow, N. N., G. G. Tiniakow, and J. E. Trofimow.
1936. "On the Morphology of the Chromosomes in Gallinaceae," *Cytologia Tokyo*, 7:466–89.

Solis, G. J. de.
1931. "Diary of a Visit of Inspection of the Texas Missions Made by Fray Gaspar Jose de Solis in the Year 1767–1768," *Southw. Hist. Quart.*, 35:28–76.

Sommers, J.
1958. "The Commission's Wild Turkey Trapping Program," *Miss. Game and Fish*, 21(8):4–5.

Sosa, Gaspar Castaño de.
1865. "*Memoria del descubrimiento . . .*" *Col. Doc. Ineditos*, 4:283–354; 1871. 15:191–261.

"Southern."
1896. "The Wily Gobbler Decoy," *Forest and Stream*, 46:313.

———.
1900. "Turkeys," *Forest and Stream*, 54:349.

Spallanzani, L.
1787. *Opuscules de physique.* J. Senbier, transl. Vol. II. Paris.

Spangenberg, A. G.
1916. *Journey to Onondaga in 1745.* In W. M. Beauchamp, *Moravian Journals Relating to Central New York.* Syracuse.

Sparks, J.
1882. *The Works of Benjamin Franklin.* Vol. X. Chicago.

Spears, J. R.
1889. "The Ozark Mountains," *Forest and Stream*, 32:490.

Spears, Mary.
1853. ["Pioneer life of] Mary Spears," *Putnam's Mag.*, 1:267–75; 1916. *Jour. Ill. State Hist. Soc.*, 9:152–71.

Speck, F. G.
1909. *Ethnology of the Yuchi Indians. Anthr. Publ. Univ. Pa. Mus.* 1(1).

———.
1915. *The Nanticoke Community of Delaware. Contr. Mus. Am. Indian* 2(4).

———.
1921. "Bird-lore of the Northern Indians," Public Lect. Univ. Pa. Faculty, 7:349–80.

———. 1925. "The Rappahannock Indians of Virginia," *Ind. Notes and Monog.*, 5(3):25–83.

———. 1927. *The Nanticoke and Conoy Indians.* Pap. Hist. Soc. Del. n.s., 1.

———. 1928. Chapters on the Ethnology of the Powhatan Tribes of Virginia. *Ind. Notes and Monog.* 1(5):225–455.

———. 1931. "A Study of the Delaware Indians Big House Ceremony," Pa. Hist. Comm. *Publ.* 2: 5–192.

Spencer, J.
1908. "The Shawnee Indians," *Trans.* Kansas State Hist. Soc. for 1907–1908, 10:382–401.

Sperling, J.
1661. *Zoologia physica.* Lipsiae.

Sperry, C. C.
1941. *Food Habits of the Coyote.* Fish and Wildlife Service, Wildl. Res. *Bull. 4.*

Spicer, R. L.
1954. "Turkey Habitat Development Evaluation: New Mexico," *P-R Quart.*, 14(4):447–48.

———. 1957. "Emigration in Merriam's Turkey," *Proc.* 37th Ann. Conf. W. Ass. State Game and Fish Comm., 230–33.

———. 1959. *Wild Turkey in New Mexico.* N.M. Dept. Game and Fish *Bull. 10.*

"Splasher."
1881. "Wild Turkey Hunting," *Forest and Stream*, 16:164.

Sprunt, A. Jr., and E. B. Chamberlain.
1949. *South Carolina Bird Life.* Columbia.

Stabler, R. M.
1938. "The similarity between the Flagellate of Turkey Trichomoniasis and *T. columbae* in the pigeon," *Jour. Am. Vet. Med. Ass.*, 93:33–34.

———. 1938.1. "*Trichomonas gallinae* (Rivolta, 1878) the Correct Name for the Flagellate in the Mouth, Crop, and Liver of the Pigeon," *Jour. Parasit.*, 24:553–54.

———. 1941. "Further Studies of Trichomoniasis in Birds," *Auk*, 58:558–62.

Stafseth, H. J.
1939. "Tapeworm Infestation in Poultry," *Vet. Med.*, 34:763–65.

Stanberry, F. W., and L. Gainey.
1950. "Florida Deer and Turkey Restoration," *P-R Quart.*, 10(4): 415–16.

Stanford, J.
1959. "Turkeys in the Timber," *Mo. Consv.*, 20(3):1–4.

Starling, E. L.
1887. *History of Henderson County, Kentucky.* Henderson.

Steele, J. L.
1957. "Wildlife and the Big Blizzard," *Okl. Game News*, 13(6): 14–15.

Steele, J. L., Jr.
1959. "Turkey Flocks Make Progress," *Okla. Wildl.*, 15(5):18.

Stegeman, L. C.
1938. "The European Wild Boar in the Cherokee National Forest,

Tennessee," *Jour. Mam.*, 19: 279–90.

Steinhart, C. V.
  1936. "Talking Turkey," *Game Breed. and Sportsm.*, 40:53, 66–67.

Stephan, J.
  1922. *"Über eine durch Leukozyntozoen verursachte Gänse- und Putenerkrankung,"* Deutsche tierärztl. Wochensch., 30:589–92.

Stephen, A. M.
  1936. *Hopi Journal of Alexander M. Stephen.* E. C. Parsons, ed. Columbia Univ., *Contr. Anth. 23.*

Stephens, F.
  1876. "Game of Southwestern New Mexico," *Rod and Gun*, 8:281.

Stevenson, M. C.
  1915. "Ethnobotany of the Zuñi Indians," *30th Ann. Rept.* Bur. Am. Ethn. (1908–1909), 35–102.

Steward, J. H.
  1941. "Archeological Reconnaissance of Southern Utah," Bur. Am. Ethn. *Bull. 128(18):* 275–368.

Stewart, J. R.
  1918. *A Standard History of Champaign County, Illinois.* Vol. I. Chicago.

Stewart, J. T.
  1913. *Indiana County, Pennsylvania.* Vol. I. Chicago.

Stewart, R. E., and C. S. Robbins.
  1958. *Birds of Maryland and District of Columbia. N. Am. Fauna 62.*

Stock, C.
  1953. *Rancho La Brea.* 5th ed. Los Angeles Co. Museum, *Sci. Ser. No. 15.*

"Stockman."
  1890. "Texas Game and Varmints," *Forest and Stream*, 34:4–5.

Stockton, K. L., and A. S. Asmundson.
  1950. "Daily Rhythm of Egg Production in Turkeys," *Jour. Poult. Sci.*, 29:477–79.

Stockwell, G. A.
  1888. "Physiological Relations of Gular Vocalization in Grouse," *Jour. Comp. Med. and Surg.*, 9:127–35.

Stoddard, H. L.
  n.d. "Management in the Southeastern Pine-lands," MS.

———.
  1932. "Experiments in Upland Game Bird Management," *Trans.* 19th Am. Game Conf., 90–100.

———.
  1935. "Wild Turkey Management," *Trans.* 21st Am. Game Conf., 326–33; *Am. Game*, 24:22, 29–30.

———.
  1940. *Eighth Annual Report, 1939.* Co-operative Quail Study Association, Thomasville.

———.
  1941. "The Carrying Capacity of Southeastern Quail Lands," *Trans.* 6th N. Am. Wildl. Conf., 140–55.

———.
  1946. *The Bobwhite Quail.* New York.

Stone, H. A.
  1908. "Domesticating Wild Turkeys," *Country Life Am.*, 14: 275–77, 320.

Stone, W.
1906. "A Bibliography and No-
menclator of the Ornithological
Works of John James Audu-
bon," *Auk*, 23:298–312.

Stork, W.
1769. *A Description of East-Florida*
... 3d ed. London.

Strachey, W.
1849. "The Historie of Travaile
into Virginia Britannia (1612),"
Hakluyt Soc., 6.

Street, P. B.
1954. "Birds of the Pocono Mountains, Pennsylvania," *Cassinia*,
41:3–76.

Stresemann, E.
1927–34. "Aves." In Kükenthal,
Handbuch der Zoologie. Vol.
VII. Berlin and Leipzig.

———.
1940. *"Die 'vor-columbischen'*
Truthähne in Schleswig," Orn.
Monatsb., 48:154–59.

———.
1941. *"Der Fall der schleswiger*
Truthähne," Orn. *Monatsb.*,
49:33–39.

———.
1959. "The Status of Avian Systematics and Its Unsolved Problems," *Auk*, 75:269–80.

Strode, W. S.
1893. "An Old-time Outing," *Orn.*
and Oolog., 18:86–90.

Strong, H. W.
[*ca.* 1926]. *My Frontier Days and*
Indian Fights on the Plains of
Texas. N.p.

Strong, Gen. W. E.
1960. *Canadian River Hunt.* Norman.

Stuart, J.
1833. *Three Years in North Amer-*
ica. Vols. I & II. New York.

Stuart, J. G.
1952. "A Journal . . . Down the
Kentucky, Ohio, Mississippi
Rivers &c. (1806)," Ky. Hist.
Soc. *Reg.* 50:5–25.

Stubbs, S. A., and W. S. Stallings, Jr.
1953. *The Excavation of Pindi*
Pueblo, New Mexico. School
Am. Res. and Lab. Anth.
Monog., 18.

Stübel, Hans.
1910. *"Beiträge zur kenntnis der*
Physiologie des Blutkreislaufe
bei verschieden Vogelarten,"
Pflügers Arch. für d. ges.
Physiol., 135:249–365.

Studer, J. H.
1903. *The Birds of North America.*
New York.

Suarez, M. F.
1940. *Sueños de Luciano Pulgar.*
Bogota, 10.

Suchetet, A.
1890. *"Les oiseaux hybrides recon-*
tres à l'état sauvage," Mem. soc.
zool. France, 3:256–360.

Sundling, F. H.
1957. "Wild Turkeys Show Up,"
S.D. Consv. Digest, 24(4):16.

Sushkin, P. P.
1928. "On the Affinities of *Para-*
pavo californicus (Loye Miller)," *Ibis*, 135–38.

Sutton, G. M.
1929. "Photographing Wild Turkey Nests in Pennsylvania,"
Auk, 46:326–28.

———.
1940. "The Breeding Birds of Tarrant County, Texas," *Ann.* Car-

negie Mus. for 1938–39, 27:171–
206.

Swanson, A., and M. Ford.
[*ca.* 1910]. *A History of Schuyler
County, Missouri.* Trenton.

Swanton, J. R.
1928. "Social Organization and
Social Usages of the Indians of
the Creek Confederacy," *42nd
Ann. Rept.* Bur. Am. Ethn.
(1924–25), 23–472.

―――.
1946. *The Indians of the Southeastern United States.* Bur. Am.
Ethn. *Bull. 137.*

Swarth, H. S.
1904. *Birds of the Huachuca
Mountains, Arizona. Pacific
Coast Avif. 4.*

Swindell, D. E., and W. L. Jennings.
1951. "Gulf Hammock Wildlife
Investigation: Florida," *P-R
Quart.,* 11(1):26.

Sylvester, W., and P. W. Lane.
1946. "Trapping Wild Turkeys on
the Kentucky Woodlands Refuge," *Jour. Wildl. Manag.,* 10:
333–42.

T., N. A.
1886. "Wild Turkey Domestication," *Forest and Stream,* 27:204.

T., W. R.
1889. "Hunting the Wild Turkey,"
Forest and Stream, 32:172.

Tabeau, P. A.
1939. *Tabeau's Narrative of
Loisel's Expedition to the Upper
Missouri.* Norman.

Taber, F. W.
1945. "Contribution on the Life
History and Ecology of the
Nine-banded Armadillo," *Jour.
Mam.,* 26:211–26.

Taber, W.
1955. "Notes on the Behavior of
the Wild Turkey," *Wilson Bull.,*
67:213.

Tabor, I. C.
1920. "Taking Texas Turkeys,"
Outing, 77:28.

Taibell, A.
1928. *Risveglio artificiale di istinti
tipicamente femminili nei mas-
chi di taluni uccelli.* Atti d. soc.
d. natur. e matem. d. Modena,
(9)7:93–102.

Taibell, G.
1934. *A la recherche du dindon
ocellé. L'Oiseau,* n.s. 4:542–53.

Tanner, J. T., and J. W. Hardy.
1958. "Summer Birds of the
Chiricahua Mountains, Arizona," Am. Mus. *Novit. No.
1866:* 1–11.

Tápia, Andrés de.
1866. "*Relación hecha por el Señor
Andrés de Tápia, sobre la Conquista de México,*" Col. Doc.
Hist. de México, Vol. II, 554–
94.

―――.
1939. *Relación de Algunas Cosas
de las que acaecieron al Muy
Illustre Señor Don Hernando
Cortés.* In A. Yáñez, *Crónicas de
la Conquista de México.* Mexico.

Taplin, Capt. C. L.
1855. "From the Sulphur Springs
of the Colorado to the Clear
Fork of the Brazos." In *Pacific
Ry. Reports,* II(iv), app. A:73–
93. Washington.

Tathwell, S. L., and H. O. Maxey.
1897. *The Old Settlers' History of
Bates County, Missouri.* Amsterdam.

Tavernier, J. B.
   1712. *Les six voyages* (1676). Vols.
   I & III. Utrecht et Paris.
Taylor, John D.
   1890. "Sketches of Pioneer Life in
   Cuyahoga County," *Ann. Early
   Settl. Ass. Cuyahoga Co.*, 2(11):
   435–43.
Taylor, N. A.
   1936. *The Coming Empire* (1877).
   Houston.
Taylor, W. P.
   1923. "Upland Game Birds in the
   State of Washington," *Murrelet*,
   IV(3):3–15; 1925. *Cal. Fish and
   Game*, 11:97–103.
——.
   1948. "The Wild Turkey—Texas'
   Grand Game Bird," *Trans.*
   Texas Acad. Sci., 30:222–26.
Teele, A. K.
   [1888]. *The History of Milton,
   Mass., 1640 to 1887*. Boston.
Tegetmeier, W. B.
   1867. *The Poultry Book*. London.
Temminck, C. J.
   1813. *Histoire naturelle générale
   des pigeons et des gallinacés*. Vol.
   II. Amsterdam.
Temple, J. L.
   1947. "The History, Status and
   Management of the Wild Tur-
   key in Oklahoma," *Proc.* 2nd
   Okla. Wildl. Conf., 94–101.
Termer, F.
   1951. *"Die 'Hühner' der Azteken,"*
   Zeits. für Ethn., 76(2):205–15.
Tertre, J. B. du.
   1667. *Histoire general des Antilles.*
   Vol. II. Paris.
"Texas."
   1891. "Deer and Turkey Shooting
   on the Río Grande," *Am. Field*,
   36:2–3.

Tezozomoc, Fernando A.
   1943. *Crónica Mexicana.* Mexico.
Thayer, G. H.
   1909. *Concealing-coloration in the
   Animal Kingdom*. New York.
[Thomas, C. A.].
   1957. "Did Utah have turkeys in
   1200 A.D.?" *Utah Fish and Game
   Mag.*, 13(5):5.
Thomas, C. H.
   1954. "The Population Unit in a
   Wild Turkey Census," *Proc.*
   Okla. Acad. Sci., 35:166–68.
——.
   1954.1. "Management Implications
   of the Social and Spatial Be-
   havior of Wild Turkeys," Okla.
   Coop. Wildl. Res. Unit *Quart.
   Prog. Rept.*, 7(2):4–11.
Thomas, E.
   1915. "Breeding Game Birds in
   California," *Outing*, 65:736–38.
Thomas, E. F.
   1934. "The Toxicity of Certain
   Species of *Crotalaria* Seed for
   the Chicken, Quail, Turkey, and
   Dove," *Jour. Am. Vet. Med.
   Ass.*, 85:617–22.
Thomas, G.
   1848. *An Historical and Geograph-
   ical Account of the Province and
   Country of Pensilvania . . .*
   (1698). New York.
Thomas, J., and H. Green.
   1957. "Something to Gobble
   About," *Texas Game and Fish*,
   15(11):9–11, 24.
Thompson, J. B. (Ozark Ripley).
   1926. *Sport in Field and Forest.*
   New York.
Thomson, G. M.
   1922. *The Naturalization of Ani-
   mals and Plants in New Zealand*.
   Cambridge.

Thoreau, H. D.
1949. *Journal*. Vol. II. Boston.

Thornborough, L.
1937. *The Great Smoky Mountains*. New York.

Thornton, D. C.
1953. *Tar Heel Wildlife*. N.C. Wildl. Res. Comm.

Thorpe, T. B.
1846. *The Mysteries of the Backwoods* ... Philadelphia.

——.
1854. *The Hive of the "Beehunter."* New York.

——.
1855. "Remembrances of the Mississippi," *Harper's Mag.*, 12:25–40.

Tibbits, J. S.
1876. "Wild Animals of Wayne County," Mich. Pion. and Hist. Soc. *Colls. for 1874–76*, 1:403–406.

Tiedemann, D. F.
1814. *Anatomie und Naturgeschichte der Vögel*. Vol. II. Heidelberg.

Tietz, G.
1933. *Über die Empfänglichkeit verschiedener Vogelarten für eine Infektion mit originärem Hühner-und Taubenpockenvirus*. Archiv f. Tierheilk, 65:244–55.

Tiller, W. K., and A. J. Springs.
1960. "How to Build a Turkey Feeder," *Texas Game and Fish*, 18(7):14–15.

Timberlake, Lieut. H.
1765. *Memoirs*. London.

Tinbergen, N.
1939. "Why Do Birds Behave As They Do?" *Bird-Lore*, 41:23–30.

Tobias, W. B.
1950. [Turkey call]. *Pa. Game News*, 21(4):22.

Todd, W. E. C.
1940. *Birds of Western Pennsylvania*. Pittsburgh.

Tomson, R.
1890. "The Voyage of Robert Tomson Marchant, into Noua Hispania in the Yeere 1555," *Hakluyt's Voyages*, 14(3):138–54. Edinburgh.

Tooker, J.
1933. "Turkey Technic," *Sat. Even. Post*, 206(Nov. 18):36, 92.

Torquemada, Juan de.
1943. *Monarquía indiana*. Vols. I & II. Mexico.

Tozzer, A. M., and G. M. Allen.
1910. *Animal Figures in the Maya Codices*. Peabody Mus. Papers, 4(3):283–372.

Trautman, C. G.
1950. "Determining the Age of Juvenile Pheasants," *S. Dakota Consv. Digest*, 17(8):8–10.

Travis, B. V., H. M. Goodwin Jr., and E. Gambrell.
1939. "Preliminary Note on the Occurrence of *Leucocytozoon smithi* Laveran and Lucet (1905) in Turkeys in the Southeastern United States," *Jour. Parasit.*, 25:278.

Trebeden, E.
1902. "*Puissance méchanique de gésier des dindons*," *Cosmos*, (2) 46:578.

Trollope, F. M.
1832. *Domestic Manners of the Americans*. 2d ed. Vol. I. London.

Trumbull, J. H.
   1903. *Natick Dictionary.* Bur. Am. Ethn. *Bull. 25.*
Tucker, E.
   1882. *History of Randolph County, Indiana.* Chicago.
Turnbo, Silas C.
   1904. *Fireside Stories of the Early Days in the Ozarks.* N.p.
Turnbull, W. P.
   1869. *The Birds of East Pennsylvania and New Jersey.* Glasgow.
Turpin, T.
   1927. "Talking Turkey," *Forest and Stream,* 97:669.

———.
   1928. "Turkey Tales and Tips," *Forest and Stream,* 98:613–15, 650.

———.
   1928.1. "December Turkey Hunting," *Outdoor Life,* 62(Dec.): 16–17, 78–80.
Tuttle, H. J.
   1946. "Weights of Turkeys Killed in Virginia," *P-R Quart.,* 6(2): 78.
Twitchell, R. E.
   1911. *The Leading Facts of New Mexican History.* Vol. I. Cedar Rapids.
Tyler, D. T. A.
   1899. "Audubon's Seal," *Bird-Lore,* 1:172–73.
Tyzzer, E. E.
   1919. "Developmental Phases of the Protozoon of 'Blackhead' in Turkeys," *Jour. Med. Res.,* 40:1–30.

———.
   1920. "The Flagellate Character and Reclassification of the Parasite Producing 'Blackhead' in Turkeys—*Histomonas* (gen. nov.) *meleagridis* (Smith)," *Jour. Parasit.,* 6:124–31.

———.
   1927. "Species and Strains of Coccidia in Poultry," *Jour. Parasit.,* 13:215.

———.
   1929. "Coccidiosis in Gallinaceous Birds," *Am. Jour. Hyg.,* 10:269–383.
Uhler, F. M., C. Cottam, and T. F. Clarke.
   1939. "Food of Snakes of the George Washington National Forest, Virginia," *Trans.* 4th N. Am. Wildl. Conf., 605–22.
Uhlig, H. G.
   1950. "Resurvey of Flock Distribution of the Wild Turkey: West Virginia," *P-R Quart.,* 10(3): 371–72.

———.
   1951. "Wild Turkey Broods," *P-R Quart.,* 11(1):98.
———, and R. W. Bailey.
   1952. "Factors Influencing the Distribution and Abundance of the Wild Turkey in West Virginia," *Jour. Wildl. Manag.,* 16:24–32.
———, and H. C. Dahl.
   1950. "Turkey Broods," *P-R Quart.,* 10(4):505.
Underhill, A. H.
   1961. "Council Highlights," *N.J. Outdoors,* 12(1):29; (2):25.
Underhill, G. W.
   1940. "Two Simulids Feeding on Turkeys in Virginia," *Jour. Econ. Ent.,* 32:765–68.
Underwood, F.
   1894. "My First Turkey and My Last," *Forest and Stream,* 45: 533.

Union Historical Co.
1881. *The History of Jackson County, Missouri.* Kansas City.

Urbain, A. *et al.*
1951. "*Rapport sur la mortalité et la natalité enregistrées au Parc Zoologique du Bois de Vincennes pendant l'année 1950*," *Bull*. Mus. Hist. Nat. Paris, (2) 23:157–72.

Usher, I. L.
1922. "Letters of a Railroad Builder," *Palimpsest*, 3:16–32.

Ussher, R. J.
1909. "On the Cave of Castlepook, near Doneraile, Co. Cork," *Rept.* 78th Meeting Brit. Ass. Adv. Sci. for 1908, p. 697.

Van Buren, A. H.
1923. *A History of Ulster County under the Dominion of the Dutch.* Kingston.

Van Cleaf, A. R.
1906. *History of Pickaway County, Ohio.* Chicago.

Van Curler, A.
1896. "Arendt Van Curler and His Journal of 1634–35," *Ann. Rept.* Am. Hist. Ass. for 1895, pp. 79–101.

Van der Donck, A.
1841. "A Description of Netherlands (1656)," N.Y. Hist. Soc. *Colls.* 2(1):125–242.

Van Dersal, W. R.
1938. *Native Woody Plants of the United States.* U.S. Dept. Agr. *Mis. Publ. 303.*

Van Roekel, H.
1929. "Diseases Observed in Game Bird Raising," *Cal. Fish and Game*, 15:301–308.

Van Tyne, J., and A. J. Berger.
1959. *Fundamentals of Ornithology.* New York.

Varro, M. T.
1533. *Rerum rusticarum* libri III. In M. P. Cato, *Libri de re rustica.* Venice.

Vega, Ynca Garcilaso de la.
1871. *First Part of the Royal Commentaries of the Yncas* (1609). *Hakluyt Soc. 2.*

Velarde, L.
1931. "*Relación of Pimería Alta, 1716*," *N.M. Hist. Rev.*, 6:111–57.

Vessels, J.
1951. "Wild Meat Comes High," *Texas Game and Fish*, 9(11): 17–18.

"Victor."
1882. "West Virginia Notes," *Forest and Stream*, 17:487.

Vieillot, L. J. P.
1817. *Nouveau dictionnaire d'histoire naturelle appliquée aux arts*, . . . 2d ed. Vol. IX. Paris.

———, and P. L. Outart.
1825. *La galerie des oiseaux.* Vol. II. Paris.

Vigueras, I. Pérez.
1931. *Nota sobre algunos helmintos de* Meleagris gallopavo, *encontrados en Cuba, con descripcion de neuva especie.* Havana.

———.
1936. "*Notas sobre la fauna parasitológica de Cuba*," *Mem.* Soc. Cubana Hist. Nat. Felipe Poey, 10:53–86.

Villagrá, G. P.
1933. *History of New Mexico . . . 1610.* Los Angeles.

Villagutierre, Juan de.
1933. *Historia de la Conquista*

Provincia del Itzá. Bibl. Goathe-mala, Vol. IX.

Villiers, Baron M. de.
1922. *"Documents concernant l'histoire des Indiens de la région orientale de la Louisiane,"* Jour. Soc. Am. de Paris., n.s., 14:127–40.

Voegelin, C. F.
1938–40. *Shawnee Stems and the Jacob P. Dunn Miami Dictionary.* Ind. Hist. Soc., Prehist. Res. Ser., 1(3):63–102; 1(9):345–406.

Volkmar, F.
1929. "Observations on *Leucocytozoon smithi*; with Notes on Leucocytozoa in other Poultry," *Jour. Parasit.*, 16:24–28.

———.
1930. *"Trichomonas diversa* n. sp. and Its Association with a Disease of Turkeys," *Jour. Parasit.*, 17:85–89.

Vulpian, A.
1875. *Leçons sur l'appareil vasomoteur.* Vol. I. Paris.

W., A. J.
1890. "Turkey Hunting in Texas," *Forest and Stream*, 34:229.

W., G. F.
1883. "Shooting and Fishing in Florida—No. 4," *Am. Field*, 20:315.

W., J. J.
1899. "Sport in the Hawaiian Islands," *Shooting and Fishing*, 25:445.

W., L. D.
1895. "Indian Territory," *Forest and Stream*, 45:206.

Wadowski, S.
1939. "Some Observations on Intestinal Worms of Polish Poultry," *Proc.* 7th World's Poult. Cong. Cleveland, 270–71.

Wagner, F. H.
1954. "Wild Turkeys in Wisconsin," Wis. *Consv. Bull.* 19(11), 11–14.

Wagner, R.
1837. *"Beiträge zur Anatomie der Vögel,"* Abh. Akad. d. Wiss. Munich, 2:271–308.

Waite, W. M.
1882. "Questions about Wild Turkeys," *Forest and Stream*, 17:487.

Wakely, W. J., and I. L. Kosin.
1951. "A Study of the Morphology of the Turkey Spermatozoa—with Special Reference to the Seasonal Prevalence of Abnormal Types," *Am. Jour. Vet. Res.*, 12:240–45.

Waldo, F.
1901. "In the Southern Appalachians," *Forest and Stream*, 56:383.

Walker, C. A.
1911. *History of Macoupin County, Illinois.* Vol. I. Chicago.

Walker, E. A.
1947. "Wild Turkey in the Live Oak–Spanish Oak Erosion Area of the Edwards Plateau Region," *P-R Quart.*, 7(1):32–33.

———.
1947.1. "Wild Turkey in the Live Oak–Spanish Oak Erosion Area of the Edwards Plateau Region," *P-R Quart.*, 7(3):145.

———.
1948. "Wild Turkey in the Live Oak–Spanish Oak Erosion Area of the Edwards Plateau Region, Texas," *P-R Quart.*, 8(2):218.

———.
1948.1. *A Study of Factors In-*

fluencing Wild Turkey Populations in the Live Oak–Spanish
Oak Erosion Area of the Edwards Plateau of Texas. Texas
Game, Fish and Oyster Comm.

———.

1948.2. Rio Grande Turkey in the
Edwards Plateau of Texas, 1946–
48. Tex. Game, Fish and Oyster
Comm.

———.

1949. "The Status of the Wild
Turkey West of the Mississippi
River," Trans. 14th N. Am.
Wildl. Conf., 336–45.

———.

1949.1. A Study of Factors Influencing Wild Turkey Populations in the Central Mineral Region of Texas. Texas Game, Fish
and Oyster Comm. FA Rept.
Ser. 4.

———.

1950. "Tips on Wild Turkey,"
Texas Game and Fish, 9(1):2–3,
28.

———.

1951. "Land Use and Wild Turkeys," Texas Game and Fish,
9(11):12–16.

———.

1951.1. A Study of Factors In-
fluencing Wild Turkey Popula-
tions in the Live Oak–Shin Oak
Divide Area of the Edwards
Plateau of Texas. Texas Game,
Fish and Oyster Comm., FA
Rept. Ser. 6.

———.

1953. "Survey of Wild Turkey
Transplanting in Texas," P-R
Quart., 13(1):88–89.

———.

1953.1. "Survey of Wild Turkey

Transplanting in Texas," P-R
Quart., 13(4):436–37.

———.

1954. "Distribution and Management of the Wild Turkey in
Texas," Tex. Game and Fish,
12(8):12–14, 22, 26.

Wallace, D.
1911. Saddle and Camp in the
Rockies. New York.

Ward, W. P.
1930. History of Coffee County
[Georgia]. Atlanta.

Wardle, R. A., and J. A. McLeod.
1952. The Zoology of Tapeworms.
Minneapolis.

Warner, Beers & Co.
1885. History of Portage County,
Ohio. Chicago.

———.

1886. History of Hancock County,
Ohio. Chicago.

Warren, B. H.
1890. Report on the Birds of Pennsylvania. 2d ed. Harrisburg.

Warren, D. C., and R. M. Conrad.
1942. "Time of Pigment Deposition in Brown-shelled Hen Eggs
and in Turkey Eggs," Poultry
Sci., 21:515–20.

———, and C. D. Gordon.
1935. "The Sequence of Appearance, Molt, and Replacement of
the Juvenile Remiges of Some
Domestic Birds," Jour. Agr. Res.,
35:459–70.

———, and H. M. Scott.
1935. "An Attempt to Produce
Turkey X Chicken Hybrids,"
Jour. Heredity, 26:105–107.

Washington, George.
1888. "Household expenses, October, 1783," Mag. Am. Hist.,
19:171.

Waters, E. R.
1937. "The Farmer's Attitude Towards Bird Protection," *Ind. Aud. Year Book*, 36–42.

Watson, J. F.
1846. *Annals and Occurrences of New York City and State*. Philadelphia.

Wayne, A. T.
1910. *Birds of South Carolina.* Charleston.

Weakley, Harraman and Co.
1885. *History of Dearborn, Ohio, and Switzerland Counties, Indiana.* Chicago.

Weatherwax, P.
1954. *Indiana Corn in Old America.* New York.

Weaver, J. B.
1912. *Past and Present of Jasper County, Iowa.* Indianapolis.

Webb, J. W.
1958. "Federal Aid Program Helps State's Wildlife Projects," *S.C. Wildl.*, 5(2):4–5, 10–11, 19–20.

Webb, L. G.
1941. "Acorns, Favorite Food of the Wild Turkey in Winter," *Ala. Consv.*, 13(4):5, 14.

———.
1952. "Coastal Plains Wildlife Experiment and Demonstration Area," *P-R Quart.*, 12(2):126.

———.
1953. "Turkey Disease," *P-R Quart.*, 13(2):136.

Wehr, E. E.
1936. "Earthworms as Transmitters of *Capillaria annulata*, the Crop Worm of Chickens," *N. Am. Vet.*, 17(8):18–20.

———.
1937. "Relative Abundance of Crop Worms in Turkeys. Macro-

scopic differentiation of species," *Vet. Med.*, 32:230–33.

———.
1939. *Studies on the Development of the Pigeon Capillarid*, Capillaria columbae. U. S. Dept. Agr. Techn. Bull. 679. 19p.

———.
1942. "The Occurrence in the United States of the Turkey Ascarid, *Ascaridia dissimilis*, and Observations on Its Life History," *Proc. Helm. Soc. Washington*, 9:73–74.

———.
1948. "A Crop Worm, *Capillaria contorta*, the Cause of Death in Turkeys," *Proc. Helminth. Soc. Washington*, 15(2):80.

———, and R. W. Allen.
1945. "Additional Studies on the Life Cycle of *Capillaria caudinflata*, a Nematode Parasite of Chickens and Turkeys," *Proc. Helminth. Soc. Washington*, 12:12–14.

———, and D. R. Coburn.
1943. "Some Economically Important Parasites of the Wild Turkey and Hungarian Partridge in Pennsylvania," *Pa. Game News*, 13(11):14–15, 31.

Wells, W. W.
1946. *The Wildlife Program. 6th Bien Rept.* La. State Parks Comm. for 1944–45.

Werner, O. S.
1931. "The Chromosomes of the Domestic Turkey," *Biol. Bull.*, 61:157–64.

Wessell, C. W.
1937. "The Wild Turkey Propagating Areas," *Pa. Game News*, 8(4):8–9.

———.
1937.1. "Propagation Progress," *Pa. Game News*, 8(5):8.

West, H. C.
1886. "Amount of Game Killed in Missouri," *Am. Field*, 25:532.

West, J. L., and L. E. Starr.
1940. "Further Observations on a Blood Protozoan Infection in Turkeys," *Vet. Med.*, 35:649–53.

Wetmore, A.
1925. "Fossil Birds from Southeastern Arizona," *Proc. U. S. Nat. Mus.*, 64(5).

———.
1927. "Present Status of the Check-list of Fossil Birds for North America," *Auk*, 44:179–83.

———.
1928. "Prehistoric Ornithology in North America," *Jour. Wash. Acad. Sci.*, 18:145–58.

———.
1931. "The Avifauna of the Pleistocene in Florida," *Smith. Mis. Colls.*, 85(2):32–35.

———.
1932. "Additional Records of Birds from Cavern Deposits in New Mexico," *Condor*, 34:141–42.

———.
1936. "How Old Are Our Birds?" *Bird-Lore*, 38:321–26.

———.
1936.1. "Game Birds of Prairie, Forest, and Tundra," *Nat. Geogr. Mag.*, 70:461–500.

———.
1940. "Notes on the Birds of Tennessee," *Proc. U. S. Nat. Mus.* 86:175–243.

———.
1944. "Remains of Birds from the Rexroad Fauna of the Upper Pliocene of Kansas," Univ. Kansas *Sci. Bull. 30(1)*:89–105.

———.
1945. "Record of the Turkey from the Pleistocene of Indiana," *Wilson Bull.* 57:204.

———.
1956. *A Check-list of the Fossil and Prehistoric Birds of North America and the West Indies. Smith. Mis. Colls. 131(5)*.

Wharton, C. R.
1939. *History of Fort Bend County, Texas.* San Antonio.

Wheat, J. B.
1955. *Mogollon culture prior to A.D. 1000.* Am. Anth. Ass. *Mem. 82.*

Wheatley, C. M.
1871. "Notice of the Discovery of a Cave in Eastern Pennsylvania, Containing Remains of Post-Pliocene fossils . . ." *Am. Jour. Sci.*, 3(1):237.

Wheaton, J. M.
1875. "The Food of Birds as Related to Agriculture," *Ohio Agr. Rept. for 1874*, 561–78.

———.
1882. "Report on the Birds of Ohio," *Rept.* Geol. Surv. Ohio 4, part 1(2):188–628.

Wheeler, H. A.
1958. "Wild Turkeys in North Dakota," *N.D. Outdoors*, 21(5): 6–7.

Wheeler, R. J. Jr.
1944. "Turkey Investigation and Management," *P-R Quart.*, 4 (3):89.

———.
1944.1. "Turkey Investigation and Management: Alabama," *P-R Quart.*, 4(4):131–32.

——.
1945. "Turkey Investigation and Management: Alabama," *P-R Quart.*, 5(4):129–31.

——.
1945.1. "Turkey Investigation and Management: Alabama," *P-R Quart.*, 5(1):1–2.

——.
1946. "Turkey Investigation and Management: Alabama," *P-R Quart.*, 6(1):1–2.

——.
1946.1. "Turkey Investigation and Management: Alabama," *P-R Quart.*, 6(4):140–44.

——.
1946.2. "Turkey Investigation and Management: Alabama," *P-R Quart.*, 6(2):40–41.

——.
1948. *The Wild Turkey in Alabama.* Ala. Dept. Cons.

Whipple, A. W.
1856. *Report of explorations . . . from the Mississippi River to the Pacific Ocean.* No. 760. 33 Cong., 2d sess., *Sen. Ex. Doc. 78*, I:136p.; III:127p.

White, A.
1899. "A Briefe Relation of the Voyage unto Maryland (1634)," Calvert Pap. Fund *Publ.* 35:26–45.

Whitman, W.
1940. "The San Ildefonso of New Mexico." In *Acculturation in Seven American Indian Tribes.* Ralph Linton, ed. New York.

Whitney, J. F.
1887. "Hunting trips in the Indian Territory," *Am. Field*, 28:218–19.

Whittlesey, Charles.
1843. "Drives," *Am. Pioneer*, II:54–57.

Wickware, A. B.
1945. "Grasshoppers: A Potential Danger to Turkeys," *Can. Jour. Comp. Med. and Vet. Sci.*, 9(3):80–81.

Widmann, O.
1896. "The Peninsula of Missouri as a Winter Home for Birds," *Auk*, 13:216–22.

"Wilhelm."
1882. [Turkeys in Texas], *Am. Field*, 17:34.

Wilkes, Charles.
1845. *Narrative of the United States Exploring Expedition during the Years 1838–1842.* Vol. IV. Philadelphia.

Williams, A. P.
1951. "Across South Central Florida in 1882," *Tequesta* No. 11:63–92.

Williams, H. L.
1930. *History of Craighead County, Arkansas.* Little Rock.

Williams, H. Z. & Bro.
1881. *History of Washington County, Ohio.* Cleveland.

——.
1882. *History of Trumbull and Mahoning Counties.* Vol. II. Cleveland.

Williams, J.
1904. "A Preliminary List of the Birds of Leon County, Florida," *Auk*, 21:449–62.

——.
1920. "Notes on birds of Wakulla County, Florida," *Wilson Bull.*, 32:5–12.

Williams, L. E., Jr.
1961. "Notes on Wing Molt in

the Yearling Wild Turkey,"
Jour. Wildl. Manag., 25:439–40.

Williams, O. L.
1931. "Cestodes from the Eastern
Wild Turkey," *Jour. Parasit.*,
18:14–20.

Williams, Roger.
1810. "A Key into the Language
of the Indians of America
(1634)," Reprint. Mass. Hist.
Soc. *Colls.* (1)3:203–38.

Willoughby, H. L.
1910. *Across the Everglades.* 5th
ed. Philadelphia.

Willughby, F.
1678. *The Ornithology of Francis
Willughby.* London.

Wilson, A., and C. L. Bonaparte.
1832. *American Ornithology.* W.
Jardine, ed. Vol. III. London.

Wilson, E. F.
1874. *The Ojibway Language.*
Toronto.

Wilson, H. L., and J. Lewis.
1959. "Establishment and Spread
of the Wild Turkey in Southwestern Michigan," *Jour. Wildl.
Manag.*, 23:210–15.

Wilson, K. A.
1945. "Wild Turkey and Other
Upland Game Survey and a
Game Management Study in
Western Maryland," Md. Game
and Inl. Fish Comm. *Ann. Rept.
1945*, 25–41.

———.
1946. [Food habits, Maryland],
P-R Quart., 6(2):56.

———.
1947. "Wild turkey . . . Game Survey and Management Study,"
P-R Quart., 7(4):204–206.

Winship, G. P.
1896. "The Coronado Expedition,

1540–1542," *14th Ann. Rept.* Bur.
Am. Ethn., Part I, 329–613.

Winslow, E.
1897. A letter . . . In E. Arber, *The
Story of the Pilgrim Fathers.*
London.

Winthrop, Adam.
1943. *Winthrop Papers.* Vol. III.
Boston.

Winthrop, John, Jr.
1863. Letter to John Winthrop,
April 7, 1636. Mass. Hist. Soc.
Colls. (4)6, 514–15.

Winthrop, Wait.
1882. "Letters to Fitz-John Winthrop," Winthrop Papers. Mass.
Hist. Soc. *Colls.* (5)8.

Wislizenus, A.
1848. *Memoir of a Tour to Northern Mexico, Connected with Col.
Doniphan's Expedition, in 1846
and 1847.* 30 Cong., 1 sess., *Sen-
ate Misc. Doc. No. 26.*

Wissler, C.
1926. *The Relation of Nature to
Man in Aboriginal America.*
New York.

Withers, A. S.
1831. *Chronicles of Border War-
fare.* Clarksburg.

Wodzicki, K.
1929. *La vascularisation des appendices cutanés de la tête chez les
oiseaux. Bull.* int. acad. polon.
sci. lett. cl. BII, Part 7:345–88.

Wolfe, L. R.
1956. *Check-list of the Birds of
Texas.* Kerrville.

Wolfson, A.
1945. "The Role of the Pituitary,
Fat Deposition, and Body
Weight in Bird Migration,"
Condor, 47:95–127.

Wolterink, L. F., E. P. Reineke, and J. A. Davidson.

    1947. "Hemoglobin Concentrations in the Blood of Normal and Estrogen-treated Turkeys," *Am. Jour. Vet. Res.*, 8:431–36.

Wolters, Albrecht.

    1867. *Konrad von Heresbach.* Elberfeld.

Wood, C., and A. Wetmore.

    1926. "A Collection of Birds from the Fiji Islands," *Ibis*, 91–136.

Wood, C. H.

    1899. "A Deer and Turkey Hunt in Mississippi," *Forest and Stream*, 53:6.

Wood, N. A.

    1951. *The Birds of Michigan.* Mus. Zool., Univ. Mich., *Mis. Publ.* 75.

Wood, W.

    1865. *New England's Prospect (1634). Prince Soc. Publ. 3.*

Woodgerd, W.

    1959. "Long Live the King," *Mont. Wildl.*, Feb.:11–13.

Woodhouse, S. W.

    1853. Birds. In Capt. L. Sitgreaves, *Report of an Expedition Down the Zuni and Colorado Rivers.* 32 Cong., 2 sess., *Senate Ex. Doc.* 59, pp. 58–105.

Woodruff, E. S.

    1908. "A preliminary list of the birds of Shannon and Carter Counties, Missouri," *Auk*, 25: 191–214.

Woods, J.

    1822. *Two Years' Residence in the Settlement on the English Prairie in the Illinois country.* London.

[Woodward, G.] "Bob White."

    1876. "Wild Turkey Shooting," *Chicago Field*, 6:226.

————.

    1877. "Wild Turkeys," *Forest and Stream*, 9:64.

Woolfenden, G. E.

    1959. "A Pleistocene Avifauna from Rock Spring, Florida," *Wilson Bull.* 71:183–87.

Worden, A. N.

    [1956]. *Functional Anatomy of Birds.* London.

Wormington, H. M.

    1947. "Prehistoric Indians of the Southwest," Denver Mus. Nat. Hist., *Pop. Ser. Bull.* 7.

Wormley, T. G.

    1885. *Micro-chemistry of Poisons.* 2d ed. Philadelphia.

Wright, R. M.

    [*ca.* 1913]. *Dodge City, the Cowboy Capital and the Great Southwest.* Wichita.

Wright, S. A.

    1942. *My Rambles.* Austin.

Wunz, J.

    1962. "The Bearded Lady," *Pa. Game News*, 33(6):13–14.

————.

    1963. "Nature's Shave," *Pa. Game News*, 34(1):20.

Wyatt, Sir Francis.

    1935. Proclamation, September 21, 1623. In *Records of the Virginia Company*, Vol. IV. Washington.

Wynne, Capt. P.

    1937. Letter, November 26, 1608. In M. P. Andrews, *Virginia, the Old Dominion.* Garden City.

"X."

    1886. "Fort Sustly, I. T., Notes," *Forest and Stream*, 26:68.

X., C.

    1881. "Wild Turkey Calls," *Forest and Stream*, 17:127.

Yorke, F. H.
　1890. "Days with the Upland Game Birds of America: Turkey," *Am. Field*, 33:73–74, 97–98.

Young, J. Z.
　1955. *The Life of Vertebrates*. Oxford.

Young, S. P.
　1958. *The Bobcat of North America*. Harrisburg.

———, and H. H. T. Jackson.
　1951. *The Clever Coyote*. Harrisburg.

Young (Yong), T.
　1856. Letters of Captain Thomas Young ... 1634. In P. C. J. Weston, *Documents Connected with the History of South Carolina*. London.

Younger, W. C.
　1960. "Wild Turkey Studies," Ala. Dept. Consv. *Ann. Rept.* Oct. 1958–Sept. 1959, 127–30.

Zanon, Antonio.
　1763. *Letters sull' agricoltura, le arti e el commercio*. Vol. I. Venice.

Zayas, F. de.
　1941. *Los malófagos de las aves domesticas en Cuba*. Mem. soc. cub. hist. nat., 15:201–209.

Zeisberger, D.
　1887. *Indian Dictionary*. Cambridge.

[Zieman, G. W.].
　1954. "Wild Turkeys Trapped and Transplanted as Sportsmen Eye Season," *S.D. Consv. Digest*, 21(2):2–3, 16.

———.
　1955. "First Merriam's Wild Turkey Season," *S.D. Cons. Digest*, 22(1):12–13.

Zinanni (Ginanni), G.
　1737. *Delle uova e dei nidi degli uccelli, libro primo*. Venice.

INDEX

The text for *The Wild Turkey* has been set on the Linotype in 11-point Granjon. Designed by George W. Jones, one of England's great printers, Granjon draws its basic design from classic sources and is further refined by modern methods of punch-cutting. The paper on which the book is printed bears the watermark of the University of Oklahoma Press and has an effective life of at least three hundred years.